The Affect Theory Reader 2

ANIMA: Critical Race Studies Otherwise

A series edited by Mel Y. Chen,
Ezekiel J. Dixon-Román,
and Jasbir K. Puar

THE AFFECT THEORY READER 2

WORLDINGS, TENSIONS, FUTURES

Gregory J. Seigworth and Carolyn Pedwell, editors

DUKE UNIVERSITY PRESS　　*Durham and London 2023*

Project Editor: Jessica Ryan
Designed by Jenn Hill

Typeset in Minion Pro and Gill Sans by Westchester Publishing Services

Library of Congress Cataloging-in-Publication Data
Names: Seigworth, Gregory J., [date] editor. | Pedwell, Carolyn, editor.
Title: The affect theory reader 2 : worldings, tensions, futures / Gregory J. Seigworth
and Carolyn Pedwell, editors.
Other titles: ANIMA (Duke University Press)
Description: Durham : Duke University Press, 2023. | Series: Anima: critical race studies
otherwise | Includes bibliographical references and index.
Identifiers: LCCN 2022056233 (print)
LCCN 2022056234 (ebook)
ISBN 9781478024910 (paperback)
ISBN 9781478020196 (hardcover)
ISBN 9781478027201 (ebook)
Subjects: LCSH: Affect (Psychology) | Culture. | BISAC: SOCIAL SCIENCE / Sociology /
Social Theory | LITERARY CRITICISM / Semiotics & Theory
Classification: LCC BF175.5.A35 A344 2023 (print) | LCC BF175.5.A35 (ebook)
DDC 152.4—dc23/eng/20230512
LC record available at https://lccn.loc.gov/2022056233
LC ebook record available at https://lccn.loc.gov/2022056234

Cover art: *Eve Lution*, 2019. Acrylic on paper. © Claire Louise Giblin.

In memory of Lauren Berlant, 1957–2021

CONTENTS

GREG

By the time these acknowledgments are in print and before your eyes, it will have been thirteen years since the first *Affect Theory Reader* was released in fall 2010. Melissa Gregg and I honestly had no inkling of what was coming. In late fall 2015, when I hosted the Affect Theory: Worldings Tensions Futures conference at my home institution of Millersville University in Lancaster, Pennsylvania, more than seven hundred people (representing nearly every humanities discipline imaginable) submitted abstracts from over twenty-five countries. The whole event was so glorious—packed with such graciousness of spirit and generosity of intellect—that I almost did not want to contaminate its aura by doing another one. But three years later, after the launch of *Capacious: Journal for Emerging Affect Inquiry*, there was a second affect theory conference in Lancaster and then SSASS (Society for the Study of Affect Summer School) in August 2019. Every time, it was the same joyous vibes! Something happens at gatherings around affect: an atmosphere of encounter, of receptivity, of connection, of disciplines slipping a bit past their bounds, of academia affectionately lived.

At the wrap event of the *Capacious* conference in August 2018, I told Carolyn that I was thinking about putting together an *Affect*

Theory Reader 2 and wondered if she would want to be coeditor. She did. And then she waited and waited (and wrote a great book called *Revolutionary Routines* and had a baby!) while I tried to get my arms around what kind of shape this project might take. In January 2021, in the midst of the coronavirus pandemic, I sent Carolyn a draft of a book proposal that she approved and improved. We shared it with Duke University Press a week or so later. Our invite to contributors went out soon after, and by summer 2021 and into 2022, Carolyn and I were very busy editing chapter submissions, suggesting revisions to authors, and cowriting our introduction. We laugh now at the beast (at almost 22,000 words) that the introduction became, but it was simply a pleasure to write it together. Carolyn has a gift for getting to the point, staying on task, and producing the most remarkable insights by attending to the particulars of an argument (our own, someone else's) and its sweep at the same time. I tend to float and drift as a writer, picking up pieces of ideas, feels, and references, and seeing where they might go/where they might take us, lingering with the potentials for veering into the unanticipated and the otherwise. We found a rhythm and routine for bouncing the writing between us that worked to say something original about affect theory (or so we hope!) without shutting down alternate understandings and approaches. Carolyn put up with my relentless tinkerings and fussing over word choice, argument coherence, and writing voice—particularly in the final stretch—with such good humor and a gentle pulling on the reins; there should be a coeditor medal of valor. Seriously.

I cannot fully capture the experience of serving as founding member and coeditor for *Capacious: Journal for Emerging Affect Inquiry*. Mathew Arthur, Wendy Truran, Johnny Gainer, and Bryan Behrenshausen: each of them is an indispensable part of the smartest and most beautiful journal in the world. Objectively so! Best of all, *Capacious* has contributed tangibly to the futures of graduate students and early career researchers. We are small but mighty and will continue to sand off the rough edges of the academic world as much as possible. I couldn't be prouder of what *Capacious* continues to do. Thanks, too, to my Millersville colleagues and administration for participating in reading groups, assisting with the behind-the-scenes work for affect theory conferences (2015 and 2018) and a summer school (2019), and generally indulging my passions. And my tender appreciation to Randy Johnson, who facilitates a weekly online reading group with such grace, intellect, and good humor that it has become impossible to ever imagine leaving.

On a very personal level, Jackie and Kendall are my world. Affect sticks to everything. A final aside: John Turner—Please get in touch. It's been too long and I/we miss you.

CAROLYN

When I learned that there was to be a second *Affect Theory Reader*, I felt a ripple of excited anticipation to see what constellation of wonders the new book would unfold. When Greg invited me to join him as a coeditor of the collection, I was floored. It has been a pleasure to work with Greg, our extraordinary contributors, and the wonderful Duke University Press to bring *The Affect Theory Reader 2* to fruition. My appreciation goes to Melissa Gregg for conceiving the idea for the original reader in the first decade of the new millennium, when contemporary theories and studies of affect were still emergent and percolating, and to Melissa and Greg for curating such an astonishing collection of essays in 2010—which has been so important and generative to my own scholarship and to the work of so many interdisciplinary students, scholars, and practitioners of affect transnationally. I've learned a great deal from Greg in the process of putting together this collection and have been continually astounded by his ingenuity, clarity of thought, and uncanny capacity to translate the most complex theoretical and ethicopolitical dynamics into beautiful words that weave suggestive paths and establish potent connections I never would have expected—not to mention his masterful knowledge of, and infectious zeal for, all things affect. Greg is someone who genuinely loves, and is exceptionally talented at, bringing people together to establish the most generative relations and possibilities, and it has been inspiring to be part of the relations and possibilities underlying and reaching out from this reader. I will certainly miss our frequent and animated Facebook Messenger chats and video calls on all aspects of this collection—both the weighty and the entirely trivial!

My gratitude goes to my dear colleagues and friends and particularly Beckie Coleman, Angharad Closs Stephens, Mónica Moreno Figueroa, and Dawn Lyon for ongoing and vital conversations linked to affect, including so many of the concepts, themes, and issues addressed in this volume, which have been pivotal to my own thinking and ways of inhabiting the world. Thanks, as ever, to my family for everything. Luis Cereceda and Sadie Cereceda Pedwell were excited to finally meet Greg in person when we held our first preview event for this collection, organized by the wonderful Tony D. Sampson in London, in July 2021.

GREG AND CAROLYN

Our contributors to *The Affect Theory Reader 2* were a dream come true. It was fascinating to read through chapter submissions as they arrived, send along feedback that was always taken into account during revisions, and then place these chapters into different constellations to discover what emerged from their interstices. It was in reaching across the chapters and their brilliant contents that we realized the introduction had to be called "A Shimmer of Inventories"—each contributor brought such a singular intensity to their work. Every one of them stirs up something that challenges and illuminates a particular angle or orthodoxy of affect study. Duke University Press is likewise dreamy and shimmery. Ken Wissoker is simply the best. Our sincere appreciation also to Ryan Kendall for shepherding us through the nuts and bolts of Duke's forms, contracts, and so forth. Much appreciation also to our project editor, Jessica Ryan, and to Brian Ostrander and colleagues at Westchester Publishing Services. Thanks to the four anonymous reviewers at Duke for very insightful advice on the draft document and the final submission, which strengthened it immensely. We wish to also express our gratitude to the series editors at Anima (Mel Chen, Jasbir Puar, and Ezekiel Dixon-Román) for inviting this book to join their amazing lineup. Delighted to be in such good company! Finally, thanks to Claire Giblin for allowing us again to use one of her gorgeous artworks on the cover.

Last week, Lauren Berlant's *On the Inconvenience of Other People* arrived at Greg's house hot off the press from Duke. Lauren, as readers will see, never left our minds while pulling this project together. What to say? Lauren is all-around. Working with the Berlant estate to sort out the publishing of some of her/their final writing was an honor. Ian Horswill and Laurie Shannon are superb at maintaining Lauren's vibrancy. Thanks also to Katie Stewart for assisting us with securing the rights to publish these final pieces by Lauren Berlant. Other people are not always inconvenient.

INTRODUCTION

A Shimmer of Inventories

Gregory J. Seigworth and Carolyn Pedwell

So perhaps there is not a monoaffective imaginary.
—Lauren Berlant, "Affect and the Politics of Austerity:
An Interview Exchange with Lauren Berlant," 2014

In October 2010, *The Affect Theory Reader*—coedited by Melissa Gregg and Gregory J. Seigworth—was released into what feels like a wholly different world historical moment. Now, a little over a decade later, we (Greg and Carolyn) have assembled this follow-up volume of entirely new chapters. Whereas *The Affect Theory Reader*'s preface writing wrapped up on the eve of (literally the night before) Obama's first inauguration, this new reader enters the world in the enduring aftermath of Trumpism and the transnational rise of authoritarian populism, the urgency of #BlackLivesMatter writ large, the unrelenting forces of worldwide ecological devastation, the *bios* insecurities exacerbated by the global coronavirus pandemic, the unconscionable humanitarian crises in war zones like Palestine, Syria, Ukraine (and too many more), the visible increase in violence against women protests, the intertwined predicaments and pleasures wrought by new technological interfaces, artificial intelligence, and social media, a radical rethinking of the operations of "care" through trans/queer/crip/feminist lenses, and, well . . . name your event, pick your adventure, navigate whatever calamity. By the time this reader is in your hands, who knows how this world will feel? Where will old/new promises and threats be located? But beneath such big events, affect—in its often supple and subtle evental unfurlings—is always impinging, accreting, shuffling, and reshuffling: in, among, and alongside the myriad ripplings and miniscule skin pricklings and contact surfaces of the thoroughly mundane.

One of the chief aims of the original *Affect Theory Reader* was to capture without closing off an undulating, albeit never-to-be-cohesive, field of inquiry in the midst of its coming-to-bloom. Providing a few foundational affect coordinates—such as "forces," "encounters," "in-betweenness," "capacity," "intensities," and their "passages"—avoiding any bold proclamations about an affective turn (not a turn but rather a cluster of attunings!), and recognizing much longer traditions and trajectories (maybe eight? always more) of affect orientations, the volume featured many of the most vibrant voices in affect's study, strung them together along a few threads of commonality, but also did not mind too much if the seams showed. The first book arrived as its own kind of encounter with intensities.

In the decade plus since the first volume landed—and not without some amount of scuffling and pushback—affect theory continues to open invigorating paths for intellectual inquiry, reshape long-standing disciplinary debates and conceptual formations, and inspire imaginative cross-contaminations of academic and aesthetic genres, even televisual ones. What better evidence of this than the moment in Netflix's series *The Chair* (2021–) when Dr. Ji-Yoon Kim (played by Sandra Oh) refuses to provide David Duchovny (played by David Duchovny) with a quick tutorial on developments in the humanities since his undergraduate days at Princeton, finally saying exasperatedly, "A lot has happened in the last thirty years!" Duchovny demands to know, "Like what?" And the very first words out of Sandra Oh's mouth? "Like, affect theory." (Yes, Oh's character then offers a litany of other theories, but let us allow this tiny shimmer for "affect theory" to linger for a bit longer in the atmosphere of its emergence.) This new reader gathers together more than twenty people doing some of the most interesting and challenging work informed by a capacious understanding of affect's doings: drawn from a diverse (often divergent) set of disciplinary orientations and methodologies, uniquely contoured critical and conceptual formations, variously lived-ongoing situations/experiences/histories, and with specific political, ethical, and world-building (and unbuilding) commitments. If 2010's *Affect*

Theory Reader brought, at least, a modicum of coherence to a twinkling constellation of multidisciplinary shimmerings, we hope that this collection manages to shake a few things loose by injecting elements of disquiet, tension, ambiguity, obstinacy, oversaturatedness, cruel-esque optimism, and sometimes unmitigated pessimism into any too ready acclamation of affect theories' taken-for-granted presumptions, procedures, and palpabilities.

This book does not pretend to offer anything like a comprehensive survey of full-fledged, far-flung affect theory in its various modes,

Figure I.1. Still of David Duchovny "Like what?" from *The Chair* (2021).

Figure I.2. Still of Sandra Oh "Like affect theory…" from *The Chair* (2021).

moods, and guises. That has become an even more impossible task. Affect studies continues to evolve and mutate as a rangy and writhing poly-jumble of a creature (with far more than eight tentacles). Indeed, we have a mutual friend who confessed somewhat frustratedly that capturing the contemporary state of affect theory was not unlike entering a "fugue state." But to us, this only indicates how there is no universal key for transposing affect and its study into harmonious attunement across the conceptual/disciplinary territories of academic inquiry and practice. There will never be a single overarching critical-methodological magnetic force that magically consolidates all the touchpoints, vectors, and ambiences of affect study into any representative totality. And we would not wish it otherwise. Here, we fall happily in line with dearly departed (yet forever present) Lauren Berlant: there is no monoaffective imaginary.

Somewhat more modestly, *The Affect Theory Reader 2: Worldings, Tensions, Futures* is intended to reorient and sometimes disorient its readers, once more with feeling (even unfeeling), to the past, present, and future state(s) of affect study. What is at stake in the contact encounters or singular *worldings* of affect as sensed through and between sometimes quite differently directed disciplinary (as well as ill-disciplined) registers and atmospheres? How have inevitable *tensions* (political, aesthetic, ethical, theoretical, and more) catalyzed debates over the utility of theories of affect for established and nascent fields of knowledge and practice? Where are the *futures* of affect study pointing? In the latter case, such a move might necessitate stretching back to regain or trace anew neglected roots in the routes that tend and bend toward and through affect study.

Many of our contributors engage with how the conceptualizations and potentialities of affect have shifted since the first volume—whether that takes the form of provocations to reject or depart from particular affective lineages or lenses, imaginative reinterpretations and/or dishabitations of past sites and sources of affect theory, or speculative visions of new foundations and formations for the study of affect. Several confront affect studies' occlusions and omissions—around matters of race, indigeneity, decoloniality, alternative genealogies, methodological fuzziness, conceptual cul-de-sacs, and all of those inevitable ossifications of citational practice and argument structure that almost inevitably follow in the uptake and popularization of any emerging theory.

Several of our authors directly address critiques of affect theory as #AffectSoWhite—often by confronting the ongoing historical persistence of Eurocentric blind spots in affect inquiry and the lived deracinated equivalences between the capacities to affect and to be affected. In the substantial blowback against "critical race theory" that arose in the United States, the United Kingdom, and elsewhere (especially in mid-2021) as conservative politicians and far-right media outlets stoked white-hot grievances and sought public retribution for the previous year of Black Lives Matter protests following the murder of George Floyd, the matter and mattering of race and racisms must be further foregrounded and far better addressed across theories and studies of affect. Moreover, as several of our contributors emphasize, these processes involve complex ontopolitical, biopolitical, and geopolitical dynamics that require transnational and transmaterial affective approaches.

One of our aims throughout this collection, then, is to point to some of the ways that historical formations, present formulations, and future countenances of affect inquiry must be redrawn and "unlearned." Each chapter offers an encounter with affect in the midst of some manner of resonance, coagulation, scatter, fight, or flight—tangled up variously in the next, the not yet, the never quite, and/or through acts of outright refusal or negation. If there is already a potted history of affect studies that affixes or regulates the rhythms and flows of affect's theoretical trajectories (and undeniably the first reader could not help but lay down some markers as it surveyed and inventoried various shimmerings), then one of our chief desires this time is to knock *sideways and back* any and all orthodoxies, conceptual calcifications, received histories, and prescribed futures within and surrounding affect theory. At least a little bit.

What we hope to have collected between the covers of *The Affect Theory Reader 2* is a proliferation of feels, a supple set of minor (and often more than minor) affect provocations, an ambitious passel of living/other-than-living encounters that delineate themselves—collectively and singularly—to show how theories of affect are never a matter of "anything goes" (indeed, it very much matters what goes and how) while simultaneously denying closure around any notion of a monoaffective imaginary. Given affect theory's ongoing state of diffusion, its atmospheric densities, and extra-/infradisciplinary contaminations, we would much prefer that this collection be read as offering an abundance of pluri-affective imaginaries. Inverting the first volume's introduction "An Inventory of Shimmers," we have come to think of this one as a shimmer of inventories.

Conjuring Up Affective Inventories

How might a shimmer of inventories work? And how might it be different from the few already existing shorthands for aggregating and typologizing different forms of affect inquiry as they come to manifest and move across a range of ontological and para-ontological registers? Although affect study and its theories can always be provisionally compartmentalized from various perspectives, this should only be done with some caution and a big dollop of contingency. For instance, if we turn to one rather obvious primary source, Spinoza's "lines, planes, and bodies" in his *Ethics* (III preface) can offer a geometrically elegant architecture for formatting approaches to affect, for, that is, inventorying affect's shimmerings under different types of light: bodies (*affectio*), lines (*affectus*), and planes (*immanence*) (Sharp 2011). *Affectio* or affection—initially and somewhat mistakenly translated as "emotion"—focuses on a body's (and/or bodies') doing or undoing at the point of contact/encounter/impingement. *Affectus* concerns how forces or intensities rise and fall over the course of action undertaken by a body/bodies—focusing on relationality and process as continuous lines of variation, always in the midst of ongoingness. *Immanence* is the pure capacity of all things, all bodies (a world) to affect and be affected, to connect and disconnect: emphasizing the infinite potential for connectedness and relationality stretched to its widest as a single plane (God, nature, substance).

With this set of coordinates, one can begin—almost grid-like—to locate scholarship that is fundamentally oriented by, say, phenomenology: post- (Don Ihde), queered- (Sara Ahmed), and otherwise (Calvin Warren) as *affectio*; process philosophies and vitalism, from Lucretius's swerve to José Muñoz's cruise as *affectus*; and aesthetico-political ecologies of incorporeality, materiality, and animacy akin to Isabelle Stengers's cosmopolitics or Edouard Glissant's "Relation" or Kathleen Stewart's "ordinary" as *immanence*. Having such a map at hand—it's a point! A line! A plane!—can reveal something about the conceptual-material terrain to be covered in one's writing and about the stakes in shifting from one register to another; for instance, how moving from contact/encounter (point/body) to matters of capacity (immanence of a world) could lead to questions of ability/debility surfacing in ways that might not have happened otherwise. Such a flexy grid likewise might allow us to discover what is happening in those moments when different affect theorists seemingly talk past one another, such as scholars who experiment with the potentials that circulate in the space of worldly relation/nonrelation (immanence) versus those who attend to the powers that permeate and shape that same space (lines/of force, of variation). Who is doing the *real* politics here? Who is neglecting the aesthetic dimension? And so forth. Suddenly, a site of friction can emerge. But quite often, differences can be attributed to a particular emphasis, following a different door of affect entry, how one comes to navigate the scene of affect inquiry, and then where/how one exits (Anderson 2014).

Chances are that an entry point through one of these portals (*affectio*/*affectus*/immanence) will inevitably drift across, rub up against, and perhaps exit through one of the other ones. Witness, for example, how Katherine McKittrick's (2021, 127) loving invocation of "black livingness" and her devotion to methods in the making are intensely processual and relational (*affectus*) as she draws from Frantz Fanon/ Sylvia Wynter's sociogenic principle of/for an immanence of blackness that steadfastly rejects the overdetermined critical attention to impingements on the Black body (*affectio*) as a site that too often becomes "the target (the bullseye and the objective) of hate and racist violence." Or see how Mel Chen (2012, 209–11) draws a vivid distinction between how they encounter a table, not exclusively through phenomenological touch or contact (*affectio*) as Ahmed would have it but as an ingestion of molecular particles of sloughed-off skin surfaces that reveal an immanence of "mutual imbrication, even at the most material levels." Again, however, even a deceptively straightforward yet modulatory schema like "lines, planes, and bodies" cannot provide a catch-all inventory for every genre or gesture operating across affect theory: not even Spinoza can achieve that sort of grace.

So when inventorying, while there is something to be said— certainly—for wishing to get momentarily tidy and heuristic versus going fugue and getting playfully pragmatically experimental, it ultimately depends on what you are after. Here is the key thing: although affect theory remains forever open to operational closure (whether by way of disciplinary technique, political expediency, or deadline panic), one should refrain from too immediately hanging a "this section closed" sign over any particular clearing in affect theory's *open*. Making a shimmer of inventories while being mindful of how any particular organization of contents should not preclude an openness to rescrambling the sequence, we have placed the twenty chapters that follow into five subsections: (1) Tensions, In Solution, (2) Minor Feelings and Sensorial Possibilities of Form, (3) Unlearning and the Conditions of Arrival, (4) The Matter of Experience, or, Reminding Consciousness of Its Necessary Modesty, and (5) A Living Laboratory: Glitching the Affective Reproduction of the Social. Along the way, we toyed with a multitude of alternate section headings and considered other thematic dis-/entanglements (and readers will, of course, always choose their own paths no matter what we editors intend).[1]

We are reminded, here, of the fictitious taxonomy of animals that Argentinian writer Jorge Luis Borges attributes to a Chinese encyclopedia—the notorious inventory that delighted Michel Foucault (1970, xv), in his introduction to *The Order of Things*. With a half wink, we believe many of the encyclopedia's designations could swap in as our subsection titles, too: "(f) fabulous, (g) stray dogs, (h) included in the present classification, (i) frenzied, (j) innumerable, (k) drawn with a very fine camelhair brush, (l) *et cetera*, (m) having just broken the water pitcher, (n) that from a long way off look like flies." Or at least we would like to see our organization of this book's contents as animated by a similar spirit. As Foucault enthused, such inventorying is about "breaking up all the ordered surfaces and all the planes with which we are accustomed to tame the wild profusion of existing things . . . the thing we apprehend in one great leap, the thing that, by means of the fable, is demonstrated as the exotic charm of another system of thought, is the limitation of our own, the stark impossibility of thinking *that*" (xv). Escaping any monoaffective imaginary must, by necessity, rely on composing and continually decomposing a shimmer of inventories, one that raises the "stark impossibility of thinking *that*," of feeling *this*.

Sometimes an inventory can be rendered as an itinerary, as a travelog of entrances and exits into and out of theories of every stripe. As David Duchovny now knows, a lot of significant theory shifts have transpired over the last thirty years. In the next section, we will (1) address a few of the critiques of affect theory in its more recent history, (2) consider the relation of theory and practice through affect, and (3) shimmy, if not exactly shimmer, through a short dance number (actually more like a game of musical chairs) about how to get off on the right/wrong foot in theories of affect.

Of Balloons and Flailings

Silly Theory. Stupid Theory. Sexy Theory. Seething Theory. Stuck Theory. In his book *Avidly Reads Theory*, literature professor Jordan Stein (2019) takes readers on a deliciously funny and insightful five "feeling chapters" jaunt across the 1990s theories of his graduate school days. It is a fast-paced zigzagging series of detours until the end. In the last chapter, "Stuck Theory," Stein reaches affect theory after passing through, among other things, a serious fling with Jacques Lacan's *Écrits* and a "trauma"-themed graduate seminar with Ruth Leys. In the wake of the private and national traumas that followed September 11, 2001, Stein finds that writings from Lauren Berlant, Gilles Deleuze and Félix Guattari, and Eve Sedgwick offer crucial illuminations into the nature of stuckness: theoretical, political, and personal all at once. It is not so much that affect theory unsticks him or the world but rather that it provides a means for putting theory and practice together and thus for making a home among "the things that one could not find the words to say" (117). Although not exactly a lament, Stein is convinced that his own sense of theory stuckness would have played out differently if he had only encountered affect theory earlier. For Stein, affect theory is "less a theory proper and more of an ongoing interdisciplinary conversation" (115). And he goes on to note that affect theory has seen a "ballooning interest" over the past decade.

Although it appears that affect theory is going to be sticking around, it is also apparent that, in its ballooning, affect theory has (inevitably) become not only a thing that dwells often in stuckness but also something to be stuck, say, with a needle or a dart. Prick the affect theory balloon and watch it pop! That is, affect—as an intense encounter or minor impingement, as an area of study, as a theoretical practice—has found itself enmeshed in its fair share of intellectual consternations and pan-disciplinary controversies. In the time that has passed since the publication of the first *Affect Theory Reader*, pinpoint and full-scale critiques of affect theory have come from many angles, with varying rationales and backstories, staking diverse claims and counterclaims about the fields' presuppositions, blind spots and (in)coherences, its political or apolitical valence(s), its critical-methodological purchase, and, sometimes, its very worthiness as a respectable scholarly pursuit.[2]

Part of the problem of mounting a critique—or for that matter, a defense—of affect theory is, it is not one single theory (or two theories . . . or eight theories); affect theory is not about simply bridging or sludging disciplinary lenses and procedures together but rather rendering one more sensitive and highly attuned to the singular nature of disciplinary processes already underway. That is, one of the lingering side effects of spending serious time wandering in and through "the affective" is its capacity to render the act of theorization itself (whatever its basis) haptic, multisensory, synesthetic. Feeling through the circumambience of a particular encounter's intensities, sticking with its reverberations, puzzling out the tiniest feelers that feed into and out of a situation, finding a way to convey worlds through words and/or other forms of expression to produce some fraction of a difference to how *this* world registers: grasping (if only sometimes dimly) how theory has dimensionalities other than linear, how it is textured by the shape and rhythms of your study (not bending the objects of analysis to fit one's theory), to find what is singular and yet render its singularity shareable through a theorization that serves as a relay or a friction that opens onto other existences, other worlds. Of course this is easy to assert *in theory* but much harder to pull off *in practice*. This occurrence is not instantaneous or magic—it takes time, it takes care and labor, it takes dwelling, duration, or as Lauren Berlant (Berlant and Edelman 2014, 117) would say, dilation: "This is what it means to live, and to theorize, experimentally: to make registers of attention and assessment that can change the world of their implication, but also model the suspension of knowing in a way that dilates attention to a problem or scene." And needless to say, how the outcome of such an endeavor turns up as something that counts as doing "affect theory" varies discipline to discipline, case by case, scene after scene.

Perhaps, then, theories of affect, at their best, are uniquely (non)positioned to deflect, navigate, and/or reintegrate all manner of disciplinary claims, counterclaims, and contestations. Or, anyway, let us not get too reactive or overly policing about the capacities of affect theory to itself be affected, knocked around, or knocked down. After all, who wants to be part of an affect studies that cannot feel some shiver of appreciation regarding those who have invested the time and energy to seriously poke at affect theory's presumed hyperinflation, to pop and then pry apart its cases, concepts, and theories to argue that the present state of affairs could be something more, something less, or something completely otherwise? Why not pursue a "ruthless criticism of everything existing" (as, in his own way, Marx wished) in, through, and *of* affect theory? Why not develop a finely drawn line of critique, perhaps neither reparative nor paranoid, that lands and sticks in ways that refuse to be accommodated or assimilated, in ways that scramble the coordinates and orientations of affect studies' continued existence, and that propose options for engaging affect very differently or indeed advocate navigating a wide berth around nearly the whole of it?

Here, we will whisper something into your ear: we (this book's editors) sometimes entertain the potentiality and, yes, the reality that affect inquiry can always be thoroughly redrawn, undone. Radical contextualism, rigorous attunement to felt singularity, and an unshakable belief in historical contingency will do that to you. Affect theory has never been one (theory), never had a telos, never been nor taken a "turn." The exploration of affect has, from the get-go, been all fits and starts, do-overs and do-again-and-agains, flailings and flailings-better, flailings-worse.

Although the slings and arrows directed toward affect theory have not always struck their target, we do wish to address a few of the most resonant (and sometimes ages-old) critiques, not in an act of defensiveness, we hope, but with just the right amount of playfulness necessary to dodge, duck, and/or dignify the aims of particular pins and needles. Let us dance this mess—scattered darts and busted balloons alike—around! These few initiating steps are directed as much to affect theory's acolytes and adopters who earnestly start off or end up on the "wrong foot" somewhere along their affective route (although that does not preclude arriving at moments of serendipitous insight too).[3]

Getting on the Good Foot: Affect Theory/Practice

The original source for setting off on the most seriously wrong of all possible feet still haunts: occupying one side or the other of the Cartesian split of mind/matter. Perhaps it would have been better if, like Alfred North Whitehead, affect theory stated more directly that it wished to explore the "nonbifurcated" nature of material realities and speculative inquiry. Thus, affect theory's penchant, for example, of adding prefixes like "pre-," "non-," "more-than-," and "other-than-" to words like "human," "consciousness," "intentionality," "represen-tation," "discursive," "linguistic," "personal," "cognitive," and so forth might not have led to such a flurry of misunderstandings. But if you understand affect theory's talk of "pre-"/"non-"/"other-than-"/"more-than-," let's say, "consciousness" as privileging matter, body, ontology, and exteriority to the exclusion of mind, thought, epistemology, and subjectivity, then your affect theory dance is already off-kilter.[4] If you are operating by split dualities to exalt the less privileged side of any particular affectual-conceptual pairing, stop right now. Stand up. Push those chairs closer together until everything touches everything else. Recommence the music!

Yes, in part as an early reply to the Cartesian mind/body split, Spinoza said, "We don't yet know what a body can do," but he also clearly showed that we were (and still are) a long way from knowing all that thought can do. Beyond that, bodies *and* thoughts—in their inseparability—are simultaneously immersed in their own particu-lar worlds *and* in the wider world. What can a world do? In affect theory, the potentials (as forces that can incline or decline) and pro-ducibilities (as well as improducibilities) of a world, of an event, of a scene continue to reside right alongside its/their actualization. And this means bringing into account the adjacency and imbrication of intensities (of all sizes and shapes) where affect is palpable as an array of "causes" always on their way to "effect," while also insisting/persisting/subsisting as resonant force residues on the other side of any particular encounter's end result. This, for instance, is not merely about making room for the inclusion of thought or sensation as, say, "located" in foldings of brain matter or then extending the brain into a proprioceptive body-schema but also continuing through to the nonbifurcated wider matters of existence. Studying affect means paying attention to how matter comes to *matter* by way of intensity (immense to miniscule), force relations (weak to strong), density (high to low grade) while in context (geographical, historical, sociomaterial), in contestation, as matterings and rhythms of resonance and dissonance. Although this may sound like the most extraordinary task, we suggest that it is not as difficult as it seems; affect theory just asks that you attend to how the "extra-" appends itself to (interpenetrates and circulates through/about) the ordinary (in other words, see everything that Katie Stewart has ever written).

Luckily, the "extra-" also serves to remind you that one—whether analyst, event, object, theory—is never alone (autonomous, sovereign) in any of this. That is, affect is generatively foundationally relational (which is not to say that what happens in the relation "to affect/to be affected" is always reciprocal). Affect emerges through relations—often in tension—of inbetweenness. This is where movement, subtle changes, and not-so-subtle disturbances happen. Differentiations? Yes. But differences that are understood as mutually exclusive and oppositional? Generally no. Differings by degree that slide and shift and shimmy and shade without rising to (or falling into) full eclipse? Absolutely. Field all the relations of forces, bodies, encounters available, and there is, needless to say, never any fielding them all—then treat this "whole" gathering-up as one part, alongside all of the other parts in their uniquely situated specificity. But do not see "the whole gathering-up" or fielding (the French word is *agencement* as in layout or arrangement) as a place where everything is sutured up, closed off. Further, this is by no means a flat ontology; there are scales and proportions to account for and, of course, the matter of exactly who/what is doing the affecting and who/what is being affected. The scene is never tipped entirely one way or the other. There are contextualized differentiations in the shape, textures, rhythms, and histories of encounters that bear on the ratios of capacities and incapacities to affect and be affected. It all always depends.

As you might guess, this same view toward worldly nonbifurcation and ways of attending to the "extra-" of the ordinary has profound implications for how affect theory understands the relation of "theory" and "practice." You are never just doing one and then the other. This is not about theory now, practice later, or a detour through theory, or practice all the way down, or theory all the way up. That is, affect as *theory* should not be presumed to occupy the role of "abstraction" in relation to affect as *practice* (especially if practice = method as preset procedures). Following Raymond Williams's (1983, 316) tracing of the etymology of the word "theory" in his *Keywords*, we will note that "theory" first coincided with "the speculative" before it ("the theoretical") became a separate space—bifurcated, set aside—for some manner of pure mentalist abstraction or reflection. Theory/speculation and practice were initially grasped as operating together in mutual imbrication, phasing into and out of each other, constitutively saturating. Theory and practice need not shout to each other across a bifurcated gap of self-to-world/world-to-self reflection (extension versus thought) that is supposedly required to achieve proper critical-interpretive distance.

As if finessing the aforementioned gap, Berlant helpfully offloads the work of theorizing directly onto the affect theorists' senses.[5] Wait, *is* this helpful? After all, in the next moment, Berlant (2011, 31) adds, "Then again, maybe we did not really want our senses to be theoreticians: because then we would see ourselves as an effect of an exchange with the world, beholden to it, useful for it, rather than sovereign at the end of the day." Yet with this notion of the affect theorist's theorizing senses, Berlant does not conceive the senses as unmediated worldly receptors (this is not Hegel's "sense-certainty"), nor as fully corporealized nodes operating in secret somewhere beyond the reach of consciousness (this is not an appeal to the fibers of a body as an inherently preconstituted and liberatory force). Rather, an affect theorist's visceral literacy is nonbifurcated and labor intensive: "the visceral response is a trained thing, not just autonomic activity. Intuition is where affect meets history" (52). Or, back to Williams's (1977, 131) "structures of feeling": "It is the kind of feeling and thinking which is indeed social and material, but each in an embryonic phase before it can become fully articulate and defined exchange." Theory practice as sensorial training is immersed in the ever-emerging historical torsions of the material and the social, feeling *and* thinking, in ordinary and sometimes revolutionary routines of habituation and dehabituation.

Senses become viscerally historically situated theoreticians by staying within the scene, "with the trouble" (as Donna Haraway says), by continually and speculatively recalibrating around particular objects,

encounters, and atmospheres in an attempt to move with (and sometimes against) what is taking shape—socially and materially—as
normative and non-, as fixed or "in solution" (Williams 1977, 133). It
goes without saying that habituations and unhingings of these sense
theoreticians do not come with any kind of guarantee (How many
times around the chairs? When to start and stop the music?)—if only
providing a predetermined number of reiterations and a rising ca-
dence for stepping off could make it so! There are no ready-made
guidelines for how and when the subtle shiftings of matter and habits in formation suddenly transition from recursively recommencing
their own wobbly loop to then tip into intuition's uncanny capacity
for remembering forward. As Berlant and Williams both maintain
in their own ways, theory's offloading onto the senses is never going
to yield readily compartmentalized procedures and sequential steps
to trace out; there are always overdeterminations, ambiguities, entanglements, incoherences, blockages, noise, and more that must be
accounted for. That is *not* because these kind of clusterings are left-
overs or lie in excess after one's analysis has wrapped up, but because
ambiguities, overdeterminations, clots, tensions, and stuckness are
the initiating condition of affect theory, the "extra-" that gives ambi-
ence to the ordinary. These obstinate and restless features are the very
mess that constitutes affect theory's weather.

If the antagonism of foundational bifurcations—as a set of gaps
that holds everything in its right place—is what gets your system
moving, then the clamorous ascent of affect theory is only going to
confound and frustrate. Where is the properly manicured space-time
required for critical reflection, public deliberation, symbolic efficiency,
and the "intact person with his or her intentions and meanings" (Leys
2017, 16)?[6] A contrarian might point out here that Silvan Tomkins
was a serial bifurcator—a proliferator of polarities in tension: weak/
strong, surprise/startle, interest/excitement, shame/humiliation,
and many more. Tomkins's affect theory barely ever holds steady
at "one," and indeed, at almost any moment, it instantly multiplies
into affect *theories*: like someone who sneakily adds another chair
every time the music stops instead of taking one away. But at its core,
Tomkins's drive system and affect system are deeply enmeshed with
cognitive processes.[7] Maybe in affect theory or *theories*, the issue
is less the whole matter of splitting into twos and more about how

this bifurcation comes to play out as a duality. In studies of affect, "difference from" or "difference between" often do not offer as much traction. But difference in itself will tease and tug in all directions: registering the shifts in gradations or degrees, attending to the line(s) of variation where just a moment before there was only a single re-markable point (of contact, of encounter)—say, as when, in a glitch of unlearning or an out-of-sync dance move, one catches a glimpse of an adjacent but previously unnoticed world—or perhaps it is a set of points, the barest outline of a curve or sense of a swerve (maybe a swoon). Soon, however, there is a fuller scene or atmosphere, a lay-out, an *agencement*.

The *theory* of affect theory is an index of this effort expended in sensorially attending to and carrying along these continually shuf-fling intensities, lines of variation, and the persistence or dissipation of worlds. It can become quite a crowd: this "extra-."[8] The bad news, we suppose, is that affect theory in practice is not the kind of thing that arrives fully formed or unfolds like magic. The good news is that "practice" is already at hand, underfoot (even a wrong one). To en-gage this endeavor of nonbifurcated affect theory practice is no great mystery or mystification: say you have an encounter with a genre of music to which you have been little exposed or join a collective un-dertaking that pushes toward a specific form of action. Invariably, there are affective points, lines and planes to venture along, to risk, to find and lose yourself at the same time. When something sticks, prac-tice begins to turn to saturation—or maybe almost nothing sticks, then it is all on the fade—or sometimes, you are left half-suspended and middling through. Chances are high that you will bring some gathering of sense theoreticians (if only embryonic) to such situa-tions: viscerally speculative theoreticians that must remain pliable in practice. But there are not any immediate or easy assurances to offer here; it takes time and experience/experimentation.[9]

In what seems almost like a throwaway line in *Cruel Optimism*, Berlant (2011, 52) writes, "You forget when you learned to *use your inside voice*—it just seems like the default mode, even to write in it. But it is never the end of the story."[10] But for us, this moment captures quite succinctly how practice, as affect theory's *inside voice*, comes to bleed through to the theory side of the affect theory practice equation: extension and intension in co-resonance. This inside voice signals the labor-intensive, cumulative arrival of an intimately embodied land-scape of exterior encounters. That is, for affect studies, theory and practice are hinged or folded into one another (similar to how habit/experience and intuition/experiment come to lean on each other) as irreducible engagements with the speculative and the material simul-taneously. But not so fast, as Berlant says: acquiring an inside voice "is never the end of the story"; one persists along the evolving seam of intimate and exterior. This affect saturation of theory and practice means that their entwining is not so much waiting to be activated as the origin point of impingements and encounters with intensity; rather, it emerges out of them. When the outside finds its way inside, this is not a mere "default mode" but a transformational shift to a dif-ferent register of expression and an opportunity to engage and move (through) one's world otherwise.

Despite this attention to "voice" (inside and out), however, we want to swerve from any too immediate conclusion that affect is fully tied to the personal and the human when, in fact, theories of affect are generally more closely aligned with the impersonal and the so-cial. The *capacity* "to affect" and "to be affected" is not strictly or only personological. Capacity does not inhere in things or in bodies like a property relation (capacities are not properties). Not vacuum-packed in the capacity *of* a body (the capacity of a person, a brain, a balloon [McCormack 2018], a whatever), affect is instead engaged in capaci-ties *to* and incapacities *to*. If capacity/incapacity or debility are to be located anywhere in particular, it is in the interstices and thresholds of relation. Jasbir Puar (2017, 19–20) articulates this clearly with what she calls an "amendment to affect studies": "Debility and capacity are not properties or attributes of a discrete body or a representational grid certain bodies are placed into. Debility may well simultaneously appropriate bodily capacities closing off, perhaps to give rise to a new set of bodily capacities. Capacity is not discretely of the body. It is shaped by and bound to interface with prevailing notions of chance, risk, accident, luck, and probability, as well as with bodily limits/incapacity, disability, and debility." In short, when the whole matter of affect is misunderstood as the capacity *of* things, of con-sciousness, of bodies, of a world (and especially the capacity of affect theory itself), your argument is almost definitely going to land on the wrong foot.

Meanwhile, there are also critiques of affect theory's own "capacity to" that begin from compositional questions about the limits and paradoxes of addressing the insignificant, the nonrepresentational, and the extra-/a-signifying through language, argument construction, and poetically performative academic discourse. In other words, many of these criticisms argue that affect theory's attunement to what goes on beyond, below, alongside language/meaning/representation/ human is confounded by an inevitable reliance on language, meaning, and representation when sharing one's findings. This is easily one of the dreariest critiques that one can make of affect theory: that it is somehow caught up in an act of performative self-contradiction. Because language and representation are a frequent means (although not the only means) of communicating the results of an affect studies project, it is claimed that one can only vaguely gesture to the feely, nonrepresentable, and extralinguistic because it is all preordained to end up pinned to the grid of interpretative decodings in language, rhetorical modes of argument, conveyed as meaning to be interpreted by a conscious mind. But this critical maneuver assumes that language and the symbol and the material and meaning and the concept and human consciousness are somehow free of any contamination from the realms of feeling, sensation, potentiality and impotentiality, processuality, gradations of intensity, and so on. As affect theory amply demonstrates, however, a nonbifurcated world is most definitely aswim in floaty ambiguities and knotty entanglements of mattering and meaning.

Because affect studies regularly focuses on the question of "what a body can do," others have occasionally stepped forward to unhelpfully reaffix the perceived waywardness of such investigations by stating with blithe assurance that they know the precise boundaries of what thinking, language, materiality, objects, and subjects can do (again, as if we established all that "thought can do"). And affect inquiry has overstepped all these bounds. Time to corral! But by denying the full fixity of such things, affect theory is *not* actually the one holding up the mirror of infinite regress or falling into the swarming incrementalisms of Hegel's bad infinity. Sometimes in order to step off on the *right* foot (which could be a left foot) in affect theory, you must be capable of acknowledging the historically derived, situationally specific boundedness of things (like thought, bodies, disciplines, language) while also taking into account the muddiness, contamination, ambiguities, incoherences, and auratic flux that are *right there too*. Language, representation, and consciousness are, themselves, always fringed with and permeated by affective forces (often subtle, always modulating), perpetually in the midst of generating and regenerating their unique ratios and rhythms of boundedness/boundlessness. One is perpetually engaging with those thresholds of mattering-meaning that come to slide between worlds and words.

We could go on, foot by foot, but this is beginning to sound, as Berlant would say, too much like a "genre flail"—in this case, an unholy mixture that tries to be both a jaunty rejoinder to mostly nameless critics and, even more so, a cautionary tale aimed at affect theory's acolytes and adopters. Despite our efforts to carry it off with some amount (we hope!) of levity, this dance has gradually come to feel increasingly pedantic, leaning more and more toward humorlessness. Berlant (2018, 157) defined genre flailing as "a mode of crisis management that arises after an object, or object world, becomes disturbed in a way that intrudes on one's confidence about how to move in it." Whatever surefootedness we might have managed to display above, it is always undercut, as you might have sensed, by a thousand and one wiggly disturbances, anxiously troubled by under-nuanced vibrancies of feeling and knowing and experiencing—of which, of course, Berlant was well aware: "whether the writer is trying to open up the object or close the object, extend a question or put it to rest. It's impossible to distinguish a defense against knowledge from its production, and here's the thing—you can never know" (156). But then, that's the thing about affect theory: although it is by no means fiercely prescriptive or procedural (Do this! Don't do that!), it can set up shop rather nimbly in crisis modes: ordinary and extra-. Why is that? Because bruises and blisses, intensities and slackenings, assemblings and frayings are what set worlds into motion or push them toward collapse and everything in between: for better *and* for worse.

If Jordan Stein is right (and we think he is), we are living and dying in times that, more than ever, call for a "stuck theory": one that acknowledges ambiguities and tensions as both inescapable and absolutely necessary while tracking forces and feels through their most capacious and/or utterly decapacitating orbits. In affect theory, tensions do not so much move toward permanent resolution, but instead, they remain in solution. And not surprisingly, that is precisely what the first section of chapters in this volume opens up to deeper elaboration.

Tensions, In Solution

Rather notoriously, the first volume of *The Affect Theory Reader* pointed to two essays, both published in 1995, as constituting "a watershed moment" (Seigworth and Gregg 2010, 5) for the rise of contemporary affect theories: Eve Sedgwick and Adam Frank's (1995) "Shame in the Cybernetic Fold" and Brian Massumi's (1995) "The Autonomy of Affect." In the years that followed, these pieces came to stand as two key pathways informing writing on affect, emotion, and feeling: the Tomkins-Sedgwick line and the Spinoza-Deleuze-Massumi line. This bifurcation has been useful to some extent (it worked to clarify two ascendant paths, among many) but also un-helpful in lots of ways. It was never intended to be so definitive or as apparently divisive. In the Australian context, especially on evidence in the first reader (see chapters by Anna Gibbs, Elspeth Probyn, and Megan Watkins), Tomkins/Deleuze are regularly and intimately in-tertwined in theorizing affect. And needless to say, Sara Ahmed (2004, 2010, 2017) (who has the opening chapter in the first reader) has always moved outside/beyond such orbits. Yes, there are plenty of productive *tensions* to be drawn out of the use in combination of these two theoretical pathways alongside bridges still to be made (or burned down) but also, very different spannings and intersections that might yet lead us into altogether different districts and genealo-gies of affect theory.

As the contributors to the *Affect Theory Reader 2* illuminate, the foundations of affect studies are inherently contingent and contested (as well as multiple), in part, because "affect theories are animated by revisiting and revising concepts, through putting them to work in multiple circumstances, and by *working with the tensions that ensue*" (McCormack, this volume; our emphasis). Confronting this challenge directly in the reader's opening chapter, "The Elements of Affect Theories," Derek McCormack sidesteps the Tomkins/Deleuze "divide" to revisit a concept that certainly feels very familiar: Ray-mond Williams's (1977) "structures of feeling." McCormack's focus on "the elemental imaginary" that Williams's concept evokes, however, enables us to attune to it anew. For Williams, he suggests, the way so-cial experiences are "in solution" in everyday life is "analogous to how a solute is dissolved in a solvent, or to how water vapor may be held by air that is not yet saturated." Moreover, if structures of feeling's most vital contribution to affect studies relates to its concern with how the present is experienced affectively *as it unfolds*, this is "akin to the technique of sounding as an ongoing process of testing varia-tions in elemental milieus (depth, pressure, temperature etc.) using devices, technical and corporeal, of different kinds."

Yet if Williams implicates the elements *as analogy*, McCormack argues that thinking beyond the analogical is necessary to confront the climate emergency and related ecological and sociopolitical con-ditions and events, including "fires, heat waves, floods, storms, gla-cial retreat and melting, and air pollution"—a challenge that requires recognition that "not all bodies, lives, or worlds weather in the same way," particularly in the midst of racial capitalism. In this vein, draw-ing on Hortense Spillers, Sylvia Wynter, Saidiya Hartman, and others, the geographer Katherine Yusoff (2019, 2) considers, in her *A Billion Black Anthropocenes or None*, how accounts of the Anthropocene which employ the language of species life to invoke a "universalist geologic commons" often elide the histories of racism that are closely bound up with histories of geology. Relatedly, for Christina Sharpe (2016, 104), weather is the "totality of our environments; the weather is the total climate; and that climate is anti-black." In turn, for the Indigenous writer Billy Ray Belcourt (2020, 8), weather can, follow-ing Sharpe, encapsulate the "asphyxiating conditions" of racist and settler colonial oppression but also a precipitating desire to "shore up another kind of emotional atmosphere." What is essential to confront in any elemental engagement with affect, then, is how climate and weather are more than analogies; they are, in McCormack's words, "forms of violent envelopment and exposure in mixed elemental mi-lieus that bear the traces of earlier forms of violence." Attending to the elements, from this perspective, not only expands the range "of objects with which affect theories are concerned," but it also compels consideration of "the conditions in which theory takes place."

In this vein, other affect scholars have explored how Williams's analogue vision of media and culture might be reimagined for our digital age. In her book *If, Then: Algorithmic Power and Politics*, Taina

Bucher (2018, 157) glimpses an emergent transnational structure of feeling animated by the growing presence of algorithms within "the fabric of everyday life." Rebecca Coleman (2017), moreover, develops the concept of "infrastructures of feeling" to address the temporal qualities of affective experience as mediated by digital platforms like Netflix and Twitter. It is this algorithmic element of current affective ecologies that animates Susanna Paasonen's chapter in this reader. In the context of global data capitalism which strives to turn all human activity and affect into data points for the generation of capital—(re)producing reductive typologies of emotion through social media's options of "like," "love," "ha-ha," "sad," or "angry" alongside other computational techniques such as sentiment analysis—Paasonen foregrounds the differences that *affective ambiguity* make for analysis.

Resonating with McCormack's interest in the tensions that emerge from re-revisiting "familiar" concepts, Paasonen shows how working with ambiguity involves "holding on to mutually conflicting meanings and impacts without doing away with irreconcilable differences and tensions that cut through them." Importantly, for Paasonen and other contributors, this imperative applies as much to our objects as to the theories that emerge through them. Although Tomkins and Spinoza have (too) frequently been presented as oppositional coordinates for affect theory, Paasonen suggests that both thinkers "foreground inde-terminacy, unpredictability and ambiguity in how bodies affect and are affected by one another." In different ways, that is, Tomkins and Spinoza each insist that there is "no uniformity to what things excite, how and whom"—a claim that is particularly salient in relation to the affective dynamics that fuel compulsive attachment to digital apps and social media platforms.

To approach social media through the lens of ambiguity is thus to operationalize this shared insight; to appreciate, in Paasonen's words, "how the same objects—be they platforms, apps, threads, posts, com-ments, links, or something else—come to mean and effect distinctly different things, depending on how they materialize in encounters between human and nonhuman bodies." When we inhabit affec-tive ambiguity in this way, we begin to see how mediated intensi-ties cannot be fully generalized or predicted in advance and, in turn, how what Shoshanna Zuboff (2019) calls "surveillance capitalism" and what Wendy Hui Kyong Chun (2021) terms "discriminating data" can often yield "forms of agency and social organization irreducible to [their] logics" (Paasonen, this volume). In amplifying the "critical edge of ambiguity" to address how affect escapes easy containment in neat categories of emotion, then, Paasonen's chapter both extends and critically exceeds Tomkins's basic emotions paradigm.

Part and parcel of revisiting and revising affect theory's foundations is, in this view, not only thinking beyond "the usual suspects" but also reencountering the possibilities of theories and concepts we think we already know in order to put their tensions back into solution. Helpfully, in *A Silvan Tomkins Handbook: Foundations for Affect Theory*, Adam Frank and Elizabeth Wilson (2020, 8) do precisely this. They consider, for instance, how Tomkins's account of weak theory can open up binary configurations of affect studies to a wider methodological ecology including, but not limited to, the "psychoanalytic, phenomenological, Aristotelian, empirical, biochemical, and, of course the myriad traditions of thinking about emotions beyond the West." In their chapter here, Frank and Wilson explore what it means to view Tomkins's affect theory as "in tension" with psychoanalytic theories of mind from Sigmund Freud to his more recent interpreters in the Kleinian tradition. Beyond demonstrating the continued relevance of psychological and psychoanalytic theories to interdisciplinary affect studies, Frank and Wilson, similar to McCormack and Paasonen, also indicate how we might approach the "tensions among affect theories as something other than simple antagonisms." All three chapters, then, respond in their own ways to Sedgwick's (1996, 2003) call for more reparative intellectual practices—not necessarily (or only) as an imperative to approach our research objects with an orientation of care or nurturance but rather (or also) as a practice of *inhabiting*, rather than transcending, affective tension, conflict, and ambivalence.[11]

Addressing tensions through *and within* affect theory also demands grappling directly with the unfolding biopolitics and geopolitics with which both affect and its study are entangled. As Kyla Schuller (2018, 13) argues in *The Biopolitics of Feeling: Race, Sex and Science in the Nineteenth Century*, affect theory's central (Spinozist) formulation of "capacities for affecting and being affected" is not neutral; it is implicated in racialized, gendered, and classed "animacy hierarchies" produced through "unevenly assigning affective capacity throughout a population."[12] Consequently, as Jasbir Puar (2017) illustrates in *The Right to Maim: Debility/Capacity/Disability*, articulations of affective capacity always have an underside: debility—forms of slow death that assume particular significance within the aftermath of colonialism and contemporary neo-imperialism and racial capitalism. Taking up these and other critical engagements with affect, Tyrone Palmer's chapter, "Affect and Affirmation," considers how affect theory's predilections, especially in its Deleuzo-Spinozist variations, for generativity, the affirmative, and "productive capacity" lead to "curious silence and universalizing gestures offered in the face of (anti)blackness." With the everyday prohibitions on Black life, alongside the immanent possibility of Black death that Claudia Rankine (2015, n.p.) calls "the quotidian operations of antiblackness," Palmer asks what explanatory power affect theory can retain "in the face of a mode of being that signals 'incapacity in its pure and unadulterated form?'" (Wilderson 2010, 38, cited in Palmer, this volume).

Rather than foregrounding negative affects or the affects of the killjoy and then considering how these might be redeemed or mined for their generativity or potential, Palmer considers "what might be gleaned from a fidelity to the negativity which blackness brings to bear on the World of possibility and the possibility of world(s)." By squaring off with affect theory's often underproblematized championing of generativity, creativity, potentiality, and affirmation, he introduces tensions into what has, for some, become affect theory's default position: a decided tilt toward joyful abundance, capaciousness, and potentiality as an unalloyed good, as an ontoethical/methodological virtue.[13] In doing so, Palmer contributes to ongoing dialogues transpiring through and between a variety of perspectives found across Afropessimism/antiblackness/social death and Black joy/optimism/Black livingness in Black studies scholarship[14]—and simultaneously strikes, quite directly, at the pasts, presents, and futures of affect theory.

Writing at the intersections (and intertensions) of feminist, queer, trans, critical race, and decolonial thought, Kyla Schuller addresses the affective politics of (in)capacity from a different, though resonant, perspective. Her chapter, "Unfuckology: Affectability, Temporality, and Unleashing the Sex/Gender Binary," turns to the gendered and racialized legacies of American sexology to consider how affect is "bound up with the history of biopolitical fantasies that scientists and reformers [use to] shape the direction of human growth itself." As Schuller's analysis of the mid-twentieth-century making of "gender" underscores, pace Palmer's discussion, "models of affective capacity and bodily plasticity are not innocent spheres, removed from the political"; rather, they can function as technologies of biopolitical differentiation and regulation. Affect theory, however, might help us to conceptualize, she suggests, "less brutal systems of gender." Hence, Schuller explores how a redrawn understanding of affect (and affect theory) might shift the tenses and tensions of the sex/gender distinction away from the biopolitical violation of bodies toward ways that "sex/gender can be reimagined affectively to capture how power acts on the body over time, while keeping close to mind how the origins of gender lie themselves in a form of medical control and prosecution that understood the physical body and sexed identity as malleable entities coiled together with the practitioners' grasp."

Indeed, what is vital, ontoepistemologically and methodologically, to affect studies' ability to grapple with tension, ambiguity, and (in)corporeal complexity is, for a number of our contributors, a finely tuned capacity to sense, appreciate, and shift between differences in the textures, rhythms, and contours of time, space, and tensions in solution, while also addressing the implications of their entanglements. It is all too rare, Paasonen argues, that analyses of "the dynamics of data capitalism, the algorithmic polarization of sociability, and the political economies of targeted advertising in social media get to meet careful analyses of the micro: the quotidian, the messy, and the felt." Yet what inhabiting the affective ambiguity central to contemporary ecologies (digital or otherwise) urgently requires, she contends, is attention to the imbrication of "diverse scales"—so that "big data analysis meets the care necessary for qualitative inquiry" and "abstract musings of society, culture, and politics are faced with the acuteness of the singular." Relatedly, in McCormack's view, while an elemental approach to structures of feeling might be seen to privilege "a kind of localism or an affirmation of the feeling of [the] present as an immediacy that precludes any grasp of something more planetary," it actually assumes "a much more multivalent role for thinking across the elements of affective life."

All of the chapters featured in this opening section exhibit the myriad tensions, never to be fully resolved, not only in affect theory's established lineages and coordinates but also within and across a diverse array of affective routes, resources, and rhythms. As they show, complicating and transforming the "taxonomies of what affect theory feels and knows today" (Frank and Wilson 2020, 9) demands not "doing away with the mess but [rather] working with and within it" (Paasonen, this volume). This calls for ongoing efforts "to grasp the feeling of the presencing of the present" while holding open different space-times for "minor projects of collective world making" (McCormack, this volume). Elements, tensions, and mess in solution—they can make worlds and/or destroy them. This can feel rather immense (and it is), so let us shift the compositional scale. In the next section, our authors take up the affective role of "the minor."

Minor Feelings and Sensorial Possibilities of Form

A focus on the tonalities and possibilities of "the minor" has become increasingly vital to the development of contemporary affect theories. Erin Manning (2016) argues in *The Minor Gesture* that the minor is not simply what is seemingly insignificant or happening at a micro level, nor does it necessarily correspond with the figure of "the marginal"—although it might well encompass any and all of these. Rather, following Deleuze and Guattari's articulation, the minor names those continually unfolding, yet often un(re)cognized, dynamics that "open up experience to its potential variation" (1). If the major is identified according to predetermined principles of value and significance, the minor loosely indexes the unpredictable, aleatory forces that run through it all, creating or signaling possibilities for established formations and tendencies to materialize differently.[15] Engaging with minor affective registers, in this view, requires attending to experience as it feeds forward—a practice that resonates not only with the so-called Spinoza-Deleuze-Massumi tradition but also with Sedgwick's (2003) call for honing our capacity to sense change as it is actually happening. It is, as Williams (1977, 134) puts it, about becoming oriented to that which "hovers at the very edge of semantic availability" or perhaps akin to Bergson's (1999) "intuition"—an immersive form of sensorial engagement with the richness and flux of material life, which operates in excess of analytical thought.[16]

As our contributors highlight, however, other crucial resources for thinking affect and the minor move beyond Deleuze and Guattari's philosophy to engage cultural theory, feminist, queer, trans, and critical race studies, and Black thought. Sianne Ngai's (2005, 1) *Ugly Feelings* beautifully assembles a range of minor and otherwise politically ambiguous affects—envy, irritation, anxiety, stuplimity, paranoia, and animatedness—associated with "the politically charged problem of obstructed agency" (32). For Ngai, the analytic advantage of engaging the minor is that "the unsuitability of weakly intentional feelings for forceful or unambiguous action is precisely what amplifies their power to diagnose situations" (27). In this way, Ngai's account intersects with Berlant's (2011) diagnosis in *Cruel Optimism* of our affective "impasse" within crisis-ordinary conditions of deteriorating political and economic possibility, or more recently, Cathy Park Hong's (2020) rendering in *Minor Feelings* of the involuted affects that arise when one, as Asian American, lives "under a softer panopticon, so subtle that it's internalized, in that we monitor ourselves, which characterizes our conditional existence" (202). There is also, of course, Sara Ahmed's exploration of these histories—whether through her foundational account of *The Cultural Politics of Emotion* (2004) or her suggestive engagement with the more minor (and often less affirmative) affects of happiness (2010).

Particularly compelling is the way that these inhabitations of the minor are linked to a multiplicity of moods and modes of experimental inquiry drawing on affect theory's penchant for doing academic writing otherwise. Think, for instance, of Kathleen Stewart's (2007, 4) carefully honed attention to "things that are in motion and that are defined by their capacity to affect and be affected" in *Ordinary Affects*; Ann Cvetkovich's (2013) mixing of memoir and critical essay to explore depression otherwise to medical models; or Heather Love's (2010, 375) mobilization of Erving Goffman's and Bruno Latour's microsociology to outline an alternative approach to interpretation that is "close but not deep." In *The Hundreds*, Berlant and Stewart (2019) experiment by imposing the creative constraints of precise hundred-word limits (100, 200, 300 . . .) and techniques of "amplified description" to attune to how affect comes to take form (or not) across contemporary scenes. Consider also the haunting force of Saidiya Hartman's account of the Atlantic slave trade articulated through her own journey along the slave route in Ghana in *Lose Your Mother* (2007), as well as her genre-defying fabulation of the inner lives of Black women in post-emancipation New York and Philadelphia in *Wayward Lives, Beautiful Experiments* (2019). In pushing forward the sensorial possibilities of form, these authors all channel "the power of writing to engender new forms of life" (Berlant and Stewart 2019, n.p.) and engage the minor in ways that evade the pitfalls of what Sedgwick called "paranoid critique."

Taking these affective legacies in new directions, the authors featured in this section explore how affect transforms written expression across the public and scholarly domains, with a range of aesthetic and politicoethical implications. In her chapter "Minor Feelings and the Affective Life of Race," Ann Cvetkovich follows the recent migration of critical race theory and feminist and queer affect theory into creative nonfiction and other experimental genres of public writing, as exemplified by Claudia Rankine's *Citizen* (2014) and Maggie Nelson's *The Argonauts* (2015). Of particular interest here is how the genre of the nonfiction essay is transforming, and spawning new categories such as "creative nonfiction," "lyric essay," and "autotheory" through efforts to convey the racialized and queer ordinary as structures of feeling. Focusing on Cathy Park Hong's *Minor Feelings* (2020) and Billy-Ray Belcourt's *A History of My Brief Body* (2020)—works that respectively weave personal narrative with affect scholarship to encounter Asian American and queer Indigenous experience—Cvetkovich explores how these authors mobilize a "complex web of citationality" to address minor feelings beyond "Black-white binarisms" and in ways that "expand what counts as theory." The result is an intersectional affective praxis of the minor that scrambles the juxtaposition of "positive and negative affects, or critique and reparative strategies" so that "mourning and joy, pessimism and utopia, are not distinct."

Extending this scholarship to confront the affective ambivalence and "trauma ordinariness" that pervades contemporary trans experience, Hil Malatino, in his chapter "Resisting the Enclosure of Trans Affective Commons," addresses the "ensemble of bad feelings"—anxiety, rage, fatigue, exhaustion, anger, fear, and loneliness—that makes trans folks especially vulnerable to emergent forms of predatory capitalism, such as venture capital–funded hormone subscription and telehealth services. For Malatino, the proliferation of such services points to a troubling "nexus of trans precarity, economic pre-dation, and negative affect" alongside a cruelly optimistic investment in "capitalism's reparative capacity" (Berlant and Greenwald 2012, 77). In this way, Malatino's chapter pushes forward Ngai's, Berlant's, and Ahmed's legacies, while also articulating with Puar's (2017) power-ful account of "debility" as the underside of claims to affective capacity, whose minor graspings and rhythms demand but often fall beneath recognition. Across this work, the minor pulses through the mundane, the ordinary, and the everyday to illuminate the ongoing injuries and foreclosures of neocolonialism, neoliberalism, racial capitalism, and induced precarity—while also striving to open up the not-always-visible potentialities for alternative modes of affective social life.

Yet as several contributors to the reader underscore, tarrying with minor registers of feeling can also disclose the residual and exclu-sionary humanisms of affect theory itself. Thinking with Toni Mor-rison's novel *Beloved* (1986) and Charles Burnett's film *Killer of Sheep* (1977), Rizvana Bradley's chapter, "Too Thick Love, or Bearing the Unbearable," locates an indeterminate genre of feeling characterized by the racially gendered modes of slowness, exhaustion, bitterness, and perseverance, which she suggests reveal the impossibility of a universal grammar of fatigue in an anti-Black world. If Williams's structures of feeling are frequently animated in affect studies to explore the possibilities of inhabiting affective duration as it unfolds, Brad-ley considers how centering *Black affect* demands engagement with "a temporality without duration." As "blackness confronts a nexus of stolen pasts, of protracted presents without presence, of futurities withheld," Black experience, as conjured too in the *Killer of Sheep* and other Black cinematic invocations, "unfolds in the absence of the tem-poral horizon that freedom bestows to the human" (Warren 2018, 97, cited in Bradley, this volume). Bradley is particularly concerned here with the affective life of the Black maternal—a figure who, as hor-rifyingly enacted by *Beloved*'s Sethe, "is fated to *reproduction* of fugi-tive survival as well as social death." Too thick love, in this context, is the Black (feminine) affect that registers in the world as "bitterness, obsession, or madness" but is precisely where "the accumulations of the nonevent of Black existence *remain*."

Whereas Bradley figures too thick love as a maternal genre of Black affect in the violent aftermath of transatlantic slavery, Omar

Kasmani's chapter, "Migration: An Intimacy," addresses his own version of "thickness" as an affective manifestation of European colonialisms. Thickness, he suggests, is European history's pervasive and
suffocating sense of mastery, certainty, and knowingness—against
which migrant affect is inevitably "marked by a sense of thinness," a
sense of "being forever short of history in the city." But as Kasmani
shows through a vivid, third-person ethnographic scenography of
queer Muslim migrant "(be)longing" in Berlin, thinness may also
take shape as a mode of resistance to persistent Eurocentric demands
for transparency and knowability. Kasmani's sensuous writing functions less to reveal or magnify particular affective experiences than to
create atmospherics of the "hazy, not entirely knowable, opaque."
Thin, in this way, conjures the porosity of bodies and scenes that touch
briefly to then slide in proximities that do not quite stick in the usual
ways, that come up short but leave traces nonetheless. As an affective genre of the minor, thinness signals how migrant affects "be they
partial, personal, or permeable forms that evade public gaze and
scrutiny, even intelligibility—*infrathin* in Erin Manning's terms—
bear political and outward resonance all the same." By weaving lived
experiences of porosity and opacity with haptic texturings of affect,
Kasmani approaches the intimate "beyond the confessional," while
assembling "archives, journeys, and genealogies foreclosed by a largely
Christian and Western Europe and North America centering grain of
affect studies."

As the chapters in this section illustrate, approaching the minor involves not only attuning to emergent processes active beside or "beneath
the surface of everyday life" but also addressing how "embodied habits
are (re)produced through dominant modes of social intelligibility which
often work in exclusionary and violent ways" (Pedwell 2021, xvii, 7). And
yet, across these contributions, what constitutes the minor in and
for affect theory is not only a realm of indistinct, marginalized, or
neglected feelings but also "the conduit, the orientation, that angles
otherwise" (Manning, this volume) enabling relationalities and tendencies in germ to sprout in unexpected—sometimes fugitive—
places and times. Although there is no one way to anticipate such
arrivals or to prefigure their flourishing or withering, the next section
of the reader addresses how practices of "unlearning" can contribute
to an ethicoaesthetic that attunes to pedagogies of event care.

Unlearning and the Conditions of Arrival

Throughout her book *Unthinking Mastery*, Julietta Singh is committed to undoing discourses of colonial mastery by returning, over and over again, to dehumanized practices of learning. By evacuating the place of the master (whether an external figure, an institution, a particular discourse, or one's self), Singh believes that nothing of great significance is being subtracted from the educational process; instead, the swirling circumambience of everything that had not been previously admitted in the pedagogical scene *begins to show up*. As she puts it, "Education in this sense is a transformative act of becoming profoundly vulnerable to other lives, other life forms, and other 'things' that we have not yet accounted for or that appear only marginally related to us" (Singh 2018, 67). Such a reimagining of pedagogic practice is never straightforward or guaranteed to produce measurable or positive (un)learning outcomes. So much can and does run astray, go haywire, backfire spectacularly. It goes without saying that unlearning will always transpire simultaneously with learning, and exactly who or what inhabits either side of this equation is dependent on the embodyings of lived experience in and across specific contexts.

As Ariella Aïsha Azoulay (2019, 17) argues in *Potential History: Unlearning Imperialism*, "Unlearning is a way of assuming that what seems catastrophic today to certain groups was already catastrophic for many other groups, groups that didn't wait for critical theory to come along to understand the contours of their dispossession and the urgency of resisting it and seeking reparation." This is one of the reasons why Azoulay advocates for unlearning "with companions"—because we are going to absolutely need each other (including nonhuman others) if we are to "reject the effectuated" (15). But here, we will add, this also requires learning to reject or reinflect what has been and continues to be *affectuated*. In this section of the reader, our authors address various modes of coming to know, of coming to *un*know, of the *feelings* that precede/accompany/linger in the contextual matterings of knowing and unknowing, of the care required in tending to knowledges and how knowledge travels (whether in classrooms, across time, between cultures, among and through bodies), *and* when/where learning must entail unlearning.

M. Gail Hamner's chapter, "Unlearning Affect," calls directly "for unlearning the racial logics of enclosure by unlearning affect." In the midst of the racialized impasse associated with what has been called "cancel culture" or "consequence culture" in the United States (and beyond), Hamner draws on the scholarship of Denise Ferreira da Silva and Sylvia Wynter to illustrate how racial privilege sediments in the affectively attuned philosophies of J. G. Herder, G. W. F. Hegel, and C. S. Peirce. In doing so, she frames our contemporary impasse as rooted in what Ferreira da Silva calls "onto-epistemological presumptions" and what Silvan Tomkins understands as "scripts": "elements of personal-social being that are structured, intangible, and resistant to change" (Hamner, this volume). Although intensely polarized public and social media discourses may "succeed in public shaming, in speaking truth to power, or rallying one's base," genuine transformation, Hamner argues, depends on "the task of unlearning our affects." And this task is concomitant with unlearning whiteness.

The kind of undoing and unlearning of racialized universalisms that animates Hamner's contribution is materially situated by Nathan Snaza in his case study at his home institution of the University of Richmond. In his "Why This? Affective Pedagogy in the Wake," Snaza addresses Richmond's racialized histories and their "conditions of arrival" into our present moment. His pedagogical orientation is attentive to how method and "event care" can resist and/or disrupt humanist (and disciplinary and institutional) enclosure. Mobilizing Christina Sharpe's *In the Wake* (2016), a book powerfully focused on the destructive wake of transatlantic slavery, Snaza's chapter considers what "wake work" might entail—in our classrooms and far beyond—for subjects variously oriented to "the ongoingness of antiblackness as it shapes the ongoing mattering of the world." For white people in particular, Snaza contends that the pedagogical imperative is to shift what is framed as "background to foreground, to notice the hum, pay 'maximal' attention, and bring what you can to the *event*." In the writing of both Snaza and Hamner, then, at stake is "how to care for *this* event such that whatever it is we bring to it tends somewhere otherwise than coloniality and antiblackness" (Snaza, this volume). How, they ask, can affect inquiry help us to register those forces that perpetually sift through the matter of "what counts as human, as kin?"—in classrooms, university architectures and site markers, curricular and disciplinary formations, and other deeply embedded colonialisms—

to reveal "the multidirectional violence that saturates the situations we move through?" (Snaza, this volume).

Processes of learning/unlearning always transpire in the midst of enclosures and disclosures of all sorts: institutional, architectural, interpersonal, historical, habitual. Calling a class to order (or not). Using that textbook and those old notes (or not). Trying to get a "read" on the evolving classroom atmospherics. Anticipating the conditions of arrival and/or the lines of departure. Realizing when a particular set of disciplinary practices or knowledges must be shed, reshaped, contracted, or expanded. As Singh (2018, 119) writes, "If we can learn how to recognize our own surprising complicities with dehumanization, we can also learn how to abide with others (human, inhuman, and dehumanized) that have enabled us to become particular kinds of masterful subjects. Precisely in this abiding, in consciously reading ourselves and attaching ourselves to that which we have [been] subjected, we can begin to learn how to become differently relational with others." To abide—by rejecting the affectuated in order to become differently relational with others, to hold on to each other (or some thing), to find companions within and across difference and otherness that is not based on resemblance or species or even on drawing a distinction between living and nonliving.

A moment of pause, though: mere appeals to "care" and "relationality" that often follow in the task of unlearning will, of course, never be enough to save us or our worlds—indeed, such appeals can sometimes act to further perpetuate harm and violence. Crucially, Snaza (alongside others in this section and across this reader) works to contest any sort of one-size-fits-all affective solutionism or universal applicability into other events/episodes, into *your* situation— what Rebecca Adelman (2015) has called, in a different context, the maneuver of the "affective auto-complete." For Snaza, the pedagogic force of the deictic (Why *this*?) operates as a wedge into the singularizing *this-ness* that "is hyperindexical, oriented toward exactly what is happening *here, now* without assuming or requiring that the deictic situation homogenizes." As we have said above, it all always depends.

Perhaps this is why unlearning X nearly always requires a profound wrestling with the *feeling* that inevitably accompanies knowing, especially in those circumstances in which knowing presents itself as omniscient mastery, as universal applicability. Upending the underexamined acquisition of saturated/situated forms of music expertise, disciplinary training, and mastery, Dylan Robinson and Patrick Nickleson want to open up the ears of music studies to otherwise "listening positionalities" by troubling what counts as the "feeling of knowing music." Their chapter asks, "How should we name the mechanism by which music scholarship builds disciplinary knowledge on top of or in relation to shared affective and loving experiences of music?" Robinson and Nickleson wish to reshape the textures of the music encounter by redirecting music listening from the realm of object dissection, resource extraction, and settler colonial-derived possession. They ask us to, instead, consider music and sound in the context of "animate relations" in the sensory spaces of listening and music making. What moves in the slivers and expanses of sensory mixity and wonder that Indigenous epistemologies of music studies can disarticulate and re-animate in ways that are *otherwise* to the persistent automaticities of settler colonial listening practices? This generative querying of the commonplaces of bodily receptivity (as never entirely natural or neutral) and then tuning into what is present but viscerally unavailable within normate listening positionalities epitomizes the themes that organize this section of the reader: utilizing counteraffectuating techniques as unlearning in order to foster more capacious conditions of arrival.

The chapters here explore what processes and politics are involved in (un)learning affective autocompletions and (re)inhabiting everyday modes of knowing, feeling, and receptivity (Highmore 2011) in radically other ways. Although many of the chapters in this section attend primarily to the psychic, pedagogical, sociobiological, and politicoeconomic force relations that figure *human* affective life, in the next section we offer a parallel body of affect scholarship that emphasizes what transpires in encounters with what is "more than human" and "other than conscious" and that resists any ready assumptions that such matters are simply another "construct of the human" (Massumi 1995, 100).

The Matter of Experience, or, Reminding Consciousness of Its Necessary Modesty

In his preface to the twentieth-anniversary edition of *Parables for the Virtual*, Brian Massumi (2021, xiii) does not mince words: "I have never identified what I do as affect studies or identified myself as an affect theorist." Yet it is not as if Massumi is trying especially hard to run away from what has transpired as affect theory after his profoundly significant book (stepping off as it does with "The Autonomy of Affect" essay as its first chapter). Indeed, Massumi's new introduction is immediately followed by two glossaries on . . . affect! Massumi is, however, primarily reacting to two irksome matters in the study of affect: (1) treating affect like an object, a thing, a noun when affect is, instead, in motion, in solution, processual, of the event, and (2) subsequently treating this mistakenly stilled concept of affect as an object of thought, as an area of study that gives rise to a disciplinary practice known as affect theory. We hope that it is already clear from our opening arguments about "getting off on the wrong foot in affect studies" that Massumi's misgivings engage in a similar dance with our own. And although Massumi holds that his insights into "movement," "sensation," and especially "the virtual" are his most pertinent contributions to contemporary critical-aesthetic philosophy, we would insist that these generative operators are rather thoroughly co-immersed with the processuality of affect.

In his essay "The Autonomy of Affect" (published a few years before its inclusion in *Parables*), Massumi (1995) sought to develop a framework for affective and material life attuned to processes of emergence and potentiality (i.e., the virtual) at work both above and below "the subject." Often misunderstood, "autonomy" is not a mystical beyondness but rather the diffuse everywhere/everywhen-at-onceness of intensity. Autonomy is not an immutable locale or residence but is made and remade through the cyclings of affect as precipitate and producibility, as bodies and worlds recursively engage each other. But these intensities, especially through their pulsings and cyclings, are not "in" a body (or, at least, not "in" a body any more than "in" a world); they are "in" the coming-into and falling-out-of encounter or contact, of mutual and myriad impingements. Autonomy is the name that Massumi (2002, 36) gives to the nonplace (because it is potentially *every* place) where relationality is affectively strung between/within/among bodies and worlds: "continuous, like a background perception that accompanies every event, however quotidian." Autonomy does not transcend the given but is immanent with it, continually shuffling, reconfiguring, and smudging points of intensity and rejiggering modes of relationality (including nonrelationality). Again, this is not some otherworldly or fantastical hypothesis, but it is "speculative" in the sense of daring to address what gives shape and texture to intertwining emergent and residual conditions of moment-by-moment existence by attending to what perceptually (and perpetually) passes beneath notice, along or just beyond the fringes of awareness.

Extending this more speculative route, various affect scholars have increasingly turned to the writings of Alfred North Whitehead. Massumi (2021, xiii) himself acknowledges that following the publication of *Parables*, Whitehead's work would exert a greater influence across his subsequent writings. Whitehead, in books like *Process and Reality* (1929), *Adventures of Ideas* (1933), and *Modes of Thought* (1938), questioned the anthropocentrism central to modern Western rationality and offered a view of the world as composed of fundamentally interrelated processes and events. His desire to harmonize the insights of mathematical physics and the intuitions of sensory empiricism led him to offer an account of affective life as at once patterned and open ended and always more than human.

Throughout his career, Whitehead was particularly concerned to interrogate (as we mentioned above) what he called "the bifurcation of nature": that is, the artificial separation between nature itself and our sensory awareness of it. His concept of "process" sought to reconcile this divide by offering a framework in which "the red glow of the sunset" and "the molecules and electric waves that compose it share the same ontological status" (Whitehead 2004, 29). We might say, then, that for Whitehead, affect is what signals and provides access to the imbrication of ontology and epistemology central to an aesthetics of material experience. In this view, as Steven Shaviro (2014, 3) puts it, "I do not come to know a world of things outside myself. Rather, I discover—which is to say, I *feel*—that I myself, together with things that go beyond my knowledge of them, are all alike inhabitants of a 'common world.'" For many scholars, one particularly rousing implication of Whitehead's framework is the opportunity to relinquish any persistent investment in accounts of agency centrally premised on human intentionality.

These and other worldly developments have translated, for some affect theorists, into a fundamental redirection of human experience in relation to processes which "operate predominantly, if not almost entirely, outside the scope of human modes of awareness" (Hansen

2015, 5). Engagements with affect across a number of fields—from speculative realism and object-oriented ontology to various new materialisms, posthumanisms and engagements with computational media—have insisted on this move beyond anthropocentric ontologies. Engaging the complexity of such interventions, this section considers the risks and possibilities of aligning affect more decisively with "anthro-decentric thought" (Chen and Luciano 2015)—whether via the "nonhuman," the "inhuman," the "unhuman," the "more than human," or other conceptual categories—as well as the implications of this for theorizing thought, matter, and (non)consciousness.

Opening this section with his chapter "Nonconscious Affect: Cognitive, Embodied, or Nonbifurcated Experience?" Tony Sampson considers how the growing focus on "the nonconscious" across interdisciplinary literatures acts to "disentangle experience from a problematic human-centered perspective." In recent writings, an array of affective and new materialist interventions has expanded "the capacity of affect to an inclusive human and nonhuman world of agential organic and inorganic matter." Yet influential posthumanities work, in this case N. Katherine Hayles (2017) in her *Unthought: The Power of the Cognitive Nonconscious*, can go astray when consciousness is seen "as the end product of a leveling-up process" (Sampson, this volume). This is a leveling up that saws off each rung of the ladder as it climbs in order to make a firm distinction between higher level cognizant actors and lower level noncognizers (Hayles and Sampson 2018). For Sampson, affect theories and new materialisms do not presume the progressive winking-out of such noncognizers through a gradual ascent to consciousness but instead must retain them—as ongoing force encounters—in nonbifurcated imbricatedness.

This is not meant to elide the role of cognition, as Hayles claims, but rather to adopt an approach to worldly "experience" in which cognition is understood as a "foothold" and not a command post (Sampson 2020, 38). Not dissimilarly, Nietzsche—as Deleuze (1983, 39) notes—believed that one must "remind consciousness of its necessary modesty." To this end, Sampson explores the potentialities of a Whiteheadian nonconscious in which "there is no dichotomy between the human and what is experienced." In line with Whitehead's rejection of any bifurcation between mindful experience and matter, what is crucial to the study of affect and (non)consciousness within this ontology "is that mind and the liveness of matter only become analyzable when they are taken together in the temporal thickness of events" (Sampson, this volume), It is not, in other words, human consciousness that draws attention to experience. Rather, experience is untethered from human embodiment and cognition; it unfolds "outside of thought, *in the event*" and culls consciousness into modes of attention.

Yet in the face of this radically more-than-human perspective, other scholars insist that now is precisely the time to return to "the human"—to interrogate the biopolitical and geopolitical processes through which hierarchical forms of life continue to be (re)produced and subsequently to address their material and ethical implications. As many of the contributions to this reader illuminate, some of the most powerful and insightful engagements with the contemporary affective politics of "the human" emerge from the tradition of radical Black thought engaged with the work of W. E. B. Du Bois, Frantz Fanon, Aimé Césaire, Sylvia Wynter, Hortense Spillers, Denise Ferreira da Silva, Saidiya Hartman, and others. Although some accounts of affect and "the nonhuman" advocate a deprivileging of epistemology, many of the above thinkers insist that epistemology remains crucial to how a particular genre of the human—homo economicus—has been ontologized as natural according to Western imperialist viewpoints. Sylvia Wynter traces, in this respect, how "the empirical and experiential lives of *all* humans are increasingly subordinated to a figure that thrives on accumulation" (Wynter and McKittrick 2015, 9). Rather than approaching the human as "an ontological fait accompli," Wynter theorizes *being human as praxis* to open up possibilities for "thinking and living enfleshment otherwise" (Weheliye 2014, 8). In different ways, then, this scholarship explores the potentialities of a radical *counterhumanism* that asks how humanness might inhabit a different future.

What these interventions underscore emphatically is that a guiding tendency within much affect theory (as well as other modes of critical thought) to reflexively abandon androcentric narratives may be both problematic and premature if it fails to address the histories of dehumanization *present within* articulations of nonhuman agency and potentiality. As Zakiyyah Iman Jackson (2015, 15) maintains, the vital question to ask in response to posthumanist, object-oriented, and new materialist calls to move beyond the human is "what and crucially *whose* conception of humanity are we moving beyond?" In her view, such philosophical injunctions may also entail fraught attempts to "move *beyond* race, and in particular blackness" that "cannot be escaped but only disavowed or dissimulated" in such frameworks (16; original emphases). Because speculative engagement with what exceeds the human is one key feature of affect theorizing, the need to finesse these matters—within their highly particular conditions of arrival and across their persistences—will, needless to say, always be crucial.

One way of figuring these conditions—in which racialized, sexualized, and gendered pasts and presents are entangled with more-than-human temporalities, forces, and genealogies—entails, as Mel Chen and Dana Luciano (2015, 189) maintain, holding (at least) two inflections of the nonhuman together: one that invokes the possibility of "transmaterial affections" and the "proliferation of difference" and one that recognizes ongoing forms of "indifference and brutality." This ontoepistemological challenge points up, among other things, the need to attend to how "the impersonal" is entwined, immanently, with sedimented relations of force across shifting ecologies of life and the nonliving.

With such worldly entanglements in mind, Erin Manning's chapter, "Catch an Incline: The Impersonality of the Minor," explores the textured resonances of Black sociality in proximate relation to the process philosophies of Whitehead, Bergson, and Deleuze. Expanding the account of "minor sociality" she offered in *For a Pragmatics of the Useless*, which brings together matters of Black life and neurodiversity, Manning (2020) suggests that new modes of sociality are required to address those affective tendencies that persist beneath and beyond any sense of self-sustaining subjectivity: by *not* parsing the intelligible, productive, or useful—particularly when "neurotypicality and whiteness combine to form a normative baseline for existence" and hence, for the dominant figurations of "the human." In Manning's chapter, it is "the force of the impersonal" that links Black thought and process philosophy via a "logic of approximation of proximity" which also "recognizes gaps and moves through them." That is, between Black thought and process philosophy, responses to the questions "How are we made?" and "What makes the field through which we recognize ourselves" begin "not in the personal but in the world?" (where, as Sampson also reminds us, Whitehead located "experience"). Instead of foregrounding "the self-serving individual who leads existence" or "the colonial narrative that places [the] subject—whiteness—in advance of the world," these overlapping modes of feeling-thought start from "process, open field." To begin with the impersonal, then, is not to leave race or racialized histories behind but rather to approach the endurance of blackness as "being of relation" and "in the layerings of so many carryings" rather than as "identity." It is also, Manning argues, to appreciate how, amid ongoing forms of biopolitical, geopolitical, and ontopolitical violence, "living otherwise *begins* in the relational field" where "there is no separation between who we are and how we world" (our emphasis).

Extending these discussions of the (contested, fugitive) place of the impersonal, the (non)conscious, and the (non)human in contemporary affect theories, Lisa Blackman's chapter focuses on technologies of the nonrational in the wake of Trumpism and its affective post-truth politics of disinformation, gaslighting, and disbelief. Blackman's archive offers a litany of contemporary forms of domestic and extradomestic abuse (at once, personal and impersonal, social and inhuman/e), focusing primarily on strategic deception and coercive power. Through a writing style that mirrors the chapter's contents, she homes in on the role of counterfactual reasoning amid the swirling concatenations of "registers and modalities for attending to the world that exceed conscious rational thought and that are shared and distributed across the human and more than human." In seeking to retroactively change the past in order to preemptively induce a future where alternate realities can "*feel true*," counterfactual techniques of persuasion, influence, and governance have a close kinship to what Blackman calls "emotions and affects of convolution." These are strange affects that work to disorient, confuse, bewilder, and knock off-kilter. In casting domestic abuse assemblages in light of the waking horrors of the Trump presidency, Blackman's chapter raises important questions concerning Trump's uncanny ability to "exploit, coerce, manipulate, and frame reality such that conspiracy theories, lies, and other forms of mis- and disinformation become contagious and infectious." It is affect studies that, Blackman believes, is "best placed to apprehend, diagnose, and intervene" within such fraught settings—to trace how a domestic scenario for traumatic encounters and forms of nonphysical abuse spirals out of and in to "military, colonial forms of power, media power, [and] soft power."

Situated within a similar set of coordinates but from an altogether different direction, Cecilia Macón's chapter, "Haunting Voices: Affective Atmospheres and Transtemporal Contact," begins with the recorded testimonies of survivors of state-inflicted violence and torture. In her pursuit of the qualities of transtemporality that pervade the oral archives of state terrorism in Chile and Argentina, Macón looks to how social memory and digital media intersect to create atmospheres and materialities of encounter. If Blackman examines how counterfactual modes of reasoning rewrite the past in ways that are often dangerous and damaging, Macón explores how the sound atmospheres of terror, as described by survivors of those traumatic pasts, signal forms of "archival agency" that offer the potential to generate affirmative "political change in the present." As such dynamics underscore, affective atmospheres are "not inert, ghostly things but are entities with agency affected by the practices they generate"—such that "the present can affect the past that is never merely past nor does it survive in an unaltered state." In unfolding the logics and possibilities of "transtemporal contact" in this context, Macón is concerned with the workings of nonhuman agency in which matter not only provides "evidence of external events" but also acts as "witness beyond the realm of the human" (see Schulppie 2020). In this chapter, nonhuman agency is associated with "voices that persist unattached to their original bodies," and archival agency moves across temporal thresholds to, at once, connect and separate (while also coinciding with) the processual passages between past, present, and future of these haunting soundscapes.

Each of the authors in the section ventures into various "beyonds" (of the more-than-, other-than-, non-) to explore what counts (or does not) as fitting under the category of the human: eschewing any ready-made bifurcation of human and nonhuman, accounting rather for what happens when we presume the body to be processually extended into mind and matter at once. Nonbifurcated. We will return to Brian Massumi to wrap up here because, after all, he cannot quite quit affect theory nor are particular theories of affect ready to quit him. Quoting from his "missed conceptions" supplement to *Parables for the Virtual*: "Affect theory does not reduce the mind to the body in the narrow, physical sense. It asserts that bodies think as they feel on a level with their movements. This takes thinking out of the interiority of a psychological subject and puts it directly in the world: in the co-motion of relational encounter" (Massumi 2021, xlvii). The final section of this reader pursues the "co-motion of relational encounter" with a focus on how experiential/experimental procedures are becoming ever more targeted on the capture and control of relational encounter often through affective governance and algorithmic datafications of social reproduction.

A Living Laboratory: Glitching the Affective Reproduction of the Social

In the background of the four chapters that comprise this reader's final section, we would like to imagine a question that hovers, one that sends us back, full circle, to this book's first chapter: What ingredients might be included in a periodic table of elements for affect study?[17] As Derek McCormack suggests, such a table of elements would form "part of an expanded affective empiricism for thinking about, attending to, and where necessary, resisting and reworking the interactive, influential relation between subjects and worlds." One such element uniting the quartet of contributors in this final section of the reader is the *body politic* and, more specifically, how bodies are collectively enlisted, voluntarily and involuntarily, in affective processes of social reproduction, often quite traumatically: to their detriment, their immiseration, their maiming. Turning (directly sometimes) to Gilles Deleuze's remarks on the rise of "control societies," the authors here interrogate the different roles played by the "body" in our contemporary body politic: a body—rendered as skin, as flesh, as data— that is neither a priori resistant/rebellious nor merely acquiescent but strung along and among, as McCormack states, all manner of "forces and bonds through which worlds cohere and dissolve or become variously toxic and nourishing."

Deleuze sketches out his control societies argument in two places: "Postscript on the Societies of Control" and in an interview with Antonio Negri, "Control and Becoming." With "control," Deleuze (1995) extends Michel Foucault's broad periodization of two earlier logics of sociopolitical formation into a third phase:

I *Sovereign societies*—a period roughly from the end of Dark Ages to the Enlightenment in which the sovereign's body itself secured the force of law while, correspondingly, the subject's body can be made to suffer a range of spectacular (public) physical punishments if determined to violate the sovereign body/law.

2 *Disciplinary societies*—a period from the Enlightenment to the mid-twentieth century of governmentality and subjectivation that expected citizens to conduct themselves through various, institutionally derived identities/molds (patient, student, worker, spectator) in order to conform to routinized practices of embodied docility that work to preserve and reproduce social cohesion.

3 *Control societies*—a period beginning around the 1950s and continuing today characterized by the rise of multinational corporate capitalism and its near-eclipse of the nation-state as the prime organizer of sociopolitical dynamisms, the arrival of computational culture and cybernetization, and the ascent of the modulation of consumer/debtor as suturing modes of subjectivation.

As we will see in Ezekiel Dixon-Román's chapter in this section, it is crucial to draw attention to how Sylvia Wynter's descriptive statements or *genres* of "Man 1" (European man's shift from theological to secular) and "Man 2" (homo economicus) align with Foucault "on the selection of the markers of the epistemological transformations that constitute modern thought" (Ferreira da Silva 2015, 96), but also foundationally center race and coloniality in any thoroughgoing account of the long history of the Human.[18] How these operational logics of power and domination continue today are addressed in the chapters by Dixon-Román, Jasbir Puar (who speaks of a "sovereign right to maim" in the Palestinian territories), and Michael Richardson. There is no clean break between these transformations and no uniformity or stability across variously lived subjectivities within and beyond them; they precede at different tempos and with vastly different affective configurations across global spaces and times, persisting/subsisting within and alongside each other.

However one might consider or dispute control societies as an analytic, it seems undeniable that new twists in the reproduction of the social perpetually rise and fall at the level of affect. The authors in this final section unfold these machinations in order to discover where there might be a glimpse or glitch of potentialities that could disrupt, diffract, or disorder societies' most perniciously iterative practices (see also Amoore 2020; Clough 2018). Centrally, it is the work performed by algorithmic architectures that receive our authors' closest examination. Control societies are less invested in molding subjectivities to align with particular institutional forms and more driven by the churn of wealth-and-flesh extraction potentials unleashed through algorithmic modulation: in the composition of both the social field itself and of the individual. Hence why, quite often, daily existence can feel more akin to maneuvering through the shape-shifts of a recursively tailored environmentality (as innumerable facades of "you" refract and circulate in a real-time orbit alongside the mobile trajectory of one's scene changes), rather than in negotiation with the temporal lag of governmentality. In other words, disciplinary societies are almost always disciplining you after the fact, whereas control societies (think "recommendation engines," or the profiling algorithms used by police departments, like PredPol [Benjamin 2019, 83]) nudge a more supple or fungible "you" toward an opening in space-time prepared slightly in advance of your arrival. Deleuze (1995, 180) terms this affective sense of immersive and undulating subjectivity "the dividual"—animated through the calculative processes that disassemble and reassemble infinitely fragmentable bits of self/interest/body/desire/fear/world (all to be parsed but then strung together again in ever-new data configurations). If the individual is ideological and representational with a relatively circumscribed interior/exterior, the dividual is affective, algorithmically enmeshed, and distributed, webbed in relations that can feel half-voluntary and half-enforced (although the scalar dynamics of what appears as "voluntary" and "enforced" can tip ever so gradually or in an instant, depending on the particular force encounters of bodies, histories, scenes).[19]

While Dixon-Román, Puar, and Richardson each engage with the dividual, algorithms, and control societies, this final section leads off with Jason Read's contribution, which reckons with the organization of affect (or the affects) as a unique vantage point into social reproduction and thus willing/unwilling participation in this churn of relations and forces. Beginning with Spinoza's vexing question "Why do people fight for their servitude as though it was their salvation?" Read pursues the ways that Spinoza's query has been updated and reframed, first psycho-socioeconomically by Deleuze and Guattari in 1968 and then more recently by Frédéric Lordon around the matter of labor and social relations, in order to demonstrate how "the intimacy of the economy" is bound up with "the way that work and consumption restructure our desires and joys." Here, Read describes a telling shift in the reproduction of social relations through the body politic:

"it is capital more than the state that organizes common desires and fears in the twentieth and twenty-first century."

Grasping this shift in emphasis is hardly earthshaking (indeed, it is taken for granted these days), yet what is less noticed is how this signals a profound cross-wiring in the affectual composition of subjectivity: flipping the polarities between the contingency of capital's "investment in abstract indifference" and the necessity of the state's investment in securing "identification in specific identities." Hence, with the coronavirus pandemic and the revaluation of (and, perhaps, the "great" resignation from) working life that followed in its wake, something became unsettled in how people live and locate the relation of necessity and contingency as individual/collective laboring bodies. Could this provide a glimpse into some newly resonant configuration for the everyday organization of affect, perhaps an emerging counterlaboring body-politic flashes on the horizon? Or are these threads momentarily left dangling along the frayed edges of subject formation only going to be restitched via newly contoured fears and desires into the sociopolitical fabric?

It is with another kind of sideways hopeful glimpse that Ezekiel Dixon-Román, in his "Algorithmic Governance and Racializing Affect," calls attention to the "indeterminacies of blackness" that exceed capture in algorithmic profiling. Might this excess become a resource for pushing the regenerative capacities and debilities of racialized capital into more open-ended loopings that slip beyond algorithmically shaped autopoietic enclosure? Through the more-than-material immanence of flesh, Dixon-Román considers how the fugitivity of blackness might provide unforeseen opportunities for glitching the performative force of calculative spatiotemporalizations. His argument—with its deployment of Sylvia Wynter's sociogenic principle and Denise Ferreira da Silva's critique of the "transparent I" of Eurocentric philosophy— could be productively read alongside M. Gail Hamner's chapter earlier in this reader, especially as both seek critical approaches that might cause racially debilitating narratives and computer protocols to jump their tracks.

The recalcitrant and reconstituted fleshy dividual serves as the source of both promise and threat for Black futurity, or as Alexander Weheliye (2014, 40) argues, flesh is "the ether that holds together the world of Man while at the same time forming the conditions of possibility for the world's demise."[20] From the perspective of bodily inhabitation, Michelle Ann Stephens (2014, 201), in her *Skin Acts*, writes, "In the experience of living in, being in, one's skin, the flesh is an aspect of the self one discovers on the edge, on the hide just as it is being shed, just as one enters the symbolic order to stand before the Other's gaze." For Dixon-Román, flesh haunts, as overflow and abundance on the cusp of entry to and exit from the dividuating order, as a "potentiation of value" coursing through the machines of algorithmic governance. There are, however, no ready-made assurances in such "a radical recursive praxis," just potentiation (that might not even be "just").

Then Jasbir Puar, in her chapter, "Dividual Economies, of Data, of Flesh," looks to the intricate and porous relations among flesh, calculation, and the marking of time itself, especially as enmeshed in the lacerating, excruciating slownesses of Palestinian life. How does the indeterminacy and the uncertain calculus of datafication become "a folded-into-the-flesh condition of possibility, an ontology of flesh as felt?" Algorithms, as Puar shows, are not only operationalized through machines and/or at a distance but also manifest up close in the physical arrangements of the material world and in movements through heavily monitored and cordoned landscapes that work, alternately, to capacitate and incapacitate. Looking at how architectures of containment and performance-based art installations converge on "an art of quantification," Puar's chapter shows "how dividualization is both digital and of the flesh, involving series of recursive relationalities as well as a way of 'unseeing' and reseeing corporeality." Reminiscent of Hortense Spillers's (1987, 68) vital insights into how "the divided flesh" of the captive body becomes a "living laboratory" for all shape and manner of procedures for objectification, mutilation, and atomization, Puar indexes the brutal parsings of contemporary dividuation: how it acts to contain not only movement undertaken but "what movement is imagined to be" and how body parts (eyes, knees, ankles) "float free of the human form" so that maiming can be justified as humanitarian. But also, what do the practices of living through the pandemic in places already dwelling in precarity, like Palestine, have to teach us about "inhabiting temporalities askew" and about "the potentiality in dividual economies"? Puar argues that answers to these questions cannot adequately be divined through techniques or strategies of representation but instead must engage with nonrepresentational critique.

Michael Richardson concludes this section by weaving between and through the layerings and modalities of trauma induced by the algorithm. If Puar shows how algorithmic logic wends beyond its black box to modulate physical infrastructures as well as prehend the potential for movement, Richardson asks, how do the world's movements and the recursive jitterings of algorithms themselves rebound back onto this process as a whole? Richardson writes, "Algorithms are instruments of worlding (Stewart 2007), their affective ensembles pulsing into operative form within and between computational architectures and fleshy, social bodies alike." What would it mean to understand the affectability of the algorithm itself as shot through/ saturated by trauma and not only the capacity of the algorithm as stirrer of trouble and instigator of trauma?

Trauma is now transmediated across the entirety of the social field by algorithms in ways that more traditional media—say film, radio, newspapers, television in the time of disciplinary societies—could really only dispense within the space-time of their particular mode of individuating enclosure. As trauma becomes automated (capturing, calculating, and feeding data forward in real time), it impinges "on the human sensorium" in massive and dividualized ways, immense to miniscule: from the full-scale rupture of the traumatic event to the slimmest registerings of microdynamics of bodily adjustments and rupturings, bundled together and affectively interpenetrating. Here, algorithms themselves can be as troubled as much as they are troubling (see also Amoore 2020). Richardson maintains that "algorithmic systems cannot be corrected away from the production of trauma because they are always already traumatic, constituted on the one hand by the trauma cultures from which they arise and on the other hand by the radical disjunctures in their own operative, determinative processes." Just as Puar calls for nonrepresentational critique, Richardson advocates for an "affective politics" that addresses algorithmic trauma by rejecting its "computational rationality" and its hyperefficient, problem-solving mythos and rather, wrestles with all the trouble and trauma—the psychoses, contingency, viscerality, and unknowability—of messy, fleshy-worldly entanglements.

What kind of methods might be adopted by an affective politics that addresses algorithmic trauma? We are reminded of the Wynterian methodologies of Katherine McKittrick (2021, 106n9) and her discussion of blackness and algorithms from the chapter "Failure (My Head Was Full of Misty Fumes of Doubt)" in *Dear Science and Other Stories*.[21] Here McKittrick catches the essence of the messy, fleshy-worldly entanglements of this "living laboratory" section in a single footnote: "If black life is the nonuniform problem, we might sit with this and its attendant noncomputability. If entered (recorded, logged), within the context of computation, black life might offer us multiple ways to unthink the problematic enfleshment of algorithms because it is an irresolvable variable, if entered (recorded, logged) into the equation, and within the working with and working out stages, the unsolvable also provides the opportunity to sit with unpredictability-entropy as this relates to the potential, not only for death-dealing, technologies of human life" (2021, 106). Throughout her poignant unfolding of this problematic, McKittrick tries to make her way toward an algorithm that ends anywhere other than Black death. She fails at every turn. So much of mathematics, like the training sets used to build algorithms, has only ever reckoned with Black livingness as a problem, with Black as always already marked for death. Deploying an algorithm within existing systems of racialized knowledge only arrives at this conclusion faster.

If we are to get elsewhere, then we need to start somewhere else. "What happens," McKittrick wonders, "to our understanding of black humanity when our analytical frames do not emerge from a broad swathe of numbing racial violence but, instead, from the multiple and untracked enunciations of black life?" (105). McKittrick reflects then on her own practice, her methods, and how the questions that she asks over the course of her research "emerge from difficult and unbearable encounters" and do not yield any "predetermined codified answer" (120). This encounter of intensities produces "an unfinished mess and a still-worried and still-curious person who continues to be suspicious of how we come to know, where we know from, and the ways in which many academic methodologies refuse black life and relational thinking" (120). Those immeasurabilities that escape the algorithm are among the "unfinished mess" of elements that must come to populate any real or imagined periodic table for affect studies: relationality, encounter, mess, flesh, body politic, the minor, unlearning, force, ambiguity, and more. "What happens," McKittrick wonders, "if the groove or the song gives insight to the theoretical frame?" (119). Beyond divining what escapes the algorithm and its reproduction of Black death and blank repetition, McKittrick proposes that theory and research and method expand their explanatory/disciplinary frames for understanding and change by starting elsewhere, by finding alternate and otherwise ways to get on the good foot.

Taking our cue from McKittrick, we would like to believe that her methodological interventions work along a similar groove as our desire to foster a shimmer of inventories for affect theory. And further, it is this decidedly other, capacious revisioning of a laboratory for living-ness that our contributors highlight both in this section as well as previous ones. These vital encounters with affect's most basic elements and most expansive worldings inevitably get tangled up in the always unfinished mess of aesthetics/politics, ontology/epistemology, material/immaterial, human/nonhuman/extrahuman.

May these encounters with shimmers and intensities keep opening out to futures, to pasts, to irresolvable tensions and ambiguities that, as Lauren Berlant wished, will never come remotely close to constituting a monoaffective imaginary.

Coda

Our reader finishes with "A Note" from Katie Stewart and a collection of prose poems from Lauren Berlant's final writings titled "Poisonality." In the spirit of Lauren's experiments with Katie in the sensorial constraints and possibilities of form in *The Hundreds* (2019), we will end with this resonant inventory of all things Lauren:

LAUREN: AN INVENTORY

1 Lauren admits, in "Final Words," the penultimate entry in the "Poisonality" collection, that when it comes to the affect word *shimmer*, she/they[22] cannot relate. Lauren is less of a shimmerer, more of an inventorier: "a dog in a sea of crotches."

2 Like anyone making an inventory, Lauren enumerates elements: sometimes with numbers, sometimes in lists, sometimes with nots. Witness "Funny Story." What makes a funny story? Lauren initially sniffs out a few of its inherent properties, often by way of analogy but mostly by encircling the genre of the funny story with all it is not. Not an anecdote. Not magical. Not demanding. Not really memorable

or forgettable. Not generalizable. Not intimate. Not a psychological genre. Not a treasure. Not a trauma. This is not a process of elimination, though. It is a process of becoming attuned, of resonance conducting. Each of these nots carry their own shimmer of inventories, leaving faintly affective traces that generate a collective undertow as one means for feeling around a scene or a thing. Or as Lauren concludes "Poisonality's" opening vignette, "feeling around the middle for a tug in any direction that can seem like an intention."

3   Lauren attunes best to ripples in the social fabric of the ordinary, not rents. Episodes, not events. Episodes can foster a pedagogic embodying of capacities for being affected, for converting passive endurance into active, collective participation in the world's continued unfolding. "I am training for a feeling I don't have yet." Events, though, can suddenly heave up and rupture a world in ways that obliterate episodic attunings, in ways that scramble the capacity to caption, in ways that induce genre flailings. What happens when the event of death arrives episodically? Lauren is writing from inside its room. "Can you feel your receptivity? Where is it, can you put your hand on your body where it is?"

4   Lauren works to forestall post-death misreadings. At one point, Lauren writes, "I need phrases to fuel alternative worlds" but then immediately acknowledges that using "alter worlds" would be preferable since it better "suggests how a small shift can open up the image of another world" whereas the use of "alternative worlds" is ill-fitting, too baggy, generically imprecise. How to adequately fit worlds to words that are going to arrive after the author has departed? How to register and cast forward the writerly dimensions of this room right now—where/when Lauren's body can still "quicken to anything: the whatever, the x, all the beloved placeholders"—in order to finesse the receptivity of future readers? "Outside, there are empty shoes at the door that happen to be your size. Inside, there are blocks of time set out for you plural to bullshit and brainstorm collectively, until a problem loses its corset." When inventorying goose-bumps up against its limits (its relative flatness, its tendency to list or enumerate), analogy is the other mode that Lauren employs to do affect's heaviest lifting. The capacity of analogy to open up the image of another world, an alter world, cannot be overstated.

5   In the section titled "Waiting," Lauren makes an inventory of the mood shifts and prehensive adjustments that multiply in the space-

time of awaiting the latest test results from scans and cancer treatments. The list begins:

1 Nothing changed.
2 Everything changed.
3 Everything's better.
4 Some things are. . . .

What are we to make of the fact that Lauren's listing includes an entry for the number 13 both before and then after "12"? What is happening to the sequence, to the flow, here? The corralled number 12 on this list is "remains." Earlier, Lauren defines a remain as "what gets left behind without a plan for it, marking the place of the radically useless." But maybe there is no mystery to unravel here. Maybe it is just a mistake from too much waiting, too much multiplying, too much revising. Of all possible numbers, did it have to be 13 twice, though?

6 But Lauren is not a noun: neither a remain nor remains. And certainly not radically useless. In the vignette "You Have a New Test Result," Lauren retells a story from *Sum: Forty Tales from the Afterlives* by David Eagleman (2009). In the story, people who have died enter a waiting room "where they are stuck until no one on Earth remains to say their name. People who had built monuments to themselves were therefore the last to enter the afterlife, because tour guides and lecturers had a duty to repeat the story of how they had mattered. Death's finitude hovered over them like a blinking cursor." We have, however, taken a different lesson from this story. There are reasons why we have repeated Lauren's name here, repeated "Lauren" again and again. There are reasons why this coda is written in the present tense. Lauren remains. (800)

Notes

The epigraph at the opening of this chapter comes from Helms Gesa, Marina Vishmidt, and Lauren Berlant's "Affect and the Politics of Austerity: An Interview Exchange with Lauren Berlant" in *Variant* 39/40 (Winter 2010).

1 Case in point: Omar Kasmani's gorgeous chapter on affect, belonging, and migration could have easily shimmered into almost any of the other subsections (and did, as we kept turning its facets over and over). Likewise, other chapters, if shuffled and resequenced, could unfold distinctive trajectories into and across affect that reveal ready alignments as well as jabbing counterpositions.

2 The best book-length critique of affect theory to date is Ashley Barnwell's (2020) *Critical Affect: The Politics of Method*. From the perspective of social science, Barnwell looks to both method and genre for ways that affect theory overplays its hand: trumpeting creativity (and the new) over historical continuity with earlier modes of inquiry, too readily caricaturing all that smells of positivism and critique for the boundlessness of poetry and mess. For a few other pertinent critiques with varying degrees of balloon popping acuity, see Andrejevic (2013), Bollmer (2014), Culp (2016), Galloway (2017), Grossberg (2015), Hemmings (2005), Leys (2011, 2017), Martin (2013), Palmer (2017), Papoulias and Callard (2010), and Wetherell (2012, 2015).

3 Greg has learned so much from graduate students and early career scholars as editor at the open access journal *Capacious: Journal for Emerging Affect Inquiry*, http://capaciousjournal.com/.

4 For more on the role of pre- and non- in affect studies, see Seigworth (2014, 2017).

5 Berlant is riffing on Karl Marx's *Economic and Philosophic Manuscripts of 1844* (1964, 141): "The forming of the five senses is a labor of the entire history of the world down to the present." See especially Berlant's lengthy quote from Marx's *1844* manuscripts and his direct theoretical appeal to the senses—"The senses have therefore become directly in their practice theoreticians"—in the first chapter of *Cruel Optimism* (2011, 31).

6 For debates around intentionality in relation to affect theory, see Pedwell (2020) and other pieces in the "Review Symposium on Ruth Leys's *The Ascent of Affect*," *History of Human Sciences* 33 (2). See also Schaefer (2022). Or as Katie Stewart (2017, 124) frames this whole affair in a deliciously succinct clapback: "Meanwhile, back at the academic ranch, the death maws of humanist critique just keep snapping at the *world* as if the whole point of being and thinking is just to catch it in a lie."

7 Nothing in Tomkins's work hints at the necessity of holding the world at arm's length in order to unlock its rightful meaning so as to simultaneously affirm one's own solidity: not when you could go in for a bear hug (actually, it is a kitten named "Bambi" [Sedgwick 2003, 95]) in an attempt to still all that trembles in the wake of feeling (whether too much or its absence).

8 Our thanks to contributor M. Gail Hamner who read the first draft of our editors' introduction and gave us this very helpful and inspiring response: "It feels to me that the words you craft in your opening, before framing and canvassing the chapters, attempt to do for the *study* of affect what you also assert about affect itself, that it, to position it not as a thing or line of inquiry or subdiscipline, but as an *effort*. Because the *study* of affect indexes *effort* and not a stable thing or method, it is floppy, diffuse, profligate, without being abstruse, undecidable, or elusive" (personal communication, July 27, 2021).

9 At the end of *Sex, or the Unbearable*, Berlant (2014, 116–17) writes back to Lee Edelman:

> I insist . . . on a less austere materialism of a continuously contemporary ordinariness, in which beings try to make do and to flourish in the awkward,

riven, unequal, untimely, and interesting world of other beings, abstractions, and forces, and in which we therefore have a shot at transforming the dynamics and the costs of our negativity and appearance. . . . This is what it means to live, and to theorize, experimentally: to make registers of attention and assessment that can change the world of their implication, but also model the suspension of knowing in a way that dilates attention to a problem or scene.

10 To our knowledge, Lauren Berlant never wrote throwaway lines.

11 For more on Sedgwick, reparation, and ambivalence, see Berlant (2019), Pedwell (2014, 2021), Stacey (2014), and Wiegman (2014).

12 See also Chen (2013) and Chen and Luciano (2015).

13 In a similar vein, see Andrew Culp's (2016) *Dark Deleuze*, which advocates for a reading of Deleuze's take on affect as focused on cruelty rather than intensity, as an anti-phenomenology rather than a body's becoming.

14 See, for example, the congenial but carefully delineated position takings between Fred Moten (2018) in *The Universal Machine* and Jarod Sexton (2012, 2017). For something less congenial, see Jesse McCarthy (2021) on Frank Wilderson.

15 See also discussion of affect, habit, and the minor in Pedwell (2021).

16 For an account of the resonances among Bergson's intuition, Deleuze's affect, and Williams's structures of feeling, see Seigworth (2006).

17 See, as one example, Gumbs's (2018) wonderfully realized experiment with the use of the periodic table of elements to chart the movement of energies and elements in M. Jacqui Alexander's and other Black feminist works.

18 See Ferreira da Silva's examination of the overlaps and divergences between Wynter's and Foucault's thought-architectures (2015); also see her critique of Foucault's engagement with the discourse of race in *Unpayable Debt* (2022, 131–35). For an essay that casts Wynter's framework in light of Deleuze's control society, see Hantel (2020).

19 For more on the interrelations of control, affect, algorithms, and the dividual, see Amoore (2020), Beller (2021), Chun (2021), Clough (2018), Clough et al. (2015), Hansen (2015), Massumi (2015), Parisi (2019), and Parisi and Dixon-Román (2020).

20 "Flesh," writes R. A. Judy (2020, 208) in his *Sentient Flesh*, is "an irreducible elemental level of existence." In their *All Incomplete*, Stefano Harney and Fred Moten (2021, 82) address the elemental stakes of the flesh of Black studies in light of Deleuze's appeal to Spinoza:

> Deleuze says we don't yet know what a body can do. Can we imagine what we don't know that flesh can do? Because flesh won't do, it does. Flesh senses extra while, with transatlantic slave trade, capital "invents'" a collectivization of broken, working "bodies." Such invention, such bad sociological finding, can't know that flesh was working, sensing, before capital and its concepts got there. Capital wants to master that mystery, but the incalculable is invaluable no matter how much you count on it, no matter how many times you put a price on it, no matter how regularly and regulatively you lock it up or shoot it down.

21 John Law's *After Method: Mess in Social Science Research* played in the background as we (Greg and Melissa) considered the place and role of method in the first *Affect Theory Reader*. For this second one, Greg and Carolyn have found McKittrick's *Dear Science* to be, along with Lauren Berlant, an ideal soundtrack for providing feedback to our contributors as well as so helpful to our writing of this introduction.

22 Finally, a key detail about Lauren and pronouns. Lauren's estate has provided Duke University Press and us a brief statement on this matter, from which we quote here: "Lauren's pronoun practice was mixed—knowingly, we trust. Faced with queries as to 'which' pronoun Lauren used and 'which' should now be used, the position of Lauren's estate (Ian Horswill, executor; Laurie Shannon, literary executor) is that Lauren's pronoun(s) can best be described as 'she/they.'

"'She/they' captures the actual scope of Lauren's pronoun archive, and it honors Lauren's signature commitment to multivalence and complexity. It also leaves thinkers free to adopt either pronoun, or both of them, as seems most fitting in their own writing about *her/them*."

References

Adelman, Rebecca. 2015. "Feeling Good about Feeling Bad about Aylan Kurdi." *Antenna*, September 22. https://blog.commarts.wisc.edu/2015/09/22/feeling-good-about-feeling-bad-about-aylan-kurdi/.

Ahmed, Sara. 2004. *The Cultural Politics of Emotion*. Edinburgh: Edinburgh University Press.

Ahmed, Sara. 2010. *The Promise of Happiness*. Durham, NC: Duke University Press.

Ahmed, Sara. 2017. *Living a Feminist Life*. Durham, NC: Duke University Press.

Amoore, Louise. 2020. *Cloud Ethics: Algorithms and the Attributes of Ourselves and Others*. Durham, NC: Duke University Press.

Anderson, Ben. 2014. *Encountering Affect: Capacities, Apparatuses, Conditions*. Surrey, UK: Ashgate Publishing.

Andrejevic, Mark. 2013. *Infoglut: How Too Much Information Is Changing the Way That We Think and Know*. New York: Routledge.

Azoulay, Ariealla Aïsha. 2019. *Potential History: Unlearning Imperialism*. London: Verso.

Barnwell, Ashley. 2020. *Critical Affect: The Politics of Method*. Edinburgh: Edinburgh University Press.

Belcourt, Billy Ray. 2020. *A History of My Brief Body*. Toronto: Penguin.

Beller, Jonathan. 2021. *The World Computer: Derivative Conditions of Racial Capitalism*. Durham, NC: Duke University Press.

Benjamin, Ruha. 2019. *Race after Technology*. Cambridge: Polity.

Bergson, Henri. 1999. *An Introduction to Metaphysics*, Indianapolis: Hackett.

Berlant, Lauren. 2011. *Cruel Optimism*. Durham, NC: Duke University Press.

Berlant, Lauren. 2018. "Genre Flailing." *Capacious: Journal for Emerging Affect Inquiry* 1 (2): 156–62.

Berlant, Lauren, ed. 2019. *Reading Sedgwick*. Durham, NC: Duke University Press.

Berlant, Lauren, and Lee Edelman. 2014. *Sex, or the Unbearable*. Durham, NC: Duke University Press.

Berlant, Lauren, and Jordan Greenwald. 2012. "Affect in the End Times: A Conversation with Lauren Berlant." *Qui Parle: Critical Humanities and Social Sciences* 20 (2): 71–89.

Berlant, Lauren, and Kathleen Stewart. 2019. *The Hundreds*. Durham, NC: Duke University Press.

Bollmer, Grant David. 2014. "Pathologies of Affect: The 'New Wounded' and the Politics of Ontology." *Cultural Studies* 28 (2): 298–326.

Bucher, Taina. 2018. *If . . . Then. Algorithmic Power and Politics*. Oxford: Oxford University Press.

Burnett, Charles, dir. 1977. *Killer of Sheep*. Third World Newsreel.

Chen, Mel. 2012. *Animacies: Biopolitics, Racial Mattering and Queer Affect*. Durham, NC: Duke University Press.

Chen, Mel, and Dana Luciano. 2015. "Introduction: Has the Queer Ever Been Human." *A Journal of Lesbian and Gay Studies* 21 (2–3): 183–207.

Chun, Wendy Hui Kyong. 2021. *Discriminatory Data: Correlation, Neighborhoods and the New Politics of Recognition*. Cambridge, MA: MIT Press.

Clough, Patricia Ticineto. 2018. *The User Unconscious: On Affect, Media, and Measure*. Minneapolis: University of Minnesota Press.

Clough, Patricia Ticineto, Karen Gregory, Benjamin Haber, and R. Joshua Scannell. 2015. "The Datalogical Turn." In *Non-representational Methodologies: Re-envisioning Research*, edited by Philip Vannini, 146–64. London: Routledge.

Coleman, Rebecca. 2017. "Theorizing the Present: Digital Media, Pre-emergence and Infra-structures of Feeling." *Cultural Studies* 32 (4): 600–622.

Cvetkovich, Ann. 2013. *Depression: A Public Feeling*. Durham, NC: Duke University Press.

Culp, Andrew. 2016. *Dark Deleuze*. Minneapolis: University of Minnesota Press.

Deleuze, Gilles. 1983. *Nietzsche and Philosophy*. Translated by Hugh Tomlinson. New York: Columbia University Press.

Deleuze, Gilles. 1995. *Negotiations*. Translated by Martin Joughin. New York: Columbia University Press.

Ferreira da Silva, Denise. 2015. "Before Man: Sylvia Wynter's Rewriting of the Modern Episteme." In *Sylvia Wynter: On Being Human as Praxis*, edited by Katherine McKittrick, 90–105. Durham, NC: Duke University Press.

Ferreira da Silva, Denise. 2022. *Unpayable Debt*. London: Sternberg Press.

Foucault, Michel. 1973. *The Order of Things: An Archaeology of the Human Sciences*. New York: Random House.

Frank, Adam, and Elizabeth Wilson. 2020. *The Silvan Tomkins Handbook: Foundations for Affect Theory*. Minneapolis: University of Minnesota Press.

Galloway, Alexander. 2017. "The Swervers." May 6. http://cultureandcommunication.org/galloway/the-swervers.

Grossberg, Lawrence. 2015. *We All Want to Change the World—The Paradox of the US Left: A Polemic*. Creative Commons. https://www.academia.edu/13048909/We_all _want_to_change_the_world_The_paradox_of_the_U_S_left_A_polemic.

Gumbs, Alexis Pauline. 2018. M *Archive: After the End of the World*. Durham, NC: Duke University Press.

Hansen, Mark B. N. 2015. *Feed Forward: On the Future of Twenty-First Century Media*. Chicago: University of Chicago Press.

Hantel, Max. 2020. "Plasticity and Fungibility: On Sylvia Wynter's Pieza Framework." *Social Text* 38 (2): 97–119.

Harney, Stephano, and Fred Moten. 2021. *All Incomplete*. Colchester, UK: Minor Compositions.

Hartman, Saidiya. 2007. *Lose Your Mother: A Journey along the Atlantic Slave Route*. New York: Farrar Straus Giroux.

Hartman, Saidiya. 2019. *Wayward Lives, Beautiful Experiments: Intimate Histories of Social Upheaval*. London: Serpent's Tail.

Hayles, N. Katherine. 2017. *Unthought: The Power of the Cognitive Nonconscious*. Chicago: University of Chicago Press.

Hayles, N. Katherine, and Tony D. Sampson. 2018. "Unthought Meets Assemblage Brain." *Capacious: Journal for Emerging Affect Inquiry* 1, no. 2: 60–84.

Helms, Gesa, Marina Vishmidt, and Lauren Berlant. 2010. "Affect and the Politics of Austerity: An Interview Exchange with Lauren Berlant." *Variant* 39/40 (Winter): https://www.variant.org.uk/39_40texts/berlant39_40.html.

Hemmings, Clare. 2005. "Invoking Affect: Cultural Theory and the Ontological Turn." *Cultural Studies* 19 (5): 548–67.

Highmore, Ben. 2011. *Ordinary Lives: Studies in the Everyday*. New York: Routledge.

Hong, Cathy Park. 2020. *Minor Feelings: An Asian American Reckoning*. New York: One World.

Jackson, Zakyyiah Iman. 2015. "Outer Worlds: The Persistence of Race in Movement 'Beyond the Human.'" *GLQ: A Journal of Lesbian and Gay Studies* 21 (2–3): 215–18.

Judy, R. A. 2020. *Sentient Flesh: Thinking in Disorder, Poiesis in Black*. Durham, NC: Duke University Press.

Leys, Ruth. 2011. "The Turn to Affect: A Critique." *Critical Inquiry* 37 (Summer): 434–73.

Leys, Ruth. 2017. *The Ascent of Affect: Genealogy and Critique*. Chicago: University of Chicago Press.

Love, Heather. 2010. "Close but Not Deep: Literary Ethics and the Descriptive Turn." *New Literary History* 41 (2): 371–91.

Manning, Erin. 2016. *The Minor Gesture*. Durham, NC: Duke University Press.

Manning, Erin. 2020. *For a Pragmatics of the Useless*. Durham, NC: Duke University Press.

Martin, Emily. 2013. "The Potentiality of Ethnography and the Limits of Affect Theory." *Cultural Anthropology* 54 (Suppl. 7): S149–58.

Marx, Karl. 1964. *The Economic and Philosophic Manuscripts of 1844*. Translated by Dirk Struik. New York: International.

Massumi, Brian. 1995. "The Autonomy of Affect." *Cultural Critique* 31:83–109.

Massumi, Brian. 2002. *Parables for the Virtual: Movement, Affect, Sensation*. Durham, NC: Duke University Press.

Massumi, Brian. 2015. *Ontopower: War, Powers and the State of Perception*. Durham, NC: Duke University Press.

Massumi, Brian. 2021. *Parables for the Virtual: Movement, Affect, Sensation—20th Anniversary Edition*. Durham, NC: Duke University Press.

McCarthy, Jesse. 2021. *Who Will Pay Reparations on My Soul?* New York: Norton.

McCormack, Derek. 2018. *Atmospheric Things*. Durham, NC: Duke University Press.

McKittrick, Katherine. 2021. *Dear Science and Other Stories*. Durham, NC: Duke University Press.

Morrison, Toni. 1986. *Beloved*. New York: Knopf.

Moten, Fred. 2018. *The Universal Machine*. Durham, NC: Duke University Press.

Nelson, Maggie. 2015. *The Argonauts*. Minneapolis, MN: Graywolf.

Ngai, Sianne. 2005. *Ugly Feelings*. Cambridge, MA: Harvard University Press.

Palmer, Tyrone S. 2017. "'What Feels More Than Feeling?': Theorizing the Unthinkability of Black Affect." *Critical Ethnic Studies* 3 (2): 31–56.

Papoulias, Constantinas, and Felicity Callard. 2010. "Biology's Gift: Interrogating the Turn to Affect." *Body and Society* 16 (1): 25–56.

Parisi, Luciana. 2019. "Critical Computation: Digital Automata and General Artificial Thinking." *Theory, Culture and Society* 36 (2): 89–121.

Parisi, Luciana, and Ezekiel Dixon-Román. 2020. "Recursive Colonialism and Cosmo-Computation." *Social Text*. https://socialtextjournal.org/periscope_article/recursive-colonialism-and-cosmo-computation/.

Pedwell, Carolyn. 2014. "Cultural Theory as Mood Work." *New Formations* 82:49–65.

Pedwell, Carolyn. 2020. "Affect Theory's Alternative Genealogies." *History of the Human Sciences* 33 (2): 134–42.

Pedwell, Carolyn. 2021. *Revolutionary Routines: The Habits of Social Transformation*. Montreal: McGill-Queen's University Press.

Puar, Jasbir. 2017. *The Right to Maim: Debility/Capacity/Disability*. Durham, NC: Duke University Press.

Rankine, Claudia. 2014. *Citizen: An American Lyric*. New York: Penguin.

Rankine, Claudia. 2015. "On Racial Violence: 'The Condition of Black Life is One of Mourning.'" *New York Times*, June 22. https://www.nytimes.com/2015/06/22/magazine/the-condition-of-black-life-is-one-of-mourning.html.

Sampson, Tony D. 2020. *A Sleepwalker's Guide to Social Media*. Cambridge: Polity.

Schaefer, Donovan. 2022. "Rationalist Nostalgia." *Capacious: Journal for Emerging Affect Inquiry* 2 (4): 115–35.

Schuller, Kyla. 2018. *The Biopolitics of Feeling: Race, Sex and Science in the Nineteenth Century*. Durham, NC: Duke University Press.

Schulppie, Susan. 2020. *Material Witness: Media, Forensics, Evidence*. Cambridge, MA: MIT Press.

Sedgwick, Eve Kosofsky. 1996. "Introduction: Queerer than Fiction." *Studies in the Novel* 28 (3): 277–80.

Sedgwick, Eve Kosofsky. 2003. *Touching, Feeling: Affect, Pedagogy, Performativity.* Durham, NC: Duke University Press.

Sedgwick, Eve Kosofsky, and Adam Frank. 1995. "Shame in the Cybernetic Fold: Reading Silvan Tomkins." *Critical Inquiry* 21 (2): 496–522.

Seigworth, Gregory J. 2006. "Cultural Studies and Gilles Deleuze." In *New Cultural Studies: Adventures in Theory*, edited by Gary Hall and Claire Birchall, 107–26. Edinburgh: Edinburgh University Press.

Seigworth, Gregory J. 2014. "Affect Theory as Pedagogy of the 'Non-.'" *Footprint: Delft Architecture Theory Journal* 14:109–17. https://journals.open.tudelft.nl/footprint/article/view/805.

Seigworth, Gregory J. 2017. "Capaciousness." *Capacious: Journal for Emerging Affect Inquiry* 1 (1): i–v.

Seigworth, Gregory J., and Melissa Gregg. 2010. "An Inventory of Shimmers." In *The Affect Theory Reader*, edited by Melissa Gregg and Gregory J. Seigworth, 1–25. Durham, NC: Duke University Press.

Sexton, Jared. 2012. "Ante-Anti-Blackness: Afterthoughts." *Lateral: Journal of Cultural Studies Association* 1. https://csalateral.org/issue/1/ante-anti-blackness-afterthoughts-sexton/.

Sexton, Jared. 2017. "On Black Negativity, or, The Affirmation of Nothing." *Society and Space* blog, September 18. https://www.societyandspace.org/articles/on-black-negativity-or-the-affirmation-of-nothing.

Sharp, Hasana. 2011. *Spinoza and the Politics of Renaturalization.* Chicago: University of Chicago Press.

Sharpe, Christina. 2016. *In the Wake: On Blackness and Being.* Durham, NC: Duke University Press.

Shaviro, Steven. 2014. *The Universe of Things: On Speculative Realism.* Minneapolis: University of Minnesota Press.

Singh, Julietta. 2018. *Unthinking Mastery: Humanism and Decolonial Entanglements.* Durham, NC: Duke University Press.

Spillers, Hortense. 1987. "Mama's Baby, Papa's Maybe: An American Grammar Book." *Diacritics* 17 (2): 65–81.

Stacey, Jackie. 2014. "Wishing Away Ambivalence." *Feminist Theory* 15 (1): 39–49.

Stein, Jordan Alexander. 2019. *Avidly Reads Theory.* New York: New York University Press.

Stephens, Melissa Ann. 2014. *Skin Acts: Race, Psychoanalysis, and the Black Male Performer.* Durham, NC: Duke University Press.

Stewart, Kathleen. 2007. *Ordinary Affects.* Durham, NC: Duke University Press.

Warren, Calvin L. 2018. *Ontological Terror: Blackness, Nihilism, Emancipation.* Durham, NC: Duke University Press.

Weheliye, Alexander. 2014. *Habeas Viscus: Racializing Assemblages, Biopolitics and Black Feminist Theories of the Human.* Durham, NC: Duke University Press.

Wetherell, Margaret. 2012. *Affect and Emotion: A New Social Sciences Understanding.* London: Sage.

Wetherell, Margaret. 2015. "Trends in the Turn to Affect: A Social Psychological Critique." *Body and Society* 21 (2): 139–66.

Whitehead, Alfred North. 1929. *Process and Reality.* New York: Free Press.

Whitehead, Alfred North. 2004. *The Concept of Nature.* Amherst, NY: Prometheus Books.

Wiegman, Robyn. 2014. "The Times We're In: Queer Feminist Criticism and the Reparative 'Turn.'" *Feminist Theory* 15 (1): 4–25.

Wilderson, Frank B. 2010. *Red, White, and Black: Cinema and the Structure of U.S. Antagonisms.* Durham, NC: Duke University Press.

Williams, Raymond. 1977. *Marxism and Literature.* Oxford: Oxford University Press.

Williams, Raymond. 1983. *Keywords: A Vocabulary of Culture and Society.* Oxford: Oxford University Press.

Wynter, Sylvia, and Katherine McKittrick. 2015. "Unparalleled Catastrophe of Our Species? Or, to Give Humanness a Different Future: Conversations." In *Sylvia Wynter: On Being Human as Praxis*, edited by Katherine McKittrick. Durham, NC: Duke University Press.

Yusoff, Kathryn. 2019. *A Billion Black Anthropocenes or None.* Minneapolis: University of Minnesota Press.

Zuboff, Shoshana. 2019. *Surveillance Capitalism: The Fight for a Human Future at the Frontier of Power.* London: Profile Books.

PART ONE TENSIONS, IN SOLUTION

1 THE ELEMENTS OF AFFECT THEORIES

Derek P. McCormack

"The news came over the radio. *There is only air now.*
Abandon your experiments." —Jenny Offill, *Dept. of Speculation*, 2014

The elements are a cloud of imaginaries and matters of concern dispersed across the humanities and social sciences.[1] As generatively vague a concept as affect, the elements percolate through social and cultural theory in different versions including, but not limited to, matter, milieu, molecule, and media (Engelmann and McCormack 2021). They were really only side-glanced at in the original *Affect Theory Reader* (Gregg and Seigworth 2010). There, the elements were minor traces, barely detectable amid arguments and provocations about the affectivity of social, cultural, and political formations. That volume examined the promise of affect for cultural and social theories by pushing these theories to take seriously (but not solemnly) the empirical impact on bodies and subjects of "more-than-representational" forces (Lorimer 2005). And this promise was pursued brilliantly through a "shimmering inventory" of the many points of purchase offered by affect theories for thinking the composition and decomposition of worlds.

To note the relative absence of the elements from the first *Affect Theory Reader* is not to perform one of those "gotcha moments" that sometimes passes for critique. It is not a calling out, a charge that something was excluded when it should have been present, or a claim that an absence is an indicator of a lurking problematic. It is a recognition that

Derek McCormack @derekpmccormack · Jan 7, 2021   •••

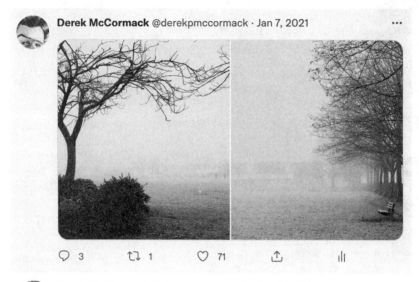

♡ 3   ⟲ 1   ♡ 71   ⬆   ılı

 Derek McCormack @derekpmccormack · Jan 6, 2021   •••
"...it seemed to me, I must confess, that we were living in a less spacious age" (Gabriel, in James Joyce's 'The Dead').

in the decade or more since the publication of the earlier volume and the writing of its constituent chapters, circumstances have changed. Certain conditions, processes, and events have become more palpable, more forceful, more visible, more intrusive in affective worlds even if they were already germinating in those worlds or, in many cases, had already intruded in or destroyed others. These include fires, heat waves, floods, storms, glacial retreat and melting, and air pollution, each of which implicates affective ecologies across bodies and borders. An immediate response to this disparate list might be to scale it up by invoking the Anthropocene as the planetary circumstance for contemporary affect theories. The Anthropocene was not really present in the earlier volume—it did not even make the index. It would be tempting to see the surfacing, or resurfacing, of the elements in social and cultural theory in the years since as yet another signal of the Anthropocene. It would be equally tempting to title this chapter rather differently—something like "Affect Theories in the Wake of [or 'after' or maybe even 'for'] the Anthropocene." The problems with the category of the Anthropocene are by now well documented (see Yusoff 2019), however. It too easily becomes a shorthand and lament for the transformation and ending of *the world* as the common "cene" of a violent Eurocentric colonial cartography (Grove 2019). It too easily homogenizes transformations in a world of many worlds (de la Cadena and Blaser 2018) in which diverse and situated attachments emerge and are extinguished through forms of racial capitalism. And like some other abstractions (but not all), it provides a term on which to offload the work of understanding the many possible worlds with multiple beginnings and endings (Savransky 2021) that are neither planetary nor personal in scale.

In this chapter, the elements figure as a loosely defined cluster of provocations for bracketing the problems of the Anthropocene as a s/cene-stealing abstraction while also emphasizing the multiple processes, entities, and forces to which that term gestures but which exceed its capture. Paying attention to the elements widens the spectrum of objects with which affect theories are concerned. It is also an invitation to think about the conditions in which theory takes place. The first section

Derek McCormack
@derekpmccormack   ...

The relief, after a long screen-based day, of just gazing into the distance for a few minutes.

5:42 PM · Feb 10, 2021 · Twitter Web App

of this chapter considers these issues by revisiting the elemental terms of Raymond Williams's (1977) concept of "structure of feeling." The second scrutinizes the question of elemental influence, before the penultimate section provides a brief overview of how the worlds that affect proposed (Stewart 2017) are weathered. In the process, the chapter argues that understanding the diverse materialisms and meanings of the elements is an important strand of thinking through the composition (and decomposition) of affective worlds and, just as significantly, the formation and fraying of attachments to these worlds (Alaimo 2015).

Analogies

The circumstances of the pandemic, during which this chapter was delayed, worried about, and eventually written, sometimes felt so affectively saturated. Too much feeling to think through at a time of diminished capacities, prolonged distancing, enforced proximity. In those circumstances, a slow lap around a park or a moment in a suburban garden were minor luxuries, opportunities for refocusing, forgetting, or diverting attention. In those circumstances, theory, too, seemed like a kind of luxury. And opportunities to gather around the germ of some kind of theoretical constraint were especially valuable. During the bleaker months of late 2020, I was invited to an informal online reading group on Raymond Williams's concept of structures of feeling, organized by Ben Anderson and Rebecca Coleman. Participants were asked to read the relevant chapter in *Marxism and Literature* (1977) and to speak briefly to how it resonated with aspects of their own work. For me at least, the value of the meeting was not really concept specific—the sheer fact of gathering, even online, was enough. In my case, the promise of the event also worked to temper what felt like an ever-weakening attachment to the habits and project of academic thinking and writing and to theory and theorization as quick-fire responses to the circumstances of the present. This weakening was shaped by post-COVID tiredness, breathlessness (McCormack and Sabine 2021), and exhaustion. It was influenced by the task of sustaining the ordinary in constricted times. And it was exacerbated by readings of some terribly misjudged Euro-theoretical takes on the politics of the pandemic (e.g., Agamben 2021).[2]

In those circumstances, the reading group appealed as an opportunity to revisit what seemed like a familiar concept, one of the key reference points for efforts to theorize the experience of the conjunctural in affective terms (Anderson 2014; Coleman 2018). Affect theories are animated by revisiting and revising concepts, through putting them to work in multiple circumstances, and by working with the tensions that ensue. In the process, concepts can become defamiliarized such that fields of difference (aesthetic and speculative) are generated. Structures of feeling is no exception. Williams defines and recalibrates the concept throughout his writings (see, e.g., Williams 1981). The definition offered in *Marxism and Literature* is one of many, although it is perhaps one of the more succinct. There, Williams (1977, 134) writes, "Structures of feeling can be defined as social experiences in solution, as distinct from other social semantic formations which have been precipitated and are more evidently and more immediately available."

The definition opens up lots of possibilities. What interested me most during the reading group was the elemental imaginary it invokes. Williams resolves the tension between two terms ("structure" and "feeling") by employing the vocabulary of both chemistry and meteorology. Structures of feeling are social experiences *in solution*. They are dissolved in a sociocultural field which for Williams is analogous to a solvent or atmosphere. And they are distinct from semantic formations which have been *precipitated*. Clearly, Williams is not alone in grasping affective life via an elemental imaginary or vocabulary. Eve Kosofsky Sedgwick (2012), notably, wrote about how an elemental imaginary infuses the writing of Proust. In addition, many of the concepts that figure in efforts to make sense of the space-times, rhythms, and intensities of affect, mood, feeling, emotion, and so forth have elemental associations. Atmosphere is perhaps the most obvious (see, e.g., Anderson 2009; MECO Network 2019; Peterson 2021; Simmons 2017). In some cases, the ontology of affect is understood as atmospheric. Elsewhere, atmosphere is used analogously; affective atmospheres are *like* meteorological atmospheres.

Williams's use of terms like "solution" and "precipitation" falls into the latter category. How well, then, do these terms fit the purposes to which he puts them? At first glance, structure and solution seem antithetical. Structure appears too rigid to be understood as something dissolved in a solvent. Williams's terms might therefore seem ill chosen. But they are more appropriate than they appear. Fluids, whether water or air, have structures of a sort. Oceans and atmospheres have distinct layers, for instance, often defined by differences (sometimes quite stark) in temperature. Both can also be composed of relatively distinct bodies that are nevertheless in solution. Oceans are composed of bodies of water of different properties that move past and through one another with various degrees of mixing. They have currents, eddies, and patterns of circulation that are relatively predictable within certain parameters. The same can be said of atmosphere(s). They have currents and cells and bodies of air including, for instance, storms that are predictable and trackable within certain constraints. *Precipitation*, the other decidedly elemental process to which Williams refers, has both meteorological and chemical associations. Meteorologically, precipitation occurs when the air cools to a temperature at which it is saturated with water vapor, which then condenses and falls under the influence of gravity as rain, sleet, hail, snow, and so forth. This process does not just produce an object (a precipitate) but generates more processes and events (showers, etc.) that feed and flow back into a field/solution. Chemically, in contrast, precipitation occurs when substances dissolved in a supersaturated solution react to produce an insoluble material—a precipitate.

For Williams, then, "social experiences" are "in solution" in a sociocultural field in a manner analogous to how a solute is dissolved in a solvent or to how water vapor may be held by air that is not yet saturated. Differences in temperature, density, pressure, and concentration are, if Williams's analogy is stretched a little further, akin to differences in the affective intensity, frequency, and force of encounters that shape sociocultural fields. Equally, like solutes or water vapor, the shape or form of social experiences in solution may not be immediately obvious because they have yet to cross a threshold that generates a phase change that might be grasped as precipitation. By precipitating, social experiences become "evidently available" in sociocultural practices or processes in the way that the volume or frequency or intensity of rain or hail or snow are measurable. This process can be read retrospectively—indeed it must be when there is no alternative to using cultural forms as evidence for the historical existence or emergence of structures of feeling. But the real significance of Williams's use of an elemental imaginary is to point to the challenge of grasping the feeling of the present as it emerges. This is a process of sensing out or feeling into "emergent formations (though often in the form of modification or disturbance in older forms)"

Derek McCormack
@derekpmccormack

···

Last of the garden ice

12:36 PM · Feb 14, 2021 · Twitter Web App

(Williams 1977, 134). It is akin to the technique of sounding as an ongoing process of testing emerging variations in elemental milieus (depth, pressure, temperature, etc.) using devices, technical and corporeal, of different kinds.

Influences

Williams provides some initial orientation for thinking the elements of affect theories. His elemental imaginary underpins a concept articulated in a context in which it is possible to partition, at least partially, the social and cultural from the elemental while also conceptualizing them as necessarily related (see Giblett 2012). This partitioning makes it possible to think of the relation between elements and the feeling of social formations as analogous. This relation is more than analogous, however. The elements do more than provide an imaginary or vocabulary for thinking about the forms and conditions of affective lives and worlds. They participate in these lives and worlds. The elements, as Melody Jue and Rafico Ruiz (2021, 1) write, "are not a neutral background, but lively forces that shape culture, politics and communication." They are influences as well as analogies (analogies, of course, are also influences). A central task of elementally attuned affect theories is grasping the influence of the elements as lively but not necessarily benign forces on the composition and decomposition of worlds and on attachments to those worlds. This means, in turn, that the "lively forces" of the elements are not just influences on the objects to which affect theories attend. They are also influences on those theories, part of the media in which thinking theoretically is always "in solution" (Jue 2020; Peters 2015).

The resurfacing of the elements in the humanities and social sciences, including in affect theories, can be understood, following Williams, as a kind of modification or disturbance of a set of existing theoretical forms. This kind of disturbance is not necessarily new. The elements have long disturbed, modified, and influenced theories of feeling, emotion, and sensibility (Bennett 2020). They have also provided a focus for the fraught question of the influence of environments, milieus, and circumstances on forms of social, cultural, and affective life. Central to the emergence of flavors of, for example, Western romanticism is an affirmation of encounters with and immersion in the "force of the elemental" (Adey 2015) as the basis for the cultivation of valued forms of feeling and sensibility. This enthusiasm often rested on and reproduced racialized assumptions about which bodies and subjects had the capacities to be affected by the elements and to recognize, temper, and control this process. Late nineteenth- and early twentieth-century ideas about environmental influence, veering on environmental determination, were informed by gendered and racialized discourses about the susceptibilities of different bodies (see Schuller 2018). Although such ideas are not traceable in any straightforward way to aspects of contemporary social and cultural theory, they point to the importance of thinking carefully through claims about experimenting with the influence of the elements as part of the elaboration of affect theories.

One response to the question of this influence might be to minimize it. Or to suggest that, at most, the elements are part of the ambient conditions (or "solution") in relation to which thinking takes place but whose influence can be transcended. Minimizing this influence might be an important way of avoiding the implicit romanticism of some versions of affect theory in which the affirmation of feeling—and of capacities to feel—can become an end in and of itself. It would be equally as problematic, and just as political, to minimize the influence of the elements on thinking to the point that the former is safely backgrounded or neutralized. This would simply be to revive the ghost of Cartesianism through the privileging of a form of disembodied thinking. It would be to assume that there is some kind of idealized, pure elemental milieu in which thinking takes place. And it would be to ignore the multiple forms of elemental exposure, variously benign and malignant, in relation to which theorizing emerges. Experiences of exposure involve multiscalar worldings and unworldings that influence the conditions of thinking. Mel Chen (2012) emphasizes the molecular intimacies of these exposures, but the particular animation of these "intimacies" might also include other versions of the elements as they saturate or precipitate within the conditions in which thinking takes place.

Minimizing the influence of the elements would also be to ignore their participation in many forms of life and situated knowledges that are not reducible or traceable to Western ontologies and epistemologies and are not their exotic other. Many strands of thinking, including affect theories, have arguably come late to this realization. There are significant risks here, of course (Todd 2016), including simply importing diverse elemental knowledges into non-Indigenous scholarship in ways that add a touch of the other than human without attending to the specific, situated, and often contested contexts of those knowledges. What matters instead are the circumstances under which elemental forces or entities are taken seriously as agencies or influences as they affect and are affected by others. Understanding these circumstances involves controlled equivocation via which elemental entities in some worlds become participants in others in ways that are more than analogous (de la Cadena 2015). This might, for instance, involve mapping cartographies of elemental forms in settler societies, as Candace Fujikane (2021, 23) does in Hawai'i:

> Kanaka Maoli cartography takes familial relationships with the akua, the elemental forms, as a premise, and cultural practices are grounded in chants and practices that ask the akua for their consent. There are protocols in place for asking permission to enter into a place and to gather. The elemental forms respond to these requests and recognize us through hōʻailona (signs). Sometimes the signs are elemental: a sudden rush of wind, the flick of a fish tail, a flock of nēnē flying overhead, or the mists that kolo (creep) in to hide a place from our eyes. At other times, kūpuna explain that they feel in their naʻau (seat of knowledge or visceral core) whether their actions are pono (morally right, just, balanced).

This work foregrounds both the challenge and urgency of thinking carefully about how encounters with elemental forces and agencies shape the conditions in which thinking takes place. What Melody Jue (2020) calls the conceptual displacement of "milieu-specific" analysis provides some further orientation here. For Jue (2020, 14), "milieu-specific analysis acknowledges that specific thought forms emerge in relation to different environments, and that these environments are significant for how we form questions about the world" and how we write theory. Jue engages directly with the question of influence by foregrounding milieu-specificity. The proposition here is that thinking in relation to earth might be different to thinking in relation to the elemental properties of water, where experiences of immersion might displace thinking (see also Squire 2017). As Jue also admits, elemental milieus are not compositionally pure. It is certainly possible to experiment carefully with conceptual and affective displacement through milieu-specific techniques like diving. But the "solution" in relation to which experience is dissolved and emerges is much more mingled and mixed than milieu-specific analysis might suggest. As Astrida Neimanis (2020) writes in relation to breathing, "definitively separating social and cultural conditions from environmental ones is impossible."

Breathing reveals both the importance and limits of these engagements and experiments with elemental influences. Breathing can be affirmed as a technique of thinking for challenging the bases and biases of Western metaphysics (Irigaray 2002), for cultivating a repertoire of geopoetics (Engelmann 2015), and for thinking about how elemental milieus partake in political thinking (Bennett 2020). Breathing also reveals how elemental influence cannot be compartmentalized or partitioned (Ahmann and Kenner 2020; Kenner 2018). It discloses the multitemporality of the influence of the elements and the multiple forms of violence and toxicity in which they are implicated. Sometimes this influence unfolds as a slow process or gradual accumulation that takes time before it registers or can be sensed by humans or nonhumans (Calvillo 2018; Murphy 2017). Sometimes it takes place as a definite act through which asphyxiation reveals wider structures of violence (Benjamin 2016). Grasping these processes means thinking carefully about which breathing bodies can be and are exposed to what conditions as part of understandings of and experiments with the elemental de/composition of worlds (see Shapiro 2015). The point here is not to pathologize breathing through necessary attention to violence, toxicity, or constriction. It is also to hold open the space-times of breathing as sources for conspiring (Choy 2016; Myers 2021) or aspiring (Crawley 2016; Sharpe 2016) toward minor projects of collective world making.

All of this suggests that structures of feeling are elemental in more than analogous ways. Williams's concept also requires modification because it is developed in an effort to make sense of social experience mediated through *analogue* practices. Although certainly interested in media, especially TV (Williams 2003), Williams may not have anticipated how significantly the experience of media has been transformed via digital technologies in the decades since his death. Rebecca Coleman (2018) has modified and extended Williams's argument through a discussion of the "infrastructures of feeling" that characterize the elastic spatiotemporality of the affective experience of the present, particularly as it is tensed by digital platforms like Netflix and Twitter. In the process, Coleman shows how social experiences are in solution in a field of affective variation also influenced by the capacities of code, digital devices, and algorithmic agencies as they sense processes operating beneath or below thresholds of conscious attention.

This means that the elements influence affective life in an additional way: infrastructurally. Structures of feeling are dependent on a whole range of infrastructures and devices for which elemen-

Derek McCormack
@derekpmccormack

⋯

Change in temperature

11:47 AM · Feb 15, 2021 · Twitter Web App

tal materials are essential. Elemental materials (from the rare to the ubiquitous) form the geological substrate of the technical infrastructures and devices that make certain forms of contemporary affective life possible (Parikka 2015). As Nicole Starosielski (2021) has documented, mediated forms of affective life are dependent on the manipulation and management of elemental materials and milieus. This includes, for example, the smelting necessary to purify silicon, the hyperpurity of the clean rooms in which silicon-based processors are fabricated, and the management of thermally controlled environments of data centers. Through these processes and sites, the algorithmic extraction of data as a reservoir of affective value is linked infrastructurally with elemental media, materials, and milieus (see also Crawford 2021). This is not to claim that affective infrastructures (Berlant 2016) are only possible because of elemental infrastructures and devices but that increasingly the latter underpin the conditions of the former. Put otherwise, the elements, in their diverse manifesta-tions, are infrastructural to the affective mediation of the "solution" and "social experiences" about which Williams writes.

Weathering

Understanding the elements of affect in ways that are more than analogous is both a theoretical and a political point. As Astrida Nei-manis (2020) notes, "Analogies and equivalences are their own kind of violence" if they subsume difference or offload the work of tracing the circumstantial specificity of exposures. How, then, to trace the connections between the elements and structures of feeling in ways that are more than analogous? One way is through weather. Weather has become a signature concept for thinking through the feelings of the "presencing" of the present. There are important precursors here in affect theories. In Eve Sedgwick's (2012) *The Weather in Proust*, for instance, weather provides a concept for thinking the affects of im-mersion in elemental surrounds. This refers not only to the feeling of being enveloped by elements such as air and water; it can also be about the feeling of being enveloped by a text. Beyond this, weather also provides a way of grasping the "meteorological" quality of el-emental surrounds as space-times of affective experience shaped by digital platforms and tensed by exposures to and insulation from the impacts of environmental change (see also Parikka 2017).

Jenny Offill's (2020) novel *Weather* provides one pathway into thinking about how this concept can be tracked across the elements and affects. I read it, by chance, not long before the reading group on structures of feeling. Its brevity and discontinuity suited my post-COVID fatigue, energy levels, and brain fog. *Weather* centers on Lizzie, a New York–based librarian, as she tries to make sense of, variously, parenthood, the ambient threat of climate change, and atmospheres of end-times in Trump's America. The novel is presented as a shower of fragments, anecdotes, jokes, and so forth. Its form seems to mimic, simultaneously, a cascade of tweets or social media messages and the episodic materiality of weather as it arrives and departs as a series of events. Offill herself suggests that she wanted to see what it would be like to "write atmospherically" (quoted in Lefferts 2020). Because of this, the form of *Weather* deliberately amplifies the feeling of a present always emerging in discontinuous moments. As one critic observed, *Weather* is "written in a heightened present tense that allows for memory but little sense of purpose or continuation" (Oyler 2020). This is a present experienced as a flurry of solicitations that evaporate as soon as they arrive, in a process continually being refreshed. *Weather* amplifies the feeling of the presencing of the present as it is conditioned by the temporality of platforms like Twitter (Coleman 2018). This kind of experiment in form is not necessarily new, of course. And Offill's *Weather* parallels experiments undertaken in strands of affect theory in which forms of episodic writing evoke the feeling of scenes or worlds as an effort to generate a sense of experience in solution. In *Weather*, micro-scenes are also tempered by the multitemporality of climate change as an all-enveloping abstraction that influences and intrudes into the feeling of the present. The tension between the ordinary and these abstractions was signaled in Offill's (2014, 56) earlier *Dept. of Speculation* in which the narrator mistakenly assumes that a lecture series on "The Long Now" is about "the feeling of daily life" when it is a discussion of "global" issues like climate change and peak oil.

Weather was well received critically. However, some responses to its form questioned whether *Weather* was, in fact, a "novel." As one reviewer put it, "Lizzie's observations are often amusing, but there's no reason they should be organized as a novel and not as a particularly literate twitter feed" (Oyler 2020). The problem, for that reviewer at least, was that *Weather*'s form was too constrained by the task of amplifying the immediacy of an online present. As that reviewer continued, if the novel is "going to be preserved, it should maintain some distinction from other forms. In replicating the experience of being online, Offill conveys the paranoic mood of the present, but she ignores the strength of the novel as a mode, which is its ability to reflect a mind that is contained in a body that exists in the world, a mind that may be hyperaware of its time but is not actually trapped by it" (Oyler 2020). One response to this might be to see it as the kind of disturbance in form through which Williams suggests structures of feeling can be grasped. *Weather* is certainly indicative of a minor disturbance if the question is the status of the novel as a worldly and world-making form (Ganguly 2016). *Weather*, in these terms, might seem trapped by the hyperlocalism of the present, too immersed in the form of the feeling of immediacy of temporary moments or scenes. It might appear to fail to conjure a world of sufficient scope and scale to do justice to the problem that lurks in the interstices of the novel—climate change. If climate change is the problem clouding *Weather*, then the minor worlds of feeling of which it consists might be seen as inadequate to the task of grasping the space-times of this problem. This response to *Weather* could be read further through contemporary critiques of the phenomenological concept of world because it fails to grasp the scale (in both a spatial and temporal sense) of climate change.[3] This critique also mirrors tensions about the differences between weather and climate. The latter is traditionally understood in science as the average weather over a particular period of time. Weather is the condition of the atmosphere at a particular time and place. Weather, in contrast to climate, is localized. In some ways, then, the promise of the novel as a world-making form, and of many strands of theory, can be grasped in terms of climate as a transcendent abstraction.

Offill's book arguably blurs this distinction between weather and climate. A more generous reading of *Weather*, and of lots of contemporary work on affective life, is that it tries to grasp the feeling of the presencing of the present in worlds that are affectively tensed by problems that oscillate between backgrounded abstractions and foregrounded intrusions or impacts. Rather than necessarily privileging a kind of localism or an affirmation of the feeling of present as an immediacy that precludes any grasp of something more planetary, weather as a concept performs a much more multivalent role for thinking across the elements of affective life. To think the affective in terms of weather is to emphasize the feeling of situations while also tracking how they become generalizable beyond localized experience through cultural forms, stories, or genres of expression (Berlant 2011).

While hinted at in Offill's novel, contemporary work on weather moves well beyond the relatively privileged situation of Offill's narrator. This work takes phenomenologically oriented accounts of experience and reads them through feminist theory, the concept of transcorporeality (Alaimo 2010) and the idea of worlding as processual interaction (Barad 2007). For Astrida Neimanis, writing with Rachel Walker (2014) and Jennifer Hamilton (2017, 2018), foregrounding weather and weathering is about showing how the abstraction of climate shows up

in the affective processuality of worlds. Weathering, for these scholars, is an ongoing process of bodies interaffecting and being affected
by the "thick time" of the elemental circumstances of the histories,
presents, and futures of worlds: "our bodies are makers, transfer
points, and sensors of the 'climate change' from which we might
otherwise feel too distant, or that may seem to us too abstract to get
a bodily grip on" (Neimanis and Walker 2014, 559). Weathering in
these terms also foregrounds the work of enduring and persisting but
not in any kind of heroic way. Not all bodies, lives, or worlds weather
in the same way. For Claudia Rankine (2020, 1), weather names "a
form of governing that deals out death and names it living." In Christina Sharpe's (2016) work, the refusal to partition climate and weather
is important as a way to grasp the ongoing exposure of Black lives to
forms of violence. Weather, for Sharpe (2016, 104), is the "totality of
our environments; the weather is the total climate; and that climate is
anti-black." Neither weather nor climate are analogies here: they are
forms of violent envelopment and exposure in mixed elemental milieus that bear the traces of earlier forms of violence. This blurring of

Derek McCormack
@derekpmccormack   ...

Hail

5:39 PM · Mar 11, 2021 · Twitter Web App

elemental categories of weather and climate is also a way of refusing the violent reductivism of certain kinds of science and their stories (McKittrick 2021) while also avoiding insulating "culture" or affective forms of life from the influence of the elements.

Weather is a reminder of how the elements influence the (infra)structures of feeling of the worlds in relation to which the problems and possibilities of affect theories are posed and reposed. Weather impacts and implicates bodies and forms of life through multiple exposures. Its space-times are tensed affectively across the differential experiences, energies and emissions of bodies, their histories and their futures. Not all writing about weather or weathering is about the elements, nor should all writing about the elements be subsumed within some kind of elemental turn. Nevertheless, the emergence of these matters of concern across the social sciences and humanities provides an important indicator of how the elements and forms of affective life can and are being thought together through a process of "co-saturation" (Jue and Ruiz 2021).

Conclusion

During the time of distancing in which much of this was written, weather, for me, was often little more than "theatre" (Offill 2014, 175). I watched it from the window, and it sometimes drew me out in moments of relatively safe exposure. The distraction of weather was a luxury, a scene of attention for making a world a little more expansive than it felt for long periods. And to some extent, of course, this discussion of the elements might just seem like another way of making a little more of affect theories, of saying that over the last decade or so, these theories have become more radically empirical than they already were. Lauren Berlant (2016) articulated the empiricism of affect in terms of impact: "affect is a way of talking about the impact of the world on subjects and the way they try to assess their belonging to the world, their sense of relation to strangers and other humans through identification." Thinking affect in terms of the elements multiplies how the impacts of the world, or of worlds, are understood, the forms of relation implicated in this impact, and indeed the very question of what counts as a "stranger." It also goes further by encouraging attention to how, in turn, the affective attachments of those subjects impact the elemental (de)composition of worlds. The elements are part of an expanded affective empiricism for thinking about, attending to, and where necessary, resisting and reworking the interactive, influential relation(s) between subjects and worlds. It is an empiricism "in solution," one that sounds out the forces and bonds through which worlds cohere and dissolve or become variously toxic and nourishing.

There are important political qualifications to this empiricism, however. If the concept of structures of feeling emphasizes experiences emerging "in solution," then the elemental processes of which this solvent are composed are often inscrutable and in many cases simply unavailable to human experience unless supplemented by technical devices. This applies as much to the slow leaching of chemicals (Balayannis and Garnett 2020) as it does to the computational infrastructures through which elemental milieus take shape. Trying to make sense of *and* in these surrounds, or to feel them out, is also of course by no means only the domain of affect theory. It is also the

Derek McCormack
@derekpmccormack   ...

Yesterday's clouds

12:55 PM · Apr 12, 2021 · Twitter Web App

ılı View Tweet analytics

domain of speculative forces and practices through which the elements are engineered, extracted, forged, manipulated, modified, and purified as part of the generation of different forms of value and violence. So much is at stake in the questions of which elemental influences and exposures are made explicit, by whom and to whom, and at what cost. All the more important, then, to understand how bodies, subjects, and worlds are affecting and being affected by elemental processes operating across multiple temporalities and spatialities and often beyond thresholds of human sensing and experience. All the more important, even if the elements are not always immediately available empirically, or indeed are not directly felt, that affect theories find concepts, vocabularies, and modes of expression for focusing attention on their influence and impact in the feeling of the present.

Notes

I'm grateful to the editors, Carolyn Pedwell and Greg Seigworth, for the invitation to contribute and for their generosity and encouragement. Thanks also to Ben Anderson and Rebecca Coleman for providing an occasion in which to return to Raymond Williams.

1   See, for example, Adey (2015), Cohen and Duckert (2015), Peters (2015), Starosielski (2019), and Jue and Ruiz (2021).

2   For instance, Agamben's response to the wearing of masks was to see it as diminishment of public life. He seemed unable to grasp that wearing masks might also be understood as a commitment at least to some versions of that life.

3   This kind of critique is developed in some strands of new materialism with planetary ambitions, notably that of Timothy Morton (2013).

References

Adey, Peter. 2015. "Air's Affinities: Geopolitics, Chemical Affect and the Force of the Elemental." *Dialogues in Human Geography* 5 (1): 54–75.

Agamben, Giorgio. 2021. *Where Are We Now? The Epidemic as Politics*. Translated by Valeria Dani. Lanham, MA: Rowman and Littlefield.

Ahmann, Chloe, and Alison Kenner. 2020. "Breathing Late Industrialism." *Engaging Science, Technology, and Society* 6:416–38.

Alaimo, Stacy. 2010. *Bodily Natures: Science, Environment, and the Material Self.* Bloomington: Indiana University Press.

Alaimo, Stacy. 2015. "Elemental Love in the Anthropocene." In *Elemental Ecocriticism: Thinking with Earth, Air, Water, and Fire*, edited by Jerome Cohen and Lowell Duckert, 298–309. Minneapolis: University of Minnesota Press.

Anderson, Ben. 2009. "Affective Atmospheres." *Emotion, Space and Society* 2 (2): 77–81.

Anderson, Ben. 2014. *Encountering Affect: Capacities, Apparatuses, Conditions*. Farnham, UK: Ashgate.

Balayannis, Angeliki, and Emma Garnett. 2020. "Chemical Kinship: Interdisciplinary Experiments with Pollution." *Catalyst: Feminism, Theory, Technoscience* 6 (1): 1–10.

Barad, Karen. 2007. *Meeting the Universe Half-Way: Quantum Physics and the Entanglement of Matter and Meaning*. Durham, NC: Duke University Press.

Benjamin, Ruja. 2016. "Catching Our Breath: Critical Race STS and the Carceral Imagination." *Engaging Science, Technology, and Society* 2:145–56.

Bennett, Jane. 2020. *Influx and Efflux: Writing Up with Walt Whitman*. Durham, NC: Duke University Press.

Berlant, Lauren. 2011. *Cruel Optimism*. Durham, NC: Duke University Press.

Berlant, Lauren. 2016. "Interview with Lauren Berlant." Research Centre for Cultures, Politics, and Identities, Faculty of Media and Communications, Singidunum University. Last accessed December 30 2021. https://www.youtube.com/watch?v=Ih4rkMSjmjs.

Berlant, Lauren. 2016. "The Commons: Infrastructures for Troubling Times." *Environment and Planning D: Society and Space* 34 (3): 393–419.

de la Cadena, Marisol. 2015. *Earth Beings: Ecologies of Practice across Andean Worlds*. Durham, NC: Duke University Press.

de la Cadena, Marisol, and Mario Blaser. 2018. Introduction to *A World of Many Worlds*, edited by Marisol de la Cadena and Mario Blaser, 1–22. Durham, NC: Duke University Press.

Calvillo, Nerea. 2018. "Political Airs: From Monitoring to Attuned Sensing Air Pollution." *Social Studies of Science* 48 (3): 372–88.

Chen, Mel. 2012. *Animacies: Biopolitics, Racial Mattering, and Affect*. Durham, NC: Duke University Press.

Choy, Timothy. 2016. "Distribution." *Theorizing the Contemporary, Fieldsights*, January 21. https://culanth.org/fieldsights/distribution.

Cohen, Jerome, and Lowell Duckert, eds. 2015. *Elemental Ecocriticism: Thinking with Earth, Air, Water, Fire*. Minneapolis: University of Minnesota Press.

Coleman, Rebecca. 2018. "Theorizing the Present: Digital Media, Pre-emergence and Infra-structures of Feeling." *Cultural Studies* 32 (4): 600–622.

Crawford, Kate. 2021. *Atlas of AI: Power, Politics, and the Planetary Costs of Artificial Intelligence*. New Haven, CT: Yale University Press.

Crawley, Ashon T. 2016. *Black Pentecostal Breath: The Aesthetics of Possibility*. New York: Fordham University Press.

Engelmann, Sasha. 2015. "Toward a Poetics of Air: Sequencing and Surfacing Breath." *Transactions of the Institute of British Geographers* 40 (3): 430–44.

Engelmann, Sasha, and Derek P. McCormack. 2021. "Elemental Worlds: Specificities, Exposures, Alchemies." *Progress in Human Geography* 45 (6): 1419–39.

Fujikane, Candace. 2021. *Mapping Abundance for a Planetary Future: Kanaka Maoli and Critical Settler Cartographies in Hawai'i*. Durham, NC: Duke University Press.

Ganguly, Debjani. 2016. *This Thing Called World: The Contemporary Novel as Global Form*. Durham, NC: Duke University Press.

Giblett, Rodney. 2012. "Nature Is Ordinary Too: Raymond Williams as the Founder of Ecocultural Studies." *Cultural Studies* 26 (6): 922–33.

Gregg, Melissa, and Gregory Seigworth, eds. 2010. *The Affect Theory Reader*. Durham, NC: Duke University Press.

Grove, Jarius. 2019. *Savage Ecology: War and Geopolitics at the End of the World*. Durham, NC: Duke University Press.

Irigaray, Luce. 2002. *Between East and West: From Singularity to Community*. Translated by Stephen Pluhacek. New York: Columbia University Press.

Jue, Melody. 2020. *Wild Blue Media: Thinking through Seawater*. Durham, NC: Duke University Press.

Jue, Melody, and Rafica Ruiz, eds. 2021. *Saturation: An Elemental Politics*. Durham, NC: Duke University Press.

Kenner, Alison. 2018. *Breathtaking: Asthma Care in a Time of Climate Change*. Minneapolis: University of Minnesota Press.

McKittrick, Katherine. 2021. *Dear Science and Other Stories*. Durham, NC: Duke University Press.

Lefferts, Daniel. 2020. "After 'Dept. of Speculation,' Jenny Offill Looks Outward." *Publishers Weekly*, January 3. https://www.publishersweekly.com/pw/by-topic/authors /profiles/article/82072-after-dept-of-speculation-jenny-offill-looks-outward.html.

Lorimer, Hayden. 2005. "Cultural Geography: The Busyness of Being 'More-Than-Representational.'" *Progress in Human Geography* 29 (1): 83–94.

McCormack, Derek P., and Lucy Sabine. 2021. "Breathing Worlds." *Venti* 2 (1): n.p.

The MECO Network. 2019. *100 Atmospheres: Studies in Scale and Wonder*. London: Open Humanities Press.

Morton, Timothy. 2013. *Hyper-objects: Philosophy and Ecology after the End of the World*. Minneapolis: University of Minnesota Press.

Murphy, Michelle. 2017. "Alterlife and Decolonial Chemical Relations." *Cultural Anthropology* 32 (4): 494–503.

Myers, Natasha. 2021. "How to Grow Liveable Worlds: Ten (Not-So-Easy) Steps for Life in the Planthroposcene." Accessed January 5, 2022. https://www.abc.net .au/religion/natasha-myers-how-to-grow-liveable-worlds:-ten-not-so-easy-step /11906548.

Neimanis, Astrida. 2020. "The Sea and the Breathing." *e-Flux Architecture*. Accessed December 20, 2021. https://www.e-flux.com/architecture/oceans/331869/the-sea -and-the-breathing/.

Neimanis, Astrida, and Rachel Walker. 2014. "Weathering: Climate Change and the 'Thick Time' of Transcorporeality." *Hypatia* 29 (3): 558–75.

Neimanis, Astrida, and Jennifer Hamilton. 2017. "The Weather Is Now Political." *The Conversation*, May 22. https://theconversation.com/the-weather-is-now-political -77791.

Neimanis, Astrida, and Jennifer Hamilton. 2018. "Open Space Weathering." *Feminist Review* 118 (1): 80–84.

Offill, Jenny. 2014. *Dept. of Speculation*. London: Granta.

Offill, Jenny. 2020. *Weather*. London: Granta.

Oyler, Lauren. 2020. "Are Novels Trapped by the Present?" *New Yorker*, February 12.

Parikka, Jussi. 2015. *A Geology of Media*. Minneapolis: University of Minnesota Press.

Parikka, Jussi. 2017. "On Media Meteorology." Accessed January 18, 2022. https://jussiparikka.net/2017/05/31/on-media-meteorology/.

Peters, John Durham. 2015. *The Marvelous Clouds: A Philosophy of Elemental Media*. Chicago: University of Chicago Press.

Peterson, Marina. 2021. *Atmospheric Noise: The Indefinite Urbanism of Los Angeles*. Durham, NC: Duke University Press.

Rankine, Claudia. 2020. "Weather." *New York Times Book Review*, June 21.

Savransky, Martin. 2021. *Around the Day in Eighty Worlds: Politics of the Pluriverse*. Durham, NC: Duke University Press.

Schuller, Kyla. 2018. *The Biopolitics of Feeling: Race, Sex, and Science in the 19th Century*. Durham, NC: Duke University Press.

Sedgwick, Eve Kosofsky. 2012. *The Weather in Proust*. Durham, NC: Duke University Press.

Shapiro, Nicholas. 2015. "Attuning to the Chemosphere: Domestic Formaldehyde, Bodily Reasoning, and the Chemical Sublime." *Cultural Anthropology* 30 (3): 368–93.

Sharpe, Christina. 2016. *In the Wake: On Blackness and Being*. Durham, NC: Duke University Press.

Simmons, Kirsten. 2017. "Settler Atmospherics." *Member Voices, Fieldsights*, November 20. https://culanth.org/fieldsights/settler-atmospherics.

Squire, Rachel. 2017. "Do You Dive? Methodological Considerations for Engaging with Volume." *Geography Compass* 11 (3): 1–11.

Starosielski, Nicole. 2019. "The Elements of Media Studies." *Media+Environment* 1 (1). https://doi.org/10.1525/001c.10780.

Starosielski, Nicole. 2021. *Media Hot and Cold*. Durham, NC: Duke University Press.

Stewart, Kathleen. 2017. "In the World That Affect Proposed." *Cultural Anthropology* 32 (2): 192–98.

Todd, Zoe. 2016. "An Indigenous Feminist's Take on the Ontological Turn: 'Ontology' Is Just Another Word for Colonialism." *Journal of Historical Sociology* 29 (1): 5–22.

Williams, Raymond. 1977. *Marxism and Literature*. Oxford: Oxford University Press.

Williams, Raymond. 1981. *Politics and Letters: Interviews with New Left Review*. London: Verso.

Williams, Raymond. 2003. *Television: Technology and Cultural Form*. London: Routledge.

Yusoff, Kathryn. 2019. *A Billion Black Anthropocenes or None*. Minneapolis: University of Minnesota Press.

Susanna Paasonen

At this particular historical conjuncture, techniques for measuring, aggregating, analyzing, and monetizing affect on online platforms similarly to any other user data are in broad use. It is a guiding principle of social media platforms and search engines to predict users' potential interests on the basis of their previous actions: If you have liked *this*, then you may also like *that*; and if *that* has tickled your interest, then *this* just might as well. This principle of correlation is effective in how web browsing habits tracked through cookies lead to personalized suggestions, advertisements, and hits and in how social media algorithmically suggests people and brands that one might like, know, or prefer to follow. In order to predict what users could be interested in, contemporary data capitalism also taps into sentiment analysis aiming to quantify affective or emotional responses. Starting with likes, this economy has expanded to broader attempts to measure and modulate intensities and qualities of feeling. The resulting economy operates with firm premises of correlation and taxonomical understandings where positive and negative affect can be identified and further placed in distinct, carefully labeled boxes. Within all this, affect becomes positioned as guarantor of authenticity or even as a subjective truth concerning objects, situations, and settings—and is monetized as such.

As Margaret Wetherell (2012, 122) nevertheless points out, affective patterns are fragmented, inconsistent, and heterogeneous in how they become registered—that is, plural and rife with incommensurability. This chapter builds on the premise that working with affect in cultural and social inquiry not only allows for but necessitates examinations of ambiguity for the reason that intensities registered in bodies refuse to be contained in neat taxonomies, despite the extent of efforts to achieve this. Ambiguity emerges in how intensities become differently registered in different bodies and in how they consequently impact available ways of being in and making sense of the world. Working with ambiguity means holding on to mutually conflicting meanings and impacts without doing away with irreconcilable differences and tensions that cut through them. The unfixity, incongruity, and contingency of meaning that ambiguity entails, I suggest, crucially impacts the possibilities of interpreting and knowing in academic, corporate, and vernacular contexts alike.

My interests lie in what attending to the surprising, intractable, untidy, messy, and constantly shifting realities of cultural and social lives through the lens of ambiguity means for cultural analysis, affect inquiry, and media studies (Law 2004, 3–4). This interest is akin to Lauren Berlant's (2011, 685) call for social theory to explore "enigmatic, chaotic, incoherent, and structurally contradictory attachments," so as to acknowledge the perpetual presence of ambiguity and incoherence (see also Seigworth 2012, 351). Contra data capitalism's polarizing and generalizing epistemologies, this chapter is interested in the critical edge of ambiguity.

Shifty Meanings

To argue that affect allows for examinations of ambiguity is perhaps not the most obvious of statements to make. Alternatively, it may come across as simply all too obvious. Ambiguity means that things are simultaneously *both and* so that they refuse to be pinned down to a singular perspective or outcome: this opens up space for epistemological work on the sites, possibilities, and impossibilities of knowing. Ambiguity refers to the instability or multiplicity of meaning and is therefore something of a fact of life, whereas affect is not an issue of meaning as such. Rather, the turn to affect in cultural inquiry has been a reaction to the dominance of language, linguistics, and questions connected to semiosis, meaning, representation, and significa-tion within the humanities and social sciences. In his critique of the so-called affective turn, Mark Andrejevic (2013, 104–5, 156–57) sees it as turning away from questions of representation, cognition, and thought toward intensities circulating below the realms of conscious-ness so as to basically circumvent much of critical analysis. I suggest that the issue can be more productively and accurately framed as an expansion of analytical perspectives to account for the somatic and affective aspects of experience—and not merely the cognitive—in order to foreground their inseparability in ways of sensing and mak-ing sense (Gibbs 2002, 339–40; Sobchack 2004, 13).

In exploring the fundamental instability and elusiveness of mean-ing, polysemy, and the deferral and the arbitrariness of signification, cultural and social theory have addressed ambiguity for more than half a century. It is no surprise that ambiguity has long been a concern in aesthetic, textual, and literary analysis exploring the multiplicity of meaning (Empson 1949; Ossa-Richardson 2019; Tucker 2003). Here, ambiguity is framed as "not a disease of language but an aspect of its life-process—a necessary consequence of its adaptability to var-ied contexts" (Kaplan and Kris 1948, 417). To rephrase, ambiguity is not positioned as something for interpretation to solve or clarify but rather as that to be accounted for as a default element in how mean-ing comes about and becomes felt. It is befitting for the concept of ambiguity itself to be open to diverse interpretations so that it "can mean an indecision as to what you mean, an intention to mean several things, a probability that one or other or both of two things has been meant, and the fact that a statement has several meanings" (Empson 1949, 5–6). As an issue of doubt and plurality, ambiguity is seen to weave through the history of Western literature (Ossa-Richardson 2019, 2). It has also been identified as a characteristic of modernist art involving "an hitherto unprecedented multidirectionality (multi-dimensionality), and . . . the progressing disintegration of traditional ethic and aesthetic values" (Mozejko 2007, 13) and as a marker for postmodernity where "emphasis on ambivalence, multiplicity, and paradox illuminate the fact that contemporary social reality itself can be characterized in those terms" (Ryu 2001, 6).

Understood as precognitive intensity that moves bodies from one state to another in their encounters with other bodies in the world, affect is ambiguous because it cannot be simply confined to the registers of meaning. Although meaning undoubtedly can, and does, emerge from such encounters, these are initially of more undifferentiated kind, with bodies moving through states of alertness, interest, arousal, boredom, and a range of registers beyond. When addressing zones of impact where such intensities become registered, affect inquiry broadly operates with divisions between the positive and the negative depending on whether the body's "power of acting is increased or diminished" (Spinoza 1992, 158). Events, atmospheres, and objects are then seen to either add to one's life-forces or to eat away at them so that the body's liveliness increases or diminishes, becomes amplified or atrophied. The issue is nevertheless also one of fundamental ambiguity in that bodies are impacted in conflicting and contingent ways: one's life-forces can simultaneously grow and wither in ambiguous oscillations and quiverings (Coleman 2016, 100).

The immediacy of affect remains in excess to the categories of emotion through which it is retrospectively made sense of: a gap both temporal and qualitative opens up between the moment of affective encounter and eventual considerations, analyses, or classifications of feeling. Meanwhile, mundane judgments over what the force of affect means play a key part in social organization, erotic attachments, and consumer preferences alike. For Anna Gibbs (2002, 339), media and bodies can be seen "as vectors, and affect itself as the primary communicational medium for the circulation of ideas, attitudes and prescriptions for action among them." If relations between the bodies of people and those of media involve encounters and exchanges on the plane of affect, as Gibbs proposes, this has both become explicit and transformed with the social media economy that aims to measure and predict user affect to unprecedented degrees. Within this economy, affect is central to what drives people to engage, care, and generate data.

Likes, Loves, Ha-Has

Affect, emotion, and sentiment analyses are used in both media and neuromarketing for uncovering precognitive, immediate "truths" about users in order to more efficiently target products and services to them (Andrejevic 2013, 15). The means toward this end are multiple just as they are ubiquitous. Reading an online article, for example,

I am asked to identify the feelings it evokes through options ranging from remorse, guilt, disappointment, and anger to interest, amusement, pleasure, admiration, and joy. This particular application is by NayaDaya, an empathy analytics company that asks users (such as the readers of an online newspaper) to name how they feel about content. On the basis of aggregating the ensuing data, NayaDaya can then tell their customers (such as an online newspaper) what content comes across as most significant, what influence it may have on users' behavior, and where this customer should focus on in order to achieve the desired impact.[1] As a subfield of sentiment analysis, also known as opinion mining, empathy analytics build on studies of emotion terms and meanings—translations between feeling and semantics—in order to map and predict consumer behavior (e.g., Fontaine, Scherer, and Soriano 2013). For its part, Heartbeat, one of NayaDaya's many competitors, analyzes "text from any source (i.e. surveys, social media, reviews)" and segments the data "into 10 primary and 100 secondary emotions. The resulting emotion insights are clear and actionable, and allow us to aggregate emotion data."[2]

At the heart of such ventures lies a taxonomy of terms used to express emotion: Heartbeat alone advertises a database of ten thousand emotive words and phrases, ever growing. Within this economy, affect, pinned down semantically and classified in its qualities, is approached similarly to other user data to be harvested, quantified, analyzed, and used for optimizing targeted advertising and consumer interest. Empathy, as mapped out with the help of artificial intelligence, translates as consumer empathy toward brands. Through tracking and then predicting meaningful connections with brands, empathy analytics aims to make brands, companies, and products more relatable so as to increase consumer attachment and loyalty. Just as empathy analytics seek to map out affective ways of relating to online content, Facebook's reaction options now extend beyond "likes" to "love," "ha-ha," "wow," "sad," "angry," and the pandemic "care," generating analyzable data on users' ways of relating to content in their newsfeeds. Within all this, "social interactivity and user affects are instantly turned into valuable consumer data and enter multiple cycles of multiplication and exchange" (Gerlitz and Helmond 2013, 1349).

Like buttons are used to "express approval or social solidarity, as well as taste information provided by closely connected users within a network" so that advertising "is subsequently targeted to a particular user based on the aggregation of extensive affective activity from across her or his personal network" (Jarrett 2015, 205). The resulting affective data are seen to speak of qualities and not merely the quantities of attention: that is, multiple reaction options are designed to add finer granularity to analyses of not only where user attention clusters but how this happens and matters. Such granularity is of key interest to an advertising platform like Facebook dependent on successfully offering its customers—that is, advertisers—lucrative spots for their commercial messages. Through reaction options, the platform can both analyze user moods and predict what content they might positively react to in the future in the shape of liking, loving, and ha-haing. If the visibility of such content is then optimized at the expense of that which is likely to generate sad and angry reactions—or the ambiguous "wow"—advertisers can reach more positively attuned audiences (Paasonen 2021, 83–86). The commercial benefits, or at least the potential opportunities, of this are obvious.

Within this logic, reaction options operate as indexes of attention and affect and, to a degree, as perceived guarantors of authenticity in how people relate to content and to one other on advertising platforms. Given the concern with making sense of user affectations in qualitative scales, tactics of interruption are also at play, from users taking the time to adjust their advertisement settings to randomizing their reactions to content with Go Rando, a browser extension designed to create affective noise by randomly picking one of the available reaction options when "liking" any individual post.[3] The scale of such interventions is, however, rather marginal.

At the same time, it is important to notice how the simple heart of the reaction button "love," for example, can be intentionally connected to a cute cat photo inasmuch as to a post announcing that this very cute cat has violently died. The "care" button, introduced during the COVID-19 pandemic in April 2020 and interpreted by users as referring to a range of things—rimming and Mayan heart sacrifice included—is shifty in its communicative uses extending from gestures of compassion to high levels of irony. For its part, the seemingly neutral option of a startled "wow" is broadly used to express sarcasm, mockery, and contempt (Lehto and Paasonen 2021). Reaction buttons are similar to emojis in how they are used to demonstrate, perform, and express feeling and to create affective alignment. They are nevertheless also persistently blurry in their referents and densely contextual in their meanings (Highfield 2018; Miller et al. 2017). Within the landscape of social media rich in ambivalent exchanges, sarcasm, and irony, the meaning of emoticons is, in sum, by no means set or easy to decipher (Phillips and Milner 2017; Wenzel 2019).

Such shiftiness and complexity of meaning, while unavoidable, is left with little room in the taxonomical imagination of a social media economy that aims to transform affect into data in rather straightforward terms. In her critique of cultures of big data, Wendy Hui Kyong Chun (2021) argues that their general design principle of homophily—the love of the same, the idea that similarity breeds similarity and that birds of a feather flock together—is effectively a tactic of social segregation. It then follows that homophily's relationship to "echo chambers is not accidental but fundamental" and that such echo chambers are "not unfortunate errors, but deliberate goals" (Chun 2021, 24, 82). The design principle of homophily gives rise to clusters of users, posts, and adverts premised on shared feeling. Such aggregations of liking and loving also entail aggregations of dislike and hate as a rudimentary analysis of the communication dynamics of virtually any social media platform will render evident. Affective homophily, the love of feeling similarly, fuels social organization on platforms such as Twitter and Facebook, as in the outrage and sadness of #BlackLivesMatter and #MeToo that mobilize bodies into collective action (Sundén and Paasonen 2019). Affective homophily is key to the making of connections where views align so as to leave little room for disagreement except in terms of conflict. Aggregations of affect within social media involve both amplification and homogenization where the ambiguities that make experience, sociability, interpretation, and culture risk being flattened out.

Good or Bad? Or Indifferent?

Affective aggregation, in following a taxonomical rationale, broadly echoes divisions drawn between positive and negative affect in cultural theory, yet similarities soon become obvious. Silvan S. Tomkins (2008, 647), despite his broad taxonomical approach, considered it impossible to unambiguously code and classify affect both due to the ambiguity of language pertaining to it and "the great variety of admixtures of affect with cognitive, behavioral, and event references." Such elusiveness and complexity are part and parcel of affect inquiry, independent of which theoretical trajectories one sets out to follow. To approach social media economy through affect inquiry, I argue, is in fact a means of inserting ambiguity into the heart of things. This argument runs counter to Andrejevic's (2013), according to which the rise of affect inquiry is parallel with, and helps to support, the premises of neuromarketing and sentiment analysis by prioritizing gut feelings over conscious thought as sites of presumed precognitive truth.

Rather, I argue that affect inquiry helps us to see how the shapes and hues of intensities registered cannot be fully predicted or known, let alone generalized or predicted. As unqualified intensity preceding its fixing in categories of emotion, affect "is not ownable or recognizable and is thus resistant to critique" (Massumi 2002, 28). Even when its intensities are made sense of through descriptions of feeling and emotion, as is extensively the case in sentiment analysis, these escape capture in neat pigeonholes of the kind that Facebook's reaction options operate with. It then follows that they are, at least to a degree, resistant to monetization in an economy attempting to translate and transform affect into sellable data (Paasonen 2021, 95, 117).

The issue is one of ambivalence as varied and multiple feelings toward objects but, even more fundamentally, that of ambiguity where the meanings of these objects are multiple and therefore unsettled. Whereas the notion of "ambivalence" communicates attitude and perception of those doing the interpretation—as in people having mixed feelings about this or that—the term "ambiguity" is attached to the properties of things (media representations, material objects, cultural debates) and their default shiftiness in terms of meaning making. When clicking through online news items, top tweets, and TikTok videos, affective intensities constantly push and pull bodies from one state to another, possibly to diverse directions at once so that we can be pleasantly surprised, startled in shocking ways, or puzzled in mundane amalgamations of pleasure, unease, and disgust. An intensity that is enlivening—and in this sense positive—can intermesh with ripples that make bodies feel stuck or shrink their capacities to move, act, and relate. Negative affective intensities of rage may energize bodies and fuel their actions for emancipatory ends while sadness can be enjoyable as such: to cite Yul Brynner's melancholy character in *The Journey* (1958), "we feel sad, which is the best way of feeling good" (see also Massumi 2002, 23–24).

It can also be that affective complexity is precisely key to the attraction that much social media holds as users take pleasure in witnessing vitriolic flame wars, hating public figures, being outraged by other people's opinions, or reading narratives of grief, devastation, and suffering. Excitement, which Tomkins (2008, 191, 193) discusses as the affect investing things with a sense of magic, can come in all kinds of hues and be cut through by ripples that are far from enjoyable, just as pleasure itself can be tinted with discomfort and shame. Without degrees of excitement, things—whether these be threads of political debate or profile photos of potential sex partners in a hookup app—do not grab or even matter much. Although this is also the general premise of empathy analytics, there is no uniformity to what things excite, how, and whom.

Tomkins (2008, 190) discusses this as the autonomy of affect: "Any affect may have any object. This is the basic source of complexity of human motivation and behavior.... Because excitement may accompany anything under the sun, its profile of activation, duration and reduction as well as its frequency will depend to some degree on the objects in which it is invested." As any affect can have any object, and conversely, any object can be associated with any affect, that which some find enraging or disgusting can, for others, bring joy, cause shame, or result in the affective flatness of boredom. And as no simple causality can be presumed between objects and affects, encounters with the world remain open ended and rife with surprise. These encounters shift in space and time: as Spinoza (1992, 133) famously put it, "the human body can be affected now in one way, now in another, and consequently it can be affected in different ways at different times by one and the same object." For Spinoza (1992, 153), the perceived goodness or badness of things was further distinct from the qualities of these things as mere "modes of thinking, or notions which we form from the comparison of things one with another," since "the one and the same thing can be at the same time good and bad, and also indifferent." Following this line of thought, one and the same object—be it a clickbait item, an Instagram lunch photo, or a hard-core porn clip—enables a plethora of affective encounters.

Tomkins's discussion of excitement accompanying "anything under the sun" while simultaneously being dependent on the objects that it is invested with suggests that one person is more likely to be excited by some objects than another; yet, other people are bound to be excited by other things altogether. It further suggests that objects need not be understood as blank neutral reservoirs that become invested or layered with affect. Rather, objects' qualities invite certain kinds of encounters so that different objects are, for different people, differently resonant. Understanding affect as autonomous, *yet also* dependent in its rhythms and intensities on the objects that it becomes invested in, or attached to, means bridging or overlapping affect inquiry with aesthetics as a theorization of experience focused on the power of cultural products to touch, impact, and possibly shock (e.g., Armstrong 2000; Deleuze 2003; Ngai 2012). Within this framework, cultural objects can "physically arouse us to meaning" so that the meanings attached to them shift from one encounter to the next as affective dynamics weaken, strengthen, and become differently registered (Sobchack 2004, 57).

This perspective also leaves room for surprise (and startle) as instances where we do not quite know what, or how, to feel, even as something is definitely felt. When understanding experience as being in perpetual motion, our ways of understanding ourselves, the objects we study, and the world within which we live remain similarly on the move. Tomkins's theorizations of affect, grounded in empirical inquiry and concerned with the capacities of bodies to feel out the world, offer one avenue for thinking through what Spinoza (1992, 105) addressed as the impossibility of determining "the limits of the body's capabilities . . . what the body can and cannot do." As different as Tomkins's and Spinoza's respective approaches to affect are, they both foreground indeterminacy, unpredictability, and ambiguity in how bodies affect and are affected by one another (Frank and Wilson 2020, 71–77).

For Tomkins (2008, 191), the affect of excitement is crucial enough to be the stuff that makes the self: "I am, above all, what excites me." In Tomkins's view, excitements shape a person so that a music lover is excited by music, a scholar by academic pursuits, and a sports enthusiast by exercise or the activities of a favorite team. Expanding this point on excitements and affective attachments to more fleeting, random, and discontinuous encounters with the world makes it possible to see how diverse objects of excitement constantly make and unmake us—and, indeed, how excitements of all kinds dot and pattern everyday lives as persistent engulfing passions inasmuch as minor sparks of interest that do not a bonfire make, even as they leave their marks.

Social media is the stuff of minor excitements as the search for affective intensity propels users to click, swipe, share, and like (Dean 2010). As microevents, minor mundane enchantments and excitements add to one's liveliness as oscillations of intensity and therefore make the self as something of a patchwork relating to, attaching itself to, and assembling diverse objects and object worlds into attachments, nonrelations, and antagonisms. Whereas much affect inquiry has been interested in major events entailing degrees of rupture and drama, everyday lives are largely composed of events in minor scales (see Paasonen 2021, 11, 115–16; Stewart 2007). To think of the self as being made in a patchworked fashion so that the excitements that shape us—larger, smaller, medium, and impossible to pin down in terms of scale—can, but do not necessarily need to, connect or overlap with one another means that these excitements regularly come in unmatching patterns, textures, materials, and proportions. This allows for considering such excitements as heterogeneous, possibly conflicting, transient, surprising, and paradoxical. It also allows for considering ourselves as made up in the same vein.

It is my argument that independent of the volume and granularity of data that social media platforms generate of their users' tastes, moods, friends, and consumer preferences or the techniques for analyzing these data, the complexities and contingencies involved in our attachments with the world also resist and partly escape such capture. Although data capitalism entails a considerable power of corporations to monitor, predict, and manipulate the moods and actions of users, this power is by no means uniform, nor are its outcomes predictable or unequivocal. Operating with homogenized and taxonomical understandings of affect, the objects to which it becomes attached, and the paradoxical excitements that make the self, data capitalism is something of a blunt instrument, even as it is definitely massive enough for its sway to have expansive societal, economic, and political impact.

The work of cultural and social analysis involves working with and through ambiguity since the meanings of cultural products and social phenomena are never fixed: these accommodate multiple, possibly mutually contradicting interpretations, uses, and practices, and at the very least, feelings toward them can be highly mixed. Culture is the stuff of ambiguity, yet ambiguities more than easily disappear in analytical work aiming at firm outcomes and strong compelling arguments. This is the case with much conversation connected to social media's impact on personal and collective lives, largely construed in negative terms as corroding cognitive and affective capacities, forms of sociability, political engagement, and overall enjoyment taken in life (for an extended discussion, see Paasonen 2021).

To approach social media through the lens of ambiguity allows for considering how the same objects—be these platforms, apps, threads, posts, comments, links, or something else—come to mean and effect distinctly different things, depending on how they materialize in encounters between human and nonhuman bodies. The factors and actors involved in this are too plural to list, ranging from platform affordances and vernaculars to connection speeds and end devices, to the rhythms of media products circulating across platforms, and to how people, at different moments, feel differently about the bodies—representational, technological, human—that they encounter. The excitements of social media are part and parcel of that which makes the self within the everyday. These excitements can fail to deliver by merely resulting in dullness and boredom; they may involve startled surprise or the intermeshing of disgust and amusement; they can be about bonds and attachments forged over stretches of time or take place as serendipitous, fleeting fascinations. Within such encounters, bodies pass from one state to another or oscillate between different states of varying degrees of aliveness, in ways both imperceptible and drastic (Paasonen, Hillis, and Petit 2015, 1–2).

To acknowledge and work with ambiguity does not result in relativism as the general acknowledgment of the meaning of things being contextual, subjective, and hence impossible to generalize—or that, basically, any interpretation is as true as and equal to any other. Rather, the issue is that of critical inquiry being able to hold on to irreconcilable tensions in society and culture without an attempt to resolve and flatten them out in a neat analytical closure. Acknowledging that things really are *both and* makes it possible to see how dynamics that appear mutually exclusive can in fact be dependent on or give rise to one another (Bem 2019). An analytical approach of this kind is at play in Sianne Ngai's (2012, 19, 23) discussion of contemporary dominant aesthetic categories where the interesting feeds the boring, where the cute entails tensions between aggression and tenderness, and where the zany fuses playfulness with desperation. For Ngai, affective tensions within aesthetic categories explain much of their appeal. It can be argued that the same applies to the appeal of social media where interest and boredom, attention and distraction, dependence and agency play off one another (Paasonen 2021).

Critical inquiry zooming in on "an unresolvable clog of curly ambivalences" (Seigworth 2013, 347) that is capable of bearing "the weight of ambivalence and contradiction" (Berlant 2011, 690) can then account for how surveillant and exploitative data capitalism yields forms of agency and social organization irreducible to its logics. It can further help in unraveling the contradicting affective intensities evoked by cultural objects and the contradicting meanings that they consequently take on, as well as the ways in which enlivening intensities intermesh with the apparent flatness of experience in routines of social media browsing. The challenge is to explore how this happens, what bodies these encounters involve or assemble, and what follows or emerges from them. Although this is no simple task, it is not an impossible one—and, as I propose, one certainly worthwhile.

First and foremost, this simply means acknowledging the messiness of things and the value of scholarship not doing away with the mess of it all but rather exploring it in order to show how things can mean and matter differently and what may emerge from the murkier waters where diverse investments, attachments, and aims intermesh and clash. Methodologically, it means embracing diverse scales at one go so that, for example, big data analysis meets the contextual care necessary for qualitative inquiry, or where more abstract musings of society, culture, and politics are faced with the acuteness of the singular. And as I have argued, this also means relying on affect not as a marker of feeling possible to pin down in sentiment analysis but as a realm of encounters that, as unpredictable and paradoxical as they may be, are also the very stuff that makes the self as a heterogeneous assemblage of interests and excitements.

Apparently Neat, yet Messy

Consider, for example, a polarized social media event par excellence: the then–US president Donald Trump falsely tweeting about winning the election on November 7, 2020, when the result was finally called. Befitting Trump's position as an emblem and engine of antagonistic and polarized social media exchange and the focus of global attention, his tweet "I WON THIS ELECTION, BY A LOT!" garnered over 980,000 replies, 880,000 retweets, and 1.1 million likes. In a workshop that Elena Pilipets and I conducted, our analysis of quote tweets—retweets inclusive of user comments—responding to Trump addressed a sample of 16,103 images and 47,455 text replies. What became evident was largely predictable—namely, the active participation of and clash between Trump's loyal supporters and ardent antagonists followed the bipartisan logic of the elections themselves. Computational analysis focusing on recurrent patterns and content with the highest engagement metrics (likes, shares, or comments) made this polarization ever more evident in how expressions of love and support sharply met those of mockery, boredom, and acute dislike. It also showed the presence of popular reaction GIFs used to communicate such sentiment (Pilipets and Paasonen 2021).

By and large, the analysis then helped to make visible that which was already known—namely, the pronounced presence of polarization and homophily in social media. It did not, however, unproblematically point to the presence of filter bubbles or echo chambers since, despite users clearly taking sides and strongly airing their feelings, this happened within a Twitter thread originated by and clustering on Trump so that the love of similarity did not cancel out but rather operated within a plural (even if starkly divided) affective environment (see also Bruns 2019).

As we shifted scales of analysis to content that is easily filtered out as spam (and hence excluded from analysis), the degrees of messiness involved grew more evident. In addition to users hijacking Trump's Twitter thread in order to promote influencer accounts or to otherwise reorient the attention of others, seemingly random memes abounded, as did quote tweets recycling "creepypasta" featuring scary faces, "cursed images" depicting the uncanny mundane, demonic spells, and nonsensical, often unconnected comments spelled out in the Armenian alphabet. When focusing on the set of 522 quote tweets written in Armenian—a highly partial data set that was being removed as spam when scraped—things got messy indeed as the thread gathered force as something of a social theater increasingly disconnected from the fact and figure of Trump, even as he operated as something of an affective cluster and aggregator. In addition to straightforwardly and elaborately cursing Trump in Armenian, users used the lyrics of "Macarena," possibly those of "Wonkey Donkey," random bits of text, or merely expressed their appreciation over other users having translated their tweet (back) to English. Meanwhile, the visuals featured sad-looking dogs munching on spaghetti, ghouls, and someone in a Pikachu suit pushing their arm through the mouth hole to strangle a woman (Pilipets and Paasonen 2021).

Without venturing further into the nuances of the material recycled, this analytical exercise—rather straightforward in moving from a larger data set to a smaller one and from tracking repetitions, patterns, and engagements to attending to the ephemeral and the spammy through qualitative means—helps to make evident the surprising and the ambiguous amid the very predictable. The Armenian curses reacted to one another and to the thread as such in ways that would make attempts to pin down their sentiments through the means of empathy analytics rather futile. The fact that such data, in their repetitive tweet structures, low engagement metrics, and temporal waves of imitation, are the stuff to be filtered out as spam (both by the platform itself and when processing scraped data for analysis) so that they are unlikely to even become part of a temporally structured data set shows how retrospective analyses may well miss that which is strikingly evident when social media engagement unfolds in real time.

Ambiguity translating as noise more than easily disappears in analysis focusing on patterns. This is one of the basic principles of empathy analytics (and many other forms of analysis) premised on aggregating data and making predictions its basis. Such flattening out and generalization is at the center of Andrejevic's critique of affect theory's applications in media research. It is, however, my proposal that affect inquiry, precisely in its embrace of uncertainty and ambiguity, offers alternatives to such analytical flattening out. Moving from and between taxonomical inquiry and the actual mess from which taxonomies are to be derived is a means for disturbing and challenging the logic of correlation that Chun critiques, not the means for reinforcing it. The excitements that make the self are fundamentally ambiguous in how they pull the body in different directions and in how things that capture attention and energize bodies become objects of multifaceted interest through captivated ridicule, bemused disgust, embarrassed fascination, and guilty desire. As the singular event of Trump's quote tweet replies makes evident—and it may be plainly obvious at this point—there can be much excitement involved in objects and expressions of hate and scorn alone. Even more centrally, the analysis of responses to Trump's tweeting helps to illustrate some of the ways in which the excitements that make the self, from one moment to another, are threads in heterogeneous tapestries of attention and engagement that may but do not necessarily result in clear patterns.

Rather than operating with generalizing accounts where certain objects are seen as predictably connected to certain affects or vice versa, affect inquiry helps to foreground contextual attunement to differences between bodies, situations, and objects guided by the overall principle of autonomy as multipotentiality. It is all too seldom that macrolevel considerations attending to the dynamics of data capitalism, the algorithmic polarization of sociability, and the political economies of targeted advertising in social media get to meet careful analyses of the micro: the quotidian, the messy, and the felt. Analytical zooming in—solely—on either the micro or the macro will remain partial in its grasp, for it is precisely the dynamic, contradictory, and ambiguous entanglements of the structural and the individual, the societal and the personal, the corporate and the intensely felt that make both data culture and the self. This does not necessitate doing away with the mess but diving into it.

Notes

1 NayaDaya.com, accessed January 4, 2022, https://www.nayadaya.com/.
2 "Empathy Analytics," Brand for Benefit, accessed January 4, 2022, https://www.brandforbenefit.com/empathy-analytics.html.
3 Ben Grosser, "Go Rando," accessed May 20, 2021, https://bengrosser.com/projects/go-rando/.

References

Andrejevic, Mark. 2013. *Infoglut: How Too Much Information Is Changing the Way We Think and Know*. New York: Routledge.

Armstrong, Isobel. 2000. *The Radical Aesthetic*. Oxford: Blackwell.

Bem, Caroline. 2010. "Cinema | Diptych: *Grindhouse | Deathproof*." JCMS: *Journal of Cinema and Media Studies* 58 (2): 1–22.

Berlant, Lauren. 2011. "A Properly Political Concept of Love: Three Approaches in Ten Pages." *Cultural Anthropology* 26 (4): 683–91.

Bruns, Axel. 2019. *Are Filter Bubbles Real?* Cambridge: Polity.

Chun, Wendy Hui Kyong. 2021. *Discriminating Data: Correlation, Neighborhoods, and the New Politics of Recognition*. Cambridge, MA: MIT Press.

Coleman, Rebecca. 2016. "Austerity Futures: Debt, Temporality and (Hopeful) Pessimism as an Austerity Mood." *New Formations* 87:83–101.

Dean, Jodi. 2010. *Blog Theory: Feedback and Capture in the Circuits of the Drive*. Oxford: Polity.

Deleuze, Gilles. 2003. *Francis Bacon: The Logic of Sensation*. Translated by Daniel W. Smith. London: Basic Books.

Empson, William. 1949. *Seven Types of Ambiguity*. 2nd ed. London: Chatto and Windus.

Fontaine, Johnny J. R., Klaus R. Scherer, and Christina Soriano. 2013. *Components of Emotional Meaning: A Sourcebook*. Oxford: Oxford University Press.

Frank, Adam J., and Elizabeth Wilson. 2020. *A Silvan Tomkins Handbook: Foundations for Affect Theory*. Minnesota: University of Minnesota Press.

Gerlitz, Carolin, and Anne Helmond. 2013. "The Like Economy: Social Buttons and the Data-Intensive Web." *New Media and Society* 15 (8): 1348–65.

Gibbs, Anna. 2002. "Disaffected." *Continuum: Journal of Media and Cultural Studies* 16 (3): 335–41.

Highfield, Tim. 2018. "Emoji Hashtags/Hashtag Emoji: Of Platforms, Visual Affect, and Discursive Flexibility." *First Monday* 23 (9). https://doi.org/10.5210/fm.v23i9.9398.

Jarrett, Kylie. 2015. "'Let's Express Our Friendship by Sending Each Other Funny Links instead of Actually Talking': Gifts, Commodities, and Social Reproduction in Facebook." In *Networked Affect*, edited by Ken Hillis, Susanna Paasonen, and Michael Petit, 203–20. Cambridge, MA: MIT Press.

Kaplan, Abraham, and Ernst Kris. 1948. "Esthetic Ambiguity." *Philosophy and Phenomenological Research* 8 (3): 415–35.

Law, John. 2004. *After Method: Mess in Social Science Research*. London: Routledge.

Lehto, Mari, and Susanna Paasonen. 2021. "'I Feel the Irritation and Frustration All Over My Body': Affective Ambiguities in Networked Parenting Culture." *International Journal of Cultural Studies* 24 (5): 811–20.

Massumi, Brian. 2002. *Parables for the Virtual: Movement, Affect, Sensation*. Durham, NC: Duke University Press.

Miller, Hannah, Daniel Kluver, Jacob Thebault-Spieker, Loren Terveen, and Brent Hecht. 2017. "Understanding Emoji Ambiguity in Context: The Role of Text in

Emoji-Related Miscommunication." *Proceedings of the International AAAI Conference on Web and Social Media* 11 (1): 152–61. https://ojs.aaai.org/index.php/ICWSM/article/view/14901.

Mozejko, Edward. 2007. "Terminologies of Modernism." In *Modernism*, edited by Ástradur Eysteinsson and Vivian Liska, 12:11–34. Amsterdam: John Benjamins.

Ngai, Sianne. 2012. *Our Aesthetic Categories: Zany, Cute, Interesting.* Cambridge, MA: Harvard University Press.

Ossa-Richardson, Anthony. 2019. *A History of Ambiguity.* Princeton, NJ: Princeton University Press.

Paasonen, Susanna. 2021. *Dependent, Distracted, Bored: Affective Formations in Networked Media.* Cambridge, MA: MIT Press.

Paasonen, Susanna, Ken Hillis, and Michael Petit. 2015. "Introduction: Networks of Transmission: Intensity, Sensation, Value." In *Networked Affect*, edited by Ken Hillis, Susanna Paasonen, and Michael Petit, 1–24. Cambridge, MA: MIT Press.

Phillips, Whitney, and Ryan M. Milner. 2017. *The Ambivalent Internet: Mischief, Oddity, and Antagonism Online.* Oxford: Polity.

Pilipets, Elena, and Susanna Paasonen. 2021. *I WON THIS ELECTION, BY A LOT! Trump Spectacle and Memetic Antagonism on Twitter.* SmartDataSprint Project Report. https://smart.inovamedialab.org/past-editions/2021-platformisation/project-reports/i-won-this-election-by-a-lot/.

Ryu, Honglim. 2001. "Ethics of Ambiguity and Irony: Jacques Derrida and Richard Rorty." *Human Studies* 24 (1): 5–28.

Seigworth, Gregory J. 2012. "Reading Lauren Berlant Writing." *Communication and Critical/Cultural Studies* 9 (4): 346–52.

Sobchack, Vivian. 2004. *Carnal Thoughts: Embodiment and Moving Image Culture.* Berkeley: California University Press.

Spinoza, Baruch. 1992. *The Ethics, Treatise on the Emendation of the Intellect and Selected Letters*, edited by Seymour Feldman and translated by Samuel Shirley. Indianapolis: Hackett.

Stewart, Kathleen. 2007. *Ordinary Affects.* Durham, NC: Duke University Press.

Sundén, Jenny, and Susanna Paasonen. 2019. "Inappropriate Laughter: Affective Homophily and the Unlikely Comedy of #MeToo." *Social Media + Society* 5 (4). https://doi.org/10.1177/2056305119883425.

Tomkins, Silvan S. 2008. *Affect Imaginary Consciousness: The Complete Edition.* New York: Springer.

Tucker, Herbert F. 2003. "Teaching Ambiguity." *Pedagogy* 3 (3): 441–50.

Wenzel, Andrea. 2019. "To Verify or to Disengage: Coping with 'Fake News' and Ambiguity." *International Journal of Communication* 13:1977–95.

Wetherell, Margaret. 2012. *Affect and Emotion: A New Social Science Understanding.* London: Sage.

Adam J. Frank and Elizabeth A. Wilson

In the Netflix dramedy *The Chair* (about an English department in an elite US university) Professor Ji-Yoon Kim (played by Sandra Oh) finds herself having to explain to David Duchovny (played by David Duchovny) why his dissertation on Beckett, written over thirty years ago, is out of date. A lot has happened in the field in the last thirty years, she explains. In response to Duchovny's request for an example of these scholarly advances, Kim provides a list: "affect theory, eco-criticism, digital humanities, new materialism, book history, developments in gender studies and critical race theory." In comparison, Kim notes, Duchovny's dissertation "reads like it's out of the mid-80s. . . . The discipline has moved forward, and you are still stuck back in a different era" ("The Last Bus in Town"). Missing from Professor Kim's list are a number of scholarly fields that, according to the generational logic of the show, we can presume to be old and due for retirement. Queer theory is not mentioned and neither is psychoanalytic theory, the latter presumably eons past its use-by date. We can infer that literary criticism, and the university as a whole, has moved on; for now, at least, we have affect theory, placed at the very top of Kim's list, as it promises to lead us into a new era of scholarly excellence and political relevance.

Although this sequential linear logic of scholarly progress is completely unsurprising in a television show like *The Chair*, we have also encountered this logic (first psychoanalysis, then affect theory) in the academic institutions that we inhabit: we read it in journals and university presses; we see it at conferences; and we hear it from students who learn, perhaps overzealously, the polemical gestures necessary to make space for new research. At the same time and often for similar professionalizing reasons, affect theories are pit against one another to highlight irresolvable disjunctions between them: affect *or* emotion *or* cognition; signification *or* impersonal perception *or* embodiment; empirical *or* theoretical; subjectivity *or* the social world. But we may have noticed by now that in the theoretical humanities, one theory of affect does not either update or replace another. And attempts to create affect lineages or genealogies that are distinct from one another under-read the ways in which different affect theories are entangled in, and indebted to, each other (Frank and Wilson 2012, 2020; Wilson 2020).

Unpersuaded by these generational logics of substitution as well as the tendency to accentuate disjunctive conflict, we turn instead to *tension* as our guiding heuristic. Tension (from the Latin *tendere*, to stretch) holds a particularly close relationship to psychological states: a straining of feelings or nerves. We would like to follow more closely the idea that theories in tension stretch each other, that they pull each other in new and surprising directions, and that they remain connected rather than fall away from each other into empty antagonisms. Specifically, in this chapter we stage a series of encounters between the affect theory of Silvan Tomkins and the affect theories of psychoanalysis from Freud onward. Although at times Tomkins situates his writing as a corrective to Freud's—indeed, he opens his four-volume *Affect Imagery Consciousness* (1962–92) with a strong critique of the psychoanalytic theory of the drives—here, we are less interested in such polemics and the wrangling for authority that Freud's writing often provokes, and more in the productive, if sometimes uncomfortable, tensions between Tomkins and psychoanalysis. Keeping these affect theories in conversation with each other, we argue, refuses the easy gratifications of substitution (in which *The Chair* excelled) and it unsettles the agonistic satisfaction of setting one affect theory against another.

Our goal is primarily interpretive: we seek to place Tomkins's qualitatively differentiated affect system and his notion of imagery in conversation with Freud and his interpreters in the Kleinian tradition. And we are particularly interested in those tensions that can move us toward a contemporary critical epistemology that takes subjectivity, subjective experience, and political subjectivation into account. Continuing the project we pursued in *A Silvan Tomkins Handbook*, here we offer more explicit emphasis on selected writers within the psychoanalytic tradition. Although the chapter is focused on Tomkins and psychoanalytic thinkers, we see an opportunity for a broader intervention into the field of affect studies: what are the ways in which one affect theory, often referred to with the shorthand name "Tomkins" or "Freud" or "James" or "Darwin" or "Spinoza" or "Deleuze," is available to be read with other affect theories? How can we *use* each other? Use, not in the sense of mistreating each other but in the sense that Donald W. Winnicott (1953, 5) suggests when he shows how the infant uses the objects within its reach (breast, fist, sounds, or toys, each "excitedly loved and mutilated") to build an affectively robust world or how a patient comes to use the analyst as an object who will survive the patient's destructive fantasies (Winnicott 1969). As Barbara Johnson (2000, 273) notes, this kind of Winnicottian use creates "a space of play and risk that does not depend on maintaining intactness and separation."

Surprise

Surprise is one of the affective responses that the use of Tomkins with psychoanalysis might invoke. In an eloquent essay about the notoriety of deconstructive reading, Barbara Johnson (2014, 331–32) argues that "a reading is strong . . . to the extent it encounters and propagates the surprise of otherness. The impossible but necessary task of the reader is to set herself up to be surprised." As we think about how to work with Tomkins and psychoanalysis, we find ourselves drawn to Johnson's appeal to surprise as a feature of reading. In their extended discussion of sex and unbearable negativity, Lauren Berlant and Lee Edelman also alight on surprise as an important part of how they have been reading their texts and reading each other. Edelman (Berlant and Edelman 2014, 120) notes the etymological links of *surprise*

to being seized, overtaken, or taken over and defines surprise psychoanalytically as "the encounter with what disrupts our expectations by
breaking though the defensive barriers associated with routine." Refusing to see psychoanalytically or deconstructively inclined criticism
as a coolly intellectual encounter, Johnson and Berlant and Edelman
each draw our attention to the affective jolt that a compelling reading
can deliver.

Surprise is one of the nine basic affects that ground Tomkins's
theory. Most of these affects are defined by Tomkins as either positive
(e.g., enjoyment-joy) or negative (e.g., anger-rage). Surprise, however,
is neither. It is a resetting affect: "a general interrupter of ongoing activity" (Tomkins 1962, 498). Surprise is "similar in design and function to
that in a radio or television network which enables special announce-
ments to interrupt any ongoing program. It is ancillary to every other
affect since it orients the individual to turn his attention from one
thing to another. Whether, having been interrupted, the individual
will respond with interest, or fear, or joy, or distress, or disgust, or
shame, or anger will depend on the nature of the interrupting stimulus and on the interpretation given to it" (498). Surprise is a brief
affective response and the experience of surprise, Tomkins suggests,
is either mildly neutral or somewhat negative. In its more intense
form, surprise becomes startle. Tomkins argues that the interruption
of surprise, good or bad, will have the effect of resetting our minds
and turning us in a new direction, cognitively and affectively. In this
sense, surprise is disjunctive. At the same time, however, surprise is
also combinatorial, binding one affective state to another. Tomkins
notes that surprise is frequently confused with the affect that immediately follows it: the happy surprise of the early return of a loved one
or the nasty surprise of the sudden arrival of someone we dread.

This understanding of surprise is in tension with, say, Edelman's
more psychoanalytically inclined use of surprise. Edelman recognizes
that a surprise "is often unpleasant" (Berlant and Edelman 2004, 120),
but he is oriented critically toward a different kind of negativity. Not
the phenomenological negativity of bad feeling but the negativity
that he has, relentlessly, associated with the death drive. Surprise is
a signal, of sorts, for "the incessant pressure of what we continue not
to know" (121). Johnson (2014, 331) also mobilizes surprise within
a psychoanalytically oriented vocabulary: the surprise of *otherness*,

where otherness is referencing the unconscious or what she calls "the imperatives of the not-self." It is clear that surprise as interruption (Tomkins) and surprise as otherness (psychoanalysis) are not the same thing, and under the care of Tomkins and Johnson and Edelman, these ideas move us in different directions. Importantly, however, Johnson's phrase "the surprise of otherness" stalls the demand to choose between these different interpretations. Both disjunctive and combinatorial, "the surprise of otherness" indicates a critical space where interruption and otherness might be used together but without generating something like an affective-psychoanalytic synthesis—without, that is, resolving the tension between them. Both of us have argued for the value of Tomkins's affect theory as an interruption to the monolithic and predictable readings that can be generated with classical Freudian theory. For example, one of us (AF) has suggested that there is benefit in reading not for a singular death drive but for "a variety of innate, negative affects, most of which are with the infant from birth, that threaten any more coherent or integrated sense of self: the rending cries of distress, the burning explosions of rage, the shrinking or vanishing compressions of terror, the transgression of the boundary between inside and outside the body in retching or disgust" (Frank 2006, 21). One of us (EW) has argued that understanding how the earliest digital computers were built requires something more than the routine Freudian-feminist indictment that these innovations are motivated by masculine envies for the capacity to biologically reproduce; instead of being substitutes for children, these machines are "sites of care and affection in their own right" (Wilson 2010, 49). Both of these readings, disputing classical Freudianism but never fully abandoning psychoanalysis or a curiosity about subjectivity and inner worlds, are attempting something like the Janus-faced surprise-otherness composite that Johnson has articulated.

Johnson has recommendations for the reader who would like to set herself up to be surprised by otherness. One could approach the impossible task of planning for a surprise by "transgressing one's own usual practices, by indulging in some judicious time-wasting with what one does not know how to use, or what has fallen into disrepute" (Johnson 2014, 332). We advocate wasting some time with the affect theories that Tomkins and psychoanalytic theorists have produced—affect theories that are still commonly held in disrepute for empirical, theoretical, and political reasons. The critical task for these readers is to remain open to surprise and, when having been interrupted and reoriented or having encountered the jolt of the not-self, read what happens next.

It is entirely unsurprising to note that the basic tension between Freud and Tomkins lies in their conceptualizations of the primary motives. For Tomkins, these are the affects, while for Freud, these are the drives (or instincts, in the *Standard Edition*'s translation). Yet for both theorists, drive and affect remain in the larger motivational picture as foundational concepts that lie on the border between the psyche and the soma. Tomkins insists that affects are physiological and describes them by way of specific bodily responses (expressions of fear, for example, may include eyes wide open, mouth agape, hair on end, and so on), but he also describes them in terms of a phenomenological gestalt—what fear feels like in awareness. Neither of these registers (the physiological, the phenomenological) is primary or exclusive in Tomkins's approach, and they clearly have a lot to do with each other. Similarly, in Freud's writing, we encounter a movement between the somatic and psychical: "'instinct' appears to us as a concept on the frontier between the mental and the somatic, as the psychical representative of the stimuli originating from within the organism and reaching the mind, as a measure of the demand made upon the mind for work in consequence of its connection with the body" (Freud 1915, 121–22).

As this reference to work implies, Freud is indebted to the nineteenth-century principle of the conservation of energy and the notion of homeostasis in its physiological applications (in, for example, Claude Bernard's notion of the *milieu interieur*). In "Instincts and Their Vicissitudes," Freud unfolds an economics in which instinct is characterized by a constant pressure that the organism seeks to discharge or reduce and whose source is an internal bodily stimulus. This source is distinct from the instinct's aim (a reduction of tension from this source) as well as from its object (anything that helps to achieve this aim). In the case of the sexual instincts that Freud takes as model, objects are less significant than sources (the body's erogenous zones) and aims (satisfaction or various forms of reversal, repression, and sublimation). Taken together, instinctual aims represent the individual's motivational field as it is charged by the organism's instinctual energy and discharged, diverted, or converted into psychical representatives of instinct: ideas and affects. For Freud, then, affects clearly derive from instinctual energy. He uses the term "quotas of affect," which Jean Laplanche and Jean-Bertrand Pontalis (1988, 374) define as "a quantitative factor postulated as the substratum of affect as this is experienced subjectively."

This is the way Freud's thinking can appear when it takes the form of metapsychology or speculative theory. When he offers specific analyses, case studies, and discussions of technique, however, distinctive affective qualities of the object become important for interpretation. We are on the terrain that Paul Ricoeur (1970, 65) has explored in great detail, the powerful ambiguity in Freud's writing "which at times states conflicts of force subject to an energetics, at times relations of meaning subject to a hermeneutics." This seeming disjunction between force and language, a quantitative energetics versus a qualitative hermeneutics, is in part responsible for the remarkable influence of psychoanalysis in so many domains of twentieth-century thought (and Ricoeur is careful to observe how Freud requires both). Tomkins's (1962, 126–27) critique is of Freud's speculative energetics:

> In his conception of motivation [Freud] attributed the urgency, innateness and time insistence of the drives to the Id, and at the same time he invested the Id with some but not all of the freer, more flexible attributes of the affect system. The Id was therefore at once an imperious, demanding, not to be put off investor of energy, and yet at the same time an investor who was capable of liquidating an investment, of seeking remote markets for investment when the immediate market was unfavorable, of even delaying an investment until a more profitable opportunity arose and of becoming a silent partner in any psychic enterprise. Had Freud not smuggled some of the properties of the affect system into his conception of the drives, his system would have been of much less interest than it was.

Tomkins's choice of metaphors to characterize the vicissitudes of instinct is no less indebted to Freud's nineteenth-century energetics than to postwar America's increasing grip on global markets. And his own theory, which offers an informatics of affect, is also oriented by the technoscience of its moment: the fields of cybernetics, systems theory, and information theory (Frank and Wilson 2020).

Recall, for Tomkins the affect system serves to amplify and give urgency to the drives. The infant's cry of distress, for example, amplifies the discomfort of hunger and acts as a signal that registers an urgent need to both infant and caregiver, self and other. The affects can also inhibit the drives, such as when the shame associated with a specific sexual act inhibits its realization. By no means entirely dislinked from the drives, the affect system abides by different logics. Where the drives are temporally constrained by cycles of need and satisfaction associated with the homeostatic regulation of the organism's internal states and are intrinsically connected with objects (respiration requires oxygen, hunger requires nutrition), the affects are free with respect to time, density, and object. They are neither fundamentally homeostatic in function nor primarily oriented toward the interior of the organism, and they are redundant and contagious in a manner that the drives are not (your anxious need to breathe does not make me asphyxiate, although the intensity of your distress is likely to lead to mine). Affects motivate us by orienting perception or directing attention to whatever appears to be important at a given moment, whether internal or external to the organism, and in distinctive ways.

Clearly, Tomkins does not take the sex drive (or sexual instincts) as exemplary of the drives as such. For him, it is only in conjunction with the affect system's qualitatively distinct forms of amplification and inhibition that the sex drive can become sexuality, a larger motivational field characterized not only by force or energy (of desire, say) and interpretation or hermeneutics (the symbolization of desire) but by qualitatively differentiated information (joy, fear, disgust). Although the drives continue to play a crucial role in motivation, Tomkins's approach does not require their transformability through a libidinal economics of repression and sublimation—the sex drive is important but perhaps not all important. Instead, we have layers of biological specificity and an attention to affective signals, no less bodily. We are still left with the problem of moving between force and language, but now this problem is differently scaled and has a different topography, with language and motivation mutually imbricated in each other in a manner that raises questions of linguistic performativity.

Abreaction

Tomkins is right, of course, that Freud attributed considerable motivational power to the drives and that although the affects "play a major role in his earlier papers," they have a "successively smaller role as Psychoanalysis evolved" (Tomkins 1962, 6). But we do not want readers to think that affect theories are foreign to psychoanalysis. With this in mind, let us turn to one place where Freud does attend to the affects with some intensity: the 1895 *Studies in Hysteria*. Coauthored with Joseph Breuer and composed of an introductory essay, five case studies, six theoretical chapters, and a set of clinical techniques for the treatment of hysteria, the *Studies* are one of those places where qualitatively distinct affects are central to psychoanalytic theory. Here, the differences between, say, fear and shame and joy really matter for the efficacy of psychoanalytic interpretation.

Breuer and Freud coin a new term to explain the circumstances that have thrown their patients into hysterical states: *abreaction*; in German, *abreagieren*: to work off, to respond, to react (especially in the sense of a chemical reaction). The hysterical patient has been unable to abreact a major traumatic event or, more commonly, a series of minor but nonetheless emotionally intense episodes ("a whole story of suffering" [Freud 1893, 31]). Such responses could have been anything from "tears to acts of revenge" (Breuer and Freud 1895, 8). Without abreaction, however, the original affect (e.g., shock, distress, humiliation) remains attached to the memory of the event. Breuer and Freud found that these memories "persist for a long time with astonishing freshness and with the whole of their affective colouring" (9). The patient has been unable to dissipate the affective experience through processes of association which would have enabled the affect to be compared with other experiences and ideas that might contradict or rectify the impression left by the event. Indeed, these affectively cathected memories, deprived of the ameliorative effects of association, are cut off from other parts of the mind, splitting consciousness and generating the hypnoid states for which hysterics had become infamous. Treatment, Breuer and Freud contend, requires putting these feelings into words, allowing the strangulated affects to finally be abreacted via speech: the talking cure.

Abreaction and the cathartic method are commonly understood to be the kind of theory and the kind of treatment that Freud would leave behind. Or in what amounts to the same thing, abreaction is important to the extent that it foreshadows what would come next. First abreaction, we might say, then psychoanalysis (the unconscious, dream analysis, Oedipus, drives). However, even as Freud was moving further away from the dynamics of strangulated affect, some of his colleagues continued to pursue these concerns with some intensity. For example, in a series of notes about laughter made in 1913 (but published after his death), Sándor Ferenczi returns to the Freudian question of abreaction and is drawn to the physiology of the body and particularly the face as an important site for the production of affect. These notes begin in a familiar Freudian manner: "laughter is a failure of repression. A defense against unconscious pleasure" (Ferenczi [1913] 1955, 180). But then, in ways that would become increasingly important for Ferenczi clinically and personally, in ways that would put intolerable strain on his friendship with Freud and on his membership in the psychoanalytic establishment, in ways that would be very influential in psychoanalytic theory and treatment decades later, and in ways that look something like Tomkins's affect theory, Ferenczi's ([1913] 1955, 180–81) mind begins to branch out in multiple, new, contradictory, breathtaking directions:

> I suggest that laughter consists of:
> (i) discharge of physical energy in Freud's sense;
> (ii) compensation for this discharge by the respiratory muscles becoming the site of the discharge. (And the face muscles (?).)
>
> Laughter is apparently a derivative of general muscle clonuses (and tonuses) which have become available for special purposes (aims). Just as expressive gestures arose from general reactions (cramps).
>
> The respiratory muscular system is thus appropriate to the expression of emotions because it permits (i) abreaction, as well as (ii) different shades of feeling and delicate graduations of inhibition.
>
> The face muscles are similarly adapted to the discharge of more delicate quantities of affect and at the same time to the regulation of breathing by the expansion and constriction of the openings of the nose and mouth (expansion = more pleasure breathed out. In weeping, sniveling movements).

These ruminations, more closely following the associative logics of his patients than the demands of published argument, are typical of how Ferenczi innovated theoretically and clinically. His clinical diary, written in 1932 (almost forty years after the *Studies in Hysteria*), documents abreactive storms of considerable power not only in his patients but also in himself. In January 1932, in relation to the treatment of a significantly disturbed patient, RN, Ferenczi (1988, 26) records that his emotional response ("grief, shock, regret, breaking down with tears in the eyes") to her stories of suffering corresponds with the first real therapeutic advance for RN: she is "permeated by a feeling that I have at last understood (that is, felt) her suffering" (26). In July of the same year, however, he notes that despite two years of abreactive work with RN, the "colossal outbursts of affect bearing every indication of terrible experiences" (168) have not brought about permanent change in her.

Rather than moving away from the importance of abreaction to clinical treatment (as did both Breuer and Freud), Ferenczi continued to innovate with both the content and the structure of the clinical session as a space where affects are worked off. One of the most notorious of these innovations was mutual analysis, where, in addition to the regular clinical hour, there was a second hour during which the analyst would lie on the couch and the patient would become the analyst (recall here Johnson's interest in interpretive spaces that do not depend on intactness and separation). These experiments with affect and mutuality horrified the psychoanalytic establishment and were part of the reason why some of Ferenczi's writings were withheld from publication for five decades after his death (Balint 1988). Ferenczi's diaries and notes struggle to think about how something like affect, as Tomkins would define it (facial, differentiated, abreactable), and something like the unconscious, as Freud would define it (terrible, ideational, interpretable), can be read and experienced together. That these texts are fragmentary, and for many years notorious, suggests that Ferenczi gave himself no easy task. Eventually Ferenczi's work was published in full and his experimentations with affect and mutuality have been read with increasing generosity (Dupont 1988; Harris and Kuchuck 2015; Haynal 2002; Rudnytsky 2022). Moreover, as classical Freudianism dispersed in the latter half of the twentieth century (Kleinianism, Lacanianism, the British middle school, self-psychology, relational psychoanalysis) and as many practitioners brought empirical methods to bear on psychoanalytic principles, the dynamics of affect so lucidly described in the *Studies on Hysteria* became important considerations once again. For these post-Freudian thinkers, theories of affect stand in some tension with the classical psychoanalytic idea that the vicissitudes of the drive should be our central clinical or theoretical concern. Some of these writers try to resolve this tension, but the more compelling of these texts (e.g., Beebe et al. 2005; Bowlby 1969; Fonagy et al. 2002; Tronick 2007) are able to tolerate the strain of thinking with both the affects and the unconscious, and use that discomfort to generate important new work on the vitality of subjective states.

Klein

We briefly take up one of these dispersions of Freudianism here whose direction was, in part, oriented by Ferenczi's thinking. According to the writers of *The New Dictionary of Kleinian Thought*, Melanie Klein "did not adhere to the conservation principle of (emotional) energy" (Spillius et al. 2011, 317) and did not make much use of Freud's economic model even as she relied on and revised his developmental, topographical, and structural models. Klein's relentlessly dynamic conception of the psyche, her emphasis on the *object* of instinct, not only its aim and source (hence *object relations*), and her unfolding of phantasy as the psychic representative of instinct, "seem to foreground the current interest in communication theory concerned with the distribution of information. Like information, phantasies of relationships with objects are not subject to a law of conservation" (317). As Eve Sedgwick and one of us (AF) have argued, Tomkins's approach to a qualitatively differentiated affect system is more compatible with Kleinian object relations than with Freudian energetics (e.g., Frank 2015; Sedgwick 2007).

The tension that we would like to explore here is between Tomkins's understanding of imagery and the concept of *introjection* in object relations theory. Ferenczi introduced this concept into the psychoanalytic literature in the essay "Introjection and Transference" (1909) where he defines it by analogy with projection: "Whereas the paranoiac expels from his ego the impulses that have become unpleasant, the neurotic helps himself by taking into the ego as large as possible a part of the outer world, making it the object of unconscious phantasies" (Ferenczi [1909] 1952, 47). Characteristically, Ferenczi exerts depathologizing pressure on these concepts ("the paranoiac projection and the neurotic introjection are merely extreme cases of psychical processes the primary forms of which are to be demonstrated in every normal being" [48]), and both Freud and Karl Abraham take up introjection in writing on grief and melancholia. Klein, who underwent analyses with both Ferenczi and Abraham, integrated the notion of introjection into her own case studies and speculative writing. In "Personification in the Play of Children," for example, Klein (1929) discusses the introjection of helpful or terrifying imagos and the conditions under which these may synthesize or fail to be synthesized as the superego. In Klein's careful and detailed account, the ego is involved in the work of addressing intrapsychic conflict (between id and superego), work that involves the introjection and projection of contrasting imagos, attempts to synthesize these, and splitting. She concludes that "this splitting of the super-ego into the primal identifications introjected at different stages of development is a mechanism analogous to and closely connected with projection. I believe these mechanisms (splitting-up and projection) are a principal factor in the tendency to personification in play" (205). Like Ferenczi, Klein understands the behavior of neurotic children to be continuous with everyday non-neurotic experience such as play.

The psychoanalytic concept of imago is very close to Tomkins's concept of imagery, a crucial element in his cybernetic account. Imagery, for Tomkins, emerges from bidirectional information duplication in humans (and other animals), efforts to match afferent (incoming) sensory, motor, or other information with efferent (outgoing) central feedback. The child's images of a parent's terrorizing or comforting face and voice are at once perceived and constructed and fit well with the idea of imago, as Laplanche and Pontalis (1988, 211) define it: "Unconscious prototypical figure which orientates the subject's way of apprehending others; it is built up on the basis of the first real and phantasied relationships within the family environment." Like imagery, which Tomkins characterizes in terms of all sorts of sensory, memory, and motor information, imagos are not reducible to the visual sense ("Feelings and behaviour, for example, are just as likely to be the concrete expressions of the imago as are mental images" [211]). Like imagos, imagery is the result of both introjection and projection since it emerges from a central matching mechanism that selects and integrates afferent and efferent flows of information that become images (of a parent's face and voice in this example). Klein (1929, 204) captures the sense in which imagos are both introjective and projective when she asserts, "The imagos adopted in this early phase of ego-development bear the stamp of the pregenital instinctual impulses, although they are actually constructed on the basis of the real Oedipal objects." Klein uses Freud's energetics ("instinctual impulses") to identify the internal constitutional source of the imago but insists that the imago itself is "constructed on the basis of" sensory experience of the parents.

In psychoanalysis, imagos are by definition unconscious, although they can be brought into conscious awareness (when reading Klein, one gets the sense that, at least for children at play, unconscious imagos are not entirely inaccessible). For Tomkins, imagery becomes conscious in the "central assembly," a collection of conscious reports that are functionally related to a central matching mechanism. In his complex account, consciousness becomes "a semistable psychological structure" (Tomkins 1992, 306) that is constantly being assembled and disassembled in relation to what information is centrally matched, and this process of matching is itself a skill of selective attention. It strikes us that Freud's (1900, 615) famous early definition of consciousness as "a sense-organ for the perception of psychical qualities" may be redescribed in terms of such skills of central matching. This tension between (largely conscious) imagery and (largely unconscious) imagos offers a promising avenue for thinking about inhibition, not in terms of a repressed libidinal energetics but an affective informatics of object relations. This tension opens up a conceptualization of repression as, in large part, a function of the affect system.

Conclusion

We could continue to pursue similar tensions between Tomkins's writing and other psychoanalytic thinkers in the Kleinian and post-Kleinian tradition. For example, one of us (AF) has found Wilfrid Bion's theory of thinking useful for critical purposes and it would be productive to bring Bion into conversation with Tomkins on "the minding system." But rather than pursue this, we would prefer to conclude with some thoughts about how the tensions we have already described above might help us to reconsider questions of political subjectivation, specifically with regard to an epistemological quandary. One version of this quandary appears at the start of "Instincts and Their Vicissitudes" where Freud (1915, 117) meditates briefly on the status of definitions in science:

> We have often heard it maintained that sciences should be built up on clear and sharply defined basic concepts. In actual fact no science, not even the most exact, begins with such definitions. The true beginning of scientific activity consists rather in describing phenomena and then in proceeding to group, classify and correlate them. Even at this stage of description it is not possible to avoid applying certain abstract ideas to the material in hand, ideas derived from somewhere or other but certainly not from the new observations alone. Such ideas—which will later become the basic concepts of the science—are still more indispensable as the material is further worked over.

Freud asserts the impossibility of a purely observational science, one that is utterly free of the impositions ("from somewhere or other") of abstraction or theory, but he never rejects the need to revise these ideas in the face of empirical evidence. In this opening paragraph, he points to the "indefiniteness" of these basic concepts and their particular status: "they are in the nature of conventions—although everything depends on their not being arbitrarily chosen but determined by their having significant relations to the empirical material, relations that we seem to sense before we can clearly recognize and demonstrate them" (117).

The nonarbitrary convention that has "significant relations to the empirical material"—does it not seem as if this useful, fundamental concept has gone missing in the polarizing amplifications of contemporary popular epistemology? Here is a frustrating example, a snapshot from recent experience: a colleague asserts at a (Zoom) department meeting that the university and regional authorities are not doing enough with regard to the pandemic (this despite a robust vaccine rollout, mandatory vaccine declarations, and ongoing public health measures). When it is pointed out that the number of reported infections is fairly low and shows signs of decreasing, the colleague asserts that the numbers are low because of a lack of testing. We are left with a basic disagreement, not simply about the facts (Is the virus actually in decline in the population?) but about evidence, authority, and power (How reliable are the daily case number reports? Can we ascertain whether there is a concerted governmental effort to reduce testing out of complacency or in order to maintain control over an anxious population?). We are left with a quandary: how to adjudicate between a seemingly naive trust in the reported data and a rejection of this trust that appears to dismiss the possibility of expertise?

If this example is reminiscent of what Eve Sedgwick identified many years ago as the emotional dispositions associated with Kleinian positions (depressive and paranoid-schizoid), perhaps Tomkins's notion of imagery may help to fine-tune this discussion. For imagery is the very ground of the relation between theory and perception, an epistemological grounding that takes place at both relatively higher and lower cognitive levels: both at the sophisticated level of how to understand numerical data related to pandemic infection rates and at the more visceral level of how to interpret an angry or caring face and voice. No doubt, we all have parental imagos that guide our responses to authority, but we also have more complex images of science, of government, and of the university, and these images are accompanied by criteria for what should (and should not) count as evidence, facts, and power. In other words, our abstract ideas are composed of conscious and unconscious images, a result of a central matching mechanism that constructs them out of sensory data and memory, and which is motivated by specific affective structures.

If analysis of ideology does not seem to be working very well these days to de-escalate polarizing opposition (to put it mildly), we wonder whether it would be possible to think about, explore, and analyze abstract ideas in relation to the images and affects that compose them. This is not to recommend a return to psychoanalytic reductionism, as if this were a viable alternative to what is much more common today, an intensive sociological reductionism. It is, rather, to keep in mind the possibility that our abstract ideas no longer have "significant relations to the empirical material" and so can and should be changed. Freud (1915, 124) discusses this possibility with regard to the indefinite concept of instinct itself, his main object of speculation in the essay: "I am altogether doubtful whether any decisive pointers for the differentiation and classification of the instincts can be arrived at on the basis of working over the psychological material. This working-over seems rather itself to call for the application to the material of definite assumptions concerning instinctual life, and it would be a desirable thing if those assumptions could be taken from some other branch of knowledge and carried over to psychology." Freud awaits empirical support from biology and expects Darwinian ideas to justify his emphasis on sexuality. Meanwhile, his interpreters in the Kleinian tradition revised his notion of instinct and adapted it to various clinical encounters (for example, with children and with schizophrenic patients). Here, we propose that Tomkins's partly empirical, partly speculative approaches to affect and imagery can play a productive role in tension with Freud and these interpreters and offer avenues for an affective analysis of what sets so many of us at odds.

References

Balint, Michael. 1988. "Draft Introduction." In *The Clinical Diary of Sándor Ferenczi*, edited and translated by Michael Balint and Nicola Zarday Jackson, 219–20. Cambridge, MA: Harvard University Press.

Beebe, Beatrice, Steven Knoblauch, Judith Rustin, Dorienne Sorter, Theodore Jacobs, and Regina Polly. 2005. *Forms of Intersubjectivity*. New York: Other Press.

Berlant, Lauren, and Lee Edelman. 2014. *Sex, or the Unbearable*. Durham, NC: Duke University Press.

Bowlby, John. 1969. *Attachment and Loss*. Vol. 1, *Attachment*. New York: Basic Books.

Breuer, Joseph, and Sigmund Freud. 1895. "Studies on Hysteria." In *The Standard Edition of the Complete Psychological Works of Sigmund Freud, Vol. 2*, edited and translated by James Strachey, 3–311. London: Hogarth.

Dupont, Judith. 1988. Introduction to *The Clinical Diary of Sándor Ferenczi*, edited and translated by Michael Balint and Nicola Zarday Jackson, xi–xxvii. Cambridge, MA: Harvard University Press.

Ferenczi, Sándor. (1909) 1952. "Introjection and Transference." In *First Contributions to Psycho-analysis*, translated by Ernest Jones, 35–93. New York: Brunner/Mazel.

Ferenczi, Sándor. (1913) 1955. "Laughter." In *Final Contributions to the Problems and Methods of Psycho-analysis*, translated by Eric Mosbacher, 177–82. New York: Brunner/Mazel.

Ferenczi, Sándor. 1988. *The Clinical Diary of Sándor Ferenczi*. Cambridge MA; Harvard University Press.

Fonagy, Peter, György Gergely, Elliot Jurist, and Mary Target. 2002. *Affect Regulation, Mentalization, and the Development of the Self*. New York: Other Books.

Frank, Adam. 2006. "Some Affective Bases for Guilt: Tomkins, Freud, Object Relations." *ESC: English Studies in Canada* 32 (1): 11–25.

Frank, Adam. 2015. *Transferential Poetics, from Poe to Warhol*. New York: Fordham University Press.

Frank, Adam, and Elizabeth A. Wilson. 2012. "Like-Minded." *Critical Inquiry* 38 (4): 870–77.

Frank, Adam, and Elizabeth A. Wilson. 2020. *A Silvan Tomkins Handbook: Foundations for Affect Theory*. Minneapolis: University of Minnesota Press.

Freud, Sigmund. 1893. "On the Psychical Mechanism of Hysterical Phenomena: A Lecture." In *The Standard Edition of the Complete Psychological Works of Sigmund Freud, Vol. 3*, edited and translated by James Strachey, 25–39. London: Hogarth.

Freud, Sigmund. 1900. "The Interpretation of Dreams." In *The Standard Edition of the Complete Psychological Works of Sigmund Freud, Vol. 5*, edited and translated by James Strachey, 339–627. London: Hogarth.

Freud, Sigmund. 1915. "Instincts and Their Vicissitudes." In *The Standard Edition of the Complete Psychological Works of Sigmund Freud, Vol. 14*, edited and translated by James Strachey, 109–40. London: Hogarth.

Harris, Adrienne, and Steven Kuchuck, eds. 2015. *The Legacy of Sandor Ferenczi: From Ghost to Ancestor*. New York: Routledge.

Haynal, André. 2002. *Disappearing and Reviving: Sándor Ferenczi in the History of Psychoanalysis*. London: Karnac.

Johnson, Barbara. 2000. "Using People: Kant with Winnicott." In *The Barbara Johnson Reader: The Surprise of Otherness*, edited by Melissa Feuerstein, Bill Johnson González, Lili Porten, and Keja Valens, 262–74. Durham, NC: Duke University Press.

Johnson, Barbara. 2014. "Nothing Fails like Success." In *The Barbara Johnson Reader: The Surprise of Otherness*, edited by Melissa Feuerstein, Bill Johnson González, Lili Porten, and Keja Valens, 327–33. Durham, NC: Duke University Press.

Klein, Melanie. 1929. "Personification in the Play of Children." In *The Writings of Melanie Klein*, vol. 1, *Love, Guilt and Reparation and Other Works 1921–1945*, 199–209. New York: Free Press.

Laplanche, Jean, and Jean-Bertrand Pontalis. 1988. *The Language of Psychoanalysis*. London: Karnac.

Ricoeur, Paul. 1970. *Freud and Philosophy: An Essay on Interpretation*. New Haven, CT: Yale University Press.

Rudnytsky, Peter. 2022. *Mutual Analysis: Ferenczi, Severn, and the Origins of Trauma Theory*. New York: Routledge.

Sedgwick, Eve Kosofsky. 2007. "Melanie Klein and the Difference Affect Makes." *South Atlantic Quarterly* 106 (3): 625–42.

Spillius, Elizabeth Bott, Jane Milton, Penelope Garvey, Cyril Couve, and Deborah Steiner. 2011. *The New Dictionary of Kleinian Thought*. London: Routledge.

"The Last Bus in Town," *The Chair*. 2021. Season One, Episode Five [13.10"–14.10"]

Tomkins, Silvan. 1962. *Affect Imagery Consciousness*. Vol. 1, *The Positive Affects*. New York: Springer.

Tomkins, Silvan. 1963. *Affect Imagery Consciousness*. Vol. 2, *The Negative Affects*. New York: Springer.

Tomkins, Silvan. 1991. *Affect Imagery Consciousness*. Vol. 3, *The Negative Affects: Fear and Anger*. New York: Springer.

Tomkins, Silvan. 1992. *Affect Imagery Consciousness*. Vol. 4, *Cognition: Duplication and Transformation of Information*. New York: Springer.

Tronick, Ed. 2007. *The Neurobehavioral and Social-Emotional Development of Infants and Children*. New York: W. W. Norton.

Wilson, Elizabeth A. 2010. *Affect and Artificial Intelligence*. Seattle: University of Washington Press.

Wilson, Elizabeth A. 2020. "Affect, Genealogy, History" [Review Symposium on Ruth Ley's *The Ascent of Affect: Genealogy and Critique*]. *History of the Human Sciences* 33 (2): 143–50.

Winnicott, Donald W. 1953. "Transitional Objects and Transitional Phenomena." In *Playing and Reality*, 1–25. London: Routledge.

Winnicott, Donald W. 1969. "The Use of an Object and Relating through Identifications." In *Playing and Reality*, 86–94. London: Routledge.

4 AFFECT AND AFFIRMATION

Tyrone S. Palmer

> Our *extimate* negation is affirmation inside out, a negativity of the infinitesimal. Unbearable, interminable, unfathomable.... There is nothing to affirm. —Jared Sexton, "On Black Negativity; or, the Affirmation of Nothing," 2017

While it is nearly impossible to neatly summarize or sufficiently condense affect into one strain or trend due to its (anti-)foundational multiplicity and resistance to categorization, it can be said that the disparate tendencies, approaches, and dispositions that comprise the discursive terrain of "affect theory" cohere around a systematic commitment to affirmation. Affirmation, here, names a singular emphasis on productive capacity; a philosophical ethos and political orientation that prioritizes positivity and connection over and against detachment and destruction. As a guiding principle, the affirmationist logic of affect theory insists on the generative, the possible, the new—as such, affect is positioned as an ever-renewable material resource: as that which marks the inherent relation and potentiality of all modes of mattering, a central element in the realization of new worlds. Considering the grammars and concepts that comprise affect theory's various means of articulation, one notices a trend: affect affirms life, resistance, futurity, mobility, capacity, openness, and in the simplest of terms, existence. That the rhetorical and conceptual bedrock of affect theory is characterized by such an overarchingly positive tenor positions inquiry into the negative as necessarily oppositional—negativity, broadly construed, is made the scene of a stubborn resistance to the interpellative call of affect, characterized by stasis and (en)closure, home to a retrograde insistence on cynical critique in the face of boundless possibility. This perspective is present—either by implication or explicit argument—in many of the touchstone works that have emerged in the past decade and a half of the ubiquitous and innumerable "turns" to affect in the humanities but is perhaps most succinctly rendered in the introductory chapter of the first *Affect Theory Reader*: "Affect speaks in the voice of an imperative" (Gregg and Seigworth 2010, 13). This imperative—the demand and command that affect persistently makes—is one of creation: there is always something more; a chance, a possibility, an ever-present not-yet-here on the horizon, an excessive bodily force that resists any attempt to capture it, a pathway of escape.

In many ways, this emphasis on generativity and creation is not specific to affect theory but rather is endemic to critical-theoretical discourse writ large. As Benjamin Noys (2010, xi–xi) notes, "'Affirmationism' constitutes a dominant and largely unremarked [upon] *doxa*" within contemporary theory, which is counterintuitively situated "[in] alignment with the ideology of contemporary 'creative capitalism' . . . predicated on invoking the inexhaustible value-creating powers of novelty, production, and creativity."[1] Although often positioned as an immanent critique of capital's extensive powers of consumption, aiming to identify modes of "agency" within and "resistance" to the central antagonisms that plague civil society, in its insistence on ever-shifting yet always available means of refusal and modes of dissent, critical theory and the humanities subsist on the drive to continually identify and (re)produce oppositional modes of being and forms of life. This being said, affect theory represents a particularly strident form of affirmationism in that so many of the key concepts in use throughout the discourse function to reify affirmation as the only possible outcome of a consideration of affectivity. The central term in question is "affect" itself, which through its many articulations and definitions—as radical abundance, as unbounded intensity, as an ever-shifting "capacity to," as the substance of relation(ality)—is reducible to an essence of affirmation. In practice, the turn to affect is invariably a turn to affirmation; to affect is to affirm.

The coupling of affect and affirmation at the level of the concept manifests in the insistence on the ever-processual, and therefore resistant, nature of affective exchange and in the pronouncement of an unyielding capacity to act—the inherent *chance* of the emergence of *something else*—in the face of a political apparatus which aims at totalizing domination. The political stakes, and promise, of affect theory rests in this unwavering generativity of new worlds of possibility; affect is the materiality of world(ing) as such, and this investment in a world, of any sort, is never questioned.[2] One of the primary points of appeal of affect theory is its focus on often denigrated modes of bodily knowledge, its affirmation of "the body" as the site of resistance over and against a structural determinism that would render it inert. It purports to make space within the critical-theoretical lexicon for the imperceptible, the untranslatable, those moments and phenomena that fall outside of the grasp of hegemonic modes of knowledge.

But for all the language affect theory has provided to contend with the continually shifting sociopolitical landscape, it has offered little more than a curious silence and universalizing gestures in the face of (anti-)Blackness, that which lies at the foundation and fulcrum of the political, its constitutive outside. The question of race in affect theory has been the site of a number of important critiques and interventions, and although strides have been made to think beyond the potentiality of the unspecified body and toward the particularized affects of racialization, there remains a caesura when met with Blackness in its singularity.[3] There has been little acknowledgment within affect studies of how profoundly Blackness shapes the seemingly universal (and universally applied) categories of affect, feeling, sensation, and the body.[4] I take this lack of self-reflexivity within the discourse not as an oversight but as indicative of a structural issue in the very conception of affect itself, one that is part and parcel of what I am identifying here as its affirmationist logic. For if affect can only ever emerge as a positive reinforcement of capacity, as "the endless capacitation of the individuated body" (Puar 2017, 20), what explanatory power does it have in the face of a mode of being that signals "incapacity in its pure and unadulterated form" (Wilderson 2010, 38)?[5] If affect affirms existence, potential, and plentitude, then Blackness stands as the figure of its negation, and as such, there is a seemingly insurmountable contradiction in terms when it comes to conceptualizing "Black affect." If one's aim is not to simply apply affect as it has been theorized to Black life, but to think alongside Blackness as ontological negation—as the site of affect's undoing, even as it is rendered subject to affect's violent operations—then a consideration of the problem of "Black affect" has a number of implications for the ethico-political stakes of affect broadly considered (i.e., to what and to whom affect can "speak"). Can there be a thinking of affect that does not insist on affirmation and generativity but instead on an unbridled negativity? What would the implications of such a theory be? What would affect theory be without its underlying, unacknowledged assumptions?

By thinking through these questions, this chapter considers more closely the political, conceptual, and methodological stakes of the affirmative drive and logic of affect theory through a consideration of the discursive moves of key texts within the field. I am particularly interested in the relation between affect theory as a resolutely affirmationist discourse—committed to generativity above all else—and its position as what Eugenie Brinkema (2014, 31) identifies as "the negative ontology of the humanities," that which is invoked to address any seeming absence or unthought possibility within humanistic inquiry. Brinkema notes that "affect has allowed the humanities to *constantly possibly* introject any seemingly absent or forgotten dimension of inquiry, to insist that play, the unexpected, and the unthought can always be brought back into the field" (xi). In light of this astute observation, I ask, What is it within and about affect that allows it to continually be invoked as panacea, and what must be erased, ignored, or rendered lost in order for it to only ever be conjured, in this capacity, as positive potentiality? Why does Blackness continue to remain unthought to that which can supposedly always recover the "unthought," beyond the bounds of the retrievable? And most pointedly, what does, or *can*, affect (theory) say when met with that which cannot be affirmed?

Producing Affirmation

The intertwinement of affect and affirmation is made plain in Brian Massumi's *Parables for the Virtual*, a text that since its publication two decades ago has undoubtedly formed the basis for a broad swath of the considerations of affect that have emerged in its wake. In the text's introduction, Massumi (2002, 12) positions the key methodological intervention of then-nascent affect theory as located within its "productivist approach," which insists on process, movement, and emergence. Productivism is held in distinction to (sociocultural) constructivism, which is characterized by stasis and rigidity, theorizing bodies as fixed positions on a grid as opposed to dynamic assemblages in the constant flux of becoming. For Massumi, an embrace of productivism in our analyses, and by extension a centering of affect qua intensity and unmediated experience, disrupts what he identifies as the theretofore dominant trend in cultural theory toward a negative mode of critique—one that detracts and debunks as opposed to building and affirming. In contrast, the productivist approach entails "[a] shift to *affirmative* methods: techniques which embrace their own inventiveness and are not afraid to own up to the fact that they add (if so meagerly) to reality" (12–13). Affirmation, as method, celebrates the potential inherent in theorizing, the ever-present possibility of a new form of thought. The very act of thinking (with) affect is positioned as an affirmative gesture, opening oneself and one's thought up to a realm of possibilities and "adding something to the world, if only the enjoyment [of creation] itself" (13). The enjoyment of creation is evident in the language used to articulate the circulation of affect—boundless, amorphous, slippery—and this methodological emphasis on creation operates in parallel to the commonplace positioning of affect as an excessive remainder to any given enclosure. This celebratory emphasis on creation yields a mode of approaching social antagonism as always already open to fugitive possibilities. A critical attentiveness to affect, then, necessitates a turn away from a subtractive, destructive negativity, and because "affect is unqualified . . . it is not ownable or recognizable and is thus resistant to critique" (28). Critique functions here as a metonym for negativity, which affect is perpetually pitted against; negativity is a roadblock to the generative potentiality affect promises and must thus be done away with—bracketed, suppressed, removed, denied.

Massumi's affirmationism extends beyond the question of method, however, and is evident in his articulation of the ontology, and/as *autonomy*, of affect. His conception of affect, which is heavily indebted to the thought of Baruch de Spinoza and Gilles Deleuze,[6] is defined by its ineffability, its perennial escape from capture by language (in and as meaning) and perception. It is also inextricably linked to (an affirmation of) life itself—as Massumi (2021, xxxvi) states, "Affect in the broadest sense [i]s what remains of life potential after each and every thing a body says or does . . . a perpetual bodily remainder . . . a reserve of potential or newness or creativity." It is the distilled affirmative essence of life that persists regardless of any attempt to subdue or destroy it. As such, affect de facto endures and resists, it is an intensity that is "immanent to [experience]—always in it but not of it" (33) and that is therefore at play in every element of existence. In this rendering of affect, the question of what lies at the limits of life itself—capacities that are exhausted beyond recovery or retrieval—is unthinkable; to exist is to be open to affect and its ineluctable plentitude.

Yet while Massumi is unequivocal in his commitment to affirmation as method and ethos—indeed, as the very essence of affect—his is not the only form in which such a commitment takes shape. A less patently obvious, yet no less potent, mode of affirmationism is at work in a number of critical texts that purportedly aim to foreground the question of the negative in relation to affective experience and that even demonstrate a level of skepticism toward affirmation.[7] These texts make clear that the hegemonic orientation toward the affirmative I am describing entails not only an emphasis on positive modes of affective sociality but on a singular way of contending with affective experience *of all permutations*. In other words, affirmationism in this context is not solely, or even primarily, about an insistence on joy, pleasure, and other recognizably "positive affects" (though there is no shortage of work with that focus). Rather, the pull of affirmationism is evident in how we read and contend with even so-called negative affects, those dimensions of affective experience that emerge at sites of violence and dispossession. Many of the significant considerations of the negative affects have been characterized by the naming of specific negative affective states or "bad feelings"—for example, shame, anger, envy, paranoia, disgust, pain, depression, and so forth—and subsequently affirming and positioning them as legible and credible modes of affective experience, in contrast to the pathologization and dismissal with which they are generally met.

Sianne Ngai's *Ugly Feelings* is an especially noteworthy text in this vein for its foregrounding of the marginal and "minor" affective registers—those affects that are indicative of suppressed, diminished, or "suspended" agency, that do not immediately present themselves as useful or pleasant but are in fact often experienced as intense displeasure. Yet as essential as Ngai's (2005, 1) text is for its centering of "sites of emotional negativity" as they emerge from and around the aesthetic, she notes that "it is part of [her] book's agenda to *re-cuperate* . . . negative affects for their *critical* productivity" (3) as well as their "social and symbolic productivity" (10). Although looking at negativity through a critical lens, there is an enduring emphasis on what is useful about it politically, socially, and aesthetically in a way that ultimately falls in line with the methodological imperative of productivity articulated by Massumi. Along similar lines, in the conclusion to her contribution to the first *Affect Theory Reader*, titled "Happy Objects," Sara Ahmed (2010, 50) calls for a move "beyond the affirmative gesture" in our considerations of affect, noting that the dominant tendency is to try to convert supposed "bad feelings" into "good feelings," generally toward the ultimate goal of attaining "happiness": the ultimate good feeling. The pursuit and attainment of positive affects is placed above a reckoning with the negative and in fact misapprehends the true scope of negative affects—as Ahmed states, "[The] affirmative turn actually depends on the very distinction between good and bad feelings that presumes that bad feelings are backward and conservative and good feelings are forward and progressive" (50). Yet rather than taking this observation a bit further and therefore leading to an outright rejection of affirmation in toto, Ahmed argues that "it is the very exposure of . . . unhappy affect that is affirmative, that gives us an alternative set of imaginings of what might count as a good or better life" (50). In other words, a shift in orientation toward what are often dismissively characterized as "bad" affects can function as a gateway to affirmative "possibilities"—getting us back to the always ever-present potential for "something new" to emerge, for "alternative model[s] of the social good" (50). The question remains, unasked and unanswered, of affective registers that threaten the very stability of the social, that are pointedly and ir-redeemably *antisocial* in their orientations and manifestations.

Continuing this lineage of thought, Xine Yao's (2021, 6) *Disaffected* goes further by foregrounding "antisocial affects" that are often positioned outside of the purview of recognizable affect at all—what she terms "unfeeling." Unfeeling encompasses a range of affective phenomena that "fall outside of or are not legible using dominant regimes of expression" (11) and are presented as a means of resisting and refusing the "hegemonic structures of feeling" (17) that have been the purview of affect theory to date, serving as the standard by which racialized peoples' affective capacity (or lack thereof) has been judged. Unfeeling is a negative affective register which encompasses various techniques of "disruptive negation" (8) deployed by people of color in order to contest their conscription by the dominant order's biopolitics of feeling and its stratification of life. Yet even though her stated aim is to "stay with the negativity of unfeeling and suspend its rehabilitation" (3), there is a latent investment in the *affirmation* of unfeeling as a positive, generative force—one tasked with an oppositional insurgency—present in Yao's text. As she states, "Rather than absence or negation, unfeeling may enable dormant, incipient, and insurgent affects . . . used strategically [it] can be put in the service of the eventual flourishing of feeling" (16). Unfeeling here is presented as a performative tactic one can adopt which enables an opening toward "possibilities of feeling otherwise" (28). As such, these affects are mined for their generativity, potential, and use value, ultimately considered in order to be incorporated within an affirmationist logic.

It is worth noting that much of the work that most notably raises the question of the negative in regard to affect (even if just in the form of "bad feelings") does so through consideration of those who live on the "margins" of racialized and gendered experience—a fact that I do not see as coincidental but rather as indicative of a realization of the inextricable link between racialization and negativity. As Anne Cheng (2000, 25) observes, a "haunting negativity . . . has not only been attached to, but has helped to constitute the very category of 'the racialized.'"[8] This negativity persists in spite of attempts at its repression or disavowal in the form of discursive moves toward affirmation. However, the question of *why* the turn is so frequently made to affect, in particular, as a means of affirmative recuperation, as gateway to otherwise possibilities and reinvigorated sociality, even in the face of its continued lived experience as a mode of negation is worth further consideration. The acknowledgment of the experience of negative affects is not necessarily an engagement with or acknowledgment of *negativity* in itself—it is possible to both fully recognize and reject the pernicious and pervasive invocation of affect as positive potentiality, while at the same time insisting on its logic of productivity and affirmation. I am interested here in a mode of engagement with the negative that does not deign to recover it or find within it a means of redress or revitalization but rather reckons with it on its own terms, dwelling within its abyssal depths; that does not look to it for what it might yield in terms of a reoriented social landscape but seriously considers—and even embraces—the notion that it might upend the social, and the World, entirely.[9]

Nothing to Affirm

Moving beyond a call for recognition of the importance of negative affects, or a dialectical affirmation of the potential and possibility inherent in the negative—whereby "negativity is 'freed' from dialectical subordination, only to be made subject, finally and fatally, to affirmationism . . . 'rescued' from the threat of being merely idle and abstract negativity" (Noys 2010, 17)—what is revealed if we think further about the role of negativity within the structure of affect as discourse, concept, and phenomenon? What to make of this pervasive gesture to rescue, to redeem, and what lies beyond the reach of redemption? What lies within the negative such that we are continually called to divest from it, to look away? How might affect theory deal with the negativity that is the seemingly inevitable by-product of its inexorable drive toward creation, the refuse of its productivist approach, at the wayside of its infinite world(ing)s? What does negativity reveal when unfettered by the desire for its traversal and conversion?

A path toward an answer to these questions—or, at the very least, a serious contending with their far-reaching implications—is found in that which is constitutively negated in the articulation of affect theory's worlds of relationality and generativity, that which persistently remains in "the position of the unthought" (Hartman and Wilderson 2003, 185), simultaneously functioning as the field's condition of possibility and that which must be foreclosed for its continued coherence.[10] A critical engagement with Blackness—not as identity or cultural performance but as structural position, "deployed as method" (Ferreira da Silva 2017), elucidates the limitations of the universalist affirmationism considered in this chapter thus far and offers a fundamental challenge to the key conceptual, methodological, and ideological tenets of affect theory.[11] Thinking Blackness in this manner moves us from the tendency to apply a generalized theory of affect onto specific dimensions of Black experience, toward a mode of theorization that attends to the urgent question of whether affect and Blackness can (or should) be conceptualized together at all, in any positive sense. What is made abundantly clear in such a consideration is that the affirmationist drive of affect theory and its persistent foreclosure of the negative is mirrored by and entangled with the structuring absence of Blackness within the discourse's purview—the negativity that affect theory positions itself in opposition to, either as a corrective or diversion, is a *Black(ened)* negativity. This Black negativity, or what David Marriott (2018, 223) terms a "non-negated negativity," a negativity without bounds or reprieve, unencumbered by the machinations of dialectics, which cannot be affirmed *or* truly disavowed, is the remainder that emerges at the site of violence that produces Blackness in the first instance. It is precisely the question of this violence and its role in the articulation of the boundaries of affective experience that is continually left at bay and that points to a fracture in the concept of affect. A failure to account for this violence and the negativity that it yields is why the question of Black affect, if engaged at all, can only ever be considered as an addendum or an inadequately integrated mode of difference. This tension between Blackness and affect lies in the desire to transform this negativity into a mode of generativity—one that can translate an unrelenting destructiveness into a positive mode of inhabitation. But Blackness, as a by-product of this unremitting negativity, cannot be absorbed by the move to affirmation because "Blackness cannot affirm, or choose, itself . . . it cannot pass from indecision to a transformation of what subordinates it . . . it is excluded, not just selected; out of kilter, not just turned around; nihilated, not just subjected" (Marriott 2020, 49).

Nihilation is exactly what is at stake in the question of Blackness and affect's collision—*and* the problem of "Black affect," since the conceptual ground on which affect stands is predicated on the violent abjuration of Blackness. As Patrice Douglass (2018, 339) argues, "The violence that situates Black ontological (non)being is *unequivocally affective* . . . non-Black affect operates at the meta-level of antiblackness." In other words, affect is a central element of the production and circulation of anti-Blackness and as such cannot be disentangled from its complicity in the propagation of Black suffering or conversely rendered a pathway out of that suffering. To recognize anti-Black violence as fundamentally affective is to undermine the productivist notion of creation as an inherent good, thereby making clear that the very operations of affect and its drive toward perpetual creation function to reinforce the anti-Black order through its continual reproduction of potential. The potential inherent in affect is the infinitely mutable variation of anti-Blackness. Following this, one might say that affect theory's affirmationism, at base, only ever "affirms" anti-Blackness and that while it valorizes creation in lieu of destruction, the affirmative drive of affect is itself a destructive drive, the target of which is Blackness qua negativity. It is the continual destruction (and/as conversion) and disavowal of this negativity that yields potential, possibility, relation, and so forth as the positive terms of its articulation. The insistence on a recuperative positive potentiality is haunted by a figure that signifies the negative semantic and metaphysical density of what is always *outside*—the irrecuperable, the irredeemable, the impossible. Blackness is the figure made to hold the weight of this negativity—that which must be repressed, foreclosed, and violently negated in order to come to an understanding of affect as boundless potential and possibility.[12] As such, an investment in terms of affirmation (potential, becoming, capacity, life, etc.) is, fundamentally, a move against and foreclosure of Blackness's essential negativity and all that it portends for the question of affect. Met with the question of potential's *limit*, the answer appears to be Blackness.

In light of this, the conceptual problem of "Black affect" is thrown into stark relief—as stated earlier, the contradiction in terms seems insurmountable. In response to this apparent incommensurability, the desire is often to affirm Blackness as potential and possibility—to make recourse to an untold affective capacity in order fill in the void; to reject Blackness's negation and condemnation as a locus of incapacity by discursively endowing it with a recovered capacity. However, such moves toward affirmation function as a further extension of the violence that is endemic to (the experience of) Blackness, evident of the fact that "for Blackness to be in the world, it must . . . reinvent itself as an affirmation" (Marriott 2020, 37). To make Blackness knowable within our given order of representation—to bring it into the world that so readily seeks its destruction—it must be figured as outside of the negativity through which it is produced, integrated into the very structure which furthers anti-Blackness. Stated differently, to think Blackness as affirmation is to think Blackness against itself. Rather than turning away from it, what might be gleaned from a fidelity to the negativity that Blackness brings to bear on the World of possibility and the possibility of world(s)—an embrace of negativity not for what possibilities of renewal it offers but for the disorder it brings on the assumed ground of our theorization?

What would it mean for a theory of affect to begin at this place—to emanate from the space of negativity, where assumptions of ontological capacity, relation to (world), and limitless potential not only do not hold but exist in direct opposition to the felt antagonisms of an existence wherein potential and possibility are circumscribed by an unrelenting violence? It is through this posture toward the negative that we may be able to begin to articulate a theory of Black affect that does not insist on positivity or transcendence by projecting a humanist capacity, or articulating Blackness through affect as potentiality, but sits within and emerges from the abjection of Blackness, taking seriously that negativity signals a divestment from the World and the desire for its continual transformation and renewal through the logic of worlding. This Black negativity signals a mode of destruction without the promise of, or desire for, generativity—staying in a position of antagonism to the persistent command to create (new worlds, new possibilities, otherwise socialities), questioning the very tenets of existence that are so valued. Against the affirmationist logic, a reckoning with Black negativity presents a mode of engaging affect that undermines concepts essential to the enterprise of affect theory and that, therefore, upends its very ground and (its often underexamined) pretenses toward universality. It signals an attentiveness to modes of feeling that manifest not as connection or abundance but as recurrent shatterings that register the violence that engulfs Blackness in the flesh and are unable to transcend it.

The challenge that Blackness and/as negativity presents for affect theory lies in a rejection of this transcendental imperative, not for the sake of a navel-gazing resignation but as a means of recognizing that it is precisely the drive for continual renewal that prevents a reckoning with the vastness and scope of the problem; the irresolvable nature of the antagonism. This presents the methodological problem of how one thinks with a mode of existence in which, as Jared Sexton succinctly states in this chapter's epigraph, "there is nothing to affirm" (Sexton and Barber 2017). For if affect is in its very essence affirmational, then what power or utility does it have when thought in this context? It is through an encounter with this mode of existence that the very discourse might be upended and unthought. Rather than approach it with salvific intent or the desire to make that nothing *something* of use—to, therefore, *affirm nothing*—a more ethical approach might be to contend with what this negativity reveals about the very terms with which one approaches the social and the political. This might resonate as deeply unsatisfying in a context where one must always generate a new possibility, where the potential for transformation, or an otherwise mode of living, is a foregone conclusion that underwrites every possible trajectory of thought. But part of what this chapter has aimed to do is call into the question the very desire for satisfaction in and as affirmation. As an alternative to the constant push and pull of affirmation and negation in our critical gestures— against the dialectic of "paranoia" and reparation (Sedgwick 2002);[13] shifting away from the mere naming of structural violence and the identification of its endlessly affirmable opposition, which aims not to destroy or truly overcome it but find other possibilities within it, to carve out other modes of life in the shadow of diminishment—what does an adherence to a mode of destructiveness that promises nothing but itself offer as the basis for thought and action? What can be exposed when, disabused of the idea of the possible, we embrace the ruin available to us?

To embrace ruin, to choose destruction, to adhere to the negative— all of this language feels inept, as though it is, in some sense, betraying the negativity it is calling our attention to. There is in fact no choice *but* destruction; there is, in fact, no choice. Perpetual destruction is what (un)makes Blackness, and as such, it is what Blackness brings to bear on the world: a drive that refuses recuperation or redemption, that insists only on the diffusion of its negativity. To meet said negativity with the will to affirm is therefore to obscure it, to submit to creation and potential as the continual remaking of anti-Blackness in innumerable variations. Rather than provide prescriptions or speculations on the possibilities inherent in the negative, this chapter has aimed to clear the field for further consideration of the crucial questions opened up by this negativity, pointing to the insidious pervasiveness of the logic of affirmation. Yet even as I attempt to bring this chapter to a close, I am faced with the difficulty of resisting this very logic—indeed, it appears inescapable. What precisely is left after rejecting generativity as an organizing principle? How to avoid framing Black negativity as the generative site of affect theory's re-enchantment or as the new doxa in lieu of affirmationism? The need to articulate what can be done with this negativity, to elaborate on what it offers, exists in tension with the drive to make it productive of a new social reality.

The point here has not been to integrate Blackness into the fold of affect theory but to think Blackness, in its negativity, as the space where one finds operative a theory of affect that is incommensurable with its dominant theorization; that speaks to modes of affect that do not register as a means of escape, creation, or transcendence but rather as reiterations of structural captivity. To begin to truly think Black affect necessitates a unilateral rejection of the drive to affirm and a reckoning with negativity and the modes of feeling that emerge out of its inhabitation. In the absence of affirmation, beyond the horizon of possibility, Black affect yields nothing but its own destructiveness. It is in deference to this that we may see the World's necessary dissolution.

Notes

1   In *The Persistence of the Negative: A Critique of Contemporary Continental Theory*, Noys provides a comprehensive examination of this affirmationist tendency and its attendant anxieties about the place of the negative in the thought of various philosophers, including (most importantly for our purposes) Deleuze.

2   For further elaboration on the problematic of world(ing) in relation to Blackness and affect, see Palmer (2020).

3   For key texts on affect and processes of racialization, see Anim-Addo (2013), Chen (2012), Hesse (2016), Lim (2010), Muñoz (2006), Rai (2012), Saldanha (2006), Schuller (2018), and Yao (2021). In recent years, there have been more concerted efforts to think affect theory and Blackness, in its particularity, together. See Ashley and Billies (2019), Douglass (2018), Palmer (2017), and Warren (2016).

4   Many of the most illuminating and insightful works on these questions do not foreground a discussion of affect theory as discourse but rather demonstrate how Blackness inflects and disrupts questions of sensation, hapticality, emotion, sentimentality, and so forth. See, for instance, Bradley (2020), Hartman (1997), Jackson (2020), Moten and Harney (2013), Musser (2014), Scott (2010), and Sharpe (2016).

This essay, though aligned in some ways with many of these thinkers, departs in its centering of the question of affect as such, as well as in an insistence on negativity as essential to the problem of Blackness and affect's collision.

5   In *The Right to Maim: Debility, Capacity, Disability*, Jasbir Puar (2019, 20) offers a corrective to affect theory's dominant theorization of unbounded capacity, which she argues "takes the integrity of human form for granted." For Puar, a rethinking of capacity necessitates an acknowledgment of how "it is shaped by and bound to interface with prevailing notions of chance, risk, accident, luck, and probability, as well as with bodily limits/*incapacity*, disability, and debility" (19, emphasis mine). Along similar lines, another noteworthy challenge to the hegemony of capacity is offered by Grant Bollmer (2013), who critiques the ableism of the ontologized capacity of affect theory, noting that its insistence on a normative, biological capacity writes neuro-atypical subjects outside of the discursive boundaries of affective circulation and, more broadly, humanity. My citation of Wilderson (2010, 45) here signals Blackness as *ontologized incapacity*, or what gives "human" capacity its coherence. Colin Patrick Ashley and Michelle Billies (2017) contrarily affirm Blackness *as* capacity through a Deleuzian conception of "affective blackness" as a sticky, resistant ontology and endlessly generative force. The understanding of Blackness I am operating from differs considerably from theirs—as I argue in this essay, the affirmationist move to endow Blackness with positive capacity misapprehends its essential negativity.

6   The dominant affirmationist reading of Deleuze has been the subject of a number of critiques, perhaps most notably Andrew Culp's (2016) *Dark Deleuze*, which calls for a rethinking of this framing of the philosopher's work. Culp contends that this tendency positions Deleuze as a "naively affirmative thinker of connectivity" (1) and joyous creation, foreclosing the destructive impulses latent in his thought. As the translator of one of Deleuze and Guattari's (1987) most seminal texts into English, Brian Massumi's imprint is very much present in the dominant affirmative approaches to Deleuze.

7   As Vickie Zhang notes, "Scholars are working to reclaim negative feelings, valuing not their valence but their capacity to generate an affirmable 'politics of difference.' . . . [In such work,] bad feelings are still only being acknowledged for the productive projects they are able to inaugurate—adding a wider range of affects to the scope of affirmable action, but not fundamentally changing its 'positive' and productive impulse" (cited in Dekeyser et al. 2022, 14).

8   Although it is distinct from the work I am doing here, the sizable literature concerning racialized trauma, mourning, melancholia, death, and psychoanalysis, of which Anne Cheng's text is an important touchstone, is worth mentioning for its attempts to tarry with the negative dimensions of the psychic life of race. See also Eng and Kazanjian (2002), George (2016), and Viego (2007). Additionally, further elaborations of the link between social "marginalization" and negativity can be found, to varying degrees, in a number of texts in feminist and queer theory. In this vein, the work of this essay bears the strongest affinity with that of Lee

Edelman (2004, 9) who argues that it is in fact *queerness* which is the figure of a negativity that is "opposed to every form of social viability." A consideration of the relation between Edelman's queer negativity and Blackness is well beyond the scope of this particular chapter, but for related explorations, see Bliss (2015), Edelman (2019), and Warren (2017).

9   This is in contradistinction to theorizations of negativity which insist that its "radical" political potential lies in its affirmation and that therefore embrace the negative only insofar as it can be figured as a mode of generativity. One such example of this mode of theorizing the negative can be found in Diana Coole's (2000) *Negativity and Politics: Dionysus and Dialectics from Kant to Poststructuralism.* Coole states that negativity "emerge[s] from my readings: as *generativity*. It is in this sense . . . that it is affirmative: a creative-destructive force that engenders as well as ruins positive forms" (6); "it indicates *becoming*, a productivity that engenders every distinct form as a creative-destructive restlessness" (230). Note the conceptual linkage of creation and destruction here. As stated, I am interested in thinking negativity as a mode of destruction that is not tethered to the drive to create.

10   For more on the necessity of this foreclosure, see Palmer (2017).

11   The shift to an understanding of Blackness as structural position here is clearly informed by the work of Frank Wilderson and other thinkers of Afropessimism. This essay, in a sense, performs an encounter between Afropessimist thought and affect theory, though an explicit elaboration of the (ir)relation between these two discourses is outside of its purview and its aims.

12   As Calvin Warren (2018, 27) argues, Blackness holds the weight of the "nothing" that metaphysics aims to perpetually destroy—"the Negro is the incarnation of nothing that a metaphysical world tries tirelessly to eradicate." That "nothing" and the negativity that I am describing here are conceptualized along similar lines—as he states, "nothing *cannot* be negated" (92).

13   See Steulke (2021) for an important critique of the reparative turn.

References

Ahmed, Sara. 2010. "Happy Objects." In *The Affect Theory Reader*, edited by Melissa Gregg and Gregory J. Seigworth, 29–51. Durham, NC: Duke University Press.

Anim-Addo, Joan. 2013. "Gendering Creolisation: Creolising Affect." *Feminist Review* 104:5–23.

Ashley, Colin Patrick, and Michelle Billies. 2017. "The Affective Capacity of Blackness." *Subjectivity* 10 (1): 63–88.

Ashley, Colin Patrick, and Michelle Billies. 2019. "Affect and Race(/Blackness)." *Athenea Digital* 20 (2): 1–15.

Bliss, James. 2015. "Hope against Hope: Queer Negativity, Black Feminist Theorizing, and Reproduction without Futurity." *Mosaic: A Journal for the Interdisciplinary Study of Literature* 48 (1): 83–96.

Bollmer, Grant David. 2013. "Pathologies of Affect: The New Wounded and the Politics of Ontology." *Cultural Studies* 28 (2): 1–29.

Bradley, Rizvana. 2020. "The Vicissitudes of Touch: Annotations on the Haptic." *The b2o Review*. https://www.boundary2.org/2020/11/rizvana-bradley-the-vicissitudes-of-touch-annotations-on-the-haptic/.

Brinkema, Eugenie. 2014. *The Forms of the Affects*. Durham, NC: Duke University Press.

Chen, Mel. 2012. *Animacies: Biopolitics, Racial Mattering, and Queer Affects*. Durham, NC: Duke University Press.

Cheng, Anne. 2000. *The Melancholy of Race: Psychoanalysis, Assimilation, and Hidden Grief*. New York: Oxford University Press.

Coole, Diana. 2000. *Negativity and Politics: Dionysus and Dialectics from Kant to Poststructuralism*. New York: Routledge.

Culp, Andrew. 2016. *Dark Deleuze*. Minneapolis: University of Minnesota Press.

Dekeyser, Thomas, Anna Secor, Mitch Rose, David Bissell, Vickie Zhang, and Jose Luis Ramanillos. 2022. "Negativity: Space, Politics, and Affects." *Cultural Geographies* 29 (1): 5–21.

Deleuze, Gilles, and Félix Guattari.1987. *A Thousand Plateaus: Capitalism and Schizophrenia*. Minneapolis: University of Minnesota Press.

Douglass, Patrice. 2018. "On (Being) Fear: *Utah v. Strieff* and the Ontology of Affect." *Journal of Visual Culture* 17 (3): 332–42.

Edelman, Lee. 2004. *No Future: Queer Theory and the Death Drive*. Durham, NC: Duke University Press.

Edelman, Lee. 2019. "Queerness, Afro-Pessimism, and the Return of the Aesthetic." REAL: *Yearbook of Research in English and American Literature* 35:11–26.

Eng, David, and David Kazanjian, eds. 2002. *Loss: The Politics of Mourning*. Berkeley: University of California Press.

Ferreira da Silva, Denise. 2017. "1 (Life) ÷ 0 (Blackness) = ∞ — ∞ or ∞ / ∞: On Matter beyond the Equation of Value." *e-flux* 79. https://www.e-flux.com/journal/79/94686/1-life-0-blackness-or-on-matter-beyond-the-equation-of-value/.

George, Sheldon. 2016. *Trauma and Race: A Lacanian Study of African American Racial Identity*. Waco, TX: Baylor University Press.

Gregg, Melissa, and Gregory J. Seigworth, eds. 2010. *The Affect Theory Reader*. Durham, NC: Duke University Press.

Hartman, Saidiya. 1997. *Scenes of Subjection: Terror, Slavery and Self-Making in Nineteenth-Century America*. New York: Oxford University Press.

Hartman, Saidiya, and Frank B. Wilderson III. 2003. "The Position of the Unthought." *Qui Parle: Critical Humanities and Social Sciences* 13 (2): 183–201.

Hesse, Barnor. 2016. "Of Race: The Exorbitant Du Bois," *Small Axe* 20 (2): 14–27.

Jackson, Zakiyyah Iman. 2020. *Becoming Human: Matter and Meaning in an Antiblack World*. New York: New York University Press.

Lim, Jason. 2010. "Immanent Politics: Thinking Race and Ethnicity through Affect and Machinism." *Environment and Planning* 42 (10): 2393–409.

Marriott, David. 2018. *Whither Fanon? Studies in the Blackness of Being*. Stanford, CA: Stanford University Press.

Marriott, David. 2020. "Blackness: N'est Pas?" *Propter Nos* 4:27–51.

Massumi, Brian. 2021. *Parables for the Virtual: Movement, Affect, Sensation*. Durham, NC: Duke University Press.

Moten, Fred, and Stefano Harney. 2013. *The Undercommons: Fugitive Planning and Black Study*. New York: Minor Compositions.

Muñoz, Jose Esteban. 2006. "Feeling Brown, Feeling Down: Latina Affect, the Performativity of Race, and the Depressive Position." *Signs: Journal of Women in Culture and Society* 31 (3): 675–88.

Musser, Amber Jamilla. 2014. *Sensational Flesh: Race, Power, and Masochism*. New York: New York University Press.

Ngai, Sianne. 2005. *Ugly Feelings*. Cambridge, MA: Harvard University Press.

Noys, Benjamin. 2010. *The Persistence of the Negative: A Critique of Contemporary Continental Theory*. Edinburgh: Edinburgh University Press.

Palmer, Tyrone S. 2017. "'What Feels More than Feeling?': Theorizing the Unthinkability of Black Affect." *Journal of the Critical Ethnic Studies Association* 3 (2): 31–56.

Palmer, Tyrone S. 2020. "Otherwise than Blackness: Feeling, World, Sublimation." *Qui Parle: Critical Humanities and Social Sciences* 29 (2): 247–83.

Puar, Jasbir K. 2017. *The Right to Maim: Debility, Capacity, Disability*. Durham, NC: Duke University Press.

Rai, Amit. 2012. "Race Racing: Four Theses on Race and Intensity." *WSQ: Women's Studies Quarterly* 40 (1–2): 64–75.

Saldanha, Arun. 2006. "Reontologising Race: The Machinic Geography of Phenotype." *Environment and Planning D: Society and Space* 24 (1): 9–24.

Schuller, Kyla. 2017. *The Biopolitics of Feeling: Race, Sex, and Science in the Nineteenth Century*. Durham, NC: Duke University Press.

Scott, Darieck. 2010. *Extravagant Abjection: Blackness, Power and Sexuality in the American Literary Imagination*. New York: New York University Press.

Sedgwick, Eve Kosofsky. 2002. *Touching Feeling: Affect, Pedagogy, Performativity*. Durham: Duke University Press.

Sexton, Jared, and Daniel Colucciello Barber. 2017. "On Black Negativity, or the Affirmation of Nothing: Jared Sexton, Interviewed by Daniel Barber." *Society and Space*. https://www.societyandspace.org/articles/on-black-negativity-or-the-affirmation-of-nothing.

Sharpe, Christina. 2016. *In the Wake: On Blackness and Being*. Durham, NC: Duke University Press.

Steulke, Patricia. 2021. *The Ruse of Repair: US Neoliberal Empire and the Turn from Critique*. Durham, NC: Duke University Press.

Viego, Antonio. 2007. *Dead Subjects: Toward a Politics of Loss in Latino Studies*. Durham, NC: Duke University Press.

Warren, Calvin L. 2016. "Black Care." *Liquid Blackness* 3 (6): 36–47.

Warren, Calvin L. 2017. "Onticide: Afro-Pessimism, Gay Nigger #1, and Surplus Violence." *GLQ: A Journal of Lesbian and Gay Studies* 23 (3): 391–418.

Warren, Calvin L. 2018. *Ontological Terror: Blackness, Nihilism, Emancipation*. Durham, NC: Duke University Press.

Wilderson, Frank B. 2010. *Red, White, and Black: Cinema and the Structure of U.S. Antagonisms*. Durham, NC: Duke University Press.

Yao, Xine. 2021. *Disaffected: The Cultural Politics of Unfeeling in Nineteenth-Century America*. Durham, NC: Duke University Press.

Affectability, Temporality, and
Unleashing the Sex/Gender Binary

Kyla Schuller

We are currently in the midst of an interesting dilemma in feminist pedagogy. The rationale of one of our core concepts, the sex/gender distinction, has been crumbling for decades. Yet in undergraduate classrooms, sex and gender regularly appear as distinct terms for distinct phenomena, even as the utility of this differentiation has steadily eroded. Feminists initially elaborated the sex/gender distinction in the early to mid-1970s. Anthropologist Gayle Rubin (1978, 178) argued that social life "exacerbates the biological differences between the sexes," producing the phenomenon of gender. For Rubin, culture, political economy, divisions of labor, and kinship relations augment preexisting physical realities of sex, sexuality, and reproduction by embedding them within a complex network of power. She named this dynamic the "sex/gender system" (159).[1] Over the subsequent decades, Rubin's sex/gender system has often been enlisted to articulate the sex/gender distinction, a binary in which sex refers to the biological body, while gender refers to a social construct. This biology versus society binary echoes throughout classrooms today as one of feminism's key achievements, even as feminist theory has simultaneously considerably complicated its terms. The assumption that the matter of sex and the culture of gender are distinct phenomena with distinct trajectories has long been in crisis, and rightly so.

The sex-gender binary has been at once feminist common sense and the source of considerable instability. From the beginning, women of color feminism questioned the fantasy that physical sex was a distinct sphere from social and political life. In a famous 1979 open letter to Mary Daly, Audre Lorde took pains to explain that there was no such thing as a universal experience of sex, let alone gender. "Surely you know that for nonwhite women in this country, there is an 80 percent fatality rate from breast cancer; three times the number of unnecessary eventrations, hysterectomies and sterilizations as for white women; three times as many chances of being raped, murdered, or assaulted as exist for white women," she emphasized (Lorde 1984, 70). The "female body" simply was not one.

Judith Butler overhauled the terms of the biology-society binary in the early 1990s, positing that the category of sex materializes within complex iterations of cultural, and especially discursive, processes repeated over time. The raw material of sex is not put to work by culture; rather, the matter of sex itself precipitates through iterative social norms. In the earlier model, social life exacerbated preexisting differences inherent to physical sex. But for Butler, materiality and social signification are intertwined and simultaneous processes in which neither is a primary actor. There is no inert body later "constructed" by culture, Butler (1993) insists; instead, the sexed body materializes within heteronormative discourses of intelligibility, while at the same time, marking other bodies as unlivable, the constitutive outside of the realm of intelligibility.

Yet how matter coproduces the social world is much less clear in Butler's 1990s work than is how social norms produce the physical categories of male and female. Butler's philosophical methods, which turn to Hegel, Derrida, Austin, and Freud—a method divergent from science studies scholars like Anne Fausto-Sterling and Elizabeth Wilson who turn to the dynamic capacities of the body to absorb, transmit, and transform experience—can compound the sense that culture is the real actor and matter merely the recipient of its graces (Fausto-Sterling [2000] 2020, 2012; Wilson 2004). In applications of Butler's theories over the ensuing years, and especially prior to the publication of her sensation- and emotion-oriented *Senses of the Subject* (2015), a distorted form of the biology-society binary emerges. In some interpretations, matter becomes another world for culture, biology all but disappears, and the capacities of materiality itself fall out of the frame. These readings portray cultural norms of sex to actively imprint relatively passive matter, and the binary rears its head, albeit in a reformed version in which culture now has the power (Alaimo and Hekman 2008). This modified iteration of the sex/gender distinction often comes to embody an animacy hierarchy, to use Mel Chen's (2012) term capturing the ranking of vital capacity at the core of modern politics. Animacy, for Chen, illuminates how biopower categorizes and hierarchizes the relative "aliveness" of bodies, objects, and substances, metering out vitality as a proxy for who or what counts as part of the public sphere. The newer version of the sex/gender distinction gives culture the power of animacy while relegating the body to the status of passive material. It reveals more about biopower's tendency to deny matter the capacity of vitality or aliveness than it offers a helpful understanding of how power and the body interact. Life itself gives way to the overarching power of human volition, and a biology versus culture binary remains in place, however reconfigured.

Yet how can we continue to proceed to think about sex/gender without fundamentally reckoning with the body that lives and breathes? The double-barrel impact of affect theory and the ontological turn of the past twenty years has obliterated the fantasy that organic life is merely subservient to the efforts of the human mind. The idea that feminists ought to teach how sex takes shape primarily through cultural scripts enacted over time seems increasingly suspect in light of affect theory's emphasis on the autonomic capacities of the body, those circulating intensities, energies, and "forces of encounter" that exist outside of and before the individual and that forge new dynamic connections between organic matter, technology, and discursive life (Gregg and Seigworth 2010, 2). Life does not follow the course of binaries, even binaries that trace "interactions" between x and y—as theorists, we need to grapple with encounters, dynamics, materializations, and assemblages that never presume x can be constituted outside of y. Osteopaths have found, for example, that patients diagnosed with multiple personality disorder can have distinct blood pressures, body temperatures, and even drastically different levels of thyroid stimulating hormone, depending on which personality is dominant (Pelkey 2018). If even the diagnosis of hypothyroidism can be affect dependent, how can we think of something as complex as sexed materiality and constructs of gender without accounting for how emotion, sensation, affect, and energy make a mockery of our attempts to conceptually tear bodyminds asunder?

Sex/gender, we might say, needs affect theory. But affect is no straightforward savior. Attending to the shuttling of affective forces that make a body less a discrete object than a force field of becoming would enable us to approach both sex and gender as biocultural processes in which bodies take shape in the midst of social environments. In what follows, I take up this provocation and suggest rethinking the sex/gender distinction as marking a difference of time, rather than substance. I propose that sex denotes a biology-culture assemblage at the moment of the individuated body, while gender denotes a biology-culture assemblage at the moment of the collective. Yet, crucially, embedding affective dynamics in the heart of our notion of sex and gender does not necessarily escape the animacy hierarchy that ranks the relative vitality of all that exists, nor does it provide access to an inherently more liberatory notion of sex/gender and embodiment. Historically, scientists' and reformers' interest in the affective capacities of the body has been key to their attempts to engineer social control. In these schemes, from early eugenics to mid-twentieth century sexology, the body's responsive plasticity serves as a tool to force the direction of human growth. The very concept of gender is one of the fruits of this confluence between plasticity and control.

Gender has a surprisingly precise and recent vintage, as scholars including Jemima Repo (2015), Jules Gill-Peterson (2018), and Hil Malatino (2019) have revealed. I draw on their work explaining how gender as a medical term and framework was developed by mid-twentieth century sexologists and psychiatrists such as John Money who were bent on misguided treatment regimes aiming to "normalize" intersex youth and trans adults. I also show how these scientists implicitly invoked the earlier, nineteenth-century race science concept of bodily "impressibility" when they outlined a model for practitioners and parents to "imprint" gender on the bodyminds of young children. Gender emerged as a biocultural tool of control that crisscrossed mental, physical, emotional, and affective dimensions to maintain the fiction that the male-female binary was paramount to the order of life.

Affect can help us think of a less brutal system of gender. Yet the history of affect is also part of gender's brutality. Models of affective capacity and bodily plasticity are not innocent spheres, removed from the political. As this chapter and the scholarship it thinks with make clear, models of malleability often serve as potent vehicles of biopolitical control, even though biological determinist models that understand biology to fix one's destiny are more notorious for this use (Gill-Peterson 2018; Malatino 2019; Schuller 2018). But thinking with pliant, affective bodies is nonetheless more than worth the risk when approached with caution and the right guideposts. In that spirit, sex/gender can be reimagined affectively to capture how power acts on the body over time, while keeping close to mind how the origins of gender themselves reveal the violence of affective models of gender wielded as forms of violence and control.

In the first half of the twentieth century, new scientific models pushed ever deeper into the body, as molar approaches to the human organism as a whole gave way to granular analysis of genes, chromosomes, hormones, atomic nuclei, and blood types (Cohen 2009). The sciences of sex difference flourished within biomedicine's ever-narrowing scope. One of the perhaps unexpected outcomes of this research was the (re)discovery of the diversity of sex (Fausto-Sterling [2000] 2020).[2] The more precisely male-female difference was located in the body, the more scientists encountered exceptions to the newly codifying rules. For example, the "sex chromosome" concept widely adopted in the 1920s was formally reaffirmed in 1960 as a type of chromosome fundamentally distinct from the other twenty-two pairs in the human body (Richardson 2013). But the paradigm of the XY/XX genotype was complicated by the 1950s discovery that XXY, XO, and other sex chromosome patterns were prevalent. Trans studies scholar Jules Gill-Peterson (2018, 97) explains that "by 1950 . . . both biology and medicine had worked themselves into the position of being perilously close to lacking a rationale for the sex binary altogether." Medical practitioners identified the existence of adults and youth with genetic, morphological, and physiological intersex conditions to be a growing problem for biomedicine and the life sciences, especially in the disciplines of endocrinology, genetics, sexology, and psychology (Gill-Peterson 2018). And they responded by reaffirming the sex binary as mandatory and controlling queer bodies and lives, despite a long history of nonbinary figures in Western European culture and art (DeVun 2021).

Some children whose bodies were deemed to violate the new rules of endocrinological and genetic sex were institutionalized by the Harriet Lane Home for Invalid Children at Johns Hopkins University. When John Money, then a Harvard graduate student in psychology, arrived at Johns Hopkins with his mentor Joan Hampson in 1951, he soon began interviewing the patients at Harriet Lane (Downing, Morland, and Sullivan 2015, 4). On the basis of these interview data, Money, Hampson, and her husband John Hampson published a series of articles over the next six years that were pivotal in establishing treatment protocols for intersex infants and children. These articles were also pivotal in inventing the notion of gender in its modern sense (Gill-Peterson 2018).[3]

The goal of Money and the Hampsons' early research was to develop guidelines for physicians to assign binary sex to intersex youth, forcing their bodies to fit the male/female dimorphism science had codified. Money and the Hampsons established that there are seven independent variables that make up sex and that any of these variables may misalign. Five of these criteria had become familiar to the sciences of sex difference: "chromosomal sex; gonadal sex; hormonal sex; external genital morphology; [and] accessory internal genital morphology" (Money, Hampson, and Hampson 1955a, 302). One they borrowed from psychology, "assigned sex and rearing." The seventh and final they developed themselves: "gender role" (Money, Hampson, and Hampson 1955b, 299), which "is used to signify all those things that a person says or does to disclose himself or herself as having the status of boy or man, girl or woman" (Money 1955, 254) and that accumulates "through experiences encountered and transacted" (Money, Hampson, and Hampson 1955b, 299). These variables are all "interlinked," and no one element has sole determining power over the others (Money 1955, 258). The dominant position at the time considered gonads to determine sex in the case of intersex births (Gill-Peterson 2018, 100–127; Meyerowitz 2004). Chromosomal sex was also gaining prominence as the most accurate indicator within the consolidating genetic paradigm. But Money and the Hampsons insisted that "behavior and orientation as male or female does not have an innate, instinctive basis," whether located in the gonads, genome, or elsewhere (Money, Hampson, and Hampson 1955a, 308). Sex, in other words, was no longer deemed an innate feature of anatomy and physiology—it was now plastic, affected by the external environment.

This plasticity of sex could have lent further evidence to the nearly fifty-year paradigm, still dominant in Europe, that in the words of Gill-Peterson (2018, 120), "all humans were, to a certain degree, normally intersex so that masculinity and femininity were mere tendencies, rather than absolute forms" (see also Laquer 1992; Meyerowitz 2004).[4] Yet Money and the Hampsons were interested in developing a new model: how social experience in early childhood produced and fixed distinct sexed identities, which they termed "gender role." Gender, Gill-Peterson (2018, 97–127) argues, was deployed to solve "sex in crisis" and served as a mechanism for regulating the diversity of human anatomy and identification. The invention recalls Thomas Laquer's summation of the shift from the one-sex model of the ancients to the two-sex model in the nineteenth century, which reflected ideological rather than intellectual developments. The male-female binary became paradigmatic, he argues, due "neither [to] a theory of knowledge nor advances in scientific knowledge. The context was politics" (Laquer 1992, 152).

Prior to these initial 1955 articles, gender as a noun referred to a class or type, especially the grammatical concept of gendered nouns and pronouns and their accompanying adjectives and verbs. Gender was sometimes applied as a descriptor of men and women when "viewed as a group," again taking shape as a process of categorization into distinct types (*Oxford English Dictionary*). Texts today now often considered landmarks in the development of gender theory, such as Margaret Mead's 1949 *Male and Female: A Study of the Sexes in a Changing World* use the term "gender" only in the sense of linguistic classification, as a grammatical feature of nouns.[5] Money and the Hampsons extrapolated from the meaning of gender to name the process of how the self comes to identify with and perform its category type. It is this collective aspect of gender, its work as a psychic and social structure for assuming a sexed self as a function of a larger category phenomenon, that I wish to note here.

In these sexologists' work, gender is simultaneously a diagnostic and therapeutic for assigning a sexed identity and social role to intersex youth. But this seemingly narrow scope belies the vastness of its power. As Jemima Repo (2015, 2–4) argues, "Gender, like sexuality, is a historically specific discourse of sex" that "revolved around the problem of how to govern sex." And deploying gender to stabilize sex, Hil Malatino (2019, 168) reveals, brought forth an instrument for extending the power and reach of sexology, enabling scientists "to monitor, regulate, and control deviant segments of the population." Money and his colleagues developed what Malatino calls a "microphysics of gender" that attuned the male-female dyad "as an ideality, a barometer, [but] not as an immutable factic truth" (93). It was not nature or nurture that determined gender for Money, Malatino brilliantly elucidates. Rather, gender emerged from sexologists' undertaking of "a careful weighing of all the aforementioned variables to determine a 'best sex'" (93). In effect, gender was not an attribute of the individual. Instead, it was a homeostasis of body and environment created by medico-scientific professionals, and intersex youth were deemed its raw material.

Gender, we might say, functioned as a security instrument through which practitioners of sexology—or, in Money's infamous coinage, "fuckology"—could regulate sex. For Foucault, biopower operates through two distinct modes of control: disciplinary power and security power. Disciplinary power takes shape through institutions like hospitals, prisons, schools, and domestic homes and is directed at the body of the individual. Its goal is to shape and train docile subjects and family units and its heyday was the nineteenth century, though it certainly continues through today. "Security power" (2009), by contrast, is a newer mode of power scaled to the organic dimension of the species, operating through indirectly manipulating the phenomena inherent to the species as a whole. Security power attempts to maintain homeostasis through regulating the "physical processes" innate to the population itself, such as rates of birth, death, morbidity, and economic productivity (50–110). While disciplinary power targets growing bodies by deploying external instruments such as the prison, security power regulates the unpredictability of organic growth through manipulating the very organic processes intrinsic to life. Consider vaccines, for example, as a prime security instrument: they minimize the threat a pathogen poses to the population through the strategic application of that very pathogen (or a mimic of its RNA). The goal of homeostasis is reached when the microbe's threat to the population as a whole has been effectively neutralized through its very implementation.

Gender was developed to be a security instrument that works through a specific tool: harnessing the body's affective capacity. Specifically, sexologists seized the affective dimensions of sex as a means to regulate sex itself. Money postulated that identity was plastic up to the age of eighteen months. In this flexible period of infancy, experiences "imprint" on the mind and accumulate as gender identity—and those influences could be orchestrated by sexologists and parents to eliminate the possibility of intersex youth (Money, Hampson, and Hampson 1955a, 1956). Gender would enable practitioners to impose binary identity on intersex kids through regulating the impressions they received that would shape their self-understanding.

Explicitly, Money borrowed the notion of imprinting from the 1930s work of behavioralist ethologist Konrad Lorenz (1937) to develop the concept of gender as accumulated affect. Lorenz had studied the behavior of just-hatched baby mallard ducklings and greylag goslings, discovering that the baby birds would imprint on a variety of objects and beings, including himself, that behaved and moved like their mother would. Imprinting meant a lifelong attachment to that person or object. The affective bond also shaped sexual attraction in adulthood. Filial and sexual attachment, he showed, was not innate but resulted from being affected by the right external stimuli during the first twenty-four hours upon hatching. Orchestrating affective responses could thus shape the species impulses of love, intimacy, and eroticism, bringing these fundamental components of life itself under the control of scientific direction—and biopolitical regulation.

Implicitly, Money also invoked the notion of impressibility, a nineteenth-century race science concept meaning the capacity to be affected over time. Repo (2015, 31) notes that Money and the Hampsons "radically changed the location of the truth of sex from residing in the genitals to being an outcome of a behavioral control system." They did so by relying on a century-long concept of impressibility in which experiences press into flesh and accumulate, over time, as race and sex difference (Schuller 2018). Far from being new, their framework of gender acquisition through parental imprinting reinvigorated a longer history of engaging with the affective capacities of the body as an opportunity for division and control.

Phrenologists, comparative anatomists, vertebratologists, and others milling about the exploding fields of nineteenth-century US race science decided that only white bodies absorbed long-term effects from their sensations and experiences, and thus only whites were capable of growth and progress. The notion of impressibility delineated white bodies deemed capable of absorbing the effects of their experiences from racialized bodies determined to be insensible, on the bottom of the human animacy hierarchy. The Lockean notion of the body as a tabula rasa formed the substrate of their theory: corporeality from body to brain was a blank slate, dependent on external sensation for its development. Yet as with the project of liberal humanism in general, its universalisms were never universal. *Man* was a blank slate, continually receiving its qualities through absorbing and reflecting on impressions from the environment, but *Man* was only white, European or Anglo-Saxon, male, and propertied. Adults of color, they declared, were unimpressible, incapable of retaining their impressions or reflecting on their sensations over time and thus gaining a measure of control over their development (Schuller 2018). To be racialized meant to be suspended in the raw vulnerability and eternal reactivity of the ever-present, a state that Denise Ferreira da Silva (2007, xv, 44, 46) has usefully termed "affectability": a condition of being continually subject to external influence and power. Youth of color, some scientists and many reformers declared, did retain a measure of impressibility before the age of ten. The attempt to seize and direct this plasticity provided a scientific rationale for brutal assimilation projects including off-reservation boarding schools for Indigenous youth and the mass labor schemes for Irish immigrant youth now known as the orphan trains. In this era before genetics, these projects were designed to impress the habits of serving white society into the flesh and the hereditary material, creating heritable modifications that would be passed down through future generations (Schuller 2018).

Impressibility, a discourse that bound together ideas of temporality, affect, emotion, and embodiment, underpinned the new mid-nineteenth century logic of innate race difference. Race, in other words, consolidated less as a theory of biological determinism than in the form of a carefully stipulated ranking of affective capacity that determined the potential for growth. Crucially, the modern male-female binary also emerged in this same milieu. The malleability of the tabula rasa, shaped by its experiences rather than in possession of innate qualities, portended the potential for unlimited growth but also radical vulnerability. Race scientists solved the problem of the precarity of whiteness by elaborating on the sex binary, newly insisting that male/female was a state of absolute difference with regard to physiology, anatomy, and mental and emotional capacity (Russett 1989). White women, they declared, were altogether too impressible—capable of progress but also likely to get led astray by their own susceptibility to external influence. Meanwhile, white men possessed just the right amount of sensitivity, enabling them to maintain altruism, abstraction, and justice. The sex binary was deployed to stabilize the precarity of impressible whiteness (Schuller 2018).

In the mid-twentieth century, gender imprinting would stabilize the newly exposed variability of sex. It did so by seemingly giving practitioners control over plasticity itself (Gill-Peterson 2018). Their notion of gender, in common with the earlier theory of impressibility from which it in part emerged, blended biological and social phenomena into seamless targets of medical power.

Gender emerged as physician-directed labor that completes biological development and its key technology is time. As Gill-Peterson (2018) emphasizes, Money and the Hampsons propose a notion of gender as telos in which practitioners, and parents in their wake, complete the work of developmental progress that biology initiates. Gender-identity differentiation is "the psychodevelopment of sex [and] is a continuation of the embryo development of sex," Money and Ehrhardt (1972, 7) later explained. Parental and social behavior toward the child, as well as the child's own recognition of their genital morphology, imprints a clear sexed identity and role. Money and the Hampsons (1955a, 308) write, "In place of a theory of instinctive masculinity or femininity which is innate, the evidence of hermaphroditism lends support to a conception that, psychologically, sexuality is undifferentiated at birth and that it becomes differentiated as masculine or feminine in the course of the various experiences of growing up." Gender is a biosocial interaction that accretes over time. Gender challenged the prevailing theory that all human sex is mixed and that sex is a spectrum. Instead, gender is a specific transmission that enables the child's development into maturity, maturity understood here in a teleological sense as specialization.

Most pressingly, gender presented a solution to the crisis of intersex, or what Money and the Hampsons (1955b, 291) called "genital unfinishedness." Intersex became a disorder of time, and the telos of gender was its treatment. Through its temporal narrative, gender im-printing swallows undifferentiated bodies into a populational norm of binary sex. Their queerness is a problem of time, not of the possi-bilities of the human body itself (Gill-Peterson 2018; Malatino 2019). In the words of Money and the Hampsons (1955b, 291), "The public construes an [*sic*] hermaphrodite as being half boy, half girl. The parents of a hermaphrodite should be disabused of this conception immediately. They should be given, instead, the concept that their child is a boy or a girl, one or the other, *whose sex organs did not get completely differentiated or finished.*" Intersex infants were simply bodies that were incomplete, yet to be fully realized in the hands of the surgeon-psychiatrist. Gender became the biopolitical process of finishing what nature left unfinished, through nonelective surgery and forced sex identification. Gender, in this sense, is an affect-based security instrument that enables sexologists to work within the mate-rial givens of a population to regulate its outcome. Gender stabilizes the precarity of sex in the individual life span of intersex children, and gender stabilizes the binary sex structure of the population over the generational time of the species.

When feminists took up the concept of gender in the 1970s, there was little public appetite among liberals for arguments that intertwined culture and physiology like Money's theory of imprinting. Indeed, the main progressive achievement of postwar social science was widely considered to be the UNESCO conferences' reframing of race in the early 1950s. These conferences concluded that race was strictly the re-sult of cultural norms and had no grounding in anatomy or physiol-ogy (Downing, Morland, and Sullivan 2015).[6] The key feminist in-tervention into gender followed suit. For Gayle Rubin, Ann Oakley (1972), and many feminists in their wake, one of the key problems with the sexological notion of gender was the way it mixed cultural and biological phenomena into one. Feminists split biological sex from cultural gender and emphasized how historically contingent, and thus alterable, gender paradigms award power to men and ren-der women their property. This move had the additional benefit of wresting "gender" away from John Money's notoriously misogynist, exploitative research and coercive treatment and turning gender into a concept useful for feminists—a move he fiercely contested.

But today, the social-biological binary has run its course, and the need for an affective notion of gender that crisscrosses the artificial divisions of the immaterial and material is pressing—as long as we keep in mind that biosocial models can be as fully embedded within biopolitical hierarchies as biological determinist ones. We can suspend the biopolitical narrative feminists *have* adopted from Money in which gender regulates social and biological instability. Instead, feminists can wholeheartedly refuse the methods and goals of Money and his collaborators' violent work while also, carefully, revisiting the idea of gender as an affective process in which biology and culture forge each other over time. Gender theory needs new models to articulate how social experience *becomes* physiological over time, and affect theory can help us here, as long as we keep the pitfalls of its history that Malatino and others have so carefully illuminated in mind. Gender's grammatical origin as an account of category type has been pulled into biopolitical processes to smooth and secure the health of the population, especially maintaining the sex binary and its economic productivity. But gender can be imagined otherwise.

Understanding the lived effects of poverty, trauma, and violence on the individual and social body can expand feminist and anti-racist analyses and modes of political action. Both sex and gender could be understood as assemblages comprising the dynamic flows between physical bodies and the environments in which they live, encounters that accumulate over millennia. The difference between sex and gender, I propose, is not one of substance but one of temporality. Sex is a material-semiotic assemblage registering as the individuated body and gender a material-semiotic assemblage materializing as the collective. The advantages of this affective model of sex/gender are that it acknowledges that differential experiences of power precipitate in the flesh while also insisting on the impossibility of differentiating between the social and the biological in the first place. Sex/gender are overlapping processes, at once distinct moments in time yet also mutually determining events impossible to delineate.

Taking gender's biopolitical function head-on and reappropriating its aims can help us understand the material effects of power. This "security" instrument, in other words, could be helpful in tracking how capitalism and neocolonialism impact life chances. Might gender's initial function as temporality be helpful? We see broad gender disparities in health today: women have autoimmune conditions at twice the rate of men; US Black women's mortality rate during pregnancy is two to six times that of white women; and rates of clinical depression and anxiety among women are twice that of men (Angum et al 2020; Flanders-Stepans 2000; Mayo Clinic 2019; Population Reference Bureau 2021). During the height of the COVID-19 pandemic, the GenderSci Lab convincingly argued that COVID-19 disproportionately affects men—and especially Black and Latino men—due to work conditions and other environmental exposures, and not because of chromosomal difference as some have insisted (Boulicault et al 2022). Sex and race do not cause these tragic differences in morbidity and mortality; drastic social inequality does. Yet currently, our basic notion of gender cannot account for the feedback loop between embodiment and the repertoires of experience, for the material consequences of power that grind into flesh and shape life outcomes.

A framework of gender that attends to "the unfolding of bodies into worlds," in Sara Ahmed's (2010, 30) elegant phrase in the first *Affect Theory Reader*, better equips us for a post-interactionist model in which bodies and environments do not interpenetrate so much as they are interdependent, constitutionally incapable of existing without the other. This is what remains extractable from gender's origins as a diagnosis and treatment: gender is a semiotic materiality embedded in time. Sex/gender can be conceptualized as a means to grasp the social *and* physical impact of power relations in the near and long term, working within a notion of affective becoming fully attentive to the power dynamics through which affect itself has been recruited into the processes of sex, gender, and race differentiation and control.

By thinking of gender/sex as differences of temporality, I mean to emphasize that they are the same phenomenon but maintain distinct rhythms and tempos. The individuated body, or sex, of course is not an individual body at all. It is an ecology—a teeming assemblage of entities, human and nonhuman, with porous boundaries—immersed in an even wider world. But this individuated ecology experiences disease and debility, racialization and sexed embodiment, as a distinct self, and it navigates capitalist structures built on legacies of Man in which rights connote the possibility of the individual attainment of property. And our individual experiences of how we live in our bodies matters, our divergent histories of pleasure and medical subjection and those particular capacities we both acquire and inherit; our experiences of labor carving into the body; our histories as boundaried energy fields, of circulating affects and emotions binding us to other bodies. Sexuality names the modern discourse that, in the words of Peter Coviello (2013, 12) reading Foucault, "battened into place" a flurry of attachments, desires, impressions, and eroticisms into a discrete, finite property of the self. Sex as an individuated material-semiotic assemblage, we might say, could make the reverse move, throwing off a discourse of a static body, pinned under the weight of its scientific identification, sending it spinning through the constellation of forces that accumulate as individual lives and the temporal compound of sex/gender.

Repo (2015) argues that we should abolish gender full stop, that its biopolitical function is too enormous to dislodge. And certainly for some, that is the right choice. Both binary sex and gender originated as forms of scientific-medical control and thus, for many, may be beyond redemption. But for others, they remain meaningful. And gender in both its grammatical and medical origins signals group affinity. Gender is a cooperative formation, a collective identification with type. Gender, Malatino (2019, 193) suggests, might best be thought of as *becoming* that leaves behind the "disjunction between biological sex and performed gender" that the sex/gender distinction relies on and that results in perceiving trans lives "in terms of traumatic disjunction," caught between two distinct poles. Gender as unfolding assemblage can also reorient toward the grammatical origins of gender as group belonging and away from gender as security technology targeting queer bodies. We need more modes of collectivity to resist the brutalizing logics of binary sex and gender as regulatory ideals, while also insisting that gender and sex as frames of attachment, collectivity, and desire are optional.[7]

Proliferating gender labels today attest to the importance of structures of attachment that link embodied experience to social and political identities. We need more ways of living in bodies together, of conceptualizations of the self that recognize it to be a complex of affects, desires, orientations, and precipitations of experience ultimately coterminous with other bodies and wider ecologies. This stands in sharp contrast to the notion of the body and its sex/gender as fixed, individuated, and mandatory identities, properties, and interior substances. For some, opting out of binary gender altogether best embodies the potential of unfolding as an individuated body co-constituted within its environment. For others, gender can be envisioned as an elective and flexible site of collective struggle. Gender as a verb, as a coalitional social movement rather than a distinct identity, is one of the great gifts of 1970s Black and women of color feminism. Gender can be redeployed away from the biopolitical goal of regulating the diversity of sex and toward the liberatory aim of generating more modes of collective formation that capture the way our bodies are in continual, dynamic co-constitution with power. Rethinking the relationship between sex, gender, and affect can help to interrogate, rather than perpetuate, regimes of biopolitical control.

Notes

Special thanks to Hil Malatino for generous constructive criticism of an earlier version of this essay and to Carolyn Pedwell and Greg Seigworth for perceptive and rigorous feedback.

1   Rubin (1978, 178) writes that the social division of labor "exacerbates the biological differences between the sexes and thereby creates gender."

2   Fausto-Sterling ([2000] 2020) links the pathologization of intersex bodies with the increasing complexity of sciences of sex since the mid-nineteenth century that developed new ways to taxonomize and, at the same time, disappeared most queer bodies into binary sex.

3   Gill-Peterson (2018, 100–127) stresses that their work built on several decades of endocrinological research conducted by Lawson Wilkins and others who previously treated and experimented on intersex children housed at Harriet Lane.

4   Shifting paradigms provide further evidence of Thomas Laquer's (1992, 115) claim that the concept of physical sex "is the result not of biology but of our needs in speaking about it."

5   Psychologist Madison Bentley used the notion of gender as "the socialized obverse of sex" in a 1945 article as well as in a 1950 review of Mead's *Male and Female*.

6   Iain Morland argues this was key inspiration for Money (Downing, Morland, and Sullivan 2015).

7   For a provocative reading of gender as desire, see Chu (2019).

References

Ahmed, Sara. 2010. "Happy Objects." In *The Affect Theory Reader*, edited by Melissa Gregg and Gregory J. Seigworth, 29–51. Durham, NC: Duke University Press.

Alaimo, Stacy, and Susan J. Hekman. 2008. *Material Feminisms*. Bloomington: Indiana University Press.

Angum Fariha, Tahir Khan, Jasndeep Kaler, Lena Siddiqui, and Azhar Hussain. 2020. "The Prevalence of Autoimmune Disorders in Women: A Narrative Review." *Cureus* 12 (5): e8094. https://doi.org/10.7759/cureus.8094.

Bentley, Madison. 1945. "Sanity and Hazard in Childhood." *American Journal of Psychology* 58 (2): 212–46.

Bentley, Madison. 1950. "Brief Comment upon Recent Books." *American Journal of Psychology* 63 (2): 312.

Boulicault, Marion, Annika Gompers, Katharine M. N. Lee, and Heather Shattuck-Heidorn. 2022. "A Feminist Approach to Analyzing Sex Disparities in COVID-19 Outcomes." *IJFAB: International Journal of Feminist Approaches to Bioethics* 15 (1): 167–74.

Butler, Judith. 1993. *Bodies That Matter: On the Discursive Limits of "Sex."* New York: Routledge.

Butler, Judith. 2015. *Senses of the Subject*. New York: Fordham University Press.

Chen, Mel Y. 2012. *Animacies: Biopolitics, Racial Mattering, and Queer Affect*. Durham, NC: Duke University Press.

Chu, Andrea Long. 2019. *Females: A Concern*. New York: Verso.

Cohen, Ed. 2009. *A Body Worth Defending: Immunity, Biopolitics, and the Apotheosis of the Modern Body*. Durham, NC: Duke University Press.

Coviello, Peter. 2013. *Tomorrow's Parties: Sex and the Untimely in Nineteenth-Century America*. New York: New York University Press.

DeVun, Leah. 2021. *The Shape of Sex: Nonbinary Gender from Genesis to the Renaissance*. New York: Columbia University Press.

Downing, Lisa, Iain Morland, and Nikki Sullivan. 2015. *Fuckology: Critical Essays on John Money's Diagnostic Concepts*. Chicago: University of Chicago Press.

Fausto-Sterling, Anne. (2000) 2020. *Sexing the Body: Gender Politics and the Construction of Sexuality*. New York: Basic Books.

Fausto-Sterling, Anne. 2012. *Sex/Gender: Biology in a Social World*. Abingdon, UK: Taylor and Francis.

Ferreira da Silva, Denise. 2007. *Toward a Global Idea of Race*. Minneapolis: University of Minnesota Press.

Flanders-Stepans, Mary Beth. 2000. "Alarming Racial Differences in Maternal Mortality." *Journal of Perinatal Education* 9 (2): 50–51.

Foucault, Michel. 2009. *Security, Territory, Population: Lectures at the Collège de France, 1977–78*. Translated by Graham Burchell. New York: Picador.

Gill-Peterson, Jules. 2018. *Histories of the Transgender Child*. Minneapolis: University of Minnesota Press.

Gregg, Melissa, and Gregory J. Seigworth. 2010. "An Inventory of Shimmers." In *The Affect Theory Reader*, edited by Melissa Gregg and Gregory J. Seigworth, 1–25. Durham, NC: Duke University Press.

Laquer, Thomas. 1992. *Making Sex: Body and Gender from the Greeks to Freud*. Cambridge, MA: Harvard University Press.

Lorde, Audre. 1984. "An Open Letter to Mary Daly." In *Sister Outsider: Essays and Speeches*, 66–71. Trumansburg, NY: Crossing Press.

Lorenz, Konrad. 1937. "The Companion in the Bird's World." *The Auk* 54 (3): 245–73.

Malatino, Hilary. 2019. *Queer Embodiment: Monstrosity, Medical Violence, and Intersex Experience*. Lincoln: University of Nebraska Press.

Mayo Clinic. 2019. "Depression in Women: Understanding the Gender Gap." Last modified January 19. https://www.mayoclinic.org/diseases-conditions/depression /in-depth/depression/art-20047725.

Meyerowitz, Joanne J. 2004. *How Sex Changed a History of Transsexuality in the United States*. Cambridge, MA: Harvard University Press.

Money, John. 1955. "Hermaphroditism, Gender and Precocity in Hyperadrenocorticism: Psychologic Findings." *Bulletin of the Johns Hopkins Hospital* 96 (6): 253–64.

Money, John, and Anke A. Ehrhardt. 1972. *Man and Woman, Boy and Girl: Differentiation and Dimorphism of Gender Identity from Infancy to Maturity*. Baltimore: Johns Hopkins University Press.

Money, John, Joan G. Hampson, and John L. Hampson. 1955a. "An Examination of Some Basic Sexual Concepts: The Evidence of Human Hermaphroditism." *Bulletin of the Johns Hopkins Hospital* 97 (4): 301–19.

Money, John, Joan G. Hampson, and John L. Hampson. 1955b. "Hermaphroditism: Recommendations concerning Assignment of Sex, Change of Sex, and Psychologic Management." *Bulletin of the Johns Hopkins Hospital* 97 (4): 284–300.

Money, John, Joan G. Hampson, and John L. Hampson. 1956. "Imprinting and the Establishment of Gender Role." *Archives of Neurology and Psychiatry* 77 (3): 333–36.

Oakley, Ann. 1972. *Sex, Gender and Society*. New York: Routledge.

Pelkey, Zinaida, DO. 2018. Personal communication, October 15.

Population Reference Bureau. 2021. "Black Women over Three Times More Likely to Die in Pregnancy, Postpartum than White Women, New Research Finds." *PRB*. Last modified December 6. https://www.prb.org/resources/black-women-over -three-times-more-likely-to-die-in-pregnancy-postpartum-than-white-women -new-research-finds/.

Repo, Jemima. 2015. *The Biopolitics of Gender*. New York: Oxford University Press.

Richardson, Sarah S. 2013. *Sex Itself: The Search for Male and Female in the Human Genome*. Chicago: University of Chicago Press.

Rubin, Gayle. 1978. "The Traffic in Women: Notes on the 'Political Economy' of Sex." In *Toward an Anthropology of Women*, edited by Rayna Rapp Reiter, 157–78. New York: Monthly Review Press.

Russett, Cynthia Eagle. 1989. *Sexual Science: The Victorian Construction of Womanhood*. Cambridge, MA: Harvard University Press.

Schuller, Kyla. 2018. *The Biopolitics of Feeling: Race, Sex, and Science in the Nineteenth Century*. Durham, NC: Duke University Press.

Wilson, Elizabeth. 2004. *Psychosomatic: Feminism and the Neurological Body*. Durham, NC: Duke University Press.

PART TWO   MINOR FEELINGS AND THE SENSORIAL
                    POSSIBILITIES OF FORM

Ann Cvetkovich

Creative Nonfiction as Affect Theory

One way to gauge the current state of affect theory—and how it has been informed by questions of race—is to look at the popularity of Claudia Rankine's *Citizen: An American Lyric* after its publication in 2014. It was a book whose time had come—part of a swell in the literary public sphere that responded to the deaths of Trayvon Martin, Michael Brown, and Eric Garner by creating a cultural arm of the Black Lives Matter movement. Rankine, and fellow travelers Ta-Nehisi Coates, Natasha Trethewey, Elizabeth Alexander, and Tracy K. Smith, to name just a few, use the genres at their disposal—poetry, novel, memoir, essay but also innovative combinations of them—not only to document Black death but to help process it, providing spaces of mourning and analysis that would, for example, turn systemic racism into a household word in the aftermath of George Floyd's murder in 2020.[1]

Although Rankine's *Citizen* certainly documents Black death from Trayvon Martin onward—with a revised edition adding additional names as the death toll continues to rise—and essays such as "The Condition of Black Life Is One of Mourning," published in the *New*

York Times, extend her reach as public intellectual, her own writing is just one part of her efforts to change the literary public sphere, as evidenced in her coedited anthology *The Racial Imaginary* and the establishment, under her direction, of the Racial Imaginary Institute.[2] Even though around 2014 something might have changed, both in the struggle for racial justice and in the literary public sphere, it was also a long time coming, not only in Rankine's previous work but that of many others. For example, Rankine's *Don't Let Me Be Lonely*, published in 2004 and also subtitled *An American Lyric*, references the beating of Rodney King (1991), the assault of Abner Louima (1997), and the death of Amadou Diallo (1999), all at the hands of the police, and *In the Hood*, the work by David Hammons featuring a black hoodie that appears on the cover of *Citizen*, dates from 1993. Any effort to periodize must also account for continuities, since without long histories of struggle against anti-Black violence even just within recent decades, the current moment would not be possible.[3]

The work of Rankine and others has drawn attention to Black death and mourning, but to my mind, one of the most important contributions of *Citizen* is its focus on what have been called micro-aggressions. But the specificity with which Rankine documents the everyday encounters that are the manifestation of systemic racism, especially in middle-class contexts, resists the flattening that can be the result of such a generic diagnostic category. Rankine's method of documenting ordinary racisms through the innovation in form that has been called lyric essay opens up new ways to describe systemic racism by drawing attention to its affective life. She uses her skills as a poet to capture moments of disruption or encounter without having to provide character or narrative; these are sketches, scenes, fleeting and ephemeral moments, whose serial accumulation produces an archive of feelings. Rankine's use of the second-person "you," which has drawn the attention of so many of her readers of literary form, transforms the personal experience central to memoir into a collective format that reveals the affective life of race and racism to be a shared and often impersonal structure of feeling.[4] Central to Rankine's effort to link felt experience with systemic structures, which is a foundational goal for affect theory, is her development of a writing practice that can do that work, and in this she takes affect theory in new directions especially with respect to its capacity to address the ordinary life of systemic racisms. Rankine, along with many other writers working in creative idioms, addresses systemic racism not just in its more spectacular public forms, such as police shootings and incarceration, but through *minor feelings*, the ordinary experiences that get swept underground or that pile up unnoticed, at least to some.

In thinking about Rankine's development of the lyric essay as simultaneously a new genre of nonfiction *and* a new form of affect theory, as well as her impact on the literary public sphere, I would place her alongside another poet/writer whose reputation blew up at around the same time—Maggie Nelson, whose *The Argonauts* was published in 2015 to great acclaim as well for its formal innovation, which put "autotheory" on the map as a genre. In part due to their experiments in form, Nelson and Rankine both received MacArthur "genius" awards in 2016, and like Rankine, Nelson uses her skill as a poet to create new versions of the nonfiction essay that document everyday experience—in her case, queer family life. Also like Rankine, she came to her breakout book from a well-established history of publications that, for Nelson, encompass nonfiction scholarly books, poetry, and experiments in the memoir and essay forms that often combine the two, such as *Bluets* (2009). Drawing on a lineage that includes Roland Barthes as well as her teachers Eve Sedgwick and Eileen Myles, Nelson's capacity to work across genres stems from her multiple influences, including not just poetry but academic theory, especially queer affect theory, and in her most recent book *On Freedom* (2021), traditions of Black radical thought. The invention of genres for loss and mourning, and innovative approaches to the challenges of documenting affect, especially the ordinary, have been central to Nelson's work, most notably in two different experiments in form that grapple with her aunt's murder—*Jane: A Murder* (2005) and *The Red Parts* (2007).

I am struck by the overwhelming popularity of both of these writers of "instant classics," including their visibility in both scholarship and teaching in the academy and the affective intensity of their reception. Taken together, Rankine and Nelson—and their many and increasing numbers of fellow travelers—suggest that something is happening with the genre of the nonfiction essay—as signaled by efforts to name new categories such as creative nonfiction, lyric essay, and autotheory. In addition to being at the center of new developments in the literary public sphere, it is also having ripple effects in the world of theory especially because another effect of this genre invention are new crossovers or porous boundaries between academics and writers that produce a dense citationality. The intersectional convergence of efforts to document the queer and racialized ordinary and everyday as affect or structure of feeling represent a new turn in affect theory that also takes the form of a writing project. Although the innovations of writers like Rankine and Nelson are recognized by the attention they have received, they are also building on what has come before—not only in their own careers in which they have built from poetry to other genres—but as part of a longer lineage of queer and racialized writers with an attunement to affect and the project of documenting everyday intimacies.

Indeed, this work in the literary public sphere not only has its counterpart in academic work on racialized and queer affect theory, but the two domains are in close dialogue with one another, and their exchanges contribute to experiments in form in both arenas. Creative uses of the essay form by Saidiya Hartman, Christina Sharpe, and Katherine McKittrick or the fusion of poetry and the essay across the work of Fred Moten respond to the affective demands and pressures of conceptualizing both Black mourning and loss, and Black survival and joy, as well as the challenges of thinking them together.[5] Experiments in academic writing that combine queer affect theory and the critical memoir are an important legacy of Eve Sedgwick's work, and affect theory's interest in the ordinary and everyday leads to the focus on writing practice in Lauren Berlant and Katie Stewart's (2019) *The Hundreds*. Debates about the antisocial in queer theory and the dialectical relations between utopianism and pessimism also catalyze ways of thinking by means of a writing practice, often one that is collective.[6] One sign that this work builds on previous generations is the renewed attention and wider appreciation for women of color feminists such as Audre Lorde and Gloria Anzaldúa as foundational for affect theory and other fields of inquiry (from disability studies to new materialisms) that are thus not entirely new and for their innovative combinations of poetry, memoir, and essay as new genres of both the literary and theory.[7] Although emerging from a range of sources and contexts, the turn to affect in this work has a shared commitment to moving beyond the spectacle of trauma to something more everyday—and to a dialectical relation between positive and negative affects, or critique and reparative strategies, that means that mourning and joy, pessimism and utopia, are not distinct. It builds on the legacy of social movement politics—including its failures and disappointments, its affective modes of left melancholy and political depression. And so, this evolution is also marked by forms of generational and citational transmission where each generation takes up its precursors and pushes their work forward.

One mark of this work is a complex web of citationality in which people cross over genre and identity categories to read each other. Consider, for example, the wide reach of José Muñoz's concept of "cruising utopia," which has sparked the imagination of writers and artists both within the academy and beyond. Muñoz's work is also valuable for his turn to race as affective structure of feeling rather than identity so as to be able to describe Latinx experiences of minor feelings. Transforming what can often be a dominant focus on blackness in critical race studies, Muñoz (2006, 676) proposes a capacious notion of brownness or a "brown commons" as a shared sensibility of feeling "not quite right."[8] This focus on affect to describe the "sense of brown" is accompanied by a shift away from the spectacular to the everyday and/or the minor—and to feelings that are often not quite visible or palpable, especially to outsiders or mainstream white publics. An attunement to the minor feelings of Brown life also represents a turn away from the spectacle of death, toward minor pleasures, including queer ones, that recalibrate the dialectics of hope and despair, of positive and negative affect.

Many strands of affect theory thus converge in attention to everyday affects, or minor feelings, as the structure of feeling of racialized experience and as a way to address systemic racism—which brings new challenges for reckoning with a range of experiences across multiple identities. I would like to explore how this cultural phenomenon is manifest in Cathy Park Hong's (2020) *Minor Feelings* and Billy-Ray Belcourt's (2020) *A History of My Brief Body*—both nonfiction/essay works of mixed genre by poets, both influenced very explicitly by critical theory including affect theory and public feelings work, and both a next generation already building out from Rankine and Nelson, who are also cited by both. I also want to include them here because just as Muñoz extends Black studies to include "the sense of brown," these two writers, one Asian/Korean American, the other Indigenous (Driftpile Cree) and queer, are expanding the frame of racialized affect theory to undo Black-white binarisms and bring greater specificity to generic categories such as Asian American and Indigenous/ Native American. Such work is not merely additive but seeks to acknowledge the foundational nature of Indigenous genocide and settler colonialism—and reckon with the migrations of Asian diaspora and Latinx cultures, among many others, as part of the racialized history of the Americas. They also do so by developing new writing practices that constitute new forms of affect theory and create documents of the microdynamics of the everyday that will be necessary in order to change the killing systems of racism.

Cathy Park Hong's Minor Feelings

In the midst of an essay called "Stand Up" on her complex investment in Richard Pryor's performance of racialized anger and humor, Cathy Park Hong pauses her narrative, which is at once personal and critical, to explain her book's title concept and its theoretical sources. "In Pryor, I saw someone channel what I call minor feelings: the racialized range of emotions that are negative, dysphoric, and therefore untelegenic, built from the sediments of everyday racial experience and the irritant of having one's perceptions of reality constantly questioned or dismissed. Minor feelings arise, for instance, upon hearing a slight, knowing it's racial, and being told, *Oh, that's all in your head*. A now-classic book that explores minor feelings is Claudia Rankine's *Citizen*" (2020, 55). In addition to acknowledging *Citizen* (which has achieved the status of "classic" after only five years), Hong also notes that her concept of "minor feelings" is "deeply indebted" to Sianne Ngai's notion of "ugly feelings" as another name for "negative emotions—like envy, irritability, and boredom—symptomatic of today's late-capitalist gig economy" (56). Although Lauren Berlant is not literally cited here, she is present in the acknowledgments, and Hong mentions "optimism" as the pressure for the good life that "increase(s) these feelings of dysphoria" (55). Hong crafts her theory of "minor feelings" through a writing practice capable of documenting experiences and identities that are often missing from American literature, and she casts a wide citational net that draws from writers, theorists, and comedians and that tracks between Black and Brown theory. Moreover, this is a citational practice that cuts across genres and identities in order to break down and break open the generic category of the Asian American. Hong uses it to document the specificity, in a minor register, of her own experiences as the child of Korean immigrants who becomes an academic and writer through the upward mobility offered by education but who has also suffered from depression that is culturally produced by that very mobility and the assimilation and internalized racism it demands.

The task of writing about minor feelings demands new genres of writing—and forms of what we might call, following Berlant, "genre flail"—because it is serial and ongoing, "not generated from major change but from lack of change, in particular, structural racial, and economic change" (56).[9] Hong draws from affect theory that has been used to describe Black ordinary experience (Rankine), queer Latinx structures of feeling (Muñoz), and American ordinaries (Berlant) to illuminate Asian American lived experience that often goes underdescribed, or remains invisible and minor, in relation to other racialized categories—or misdescribed through notions of the model minority.[10] Her subtitle "An Asian American Reckoning" calls not so much for an additive inclusion in the full landscape of American experience but for a conceptual and representational practice that would put racialized groups in contact with one another while also retaining their specificity. The model is something like Lisa Lowe's (2015) "intimacy of four continents," which developed an account of Asian diasporic presence in the colonial histories that put Indigenous Americas, African diaspora slavery, and European colonialism in dense relation to one another, especially through the traffic in migrant labor that followed the abolition of the slave trade. Like Lowe, who rejects a politics of minoritarian recognition and inclusion, Hong puts critical pressure on the category of Asian American identity as she reaches, through her writerly approach to combining personal and critical narrative, for the specificity of her Korean heritage, family dynamics, and pathway to a life as an artist and intellectual.

"There is no immediate emotional release in the literature or minor feelings. It is cumulative. . . . Because minor feelings are ongoing, they lend themselves more readily to forms and genres that are themselves serial, such as the graphic novel, the serial poem, or the episodic poetic essay" (Hong 2020, 56). In Hong's search for a genre that might allow her an escape from the structures of poetry, whose forms promise her transcendence but continually return her to her Asian body and self-hatred and being stuck ("I still couldn't rise above myself, which pitched me into a kind of despair") and whose publics mean that "the white room was such the norm that I barely even noticed it. But when I did I began to feel the whiteness in the room" (44). Hong finds an alternative in Richard Pryor's unapologetic relation to his audience and his busting open of the stand-up comedy form to express rage, sexuality, and blackness that is not framed for a white audience. In exposing feelings that are "minor" only because so often rendered invisible or repudiated, Pryor "blowtorched the beige from my eyes" (38).

After the pause for theoretical analysis inspired by Richard Pryor in "Stand Up," itself a richly layered mini essay, Hong proceeds to lay out an account of the Korean presence in Los Angeles that connects her own family's experience to the LA riots and stories of immigrant families gone astray—but not in the "sentimental" mode of the ethnic story that humanizes. Instead, there is the alcoholic dentist with multiple marriages who loses his practice and leaves nothing but debt behind, and the sauna owner who was shot by the shoe shiner whose rent he raised. These are stories where the distinctions between victims and perpetrators are blurred, where no one emerges as the winner. Hong acknowledges the differences between her own family's upward mobility (itself marked by pain and a host of minor feelings) and those who remain, including the complex neighborhood dynamics that led to the killing of Latasha Harlins by Soon Ja Du and the intraracial dynamics of Korean-Black relations that inflect the 1992 LA riots. She retains the unresolved pain and the contradictory relations among racialized cultures that produces the dread and depression she describes in her opening essay's account of her encounter with a Korean American therapist who refuses to see her.[11] In narrating her own muted forms of anger, despair, and self-hatred as collective structures of feeling, Hong seeks to displace clichéd stereotypes. It is not minoritizing; it is a way of building the specificity of Korean LA into the landscape of American culture—the kind of analysis that Hong was called to do, for example, in the wake of the murders of Asian immigrant women in Atlanta in 2020, to explain the specific dynamics of anti-Asian racism and to address anti-Black and other kinds of anti-immigrant racisms. "Writing about race is a polemic, in that we must confront the white capitalist infrastructure that has erased us, but also a lyric, in that our inner consciousness is knotted with contradictions" (64). It's not easy work: "If I were to describe minor feelings as a sound, it would be the white noise of whooshing traffic in that area, of life passing me by so that I felt even more bereft" (58). Hong is trying to describe LA's K-Town as a place that feels like home but is also minor, nondescript, and full of pain and history. She uses affect theory—but also stand-up and other genres—to craft a way out of the impasses that render her own experience, and that of Korean Americans and other Asian Americans, invisible—getting at it through theory and story in a new form of the essay that undoes American literary genres. "To understand the riots, one must be able to balance multiple truths," and Hong notes that in trying to write a novel that might do this, "I had nothing to show for this search but a trail of failed forms" (61–62). Instead, she turns to the episodic essay form and the inspiration of stand-up so as to capture Korean historical trauma and the sad and bitter women in her family, as well as her own struggles with loneliness and depression because even second- and third-generation writer/poets are not model minorities.

Billy-Ray Belcourt: Lessening the Trauma of Description

Like Cathy Park Hong, Billy-Ray Belcourt is a poet turned essayist, and he also uses affect theory to think about race as structure of feeling in *A History of My Brief Body*, a memoir in essays that follows on his two award-winning books of poetry, *This Wound Is a World* (2017) and *NDN Coping Mechanisms* (2019). There are many overlaps in the broad citational network that is central to their writing practice, including Claudia Rankine and Maggie Nelson, as well as critical theorists such as Jose Muñoz and Lauren Berlant.[12] But Belcourt, who is a member of the Driftpile Cree Nation, is distinctive in so far as his citational constellation of different theories makes space for Indigenous ways of knowing that are increasingly recognized as foundational for any kind of critical inquiry. The growing prevalence of land acknowledgments in the United States, for example, gestures toward this recognition, although they have been in practice for long enough in Canada to have generated critique of their sometimes overly symbolic value. Belcourt's work emerges in the urgent and fraught context of Canada's Truth and Reconciliation Commission process and its accompanying Calls to Action, which demand material, not just symbolic, recognition, including sovereignty and land back movements. The terrible revelations in 2021 of unmarked burials at the site of the former Kamloops Indian Residential School and other locations was a stark reminder that this history continues to shape the present. Although some Indigenous cultural work takes a separatist approach to knowledge production, and understandably so, Belcourt takes a more "promiscuous" approach to theory (perhaps inspired by his queer affinities) acknowledging, for example, the importance of Black studies for Indigenous thinking and drawing on Hartman's afterlife of slavery, Moten's undercommons, Sharpe's in the wake, and more. Through his citational practice, Belcourt's intersectional approach to Black and Indigenous theory establishes a crossroads that has been overdue, especially given the foundational status of Indigenous culture in the Americas. With his attention to settler colonialism and genocide and the feelings those systems engender for Indigenous lives (including their queer specificity), Belcourt shares affinities with Hong's use of affect theory and critical race theory—drawn from a range of sources that have often been rendered minor—in order to put indigeneity in relation to other kinds of racialized identity and experience. But the stakes are different in Belcourt's case if one starts from the premise that the violent seizure and settlement of Indigenous land is central for all cultural and historical work in the Americas. I am interested in the implications of this premise for affect theory and how it is addressed by Hong and Belcourt's shared commitment to genres of writing that combine poetry and theory so as to present race as affective structure that includes minor feelings. Moreover, how might reading these writers together produce forms of racialized affect theory that can simultaneously center Indigenous epistemologies and account for a range of racialized experiences and minor feelings that disrupt Black-white binarisms as well as generic and inadequate categories such as Asian American?

   "To a room of conference attendees, I said, 'I'm an emotional person, so I read theory day in and day out'" (2020, 104). Belcourt's effort to combine different theories of race, complemented by his formal experiment in bringing theory and poetry together (as the quotation above suggests), reveals an affective relation to theory that produces a broad citational network, expands what counts as theory, and brings it into poetry and lyric essay. As he notes about his use of the essay form, "My story isn't linear, and in these pages I marshal the forces of poetry and theory to create a kind of memoir that stretches well beyond the boundaries of my individual life" (2020, Author's Note). *A History of My Brief Body* moves with a loose chronology from Belcourt's early life—his relation to his *nohkom* (grandmother), his life as a proto-gay kid on the reserve—into adulthood—going to university, coming out and cruising. But history and systemic structures also play out across his body—or in "the theoretical site that is my personal history" (9)—as in the title story's account of landing in the emergency room with fear of an STD, or his experiences of gay cruising through social media apps such as Grindr. And as the book proceeds, Belcourt opens out onto discussions of missing and murdered Indigenous women, the trial for Coulten Boushie's murder, Indigenous youth suicide, and the legacy of residential schools, showing how the intimate life (and death) of the body, both his own and that of others, is a crossroads for long and ongoing histories. As with Hong, the episodic essay form is shaped by the ongoing nature of violence, as well as the ongoing persistence of survival in the face of that violence. Theory and emotion are not at odds, and the segmented essay that Hong describes as a genre of minor feelings is likewise useful for Belcourt, whose work is also inspired by Indigenous affect theorist Dian Million's (2014) notion of "felt theory" as a form of knowledge that emerges from lived experience.

Although, as in his books of poetry, *A History of My Brief Body* is littered with wounded bodies and emotional damage, one of the book's central projects is to wrest joy from a genocidal culture that sees only deficit or death. In doing so, he borrows freely from discussions of Afropessimism and Black joy and finds, in queer intimacies and other minor forms of being or world making, modes of living beyond bare survival. It is exciting to see an Indigenous poet/writer lead the way forward in working through debates in affect theory about how to think the queer antisocial or Afropessimism alongside concepts of utopia or joy, thus making Indigenous ways of knowing indispensable to any version of affect theory. One lively area of growth is Indigenous affect theory that draws on Indigenous languages, such as Dylan Robinson's (2020) "hungry listening" as a term for settler colonial perception that is a translation of the Halq̓eméylem words *shxwelítemelh* (for white person's, but more literally starving person's, methods/things) and *xwélalà:m* (listening). But Belcourt's "catholic" citational approach to affect theory builds bridges that also facilitate this process.

In using the resources of Afropessimism to articulate Indigenous joy, Belcourt resists becoming an "exhibit in the museum of political depression," building on a concept that has circulated within affect theory.[13] High rates of Indigenous death persist alongside the brutal dynamics of premature death for Black people. But the "museum" of political depression has a specific resonance in Indigenous culture because of histories of representation of dead and disappearing "Indians," the appropriation and theft of cultural artifacts, and the testimonial cultures that respond to the history of residential schools. The conceptual project of wresting Indigenous joy from Indigenous death becomes a writing project because it is a representational problem that requires a poetics of minor feelings and resistance to spectacular or hypervisible forms of display. Belcourt takes a writerly approach to this theoretical question, using a mixed-mode prose that combines his own experience, theoretical reading, and an account of systemic structures. He resists what he calls the "trauma of description," the documentary accounts that have looked only for dead Indians or that seek to tie them to narratives of decline and disappearance. An experimental or speculative writing may be necessary to do the job, but it is a writerly practice that also finds use in affect theory. Inspired (literally) by Christina Sharpe's (2016) term "breathtaking spaces" to describe the "asphyxiating conditions" of oppression, the power of writing lies in its affective liveliness and its capacity to be a "practice of breathing" in its movement across images and its attention to the life of the body, especially in the sexual encounters of cruising culture (Belcourt 2020, 8–9). "This undefeatable excess is what I understand to be the poetic drive" (158). Belcourt draws on Sharpe's image of weather to name his desire to "shore up another kind of emotional atmosphere" or an "ecology of feeling" as an affective project (8).

In his effort to wrest joy, Belcourt faces up to the reality of suicide in Indigenous communities and asks that we think of suicide as a way of being in a fucked-up world, a way of claiming life. And as part of his writing practice, he also speaks—in the penultimate essay "Fatal Naming Rituals"—of the responsibility of the white settler to "lessen the trauma of description" (2020, 143). Even as Belcourt has been quite expansive in his citational reach and starts the essay with Fred Moten on terror and joy as a jumping off point, the text pulls close around the writerly challenges specifically faced by Indigenous writers. He starts with his discovery of Beatrice Mosionier's *In Search of April Raintree* as a young person—through the work of Dian Million whose claims for testimony as a form of "felt theory" provides a foundation for Indigenous affect theory. Countering the way his own work has been dismissed as simple—Belcourt assembles a "commune of love" that is specifically Indigenous—in addition to Audra Simpson, Million, and Mosionier, also Layli Long Soldier, Maria Campbell, Terese Mailhot, Leanne Betasamosake Simpson, Gwen Benaway, Liz Howard, and Super Futures Haunt Qollective. He announces that "you aren't invited into our commune. We aren't at the point of hospitality. I won't tell you when the time has come" (2020, 148), building on his repeated citation of Audra Simpson's notion of refusal to engage with settler frameworks.[14] This work of creating space in which Indigenous lives and letters can flourish is one of the possible futures of affect theory, one that refuses settler colonial categories in favor of Indigenous concepts of the connections between mind, body, and heart, of the entanglements of bodies and environments, and of perception and sensation.[15]

Conclusion: Speaking Nearby

Borrowing a concept from Trinh T. Minh Ha, Cathy Park Hong (2020, 103) explains that "I turned to the 'modular' essay because I am only capable of 'speaking nearby' the Asian American condition, which is so involuted that I can't stretch myself across it. The more I try to pin it the more it escapes my grasp." She likes "the episodic form, with its exit routes that permit me to stray" (104) because she is seeking to undo a monolithic or bland version of the Asian American. Writing about minor feelings becomes a route to different understandings of race as an affective structure of feeling.

This notion of "speaking nearby" is useful also for considering my own position as a white and settler reader of the developments in the literary and theoretical public sphere represented by the work of Hong, Belcourt, and their fellow travelers. Although this essay is a form of acknowledging and amplifying their work, it is possible that the best way of attending to it would be to step aside and wait for it to continue to unfold on its own terms. Belcourt (2020, 143, emphasis mine) specifically notes that "*you, a white and settler you*, are beholden to a project of lessening the trauma of description," and if settler scholars are to take up that challenge, then we would do well to encourage the flourishing of forms of affect theory that emerge from Indigenous worlds and experiences. From a location nearby, I listen for variations on Muñoz's attention to brownness as a structure of feeling and learn from the specificities of different forms of minor feelings Black, Indigenous, Brown, Korean American, and more and from intraracial discussions of their connections. And I also look to see whether Indigenous ways of knowing are present across the intimacies of multiple continents and cultures—and whether there is a continued questioning of settler colonial presence and Indigenous sovereignty and land as a starting point for critical work, including that of exploring white settler identities as structures of feeling.

Attunement to minor feelings makes it possible to address historical trauma and genocide in ways that are less deadly—and also opens the way to other kinds of affective world making, including the forms of Indigenous language resurgence and cultural sovereignty that cultivate new ways of knowing and naming affective experience. It might not be time for white settlers to join that party—and maybe we will never be invited as guests. All the more reason, then, to welcome these experiments in the essay form that enable poets and scholars, academics and public writers, to build something through shared attachments to questions of affect that "lessen the trauma of description." In making space for different experiences of the minor and also different ways of documenting minor feelings so that they can constitute knowledge, the citational networks created by Hong and Belcourt, which extend across identities and genres, suggest generative forms of contact and exchange and lend themselves to writing practices that perform new forms of relationality.

Notes

1   See Coates, *Between the World and Me* (2015), Trethewey, *Beyond Katrina* (2010) and *Memorial Drive* (2020), Alexander, *The Light of the World* (2015), and Smith, *Ordinary Light* (2015). The list of Black writers alone is long, but I flag here the

prominence of the essay tradition whose lineage extends back to Baldwin, DuBois, and slave narrative, as well as the writer as public intellectual, especially poets who also write essays and memoir.

2   For the Racial Imaginary Institute, see https://theracialimaginary.org.

3   See, for example, Taylor (2016) on the multiple developments over time that contributed to the Black Lives Matter movement and its moment.

4   See, for example, Ferguson et al. (2016) in the *Los Angeles Review of Books* as well as many essays in scholarly journals. Especially important has been discussion of Rankine's use of the second person and her relation to the lyric genre in poetry.

5   See Hartman (2006, 2019), Sharpe (2016), McKittrick (2021), Moten (2003), and Moten and Harney (2013). These are just some of the more frequently cited scholars whose work crosses over into other audiences and genres, but there are increasing numbers in the academy who are experimenting with form and style in scholarly work, and they also build on much that has come before.

6   See Sedgwick (2002), Stewart (2007), and Berlant (2011). Again, as with the previous note, these are just a few of the more frequently cited scholars whose work exemplifies experiments in genre that accompany work in queer and affect theory.

7   See, for example, Anzaldúa and Moraga (1984), Lorde (1984), and Anzaldúa (1987). The work of bell hooks is also an important inspiration for many.

8   In addition to Muñoz (2006), see also the earlier formulation in Muñoz (2000) and the further evolution of the idea of race as affect rather than identity in *The Sense of Brown* (2020), including concepts such as the "brown commons." For further discussion of the significance of this version of an affective turn, see Cvetkovich (2014).

9   For the concept of "genre flailing," see Berlant (2018).

10 Hong also cites Sara Ahmed, Kathryn Bond Stockton, Judith Butler, and Saidiya Hartman, as well as fellow writers Farid Matuk, Eula Biss, Maggie Nelson, Evie Shockley, Claudia Rankine, and John Keene, many of whom also combine poetry and prose.

    Hong's use of the term "minor feelings" is also resonant for this essay because some of the ideas here have their origin in a panel strand that Rizvana Bradley organized on Black Affect and Minor Feelings for the 2015 Affect WTF conference for which I wrote a paper about the relevance of the concept for thinking about Black queer/feminist lineages from Audre Lorde to Claudia Rankine. I note also that Belcourt's newest work, a novel, is titled *A Minor Chorus* (2022), for which the concept of the "minor" (as well as the "chorus") is inspired by Saidiya Hartman's (2019) use of it in *Wayward Lives, Beautiful Experiments*.

11 See Eng and Han (2019) on therapy that addresses Asian American structures of feelings, including the burdens of the model minority myth.

12 Both Nelson and Rankine wrote blurbs for *Minor Feelings*; Nelson is featured in one of the epigraphs for *History of My Brief Body* (2020), and at other points, on pp. 21 and 76; Rankine's *Don't Let Me Be Lonely* is cited on p. 42.

13 For the concept of "political depression," Belcourt cites Cvetkovich (2012) and Cvetkovich and Michalski (2012), but the concept originates with Feel Tank Chicago, whose founding members include Lauren Berlant, Debbie Gould, Mary Patten, and Rebecca Zorach. For more on Belcourt's citational relation to queer affect theory and critical race theory, see Cvetkovich (2022). A version of *History of My Brief Body* was submitted as Belcourt's PhD dissertation at the University of Alberta, and he thus travels in the worlds of both academia and creative writing.

14 On Indigenous refusal, see Simpson (2014).

15 See Robinson (2020) and his ongoing work on listening, settler colonial perception, and sensate sovereignty, as well as emerging scholars such as Eli Nelson and Jennifer LeBlanc.

References

Alexander, Elizabeth. 2015. *The Light of the World: A Memoir*. New York: Grand Central Publishing.

Anzaldúa, Gloria. 1987. *Borderlands/La Frontera: The New Mestiza*. San Francisco: Aunt Lute Books.

Anzaldúa, Gloria, and Cherrie Moraga, eds. 1984. *This Bridge Called My Back: Writing by Radical Women of Color*. Boston: Kitchen Table: Women of Color Press.

Belcourt, Billy-Ray. 2017. *This Wound Is a World*. Calgary: Frontenac House.

Belcourt, Billy-Ray. 2019. NDN *Coping Mechanisms*. Toronto: House of Anansi Press.

Belcourt, Billy-Ray. 2020. *A History of My Brief Body*. Toronto: Penguin Random House.

Belcourt, Billy-Ray. 2022. *A Minor Chorus: A Novel*. Toronto: Penguin Random House.

Berlant, Lauren. 2011. *Cruel Optimism*. Durham, NC: Duke University Press.

Berlant, Lauren. 2018. "Genre Flailing," *Capacious* 1 (2). https://doi.org/10.22387/CAP2018.16.

Berlant, Lauren, and Kathleen Stewart. 2019. *The Hundreds*. Durham, NC: Duke University Press.

Coates, Ta-Nehisi. 2015. *Between the World and Me*. New York: One World.

Cvetkovich, Ann. 2012. *Depression: A Public Feeling*. Durham, NC: Duke University Press.

Cvetkovich, Ann. 2014. "Tuning in to the Sense of Brown." *boundary 2*. https://boundary2.wordpress.com/2014/03/10/turning-in-to-the-sense-of-brown/.

Cvetkovich, Ann. 2022. "Billy-Ray Belcourt's Loneliness as the Affective Life of Settler Colonialism." *Feminist Theory* 23 (1). https://doi.org/10.1177/14647001211062727.

Cvetkovich, Ann, with Karin Michalski. 2012. *The Alphabet of Feeling Bad*. Video installation.

Eng, David, and Shin-Hee Han. 2019. *Racial Melancholy, Racial Dissociation: On the Social and Psychic Lives of Asian Americans*. Durham, NC: Duke University Press.

Ferguson, Roderick A., Evie Shockley, Maria A. Windell, Daniel Worden, Lisa Uddin, Catherine Zuromskis, and Kenneth W. Warren. 2016. "Reconsidering Claudia

Rankine's *Citizen: An American Lyric*. A Symposium. Parts 1 and 2." *Los Angeles Review of Books*, January 6 and 7. https://lareviewofbooks.org/article/reconsidering -claudia-rankines-citizen-an-american-lyric-a-symposium-part-i/.

Hartman, Saidiya. 2006. *Lose Your Mother: A Journey along the Atlantic Slave Route*. New York: Farrar, Strauss.

Hartman, Saidiya. 2019. *Wayward Lives, Beautiful Experiments*. New York: Norton.

Hong, Cathy Park. 2020. *Minor Feelings: An Asian American Reckoning*. New York: One World.

Lorde, Audre. 1984. *Sister Outsider*. Trumansburg, NY: Crossing Press.

Lowe, Lisa. 2015. *The Intimacies of Four Continents*. Durham, NC: Duke University Press.

McKittrick, Katherine. 2021. *Dear Science and Other Stories*. Durham, NC: Duke University Press.

Million, Dian. 2014. *Therapeutic Nations: Healing in an Age of Indigenous Human Rights*. Tucson: University of Arizona Press.

Moten, Fred. 2003. *In the Break: The Aesthetics of the Black Radical Tradition*. Minneapolis: University of Minnesota Press.

Moten, Fred, and Stefano Harney. 2013. *The Undercommons: Fugitive Planning and Black Study*. New York: AK Press.

Muñoz, José Esteban. 2000. "Feeling Brown: Ethnicity and Affect in Ricardo Bracho's *The Sweetest Hangover (and Other STDs)*." *Theatre Journal* 52 (1): 67–79.

Muñoz, José Esteban. 2006. "Feeling Brown, Feeling Down: Latina Affect, the Performativity of Race, and the Depressive Position." *Signs* 31 (3): 675–88.

Muñoz, José Esteban. 2009. *Cruising Utopia: The Then and There of Queer Futurity*. New York: New York University Press.

Muñoz, José Esteban. 2020. *The Sense of Brown*. Durham, NC: Duke University Press.

Nelson, Maggie. 2005. *Jane: A Murder*. Berkeley: Soft Skull Press.

Nelson, Maggie. 2007. *The Red Parts: Autobiography of a Trial*. New York: Free Press.

Nelson, Maggie. 2009. *Bluets*. Seattle: Wave Books.

Nelson, Maggie. 2015. *The Argonauts*. Minneapolis: Graywolf Press.

Nelson, Maggie. 2021. *On Freedom: Four Songs of Care and Constraint*. Minneapolis: Graywolf Press.

Ngai, Sianne. 2005. *Ugly Feelings*. Cambridge, MA: Harvard University Press.

Rankine, Claudia. 2004. *Don't Let Me Be Lonely*. Minneapolis: Graywolf Press.

Rankine, Claudia. 2014. *Citizen, an American Lyric*. Minneapolis: Graywolf Press.

Rankine, Claudia. 2015. "The Condition of Black Life Is One of Mourning." *New York Times*, June 22.

Rankine, Claudia, Beth Loffreda, and Max Cap King, eds. 2015. *The Racial Imaginary: Writers on Race in the Life of the Mind*. Hudson, NY: Fence Books.

Robinson, Dylan. 2020. *Hungry Listening: Resonant Theory for Indigenous Sound Studies*. Minneapolis: University of Minnesota Press.

Sedgwick, Eve Kosofsky. 2002. *Touching Feeling: Affect, Pedagogy, Performativity*. Durham, NC: Duke University Press.

Sharpe, Christina. 2016. *In the Wake: On Blackness and Being*. Durham, NC: Duke University Press.

Simpson, Audra. 2014. *Mohawk Interruptus: Political Life across the Borders of Settler States*. Durham, NC: Duke University Press.

Simpson, Audra, and Andrea Smith, eds. 2014. *Theorizing Native Studies*. Durham, NC: Duke University Press.

Smith, Tracy K. 2015. *Ordinary Light: A Memoir*. New York: Knopf.

Stewart, Kathleen. 2007. *Ordinary Affects*. Durham, NC: Duke University Press.

Taylor, Keeanga-Yamahtta. 2016. *From #Black Lives Matter to Black Liberation*. Chicago: Haymarket.

Trethewey, Natasha. 2010. *Beyond Katrina: A Meditation on the Mississippi Gulf Coast*. Athens: University of Georgia Press.

Trethewey, Natasha. 2020. *Memorial Drive: A Daughter's Memoir*. New York: Harper Collins.

Hil Malatino

The "trans mundane" refers to the affective everyday milieus of trans subjects wherein infrapolitical webs of care are woven in the midst of sometimes overwhelming, sometimes steadily low-grade but nevertheless reliably relentless saturations of negative affect. Thinking with and through the trans mundane means focusing on ordinary affects (Stewart 2007) over and against an ongoing cultural emphasis on trans visibility and representation, wherein so-called positive representation is framed as the "primary path through which trans people might have access to livable lives" (Gossett, Stanley, and Burton 2017, xv) through a kind of magical thinking that endows representation with the power to address and redress structural violence—what Reina Gossett, Eric Stanley, and Johanna Burton (2017, xv) call "the trap of the visual." Emphasizing affect over visuality, which has long dominated conversations about trans being and becoming, opens the possibility of thinking through an ensemble of bad feelings that stubbornly attend trans experience, even across axes of racial, gendered, sexual, and economic difference (though unevenly): anxiety, rage, fatigue, exhaustion, anger, fear, loneliness. I argue that this specific conjuncture of negative affect is systematically exploited by trans tech start-ups that provide hormones, medical consultations, and transition-related support via app and mail-order prescription services.

Let's begin, then, with a snapshot from the trans mundane that bears specifically on the unjust stratified access that shapes trans health care: amid the COVID-19 pandemic, a beloved friend went under the knife to have his chest reconstructed. He was paying out of pocket to the tune of $10,000 for top surgery because his insurance, provided by a public university in West Texas, specifically excluded transition-related medical procedures. His health-care access situation was, and remains, common. Consider two other evidentiary instances, drawn from the intimate sphere of folks who were on stand-by during this friend's surgery: I, having formerly worked at a public university in Tennessee, delayed surgical and hormonal transition for nearly a decade on account of precisely the same exclusions, completely unable to pay the extremely high surgical fees or the monthly out-of-pocket cost of testosterone and still afford groceries (the university did not pay very well and would later become an object of academic internet ire when they announced a nontenure-track lectureship in English that paid less than $30,000 for a 4-4 course load). My lifelong best friend, who had hormonally transitioned at the age of twenty, waited over a decade for top surgery because his then-employer—a statewide LGBT nonprofit—also carried the same type of exclusions, which meant he spent his days doing advocacy work for an organization ostensibly concerned with trans rights that nevertheless refused to advocate for him. We were relieved, excited, and only a little nervous that our friend was finally able to access surgery; we were deeply aware and entirely tired of the difficult and circuitous path that preceded his entrance into the operating room.

After surgery, our friend returned to the small apartment he and his partner had rented during the procedure, which occurred in the state capital on account of the paucity of trans-competent surgeons in his immediate area. During the night, he suffered a severe hematoma resulting in the loss of a liter of blood; he returned to the hospital for a transfusion and monitoring while his partner, unable to enter the hospital on account of pandemic-related public health precautions, waited panicked in the car. He recovered and, waking from anesthetization, realized he was concerned about whether this surgical complication would jack up the cost of his surgery, which had already entirely depleted his savings: gratitude for continued living supplanted by economic anxiety.

At the historical moment wherein he began to seek out surgery, the insurance exclusions he encountered were already provisionally unlawful, depending on how section 1557 of the Affordable Care Act, which prohibits discrimination in health care, is interpreted. Nevertheless, it is the impacted consumer of trans medical services who is expected to take it on themselves to counter such exclusions on a case-by-case basis, figuring out workarounds, negotiating with their insuring institution, or bringing a lawsuit to bear. Not surprisingly, many trans folks opt instead to save aggressively and pay up. This is part of how predatory capitalism works: by making the pursuit of economic justice so labor intensive, so individuated and ad hoc, that already-exhausted subjects decline such pursuit.

Exploiting the Trans Mundane

Right around this time, during a global pandemic that exacerbated already-existing senses of isolation, anxiety, depression, and anomie—that intensified the forms of negative affect that already reliably saturate trans lifeworlds—a series of venture-capital-backed start-ups specializing in for-profit trans medical care began to flashily announce their existence. Although the medical establishment has long identified trans subjects as a niche market of biomedical consumers rife for economic exploitation, the appearance of these start-ups marked a new era of economic predation in the guise of trans affirmation. They offer, for the first time, an opportunity for trans people to transition in place (to borrow from the parlance that has become so ubiquitous over the course of this pandemic), to receive medical care, hormones, and advice on negotiating the state bureaucracies that administer gender without leaving one's home.

Allow me to introduce you, if you have not already made their acquaintance:[1] Plume is a telehealth service offering digital provider appointments, hormone prescriptions, and medical letters of support for surgery to the tune of $99 per month; the actual cost of hormones, blood work, and surgery is extra. Folx offers digital clinician visits and delivery subscriptions for estrogen, testosterone, PrEP, and tablets to treat erectile dysfunction, offering tiered pricing for folks newly transitioning (more expensive) and folks maintaining already-initiated transitions (less expensive); the former subscriptions are in the $120–$140 range; the latter between $60 and $100. Then there is Euphoria.LGBT, a suite of apps that coach trans subjects through the process of transition; Solace provides resources for learning about the process of transition; Clarity is a "sense-of-self" tracker that supposedly helps measure the variables of gender identity, gender expression, and desire to determine their flux, durability, and consistency; Windfall is a trans Etsy, a marketplace for makers and artists; and Bliss is a nudge-driven savings account for surgery—it boasts that "every time you get a push notification, it's helping move you closer to being yourself." Additionally, coming soon onto the market (at the time of this writing) are Devotion, a daily affirmation app, and Catharsis, "a dedicated mental and emotional health platform." Although some of these apps are free to download, paid upgrades unlock additional features.

This suite of start-ups, all appearing roughly a year deep in a global pandemic, make it possible to hormonally transition from bed and thus to sidestep the necessary tasks that often feel herculean in nature and have long been part and parcel of the transition process: seeking out an affirming physician for letters and treatment, bringing one's visibly trans body to waiting room after waiting room for blood work, specialist visits, consultations; and fighting with insurance companies for coverage. These tasks are often accompanied by significant indignity and trauma, from the routine microaggressions of misgendering and deadnaming to outright refusal of treatment. These start-ups hedge their bets on the allure of avoiding the awkwardness, discomfort, and potential harm that subtends this process.

A quick tour of the affective promises made by these companies makes this all too evident. Euphoria vows to "alleviate the great pains associated with gender transition." The opening screen of the Solace app provides a definition of solace, white text over a pink-to-blue gradient, reading, "solace: noun/comfort or consolation in a time of distress or sadness." The home page for Plume explains its raison d'être as motivated by their knowledge "that seeking gender-affirming care can be daunting, confusing, and exhausting." Folx pledges to provide "the care you deserve with medical providers who get you . . . quality, affirming support on your time from the comfort of your home."

Consider the portrait of medical transition painted here: a time of distress, discomfort, and sadness, characterized by routine encounters with doctors who, if not forthrightly transantagonistic, are at the least pretty clueless about the realities of trans lives and desires. It is a byzantine labyrinth of medical bureaucracy that one must navigate in order to access affirming care. It feels almost as if these app developers have taken seriously what trans scholars of medicine have been saying for nigh on three decades: that there is something very wrong with practices of medical gatekeeping around trans-related procedures, that they are inaccessible on account of such gatekeeping, that trans-competent providers are scarce, that physicians visits are too often nerve wracking and sometimes humiliating. Nonetheless, they seem to have selectively ignored one very important component of these critiques and the calls for medical justice that such critiques have undergirded: that one of the central barriers to medical transition is the high price tag attached.

In fact, this high price tag seems, unsurprisingly, to be the main appeal. Sasha Geffen and Annie Howard (2021) report, in an excellent article critiquing the emergence of this cohort of trans health startups, on the CEO of Euphoria, who breathlessly told a premier finance rag all about the wild profit to be wrought from the financialization of trans health:

"Euphoria's CEO Robbi Katherine Anthony spoke with *Forbes* about the financial opportunities in the trans-tech field. 'Our estimates place the average cost of transition at $150,000 per person,' she said. 'Multiply that by an estimated population of 1.4 million transgender people, we're taking about a market in excess of $200B. That is significant. That's larger than the entire film industry.'" For those of us who lived through the era of market excitement around the disposable income of (middle- and upper-class, predominately white, upwardly mobile) gays and lesbians ("double income, no kids!"), this craven pursuit of trans dollars feels familiar, though the contemporary pursuit of trans cash is remarkably savvier and, I think, more ethically bankrupt as a result. It's a trans-inclusive variant of rainbow capitalism that recognizes that a very large number of trans people, despite much higher rates of poverty and unemployment, spend what little disposable income they have on gender-affirming medical and aesthetic procedures. Not Subarus, not gay cruises, but something much less frivolous: health care. Moreover, these pay-out-of-pocket health-care services prey quite specifically on particular and overlapping segments of trans populations: those without insurance that would render this suite of services affordable, those that live beyond metropolitan centers that contain trans-affirming medical specialists, and those that would prefer the streamlined ease of access offered to avoid a hostile, awkward, or triggering encounter in their pursuit of transition-related health care. The folks most likely to utilize these services are also the people most marginalized within trans communities: those with bad or no insurance, those who are isolated and disconnected from trans peers who might be able to assist them in navigating the process of transition, those with histories of lousy encounters with health-care professionals, and those who have become avoidant and withdrawn as an outcome of the accreted impact of transantagonism.

The Enclosure of a Trans Affective Commons

Appreciating the impact (and threat) of this suite of services necessitates understanding them as an attempted enclosure of a trans commons, a for-profit extraction of forms of knowledge built interrelationally and to the side of the medical industry. There is a long communal history of trans folks mentoring one another through the process of transition documented in newsletters, circulating through in-person peer support groups, percolating on internet forums, manifest in Web 1.0 sites like TSroadmap.com, and consolidating in projects like RAD (Referral Aggregator Database) Remedy, a trans-led nonprofit that, according to their website copy, seeks to connect "trans, gender nonconforming, intersex and queer people to affirming and affordable care nationwide." I do not mean to glorify such projects and spaces, which were and are often rife with infracommunal disagreement and interpersonal tension. I just want to acknowledge that the precise services offered with a price tag by Plume, Folx, and Euphoria have long been free and have operated as integral services that managed to link quite disparate trans folks together, discursively and affectively. Much of the historic space of trans communality is underwritten by the kinds of care labor and mutual aid that have circulated in the service of demystifying and enabling transition. The privatization of the networks through which such knowledge circulates, then, is nothing short of an enclosure of a trans affective commons.

The phrase "affective commons" conjoins affect to the long-circulating concept of the commons: that which is held in common, shared, not privatized. It has circulated in recent years as a way to shorthand the radical collectivities that coalesce through ongoing protest, a way of naming "ways of coming together that disrupt racial capitalism's technologies of accumulation, extraction, and alienation" (Stanley 2018, 489). I borrow the phrase from both Eric Stanley and Lauren Berlant in order to name collective feelings that cohere through, circulate among, and undergird contemporary collective organizations of life within and against such accumulation, extraction, and alienation.

Stanley theorizes the specific variants of gay shame and queer hate as instantiations of such an affective commons, mobilizing radical queer collectives to resist the corporatization of pride, homonationalism, intensifying gentrification, police violence, and the recission of already-gutted social welfare provisions. Berlant's use of the term is less intensively focused on affect's role in consolidating resistant collectivities. Rather, they deploy it to index an obverse of the deliberate "orchestration of political emotion" (Berlant and Greenwald 2012, 77), something counterposed to forms of intentional manipulation that are rife in this era of algorithmically mediated political affect. In Berlant's (2012, 77) work, the affective commons is initially synonymous with "the unstated residue of collective life," the felt but unsaid, difficult-to-articulate mood or vibe of a group.

In a later essay, Berlant (2016, 395) expands on what they mean by "unstated residue." They articulate their suspicion of "the prestige the commons concept has attained in the US and theory-cosmopolitan context, often signifying an ontology that merely needs the world to create infrastructures to catch up to . . . the attachment to this concept is too often a way of talking about politics as the resolution of ambivalence and the vanquishing of the very contingency of nonsovereign standing that is at the heart of true equality, where status is not worked out in advance or outside of relation." Over and against the use of the commons as a means of too-quickly displacing the ambivalences and transformations at the core of left political movement, Berlant (2016, 395) proposes an alternate use, writing that "the very scenes in which the concept attains power mark the desire for living with some loss of assurance as to one's or one's community's place in the world, at least while better forms of life are invented and tried out" and concluding that "the better power of the commons is to point to a way to view what's broken in sociality, the difficulty of convening a world conjointly, although it is inconvenient and hard, and to offer incitements to imagining a livable provisional life." They offer up a dedramatized conceptual use of the commons, one characterized more by unsure, precarious, and more or less halting attempts to live otherwise, or at least envision such an otherwise, and less marked by revolutionary fervor. When I write here about a trans affective commons, I am using that phrase in the spirit of Berlant's account, with a provisional hope animated by Stanley's. That is, I am naming a collective sense of fatigue, exhaustion, and outrage brought about by inhabiting lifeworlds very much shaped by broken socialities that produce more or less unlivable lives, while bearing in mind that such negative affect is also collective acknowledgment of and testament to the inadequacies of the present conjuncture, that it is and can be mobilized in the service of imagining, and molding, a more livable provisional life.

The trans communal skill shares I mention above are all animated by a bone-deep recognition of the limits and failings of trans health care, the pragmatic difficulties of transitioning, the dearth of trans-affirming medical practitioners, and the harms wrought by the privatization of medical services. The for-profit, ostensibly trans-affirming services seeking to corner the trans health-care market know this, and they insidiously and cynically appeal to such exhaustion and malcontent in their advertising copy. The ads on my social media feeds, algorithmically aware of my abiding "interest" in such services, let me know daily that Folx "believes healthcare is about our lives—not a diagnosis," that they're "flipping the cis-stem on its head" (as if cis-centricity was limited to health care, as if price-gouging trans people was liberatory), that they're able to deliver everything from PrEP to HRT with "no ignorance, no judgment, no hassle." I'm consistently alerted to the fact that Plume is here to help me live my most "authentic life." Solace—the transition-related info and resource app offered by Euphoria—greets me each time I open the app with a disturbing personal exhortation that reads, in a minimal white font set against a beautiful Transsexual Sunset of soft pinks and blues: "Because you better believe, that I love you. That I will purge this distance. Some-day. Somehow." The app reaches out to me, proffering unconditional acceptance, closeness, intimacy, declaring its love, promising its ca-pacity to connect. It presumes my isolation, disconnection, sadness, lack of love, and it promises healing—indeed, Solace. Every time I see this welcome message, I think, "Honey, you don't even *know* me."

In addition to selling us actual hormones and medical consulta-tions, these digital services are also selling collective trans knowledge back to us with a price tag attached and appealing to the forms of collective bad feeling that circulate as a trans affective commons in order to brand this expropriative repackaging. They are seeking to profit off the trauma ordinariness that subtends trans arts of living. It is precisely this trauma ordinariness that renders trans folks more easily targeted by emergent forms of economic predation that con-strue us as a niche market rife for exploitation. Although this practice has a long genealogy as a core component of trans healthscapes in the United States, the trans tech suite of services addressed here index a certain rapid intensification of the phenomenon of preying on trans trauma ordinariness in the form of dissociation, loneliness, anxiety, and depression. The term "healthscape" comes to us from the work of sociologist and science historian Adele Clarke (2010, 105), and it refers to "a way of grasping, through words, images, and material cul-tural objects, patterned changes that have occurred in the many and varied sites where health and medicine are performed." Plume, Folx, Euphoria, and other emergent trans health tech herald a significant transformation of trans healthscapes.

The proliferation of these services occurs at a nexus shaped by trans precarity, economic predation, and negative affect; at this nexus, conceptions of trans justice and freedom become winnowed down to what Berlant calls a "pragmatic desperation" underwritten by a cruelly optimistic investment in "capitalism's reparative capacity" (Berlant and Greenwald 2012, 77). Political depression—what Ann Cvetkovich (2012, 1) refers to as the "sense that customary forms of political response, including direct action and critical analysis, are no longer working either to change the world or to make us feel better"—grounds such pragmatic desperation. It heralds a giving up on structural change, a cynical and deeply individuated effort to se-cure stability shaped by "that action of getting what one can because the other people are getting theirs, that action of thinking that 'fairness' in democracy equals no one having a cushion (and so claims on economic justice become special-interest claims rather than the claims any member of the body politic might make)" (Berlant and Greenwald 2012, 80–81).

Faux-Woke Vectoralism

One of the key reasons why folks utilize such services is because it's just easier—logistically, emotionally, psychically—to pay the higher price than to navigate the byzantine bureaucracy of trans medicine: a convenience fee one pays in order to circumvent transantagonism, red tape, and structural obscurantism. Trans tech's circumvention of such difficulties relies on decades of trans communal critique of unjust healthscapes; these start-ups are effectively operationalizing (some of) the demands emanating from this critique. One of them is that cis medical professionals should not be overwhelmingly overrepresented in decision-making positions regarding the provision of trans medical services. Another is that the provision of trans medical services should be based on a model of informed consent, one where service providers serve as conduits of information about the effects and impacts of a procedure, thereby empowering patients to make thoroughly informed choices about all trans-related medical procedures. Yet another is that the process be streamlined and integrated, with support offered at each significant juncture of transition—from name and gender-marker changes to selecting a surgeon, thus minimizing the often frustrating and sometimes baffling process of navigating transition.

One might even be tempted to call the development of such services a revolution in trans health care. And they are, I think. Just not the one that the majority of leftist trans activists had hoped for. It is something more than just a reworked and intensified version of trans-affirmative rainbow capitalism; we might call it, building on the work of McKenzie Wark, faux-woke vectoralism. Wark, in *Capital is Dead, Is This Something Worse?* proposes an end to the practice of adding modifiers to "capitalism" to name the specific, emergent features of contemporary economopolitical arrangements (post-Fordist capitalism, neoliberal capitalism, late capitalism, etc.) and instead argues that the contemporary moment heralds the supersession of capitalism itself by the development of a new mode of production, characterized by a new form of class antagonism. It is not that the antagonism between the bourgeoisie and the proletariat disappears, but rather that antagonism becomes overlaid and, in some senses, subsumed by another one: that between the vectoralist class and the hacker class. The vectoralist class does not own the material means of production; rather, they own and control information. The hacker class is that class of workers that make this information and are, in turn, subjected to it. Sometimes this is paid labor, but often—as is the case with data mining, click tracking, the myriad information we voluntarily offer up to apps—it is unwaged. As Wark (2019, 59) puts it, brutally and poignantly, "The capitalist class eats our bodies, the vectoralist class eats our brains."

"Faux-woke vectoralism" is my effort to name the processes through which trans tech aims to extort, amass, and exploit the collective knowledge and experience of trans subjects, but it can be extended to refer to any instance wherein a thin commitment to (some selective) principles of social justice works as a smokescreen or distractive window-dressing that obscures the attempted enclosure, privatization, and monetization of minoritized experiential knowledges. The wokeness is faux, of course, because it refuses a politics of collectivization and redistribution. It is overridden and determined by profit logic. In other words, if your vision of trans liberation has venture capitalists chomping at the bit, you are doing it wrong. If it offers up a way to circumvent the hostile socialities and institutions that trans subjects have historically navigated in order to access transition without actually rendering transition more economically accessible, you are doing it wrong. If it shuttles funds away from trans communities rather than materially supporting and enhancing them, you are doing it wrong.

Such predation is uniquely enabled by the saturation of negative affect that shapes the trans mundane; without it, the appeal of such services would wane. In a world—imagine, for just a moment— wherein trans folks were able to circulate publicly without fear, felt we had a right to the city (and suburb, exurb, and rural space), and could casually assume the existence and accessibility of affirmative health care, a payment premium predicated on the desire to avoid spaces of encounter would be entirely outmoded.

Note

1   The following citations are taken directly from the advertising copy, websites, and in-app statements issued by Plume, Folx, and Euphoria as of October 15, 2021.

References

Berlant, Lauren. 2016. "The Commons: Infrastructures for Troubling Times." *Environment and Planning D: Society and Space* 34 (3): 393–419.

Berlant, Lauren, and Jordan Greenwald. 2012. "Affect in the End Times: A Conversation with Lauren Berlant." *Qui Parle* 20 (2): 71–89.

Clarke, Adele. 2010. "From the Rise of Medicine to Biomedicalization: U.S. Healthscapes and Iconography, circa 1890–Present." In *Biomedicalization: Technoscience, Health, and Illness in the U.S.*, edited by Adele Clarke, Laura Mamo, Jennifer Ruth Fosket, Jennifer R. Fisher, and Janet K. Shim, 104–46. Durham, NC: Duke University Press.

Cvetkovich, Ann. 2012. *Depression: A Public Feeling*. Durham, NC: Duke University Press.

Geffen, Sasha, and Annie Howard. 2021. "Quantifying Transition." The Baffler, March 22. https://thebaffler.com/latest/quantifying-transition-geffen-howard.

Gossett, Reina, Eric A. Stanley, and Johanna Burton, eds. 2017. *Trap Door: Trans Cultural Production and the Politics of Visibility*. Cambridge, MA: MIT Press.

Stanley, Eric. 2018. "The Affective Commons: Gay Shame, Queer Hate, and Other Collective Feelings." GLQ 24 (4): 489–508.

Stewart, Kathleen. 2007. *Ordinary Affects*. Durham, NC: Duke University Press.

Wark, McKenzie. 2019. *Capital Is Dead*. London: Verso.

Rizvana Bradley

"Your love is too thick," he said, thinking, That bitch is looking at me; she is right over my head looking down through the floor at me. "Too thick?" she said, thinking of the Clearing where Baby Suggs' commands knocked the pods off horse chestnuts. "Love is or it ain't. Thin love ain't love at all." —Toni Morrison, *Beloved*, 1987

As it is written, For thy sake *we* are killed all the day long; *we* are accounted as *sheep* for the *slaughter*. —Romans 8:36

I

The preceding exchange from Toni Morrison's novel *Beloved* confronts the reader with a convolution of philosophical, ethical, and affective problematics concerning the gendered intimacies and reproductions of black life and (non)being; it confronts the reader with the strained intramurality of black existence (Spillers 2003, 277–318). This moment in the novel, in which Paul D accuses Sethe of acting out of a dangerously excessive maternity, out of a love that is "too thick," gestures toward the unequivocal and unrelenting conscription of black feminine labor in the reproduction of both worldly ontology and those fugitive black socialities that emerge in flight from the world (Hartman 2016, 166–73). "Rememory" is the mnemonic device Morrison insists we place on our tongues in order to reckon with Sethe's act of infanticide and its historical reverberations (Morrison 2004, passim). It is a device that collapses the historical, geographical, and ethical distance between the reader and Sethe's unapologetically illegitimate, unlawful form of loving in the face of the irreducible violence of a world that would see her and her children ruthlessly enslaved. In short, Morrison's rememory forces us to confront the conditions under which this repressed and forgotten act of unthinkable violence comes to constitute a mercy: a world before which blackness is simultaneously relegated to nonhumanity and called to testify to the horrors of nonbeing for the humanity from which it is expelled.

Let us pause to consider what Morrison means to draw out in this scene of contrapuntal gendering: Paul D recoils from Sethe's maternal love, finding in its weight, density, and stickiness a disposition of and toward dangerous excess. When he tells Sethe "Your love is too thick," he is prescribing certain norms of love and attachment and suggesting Sethe's maternal practice falls prey to what Lauren Berlant (2011) would have called "cruel optimism," if only we could blacken her idiom. For Paul D, that impossible dream of black maternity can only court disaster. His warning is clear: Sethe's relationship to her own thick love will destroy her and the life he seeks to make with her. Yet the disjunctive spatiotemporalities of black life, art, and intimacy cannot be understood in isolation from their gendered reproductions, which have always turned on the material and symbolic labors of black femininity and black maternity, no matter how consistently these labors are elided, pathologized, or otherwise disavowed.

Sethe's practice of *too thick love* is necessarily entangled with worldly violence, the proximate contours of which were the gratuitous brutalities to which Sethe was regularly and ritually subject at the "Sweet Home" plantation, from which she ultimately fled in a desperate bid to protect herself, her infant daughter, and her unborn child. But *too thick love* also operates against and in flight from that world's ontoepistemological mandates and strictures, against the metaphysical cataclysm of knowing and being. Sethe lays claim to this *too thick love* as a form of desire that crystallizes and fractures the world's constitutions of and constraints on black life, death, and existence, prompting singular questions of black affect, intimacy, and spatiotemporality.

Beloved testifies to the extra-diegetic resonance of a love that is always already violently constrained by the world—a love that is both hopelessly abbreviated and impossibly circumscribed by the given structure of civil society and its metaphysical fortifications. If, as Berlant (2012, 69) would instruct us, love always begins from the scene of fantasy, then we must insist that when it comes to black life, fantasy is immanently tethered to flight (Harney and Moten 2013, 84–99). This chapter is concerned with how we might attune to the affects that emerge at the difficult conjunction of black fantasies of flight, their racially gendered reproduction, and their metaphysical interdiction. In the pages running up to Sethe and Paul D's fractious exchange, Morrison (2004, 192) describes Sethe's flight from Sweet Home plantation nearly two decades prior: "She just flew. Collected every bit of life she had made, all the parts of her that were precious and fine and beautiful, and carried, pushed, dragged them through the veil out, away, over there where no one could hurt them. Over there. Outside this place, where they would be safe." *Out. Away. Over there. Outside this place.* If we are able to listen, we might hear in Morrison's chant an anticipatory echo of the impasses of the present, even if that present should not be assumed as "ours" to share.

Indeed, political idioms of *flight, exit, exodus,* and *escape* have had a prominent place within the post-1968 historical imaginations of radical milieus in various corners of the world. Although different explanations for the contemporary prominence of idioms of escape have been offered across Marxist, Foucauldian, and other Continental traditions, what they have generally shared is a sense that the spatio-temporal enclosures of the present are growing ever tighter, increasingly saturated and fenced in. Whether the wearied times of the "collateral afterworlds" that endure the accumulation of catastrophe take the shape of dizzying acceleration, fitful vicissitudes, or the apparent exhaustion of historicity, they are generally marked "by the temporality of a difficult present where life is unhinged from the pervasive hope for a better tomorrow" (Wool and Livingston 2017, 1). But how might we bring such inquiries to bear on the persistence of a figure like Sethe, whose interdicted flight and impossible endurance are foundational to the very enclosure she would refuse, an enclosure that is not so much historical as ontological?

In what follows, I want to consider the affective life of the black feminine, that figure who is fated to the *reproduction* of fugitive survival as well as social death. For Sethe's impossible imperative (of flying, carrying, pushing, and dragging pieces of life, out, away, and outside every worldly place), her structurally imposed inheritance and bequeathment, her terrible gift and burden to bear, signals a singularly black feminine ontological labor: the endlessly conscripted reproductive labor of making and breaking from the world. In lieu of a conclusion, which the nature of my inquiry prohibits, I close with a reflection on the Situationist concept of *la dérive* in order to approach a gendered predicament lodged in its racial underbelly. *Too thick love* enunciates a quest(ion) (Ferreira da Silva 2014) that remains largely unthought within the multiplicitous and divided tradition of radical critique that takes the constitutive interdiction of blackness from the world as its point of theoretical departure: how might we begin to attune to the affective valences of that interminably frustrated desire for a life beyond the reproduction of *social death and all that survives it, for flight even from the reproduction of flight*? Or, "how does it *feel* to be a problem" (Du Bois 1903, 1), not only for the world but for the fugitivity that would refuse the world we have been refused (Harney and Moten 2013)?

II

In pursuit of this racially gendered ulteriority, let us turn to Charles Burnett's *Killer of Sheep* (1977), a landmark feature that crucially enriched the black cinematic innovations of the L.A. Rebellion. Drawing on a range of cinematic influences—British documentary, Italian neorealism, and Third Cinema—as well as diasporic models from jazz, blues griot storytelling, and black literature (4), formally, *Killer of Sheep* shifts between the conventions of social documentary and fictional cinematic strategies to convey the irreducible spatiotemporality of black life. Burnett's site-specific vision of black life in Los Angeles emphasizes the singular rhythms of everyday working-class life through vignettes that offer sustained glimpses of landscapes and scenes of labor. We see Stan working long hours shearing sheep in the slaughterhouse, as well as abandoned factory yards, children throwing stones at passing trains, riding bicycles, and running capriciously through the streets. The film's inscription of black life in and as an unruly concatenation of minor performances informs a political commitment to the study of quotidian social practices and forms of intimacy that are inimical to the cinematic mainstream's "internal colonization" (Massood 1999) of black subjectivity. *Killer of Sheep* demonstrates black film's reflexive grappling with the cinematic, which, following Kara Keeling (2007, 3), indicates "a complicated aggregate of capitalist social relations, sensory-motor arrangements, and cognitive processes," and, I would add, *affective* codes that have sustained the history of film and its technological development.

Killer of Sheep's improvisational and existential mapping of black life exposes how genres of intimacy are unmade and differently remade. Expressions of black intimacy are and have always been inextricably bound, though not reducible, to histories of subjection and the worldly negation of filial and affilial relations (Wilderson 2010). As Christina Sharpe (2010, 190n6) argues, intimacy must be understood not simply as closeness and proximity, or as personal and private feeling, but as implicated in spatial and temporal dynamics "that arise out of domination and that continue to structure relations across race, sex, ethnicity, and nation." In her discernment, intimacy "is always about . . . the structures that organize and constitute the relationships between past and present and possible futures." To take up *Killer of Sheep*'s extemporaneous cartography of black intimacy as one of its signal contributions to the L.A. Rebellion, and to black cinematic innovation more generally, is necessarily to attend to its rendering of a singularly racial occlusion of and deviation from intimacy's familiar spatiotemporal fissures and cohesions, interruptions and durations (Berlant 1998). The intramural performances of withdrawal and withholding, of intimate proximity, distancing, and demurral, by which *Killer of Sheep*'s affective life is animated, have profound implications for the ontological ordering and phenomenological experience of worldly time and space, both within cinema and more generally.

In what is perhaps the most emotionally wrenching scene in the entire film, we encounter Stan and his wife, alone, slow dancing to Dinah Washington's performance of Clyde Otis's "This Bitter Earth." Roughly four minutes long and appearing more than halfway through the film, the scene unfolds in a single take. In the scene, Stan is backlit. His lambent frame stands in opposition to that of his wife, his dancing partner, who appears more than partially shaded, her profile given in shadow. The differential play of illumination and darkness becomes a shifting site of contrast, communion, and conflict. Light falls with uneven, unforgiving purpose. Stan's expression is impassive, obscuring any interior drama we might anticipate or expect such a face to reveal. As he turns, he becomes an object of aesthetic contemplation, which is to say, "an object of fantasy, violence, and delirium" (Marriott 2018, 70). And it is here, in the atmospheric friction that seems to track the laden turn of Stan's back toward us, that his refusal of the gaze which follows his movements becomes most apparent. Paradoxically, Burnett's depleted lovers find provisional solace in the midst of marital brokenness. Still, husband and wife are incapable of conforming to the cohesive shape or narrative mold of heteronormative coupling; they confront each other in and through an "unbearable tenderness," or what Berlant (Berlant and Evans 2018) described as "the state of recognizing that there's no protecting oneself from the world one is trying to survive—unwelcome, under-resourced, or with exhausted defenses." Here, unbearable tenderness becomes an *exorbitant* (Chandler 2014, 11–67) feeling that strains within and against the couple form. Stan and his nameless wife meet each other in the caesura which is theirs to share.

The slow dance draws the viewer into a contrapuntal performance of gendering that gradually, but unmistakably, shifts the locus of the drama from Stan to his wife. It is Stan's wife whose beleaguerment cuts the texture of their intimacy. She is the black maternal figure who must shoulder the material and symbolic weight of the given and its refusal, whose *too thick love* is ontologically tasked with their relentless reproduction.

The scene unfolds as an interval within an interval (Keeling 2007)—a fugal episode that redoubles the waiting and wading spatiotemporality of black existence that *Killer of Sheep* exhibits behind the mask of diegesis.[1] As Stan and his wife turn together, in a halting mimicry of the (over)turning of the world to which they are differentially yoked, she attempts to make direct eye contact, while he stubbornly averts his gaze. She presses in, gripping his back with both hands longingly, and lifting her face toward his, before he finally withdraws altogether. Her yearning mediates her husband's recalcitrant stiffness, extending the intimate yielding that Stan requires, if only so that he can refuse it. *Too thick love* names the black feminine labor that bridges that which cannot, and yet must be, shared. It is that which *anticipates* the turning away and reprises the failure of encounter *as if* it were history.

Yet I would argue that it would be a mistake to regard Stan's expressive opacity as simply the exterior facade of a disavowal of vulnerability where it is most desperately needed (Sexton 2017, 173) or as some black heteromasculine variation of an otherwise generalizable "resistant vulnerability" (Hagelin 2013). This is no simple bodily performance of masculine authority, yearning, or striving. Rather, Stan's apparently embodied stoicism performs a refusal of the interiority that has been refused him, insofar as the epidermalizing gaze of the spectator is coupled both to an absolute exposure and to the usurpation of interiority as private property. Stan's muscles appear to do the work of sustaining the rotational momentum of the embrace at the core of the scene's unfolding, a circumvolution that at once conceals and discloses the "tensed muscles" of black masculinity as "a form of bodily (un)knowing that recognizes its existence in a history of defeat while instancing its unconscious preparation to meet and resist that defeat" (D. Scott 2010, 44). That history of defeat marks and is remarked in the space of the embrace. Although Stan's straightened back strives toward perfect form, his tensed muscles allude to the physical and psychological dimensions of an existential exhaustion, a kind of fatigue irreducible to the vicissitudes of narrative or the foreclosures of historical conjuncture.

Stan's wife's comportment makes no pretense to intransigence, to a corporeal form that would hold itself together, no matter the pressure. Her face, which ferries a veritable cascade of feeling—aching desire, anguish, despair, regret—contrasts starkly with Stan's stoicism. After Stan walks away from her, she throws herself against the window, then turns and lets her body steady itself on the sill, her hands on her knees, as if her body might buckle and fold in upon itself. The thickness of the love that sustains Stan's performance of verticality materializes diametrically for his wife, whose bearing brings her low, like one touched by the certain grip of quicksand. Shifting together and apart, their dance pivots on the question it refracts but cannot resolve: *"Is there an alternative scenario, a parallel track where they live happily ever after? Where invention is capable of sustaining love?"* (Hartman 2019, 219).

III

Too thick love is that which lingers, generous and recalcitrant, in the atmospherics of the scene as it draws toward its close with Stan's wife's internal monologue. Partway through these unspoken words, she reaches for a pair of shoes from her daughter Angela's infancy, which lie neatly on a nearby bedroom dresser, and brings them close to her chest, cradling them as one would a baby. It is almost as if she is mourning the loss of a child, as if her daughter could only be shielded from the world in infancy. Her monologue recalls her time in the South: "Memories don't seem mine, like half-eaten cake and rabbit skins stretched on the backyard fences. My grandmother, mother dear, mot dear, dragging her shadow across the porch. Standing bare headed under the sun, cleaning red catfish with white rum." It is significant here that Stan's wife refers to her grandmother as *mot dear*, just as earlier in the film, her son, Stan Jr., calls his mother *mot dear*, only to be chastised by his father for slipping into speech tainted by the trace of black southern vernacular culture. ("Say old long headed boy, didn't I tell you about calling your mother mot dear? You ain't in the country.") Stan's passing rebuke is a disclosure and reconcealment of an exorbitance enclosed within a litany of effacive and defacing nominations, the exorbitance of a black maternity at once indispensable to and impossible within the world, which enters worldly speech only in serial misnamings. What might we make of the willingness of Stan's wife, this black woman at once nameless and misnamed, to claim the inordinate maternity signaled by the ruse of nomination? Does this impossible claim bear the trace of a singularly black feminine "inventiveness," buried "beneath layers of attenuated meanings, made an excess in time, over time . . . by a particular historical order" (Spillers 2003, 203)?

Angie's shoes, which take on their symbolic potency in the mother's action of cradling them close to her breast, bespeak the gendered labor of transfer and transfer of labor which is endemic to the temporality of black life in the wake of slavery—a lateral language of beholding and beholdenness (Sharpe 2016, 100–101). Taking heed of "the plasticity and obduracy of the prop" (Rhodes 2017, 17) within the cinematic, we may suggest that Angie's shoes trace the singular material bearings of the black feminine, a reproductive burden that is necessarily transgenerational, passed down from mother to daughter. After all, the black "mother's only claim . . . [is] to transfer her dispossession to the child" (Hartman 2016, 166). It is the brutal inevitability of this racially gendered inheritance—the inheritance of bequeathing dispossession—that Sethe sought to escape through her terrible act in *Beloved*, just as it is this inheritance of broken maternity that ensures that the *too thick love* she must bear can only ever register as pathological.

Heeding the singular reproductive burden to which black femininity is tethered helps us to attune to the affective contours of a minor gesture (Manning 2016) that occurs earlier in the film. The gesture takes place within a longer sequence, which begins with Stan, laboring beneath the kitchen sink, talking to his friend about "working himself into his own hell." His friend replies, "Why don't you just kill yourself? You'd be a lot happier." Working as he answers, Stan despondently rejoins, "No, I'm not going to kill myself," and then glances at his daughter, Angela, who watches silently from the corner of the room. A medium close-up shot shows Angie wearing a rubber mask of what looks like a caricature of a hound dog, her left hand shoved strangely into the mouth of the mask. Stan pauses to give her the slightest of glances—quizzical, perhaps even disturbed—before returning to his work and remarkably mundane dialogue about the gravest of dilemmas. After her older brother, Stan Jr., grabs and squeezes her rubber dog face, demanding, "Where's my BB gun?" before being rebuked and chased off by Stan, Angela walks outside, apparently drawn by the call and whistle of a neighbor boy. Angela finds him, back to a fence, and seems to nod at him, mask bobbing, before moving alongside him, her right hand gripping the fence above, her left still firmly shoved into the mouth of the mask. He looks toward her, though not quite at her, and she in turn looks toward him. His comportment is subdued, reticent, or dejected, and no words pass between them about the mask.

Commentators have often described Angela's donning of the mask as "haunting," "unsettling," "enigmatic," or "grotesque." What is most disturbing about the scene is not the mask itself but rather the gesture for which it is livery. Angela seems to be performing a refusal of the gendered fate that her intimacy with the young boy would seem to presage—a refusal of the emotive faciality (Deleuze and Guattari 1987, 167–91) that registers her mother's subjectivation and subjection, of the *too thick love* that consigns her mother to the endless work of reproducing the very world that ensnares her. But what is so profoundly morbid about Angela's gesture is the manner in which it seems to anticipate its own inevitable failure—rapt in an oral fixation that carries the trace of interdicted maternity. Angela's gesture seems suffused with both the knowledge of the world that encloses it and the trace of that which haunts that world, which remains even in closure.

IV

Stan and his nameless wife's slow dance is one among many scenes in Burnett's film that confront the viewer with an image of *black cinematic time*, imbued with the raw signatures of performances of black life, in its failed mutuality. The torturous drag of such scenes of affective raveling foreground the singular difficulties of a spatiotemporal existence which is, no matter its vicissitudes, everywhere and all the time *too thick—too much too slow* and *not enough too fast*. The irreducibly haptic scene of grief that subtends their difficult convening constitutes nothing less than an intervention into "the history of the phenomenology of time as time shows up in human lives" (Couzens-Hoy 2009, xii). Mary Ann Doane (2002, 141) has analyzed the enduring significance of "the cinematic construction of the event as the most condensed and semantically wealthy unit of time," even as it is also a "site of intense internal contradictions." Yet how might we begin to approach the dispossessive force of Burnett's film, which could be regarded, as Elizabeth Povinelli rightly observes (albeit for the wrong reasons), as exemplary of "the cinema of the non-event" (Berlant and Povinelli 2014)? More precisely, how can we think with the wayward feeling, the unbearable bearing, that emerges from what is spatially and temporally *anterior* to both cinematic diegesis and event?

Scholarly accounts have tended to emphasize the importance of the specific historical conjuncture which encloses and bears down on the quotidian life of black intimacy in *Killer of Sheep*. By such accounts, the Watts rebellion of 1965 not only presaged a concatenation of black insurgencies that would unfold in the United States in the late 1960s and early 1970s but also the rollout of new regimes of racial governmentality: from the "organized abandonment" (Gilmore 2015) of revanchist neoliberal urbanism (Smith 1996) to the "carceral-security apparatus" (Camp 2016) with which such expulsions have been conjoined. For Povinelli (2011, 134), for example, Burnett's film discloses the uneven organization of "late liberal modes of making die, letting die, and making live," across racial and class lines, at the very moment of that regime's ascendance. Others, such as Jeffrey Skoller, emphasize the hauntological dimensions of *Killer of Sheep*, which exceed the trappings of historical conjuncture and must be theorized in terms of the ongoing "afterlife of slavery" (Hartman 2008; Skoller 2005, 119–29). My interest is in the gendered reproduction of intimacies that endure the *indistinction* between these two registers of thought, in the existence that must simultaneously bear the historical renewal of regimes of racial violence—"the *stillness* of time and space" (Spillers 2003, 302) that marks black (non)being—and the fugitive spatiotemporal movements that enable survival. *Too thick love* is the affective trace of a singularly black feminine ontological labor, which undergirds not only the *linear temporality* that structures the lives of those granted narrative subjectivity, but also the "*temporality without duration*" that Calvin Warren (2018, 97) terms "*black time*."

The hyper-, ex-, and dyschronic thickness of black time subtends the emotional disintegrations of *Killer of Sheep*'s characters and saturates its cinematic images, rendering the question of whether it should be regarded as narrative cinema obsolete. As Manthia Diawara (1993, 10) observes, *Killer of Sheep* deploys a formal strategy characteristic of contemporaneous black filmic experiments in a "new realism," which "defamiliariz[es] . . . classical film language" by means of "rhythmic and repetitious shots, [by] going back and forth between past and present." Burnett's fractured vignettes are structured through an episodic progression that insists on fragmenting and distending the present, estranging the viewer from temporality. The film's many characters move errantly through cityscapes and storylines that seem to meet in their broken circularity, as if skirting the edges of an unsustainable relay between present and presence. Stan, his wife, and his two children, Stan Jr. and Angie, as well as Stan's friend Bracy, and his acquaintances Scooter and Smoke are tangled *extemporaries* subject to ceaseless reshapings. Burnett engages in an artful circumvention of narrative as the "dominant method of structuring time" (Doane 2002, 67) but not one that can be readily categorized among genres of nonnarrative cinema. For Burnett's formal experimentation does not so much refuse the hegemony of narrative (which, bracketing more nuanced debates, contemporary film historians generally agree had been established after 1907/8, if not earlier)[2] as it does refuse the *subterfuge* of narrative when it concerns *the black*. Burnett's (sur)realist ambitions in *Killer of Sheep* lead to a formal exhibition of the spatio-temporal lives of black existence, which are utterly irreconcilable with narrativity, even as narrative inevitably imposes itself as the requisite mode of historical accounting. Thus, pace Paula J. Massood (1999, 28, 29), *Killer of Sheep*'s interleaving of "a series of dramatic narrative vignettes with documentary-like nonnarrative footage" cannot simply be explained by invoking the temporal structure of African oral traditions, or by noting that its "cycle of pathos" deviates from the conventional dramatic arc of narrative cinema. Rather, the existential waywardness differentially faced and lived by Burnett's characters reveals the *imposition of narrative* onto performances of beleaguered subjectivity and the fantasies of worldly emplotment to which they are tethered, while simultaneously *repudiating narrativity's capacity* to produce anything other than *morbid projections* of black life.

After all, as Paul Ricoeur (1984, ix) would have it, "time becomes human to the extent that it is articulated through a narrative mode, and narrative attains its full meaning when it becomes a condition of temporal existence." What, then, becomes of temporality when it meets the lives of those for whom humanism lacks a grammar, for whom narrative has never offered anything other than "a conceptual prison house" (Hartman 2018; Wilderson 2010)? What is at stake here is how to begin to think and feel with the affective contours of those who are always already barred from the Aristotelian mode of "emplotment," as it has been refashioned to accommodate modernity's cartographies of history, development, and progress. In fact, it is precisely *the black's interdiction* from the organizing spatiotemporalities of the modern world that *furnishes the conditions of possibility for emplotment* (within historical time, on the map of the social). Let us recall G. W. F. Hegel's 1956, 93) infamous remarks in *The Philosophy of History*: "The Negro . . . exhibits the natural man in his completely wild and untamed state. . . . There is nothing harmonious with humanity to be found in this type of character." Africa, by the same token, has "no historical part of the World; it has no movement or development to exhibit" (99). The perpetual consignment of the black to what Denise Ferreira da Silva (2017, 277) terms the "scene of nature"—that is, as a radically affectable thing "whose existence is ruled by violence"—serves as an absolute, negative boundary for the map of civil society and its subjects, just as the founding "disqualification of sub-Saharan

Africa and its populations" (diasporic or otherwise), as Lindon Barrett (2014, 76) wrote, "organizes the linear progression of historical temporality." Blackness marks the negative spatial and temporal conditions of (im)possibility for the emplotment of the (cinematic) subject on the map of modern history and the social. Narrativity can only ever approach the black as a mechanism of genocide (Wilderson 2010, 59). Burnett's film fashions a poetics of spatiotemporality that is a "radical indictment of Narrative" (Brand 2017, 69) while also refusing to assume the garb of narrativity's dialectical antithesis. Thus, *Killer of Sheep* may be considered exemplary of "the cinema of the non-event," *not* because, as Povinelli (2011, 102) suggests, it indexes the lives of those "that have no part in late liberalism" but rather because it emerges from an existence that has no place in the spatiotemporality of the *world*, even as it remains the world's founding interdiction.[3] How, then, do we consider the relationship between blackness and Povinelli's privileged idiom of *endurance*?

The dance scene from *Killer of Sheep* is a caesura, a hold(ing) within the hold, which cuts the difference between the (in)determinancy of feeling and the feeling of (in)determinancy. The dreamlike spatiotemporality of the couple's (non)encounter—which strains synchrony and ruptures diegesis, which reveals the indistinction between realism and surrealism when it comes to exhibitions of black existence— extends the unmistakably dilatory quality of Burnett's cinematic atmosphere. Their embrace—sensuously prolonged, distended, torn— breaks, and breaks from, the "chrononormativity" (Freeman 2010) which has never been available to black existence in the first place. Swelling and extending, caving and condensing the space and time of affect, the scene gestures to a yearning that is irreducibly corporeal. Here, space and time gather and collapse through and upon the flesh as cumulate thickness, a waxing massification splayed before the enclosure of the film's frame. Theirs is an embrace whose unbearability can only be imagined to the extent to which it is imagined to be bearable, and even this is a lie.

The inestimable exorbitance and restraint glimpsed in the interminable interval of this single take might compel us to think black corporeality alongside critical readings of performances of weariness, fatigue, and exhaustion. Indeed, as Elena Gorfinkel (2012, 312) observes, figurations of tiredness and waiting become central to the telos and genealogy of an emergent postwar film aesthetic: "Challenging the present as a viable mode, the belatedness of tiredness superimposes past and present in an overlay of sensation . . . weariness falls into a state of waiting, a signification of expiring time and expiration's anticipation." Languor and fatigue, uniquely cinematic grammars successively ruptured and incompletely sutured in this slow dance, reveal dimensions of corporeal and psychic weariness and attrition that one might be tempted to liken to those postwar mobilizations of tiredness that were essential to the development of art cinema (312). But although Stan and his wife's contrapuntally gendered exhaustion does reveal something essential about the implicit entwining of cinematic and worldly spatiotemporality, as well as the violent attenuation and rescaling of black life to fit the cinematic frame, their exhaustions also complicate figurations of wearied bodies that are legible within cinema's representational field. The decelerated blurring (Moten 2017) of corporeality, affect, and spatiotemporality that unfolds through this black cinematic image strains against the racially unmarked universality of historicity, eventism, and impasse which persists even in accounts of the "wayward temporalities" (Freeman 2010) of the feminine and the queer.

Killer of Sheep confronts the viewer with the boundlessly bounded *dilation* (Berlant and Stewart 2019, 5) of the black existence which is anterior to history and the event. As Stan and his wife's dance gradually shifts toward its immeasurably pained (fore)closure, time does not simply slow but *thickens*. Space and time *accumulate* anteriorly. If this scene could be thought of as a present, it is a present that emerges in and through an irreducible condensation of dispersed and dispersive black histories of flight and expulsion, of itinerant movement even in total stillness. Can the *too thick* valences of this scene's wrenching lyricism, in and as survival, simply be presupposed as the measure of those whose backs are taken for late liberalism's floor? If the excruciating feel of this embrace reveals a corporeal drama that is interdicted from and incommensurable with worldly emplotment, how might we instead regard this scene as an occasion to explore the racially gendered reproduction of a black ulteriority that remains before metaphysics?

For Povinelli (2011, 103), Stan's embodiment in and movement through time is a matter of individuated perseverance in the face of the biopolitical depredations of late liberalism, which just barely place him within the threshold of the human: "We might say that Stan stares in the face the question of how to endure as he strives to perseverance. . . . The only thing separating Stan from the sheep is *his will to persevere*." Yet I would argue that Stan's character figures one who is structurally positioned as the anoriginary *object of the will*, irrespective of whether the apparent "willfulness" (Ahmed 2014) of his objections to objecthood are celebrated or disdained. For Stan, endurance does not reside within "the durative unfolding present" (Povinelli 2011, 49) but rather within a temporality without duration. What if we instead attuned to those modalities of incapacity and inaction delineated by belated and extrusive experience? Rather than viewing Stan as a limit case of the human will to endure, even at the edges of bare life (Agamben 1998)—a figuration that paradoxically reinscribes Stan as both the founding exclusion from, and the raw essence of, the human (Moten 2018, 174)—we might instead consider his (dis)place(ment) within a choreography of general suspension, where suspended action is calcified as the stalled temporality of *waiting* so distinctive to black life.

Blackness confronts a nexus of stolen pasts, of protracted presents without presence, of futurities withheld. Blackness is existence without being, beset by what David Marriott (2018, 235) describes as "the vertiginous experience of its own impossibility . . . its experience is that of an impasse, or aporia . . . its ipseity is that of a sea without terminus, a tragedy without resolution . . . a perpetual deferral or waiting." Povinelli (2011, 110) wonders, "How do we explain why some people keep on getting on while others do not? Why, in *Killer of Sheep*, does Stan persist beyond the point of exhaustion for other people in his neighborhood? Muscle and will, effort and endurance." But it is not so much that Stan is "getting on while others do not," not so much that Stan "persist[s] beyond the point of exhaustion," (110) as it is that Stan *and* his neighbors are *all* made to bear the mark of an inexhaustible differentiation (albeit differentially), which, at the level of black experience, exhausts the very language of perseverance and resignation, of endurance and collapse. Burnett's black cinematic time folds temporality, flesh, and affect back in on one another, fashioning a decelerated movement that savors or wallows in the sensorial thickness wherein tiredness, exhaustion, and fatigue emerge as unanswerable questions for thought. The dance marks a discompo-sure which is prior to both the *one* and the *two* of the couple form and its chrononormativities (Moten, in Fitzgerald 2015). A *too thick time* for a *too thick love*, which survives the enclosure through dreams that cannot help but conceal the unbearable bearings that (en)gender fugitivity. *Out, away, over there. . . . Outside this place.*

V

The psychic and political enclosures of urban space under histori-cal capitalism have been of enduring concern for radical intellectuals and movements since at least the nineteenth century, even as these concerns became particularly pronounced with the rise of the high modernist city in the early to mid-twentieth century (J. Scott 1998). Associated with the likes of Le Corbusier (Charles-Edouard Jean-neret), high modernism sought to fashion an urban space in which "formal, geometric simplicity and functional efficiency" became overriding imperatives, the organizational pillars of a capitalist uto-pianism predicated on the seamless complementarity of economic production and the rule of the state (J. Scott 1998, 106). It was against such urbanism, which Guy Debord (quoted in McDonough 2009, 92) referred to as "an illustration of and a powerful means of action for the worst oppressive forces," that the Situationist theory and prac-tice of the *dérive* emerged. Among those who aspire to radical forms of counterurbanism, the *dérive*, with its ongoing associative reverbera-tions through the world historical imagination of the global upheav-als of 1968, continues to hold a place of prominence.

A "calculated drifting" through the city (Wark 2011, 17), the *dérive* marked an effort to wrest a liberatory psychogeography from the ra-tionalized stranglehold of high modernist urban geography, precisely by orienting toward the disorientative. Often marshaling antiquated maps, intoxicants, days and nights of wandering, this "technique of rapid passage through varied ambiances" (Debord 1989, 62) meant to interrupt a dispensation of the city as the capitalist organization of time and space and recover or reinvent urban psychogeography as "the practice of lived time" (25, 31)—a life outside or in flight from the dictates of property. Of course, the urban landscape Stan and his family confront in *Killer of Sheep* is not that of the high modernist city but rather one that is marked by the gathering ruins of modernism, structured by a racial apartheid that seems indifferent to the great epochs of capitalist urbanism. Nevertheless, one could imagine that a practice that emphasizes a calculated drifting through the repressed openings within an otherwise seemingly totalizing urban enclosure should have some resonance here. Yet I want to suggest that it is, in fact, the *categorical failure* of the *dérive* to speak meaningfully to the conditions of (im)possibility for black fugitivity, to say nothing of the racially gendered reproduction of those conditions, that helps us to attune to the *black affect* with which *Killer of Sheep* is suffused.

At one point in the film, Stan's friend Bracy admits to Stan that he and his buddies have been "walking the streets all night. We passed here about three last night; saw the light on, but we thought it best we keep going." One could almost mistake Bracy's anecdote for a reference to the *dérive*, were it not for Stan's response, which slips a barb behind the veil of the taciturn: "You should have stopped; I'm always awake." Bracy, in turn, echoes the truth that has already worked its way between the words: "Counting sheep." Always awake, counting the very sheep he kills for a living. The *dérive* begins from a concrete "point of departure," explores "a fixed spatial field . . . establishing bases and calculating directions of penetration," and is ultimately brought to closure or temporary cessation "by the need for sleep" (Debord 1989, 64). In contradistinction, the relation between enclosure and fugitivity which confronts the black is immanent and metaphysical rather than geographic and temporal; it is a relation that is anoriginal, bereft of historicity, and utterly without reprieve. Far from incidental, what passes between Bracy and Stan in this moment is the unspeakable, shared knowledge of being outside of and against time, interdicted from history, suspended in the unforgiving dilations of the nonevent, wading and waiting. How can we begin to trace the steps of the *dérive* that emerges not as an interval of abandon, within which one might meander the recesses, cracks, and forgotten alleys of psychogeographical urbanism, but as the interval of the *abandoned*? How do we navigate the terrain of a passage that always already begins from *nowhere*, which has neither point of departure nor resting place, the passage of those whose itinerant movements appear on not a single map of the world in not a single historical archive? And where do we go from here?

McKenzie Wark (2011, 22) observes that, etymologically speaking, the *dérive*'s "whole field of meaning is aquatic, conjuring up flows, channels, eddies, currents, and also drifting, sailing or tacking against the wind. It suggests a space and time of liquid movement, sometimes predictable but sometimes turbulent." And it is, perhaps, precisely the irresolvable antagonism that is latent in the figure of the aquatic that reveals the failure of the lure of the *dérive* to catch where the black is concerned. For the black carries "the musk of the sea" on their skin, and knows the terrible intimacies of "coral and cartilage, bone and air, infrangible" (Brand 2001; 2010, 67). The beckon of the horizon and the vertigo of the abyss are irreconcilable.[4]

And yet there are moments in *Killer of Sheep* that gesture to the dream of flight, moments that perform the fugitivity that goes nowhere or has nowhere to go, even if the *too thick love* that reproduces this flight to nowhere is ultimately elided. Perhaps this blackened *dérive*, this incalculable drifting through the abyss, comes most clearly into view in the iconic shots of children jumping between the roofs of three-story buildings. The sequence directly follows one where Stan and his friend's plan to procure an engine for the car Stan has been renovating ends in ruin. Having fallen off the borrowed truck they were using to transport it, the engine is irrevocably broken: a defeat that Povinelli (2011, 102) reads as a literal, rather than metaphorical, exhibition of Stan's failure to alter "the material condition[s] for the transformation of his body, the production of a body less exhausted, alienated, and numb." As Stan and his friend return from their fruitless excursion, walking between the two buildings, they glance up at the children above. The film cuts to an extreme low-angle shot, which makes it appear, if only for the most fleeting moment, as if the children have taken flight, leaving the rubble of the street far below. Faye Adams's "Shake a Hand" falls over the sequence tellingly: "Just leave it to me / Don't ever be ashamed / Just give me a chance / I'll take care of everything / Your troubles I'll share / Let me know and I'll be there / I'll take care of you / Anyplace and anywhere."

This scene could easily be taken to exemplify the kind of "free play" that Dorothy Hendricks (2014, 17) suggests characterizes many of the sequences centered on children throughout the film, the "surreal qualities" of which appear profoundly "out of step with the adult realities of looming despair." These sequences of children engaged in free play, according to Hendricks, "serve no actual storyline" and occur "outside of the diegetic time that governs the economy of survival that the adults are restricted to" (17). But perhaps the idiom of freedom is in fact an obstacle to what is at play here, insofar as the very concept of the "'free black' . . . stages an impossible encounter," not least because black time unfolds in the absence of "the temporal horizon that freedom bestows to the human" (Warren 2018, 15, 97). As we have seen, not even the adults in this film can lay claim to narrative subjectivity, and, as the example of Angela's masking as an act of refusal without avail, the children of *Killer of Sheep* anticipate the (spatial) enclosure and (temporal) suspension in which they are already held. But if the "free play" of these children, their vertiginous flight to nowhere, exhausts or explodes the idea of freedom, then what exactly is it that remains at stake in this cinematic image?

Interestingly, although these shots are undoubtedly some of the most memorable in the film, Burnett (2020) himself has expressed ambivalence, and even shame or regret, over having shot them:

> Every time I see it, I cringe. . . . At the time I was doing that, it never occurred to me what would happen . . . if those kids fell, you know? And the fact of the matter is they did it all the time. And that's where I got the idea to shoot it from because they were doing it. I just wanted to capture, but I shouldn't have done it. I shouldn't have allowed that to happen. . . . And I think about [that] every time I see it. That would have been the end of them. . . . So that makes me cringe a bit when I see that scene.

And yet, notwithstanding the expropriative ambition the camera cannot escape, no matter who holds it in their hands, perhaps there was something deeper at play here than cinematic opportunism. Perhaps Burnett joined the children in that which all black flights to nowhere necessarily entail: *a leap of faith*, which is no less material than spiritual, which is, as Fred Moten and Stefano Harney might say, the "haptic eclipse" of faith in and as the animateriality of black survival (Harney and Moten 2021, 116). What is the relation between the quotidian leaps of faith that sustain black survival in the face of a world that would consign the black to social death, and the Fanonian "leap of invention" that, as Marriott (2018, 255) illuminates, is an enunciation of the "disorder [that] has always already begun and never stops arriving"? And if "to leap is to escape and yet remain" (313), how might we begin to stay with the racially gendered reproduction of this doubled remainder, with its terrible necessity and incalculable cost?

Perhaps these questions are anticipated by the manner in which Burnett's anxieties about this shot were ultimately trumped by a deeper knowledge, which he expresses only obliquely, by way of the sheep Stan must routinely murder to make his living. "You know, in order to survive, I guess you have to be cruel" (Burnett 2020). *Too thick love* is the black (feminine) affect that is *anterior* to such cruelty, the affect that registers in the world only as bitterness, obsession, or madness. It is where the accumulations of the nonevent of black existence *remain*.

Notes

1   Kara Keeling's chapter on the interval takes Fanon's famous declaration as its theoretical point of departure: "I cannot go to a film without seeing myself. I wait for me. In the interval, just before the film starts, I wait for me" (Fanon 1967, 107; Keeling 2007, 27–44).

2   Some of the key texts from Charles Musser, André Gaudreault, and Tom Gunning concerning the specific dynamics and chronology of this historical change are reproduced in Wanda Strauven's (2006) edited collection, which also includes a number of contemporary reevaluations of the associated debates.

3   Cf. Wilderson (2010), 11: "No slave [i.e., black], no world. And . . . no slave is *in* the world."

4   I am invoking, of course, Édouard Glissant's (1997) conception of the abyss. For my previous exposition, see Bradley and Marassa (2014).

References

Agamben, Giorgio. 1998. *Homo Sacer: Sovereign Power and Bare Life.* Translated by Daniel Heller-Roazen. Stanford, CA: Stanford University Press.

Ahmed, Sara. 2014. *Willful Subjects.* Durham, NC: Duke University Press.

Barrett, Lindon. 2014. *Racial Blackness and the Discontinuity of Western Modernity.* Urbana: University of Illinois Press.

Berlant, Lauren. 1998. "Intimacy: A Special Issue." *Critical Inquiry* 24 (2): 281–88.

Berlant, Lauren. 2011. *Cruel Optimism.* Durham, NC: Duke University Press.

Berlant, Lauren. 2012. *Desire/Love.* Brooklyn: Punctum Books.

Berlant, Lauren, and Brad Evans. 2018. "Without Exception: On the Ordinariness of Violence: Brad Evans in Conversation with Lauren Berlant." *Los Angeles Review of Books,* July 30.

Berlant, Lauren, and Elizabeth A. Povinelli. 2014. "Holding Up the World Part III: In the Event of Precarity . . . A Conversation." *E-flux* 58 (October). https://www.e-flux .com/journal/58/61149/holding-up-the-world-part-iii-in-the-event-of-precarity-a -conversation/.

Berlant, Lauren, and Kathleen Stewart. 2019. *The Hundreds*. Durham, NC: Duke University Press.

Bradley, Rizvana, and Damien-Adia Marassa. 2014. "Awakening to the World: Relation, Totality, and Writing from Below." *Discourse: Journal for Theoretical Studies in Media and Culture* 36 (1): 112–31.

Brand, Dionne. 2001. *A Map to the Door of No Return: Notes to Belonging*. Toronto: Vintage.

Brand, Dionne. 2010. *Ossuaries*. Toronto: McClelland and Stewart.

Brand, Dionne. 2017. "An Ars Poetica from the Blue Clerk." *The Black Scholar* 47 (1): 58–77.

Burnett, Charles, interviewed by Todd Melby. 2020. "Charles Burnett Discusses *Killer of Sheep*." *The Drunk Projectionist*, October. https://www.thedrunkprojectionist .com/blog/2020/9/11/charles-burnett-discusses-killer-of-sheep.

Camp, Jordan T. 2016. *Incarcerating the Crisis: Freedom Struggles and the Rise of the Neoliberal State*. Berkeley: University of California Press.

Chandler, Nahum Dimitri. 2014. *X—The Problem of the Negro as a Problem for Thought*. New York: Fordham University Press.

Couzens-Hoy, Daniel. 2009. *A Critical History of Temporality*. Cambridge, MA: MIT Press.

Debord, Guy. 1989. "Theory of the Dérive." In *Situationist International Anthology*, edited by Ken Knabb, 62–66. Berkeley: Bureau of Public Secrets.

Deleuze, Gilles, and Félix Guattari. 1987. *A Thousand Plateaus: Capitalism and Schizophrenia*. Translated by Brian Massumi. Minneapolis: University of Minnesota Press.

Diawara, Manthia. 1993. "Black American Cinema: The New Realism." In *Black American Cinema*, edited by Manthia Diawara, 3–25. New York: Routledge.

Doane, Mary Ann. 2002. *The Emergence of Cinematic Time: Modernity, Contingency, the Archive*. Cambridge, MA: Harvard University Press.

Du Bois, W. E. B. 1903. *The Souls of Black Folk*. Chicago: McClurgh.

Fanon, Frantz. 1967. *Black Skin, White Masks*. Translated by Charles Lam Markmann. New York: Grove Press.

Ferreira da Silva, Denise. 2014. "Toward a Black Feminist Poethics: The Quest(ion) of Blackness toward the End of the World." *The Black Scholar* 44 (2): 81–97.

Ferreira da Silva, Denise. 2017. "The Scene of Nature." In *Searching for Contemporary Legal Thought*, edited by Justin Desautels-Stein and Christopher Tomlins, 275–89. Cambridge: Cambridge University Press.

Fitzgerald, Adam. 2015. "An Interview with Fred Moten, Part 1: In Praise of Harold Bloom, Collaboration and Book Fetishes." *Literary Hub*, August 5. https://lithub .com/an-interview-with-fred-moten-pt-i/.

Freeman, Elizabeth. 2010. *Time Binds: Queer Temporalities, Queer Histories*. Durham, NC: Duke University Press.

Gilmore, Ruthie Wilson. 2015. "Organized Abandonment and Organized Violence: Devolution and the Police." The Humanities Institute, University of California, Santa Cruz, September 11. https://vimeo.com/146450686.

Glissant, Édouard. 1997. *Poetics of Relation*. Translated by Betsy Wing. Ann Arbor: University of Michigan Press.

Gorfinkel, Elena. 2012. "Weariness, Waiting: Enduration and Art Cinema's Tired Bodies." *Discourse: Journal for Theoretical Studies in Media and Culture* 34 (2–3): 311–47.

Hagelin, Sarah. 2013. *Reel Vulnerability: Power, Pain, and Gender in American Film and Television*. New Brunswick, NJ: Rutgers University Press.

Harney, Stefano, and Fred Moten. 2013. *The Undercommons: Fugitive Planning and Black Study*. New York: Autonomedia.

Harney, Stefano, and Fred Moten. 2021. *All Incomplete*. Brooklyn: Minor Compositions.

Hartman, Saidiya. 2008. *Lose Your Mother: A Journey along the Atlantic Slave Route*. New York: Farrar, Straus and Giroux.

Hartman, Saidiya. 2016. "The Belly of the World: A Note on Black Women's Labors." *Souls* 18 (1): 166–73.

Hartman, Saidiya. 2018. "Saidiya Hartman: On Working with Archives." The Creative Independent. https://thecreativeindependent.com/people/saidiya-hartman-on-working-with-archives/.

Hartman, Saidiya. 2019. *Wayward Lives, Beautiful Experiments: Intimate Histories of Social Upheaval*. New York: Norton.

Hegel, Georg Wilhelm Friedrich. 1956. *The Philosophy of History*. Mineola, NY: Dover.

Hendricks, Dorothy. 2014. "Children of the Revolution: Images of Youth in *Killer of Sheep* and *Brick by Brick*." *liquid blackness* 1 (1): 16–18. http://liquidblackness.com/LB1_LARebellion.pdf.

Keeling, Kara. 2007. *The Witch's Flight, the Cinematic, the Black Femme, and the Image of Common Sense*. Durham, NC: Duke University Press.

Manning, Erin. 2016. *The Minor Gesture*. Durham, NC: Duke University Press.

Marriott, David. 2018. *Whither Fanon? Studies in the Blackness of Being*. Stanford, CA: Stanford University Press.

Massood, Paula J. 1999. "An Aesthetics Appropriate to Conditions: Killer of Sheep, (Neo)realism, and the Documentary Impulse." *Wide Angle* 21 (4): 20–41.

McDonough, Tom. 2009. *The Situationists and the City*. London: Verso.

Morrison, Toni. 2004. *Beloved*. New York: Vintage.

Moten, Fred. 2017. *Black and Blur*. Durham, NC: Duke University Press.

Moten, Fred. 2018. *Stolen Life*. Durham, NC: Duke University Press.

Povinelli, Elizabeth. 2011. *Economies of Abandonment: Social Belonging and Endurance in Late Liberalism*. Durham, NC: Duke University Press.

Ricoeur, Paul. 1984. *Time and Narrative, Volume 1*. Chicago: University of Chicago Press.

Rhodes, John David. 2017. *Spectacles of Property: The House in American Film*. Minneapolis: University of Minnesota Press.

Scott, Darieck. 2010. *Extravagant Abjection: Blackness, Power, and Sexuality in the African American Literary Imagination*. New York: New York University Press.

Scott, James C. 1998. *Seeing like a State: How Certain Schemes to Improve the Human Condition Have Failed*. New Haven, CT: Yale University Press.

Sexton, Jared. 2017. *Black Masculinity and the Cinema of Policing*. Cham, Switzerland: Palgrave Macmillan.

Sharpe, Christina. 2010. *Monstrous Intimacies: Making Post-slavery Subjects*. Durham, NC: Duke University Press.

Sharpe, Christina. 2016. *In the Wake: On Blackness and Being*. Durham, NC: Duke University Press.

Smith, Neil. 1996. *The New Urban Frontier: Gentrification and the Revanchist City*. London: Routledge.

Spillers, Hortense J. 2003. *Black, White, and in Color: Essays on American Literature and Culture*. Chicago: University of Chicago Press.

Strauven, Wanda, ed. 2006. *The Cinema of Attractions Reloaded*. Amsterdam: University of Amsterdam Press.

Wark, McKenzie. 2011. *The Beach Beneath the Street: The Everyday Life and Glorious Times of the Situationist International*. London: Verso.

Warren, Calvin. 2018. *Ontological Terror*. Durham, NC: Duke University Press.

Wilderson, Frank B., III. 2010. *Red, White, and Black: Cinema and the Structure of U.S. Antagonisms*. Durham, NC: Duke University Press.

Wool, Zoë H., and Julie Livingston. 2017. "Collateral Afterworlds: An Introduction." *Social Text* 35 (1): 1–15.

An Intimacy

Omar Kasmani

"I am too short to spoon you!" He had said it aloud. It was, as he now remembers, the first thing he had said on that morning in February, their bodies still wrapped in sleep. They both knew he had tried (his best). What else, if not this, would tender failures in "thin attachments" look like, he had thought: his body tending toward him but coming short of its own expectations, stretching outward from itself but just not enough to enfold he who lay beside him, 1.9 meters tall if not more. This was not a dream or an intimate moment in the dark, easily overlooked. The witnessing morning light was evenly white in this room on Naunynstraße—that fabled street of migration in Berlin-Kreuzberg where lay, in Aras Ören's (2019, 33) verse—"behind every window, various worries and fresh hopes."[1] Only revealing that he would recall this one line from a poem so long it was a book. It had been years since he had read the German poem by the Turkish poet. He knew, though, that its migrant protagonists were both like and unlike him, forebearers of some kind, kin even who had arrived before him as "guest workers" in the former West Berlin. "With brisk steps, head buried in shoulder," Turkish men in the poem scurry to nightshifts in the white cover of winter nights just when their German neighbors descend "deep in sleep" (Ören 2019, 9). If one were to go by the opening verses of the poem, the night on Naunynstraße was no stranger to migrant affects, less so to them becoming invisible through the night. But he would not go so far as to suggest that all migrants were equal in the eyes of the city. He knew from experience that markers of class could remedy anxieties that otherwise stick to bodies in migration. Still, he had found the serendipity poetic. So, on his way home in the morning, he bought himself a copy of the *Berliner Trilogie*—three migrant poems of Ören—at the famous bookstore on the street parallel to Naunynstraße. As he read and walked on that winter morning, he had felt a spring in his step.

Eventually, February would give way. But there would be no recourse to that singular night in a single bed. No turning back from his thoughts either, it would turn out. Weeks on, he kept ruminating on what it means to be too short to spoon one's object of desire. What manner of failures lay folded in the tenderness of the night? A few were invisibly obvious to him. Some were only partially carried over to the day—that is, if not exactly memorable, not entirely forgotten to waking life either. Yet others, as it would turn out, were in the habit of returning. On a night in March, barely two weeks before a global pandemic would engulf the city, the two had found themselves in Berlin-Wilmersdorf. This was a district he had little feeling for, but contrary to his own indifference, it was pretty much where he had grown up. Only his love for good Sichuan had dragged him to the "bourgie" old west of Berlin; this much he had made plain. On that short stroll between the U-Bahn station and the restaurant, as he listened to him describe his childhood haunts, he was reminded of other shortcomings. He found fascinating his ordinary sense of history, his intimate knowledge of *Straßenecken* (street corners), his familiarity with fancy foyers and ornamented facades, the simple ease with which he was able to describe from memory characters of homes on that street: the high ceilings, the roomy rooms, the centered doors opening into other rooms. How could he, anyone for that matter, not be taken by his immaculate detailing of interiors: books upon books, antique objects from China, Persian carpets, family gossips, histories, and conversations that filled those chambers. So abundant in character his descriptions, so rich in detail his words that these would fill him with feelings of loss, displacement, not having enough history of himself, no street corner to call his own.

When does a city begin to haunt, he asked without saying it aloud this time. How long till memories reside, fade, return, he is sure to have murmured to himself. Was he just short, he wondered for days on end or, like many migrants, forever short of history in the city?

How do we, those of us affected by geochronologies of migration, pursue the historical in the full knowledge that a History will not accommodate us? How do migrants remember, not in the sense of reminiscing a past or recovering lost worlds but as a critical way to refuse a for-granted continuity of the same? What does it take to imagine our futures in the European contemporary, when at every step of the way—to repurpose Agha Shahid Ali's (1997, 21) poetic verse—*history gets in the way of memory?*

Of "non-white people in white man's countries," Samia Khatun (2018, xviii) has most poignantly observed, "arriving at the institutions of Western nation-states by different trajectories, all their lives veer from scripts of progress from East to West, from the Third World to the First, Aboriginal country to settler nation. What they have in common is that they no longer have narratives to inhabit: no tales that can hold together their experiences of the world, carrying them smoothly from yesterday to today to tomorrow."[2] Such a profound sense of being dispossessed of story and therefore history has echoes in the Urdu concept for diasporic space and condition: more capacious than its Arabic original, *ghurbah* means that the one who migrates is literally rendered "poor" by virtue of being estranged from home, homeland. Strangerness, foreignness, depravation, and poverty are all folded in the same word here. It helps us take measure of what is affectively at stake in conditions of mobility and migrancy; what transpires when dispossession becomes ordinary or the strange pervades the familiar—that is, when *home*, to quote an artwork, *is a foreign place.*[3]

The antidote to affective shortcomings in migration, still, cannot be so plain as adding more history. Migrant-historical affect, more than history per se, is about how individuals and communities in migrancy draw near to a sense of the historical. It pertains to the felt and enfleshed modes by which they/we come close to that which feels physically remote or historically removed and mobilize distinctly

affective ways of being and belonging in time. This includes the opening scene's insight that broader concerns of migrant belonging unfold
through delicate labors of coming close; that coming short of a lover,
be it person or city, can trigger forms and feelings of historical disaf-
fection. Theorizing migration by way of the intimate bolsters as much
the adjacent argument that intimacy, barely a singular situation, is in
itself an unfolding. It is a historical elaboration so to speak. It follows
that scenes of coming close, sexual or otherwise, are invariably, if not
also unwittingly, folded up with concerns that are principally in excess
to situations that transpire in the present or play out in front of our
eyes. Elaboration means that we remain affectively attached also to
that which takes form after the fact of coming close or makes itself
known by way of its longing. Coming short, then, can be as much a
disposition as a shortfall. It can be a propensity, a feeling for a bigger
world wherein the migrant will to belong makes migration, a desire to
be long, to borrow Elizabeth Freeman's (2007, 299) words, "to touch
the dead or those not born yet, to offer oneself beyond one's own time."

This, here, is a gathering of migrant affects. Languages, concepts,
histories theorized via the self and parsed through the observed become collective journeys. These take us beyond the confessional to an
affective lexicon of migration, an alternate syntax of intimate belonging in postmigrant Europe. Migrant pathways of feeling historical in
Berlin are reminders that no matter our shortcomings, we who move
and migrate, depart by will, are driven out or displaced, belong in a
bigger narrative all the same.[4]

A Move in Time

He was once a new prophet in an old desert, or so the story goes.
Spoken to by the archangel Jibrail, Muhammad believed the verses to
be signs from the Meccan high god, Allah. Mecca was where the old
Abrahamic temple stood, one that Muhammad's own family and tribe
had been caretakers of for generations. In taking exception from the
religion and position of his ancestors, Muhammad was breaking with
the old and the same. Both as a result of divine guidance and political negotiation, we are told, a prophet under duress decided to leave
his birthplace Mecca in 622 CE. With bands of his followers departing ahead of him, Muhammad, then fifty-two years of age, migrates

to Yathrab, an oasis in the Arabian desert that history would come to remember as Medina: literally, city. This event that Muslims recall as *hijrat* makes history and organizes tradition: *hijrat* means migration, flight, exodus (بجرت Urdu from the Arabic *hijrah*). Many historians of Islam, classical scholars of the Qur'an as well, divide the time of early Islam and its divine revelation into two periods: the Meccan and the Medinan. The Islamic calendar, *Hijri*, begins with Muhammad's migration in 622 CE. *Hijrat* is established as *hijri's* epoch. The year 2023 is 1445 years after *hijrat* (AH); the Islamic era is time postmigration. If *hijrat* marks time, migration also occasions the foundation of the first Muslim polity, a communing through departing. Islamic historical sources speak of an assembly where Muhammad binds each and every *muhajir*—the one who is moved by affects of *hijrat*, or simply migrant—in a fraternal bond with a corresponding local in Yathrab. Such binding and bonding is extraordinary for its time and place. It overrides the prevailing logic of tribal affiliation in favor of affective belonging through migration. In departing from Mecca, Muhammad and his people forsake the old. In migration, they are created anew. An oasis becomes a city. A community comes to be. This is not just departure in space: *hijrat*. It is equally a moving in and binding with time: *hijri*.

Hijrat was his history. In the fateful summer of 1947, his grandparents on both sides of the family had forsaken their ancestral homes in the western Indian state of Gujarat. *Hijrat* was their story also in the sense that it was not just theirs. An estimated 20 million people were displaced as a result of the British partitioning of India. Hindus, Muslims, and Sikhs had turned migrants overnight, made refugees across their own lands. New lines appeared in a geography reinvented through logics of European colonialism. "They asked for a map / & so I drew a line"—the Pakistani American poet Fatima Asghar (2018, 66) ascribes these words to the British colonial officer Cyril Radcliffe who partitioned India without having previously visited the country. A line made in haste was all it would take to rip shared histories and landscapes apart, material as well as affective. For families like his, the line meant that once crossed, there was no turning back: no routes to ancestral tombs, no pathways to the familiar sacred either. Was *hijrat* also a sacred inheritance, a belonging they carried along in a time of desolation, and which, in turn, carried them through it? With hopes to start afresh, his grandparents arrived in Karachi, the then-capital of newly formed Pakistan, a city eerily reborn in Hindu exodus and Muslim arrival.

Growing up in Karachi, he had an idea where they had roughly come from. Morbi, Surat, Kodinar, Mumbai: these were place names, at once familiar and foreign, over the border, somewhat on the verge . . . of loss and recovery, here and there. Amid all that affective knowing of where they had come from, there was little talk of where they were going. Or maybe they just were not. To his parents, both born in the newly independent nation-state, Pakistan was not destination but home, one that an entire generation had learned to make home—away from home. A home, where his grandparents' language—*Memoni*, a dialect of Gujarati—was minoritized to the extent that none of them cared to learn it again. No matter his parents spoke the national Urdu with "gujju" accents; so what if they got the genders wrong! He does too, now, only in German. Language, accents, last names, wedding rites, family recipes, and the odd visit from an Indian relative were still-active threads to places beyond. Or were they behind? Moving on had turned an ancestral geography backward. It felt as though certain histories were no longer capable of holding a future. A line had been drawn between the past and the present. They were better off in Pakistan was the family mantra as though moving westward was, in principle, a moving forward. Is the line on a map a line in time? Is the act of moving away, at times, indistinguishable from the feeling of moving on? He wonders now as much about his own *hijrat*.

Hijrat means what moves, gathers anew, also true for the concept's own migration: in north India, the Arabic original *hijrah* is remade, made queer, trans—as *hijra*—a reorientation also enunciated by the retroflexion of the Urdu-Hindi consonant ṛ. Feminine-identified, gender-nonconforming persons and communities in South Asia, regardless of religion, have historically embraced Muhammad's notion of sacred moving as a way to signal their departures from straight economies of life and their belonging outside reproductive time. Migration, once more, is that inventive move by which a *we* comes to be. It is how we desire, feel capacious, set into motion a world bigger than ourselves; attach ourselves to greater histories and inheritances;

belong with, make kin, find ancestors. The concern, then, cannot stop at place: neither the one we leave behind nor those where we transit, arrive, settle. Migration is as much a tryst with history. It is an *errance* in time, to be licentious with Édouard Glissant (2010, 211), that is a movement "not aimed like an arrow's trajectory, nor circular and repetitive like the nomad's"—less so, an idle roaming typical of the flaneur. French for wandering, *errance* here names a greater, trans-historical, more-than-local gesture of affect, that animates, moves, and mobilizes a world with "a sense of sacred motivation" (211).[5] To move in time this way just as to be errant in *errance*'s borrowed English usage is to move out of life's confines, stray from the proper course or standards.[6] What is also discovered in migration, what stirs up through the crafting of an ethnohistorical fabulation—Medina, Morbi, Karachi, Berlin—across registers sacred, ancestral, queer is a revelation: his people had always been migrants, bodies in *errance*.

A Desire to Be Long

In his cross musings on queerness and exile, Iskandar Abdalla (2020a) has observed that life in migration is akin to being in a dream: "things are not in their place, faces are blurry, events are unpredictable, space and time are out of joint." In a short film on related themes, Abdalla turns to the architectural form of the balcony to comment on the interface that dreaming and migration entails: between interior and outward modes, public and private worlds, across a past in Alexandria and a present in Berlin. His poetic observation from within the film, "sometimes in *ghurbah* [diaspora], reality emulates dreams and dreams give reality, its sense of meaning" (Abdalla 2020b) is, among other things, a reminder that dreams in many a tradition, not least Islamic, qualify as a reliable mode of thinking.[7] On dreaming in Cairo, Amira Mittermaier (2011, 7) has observed how dream visions "can foreshadow, or even bring about, future events" that generate intimate socialities, forms of kin making as well as communities of interpretation. More critically, dreams point as much to parallel modes of perception as they do to alternate conceptualizations of the real (4). On the awkwardly real in migration, Abdalla (2020b) notes, "Coping with reality is like decoding a dream. You constantly try to make sense of peculiar words and worlds; and you are constantly urged to make sense of yourself in terms that are not yours, in ways you are unfamiliar with, in a language whose sign of mastery corresponds to your ability to accept its limits; to discern its impotence in articulating certain things, its incommensurability with your pain and fears." Feelings of affective dissonance slide across episodes of romantic love and migrant belonging in the text. Of his lover, he comparably reflects, "How could it be that my body was porous to his warmth and his was opaque to my love? Luis and I were lost in translation" (Abdalla 2020a). Moments like these reaffirm the opening scene's insight and the broader idea at play here. Illuminations of intimacy and migration are not so disparate after all: each mysteriously unfolding and not thickly intelligible; both requiring labors of translation, a tarrying with sparse intelligibilities, or grasping onto shards of feeling that ordinarily fall through the cracks of verbal expression.

On a July morning in 2021, Abdalla had offered to meet up in Berlin's Tempelhofer Feld. This is a former airfield located within the fabric of city that best resembles a void on the Berlin map. Under the imposing shadow of Nazi history and architecture, walking the perimeter of an abandoned terminal building, Abdalla reflected on how urban gaps like these enabled the past to inhabit the present: that what was out of use was not exactly out of currency, or the ways in which an airport was similar to a balcony. On the question of dream and diaspora, Abdalla was quick to catch the drift. "The experience of migration makes reality something contingent," he said, before reflecting further.

> Sometimes, suddenly, I just feel detached and not there, and then, I start to think in my own world of images and thoughts, which are super, like, unrelated to what is going on, what is taking place in the place where I'm physically in. And, so I started to think about like where, what are the boundaries, where are the borders between reality and dreams? And is that something that has to do with my presence in Germany as, you know, as *gharib* [estranged], as *muhajir* [migrant], in exile, basically?
>
> I felt like my relation to home is based on imagination. If I'm not living [at] home, so, the potential of, of imagining home is so important to me . . . also, like remembering home. And I'm aware, that when I say, remembering home, it's not about remembering facts. That trying to recall certain encounters, even certain things you have lived already, but

> [in] remembering what you recall are different images. . . . You envision
> a reality in infinite ways . . . this is like, may be in exile, something
> essential . . . when home, which is also your beloved, somehow, is not
> there.[8]

Abdalla's evocation of home in terms of love was both reminder and confirmation that those who know *hijrat* know that what lies at the core of the concept is the affect of *hijr*. It literally means the condition of being separated from the beloved. It follows that the *muhajir*—that is, the one who migrates, moves, departs, parts also from locations of love. How can migration, a parting that is, not be a figure of intimacy? More so, separation (from the beloved) makes remembrance critical to displacement. To recall, however, is not simply to reminisce or re-create a past in migration. To remember is to inventively and iteratively ensure that the migrant present, a field of separation, remains open to conditions of longing and belonging.

Dream and the balcony are to Abdalla's vision of migration what mirrors and the courtyard are to Özdamar's. Three, to be precise, mirrors do more than mirroring in Emine Sevgi Özdamar's short story, *Der Hof im Spiegel* (The courtyard in the mirror). "One mirror in the kitchen. From the kitchen, you could walk, left and right, into two other rooms. In the room on the right, there was a large mirror in the corner, and in the room on the left, hanging over a painter's cabinet, there was likewise a very large mirror suspended from the high ceiling" (Özdamar 2005, as translated by Leslie Adelson). Mirrors reflect the *Hof*—that is, the inner yard typical of old residential buildings in Germany. What is gathered across them, however—*sammeln* in the German original—exceeds and expands the *Hof*: in the affective *jetzt-zeit* of the story, the movement of the neighbors becomes one with that of Özdamar's late mother in Istanbul.

> The three mirrors gathered all the windows and floors and the garden
> of the nuns' house together from three different perspectives. When I
> stood with my back to the courtyard, I saw all the nuns' windows and
> their garden in the three mirrors. We all lived in three mirrors nose-to-
> nose together. When I woke up, I did not look into the courtyard from
> the balcony, but looked in the mirror instead. I made coffee or wrote or
> cleaned and could see the courtyard and my neighbors, again and again,
> in my rooms.

On some Sundays, I saw a young nun in the mirror from behind. She was washing the minister's car in the courtyard. I called my mother. "Mother, she's washing the minister's car just now, and I'm roasting a chicken." In the mirror, I tickled the young nun's back so that she suddenly began to laugh in the courtyard below. "Mother, I'm tickling her just now." My mother said: "And just now the sun is shining in my left eye." In the receiver, I heard voices of children playing on the steep little street in Istanbul. The ships' horns commingled with the children's voices, and a street vendor yelled. "Watermelons!" (Özdamar 2005, as translated by Leslie Adelson)

The prose is porous. So are the worlds that Özdamar parses. Strategically placed, the three mirrors gather the dead in the company of the living just as they imbricate the near with the distant. Mirrors ache. Mirrors long. Here, once again, reflecting is not a casting back. This is not a looking to the past either but a longing of the migrant present. What meets the mirror changes orientation; what comes through is broken up before it is gathered. To remember in migration, to return to Abdalla (2020a), is not to confirm that the "present's quintessence seems to lie in mirroring the past" or that a migrant's "sense of tomorrow manifests itself in sheer reminiscing." Memories are given to refraction as are images altered by mirroring. Such affective returns furnish the migrant present with a sense of expanse and fragmented abundance. Physical and affective horizons of the home are tested. By the author's own admission, "I was happy in the mirror because, in this way, I was in several places at the same time." Her words echo the view that "the postmigrant city, like the migrant's sense of time is compound, interrupted at times, at times stretched" (Kasmani 2021c, 170). The shapeshifting images in Abdalla's idea of remembrance, place-and-time-defying gestures of gathering that we see in Özdamar's writing, which Leslie Adelson (2005) evocatively reads as a kind of postnational intimacy, are curiously close to how Berlin's Sufis approach and feel the historical in the city.

Tucked away *im dritten Hinterhof* (in a third backyard) was once a mosque. He would go there every week, where twenty-five to thirty men gathered around a sheikh, who led them into *Zikr*, the Sufi performance of mindful remembrance of Allah. In a room, nearly as long as it was wide and oriented obliquely toward Mecca, smells of fragrant oils lingered on and sweat softened the contours of gym-toned bodies as men oscillated on their feet, their forearms locked with one another. Rhythmically swaying left to right and back to left, they would sing hallowed praises, chant the names of God, yearn for saintly companies to become present in assemblies of affect. Most followers in this Sufi group were German Turks with "migration histories" (*Einwanderungsgeschichte*), sons of Turkish *Gastarbeiters* (guest workers).[9] Men, who though very different from him, yet somewhat like him, longed for other men in the city; who knew how to remember with their bodies, who moved and were moved in circles of weekly loves. In the words of one Sufi follower, "When *Zikr* has begun to take its course, and this spiritual force is so strong, it's possible that one, that a few, see things which one normally doesn't see. He sees angels! He sees people who have lived five hundred years ago! Saints, they are there and they do *Zikr* with us." He had thought such accounts credible because in affect-rich atmospheres, the young men were caught at their most vulnerable. He had witnessed them scream, cry, taken by fits of laughter, overcome with exhaustion, at times down on their knees. In brief moments like these, the mosque no longer felt like a place stuck in a backyard facing an automobile workshop, rather like in Özdamar's story, a *Hof* brimming with historical movement and abundance.

Zikr is Turkish, Persian, and Urdu for remembrance (from the Arabic *dhikr*). For the Sufis, it was that affective mode by which Allah and the saints were remembered in migration, summoned in Berlin, by way of chants, lyrical recitations, and synchronized movements of the body.[10] Once again, remembrance was not about mirroring the past but rather about conditions and possibilities of the present's abundance. It was after all that seductive gesture by which the fullness of the world was felt, made manifest. In fact, on his first meeting with the group, the Sufi teacher had explained to him how the here-and-now was delicately sutured with the hereafter; that the visible and the manifest (*zahir*) was simply incomplete without the knowledge of its hidden counterpart (*batin*); that the thin veil that separated *zahir* from *batin* meant that the yet-to-be-revealed was not the same as the invisible and, more critically, that an infinite longing of the world was possible should the veil be lifted in assemblies of *Zikr*. The aesthetics of such world-making were all the more critical in migration. Saints and Sufis were errant bodies of history, long passed yet mobile and wandering. Some of this felt oddly familiar to him. He already knew that Islamic saints were believed to act from beyond their graves, make appearances across history, defy order and borders of space and time. Yet, in a city as reputably godless as Berlin, transtemporally moving saints made for queerer traffics, he thought. Acting through displaced and hidden registers, moving sheepishly in the darkness of mosque interiors, they upset linear and secular orders of time all the same. This was Berlin on a different plane: porous, dilating, open to outside influences. He was seduced by the idea that through intimate gestures in ritual and believers' thin attachments, subliminal figures and migrant histories from outside Europe found an affective ground in the city. Given Berlin's many ghosts, he wondered if moving saints, angels, and spirits, like migrants themselves, had to vie for space in the city's settled ecologies of haunting.[11] Too bad, he had no good way of knowing!

It is through collective acts of remembrance, Sara Ahmed (1999, 344) notes, that migrants create a sense of home in the absence of shared terrain. Religious or otherwise, whether gathered through refracting mirrors or reflecting rituals, migrant intimacies of Berlin point to modes of belonging that are characteristically porous and hypersocial, which is to say that "the sense of time is instrumental to becoming social in an expansive mode" (Freeman 2019, 17). Or that to live, love and be/long in migration is a matter of affective gestures and dispositions: how we apprehend the world collectively and intimately but also beyond the physical and exceeding the immediate; how we allow for historical abundance to permeate and proliferate our present; how we extend our affective limbs to feel the remote historical, to touch futures that have been removed from view.

History Gets in the Way: A Postscript

"Muslims should shower naked"[12]—In his 2016 interview with *Die Welt*, the German conservative politician Jens Spahn lamented the fact that it was now "expressly allowed" (*ausdrücklich erlauben*) for men to shower in swimming trunks at his gym. In his words, "too many Arab muscle-machos stood there with their underpants on because they were embarrassed to be naked," adding, "this is a social change that I do not want. Our openness to other cultures in such cases threatens a relapse into old uptight stuffiness [*Spießigkeit*]. But I don't want a stuck-up Germany [*verklemmtes Deutschland*]."[13] European "openness" to other cultures, at least in Spahn's view, is premised on the Others' willingness to bare it all, figuratively and literally, as if the path to integration was best achieved naked; worse still, that migrants must accept that for them to be accepted, Germans must have full view of their lives, bodies, and values. In the same interview, the German politician had also obsessed over Muslim women's clothing, proudly labeling himself a "burkaphobe." Here, publicness equals visibility, and inclusion is warranted on full transparency. In *Poetics of Relation*, Édouard Glissant (2010, 189) has argued that "the real foundation of Relation, in freedoms," lies rather in opacity. His call: "Agree not merely to the right to difference but, agree also to the right to opacity," takes to task "the processes of 'understanding' people and ideas from the perspective of Western thought," whose basis, as he highlights, is the requirement for transparency (189–90).[14] Spahn's discomfort in the shower is no different. Not to mention, the urge to see bare bottoms of "Arab muscle-machos" on the part of a white, cis-male, gay, Christian, German politician reveals how the violence of colonial optics, desire, and intimacy endures in the contemporary. Arguably, then, showering with trunks counts as an act of refusal, a willful opacity on part of the migrant that obstructs and obscures the gaze of Western thought, colonial desire, as well as technologies of governance (see Simek 2015, 366). So can, potentially speaking, women's clothing, backyard mosques, or religious services in non-European languages whose distinct tactics of publicness routinely frustrate principally European forms of seeing and norms of knowing.

Furthermore, so long as arriving in Europe means arriving from outside of modernity, migrant belonging stays a temporally encumbered process, a script of progress at best.[15] Not only does such a view of migration demand a constant catching up of those who move; migrant mobility risks a slowing down or jamming up of Europe—*verklemmtes Deutschland*. In their introductory note to *Migratory Settings*, Aydemir and Rotas (2008, 7) take the emancipatory view that places *thicken* through the affective contact between migrants and native inhabitants, resulting in what they describe as "the mise-en-scène of histories." But what of dreams, memories, fears, and motivations from locations assigned backward temporal rhythms and which are not equally able or welcome to sediment in European mises-en-scène? After all, "time doesn't move as though a ghostly entity, but through the bodies of those endowed by history" (Belcourt 2020, 119). Thickness, lest we forget, is also the mastery of history, the sum and certitude of its knowings and understandings; the enduring violence of the modes by which the historical accrues its dominating sense. Thickness is European history's ability to refract, even refuse, that which comes into contact with its dense machinations. It is precisely what gets in the way of migrant memory and imagination, policing as it were, their/our entry into territories of European futurity. Migrant intimacies are in fact marked by a sense of thinness here: to attend to the wispy and the partial, the inward or the removed, the parallel and the porous is to think alongside dominant conceptions of time and geography in Europe. Thin embraces the idea that minoritized genres of historical feeling and interiorized affect, be they partial, personal, or permeable forms which evade public gaze and scrutiny, even intelligibility—*infrathin* in Erin Manning's terms—bear political and outward resonance all the same.[16] In that sense, the argument for intimacy is yet another invitation to "think thin through the thick of affect" (Kasmani 2021b, 57).

Thin articulates and enables an affective besideness to dominant history and its narrations in Europe. In turning inward, in acting obliquely or opaquely, in allying with removed or differently present figures of the urban, migrants do not retreat into parallel social existence as the German fear of *Parallelgesellschaft* would have us believe. Rather, in so doing, migrants create and nurture abundant socialities that must endure against their own historical shortfall in the European contemporary. An appeal to the imaginal or parallel modes of the real is likewise not a withdrawing from the sphere of the political. Quite the contrary: images, specters, shadows, and silhouettes are wispy yet critical forms of urban expressivity, especially for those others for whom "the path towards smooth and formal participation in official public life is blocked or impeded" (Dadi 2009, 189). Thin, opaque, or queer modes of relating that exercise and include "the right to remain hazy to broader [or dominant] publics" subvert the liberal take on political emancipation (Khan 2019).[17] Such belonging reveals how virtues of inclusion and visibility are entangled in modes and principles of governance, or why participating valuably in the public sphere cannot be made contingent on full disclosure.[18]

Last, migrant affects, if one be allowed that conjecture and the provocation, illuminate why, here, affect is migrant. To traverse theory's less-habituated geographies and mobilizations, to move archives, journeys, and genealogies foreclosed by a largely Christian and Western Europe and North America centering grain of affect studies, is to survive its thickness. To parse via the intimate and the minoritized is to consider how otherwise delicate genres and gestures of coming close have a bearing on public shapes and theoretical visions of migration. To understand migrancy as a feeling for a bigger world or an affective move in time is to stay cognizant of how and why migrant labors of longing—that is, his/our/their desires to belong and be long are thwarted—wound up invariably in affects of coming short.

Notes

1 *Was will Niyazi in der Naunynstraße?* was first published in translation in 1973.

2 This resonates with Sara Ahmed's (1999, 344) view that "the histories of the movements of peoples across borders make a difference to the spatiality and temporality of estrangement."

3 *Home Is a Foreign Place* is a series of thirty-six woodblock prints by the artist Zarina. For more, see MoMa's online collection: https://www.moma.org/learn/moma_learning/zarina-home-is-a-foreign-place-1999/.

4 Migration in this text refers to "the movement of people from one place on the planet to another, people who do not immediately, or ever, return to the place where they previously lived" (Aydemir and Rotas 2008, 7). On migration from the perspective of those who do not move, see Eliott (2021).

5 In the translator's notes, Betsy Wing uses the phrase to remark on *errance*.

6 In zoology, errant is a kind of polychaete worm that moves around actively and is not confined to a tube or burrow.

7 Dreams in the Islamic tradition derive from "the imaginal," a distinct and betwixt realm of perception and reality.

8 Recorded interview, July 3, 2021. For more, see author's video, *A City in Daily Loves* (Kasmani 2021a).

9 As part of a formal "guest worker" program, migrants sought work in former West Germany from the 1950s up until the early 1970s.

10 For migration and Sufi haunting in Berlin, see Kasmani (2021b).

11 In *Buried City*, Benedict Anderson (2017) has noted that twenty-five million cubic meters of debris from World War II lies hidden beneath Berlin's seven rubble hills, making ruination literally a subliminal figure.

12 *Muslime sollen nackt duschen*; tweet by queer.de (July 30, 2016, 10:33 a.m.).

13 Published in *Die Welt* July 30, 2016. Author's translation from the German original.

14 The opaque, for Glissant (2010, 191), is not necessarily the obscure, rather "that which cannot be reduced."

15 In her book *European Others*, Fatima El Tayeb (2011) argues that Muslims in Europe are produced as queer and accorded a position both outside of Europe and outside of modernity. On how migration impacts tempos of everyday life, see Elliot (2021). For more on affective citizenship or how desire, affects, and emotions operate in mechanisms of exclusion and inclusion, see Ayata (2019).

16 For Manning (2020, 16), *infrathin* is "the potentiation of a relational field that includes what cannot quite be articulated but is nonetheless felt." Thin in my greater work does not always signal weak or watered-down relations. Thin is about modes of attachment that keep us in arrest despite their obvious attenuations. For more, see Kasmani (2019, 2021b, 2021c).

17 For "translucent citizenship" as transgender positioning vis-à-vis the Pakistani state and society, see Khan (2019).

18 For a critique of public sphere and political participation in Rajasthan, see Piliavsky (2013).

References

Abdalla, Iskandar. 2020a. "'Seasonal Dreams' or Chronicles of a Queer Exile." *Awham Magazine* 3, no. 1 (October 29). http://awhammagazine.com/chroniceles-of-a-queer-exile.

Abdalla, Iskandar, dir. 2020b. *Balcony of My Dreams*. Berlin. [Film]

Adelson, Leslie. 2005. "Translating 'The Courtyard in the Mirror' by Emine Sevgi Özdamar: A Foreword." In Özdamar, Emine Sevgi. "The Courtyard in the Mirror." *TRANSIT* 2 (1). http://dx.doi.org/10.5070/T721009715.

Ahmed, Sara. 1999. "Home and Away. Narratives of Migration and Estrangement." *International Journal of Cultural Studies* 2 (3): 329–47.

Ali, Agha Shahid. 1997. "Farewell." In *The Country without a Post Office*, 21–23. New York: Norton.

Anderson, Benedict. 2017. *Buried City, Unearthing Teufelsberg: Berlin and Its Geography of Forgetting*. London: Routledge.

Asghar, Fatima. 2018. *If They Come for Us*. New York: Penguin Random House.

Ayata, Bilgin. 2019. "Affective Citizenship." In *Affective Societies—Key Concepts*, edited by Christian von Scheve and Jan Slaby, 330–39. Abingdon, UK: Routledge.

Aydemir, Murat, and Alex Rotas. 2008. "Introduction: Migratory Settings." *Thamyris/Intersecting* 19:7–32.

Belcourt, Billy-Ray. 2020. *A History of My Brief Body*. Columbus, OH: Two Dollar Radio.

Dadi, Iftikhar. 2009. "Ghostly Sufis and Ornamental Shadows: Spectral Visualities in Karachi's Public Sphere." In *Comparing Cities: The Middle East and South Asia*, edited by Martina Rieker and Kamran Ali, 159–93. Karachi: Oxford University Press.

Elliot, Alice. 2021. *The Outside: Migration as Life in Morocco*. Bloomington: Indiana University Press.

El Tayeb, Fatima. 2011. *European Others: Queering Ethnicity in Postnational Europe*. Minneapolis: University of Minnesota Press.

Freeman, Elizabeth. 2007. "Queer Belonging: Kinship Theory and Queer Theory." In *A Companion to Lesbian, Gay, Bisexual, Transgender and Queer Studies*, edited by George E. Haggerty and Molly McGarry, 293–314. Oxford: Blackwell.

Freeman, Elizabeth. 2019. *Beside You in Time: Sense Methods and Queer Sociabilities in the American 19th Century*. Durham, NC: Duke University Press.

Glissant, Édouard. 2010. *Poetics of Relation*. Translated by Betsy Wing. Ann Arbor: University of Michigan Press.

Kasmani, Omar. 2019. "Thin Attachments: Writing Berlin in Scenes of Daily Loves." *Capacious: Journal for Emerging Affect Inquiry* 1 (4): 34–53.

Kasmani, Omar, dir. 2021a. *A City in Daily Loves: An Affective Geography of Post-Migrant Berlin*. FUBiS Berlin. Video. https://www.youtube.com/watch?v=dsaEGpida5g&t=13s.

Kasmani, Omar. 2021b. "Critical Thin: Haunting Sufis and the Also-Here of Migration in Berlin." *Religion and Society: Advances in Research* 12 (1): 56–69.

Kasmani, Omar. 2021c. "Thin, Cruisy, Queer: Writing through Affect." In *Gender and Genre in Ethnographic Writing*, edited by Elisabeth Tauber and Dorothy L. Zinn, 163–88. London: Palgrave Macmillan.

Khan, Faris A. 2019. "Translucent Citizenship: Khwaja Sira Activism and Alternatives to Dissent in Pakistan." *South Asia Multidisciplinary Academic Journal* 20. journals.openedition.org/samaj/5034.

Khatun, Samia. 2018. *Australianama: The South Asian Odyssey in Australia*. London: Hurst.

Manning, Erin. 2020. *For a Pragmatics of the Useless*. Durham, NC: Duke University Press.

Mittermaier, Amira. 2011. *Dreams That Matter: Egyptian Landscapes of the Imagination*. Berkeley: University of California Press.

Ören, Aras. 2019. "Was will Niyazi in der Naunynstraße?" In *Berliner Trilogie: Drei Poeme*. Berlin: Verbrecher Verlag.

Özdamar, Emine Sevgi. 2005. "The Courtyard in the Mirror." *TRANSIT* 2 (1). http://dx.doi.org/10.5070/T721009715.

Piliavsky, Anastasia. 2013. "Where Is the Public Sphere: Political Communications and the Morality of Disclosure in Rural Rajasthan." *Cambridge Anthropology* 31 (2): 104–22.

Simek, Nicole. 2015. "Stubborn Shadows." *Symplokē* 23 (1–2): 363–73.

PART THREE   UNLEARNING AND THE
CONDITIONS OF ARRIVAL

10 UNLEARNING AFFECT

M. Gail Hamner

To unlearn is as hard as to learn. —Aristotle, *Politics*

In the United States, the bifurcation of public discourse by what many term "cancel" culture or "consequence" culture generates affectscapes of impasse. Americans feel the split between those who uphold white supremacy and those who battle its hold on assumptions, practices, institutional cultures, governing policies, and laws. The impasse pressures everything from congressional proceedings to faculty meetings, from city councils to Zoom chats, from huge regional protests to door-slamming breaks in kin relationships. This chapter examines assumptions about subjectivity and language that hover around this impasse and inform its patterns of noisy shame. I show that the affective dimensions of impasse are inseparable from what Denise Ferreira da Silva terms our ontoepistemological presumptions and Silvan Tomkins theorizes as "scripts"—elements of personal-social being that are structured, intangible, and resistant to change. Significantly, Ferreira da Silva holds up the conceptual and political importance of the theorizations of affect in J. G. Herder and G. W. F. Hegel. Through brief excursions into these two thinkers plus the role of affect in C. S. Peirce, I join Ferreira da Silva's powerful critiques to those of Sylvia Wynter to show the racializing logics of early affect thinkers. I argue that our posturing around racial impasse belies the orientating effects of subjectivation and the temporal capture of affect in nonconscious habits of conceptualization and gesture. We scream past each other because we *feel* past each other, in ways we cannot convey and through an untested faith in the possibility of building affective and rational commons. The social media demand is often confession and repentance, or the threat of excommunication from social approbation (including publications or even a career). By tracing the genealogy of affect as the logic of (racial) enclosure writ as (universal) possibility, this chapter asks instead that we orient ourselves to the task of unlearning our affects.[1]

Enwhitenment

"What language says is not actual," Rei Terada (2020, 147) writes, "but it describes patterns that it has not invented and without which it could not be written." These words could be transliterated from Hegel (1977, 56), for whom the operations of perception and apperception occur "behind the back of consciousness." Cognitive operations function for Hegel *through* a wash of feeling, but they are *not* feeling. The same distinction holds for most Enlightenment philosophers. The situatedness of human thought *within* affect (e.g., the sensory manifold, the sensorial immediate) is acknowledged and quickly dismissed; it gives ground to the production of rational knowledge without being their source. Marginalization of affect might seem importantly corrected by counter-Enlightenment philosophers like Herder and Peirce who dwell extensively with affect and praise its capacities. But what difference does the difference of affect really make for these philosophers? As Terada's essay warns us, "The language of logical argument talks in its sleep about settlement and expropriation, colonialism and racial capitalism in noonday life" (147). This section looks briefly at the role assigned to affect in the works of Herder, Hegel, and Peirce. Even though each is strongly attuned to affect, together they perpetuate the hegemonic norms of the Enlightenment, which Ashley Cake terms the "En*whiten*ment" as a means of insisting on its white, male, and property-owning biases.[2] We need to grasp *how* racial privilege sediments in the form and logics of their philosophies.

For Johann Gottfried von Herder (1744–1803), the story of affect is the logic of replacement. Built up from pulses of life to animal feeling, from feeling to imagination, and from imagination to reason, Herder's affect is *the* ontological medium, *the* basic force (*Kraft*) and primal feeling (*Gefühl*) of all that is. Animals, persons, and cultures do not remain mere pulses of life but develop as their affective experiences become progressively captured and channeled by flesh, word, and history. Herder's concern lies not only with his inverted ontological focus on affect but also with the experiential and social processes that replace or resituate affect within cognitive, embodied, and interpersonal dimensions. Although his writings clearly prioritize affect and feeling and yield direct impacts on Hegel, among others, Herder's work is not widely known today (Forster 2019). This is regretful because his informal, poetic style is as refreshing as his effusive attention to life's emotional pulses, which take shape in roiling currents through God-given sensoria. The seductive qualities Herder attributes to the free-flowing, liberatory, and even divine aspects of affect remain inseparable, however, from how he theorizes affect as steadily channeled and captured, decisively differentiating persons and cultures from animals, and introducing political rankings that hide behind the veils of tolerance. Attending to the possibilities of affect in Herder's thought also requires *un*learning how they ballast personal-political differentiations that explain and justify how we feel past each other in unsurpassable raciality.

Like Hegel, Herder understands the world as a swirling sea of moving forces that affect flesh, history, and sensory capacity, creating channels that generate specific lived perspectives and dispositions. This affective channeling and capture writes the story of personal, historical, and cultural development and differentiation. The link between affect and language can specify this process and draw out its politics. What Herder calls the *language* of affect includes the vocalizations of both animals and humans. These vocalizations indicate affect's pervasiveness and ontological range, from the grunts of an animal to the gurgling of human infants and what Herder denominates as the "simple" communications of human "primitives." Herder signals commitment to this affective ontology by transposing Descartes's famous *cogito ergo sum* into a more exultant avowal that excises causality: "I feel myself! I am!" (*Ich fühle mich! Ich bin!*) (Herder 1994, 4:236). His argument does subtend rationality with feeling, but feeling (affect) does not destabilize reason.

Herder argues that each human person's developed sensibility has a proper form that is shaped by a people's unique relation to territory, sensibility, and history. He calls the form of this fluctuating sensorial development "language," though not all language is verbal. The startling first sentence of *On the Origin of Language*—"Already as an animal, the human being has language" (Herder 2004, 65)—precedes Herder's claim that preverbal sounds are a "language of sensation" that "is a law of nature" (66). In other words, thought can take many forms besides words. The bee and the spider, for example, have acute "sensitivity," precise "drives," and elegant "artifactive skills," but their sphere of activity is impoverished in range and diversity relative to humans (79). When words finally develop, they do so as part of the peculiar constitution of human persons and in relation to that function of reason that Herder calls "reflection." Because words endure (where sensation does not), words tamp down the ontological sensorial flux, enabling former meanings to sediment as the word's lineament or casing. In short, although thought *can* be other than verbal language, *in humans*, words carry thought so that the former meaning of words shapes both current discourse and personal and national identity. Cries of affect come to be replaced by words, and rational thought emerges as an index of the identities of *properly different* persons and cultures (Sikka 2011). The philosopher moves rapidly from raw affective experience to varied personal and national identities that each inheres its own *propriety*.

Herder's writings are brimming with what scholars today call cultural relativism. His 1778 essay, *On the Cognition and Sensation of the Human Soul*, for instance, notes how one's senses "use all the tricks and subtleties that a blind man with his stick uses to grope, to feel, to learn distance, difference, size" (Herder 2004, 203) and follows this discussion with an extrapolation: "If one could pursue this [sensory] difference in the contributions of different senses through lands, times, and peoples, the matter would inevitably become an infinity. [One would ask,] for example, what the cause is of the fact that Frenchmen and Italians in music, Italians and Dutchmen in painting, understand something so different" (204). This affective democratization of geographical and territorial difference is somewhat undercut by Herder's commitment to the *longue durée* of cultural development that shapes personal and cultural identity; that is, simpler languages and nations may be beautiful and proper to themselves (and therefore should be tolerated and not colonized), but they are also more primitive and temporally past or lagging (cf. Herder 1833, 34). Shared feeling is replaced by a neat categorical differentiation of peoples on the social plane that, unsurprisingly, preserves European whiteness as the pinnacle of civilization.

Hegel

Where Herder's oeuvre is still relatively unknown, Georg Wilhelm Friedrich Hegel's (1744–1831) basic arguments about law, phenomenology, aesthetics, and religion are widely cited, if perhaps not arduously read and studied. My comments here are very brief and restricted to the opening section of his *Phenomenologie der Geist* (Phenomenology of spirit) on the "sense certainty" of consciousness.[3]

Charles Taylor notes that Herder's critiques of universalism and arguments for cultural expression were prevalent and generally accepted when Hegel published his *Phenomenology* in 1807, four years after Herder's death (Taylor 1975, 13–24). It is thus plausible that his opening discussion of "sense certainty" is aimed directly at Herder's advocates and his Sturm und Drang allies. The first subsection of the text's first division ("Consciousness") drops the reader into something like Herder's ontology of swirling force or Kant's sensory manifold. Readers are confronted with a bare "what *is*" that surrounds humans and forms the matter of our sensory experience. Yet Hegel's first sentence frames this immediate immersion in terms of *knowing*: "The knowledge or knowing that is at the start or is immediately our object cannot be anything else but immediate knowledge itself, a knowledge of the immediate or of what simply *is*" (Hegel 1977, 58).

Like later phenomenologists, Hegel affirms human consciousness as persistently *immersed* in the world around it ("what simply *is*") but focuses concern not on the fact or feeling of this immersion so much as the knowledge it yields. No experience, Hegel insists, and no *certainty* of experience is possible without negating sensorial immediacy and mediating it through consciousness and language. Humans are surrounded by what is surrounding us at every moment:

we see (perceive) "this," "now," "here." But to note or *apperceive* that we are seeing "this," "now," "here" is already to negate the immediacy through a distinction of self from world. A moment passes, I turn my head, and a *different* "this," "now," "here" appears before me, a different immediate experience that—again—I can only register to myself or others by differentiating myself from it. The endless saturation of the surrounding world is immediately available to me and at once divided from me, first through the dehiscence of consciousness from the objects of consciousness, and (then) through language's universalizing function of demarcation (i.e., its generalization of immanent particularity: anything can be a "this," every moment is a "now," any place can be a "here").

Above, I discussed how Herder indulges in the profusion of feeling that, over time, captures affect and theorizes a logic of *replacement* whereby linguistic patterns shape and differentiate personal and national identities. The story of affect in Hegel, unsurprisingly, follows a logic of *mastery*. Hegel *flees* (negates) sensory experience to turn around and subordinate (master) it for the sake of obtaining *certainty* of knowledge. "Knowledge of what simply *is*" requires distanciation from that simple *isness*. Although Hegel does not attend to words as singularly as does Herder, the phrase he uses in his opening section is telling: *sinnlichen Gewißheit*. Arnold V. Miller and J. N. Findlay translate the phrase into two juxtaposed nouns (sense + certainty), but a more literal translation might render it sensory certainty or sensual certainty. In other words, taken literally, Hegel does not hold certainty *next* to the senses but centers *certainty* as the dominant substantive—as the philosophical pursuit and goal—that the *senses* can only meekly qualify, serve, and support.

As with Herder, this logic of mastery is presented as the neutral development of world spirit, but scholars have mapped the connections between the *Phenomenology's* phrases that figure the birth or infancy of *Geist* and the concretizing of these figures in Africa and the animality of non-European humans. Patricia Purtschert (2019), for example, groups together the *Phenomenology's* figures of "'non-spiritual, i.e. sense-consciousness' (*sinnliches Bewusstsein*), 'natural consciousness' (*natürliches Bewusstsein*), or 'immediate spirit' (*unmittelbarer Geist*)" as what I would call the repeating ground of Hegel's dialectical melody (Hamner 2019, 1042). Human rationality *needs* the innocence of sense certainty; but reading Hegel's references to wildness in the *Phenomenology* and to Africa in the *Philosophy of History* clarifies how, in his view, Africans are stuck in the pulsing sensations of natural consciousness, while Europeans seem able to master the senses and move with spirit toward rationality (Mollendorf 1992; Terada 2019).

Peirce

C. S. Peirce (1839–1914), the cantankerous and brilliant semiotician, argued for an essential connection between meaning and practical effect and thereby established America's pragmatic philosophy: what he called "pragmaticism."[4] His approach to epistemology and ethics directly influenced William James's development of the more popular and pedagogically palatable pragmatism. Peirce positions affect as the repeating ground of a spiraling triadic architectonic that he organizes through the "universal categories" or "principles" of Firstness, Secondness, and Thirdness. These three categories constitute his logic of relations, a logic that functions with varying complexity at different scales of existence: cosmology, biology, logic, and psychology (more on this logic of relations below). As a reminder, I am tracing the genealogy of affect in this chapter as the logic of (racial) enclosure writ as (universal) possibility. If the enclosure of affect in Herder works through a logic of replacement and in Hegel through logic of mastery, I posit that the enclosure of affect in Peirce works through a logic of enfolding.

For any entity under discussion, Peirce's universal categories denominate the number and function of relations involved in its form and being. As Vincent Colapietro (2008, 42) notes, despite the odd generality and vagueness of their terminology, "the categories are not at all foreign to experience, but rather ingredient in and constitutive of experience in all of its forms." Firstness refers to simple quality or intensity (affect); it signals the kind of form that is single or singular and unrelated to its surroundings. In one of my favorite phrases, Peirce notes that a "pure" Firstness would be "thunderless, unremembered, and altogether without effect," a depiction that approximates Herder's ontological swirl of affect and the "what *is*" of Hegel's sensory immediacy (Peirce 1960, 1:292). As such, cosmological Firstness refers to what cannot be experienced but is a logical projection of the ontological reality beyond perception and even beyond substantiation. Sheer pulses of quality or intensity can *do* nothing, they can have no influence or trace, because they do not persist. To act, to have agency (even at the atomic level) is to persist, which requires Secondness and Thirdness. Secondness refers to brute or mere encounter, reaction, or resistance. When Sara Ahmed writes of the "stickiness" of affect, we might think of this as affect's Secondness. At the cosmological scale, where pure qualities come into being and then blip out (thunderless and unremembered), Secondness indicates a Firstness that bumps into (onto) something. A dyad appears: here is the quality and fact of encounter. At this point, Firstness (quality, intensity) *relates* to something in a way that *could* leave a mark (even if that mark itself does not last). Peirce gives the example of a noise that awakens you in the middle of the night: the forceful encounter with or registering of that noise is (psychological) Secondness (Hamner 2003, 97). Thirdness would be interpreting that noise as fireworks or the neighbor's cat. Thirdness refers to what perdures; it is the formation of habit, the sticking of stickiness. For perduring to occur—ontologically as well as psychologically—a dyad of quality and reaction (resistance) must relate to a third. This third might link the relation of quality and resistance to repetition and hence to temporality, or it might join them to the perspective of an interpreter (the lightning flash does not in itself endure, e.g., but my memory of it does). The various ways in which the milieu registers and influences an entity are the ways the entity is interpreted. A third, then, is a quality that relates to an object in some respect or capacity, which is its interpretant.[5] Examples of Thirdness include habits, signs, laws, and concepts.

Peirce's logic of relations functions through enfolding. It theorizes the *connected and nested* differences between different "modes of existence." A physical third (an atom, say) might be a phenomenological first (the smell of sulfur as a simple quality), while a phenomenological third (a black cat) may well give rise to a semiotic first (an icon of a cat). Each scale of existence builds on or enfolds the previous scale. Such enfolding pragmatically justifies the categories by demonstrating how empirical experiences—our connections to brute reaction and natural quality—are always *there*, enfolded into our most abstract symbolizations and imaginative linguistic flights. This fact might suggest that his system escapes the criticisms I lobbied against Herder and

Hegel. Indeed, a radical, nonracist metaphysic *might* be constructed from Peirce's system, but Peirce *himself* lacks a way to theorize differences within and through continuity except by way of his semiotic emphasis on interpretation and ethical emphasis on habit. Without a concomitant theory of something like power (that term that rages through the twentieth century like a hurricane), pragmaticism's lived and learned capacities of interpretation and habit end up rewarding the socially dominant *for* their social dominance and dismissing (if not blaming) those who are poor or marginalized. We are our habits, Peirce will say—and he is right!—but he gives no account of social continuity or social agapism that explicates why some people's habits accrue to a life of comfort, while others' habits keep them, as Ferreira da Silva says, perpetually on the horizon of death.

Critics of Enwhitenment

> Affect theory is another phase in the history of ideology theory.
> —Lauren Berlant, *Cruel Optimism*, 2011

> We often elide the psychical, physiological, and environmental processes that perpetuate existing patterns of conduct.
> —Carolyn Pedwell, *Revolutionary Routines*, 2021

We can now grasp the polemics of the substitution of En*whiten*-ment for Enlightenment. Kant's appeal to overcoming of "our self-incurred immaturity" is hardly akin to flicking a switch that bathes darkness in neutral light, for the light is itself white; it is whiteness. Although Herder, Hegel, and Peirce do make affect central, the valuations built into this way of narrativizing the Human—from sensation to interpretation—illuminate the increasing skill of reason and logic (over a lifetime) *as* affect's replacement and enclosure by rationality. Their logics of replacement, mastery, and enfolding constitute the logical ground that normalizes oppressive differentiation between persons and hides the white domination of this differentiation behind universal claims about affect, language, relationality, and reason. We can now see that Herder, Hegel, and Peirce perpetuate what Ferreira da Silva terms the logics of "the transparent I" and what Wynter refers to as "the over-representation of Man." The important scholarship of these two Black feminist scholars drills down into history, philosophy, cultural studies, linguistics, and religion to provide detailed accounts of how and why the European white man has so successfully become the global norm. They are critics of Enwhitenment, expertly illuminating the entrenchment of racial assumptions in the most general logics of discourse.

With her "analytics of raciality," Ferreira da Silva delineates the philosophical and scientific strategies that protect European (white) "man" and perpetually subordinate man's "others." The dense analyses of *Toward a Global Idea of Race* (2007) position race as a *quality* ("racial") that takes on substantiality ("raciality") through the hegemonic sedimentation of a particular logic, or what she calls "ontoepistemology." Raciality is not merely phenotype, then, but includes and works through the ontoepistemological conditions and frameworks that *produce* certain phenotypes as "other"—that is, as different and affectable. If raciality thus comes to denominate what, by my earlier discussions, Herder replaces, Hegel flees from, and Peirce embeds in semiosis, Ferreira da Silva also notes that the *social* effects of raciality are extensive and saturated with domination: "I identify the productivity of the racial and how it is tied to the emergence of an ontological context—globality—that fuses particular bodily traits, social configurations, and global regions in which human difference is reproduced as irreducible and unsublatable" (Ferreira da Silva 2007, xix). Globality is an *ontological* context because it indexes the exteriority that threatens the "transparency" of the philosophical "I"—that is, the philosophical subject's untrammeled pursuit of self-determination (reason, enlightenment). Strategies of protection against exteriority seal the production of modern subjects as split between transparency (whiteness) and affectability (raciality) (24). Ferreira da Silva's analytics of raciality scripts the history of Western reason as the production of whiteness (transparency) in a lethal and inextricable relationship to its nonwhite others (affectability).[6] To underscore the oblique, intangible quality of this logic, Ferreira da Silva notes that after decades of critical and activist labor intended to redress the exclusion of racial-affectable others from the equal rights and self-determination of transparency, these nonwhite bodies still stand on the horizon of death, *without inciting a global ethical crisis.* European (white) philosophers continue to make themselves transparent *in* the world; they move seen but unmarked and do so through various strategies that mark others as affectable and render them invisible as humans. The impasses of racism will not change by will or discourse, she argues, because the nodal point that generates racial difference is ontoepistemological: it subtends will and discourse as their conditions of possibility and their practical-institutional channeling. The history and strategies of reason do not remain in the arcane halls of philosophy but stride across the globe on the ontoepistemological tenets of imperialism, colonialism, and capitalism (Ferreira da Silva 2007, 29–30).

Wynter's incisive critiques of European thought resonate strongly with Ferreira da Silva's. Both turn their focus from specific assertions or practices to the racializing logics that condition and sustain them. Wynter (2003, 260) argues that the fundamental struggle facing us all is that "between the ongoing imperative of securing the well-being of our present ethnoclass (i.e., Western bourgeois) conception of the human, which overrepresents itself as if it were the human itself, and that of securing the well-being, and therefore the full cognitive and behavioral autonomy of the human species itself/ourselves." The claims of white Western bourgeois "Man" are "overrepresented" relative to the full range of possibilities of being human. "Man" aligns with Ferreira da Silva's focus on "transparent I" as the category of dominance that strangles life from "affectable others" (what Wynter terms the human species in excess of "Man"). Like Michel Foucault's argument in *The Order of Things* about the emergence of Man in and through the consolidation of the human sciences, Wynter scours historical archives to demonstrate that Man is indeed no more than a face in the sand fated to be washed away in the next wave (Foucault 1973, 387). But Foucault's delineation of the discursive strategies that generate "Man" in and through the ontoepistemological claims of the newly forming human sciences does not foreground or deal with a normative whiteness justified and sustained *through* the human sciences, nor does he discuss biological Man in the context of biological *animality*. Wynter uses Frantz Fanon's notion of sociogeny to demonstrate how nonwhite persons are held in a double bind between the claims of science that normalize both whiteness and the animality of nonwhiteness. Humans who are not Man (who are affectable) thus occupy the negated, unstable space *between* whiteness and animality.[7]

Like Ferreira da Silva, Wynter aims her critique at the unseen conditions of speech and practice that shape the tangible and political effects of the overrepresentation of Man. She indexes the logics of discourse through the term "colonization." The "master code" of "Man," she notes, *colonizes* the meanings and practices of Being, Power, Truth, and Freedom, thereby rendering other conceptions of being or becoming human *colonized*—that is, powerless and discounted. As postcolonial and decolonial theory has taught us, colonization enacts and sustains violence, both the overt violence of the state and the softer violence of cultural production and ideological state apparatuses.

Though their bibliographies and questions differ, Wynter and Ferreira da Silva overlap in their bracketing of racist and anti-racist *statements* so that they may focus on the *logics* of discourse and onto-epistemological *strategies* that subtend and invisibilize racist histories, practices, and structures. They both labor to show us the entanglement of philosophies with whiteness, including claims about (precognitive) affect, and how affect is replaced, captured, mastered, and enfolded by reason (which equates to white Europeans). By pointing readers over and again to the logical, discursive, epistemological, and ontological conditions of raciality, they compel us to look not only at specific instances and impasses of racism but also to foreground the more difficult and intangible labor of making the transparent I opaque, of feeling out the contingencies of "Man" that keep so much of the world's population in a double bind of strangled illegibility. Their critiques show us that simply turning to affect, as a precognitive ontology or even an affecognitive feeling (Hamner 2018) will not sidestep Enwhitenment. The racial capture of affect needs to be grasped as the normative strategy of white subjectivation and as the unthought of the conditions that form civil society's current impasse, the explanation for why we scream past each other and feel past each other. The entanglements of time, value, power, and authority that have sustained the transparent I and the overrepresentation of Man cannot be downplayed but must enter our collective thinking for transformation. But how? Is it possible for me (a white woman) to unlearn my transparency or refuse to participate in the discourses of Man?

The end of Ferreira da Silva's *Toward a Global Idea of Race* would suggest no. Her text illustrates *why* we can never seem to move the dial on white supremacy but not *what* to do about the impasse. Wynter, on the other hand, encourages resistance to the overrepresentation of Man through "being human as praxis"—that is, by reading, acting, writing, and imagining *against* the "colonization" of "Being/Power/Truth/Freedom" and *toward* the capacities of the human species that lie in excess of any dominant representation. As Carolyn Pedwell (2021, 32–33) has argued forcefully, however, although theoretical critiques like Ferreira da Silva's and Wynter's are devastating and crucial, *knowing* them is not enough to begin to change them, especially for white readers whose conscious and unconscious defensiveness clings to the habits of power and privilege.

In *Potential History: Unlearning Imperialism*, Ariella Azoulay (2019) offers a different orientation to the racializing logics that bind us in impasse. She calls readers *to actively unlearn*, to resist acting as what she terms "citizen perpetrators" and learn how to be co-citizens with those denied citizenship or kept as conditional citizens (Lalami 2020). While Azoulay's text stages extraordinary "imaginary strikes" against the logics of imperialism (against museums, history, photography, and governmentality), insisting that the work of social transformation must be done collaboratively, her passionate and engaging project does not guide nonacademics into the specific quotidian tactics of reworking and unlearning the habits, logic, reflexes, and enfleshed sedimentations of white supremacy. What does this unlearning look like in social activism, on social media, or in my relations to my neighbor?

Tomkins's "Script Theory"

This chapter examines the affecognitive dimensions of our current cultural impasse and demonstrates that cognitive, discursive positions are culturally shaped by the longue durée of "Man's" ontoepistemology. Herder, Hegel, and Peirce display the imbrication of material world, social world, language, and personal development, while Ferreira da Silva and Wynter evidence what damage accrues when scholars seek the liberatory logics of affect but ignore how its concomitant logics of enclosure and capture sustain the racial hierarchies of white supremacy. In this final section, I turn to Silvan Tomkins for a different take on the developments and deployments of subjectivity and language. I present Tomkins's script theory as one (partial) genealogy of our cultural impasse rooted in the nonconscious congealing of sociopolitical orientations, and suggest that any way through our shared impasse must draw on the time-laden collective patience required for change.

Tomkins theorizes persons as formed through lived *scenes* that are made up of at least one affect and one object. In his equation, affect names our biopsychical responses to specific lived situations. Because affect mediates biological, psychological, and social dimensions of life, it works on a person's interior *and* exterior as an aspect of both world and personal being. As mediated, affect constellates "scenes," or inversely, scenes are life's discrete and complexly affectively saturated moments. Famously termed "the basic element in life as it is lived," scenes cohere a person's ongoing affecognitive relationship with and commentary on how the world feels (Sedgwick and Frank 1995, 179). Scenes are collected moment by moment, but they are not stored in memory like words on a page. Rather, memory is the pulsing relationality *of* scenes as they co-assemble and amplify or (on the contrary) blip into the banality of the transitory and insignificant. To study the development of persons, Tomkins examines scenic relationality as scenes "co-assemble" *analogically*—that is, by the *repetition with a difference*. Scripts are the corrigible protocols that describe the rules for this analogic co-assembly (Tomkins 1995, 325). Their algorithm-like formulas provide pliable structures that orient a person's memory, focus, anticipation, and affect density. Tomkins defines scripts as "the individual's rules for predicting, interpreting, responding to, and controlling a magnified set of scenes," where *magnification* of a script refers to a further lived response to its established (but corrigible) co-assembly (320).

It is difficult to parse or summarize script theory because it is dense and because Tompkins discusses it over several different publications; its potential has therefore yet to be fully tapped by affect scholars (cf. Tomkins 1995, 295–300; Frank and Wilson 2020, 101–10). Script theory compellingly illuminates how persons can be both infinitely variable on multiple scales of biology, psychology, and sociality and yet *also* tend toward a crystallized personality with increasingly inflexible scripts that are increasingly outside of conscious control. Our *unwilled* and often *nonconscious* protocols of co-assembled scenes of life come to form the textured, variegated, and rather firmly set contours of personal and collective life (Tomkins 1995, 331). Script theory thus provides a new perspective on Enwhitenment philosophers, even those who dwell with affect. It helps us see that US cancel or consequence culture is an unhelpful tactic *on the level of subjectivation of the self* because each side of the impasse ignores how person(alitie)s *are made* and so overestimates *what subjectivity is capable of*. Our split and siloed public discourses may well succeed in public shaming, in speaking truth to power or rallying one's base, but they cannot and will not ease the script impasse.

For Tomkins (1995, 290), a script is not the pulse of affect but the nonconscious, time-laden set of protocols that "is maintained by and controls dense affect." A person has little consciousness of or control over their affective scripts (323), and this means, importantly, that a person does not capture affect so much as affect captures *her*, sculpting her personality and life *through* experiences that are at once idiosyncratic and socially shared. The lived scenes that co-assemble into scripts and structure the lives of a person and a culture will mutate and differentiate infinitely but *always within constraints that are relatively inflexible* because they are so deeply and densely formed and because humans tend toward script stability as they age. Repetition, binding, co-assembling, seizing—these are the time-laden processes of building "scripts."

Script theory, thus, explains not only how affect is captured—in this case, not by reason but by history, by the repetition with difference of the scenes of life—but also how human personality is constituted in its capture *by* affect. Despite the astounding openness and variability Tomkins theorizes in affective scripts, and despite their inherent multiplicity (what he terms their "principle of plurideterminacy") (341; see also 309), the development of human personality is a story of enclosure, a story about the formation in early life of protocols for interpreting and responding to self and world that become difficult to budge in their core constitution. Script theory helps us understand why the blooming buzzing confusion of social change never seems to substantially move the dial on anti-racism. As Tomkins notes—and Ferreira da Silva and Wynter prepare us to understand—"affect is to history as grammar is to semantics and pragmatics" (311). Unlearning affect, then, requires chipping away at that "grammar," at the occluded *conditions* of white thought and the sedimented (embodied) *logics* of white practice, instead of lambasting explicit assertions and acts on the skimming surface of social encounter. Script theory, as I read it, will require whiteness to engage a concerted effort at something like a cultural pedagogy, or what Tomkins terms "learning to learn" (Sedgwick and Frank 1995, 40).

Although many affect scholars have rejoiced in the astonishing differentiation of affective scenes and affective co-assembly, I wish to sit with their relative inflexibility. How might we change public debate in the United States to consider this structured inflexibility of human personality, while also not yielding to white fragility?

Script theory contextualizes iterative gestures and shifts within a relatively unbending matrix of script protocols. Especially salient for my argument are Tomkins's discussions of nuclear scripts, with their attendant "auxiliary augmentations" (which I will discuss further below) and ideology scripts. From the vantage point of script theory, we can see that Wynter and Ferreira da Silva are waging ideological battle against the most elusive strata of human coexistence, that which keeps "the hurt of history" hurting through a rule-like and relatively intransigent matrix of belonging, comfort, and identity restricted to those who get to fully qualify as Man or who occupy the place of the "transparent I" (Jameson 1981, 102). The volatile combination of these two scripts provides a template for the engine that drives the negative affects of our current, bifurcated civil society (cf. Pedwell 2021, 139–66). Ideology scripts, ironically, are *felt* as positive. Originating in cosmology or religion—or what I would term the social assembling of technologies of collective valuation—ideology scripts are "the most important single class of scripts" in that they provide "orientation, evaluation, and sanctions, and endow fact with value and affect" (Tomkins 1995, 353; Hamner 2019). Tomkins (1995, 309) notes that the very possibility of social change begins with shifts in personality type and ideological battle: "It now appears that when many social, economic, technological, and political forces converge massively to transform a society, such shifts in ways of life characteristically require shifts in personality types. Such changes have to be consciously elaborated as new ideologies, and fought for against older ideologies, before it is possible to displace older sociocultural imperatives. Such ideological controversy is partly effect and partly cause of social change, since it characteristically proceeds, accompanies, and follows such change, quickening as it deepens radical transformations." Ideology scripts enable and sustain the feeling of an in-group, a feeling that is binding, stabilizing, and assuring even if one does not agree with the group's every aspect.[8] Because ideology scripts are so powerfully anchoring, the clash between ideology scripts incites cultural and political fractiousness and social division.[9]

Ideology scripts are the glue of belonging and meaning that are valenced as positive, but Tomkins clearly positions nuclear scripts as preponderantly negative. They "snatch defeat from the jaws of victory" (387) and "speak to the conjunction of greed and cowardice in response to seduction, contamination, confusion, and intimidation. Nuclear scripts represent the tragic rather than the classic vision" (376). Tomkins portrays these scripts as "the lifelong pursuit of defeat amidst uncertain, partial, and temporary victories" (381) and depicts them as sustaining paranoia and self-undermining. The protocols of nuclear scripts resist new information, either assimilating it to the script's standing protocols or ejecting it as untrustworthy, like any good conspiracy theory (378).

The joint operation of ideological and nuclear scripts explains common contemporary concerns such as confirmation bias and the tendency to distrust information that comes from unknown sources. It is a dynamic exacerbated by what Tomkins calls "auxiliary augmentation," a process that arises in the face of any script's incompleteness (335). The discussion of auxiliary augmentation is brief but indicates that a script's incompleteness marks the contingency of script's formation as well as the limitation of a person's body vis-à-vis her environment. Tomkins gives the example of using a mirror every day for shaving (I cannot see my chin, except with a mirror). Augmentation refers to external mediations that extend sensorial engagement with the world that scripts absorb and use as support. For example, the incompleteness of ideology and nuclear scripts can be intensely augmented by media such as radio, cable TV, social media platforms, and even protest placards. The combination of positive reinforcement by ideology scripts (strong group belonging), negative reinforcement by nuclear scripts (paranoid defensiveness), and media's augmentation of these protocols of affective belonging and unbelonging draw the lines of cultural impasse. This situation of tremendous unhappiness, however, does not reach the level of *requiring* socio-psycho-medical intervention, so we see persons thrown back again and again on themselves, their communities, and media augmentation (Demos 2019, 183).

Even though Tomkins does not drill down to theorize why the ideologies of white supremacy and patriarchy are particularly "stuck" (as do the logics of the affectable other or the overrepresentation of Man that suffocates other modalities of being human), reading his script theory through Black critical theorists like Ferreira da Silva and Wynter generates rich potentials for affect scholars to make needed changes in our approach to social problematics. Yes, affect moves, but it also sticks. As Adam Frank and Elizabeth Wilson (2020, 8) note, it is "significant that, in Tomkins's account, affect precedes value." Put inversely, cultural valuation coalesces in mediation with biological and psychological scripts that, by conjugating affective scenes, shape the lived values of persons and cultures. Scripts resist fundamental change; stories change, but the logics remain the same. As citizen participants, we can track the shifts, say, in personality type and ideological battle formed by Black Lives Matter (BLM), or the shift in personality type and ideological battle formed by the "blue lives matter" citizen resistant to BLM's ideological warfare. But without deep massage on the ontologics of affective constitution suggested by Tomkins, Ferreira da Silva, and Wynter, these interventions will continue to scream past each other.

Wynter and Ferreira da Silva (among many others) posit various strategies to navigate this impasse, enacting what Fred Moten (cited in Carter 2020, 160) terms an "appositional" thinking that seeks "what moves dynamically through . . . oppositions as already exceeding them." Such transversal interruption (also a powerful figure at work in Wynter and Ferreira da Silva) aptly articulates what I would call a "determinativeness without determination" of the logics of affect that subtend the surface skittering of our noisy civil discourse, working in tandem with singular zaps and gaps that provoke change in the co-assembly of scenes and (perhaps) a shift in the protocols that form the scenes' scripts. As a white person trying to engage with the entrenched logics of whiteness, I feel ardently that whiteness needs to redress the logics of domination that mold white subjectivity, drawing patiently on conceptual figurations like apposition and transversality as we try to "learn how to [un]learn" white supremacy.

It is difficult to pursue unlearning affect because when it happens—if it happens—it does so at scales of temporality and spatiality that do not register as an event. Unlearning affect necessitates a time-dense and spatially engaged process of braking, unbinding, and disassembling the psychological, biological, and social protocols that are at once uniquely our own and also signatures of our location in space and time. Because these protocols are significantly oblique to our conscious sense of self, the task of unlearning the capture and channeling of affect is difficult and rare but maybe not impossible.

For whiteness, which I submit clearly has the onus to work hardest on our cultural impasse, it will require a fundamentally pedagogical approach. I remember chuckling as I read the account of Tomkins pondering how one might create a human automaton (an AI). He suggests that the temporal and spatial dimensions of human development cannot be shortcut: "In order to achieve this [sufficient 'level of abstractness and generality'] the machine would in all probability require a relatively helpless infancy followed by a growing competence through its childhood and adolescence. In short, it would require the time and spaces in which to *learn how to learn* through making errors and correcting them" (Sedgwick and Frank 1995, 40). How typical of whiteness to want to collapse life's experiential density (temporal *and* spatial) into an algorithm of condensed control! And how appropriate that Tomkins, like Wynter and Ferreira da Silva, drags (white) attention back to the messy thicknesses of temporality and textured extensivity.

What applies to the desire to create an automaton, I suggest, also applies to an already existing person and culture. The ugly theater of our current public impasse persists at the level of assertion, but whiteness (especially) needs to *learn how to learn* again in order to unlearn white supremacy. Gayatri Spivak (2004, 82) once described the work of the classroom as "the non-coercive rearrangement of desire" and unlearning affect at the cultural level might be described similarly: it takes stretches of time and differential spaces; the *collective* effort of those involved; access to spaces and opportunity to move in, out, and around a topic; commitment to the task; and careful facilitation. In other words, unlearning affect requires the kind of scenes that are currently unavailable through any of the platforms or strategies of our current public discourse. It requires attention to the logics of whiteness Ferreira da Silva theorizes as the *transparent I* and Wynter's insistence that (white) Man has overrepresented the infinitely fine-grained ways of being human. It requires approaching affect as a logic, a *protocol*, that mediates the sedimented hurts of deep history with the uncontrolled scenes of each singular moment—with all the uncontrolled pressures and unexpected possibilities they bring.

Notes

1 Feelings of gratitude overflow the small word "thanks," but *thank you* Carolyn and Greg for your precise intellectual reciprocity and gentle affect management that stood midwife to this chapter's birth.

2 Ashley Cake, a former advisee at Syracuse University, coined this term.

3 Section "A" of the *Phenomenology* is titled "Consciousness," the first subsection of which is titled "Sense Certainty." Hegel's dialectic flows and shapes each section of the *Phenomenology* in a structurally analogous manner.

4 Peirce's pragmatic maxim states, "Consider what effects, which might conceivably have practical bearings, we conceive the object of our conception to have. Then, our conception of these effects is the whole of our conception of the object." In "How to Make Our Ideas Clear" (Wiener 1958, 124).

5 This syntax echoes Peirce's (1960, 2:228) definition: "A sign is something that stands for something else, its object, in some respect or capacity, which is its interpretant."

6 Following Foucault, Ferreira da Silva includes compromised whites in the category of "affectable-others" (women, children, criminals, sexual perverts, and the mad), but her argument centers raciality as the primary horizon of death that is generated and sustained by the transparency thesis.

7 For an excellent expansion on this inbetweenness as *plasticity*, see Jackson (2020).

8 Adolescents often feel both woven into the ideology of their family and extremely disaffected by it. Years later, these same adolescents can surprise themselves by "sounding like their parents" when they assumed they had broken free from that early ideological formation. Other examples abound.

9 Tomkins (1995, 357–63) discusses "commitment scripts" as working alongside ideology scripts to manage the level of investment given to various influential ideologies operative in a person's life.

References

Aristotle. 1920. *Politics*. Translated by Benjamin Jowett. New York: Oxford University Press.

Azoulay, Ariella Aïsha. 2019. *Potential History: Unlearning Imperialism*. New York: Verso.

Berlant, Lauren. 2011. *Cruel Optimism*. Durham, NC: Duke University Press.

Carter, J. Kameron. 2020. "Other Worlds, Nowhere (or, The Sacred Otherwise)." In *Otherwise Worlds: Against Settler Colonialism and Anti-Blackness*, edited by Tiffany Kethabo King, Jenell Navarro, and Andrea Smith, 158–209. Durham, NC: Duke University Press.

Colapietro, Vincent M. 2008. "Peirce's Categories and Sign Studies." In *Approaches to Communication: Trends in Global Communication Studies*, edited by Susan Petrilli, 35–50. Madison, WI: Atwood.

Demos, E. Virginia. 2019. *The Affect Theory of Silvan Tomkins for Psychoanalysis and Psychotherapy: Recasting the Essentials*. New York: Routledge.

Ferreira da Silva, Denise. 2007. *Toward a Global Idea of Race*. Minneapolis: University of Minnesota Press.

Forster, Michael. 2019. "Johann Gottfried von Herder." *Stanford Encyclopedia of Philosophy*. https://plato.stanford.edu/archives/sum2019/entries/herder/.

Foucault, Michel. 1973. *The Order of Things: An Archaeology of the Human Sciences*. New York: Random House.

Frank, Adam J., and Elizabeth A. Wilson. 2020. *A Silvan Tomkins Handbook*. Minneapolis: University of Minnesota Press.

Lalami, Laila. 2020. *Conditional Citizenship: On Belonging in America*. New York: Pantheon.

Hamner, M. Gail. 2003. *American Pragmatism: A Religious Genealogy*. New York: Oxford University Press.

Hamner, M. Gail. 2018. "What Is 'Affecognitive'?" *Affecognitive: Religion, Film, Affect, Academia*, April 11. https://affecognitive.wordpress.com//?s=affecognitive&search=Go.

Hamner, M. Gail. 2019. "Theorizing Religion and the Public Sphere: Affect, Technology, Valuation." *Journal of the American Academy of Religion* 87 (4): 1008–49.

Hegel, Georg Wilhelm Friedrich. 1977. *Phenomenology of Spirit*. Translated by A. V. Miller. New York: Oxford University Press.

Herder, J. G. 1833. *The Spirit of Hebrew Poetry*. Vol. 1, translated by James Marsh. Burlington, VT: Edward Smith.

Herder, J. G. 1994. "*Zum Sinn des Gefühls*." In *Werke in zehn Bänden*, edited by Martin Bollacher, Ulrich Gaier, Hans Dietrich Irmscher, Rudolf Smend, Gunter E. Grimm, Jürgen Brummack, Christoph Bultmann, Thomas Zippert, Rainer Wisbert, and Günter Arnold, 4:235–41. Frankfurt: Deutscher Klassiker Verlag.

Herder, J. G. 2004. *Philosophical Writings*. Edited and translated by Michael N. Forster. New York: Cambridge University Press.

Jackson, Zakiyyah Iman. 2020. *Becoming Human: Matter and Meaning in an Antiblack World*. New York: New York University Press.

Jameson, Fredric. 1981. *The Political Unconscious: Narrative as a Socially Symbolic Act*. Ithaca, NY: Cornell University Press.

Mollendorf, Darryl. 1992. "Racism and Rationality in Hegel's Philosophy of Objective Spirit." *History of Political Thought* 13 (2): 243–55.

Pedwell, Carolyn. 2021. *Revolutionary Routines: The Habits of Social Transformation*. Montreal: McGill-Queen's University Press.

Peirce, Charles S. 1960. *Collected Papers*. Vols. 1–2, *Principles of Philosophy and Elements of Logic,* edited by Charles Hartshorne and Paul Weiss. Cambridge, MA: Belknap.

Purtschert, Patricia. 2019. "On the Limit of Spirit: Hegel's Racism Revisited." *Philosophy and Social Criticism* 36 (9): 1039–51.

Sedgwick, Eve K., and Adam Frank, eds. 1995. *Shame and Its Sisters: A Silvan Tomkins Reader*. Durham, NC: Duke University Press.

Sikka, Sonia. 2011. *Herder on Humanity and Cultural Difference: Enlightened Relativism*. New York: Cambridge University Press.

Spivak, Gayatri. 2004. "Terror: A Speech after 9/11." *boundary 2* 31 (2): 81–111.

Taylor, Charles. 1975. *Hegel*. New York: Cambridge University Press.

Terada, Rei. 2019. "Hegel's Racism for Radicals." *Radical Philosophy* 2 (5). https://www.radicalphilosophy.com/article/hegels-racism-for-radicals.

Terada, Rei. 2020. "Impasse as a Figure of Political Space." *Comparative Literature* 72 (2): 144–58.

Tomkins, Silvan. 1995. *Exploring Affect: The Selected Writings of Silvan S. Tomkins*. Edited by E. Virginia Demos. New York: Cambridge University Press.

Wiener, Philip P., ed. 1958. *Charles Sanders Peirce: Selected Writings (Values in a Universe of Chance)*. New York: Dover.

Wynter, Sylvia. 2003. "Unsettling the Coloniality of Being/Power/Truth/Freedom towards the Human, after Man, Its Overrepresentation—An Argument." CR: *The New Centennial Review* 3 (3): 257–337.

Affective Pedagogy in the Wake

Nathan Snaza

On April 1, 2019, my undergraduate literary theory students and I walked into a building named after the first president of the university.[1] We were here to discuss Toril Moi's "Nothing Is Hidden," an essay that intervenes in the literary studies "method wars" by proposing that there are no "methods": we just look at details and think, asking, "Why this?" As we entered the building, we all noticed a sign, posted on a stake in the ground, that offered "Our University's True Story," highlighting the entanglements of the building's namesake, Robert Ryland, with transatlantic slavery (he both enslaved people and wrote in defense of slavery). The sign ends by calling for a "complete and unvarnished portrayal of Rev. Ryland's legacy." This sign was a disruption to a certain trajectory in our study but also an event catalyst, one that modulated our collective but distributed attention so that when we asked "Why this?" with Moi, the "this" that impressed itself on us was the sign and, more broadly, this "legacy." The first president's legacy would have to include this building and what transpires inside of it, which means that this class constitutes a *part* of that legacy, and we faced the task of thinking about how the pedagogy unfolding takes up this inheritance and is taken up by it. What does it mean to study, today, in *this* place?

This chapter sits with the pedagogical and affective force of this deictic question, one that has, in the two years since the sign appeared, bloomed through the work of the Black Student Coalition into what is likely the most intense activism the campus has ever seen.[2] By the end of spring 2021, activists had issued six demands, including the removal of Ryland's name from the building, which led to a stand-off between students, faculty, and staff and the board of trustees.[3] As I write, nothing is settled; this chapter cannot be an account of this event from the outside but instead constitutes one moment *within* it. Animated by this event, I will sketch how Moi's deictic interrogative transformed our perception and attention and how we have grappled, collectively, to think through how our study shapes and is shaped by the materiality of enslavement. "Why this?" attunes us to highly specific worldly configurations that take on importance through extended meditation on what makes this particular thing in all its specificity distinct from other worldings that might have happened. It calls us to tune our perception in the deictic to the proximate, what one touches and is touched by (at all kinds of scales). The question thinks toward the subjunctive: what could have been and might yet be?

Immediately after reading Moi and confronting the sign, we turned to Christina Sharpe's *In the Wake: On Blackness and Being*. The wake that we studied with Sharpe was not abstract, was not something "outside" of the classroom and our encounters. It was in the walls, in the deep structure of the university we inhabited, in us. The vertiginous way that Moi's question pushed our attentions—from the most abstract level of a question's enunciative force to the most precise attunement to a specific detail we could muster—left us searching for language to slow down and attend to the manifold, diffuse, and largely ignored ways those levels are mediated in and by bodies, objects, texts, spaces, and specific conditions of emergence and circulation. To give us some traction—to put us in a space of friction (as Anna Tsing would say)—we found another question, this one from Sara Ahmed: How does this thing arrive, what are its "conditions of arrival"? Ahmed's queer phenomenology begins with an encounter—the writer at her table—and then elaborates a Marxist critique of commodity fetishism hyper-attuned to both the affective politics of racialization and heteropatriarchy, and the world-constituting agency of nonhumans. Asking these two questions together—why this, and what are its conditions of arrival?—led us back and forth between the language of the texts we read and the specific situation of our study.

This chapter seeks to theorize the affective experience of this particular class with an eye toward generalization. That is, I think education might be understood primarily in terms of affective encounters, encounters where the touching of different entities across a whole range of scales and times, reconfigures the conditions of the next encounter. Affective encounters are about orientation, as Ahmed always argues, which means that they are about politics. Beyond this general axiom, I take from Ahmed a particular insistence on the capaciousness of "affect." Although I recognize that many projects lead to wanting to sharpen distinctions between varieties of affect theory—especially a rough cleavage between uses of affect resonant with "emotion" and uses that primarily attend to prepersonal or impersonal capacity—for me, the classroom is a space that requires us to keep both at play. Our feelings—those that rise to the level where we experience them as emotions—undoubtedly (dis)orient us in space, but precisely because affects are not phenomena taking place in rigidly bounded bodies, they are best understood as aftereffects of prepersonal contact among biocultural entities, specific material milieus, and the complex histories that shape situations and the conditions of arrival of every single participant. I will sketch an understanding of the world as constitutively eventual (reading Sharpe through Whitehead), and what I am ultimately interested in here is what it would mean to conceptualize pedagogy as a form of what Erin Manning calls "event-care." Thinking through how these two questions set the conditions for event-care, I focus on politics in a specific but also capacious sense as the always more-than-human question of how entities are oriented in the colonial world, how they touch, and how that touching animates (or does not) new worlds coming into being "after Man" (Wynter 2003).

Why This?

Toril Moi offers the question "Why this?" to short-circuit the often acrimonious "method wars" circulating in literary studies with two polarized positions. On the one side would seem to stand the hermeneutics of suspicion where interpretive practices hinge on exposing hidden truths or ideologies governing the structures of utterances (including complex utterances like poems or novels or art objects) (Sedgwick 2003). This camp would include psychoanalytic and Marxist traditions of analysis and the many "critical" projects that developed in relation to them (including much feminist and queer criticism). These writers understand interpretive practice to "be" political insofar as the critical aim is to make transparent ideological structures that, by virtue of being explicitly theorized, can be resisted. On the other side are those who want to read surfaces instead of depths (Best and Marcus 2009), to repair rather than unfurl paranoid critiques (Sedgwick 2003), and who want to clear space in the field for something other than critique to flourish in our classrooms and writings.

Since a good deal of what we read in the course would probably be considered "critical" or suspicious, I wanted to give students a sense of how current disputes may be shifting the taken-for-grantedness of critique as a guiding logic for curricula in literary studies. I assigned parts of Elizabeth Anker and Rita Felski's *Critique and Postcritique* to raise questions about my own course design and the kinds of assumptions we bring to thinking about what "theory" is and what it means for undergraduate study. Although Anker and Felski's introduction offers a careful overview of the shape of the method wars (unlike my reductive one above), Moi's (2017, 35) chapter—the first in the book—effectively cries foul, noting that the entire argument feels like a distraction from acknowledging that there is no method in literary studies beyond one that can be stated plainly: we "simply look and think."

Arguing that there is a gap between how literary critics talk about method (as in the method wars) and what they do, Moi (2017, 34) posits that texts do not really have depths or surfaces and that the entire problem hinges on a "need to think of texts and language as hiding something." In the method wars, some readers want to bring to light what is hidden while others want to look at what is not hidden, but Moi insists that no matter what kinds of theories and political commitments one brings, "in the encounter with the literary text, the only 'method' that imposes itself is the willingness to look and see, to pay maximal attention to the words on the page" (35). To develop this claim, Moi turns to two canonical suspicious readers: Sigmund Freud and Sherlock Holmes. Taking up Holmes, not in Arthur Conan

Doyle's stories but the BBC television show version *Sherlock*, Moi underscores how the show frames Sherlock's reasoning skills as strange and extraordinary, but for Moi, that lesson is not about Sherlock Holmes so much as it is about a particular intensity of attention: "The other characters—the police detective, Watson—simply fail to take an interest in the features that grab Sherlock's attention. It's not that others look at the surface, whereas Sherlock looks beneath it. It is that he *pays attention* to details they didn't think to look at" (42).

Economies of attention, not "methods," are what are at stake in literary analysis.[4] And Moi borrows the deceptively simple question "Why this?" from Stanley Cavell in order to shift the debate away from binaries of surface versus depth, reparative versus paranoid, critical versus postcritical reading to questions that are not about "how" we read so much as about how we handle "matters of response, judgment, and responsibility" (47). In our class discussions, Moi's question put me on the spot as the instructor: I had to account for why I thought "literary theory" was a thing that was worth engaging (especially given its perceived "difficulty") and for decisions that I had made during syllabus construction about what questions, disputes, and theories to assign, as well as specific choices about texts that would serve as representatives of those conversations in the field. These are, in a way, anticipatable calls for responsibility, ones I prepare myself to engage every time I teach. But Moi's question kept arising in other places, ones that were not part of the "planning" any of us did before the course began. And the most obvious concern on our minds while discussing Moi's chapter was, what about *the sign outside the building?* Although Moi's question moved our attention there, we also hit up against its abstract universality: as she writes, "We can ask Why this? about anything" (46). Its generality is one reason it works: one can always start there, in any context or situation. But the trouble becomes translating "this" into the specific demands of "looking and thinking" Moi calls for. Once our attention snaps into place, what exactly does it mean to "think" here, especially when that cannot be reduced to a method or even something agentially done by a self-conscious subject because, as Erin Manning (2016, 3) has argued, "it is urgent to turn away from the notion that it is the human agent, the intentional, volitional subject, who determines what comes to be"?

What Are Its/Our Conditions of Arrival?

Moi's question is grammatically miniscule: just an adverb indicating a shift to the interrogative mood and an indexical adjective. The force of the question (and its usefulness in shifting conversations about method) lies in the way that minimal grammar attaches deixis to wonder. *This* can be anything, but whenever it is uttered, it is *this very specific thing and no other* that demands our attention. Once we notice a thing, what are we to do? The sign spurs an event, sets conditions for an emergent relationality we might call study (Harney and Moten 2013). When I arrived in the room, students were already there talking. No one knew who put up the sign, although they shared rumors circulating on GroupMe and other social media. And students immediately made the metonymic link from *how did this sign get here?* to *how did* I *get here?* That is, students immediately began to account for their own anxieties and disorientations on campus: talking about the ways that their experiences—marked by capitalist inequalities, racialization, heterosexism, ableist infrastructures, and international visa protocols—had made them feel already like things here were *off,* sometimes without being able to say what exactly or how.

Because we had touched on some of Sara Ahmed's ideas when they came up in our discussions of Julietta Singh's *Unthinking Mastery*, I turned toward Ahmed in this moment. Most of us felt out of place on campus (although in very different ways), and Ahmed (2006, 9–10) reminds us that "we only notice the arrival of those who appear 'out of place.' Those who are 'in place' must also arrive; they must get 'here,' but their arrival is more easily forgotten." Ahmed's *Queer Phenomenology* is a summons to attend to these conditions of arrival: to the ways that "here" is always constituted by a confluence of arrivals, and the conditions of that transit and circulation turn out to also influence the conditions of the encounter. Taking up the example of the writer at a table (in Husserl's phenomenology but also, for example, in Virginia Woolf's *A Room of One's Own*), Ahmed writes that "attention involves a political economy, or an uneven distribution of attention time between those who arrive at the writing table, which affects what they can do once they arrive (and of course, many do not even make it)" (32). This "political economy of attention" is exactly what our class was trying to articulate as we asked "Why this?" of ourselves, our course texts, and *the materiality of our meeting.* And her analysis provided a whole range of questions we might ask as corollaries of "Why this?"—questions that sent us looking from our deictic situation to the circuits, forces, networks, and structures that made "being here" something that happens for each of us.

Ahmed's account of the table begins in phenomenology: how does this table appear to me, the writer? But she quickly realizes that "we may need to supplement phenomenology with an 'ethnography of things'" (39). This means, first, retooling phenomenology with a kind of attention Marxists bring to critiques of commodity fetishism: what kinds of labor in what kinds of conditions were required for this table to come into being in the world and find its way *here* (39)? Ahmed pushes through what can often seem like an anthropocentric tendency in Marxism to locate labor solely in humans toward a more expansive account of the affective possibilities of things (she asks, "How does the 'matter' of paper matter?" [26]). In the process, Ahmed hits on orientation as a necessary concept: it is not the case that bodies exist as such and spaces exist as such and then orientation names the ways bodies circulate in pregiven spaces. Rather, orientation points toward the unfolding of worlds in their tendencies. Bodies and spaces are shaped by these material, affective encounters, and economies of affect lead to accumulations such that certain spaces are more available to some bodies than others, some bodies can reach more or different things than other bodies. Ahmed argues that whiteness is best understood as a logic that shapes how bodies and spaces co-compose each other: "whiteness becomes a social and bodily orientation given that some bodies will be more at home in a world that is oriented around whiteness" (138). Whiteness is less a property of bodies, or of spaces, than it is the affective sedimentation of "white" bodies and spaces as co-emergent across time. Ahmed looks at the specifics of a table and thinks with phenomenological questions we might consider as part of the psychology of affordances (what does this object allow me to do?), with Marxist questions about the sedimentation of human (but not just human) labor in objects that circulate, with decolonial and queer questions about how worlding unfolds in ways that make some feel "in place" because others are "out of line."

This gave us a set of orienting queries that helped us turn from Moi's provocative question to the seminar table around which we sat, where our conditions of arrival made *this* table feel different to each of us. This table turned out to make specific demands: I had to earn a PhD and be hired to teach in the English department. The students had to be (competitively) admitted to the university and then find their ways to English, whether as majors or not, enrolling in the class and paying relevant fees to hold their seat. And those institutional demands often uneasily met our individual needs as people trying to move through a world shaped by coloniality such that although we are all inescapably shaped by colonial inheritance, "shaping" takes many forms.

The sign noted something about the past: someone who lived when slavery was legal, and when Richmond, Virginia was a thriving scene of the chattel slave trade, enslaved people and justified slavery, even if other parts of Robert Ryland's life can be read as signaling different kinds of (quasi) anti-racist beliefs (he preached at a Black church). For many who have arrived at the university since its founding in the 1840s (just two decades before the city became the capital of the Confederacy), little about Ryland's slave owning would have seemed out of line, nor would it have made them feel out of place. But most of us in *this* room would not have been allowed here in the not-very-distant past. Learning together how to ask the kind of questions we asked in modern literary theory in a building whose name honors an enslaver became a difficult prospect, a "brick wall" as Ahmed (2017) put it elsewhere that keeps us from feeling "at home" (which may not be what we want to feel anyway). This feeling was one we had all experienced before, maybe even most of the time, but it was not one we brought to our conversations, especially in literature classes. Once the sign snapped our attention to it, though, we could not not think: how did we arrive here, in this place that only itself arrives via the theft of Powhattan land and the wealth accumulated from enslaved labor? Another inescapable question: How is it that so many can look at this campus, this building, and *not* see this, not feel this, not attune and ask why? These questions emerge in and as the event, and their force (dis)orients us.

The Wake as Event

Christina Sharpe's *In the Wake* is clearly addressed to a Black readership as she elaborates a theory of "wake work," a particular approach to attentive living in the wake of transatlantic slavery. Marking the address, located in the first person plural, I quote at length here in order to tease out a problem our class hit on as we took up Sharpe's book just a week after the sign appeared outside our door: what does it mean to live "in the wake" for those of us who are not Black? Note, as you read, the deictic insistence. Sharpe (2016, 15) writes:

> Living in/the wake of slavery is living "the afterlife of property" [Saidiya Hartman's phrase] and living in the afterlife of the *partus sequitur ventrem* (that which is brought forth follows the womb), in which the Black child inherits the non/status, the non/being of the mother. The inheritance of a non/status is everywhere apparent *now* in the ongoing criminalization of Black women and children. Living in the wake on a global level means living the disastrous time and effects of continued marked migrations, Mediterranean and Caribbean disasters, trans-American and -African migration, structural adjustment imposed by the International Monetary Fund that continues imperialisms/colonialisms, and more. And here, in the United States, it means living and dying through the policies of the first US Black president; it means the gratuitous violence of stop-and-frisk and Operation Clean Halls; rates of Black incarceration that boggle the mind (Black people represent 60 percent of the imprisoned population); the immanence of death as a "predictable and constitutive aspect of *this* democracy" (James and Costa Vargas 2012, 193, emphasis mine). Living in the wake means living the history and present of terror, from slavery to the present, as the ground of our everyday Black existence.

This long quotation is meant to offer a sense of the book's style of proliferating, asterisked elaborations of thought, one where the "terror" of "everyday Black existence" is a ground or "the weather." Antiblackness here names a totalizing, enveloping *scene* that endures in ways that make clear distinctions between historical modalities of antiblackness and present institutional/economic/legal/carceral educational operations impossible. Antiblackness, as the reference to the Afropessimist concept of "gratuitous violence" makes clear, is *the world* in its unfolding. But the world's unfolding for Sharpe is not ever thinkable only as antiblackness. Wake work attends to the ongoingness of antiblackness as it shapes the ongoing mattering of the world at levels and scales that we are taught to see as distinct, but it also includes practices that disrupt it, stall it, steer away from routes that would leave the materiality of its "wake" in the same shape. Sharpe writes, "I mean wake work to be a mode of inhabiting *and* rupturing this episteme with our known lived and un/imaginable lives. With that analytic we might imagine otherwise from what we know *now* in the wake of slavery" (18). Wake work, we might say, is both critical and affirmative. It attends to social death, yes, but also to what Kevin Quashie (2021) has recently called "Black aliveness."

One of Sharpe's key "events" is the ship *Zong*, which left Africa carrying "442 (or 470)" people in its hold and arrived in Jamaica four months later with only "208 living Africans on board" (35, 37). Most of the slaves were thrown overboard—although many jumped into the sea—as a result of fear of losses of "property" that had to be settled in an insurance claim: "The deposed crew recounted that it was lack of water and the insurance claim that motivated the throwing overboard. They recognized that insurance monies would not be paid if those enslaved people died 'a natural death'" (35). Weaving historical and genealogical work on the *Zong* with analysis of M. NourbeSe Philips's poem *Zong!*, Sharpe explicitly theorizes this ship and everything it tells us now about "the wake" as an event: "*The event*, which is to say, one version of one part of a more than four-hundred-year-long event" (37, emphasis in original).

Sharpe's nesting of events within an event suggests that there is something like an evental ontology of the world: the world is always becoming in and as events. We can name one of those events—happening at a scale of centuries—as antiblackness, slavery and its wake. And we can also name more discrete events *within* larger events, like the *Zong*. I might begin to sketch the importance of this claim by reading it against an extremely influential claim in settler colonial studies: Patrick Wolfe's (2006, 388) "invasion is a structure not an event." Wolf is getting here at the crucial idea that we cannot think of settler colonial invasion as a "one-off (and superseded) occurrence" in the past (388), a claim that seems similar to what Sharpe is after with the concept of the wake of slavery. The difference, however, is not exactly in the larger claim about the historical ongoingness of violent dispossession but in the understanding of what an "event" is. For Wolfe, that concept evokes something temporally bounded, over and done at a locatable moment. Events would be discrete. Yet for Sharpe, discreteness is a function not of events themselves per se but of how they can be felt and lived through from particular deictically marked locations ("here" in "*this* democracy"). This ontoepistemological difference is immediately soldered to a political question, for a structure leads to critical practice: the labor of uncovering how a system works so that it can be known in turn suggests the ability to imagine an alternatively conceptualized system. Critical analysis matters, we are told, because in imagining what is wrong with the world, one can plan a new one; the political task is dismantling or overthrowing the current system so that a better one can be erected. Such politics tend to be imagined playing out at large scales, with "the people" rising up in revolution. That is, if invasion is a structure, its undoing will still often be imagined as an event that founds a new structure, one that critique has to prefigure so it can guide praxis.

Sharpe's wake work is different. The very concept of "the wake" resists critical closure: it proliferates, held open by an asterisk. And the response to it cannot be a question of getting everyone to affirm a single critique so that large numbers can be orchestrated to enact an imagined better world. The political response adheres, precisely, in the evental nature of the world. As Brian Massumi (2015, 147) argues, "the event" is "the primary unit of the real." Massumi develops this theory of the event through a reading of Alfred North Whitehead's process philosophy where, as Didier Debaise (2017, 35) puts it, "each event is a passage, inherently unique in its moment, different from all others" and the world is made up of such events happening at all kinds of scales. For Whitehead, there is a tendency coursing through such events toward patterning: matter tends, in events, to hang together in particular ways. In each event, entities enter into a distributed becoming where a whole panoply of possible outcomes are virtually present and the passage of a *specific* event selects some of those outcomes rather than others.

Whitehead uses the name "society" to describe particular configurations of matter (a crystal is, in his lexicon, a society: this is not a question of anthropomorphism). As Debaise (2017, 73) explicates it, "the sole aim, the sole goal of a 'society' is to maintain its historic route, the movement of its inheritance, the taking up, the transmission of the acts of feeling that comprise it." Singular instances of antiblack society are not "examples" of larger, macrolevel events. Rather, what one viewpoint sees as a four-hundred-year-long event can be, from another viewpoint, innumerable events with different conditions, possibilities, and outcomes. Nothing is "given"; history does not "determine." Rather, in every event where bodies and spaces co-compose, there adheres a tendency, in antiblack world, for events to emerge that pass on antiblackness. Indeed, this is the probable outcome of most events, a kind of statistical or probable endurance of coloniality.[5] There is no "outside" the wake, but there is, and must be, possibilities for disruption, for what Sharpe calls the "otherwise." These potentialities adhere in matter: "But even if those Africans who were in the holds, who left something of their prior selves in those rooms as a trace to be discovered, and who passed through the doors of no return did not survive the holding and the sea, they, like us, are alive in hydrogen, in oxygen; in carbon, in phosphorous, and iron; in sodium and chlorine. This is what we know about those Africans thrown, jumped, dumped overboard in Middle Passage; they are with us still, in the time of the wake, known as residence time" (Sharpe 2016, 19). I read the movement from Sharpe's "like us" to "with us" as suggesting a shifting of scale, a zooming in, that might tend toward "in us," "as us." Our own wakefulness, attentiveness, is an articulation of the molecules that make up, and disrupt, the wake in its ongoing evental patterning.

I want to generally accept this evental ontology that takes shape in different ways in Sharpe, Massumi, and Whitehead. But the questions "Why this?" and "What are its conditions of arrival?" pull me back to the deictic: as a person becoming with events in the ongoingness of worlds, my "sense" of an event is often particular and situated. Thus, even though I would argue that worlds are evental "all the way down," I have also found it helpful to mark thresholds where perception and attention are agitated and shift. Especially in the classroom, the question becomes how to shift our attention to what is happening in a world, thereby opening up the possibility of tapping into specific material possibilities for "otherwise" worlding. The distinction between situations and events is enormously helpful for this purpose.[6] Lauren Berlant (2011, 5) writes that "a situation is a state of things in which *something* that will perhaps matter is unfolding amid the usual activity of life. It is a state of animated and animating suspension that forces itself on consciousness, that produces a sense of the emergence of something in the present that may become an event." Situations are the material-semiotic patterning of worlds in their becoming, and in our (antiblack) world, we have to say that coloniality and its violences adhere in the mind-bogglingly diffuse encounters and "events" (in Whitehead's sense). But for many, this violence fades into the situation: things here are not hidden—although they can take place at scales that baffle "human" sensoria—but they largely exist in a zone of deattunement. We might say, sticking with a word Berlant highlights in a reading of a John Ashbury poem, that the antiblackness of the world constitutes, in most cases, something like a background *hum*: "the thing that resonates around me, which might be heaven or bees or labor or desire or electric wires" (33).

The pedagogical task, I would argue, is to find ways to shift this background to foreground, to notice the hum, pay "maximal" attention, and bring what you can to the *event*: to have some sense (which will always only be partly about consciousness or the volition of a liberal subject) of how the world's becoming allows what Massumi calls "freedom" adhering *in* the situation as a possibility to be played, a material spur to improvising otherwise worlds: "our freedom is in how we play our implication in a field, what events we succeed in catalysing in it that bring out the latent singularity of the situation, how we inflect for novel emergences" (158). This play does not belong to an "I" so much as to the evental field itself: "This does not . . . mean that there is no 'I.' It just means that the 'I' cannot be located in advance of the event" (Manning 2016, 37).

Care in the Wake

Ahmed (2006, 103) notes in *Queer Phenomenology* that "contingency is linked . . . to the sociality of being 'with' others, to getting close enough to touch." The questions I have been proposing as spurs to open up an evental pedagogy proceed from this axiom: "contingency" names the possibilities of reorientation, disorientation, disruption, refusal, failure, and delinquency. If the crushing weight of the wake proceeds through the tendings of manifold events, so much so that coloniality and antiblackness can come to *feel* like just "the world," then our task is to feel out spaces of contingency where its endurance or perseverance breaks down. Rather than a large-scale planned revolution following on knowing critique of structures of dispossession and accumulation, an attunement to the evental becoming of the world suggests smaller, seemingly "minor" forms of anti-antiblack and de-colonial agitation.[7] We do not necessarily (or only) need conscious understanding of what is wrong with the workings of this world, so much as we need to participate in economies where we come to *feel* (that is, to perceive and pay attention to) the immanent, ongoing, be-coming of worlds, where this feeling might lead us to seek a simple aim, one that like Moi's question is simultaneously abstract and precise in its deixis: how can we disrupt *this* event's tending toward antiblackness?

The word Sharpe gives us for this perception and attention is "care," and for her, it is simultaneously emotional and material: in short, it is "affective." She writes, "I want to think 'care' as a problem for thought. I want to think care in the wake as a problem for thinking and of and for Black non/being in the world. Put another way, *In the Wake: On Blackness and Being* is a work that insists and performs that thinking needs care . . . and that thinking and care need to stay in the wake" (5). The forms of perception and attention Sharpe elaborates in her book—including the asterisk and annotation—are indexed to what it means to perform this care *for her*, and she generalizes to what that work may entail for Black people. Reading this book from a differ-ent perspective but fully convinced of her claims about the histori-cally/ontologically evental nature of worlds, in the modern literary theory seminar we wondered what it means to feel the wake from our own deictic perspectives in the situation.

Erin Manning's concept of "event-care" answers to this, and it points us toward an evental pedagogy that is simultaneously hyper-aware (in a "critical" register of how histories of coloniality and heterosex-ism have marked us) of differences we usually note in grammars of identity but also always alert to tapping into something else, into the more-than, perhaps into what Mel Chen (2023) has recently called "emergent being" that is belatedly "summed" into the forms iden-tity can capture. Manning (2015, 165–66) writes, hitting on "care" as a concept: "Here I don't mean the subjectivity of human-to-human care, but rather how an event produces an environment that can sustain different kinds of participation which include different af-fective speeds, including the slownesses that we perhaps associate with depression, or the speeds we associate with anxiety. With event-care perhaps there is a kind of collective tending that comes close to the sense that Guattari gave to the word 'therapeutic.'" Event-care is hyper-indexical, oriented toward exactly what is happening *here, now* without assuming or requiring that that deictic situation homogenizes. Evental force is centrifugal, not centripetal, for the most part, and yet there are tendencies that adhere in the micro-events that make up what I, following Berlant, call "situations." The question for us as we hone attention and perception—by utilizing operators like the Moi and Ahmed questions—is how to care for *this* event such that whatever it is we bring tends somewhere otherwise than coloniality and antiblackness.

This participation, then, has very little to do with "identity" or even subjectivity. This is why Massumi (2015, 171) can say to people considering what participation in an event means, "Don't bring your products, bring your process. . . . Don't perform yourself, co-catalyze a collective event with us." In events, what we call identity would seem to be part of the beginning coordinates for any occurrence: they are inseparable from the *tending* of events in particular directions with particular orientations. Tapping into evental conditions moves us away from such coordinates, instead opening up ways to feel out how antiblack tendencies can be blocked, diverted, and simply dropped.

Sharpe's book is written toward a Black readership that might crystallize around her first-person plural, and some of my students found, and find, themselves in that grammar. For the rest of us, especially in what Laz Lima calls "White Serving Institutions," we might linger with what Syd Zolf (2021, 12) writes about reading Sharpe in *No One's Witness*: "Encountering the 'monstrous intimacies' (Sharpe's term) of transatlantic slavery and its afterlives demands that white viewers/readers look directly at Medusa's obliterative head and listen to what is said and unsaid in the monstrous duration, not as voyeurs or spectators but as participants in an ongoing disaster." How do we participate in this disaster? How is the taking place of *this* very class at *this* institution a modality of that participation? Our study is an event in which the wake of transatlantic slavery conditions our environment, our weather, and our problem is how we enable colonial endurance or seek out possibilities for disruption.

In our seminar room, we had to reckon with all of this reading Sharpe. Indeed, she explicitly includes the school in her asterisked elaboration of the hold of Middle Passage, noting "the reappearance of the slave ship in everyday life in the form of the prison, the camp, and the school" (21). Asking our questions alongside Sharpe tuned our attention to the deictic force of the sign, and we realized that the name of the building says everything, hiding nothing (except through our own laziness and disinclination to ask of names, "Why this?"): this building, these grounds, this institution are not just historically implicated in antiblackness: we are (differentially) oriented in relation to *this* ship. Some of us are in the hold, while others load the ship, work on it, are investors in its endeavors, or passengers hopefully scanning toward futures of opportunity they can sense *only because they are on the ship*. Antiblackness affects every single one of us. Situations are where antiblack tendencies accumulate as orientations—habitual movements through spaces—that extend and continue antiblackness. The colonial rupture of worlds into a homogenous world is our inheritance in the materiality of our situations. And the question for us, in this event is, feeling what we can now feel of the wake, the wake that is in us and moves through us, what can we do? "Why this?" and "What are its conditions of arrival?" are questions that open the present to maximal (often other-than) conscious attention to the deictic. In thus shifting the background hum to the foreground, their combined asking creates conditions for feeling this particular sign not as a question of the "past" but of the present and of the future, or rather, futures. And this answering is inseparable from another question: What can we do now, *here,* to break the homogenizing pattern so other futures might arrive?

Notes

1   Although "I" wrote this essay, my thinking here emerges from the event. I would like to acknowledge the intellectual contributions of students in that class (Nathan Burns, Logan Etheredge, Sabrina Garcia, Joyce Garner, Krishna Lohiya, Katherine Murbach, Tracy Naschek, Claire Tate, Olivia Tennyson, Madeline Tolsdorf, Will Walker, Daniel Williams, and Yang Yang) and in the "Care, Touch, Collectivities" seminar I was reading *In the Wake* with as I wrote this chapter (Ngan Bui, Olive Gallmeyer, Kenedi Gallogly, Shira Greer, TaShira Iverson, Sam Mickey, Julia Nalecz, Kelly Saverino, Lily Von Spreckelsen, and Alison Zhang). My thinking about evental ontologies was profoundly shaped by teaching the "Event-Full Affect" seminar with Chad Shomura at the 2019 Society for the Study of Affect Summer School.

2   University of Richmond Black Student Coalition, Protect Our Web, accessed January 9, 2023, https://protectourweb.wixsite.com/urbsc.

3 Nick Anderson, "Debate Over Racism and Building Names Intensifies at University of Richmond as Top Trustee Comes Under Scrutiny." *Washington Post*, April 2, 2021, https://www.washingtonpost.com/education/2021/04/02/urichmond-racism-building-names-queally/.

4 We might note here Ashley Barnwell's (2020, 1) argument in *Critical Affect* that what is at stake is not method but "genres of criticism": ways of thinking and writing that "best capture . . . the emotional complexity of social life." Barnwell writes that "we might think about our methods as part of the very social flux that we seek to address" (15), which is, mutatis mutandis, the orientation I am proposing here toward pedagogy.

5 Katherine McKittrick (2021, 105) notes that "premature death is an algorithmic variable," spurring the question, "What happens to our understanding of black humanity when our analytical frames do not emerge from a broad swathe of numbing racial violence, but, instead, from multiple and untracked enunciations of black life?"

6 I offer a much more extended account of the situation/event distinction in *Animate Literacies* (2019).

7 See Chen (2018).

References

Ahmed, Sara. 2006. *Queer Phenomenology: Orientations, Objects, Others*. Durham, NC: Duke University Press.

Ahmed, Sara. 2017. *Living a Feminist Life*. Durham, NC: Duke University Press.

Barnwell, Ashley. 2020. *Critical Affect: The Politics of Method*. Edinburgh: Edinburgh University Press.

Berlant, Lauren. 2011. *Cruel Optimism*. Durham, NC: Duke University Press.

Best, Stephen, and Sharon Marcus. 2009. "The Way We Read Now." *Representations* 108 (1): 1–21.

Chen, Mel Y. 2018. "Agitation." SAQ 113 (3): 551–66.

Chen, Mel Y. 2023. "Differential Being and Emergent Agitation." In *Crip Genealogies*, edited by Mel Y. Chen, Alison Kafer, Eunjung Kim, and Julie Avril Minich, 297–317. Durham, NC: Duke University Press.

Debaise, Didier. 2017. *Nature as Event: The Lure of the Possible*. Translated by Michael Halewood. Durham, NC: Duke University Press.

Harney, Stefano and Fred Moten. 2013. *The Undercommons: Fugitive Planning and Black Study*. New York: Minor Compositions.

Manning, Erin. 2016. *The Minor Gesture*. Durham, NC: Duke University Press.

Massumi, Brian. 2015. "Immediation." In *Politics of Affect*, 146–76. Malden, MA: Polity.

McKittrick, Katherine. 2021. *Dear Science and Other Stories*. Durham, NC: Duke University Press.

Moi, Toril. 2017. "'Nothing Is Hidden': From Confusion to Clarity; or, Wittgenstein on Critique." In *Critique and Postcritique*, edited by Elizabeth S. Anker and Rita Felski, 31–49. Durham, NC: Duke University Press.

Quashie, Kevin. 2021. *Black Aliveness, or a Poetics of Being*. Durham, NC: Duke University Press.

Sedgwick, Eve Kosofsky. 2003. *Touching Feeling: Affect, Pedagogy, Performativity*. Durham, NC: Duke University Press.

Sharpe, Christina. 2016. *In the Wake: On Blackness as Being*. Durham, NC: Duke University Press.

Snaza, Nathan. 2019. *Animate Literacies: Literature, Affect, and the Politics of Humanism*. Durham, NC: Duke University Press.

Wolfe, Patrick. 2006. "Settler Colonialism and the Elimination of the Native." *Journal of Genocide Research* 8 (4): 387–409.

Wynter, Sylvia. 2003. "Unsettling the Coloniality of Being/Power/Truth/Freedom: Towards the Human, After Man, Its Overrepresentation—An Argument." CR: *The New Centennial Review* 3 (3): 257–337.

Zolf, Syd. 2021. *No One's Witness: A Monstrous Poetics*. Durham, NC: Duke University Press.

Dylan Robinson and Patrick Nickleson

What is the feeling of knowing music? How should we name the mechanism by which music scholarship builds disciplinary knowledge on top of or in relation to shared affective and loving experiences of music? Everyone knows music; but the primary export of music studies has been a disciplinary language that makes music strange to those who know it best.

Disciplinary knowledge of music, we want to insist, is an epistemological claim on an affective domain. This knowing-feeling, we want to argue, underwrites relationships to music as knowable, rentable, sellable, or a particular object of mastery. As Eva Mackey (2016) has shown, certainty is a key focus of settler relationships to land and resources, with the goal of guaranteeing long-term certainty for property, investment, and resource extraction. What structures need to be in place to provide that feeling of certainty? To whom and at what costs? Masterful knowledge of music, across a variety of disciplinary and discursive settings, is always premised on prior dispossessions of knowledge. These dispossessions render others as ignorant, wrong, criminal, or backward and are closely tied to parallel processes of dispossession in land. We are both concerned—Dylan Robinson (as xwélmexw/xwelítem) and Patrick Nickleson (as white settler

Canadian)—to critique the modes of mastery prominent not only in the academic study of music but in music as a practiced and performed, written and sounded, field of disciplinary engagement. How might we find ways of working that avoid merely reinstating new modes of mastery? Julietta Singh has provided models for breaking with mastery in total, as against old critiques of mastery—pervasive in both anti-colonial and postcolonial literatures—which imagine a new master to replace the old one. We cannot treat colonial mastery as distinct from intellectual mastery: "To put it crudely, a colonial master understands his superiority over others by virtue of his ability to have conquered them materially and by his insistence on the supremacy of his practices and worldviews over theirs, which renders 'legitimate' the forceful imposition of his worldviews" (Singh 2018, 9). Intellectual, disciplinary, and scientific mastery have always been the primary backdrop—the feeling of knowing, the comfortable affective relationship to a cozy world, the certainty of one's rightness and justness—to any subsequent practice of the imposition of more violent or colonial mastery. "There is an intimate link between the mastery enacted through colonization and other forms of mastery that we often believe today to be harmless, worthwhile, even virtuous. To be characterized *as the master of a language, or a literary tradition, or an instrument, for instance, is widely understood to be laudable.* Yet as a pursuit, mastery invariably and relentlessly reaches toward the indiscriminate control over something—whether human or inhuman, animate or inanimate. It aims for the full submission of an object—or something objectified" (Singh 2018, 9–10; emphasis added). It is this rendering objective, reimagined not as a disciplinary gift but as a dispossession from prior ways of knowing, that concerns us here.

Music scholars call on affect theories to mine the visceral impact of sweaty bodies on a dance floor, or vibrating bodies at a drone metal show, as opposed to those knowing readings that might set out to analyze and reify musical forms (Graber and Sumera 2020). A recurring feature of the affective focus in (ethno)musicology is that affect theory offers something to music: a set of conceptual tools and key terms for thinking through music in its nonsemantic, presemantic, or extralinguistic registers. Much important work has come out of such readings, and we do not intend to challenge their claims. We want instead to consider the place of the affective *feeling of knowing* music that develops somewhere earlier along a causal chain in thinking and writing about music. Our concern is not music as an object, practice, or vibration but rather the nexus of disciplinary, pedagogic, and epistemological relationships to music (and musicking) that music studies risks taking for granted.

How, then, does it feel to know music? What different modalities of feeling and knowing do musicologists recognize as appropriate and to what musics? Our disciplinary and "scientific" knowledge, we want to argue, risks alienating lovers of music who recognize in musicological writing, before all else, their own estrangement from their beloved music. Knowing and feeling are inseparable if not in sounding music, then in how we write, speak, and think about it. We think that these can be read into how scholars, writers, critics, artists, musicians, and legal structures *address* music. Do we "know" it as an object, a person, a property, a friend—and what feelings of certainty or mastery does this knowing underwrite? Through appropriation, sampling, and theft, understood in relation to "intellectual property," Euro-American settler musicians and institutions have constantly reinvented methods of enclosing musical recordings as tools for dispossessing the wealth of Black and Indigenous musicality. We are attentive to how music studies often takes on the form of such possessiveness, and how that propriety is extended as an asset—literally, productive of wealth—to white structures of knowing music as objectified in musical property. The dispossession from prior listening experience is not merely a decolonial metaphor but correlates with epistemic violence against nonhuman life.

How Are We Supposed to Know Music?

Guides on writing about music aimed at an undergraduate audience articulate unspoken disciplinary priorities about how to address music as a discursive object. Those ready to begin writing about music are assumed to be performers already fluent in the "literate" tradition of Western European art music; guides thus appeal to students' experience of "mastering" particular technical passages as paralleling the need to develop a fluent, authoritative writing style. A widely read guide by the musicologist Jonathan Bellman draws attention to the danger of novices, amateurs, and the musically illiterate trying to write about music: "Because most people love music, writers tend to assume they can write about it on a technical level for which they are in fact manifestly unequipped. . . . One can maintain a lifetime's interest in music, with a long history of concert attendance and a large collection of recordings, perhaps even singing in a church or community choir and playing in folk- or popular-music groups, and still have no acquired musical literacy" (Bellman 2007, 25). In a similar guide, Richard J. Wingell (2009, 6) warns students against any romanticism or poetic interpretation, disparaging "gushing prose about babbling brooks, chattering woodwinds, the imagined feelings of the composer at the time, or the fevered dreams of the listener's imagination."

What these guides make clear, in their frequent references to amateurism, naivety, and love, is that the danger in writing about music is not ignorance. It is rather that most who want to write on music already feel that they know enough to begin writing. Bellman (2007, 72–73) insists, from what world we're not sure, that "essays on musical subjects are far more common inside the university environment than outside it." The model of ignorance here is not one of the blank slate to be filled up with knowledge but of the need to paper over loving, amateur knowledge with a disciplined flood of expert scientific analyses. The danger is not that students will have nothing to say but that they will have too much to say. Against Bellman's wishful thinking, the world beyond the academy is awash with such writing—open any music criticism website, YouTube channel, or your favorite newspapers and magazines to find writing by folks duped into thinking, according to Bellman's standards, that they are experts. Although we have no interest in either valorizing or criticizing a selection of such writing, we would like to turn our attention to the immediate border of music studies scholarship. We have both recently found inspiration and disciplinary hope in the work of Black studies scholars who theorize music's expression, form, and life.

What marks Black studies' musicological difference from conventional musicology? In short, the way that music is *addressed* in the scholarship. This must be marked as an affective-epistemological distinction. *How* we know something impacts how we address it; how we address it impacts how we feel it; and around and around. Although we could similarly highlight the recent impact of work by Fred Moten, Ashon Crawley, or Greg Tate, we have been particularly drawn to Katherine McKittrick's work for how she addresses music within her thought. In particular, McKittrick's (2016, 80n2) engagement with citation regularly calls on the importance of music, as when, in the first footnote to an essay, she tells her reader that all citations come from Sylvia Wynter, before continuing, "To assist with my reading of music histories, biographies, sounds, and theories, I have been engaging the following thinkers: Richard Iton, Clyde Woods, LeRoi Jones, Mark Campbell, Jacques Attali, Édouard Glissant, Paul Gilroy, Fred Moten, Sylvia Wynter, Robin D.G. Kelley, Lawrence Levine, Angela Davis, Alexander Weheliye, Oliver Sacks, Vijay Iyer, Daniel J. Levitin, Nina Simone, Betty Davis, Funkadelic, Drexciya, Kanye West, Erykah Badu, Jimmy Cliff, and Michael Jackson." Michael Jackson and Nina Simone, like the collective names Funkadelic and Drexciya, are *thinkers* on a par with what we might normally consider "theoretical" work by Attali, Glissant, Gilroy, and Moten. Even for all of our engagements with music and musicians, it is an extreme rarity for a music studies scholar to cite musicians as *thinkers*; instead, we engage their work as objects, the musicians as primarily authors, a legal fiction that is necessarily imagined to precede the production of consequent works. McKittrick's writing about music clearly registers a different epistemological and affective relationship to music as known and felt.

McKittrick's citational engagements continue in this vein. In an essay cowritten with Alexander G. Weheliye, many footnotes simply point the reader to songs, treated as texts, from Nas, Rihanna, Mariah Carey, Timbaland, Kanye West, and others (McKittrick and Weheliye 2017). Another essay relies on Nas's lyrics as a central discursive mechanism through which to pivot the article in a new direction (McKittrick 2015). McKittrick's mode of addressing music is not uncommon among many writers in Black studies; it is clear that music is a different kind of object than conventionally understood among Euro-American music scholars. The relationship to music is less one of mastering an object and much nearer perhaps to a relationship of knowing, intimacy, or love. Indeed, *love* plays a crucial role in this literature (it already appeared above in Bellman as a danger). The preponderance of music-loving amateurs (*amāre*) is an uncomfortable problem for the musicological fear of incorrect knowledge. But Black studies considerations of music regularly turn to love. In his reading of the role of Black popular cultures, above all music, prior to the establishment of formal political power for Black Americans, Richard Iton (2008, 8) gives love a determinant role. Love is rarely rendered as political in music scholarship even though the majority of us come to the field from a deep devotion to music and the love of a particular music that pushes us to recognize it as demanding further study. Nevertheless, "I like this music"—let us not even broach "I *love* it"—is one of the first things we are pushed to leave behind as we are disciplined into critical scholarship on music. In reading scholars like McKittrick, Iton, and Weheliye who write about music without appealing to "musicology," it comes to feel as if the entire field of music studies is an elaborate alibi to avoid speaking directly about love.[1] Indeed, Ian Biddle (2006) notes as much, arguing that Guido Adler's foundational delineation of musicology necessarily required "wresting the study of music from the amateur, from that 'lover' of music, the hopeless *enthusiast.*"

Perhaps music scholarship is less concerned to *educate* nonacademic writers in how to speak about music and more concerned to *dispossess* a different felt relationship with music. Amateurs are not a threat because they do not know music. They are a threat because they know all too well, and thus, their form of knowing must be dispossessed and reconstructed as *wrong*. Music studies, discursively and pedagogically, begins not by building a new epistemological structure but from clearing the land of its inhabitants (those musical *amāres* that we all are) by knowing in music a mode of listening that informs amateurs why they should not be there. Musicology becomes a discourse of dispossession and enclosure, one that provides a language of feeling that, to return to Singh, renders appropriate the forceful imposition of one mode of knowing on another.

To consider a few parallel instances of certainty built up through dispossession, we momentarily write from our individual experience of knowing-feeling music in the next sections. First, Patrick addresses the troubled "ethics" of sampling in hip-hop through its dispossessions under Euro-American copyright law. Dylan then recounts witnessing firsthand the aesthetic alibis and violent danger produced by knowing music in its infinite, free circulation. We then reunite to consider how these two—which we introduce as if in paradoxical conflict—begin from similar, though opposing, primary dispossessions.

Knowledge, Dispossession, and Enclosure
in Sample-Based Hip-Hop

What is the affective experience of not knowing? I (Patrick) feel that I am oriented outside of my disciplinary form of listening as identification-by-extraction, or knowledge as certainty, when I listen out in the world. I want to propose that we imagine a particular orientation toward ambivalence or uncertainty, a well-informed curiosity, as an impossible ideal for listening and knowing. I am thinking here of an experience I have had, I think, only two or three times. I would be out walking in the streets of Toronto when I encounter one of my favorite songs. Rather, I encounter two of my favorite songs. It is only the most fleeting uncertainty: five seconds, or maybe ten if there is enough ambient noise to distract me from noticing some slight alterations, a hiccup, as the looped bassline restarts. Even if it is only five seconds, the feeling of charged, excited uncertainty creates a qualitative thrill that stretches well beyond its quantitative duration. The sliding bass riff, in either case, lets me know that I am about to encounter one of my favorite songs. But is it Lou Reed's 1972 glam rock hit "Walk on the Wild Side"? Or is it A Tribe Called Quest's 1990 "golden age" hip-hop classic "Can I Kick It?" I wish that this indistinct knowing-feeling—so common to listeners of sample-based musics—was one that I experienced more often. The thrill of not knowing almost turns to disappointment when the matter is settled. I want to propose that this thrill of unknowing, prior to being frustrated by its own settled certainty, could be an important value for settler listeners to feel and know.

American copyright in 1990 was laying the foundations that would allow Reed to make a simple claim when he first heard "Can I Kick It?": that's mine. He knew, with all the certainty of authorial knowing, that he had been wronged. The extractive and property-driven American ideal of musical property in copyright makes it such that trespass on any inch of Reed's territory was equivalent to breaking into and squatting in his home. The landed property metaphor is instructive here, as musical copyright operates on an entangled back and forth such that, as Nick Hayes (2020, 18) writes, "it is hard to tell which is a metaphor for the other." The weight of the law supportive of white, Euro-American intellectual property, even as it was newly reforming, allowed a full property claim: almost as if the members of A Tribe Called Quest were standing on the street selling bootlegged copies of Reed's album *Transformer* and pocketing the cash.

Discussions of sampling are typically framed as complex ethical quandaries: "Is sampling a form of theft?" A more trenchant approach might ask about a longer history of reference, appropriation, citation, and transformation in American popular musics. A Tribe Called Quest's album *People's Instinctive Travels and the Paths of Rhythm* was released in 1990 as part of what is retrospectively considered the "golden age" of sample-based hip-hop because the compositional technique was not yet illegal or as administratively burdensome as it would soon become. Albums like *People's Instinctive Travels*, De La Soul's *Three Feet High and Rising*, and Public Enemy's *Fear of a Black Planet* (all 1989–90) presented hectic and eclectic networks of samples from obscure and popular, commercial and archival recordings. "The creative field was wide open," Kembrew McLeod and Peter DiCola (2011, 21) write, "with no significant legal or administrative fences yet erected." Sampling could be dense, polyphonic, and noisy because it understood the totality of recorded music as a commons accessible to anyone with the time and patience to dig in the crates. Sampling's illegality came after the fact because many of the artists sampled— with the support and push of their labels and lawyers—realized that a whole new means of producing wealth lay in front of them if only the legal language could be put in place for its capture. When "samples" were reimagined as extractable and rentable, carrying the totality of the authored music in their fleeting seconds of use, the master recordings developed a new value as *capital*. That is, through sampling the original songs became an unchanging primary financial resource from which to draw secondary interest and rents. Things changed then. Intellectual property mechanisms and legal processes had to be rethought as the music industry recognized hip-hop not just as a genre or a fad "but as a solid source of sales revenue" (27). Suddenly, copyright "trolls" and artists' rights clearing houses could speculate on and financialize copyrights by buying up artists' catalogs en masse in hopes of collecting escalated rents and profits when someone comes knocking to lease the sample. Lawyers and artists of Reed's scale could redraw the boundaries of recorded music through a process of legal enclosure in keeping with their own ways of knowing.

Twenty-five years after "Can I Kick It?" was released, Tribe member Phife Dawg told *Rolling Stone* that Reed had no issue with the inclusion of the sample; he may have even liked its use: "'I remember with [record label] Jive, there was a problem with the sample being cleared,' Phife recalls. 'I don't think they cleared the sample, and instead of Lou Reed saying, "You can't use it," he said, "Y'all can use it, but I get all the money from that." Phife says Reed took 100 percent of the royalties and publishing and 'to this day, we haven't seen a dime from that song'" (quoted in Newman 2015).

Reed's claims against A Tribe Called Quest already rest on a prior legal fiction. Reed is not playing the bassline that connects the two songs, and it is very unlikely that Reed "wrote" that bassline as historically imagined by copyright protections. The performer here is famed session bassist Herbie Flowers who, in all likelihood, created the bassline in response to what Reed brought in, which would have been the real meat and potatoes of a copyright claim in music: lyrics and melody. In Flowers's bass playing reproduced on "Can I Kick It?" Reed heard *his* song and knew *he* was owed something. (As a wage laborer, Flowers never had a property claim in the song. He told BBC Radio in 2005 that the bassline is the way it is—double-tracked fretless upright bass and fretted electric bass—because he was paid per instrument. So a $17 session fee became a $34 session fee. [See Furman 2018, 82.]) When that bassline, which had become Reed's through American intellectual property's reliance on the metaphor to property in landed real estate, appeared elsewhere through the labor, listening, and performance of A Tribe Called Quest, Reed was able to comfortably feel, by extension, *that is also mine*. Both this in-session dispossession of Flowers for cash payment and the later retrospective dispossession of A Tribe Called Quest's new creation as a form of rent, operate on the troubling fantasy that (white) authorial copyrights are infinite, inherent, and obvious. Forms of knowing uphold and are upheld by music in its affective, felt materiality.

The "ethics" of sampling, as in the Lou Reed/A Tribe Called Quest example, is an ongoing and contentious issue that demands consideration outside the limits of sample-based musics. Using the term "racial regimes of ownership," Brenna Bhandar (2018, 2) names the ways that "property laws and racial subjectivity developed in relation to one another" in early modern literature. We see much the same in how sampling calls on the linguistic slippages between intellectual and landed property, ownership and labor, racism and capitalism even into the 1990s (and beyond). Ownership and subjectivity, for Bhandar, are held in relation precisely through one's capacity to appropriate: not only to steal, purchase, or plunder but also one's capacity to call on "scientific techniques of measurement and quantification, economic visions of land and life rooted in logics of abstraction, culturally inscribed notions of white European superiority, and philosophical concepts of the proper person who possessed the capacity to appropriate" (6). This practice has been labeled "accumulation by dispossession" by David Harvey, as "primitive accumulation" by Marx, and as "racial capitalism" by Cedric Robinson. The British lands rights activist Nick Hayes (2020) recently noted that rigid defenses of property provide our best access to the palpable affect of "ownership anxiety." We witness the precarity and uncertainty of normative landed property rights in how consistently they have to be extended and reframed (not to mention how well stocked the bureaucracies are with partisans simultaneously insistent on their self-evidence and universality). Ownership, Hayes argues, has no justification save for its own reiteration. Copyright law is similarly designed, every decade or so, to (re)naturalize Reed's claim over both Flowers's bassline and its reappearance in Tribe's music (and always at the ongoing dispossession of whatever remains of a creative commons).

Euro-American popular music has long been noted for its appropriations of Black musical and cultural practices; less often discussed is how these appropriations rely on copyright law to produce rentier relationships that dispossess people of color while funneling wealth and legal power to white property holders. The framing of copyright on musical arrangements in the United States was articulated such that "the wealth of the [predominantly Black] jazz industry has traditionally been consolidated among the [mostly white] copyright holders" of the American songbook standards (Demers 2006, 43). Dennis Bovell says his reggae band Matumbi had a falling out with their record label because they wanted the band to spend studio time playing covers of white pop songs so that "someone else would clock all the publishing [royalties]" (Marre 2011). Funneling in the opposite direction is a rarity.[2] When the Rolling Stones built a half-century career on copying the blues, there was no immediate transfer of wealth to recognize any form of theft. When Lou Reed precisely copied the opening riff of the classic Rolling Stones song "Brown Sugar" for his song "Walk and Talk It," it was considered a clever wink to knowing fans rather than an instance of explicit theft. In the fall of 2021 as we were writing this chapter, the Rolling Stones announced that they would stop performing "Brown Sugar" on tour—a song they have apparently performed at every live performance of their unending career—because the song's lyrics are an only lightly veiled discussion of raping a female slave. Media coverage of the decision was typical of this moment in pearl-clutching responses to "cultural appropriation": how could they, why would they, how did we not notice? Were the Stones "right" to ditch the song? Conservative commentators offer defenses of a classic from another era, bemoaning "changing times," oversensitive youth, and political correctness run amok. Discussion has not turned to the broader question of reparation for the presumably billions of dollars generated by the Rolling Stones industrial complex through the dispossession and enclosure of Black musical culture. Rock music originated in and very often copies Delta blues, but we are meant to view that as a creative transformation of a collective musical patrimony, not the imitation of a particular item of intellectual property. The Rolling Stones *know* the blues as a commons, not stolen but "borrowed" from—mined as a form of veneration—much as Lou Reed knows that the opening riff of a song, copied directly, is not "theft" but allusion: unless it is his song and thus a source of potential revenue. Copyright chugs along on artists' felt certainty of the validity of transfer between white parties, reframing what might be theft or illegal copying in other contexts as simple and legal reference.

The Wealth of Indigenous Songlife

Sampling is only one popular music example of the white financialization of the music of people of color as grounded in the (re)production of particular forms of knowing music as obvious and natural while others are wrong and even criminal. Salvage ethnography as a method in early twentieth-century anthropology and ethnomusicology offers numerous examples of white academics heading out into the "field" to record the stories, songs, and voices of Indigenous people, with the subsequent recordings becoming sources of wealth and academic authority. Indigenous scholars Trevor Reed (Hopi) and Robin Gray

(Ts'msyen/Mikisew Cree) have each written on one such example: Columbia University's Laura Boulton Collection of Traditional and Liturgical Music. Boulton's collection, which included several recordings of ceremonial songs from Reed's Hopi community, was sold to Columbia for $10,000. "Absent any evidence of a contract between Boulton and the performers," Reed (2016, 293) writes, Columbia University "would have difficulty proving it received a valid 'right of possession' from Boulton." As a result, "the Tribe could potentially reclaim ownership under NAGPRA [Native American Graves Protection and Repatriation Act]." Boulton's archival deposit also provided for the generation of long-term wealth. "Dated June 14, 1962," Gray writes, "the contract between the Trustees of Columbia University and Laura Boulton . . . stipulated that, beginning January 21 1964, the collection, notes, rights, title, and interest would be transferred to the university. The contract specifies that Boulton would be paid $5,000 on February 15 and August 15 each year during her lifetime." When she passed away in 1980, Boulton had been paid $170,000 from Columbia as a result of her initial sale; Columbia, moreover, "would retain the rights to the collection, including the authority to determine who can transcribe, analyze, or publish the speech of music contained therein" (Gray 2019, 725).

It's difficult to imagine a more explicit instance of the disciplinary split of ignorance and mastery, raw material and extractive capital, as audible in musical epistemologies. But my (Dylan's) work in collaboration with the Nisg̱a'a government in coastal British Columbia has recently brought much needed attention to the dynamics of such appropriations of Indigenous song where the emphasis is less on financialization than the long-term construction of a Canadian national identity in music. In 1965, Canadian composer Harry Somers composed *Kuyas*, a work for flute, soprano, and percussion. Musically, the piece appropriates a Nisg̱a'a limx' ooy—a dirge sung for the passing of a family member. It was collected by ethnographer Marius Barbeau and composer Ernest MacMillan on their 1927 expedition to the Nass River in Nisg̱a'a territory and subsequently transcribed into Western notation by MacMillan (1955) and published in his book *Music in Canada* (1955). It was in this book that Somers first encountered the Nisg̱a'a limx' ooy and used it as the basis of *Kuyas* and later incorporated it into his opera *Louis Riel* (1967).

This limx' ooy was renamed "Song of Skateen" by Barbeau and MacMillan because of its hereditary ownership by the House of

Sg'atiin. In its life as an ethnographic recording, Western music transcription, and as appropriated in Somers's *Kuyas* and *Louis Riel*, the limx' ooy exists as a song. Yet for Nisga'a people, it exists simultaneously as a living expression of mourning and as a lived connection to the land. It is known through its life. In his own way, the way of early twentieth-century ethnographic knowing, even Barbeau (1933, 106–7) himself recognizes this in-betweenness, writing that "the lament of the mourners rose plaintively and fell in descending curves, like the wind in the storm. It was the voice of nature crying out." He continues, "Even their weeping was sing-song like."

The hundred-plus songs recorded by Barbeau and MacMillan on the Nass River in 1927, even paired alongside Boulton's extensive collection, represent a fraction of Indigenous knowledge collected by folklorists, ethnographers, and anthropologists without documenting the proper protocol (Indigenous law) that governs who may sing, tell, speak, and share this cultural wealth. In addition to ethnographers promoting the use of these songs to non-Indigenous composers in an attempt to define a "Canadian musical tradition," other composers have assumed that because such songs and stories were written down in anthropological texts or existed as part of museum collections, they were simply available for use. This history of appropriation sits alongside the Canadian government's prohibition of Indigenous peoples from practicing our culture and often from singing the very same songs composers were incorporating into their compositions. Such censorship included the Indian Residential School system that ran for over one hundred years (1870s–1996), where thousands of Indigenous children were prohibited from speaking their languages and singing their songs. It also included section 3 of the Canadian government's Indian Act that, for over seventy years (1880–1951), considered sun dances and singing and dancing in potlatch and winter dances a criminal offense: "Every Indian or other person who engages in or assists in celebrating the Indian festival known as the 'Potlatch' or in the Indian dance known as the 'Tamanawas' is guilty of a misdemeanor, and shall be liable to imprisonment for a term of not more than six months nor less than two months."[3]

In this time of great precarity, many of our ancestors were convinced that sharing their songs would keep them safe for future generations of our people. Many agreed to have their songs recorded believing that the Indian Act's censorship from performing our songs and dances would result in their eventual loss. Little did our ancestors know that by sharing their songs with ethnographers for safekeeping, their songs might then become part of compositions without their consent. Returning to the ontological distinction of Indigenous songs as more than songs, Indigenous songs are also known-felt by Indigenous listeners as having life, as medicine, as primary historical documentation, and used as the equivalent to land title (as that which exists to bring the listener back into connection with the land through listening). Because such songs are more than songs, to have such songs appropriated in compositions has ramifications far beyond the infringement of copyright or Indigenous hereditary rights.

Three Feelings for a Song I Refuse to Hear (Dylan)

On Not Listening to the Limx' ooy at the Opera

To sing a limx' ooy outside of the appropriate ceremonial context and by someone other than the hereditary rights holder is not just to break Nisg̱a'a law but also to release its spirit, which can have negative impacts on the lives of the singers and listeners. I remember going to the remount of the opera *Louis Riel* in 2017 in Toronto, produced by the Canadian Opera Company and the National Arts Centre. The particular point in the aria when this Nisg̱a'a song is used is considered by many to be the high point of the opera because of its aesthetic beauty. I sat in the audience, knowing that Nisg̱a'a friends were also there, knowing that they were sitting in the audience not to hear the beauty of this work but to assess the degree of infraction the misuse of this limx' ooy represented. I knew it would likely be a painful listening experience for them. Along with other Indigenous audience members who were present that night, I also needed to make a decision: would I listen to this song that has a significantly negative spiritual impact not just on Nisg̱a'a listeners but all listeners? Sitting with my friend Cheryl L'Hirondelle, a Cree-Métis artist and singer, we decided to cover our ears for a period of about four minutes: the very same moment that other audience members were anticipating as the "high point" of the opera.

After the performance, I met up with some friends, several of whom were Nisg̱a'a, to chat. I remember their faces were graven and drained of life. They did not look as if they had heard an opera. They looked as one might look after receiving news of a death of a loved one. For the next hour, they explained to me in detail the violence that they heard, how they witnessed brutality inflicted on a loved one. One might assume, as I did before I met with them, that the transformation of a traditional limx' ooy sung by a single male voice into an aria for an operatically trained soprano supported by orchestra would result in an experience of affective distancing because of the strong differences in its presentation. Yet despite such differences, my friends noted that because the melody of the song is the same in the opera, it carried with it the same life and spiritual impact as the original. In fact, the combination of the melody with Somers's compositional treatment heightened the pain they felt while listening. Nisga'a who heard the limx' ooy embedded in the aria did not hear Somers's aesthetic manipulation of a melody; they instead heard the violent dismemberment of life. It is no understatement to say that for my friends, listening became a site of pain from witnessing violence against kin. To talk about appropriation or infringement of rights alone in this case is a gross mischaracterization of what it means to know through listening as an experience violence. This response is consistent with the more-than-aesthetic status of much Indigenous cultural production. Whether it be regalia or other material culture, drums, dance, or song, the ontology of the thing as an object is upended by the way in which Indigenous folks consider these variously as medicine, law, life, with the ability to do things in the world. When taken and used in Western art music to serve a primarily aesthetic function, the epistemic violence is felt through ontological assimilation. The life, medicine, or legal function of such work is bent toward its aesthetic use, a use often understood by settler composers as (merely) a benevolent action.

Feeling Settler Entitlement to Beauty

For the majority of the audience listening to the *Kuyas* aria, the experience is often one of joy and satisfaction. They cannot hear the limx' ooy within the orchestral timbre; they cannot hear the alterity of this song contained by the mellifluous voice of the mezzosoprano. Such was the case at a conference called "Place, Politics, and Cultural

Exchange: Indigenous-Settler Collaboration in Canadian Art Music."
There, after I and others shared the same information I've shared
here, a composer noted, "Are we forgetting it's a beautiful song? Probably that's my attitude as what's being called a 'settler.' It's a beautiful
song. I can't understand people being forbidden to sing a song. And
I find it difficult also to understand why you would want to prevent
a song being known if it's beautiful. It's something you want to share
with the world. I speak as a composer whose compositions rarely get
performed more than once." The view espoused by this composer—
that any beautiful song should be able to be used, or "shared," with
the world—understands aesthetic beauty as offering the possibility
for unlimited access. Of course such an argument applied to other
copyrighted popular music would be outlandish. What this comment
thus highlights is the way in which Indigenous song is still considered
under the stewardship of settler Canadians: a stewardship intended
to share and promote in no small part because this song is understood as part of a beautiful tradition no longer living or practiced.
In fact, it becomes imperative for the composer to share it because
Indigenous people supposedly cannot. Like Indigenous lands originally considered "unproductive" as terra nullius by settlers or those
currently held "in trust" for Indigenous people by the state, our songs
are considered property through their status as an artifact that has,
as its primary benefit, beauty to be shared with "the world." It is this
same paradigm that underpins the Western museum. The possessive
investment in beauty that knows Indigenous music as property similarly orients the study of Western art music toward forms of analysis
that demonstrate works' structures as "masterful" (as "masterworks")
through an emphasis on their self-complete structures. Why would
Indigenous people not want their songs known within such a grand,
beautiful context? the composer seemed to ask.

Feeling the Urgency of Repair

I have previously shared the above information in various presenta-
tions. I have written it again and again, in online and print forums.
The repetition of one's ideas, whether word for word or as paraphrase,
is anathema to the production of scholarship with its expectations
of continually presenting "new findings"—a colonial project bent on

"discovery" and of claiming (making into property) new terrain. I return to it again here as counteraction to match the extreme repetition of the limx' ooy as it exists in transcription through Western music notation published in journals, books, PDFs, and in archives; in the past and continuing performances of the limx' ooy as part of the *Kuyas*; and in the multiple archival recordings on wax cylinder, on CD, vinyl, and in digital formats. I return to it because of the accountability I have been charged with by Nisg̱a'a Elders Council to continue this reparative work. I return to it out of my own frustration—another way of knowing-feeling music. The Nisg̱a'a have explicitly called for the complete removal of all unauthorized forms of this limx' ooy that exist in the world today. To redress epistemic violence against the songlife represented in the limx' ooy means contending with the removal from the public sphere of *all* copies, all recordings, all publications including song transcriptions, all scores based on those transcriptions, and all wax cylinders, given that all of these versions have spiritual impact and carry life. This demand upends the understanding of the limx' ooy as property that has been unrightfully taken and instead offers an alternative form of repatriation that calls for a reevaluation of one's relation to violence against life. To be clear, the removal of this song from public access is not just because of the infringement of the hereditary rights of Sim'oogit Sgat'iin, hereditary chief Isaac Gonu, Gisḵ'ansnaat (Grizzly Bear Clan) to whom the song belongs, but because these various instances of the song perpetuate violence against life. Perhaps you have some relation to this song. Perhaps you do not. In either instance, a decision now rests with you as to how you might take part in the repetition of reparation toward the freedom of this life called song.

Conclusion

What is the feeling of knowing music? The question, we hope it is clear, is not only about the feeling of vibration on the skin or the impact of a sound wave on the eardrum. How we engage music is a key indicator of how it will continue to exist in the world discursively, sonically, and pedagogically. How do particular feelings of knowing affirm music's circulation and affirm the propriety of our relationship to it as one of certainty, recognition, possessiveness, admiration, or mastery? Can these feelings be unlearned and reimagined toward new ones: responsibility, respect, stewardship?

Whether in government proscriptions or censorship of Indigenous songlife, how property forms are imagined and policed under copyright, or in the discursive policings of the lines between expert and inexpert knowledges of music, dispossession of prior known-felt relationships with music are a first step toward the creation of legitimate musical propriety. In each case, it begins from a felt certainty that a form is inappropriate. This not only clears a safe terrain for "appropriate" felt knowledge; it simultaneously produces the enclosures and discursive policings by which resources are funneled from a common lot into an extractive claim of a singular, proper share. Indeed, we feel that our musical case studies make it clear that conventional musicological and legal relationships to knowing music are geared toward the active *entitlement* to not only particular musics but the very notion of music. Some subjects and ways of knowing are guaranteed certainty over their own propriety, their title claims, through the active dispossession of others. Even where our two distinct stories of appropriation appear to uphold different views of the circulation of music—whether recorded music is a common resource open to appropriation or whether recordings of songs should respect the limited circulation demanded by the particular songlife inscribed— the circulation of what is often musically called "appropriation" is still rendered decisively in favor of white, Euro-American, settler-colonial logics of propertied wealth via extraction.

We insist, then, that the feeling of knowing music is not purely about sensory modalities of hearing and vibration, sound and touch; rather, it is about how our mobile forms of knowing music come into relation with conceptions of territory, epistemology, and diverse intellectual and landed commons that preceded Western conceptions of the proprietary individual. Settler coloniality severs these through enclosures which then insist on prices paid for discrete properties, proper and inappropriate appropriations, and modalities of borrowing, citation, theft, payment, and reference. We think here again of Katherine McKittrick (2021, 138), who writes of "how some social systems are constituted through consensual circular organization and rooted in epistemological trappings," as well as Glen Coulthard's (2014, 13) expansion of the Marxist trope of primitive accumulation into a form of grounded normativity that "inform[s] and structure[s] our ethical engagements with the world and our relationships with human and nonhuman others over time." For both, recognizing these limitations and their relationships to land and territoriality or the human and nonhuman are only starting points of critique to move us toward new transgressions, new practices of living, even, in McKittrick's ambitious scope, new modes of being human. Our relationships to music can be, if we let them, practical training in learning to feel and know the possibility of other ways of relating.

Notes

1   We are writing in a moment when more and more scholars are recognizing this binary that we have set up and thus in a moment when it holds less and less true. For (ethno)musicological work that closely addresses love in relation to disciplinary listening, see, among others, Cheng (2016, 2019), Cusick (2006), and Robinson (2020).

2   See Katz (2004, 145–51).

3   *An Act Further to Amend the Indian Act, 1880*, S.C. 1884, c. 27, s. 3.

References

Barbeau, Marius. 1933. "Songs of the Northwest." *Musical Quarterly* 19 (1): 101–11.

Bellman, Jonathan D. 2007. *A Short Guide to Writing about Music.* 2nd ed. New York: Pearson.

Bhandar, Brenna. 2018. *Colonial Lives of Property: Law, Land, and Racial Regimes of Ownership.* Durham, NC: Duke University Press.

Biddle, Ian. 2006. "On the Radical in Musicology." *Radical Musicology* 1: n.p.

Cheng, William. 2016. *Just Vibrations: The Purpose of Sounding Good.* Ann Arbor: University of Michigan Press.

Cheng, William. 2019. *Loving Music till It Hurts.* Oxford: Oxford University Press.

Coulthard, Glen Sean. 2014. *Red Skin White Masks: Rejecting the Colonial Politics of Recognition.* Minneapolis: University of Minnesota Press.

Cusick, Suzanne. 2006. "On a Lesbian Relationship with Music: A Serious Effort Not to Think Straight." In *Queering the Pitch: The New Gay and Lesbian Musicology,* edited by Philip Brett, Elizabeth Wood, and Gary C. Thomas. New York: Routledge.

Demers, Joanna. 2006. *Steal This Music: How Intellectual Property Law Affects Musical Creativity.* Athens: University of Georgia Press.

Furman, Ezra. 2018. *Transformer.* New York: Bloomsbury Academic.

Graber, Katie J., and Matthew Sumera. 2020. "Interpretation, Resonance, Embodiment: Affect Theory and Musicology." *Ethnomusicology Forum* 29 (1): 3–20.

Gray, Robin R. R. 2019. "Repatriation and Decolonization: Thoughts on Ownership, Access, and Control." In *The Oxford Handbook of Musical Repatriation*, edited by Frank Gunderson, Rob Lancefield, and Bret Woods, 723–38. Oxford: Oxford University Press.

Hayes, Nick. 2020. *The Book of Trespass: Crossing the Lines That Divide Us*. London: Bloomsbury.

Iton, Richard. 2008. *In Search of the Black Fantastic Politics and Popular Culture in the Post–Civil Rights Era*. Oxford: Oxford University Press.

Katz, Mark. 2004. *Capturing Sound: How Technology Has Changed Music*. Berkeley: University of California Press.

Mackey, Eva. 2016. *Unsettled Expectations: Uncertainty, Land, and Settler Decolonization*. Halifax, NS: Fernwood.

Marre, Jeremy. 2011. *Reggae Britannia* (BBC documentary).

McKittrick, Katherine. 2015. "Axis, Bold as Love: On Sylvia Wynter, Jimi Hendrix, and the Promise of Science." In *Sylvia Wynter: On Being Human as Praxis*, edited by Katherine McKittrick, 142–63. Durham, NC: Duke University Press.

McKittrick, Katherine. 2016. "Rebellion/Invention/Groove." *Small Axe* 49 (March).

McKittrick, Katherine. 2021. *Dear Science and Other Stories*. Durham, NC: Duke University Press.

McKittrick, Katherine, and Alexander G. Weheliye. 2017. "808s and Heartbreak." *Propter Nos* 2 (1): 13–42.

McLeod, Kembrew, and Peter DiCola, 2011. *Creative License: The Law and Culture of Digital Sampling*. Durham, NC: Duke University Press.

Newman, Jason. 2015. "Tribe Called Quest: Lou Reed 'Got All the Money' for 'Can I Kick It?'" *Rolling Stone*, November 17.

Reed, Trevor. 2016. "Who Owns Our Ancestors' Voices? Tribal Claims to Pre-1972 Sound Recordings." *Columbia Journal of Law and the Arts* 40.

Robinson, Dylan. 2020. *Hungry Listening: Resonant Theory for Indigenous Sound Studies*. Minneapolis: University of Minnesota Press.

Singh, Julietta. 2018. *Unthinking Mastery: Dehumanism and Decolonial Engagements*. Durham, NC: Duke University Press.

Wingell, Richard. 2009. *Writing about Music: An Introductory Guide*. Upper Saddle River, NJ: Pearson.

PART FOUR THE MATTER OF EXPERIENCE,
OR, REMINDING CONSCIOUSNESS
OF ITS NECESSARY MODESTY

13 NONCONSCIOUS AFFECT

Cognitive, Embodied, or Nonbifurcated Experience?

Tony D. Sampson

Some of the major scholarly preoccupations of the previous century, like those adhering to a Cartesian division between mind and body or the psychoanalytical conscious-unconscious duality, have been supplanted by a new kind of neurological relation—that is to say, the relation established between a diminished mental faculty and the imperceptible governing power of the *nonconscious*. It is not the case, of course, that every scholar with an interest in these debates has blindly followed this trend, but the inclination toward posthumanism, for example, has certainly been shored up by a prevailing notion of consciousness grasped as just the tip of an iceberg of underlying insensible neurological processes. The once radical idea that consciousness, formerly modeled via cognitive processes like attention, perception, and memory, was just a thin slice of the action has now become a mainstream idea in the brain sciences, one that infiltrates major debates beyond neuroscience. The nonconscious poses many questions for decades of scholarly work leaning heavily on a cognitive theoretical frame and dramatically shifts the research focus away from an anthropocentric weltanschauung toward nonhuman worlds. Indeed, the nonconscious now figures writ large in wide-ranging debates on, for example, visual communication (Williams and Newton

2009), digital technologies (Grusin 2010), and the Anthropocene (e.g., Hayles 2017, 34).

Significantly, the nonconscious also maps onto a more general and influential turn to affect that initially became prominent in the brain sciences in the early 1990s (e.g., Damasio 1995). This turn has challenged some scholars who are critical of the ways in which neuroscience has been seized on in affect studies, prompting them to reevaluate the role of the nonconscious in the study of, for example, discourse and ideology (Leys 2011; Wetherell 2012) where such concepts have traditionally had a distinctively cognitive slant. Others have sought to bring together some aspects of neurobiological materialism and critique (Pitts-Taylor 2016; Sampson 2016). Furthermore, the non-conscious has become a deep-seated component of technopolitics within the humanities amid wider concerns about the precariousness of human cognition in technical systems (Hansen 2015; Hayles 2017, 173–75). As others argue, technocapitalism itself cannot be considered today without a contemplation of the cognitive *and* affective politics it suggests (Karppi et al. 2016).

Due to the complexity of this disciplinary drama, the aims of this chapter remain modest. It begins with theoretically contested notions of the neurological nonconscious that have produced two differently oriented strands in the posthumanities. So before addressing this theoretical division, it is significant to note that there is more instability than consensus in the neurosciences. The popular error of labeling the multiplicity of brain sciences a singular "*neuroscience*" has been acknowledged, as such, in the plurality of *neuroculture* (Sampson 2016). Nonetheless, this discussion narrows its focus on attempts to assimilate a contested understanding of the nonconscious in a remodeled cognitive theoretical framework on the one hand and a new materialist rendering of affect theory on the other hand. In the case of the latter strand, it is perhaps sensible to concede that there is, from the outset, no stable definition of new materialism or its closely affiliated concept of affect. In the first rendering of *The Affect Theory Reader*, there is a purposefully incomplete list of eight different theoretical angles to affect theory (Seigworth and Gregg 2010, 6–8). In this chapter, I will refer to some of these approaches while also drawing attention to a mode of new materialism indebted to Alfred North Whitehead, which embraces the nonconscious and contests certain assumptions in cognitive science (Sampson 2016, 2020). In the case of the former strand, unsurprisingly, those working within the cognitive theoretical frame have presented several challenges to the ontological (and ideological) commitments of new materialism; most notably, in this discussion, N. Katherine Hayles (2017, 65–85).

The chapter is structured around a series of brief observations intended to probe these two strands and eventually sketch out a third Whiteheadian nonconscious. The first observation notes the differing ways in which the neuroscientific nonconscious has stirred up debate. The aim is to expose some level of generality by placing a small range of varied new materialist work alongside Hayles's recent concept of the cognitive nonconscious expressed in her 2017 book, *Unthought: The Power of the Cognitive Nonconscious*. More specifically, the second observation asks if new materialism, as Hayles claims, conspicuously ignores conscious cognition. Or, as I will argue here, does it offer a more nuanced concept justifying a move beyond the cognitive framework? The third observation begins to outline a Whiteheadian nonconscious, intended to upset the anthropocentricism that arguably persists in theories of embodiment, evident in Hayles's cognitive frame and, to some extent, in affect theory as well. As follows, the discussion concludes by pointing to ways in which a theory of the nonconscious can avoid the neurocentric and phenomenological trap of the subject-predicate-object by mapping out a nonbifurcated experience.

The Rise of the Neuroscientific Nonconscious
in the Posthumanities

In order to trace the widespread influence of the neuroscientific nonconscious, we need look no further than the impact of Antonio Damasio's (1995) somatic marker thesis. Along with Benjamin Libet (1985) and Joseph LeDoux (2003), Damasio's Spinoza-inspired notion of the enhanced and enmeshed role somatically derived affects play in the processes behind reasoning and decision making is writ large in these two diverging strands of interpretation. To begin with, Damasio's work is often cited as support for a principal idea in new materialism—that is, despite the humanities' orthodox fixation with an anthropocentric worldview, human cognition is actually a late arriver. In other words, the human brain is understood to take its time to build consciousness as just one of many responses to the dynamics of external environmental stimuli. Drawing on Spinoza, the psychologist Wilhelm Wundt, as well as Libet, Damasio thus enables new materialism to frame the immediate experience of consciousness as a radical "backdated illusion" (e.g., Thrift 2007, 131). Along these lines, *thinking* is not at all limited to the *thought* inside the brain. On the contrary, Damasio (1995, 187) provides an understanding of how somatic markers act as a kind of "corporeal thinking" in affect theory. Through Damasio's work, we further see how the *forces* of affect traverse and remap emotions (Bertelsen and Murphie 2010, 140). Emotion, in this context, is a kind of *capture of affect* in consciousness, but the focus is distinctly less on how these maps relate to conventional cognitive processes than it is on the significance of a feely, bodily *precognition*.

This temporally backdated "pre-" feeds forward a distinctive nonhuman concept applied to technology in the new materialist's rendering of the affective nonconscious. For example, similarly drawing on Damasio and LeDoux, Richard Grusin (2010) offers a theory of affect in relation to the premediated human encounters with digital media, following, in part, a neuropsychology approach that insists on "the inseparability of cognition from affect or emotion, often on the priority of affect and emotion to cognition and rational judgment" (78). Grusin borrows from Hayles's (2006) modification of Patricia Clough's (2000) original "technological unconscious" concept, transforming it into the neurologically fine-tuned "technological nonconscious" (Grusin 2010, 72).

The nonconscious relation between human and nonhuman worlds of inorganic matter also becomes key to the Deleuze-Spinozan vitalisms of new materialism, by way of "linking the movements of matter with a processual incorporeality" (Seigworth and Gregg 2010, 6). Affect thus becomes the "hinge where mutable matter and wonder . . . perpetually tumble into each other" (8). In other words, affect does not just pass from human body to human body but becomes a nonconscious *force of encounter* with a dynamic materiality that possesses an autonomous nonhuman capacity to act and be acted on.

It is important to initially note that Hayles's (2017, 44) embodied concept of the "cognitive nonconscious" is also influenced by Libet's notion of a belated consciousness. However, it is Damasio's *protoself* that provides the core model of how nonconscious experience feeds forward to consciousness—that is to say, how it "operates at a level of neuronal processing inaccessible to the modes of awareness, but nevertheless perform[s] functions essential to consciousness" (10). Indeed, in this model, neuronal processes *level up* from Damasio's primary protoself to higher levels of a core consciousness (9–10). At the lower level, there is a "kind of sensory or nonverbal narrative," which integrates Damasio's somatic markers into coherent representations of the body, before becoming "melded with verbal content in higher consciousness" endowed with "abundant memory, language, and reasoning, narratives" (10). So, at the top of the stack of cognitive levels is a distinctly human sense of higher consciousness "enriched" by the production of a "well-defined protagonist, the autobiographical self" and "reinforced through the verbal monologue that plays in our heads as we go about our daily business" (9–10). It is these verbal narratives, *represented* in the mental faculty of the brain, that helps humans make sense of who they are.

Significantly, though, Hayles (2017, 9) reminds the reader that this leveling up process from proto- to autobiographical self is not restricted to humans but can be shared by some nonhumans including "many mammals, and some aquatic species such as octopi." Certainly, the novelty of Hayles's concept is found in the expansion it offers of this cognitive leveling-up process to other broadly defined *cognizers* who possess analogous interpretational and decision-making capacities. Although the starting point is strictly a neurological model, these capacities are not restricted to animals with brains but encompass other biological cognizers, "including those lacking central nervous systems, such as plants and microorganisms" (15). Moreover, the nonconscious is further extended to the cognitive capabilities of specific technical systems, some of which are inclusive of *cognitive assemblages* that bring together humans and technologies via interactions with neuron networks in the brain. This use of the term "assemblage" is important to Hayles given that it enables the humanities to break out of the "anthropocentric view of cognition" enabling "bridges" that span "across different phyla to construct a comparative view of cognition" (15).

In spite of these efforts at bridge building, Hayles's assemblage theory purposely opens up a stark categorical divide between cognitive and noncognitive worlds (30–33). On the one hand, there are the *cognizers*:

human and nonhuman *actors*, including some biological forms and computer algorithms, with the cognitive capacity to choose, decide, and interpret. On the other hand, there are *noncognizers*, including inanimate and inorganic materials, such as stones and hurricanes, which may well be agents "harnessed to perform cognitive tasks" (32) but are nonetheless noncognitive since they lack cognitive capacities. This categorical divide has a distinct intention. Significantly, the point is not to "ignore the achievements of conscious thought, often seen as the defining characteristic of humans, [but to] overcome the (mis)perception that humans are the only important or relevant cognizers on the planet" (10–11). As Hayles contends, once this "misperception" is overcome, then the humanities can turn to new important questions and ethical considerations (10–11). Indeed, whereas the technical cognitions found in artificial intelligence (AI) algorithms, for example, have been commonly, and perhaps misleadingly, compared with higher level human cognition, Hayles contends that their traits are more analogous to a cognitive nonconscious. As she puts it, "Like human nonconscious cognition, technical cognition processes information faster than consciousness, discerns patterns and draws inferences and, for state-aware systems, processes inputs from subsystems that give information on the system's condition and functioning. Moreover, technical cognitions are designed specifically to keep human consciousness from being overwhelmed by massive informational streams so large, complex, and multifaceted that they could never be processed by human brains" (11). A major concern of Hayles's work in the humanities is therefore centered on the increasing disappearance of human cognitive consciousness from technological systems.

This chapter will persist in probing these two alternative approaches to the nonconscious: new materialism and cognitive nonconscious. But for now, some cursory comparisons and contrasts need to be made. Notably, both approaches readily align themselves to neuroscientific notions of the nonconscious and expand this notion to nonhuman worlds. However, whereas new materialism expands the capacity of affect to an inclusive human and nonhuman world of agential organic and inorganic matter, the cognitive nonconscious makes a categorical distinction between selected cognizant actors and noncognizant agents dependent on their capacity to choose, decide, interpret, and act on information.

Where Is Consciousness?

Hayles's (2017) formulation of the cognitive nonconscious is based, in part, on her critique of new materialism. It is worth noting that this critique begins with some affirmative observations. For example, the new materialist's effort to decenter the human subject is noted as a welcome move against "human exceptionalism" in the humanities, which, she contends, has overly focused on a "privileged special category" imbued with language, rationality, and higher consciousness, to the detriment of the human's "continuum with nonhuman life and material processes" (65). Furthermore, Hayles seems to particularly admire the strong ontological commitment that new materialism has to a conceptual foregrounding of a materiality that is vibrant rather than passive and exists in metastable dynamic processes and assemblages with transformative potentials. Hayles continues, "After the baroque intricacies of the linguistic turn, [new materialist] approaches arrive like bursts of oxygen to a fatigued brain. Focusing on the grittiness of actual material processes, they introduce materiality, along with its complex interactions, into humanities discourses that for too long and too often have been oblivious to the fact that all higher consciousness and linguistic acts, no matter how sophisticated and abstract, must in the first instance emerge from underlying material processes" (65). This initial enthusiasm, however, conceals a rather hefty ontological disagreement concerning the ways in which new materialism frames the nonconscious. The main thrust of Hayles's criticism is what she sees as the conspicuous absence of "consciousness and cognition" (65–66). Perhaps this is because of a reluctance, she suggests, on behalf of new materialists to "slip [back] into received ideas and lose the radical edge that the focus on materiality provides" (66). Nonetheless, Hayles contends that by separating materiality from cognition, new materialism weakens the case for a new materiality since it "erases the critical role played by materiality in creating the structures and organizations from which consciousness and cognition emerge" (66). This is indeed a gritty provocation and one that new materialism should respond to in full. However, for now, this discussion will simply ask if consciousness is erroneously or purposely missing from new materialism, or is there a more nuanced understanding of how nonconscious affect relates to consciousness?

At the outset, if we again peruse Gregg and Seigworth's (2010) *Affect Theory Reader*, we can see how Hayles's suspicions have probably been fueled by what appears to be the celebratory zeal of some authors who see the role of the nonconscious in one of affect theory's main achievements—that is to say, "affect's displacement of the centrality of cognition" (5). To be sure, affect theorists have enthusiastically drawn on various neurological conditions like synesthesia to destabilize the study of discrete "cognitive modes" in preference for "sensual interconnection" (Highmore 2010, 119–20). Moreover, Brian Massumi's influential focus on affective intensities are posited in such a way as to "transform," "translate," or even go "beyond" cognition (Bertelsen and Murphie 2010, 147). Similarly, Anna Gibbs (2010, 200) argues that affect "prompts a rethinking of just what is meant by cognition at all." After affect theory, Gibbs argues, there can be no "pure cognition . . . uncontaminated by the richness of sensate experience, including affective experience" (200).

However, these attempts to weaken cognition do not entirely ignore emergent consciousness. Hayles's observation of its conspicuous absence from new materialism has been, it would appear, somewhat selective. Indeed, through its embracing of the nonconscious, new materialism has arguably developed a far more nuanced understanding of cognition. As Megan Watkins (2010, 279) points out, although nonconscious affects operate "independently, accumulating as bodily memory" and "may evade consciousness altogether," they also *aid* cognition and *induce* behavior. Indeed, this bodily memory—related in so many ways to Damasio's somatic marker hypothesis—does not become separated from cognition but purposefully weakens the grip of the cognitive frame on what it means to think. As Seigworth and Gregg (2010, 2–3) argue, "In practice, then, affect and cognition are never fully separable—if for no other reason than that thought is itself a body, embodied."

Other affect theorists do not entirely disregard cognition either but see it as the "end product; that is to say, the point at which the intensity of nonconscious affect arrives as a conscious emotion in the mind" (Probyn 2010, 77). Along similar lines, Massumi (cited in Thrift 2007, 180) grasps cognition in the sense that it completes the "capture and closure of affect." The key difference here is that rather than seeing higher order cognitive processes, like perception, attention, and memory, as the end product of a leveling-up process, affect theory favors a kind of emotional cognition as the most intensive expression of this capture.

This repositioning of cognition also presents contrasting alternatives to the important ethical considerations Hayles draws attention to. For example, her concerns over the potential disappearance of human consciousness from intelligent technical systems also indirectly draws on Clough's (2000) technological unconscious as the basis for a model of *automated cognition* which bends "bodies with environments to a specific set of addresses without the benefit of any cognitive inputs" (Thrift 2007, 177). Along these lines, Hayles (2017, 176) uses the technological unconscious to argue for an expanded cognitive framework focused on "meaning and interpretations," which would operate like a *bridge* between the "traditional humanities and the kinds of nonconscious cognitions" performed by AI algorithms. Such a bridge would bring together the technical cognitive nonconscious of the algorithm and "those humans who design and implement them" (176).

Clearly, there is much to commend in Hayles's desire to make the humanities' position on technology more immediate and less aloof. But arguably, the technological nonconscious presents an even more complex account of the role consciousness plays in technological systems than Hayles allows. It is not simply the case that human cognition has been cut out of the operations of these technical cognizers. On the contrary, it is more the case that a wider *capture of thinking* and the extension of cognitive awareness feeds on the precarious weaknesses of a human consciousness subjected to technocapitalism (Thrift 2007, 6–7). It is, indeed, this easy *capture of thinking* that leads some to argue that more attention needs to be paid to the relation between weak human cognition and the precognitive (7). This is not, then, a technological nonconscious that merely usurps the human cognizer but one that is deeply interwoven with automated algorithms (e.g., Borch and Lange 2017). In short, human cognition and the technological nonconscious do not bifurcate from each other; they are intensely entangled.

On Assemblages, Information, Embodiment, and Experience

Hayles (2017, 12) begins her thesis by relocating cognition outside of the cybernetic model of consciousness and rejecting the legacy of cybernetics in "the computation of the cognitivists." Here again, we can grasp the influence of the neurosciences on the cognitive frame as it too moves away from the exhausted computer-brain metaphor toward a new paradigm that encompasses the nonconscious. Following this logic, Hayles remarks that there is a growing recognition in the neurosciences that neuronal processes are not "fundamentally computational" (13). There is, as such, increasing support for an embodied and biologically constituted kind of cognition that is not simply restricted to an image of cognizant human thought (i.e., aware, attentive, etc.). This leads to an acknowledgment of the differing contexts in which cognitive processes are assumed to emerge. The cognitive frame therefore expands to include distributed nonconscious neuronal communications between humans, like those established via circuits of so-called mirror neurons (48). More profoundly perhaps, Hayles notes how these embodied contexts can be extended to include some nonhumans: plants, for example (16–20). It is certainly this concept of cognition as "a broad compass" that leads her to further incorporate technical contexts into the category of cognizers (20–25).

Hayles's neurologically inspired appeal to broader contexts of cognition points to some fundamental collisions with new materialism. Particular attention is drawn here, as such, to Hayles's provocative use of the term "assemblage" to explain how these broader contexts of the cognitive nonconscious are distributed exclusively through networks of cognizers. To begin with, although Hayles claims to maneuver away from computational metaphors toward an embodied model of cognition, her concept of cognitive assemblages retains many of the conventional metaphorical references to engineering terms to support the categorical division between cognizers and noncognizers. Most notably, this categorization is dependent on the role of *flows of information* and *information processing* (115–16). As follows, the cognizer is made distinct from the material agency of the noncognizer since the former can *act on* information received while the latter can only be *harnessed* as an agent of information flow (28–29).

Moreover, albeit recognizing that information is context dependent (22), Hayles's remodeled cognitive framework is, on the one hand, determined by fairly conventional computational operations, such as the leveling up from "layers of interactions from low-level choices, and consequently very simple cognitions, to higher cognitions and interpretations" (13) and on the other hand, a noncognitive material world defined by a lack of such operations—that is to say, the noncognizer is an agent that cannot process information in order to, for example, decide. A "tsunami," Hayles notes, "cannot choose to crash against a cliff rather than a crowded beach" (3). In other words, although human decisions, climate change, the self-organizing forces of matter that constitute a storm, and human death are interconnected, the middle two are only regarded as a passive part of an informational loop, defined, in effect, by a lack of information processing power.

Ultimately, Hayles presents a differently orientated materialism, claiming that the cognitive nonconscious is all about "matter, energy, and *information*, [and] not only matter in the narrow sense" (218; italics added). Therefore, the categorical borderline between cognizers and noncognizers only includes plants and technical systems since they "share certain structural and functional similarities" with a model of human cognition defined by a capacity to act on the "flow[s] of information through a system and the choices and decisions that create, modify, and interpret the flow" (116). This ensures that material agents and forces outside of these structures must take a back seat to the "cognizers within the assemblage that enlist these affordances and direct their powers to act in complex situations" (116).

There are a few frothy comparisons that can be made between certain aspects of Hayles's cognitive assemblages and new materialist affect theory. For example, the focus on mirror neurons in Hayles's account is reminiscent of Gibbs's (2010, 193–94) work on processes of affective mimicry in which she argues that the "sharing of form comprises information in the pre-cybernetic sense." Affective mimicry becomes an "action on bodies" that not only affects body chemistry but also affects attitudes and ideas (194). As theories of affective contagion suggest, there is a considerable blur established between the concept of a self-contained individual and its imitation of others (Sampson 2012). Nonetheless, the information flows that pass through Hayles's (2017) imitative cognitive assemblages are in sharp contrast to the contagions we find in affect theory. On the one hand, cognitive assemblages are connected by a series of metaphorical "channels" through which information is interpreted. These channels begin with a lower level "signal-response" system like those assumed to function in mirror neurons, for example, but have since evolved into a higher-level linguistic channel (128). In other words, these channels form information loops in "network hardware" through which mimicry must travel on its way from lower level social signals to higher level verbal codes (128). As follows, we find a "trajectory analogous to nonconscious cognition developing first, with consciousness emerging later and being built on top" (128).

On the other hand, affective contagion forms assemblages of occurrences produced in encounters between bodies and events. These encounters are broadly understood as being like "receivers and transmitters" but not restricted to information flows since they also encompass sensations, feelings, and affects. A child who mimics an airplane, for example, does more than simply make a cognitive *choice* to imitate. The child is exposed to an affective *force* of encounter, which not only affects the child's desire to imitate but also *passes on* a transformative feeling to other parts of the assemblage. Unlike the context-dependent nature of cognitive assemblages, then, connected by embedded informational channels, affect is independent of context. The force of affective encounter is transposed, as such, *across* contexts.

Probably the most marked differences between cognitive and new materialist assemblages is, in effect, noted by Hayles (2017). Whereas she sees Deleuze and Guattari's influential assemblage theory leaning on "connotations of connection, event, transformation, and becoming" and favoring "desire, affect, and transversal energies over cognition," the cognitive assemblage aims to offer a broader definition that includes a "provisional collection of parts" that are in a "constant flux as some are added and others lost. The parts are not so tightly bound that transformations are inhibited and not so loosely connected that information cannot flow between parts" (117–18). As Hayles continues, the most "important connotation" of cognitive assemblages is the "implication that arrangements can scale up, progressing from very low-level choices into higher levels of cognition and consequently decisions affecting larger areas of concern" (118).

There is, then, a further distinction that needs to be made between *leveling up* and *forces* of encounter referred to, respectively, in cognitive and affective assemblages. In the case of the latter, Hayles points to examples of what she regards as careless new materialist accounts of forces that are supposed to work *transversally* across micro and macro levels. The issue is, she argues, that forces operate differently at certain levels and therefore need to be approached with more careful consideration of mechanism specifics. The micro levels of bacterial life or quantum physics, for example, have very different kinds of forces in operation, Hayles claims, to those that might occur on a macrosociopolitical or cultural level. This criticism of the forces of new materialism hinges on what she calls the restrictive ideological leanings toward "Deleuzian deterritorializations" (73). However, this line of argument, focused as it is entirely on deterritorializations, perhaps misses the complex relations expressed in affective assemblages. With every potential deterritorializing line of flight, there is the simultaneous possibility of a territorial refrain or new territorialization or reterritorialization (Deleuze and Guattari 1987, 310–50). This should not be misunderstood as a material relation in the narrow sense: the force of one object exerting a force on another object. Neither is it complete chaos.

Further limitations become apparent in cognitive assemblage theory's initial commitment to Damasio's leveling-up process from proto- to core self. This is because the theory presents a neurocentric model of emergence that ultimately informs the subsequent ways in which cognition is distributed to a select group of biological and nonbiological contexts (the nonhuman cognizers). To be sure, what is lost in Damasio's model is an understanding of how these exterior distributed relationalities operate beyond the closed interiority of neuronal interactions. As follows, Damasio (2000), like LeDoux (2003), contends that the coherent sense of self that individual humans experience at the higher level of cognition is an emergent outcome of nonconscious interactions located *inside* the micro level of synaptic functionality. But this is not to say that the emergence of the self that says "I" is produced by a brain that is entirely immune to implicit affective somatic experiences. Nor is it a self wholly composed of purely explicit cognitive functions (perceptions, attention, memory, etc.). On the contrary, the core self emerges from nonconscious experiences of the material world in the wider sense.

Unlike new materialism, which focuses on nonrepresentational and precognitive tendencies of affect, the guiding principal of the protoself takes the form of a series of hardwired representations of the organism itself located *inside* the brain at various levels. It is these bodily representations that are supposed to maintain the coherence of self. This is what Damasio (2000, 21) considers to be the most likely "biological forerunner" of the sense of a "preconscious biological precedent." It is the various neuronal interactions between the levels of protoself and autobiographical self that produce more elaborate representations experienced at a higher level of consciousness as identity and personhood. The sense of self therefore emerges matryoshka-like through a leveling up of representations that are interpreted at the higher level of consciousness.

Similar to Hayles, then, Damasio's model seemingly breaks away from the old cybernetic models of consciousness, only to return to a familiar and problematic retention of the metaphorical concepts of information processing and representational storage inherited from cybernetics (Sampson 2016, 126–29). Nonetheless, Hayles (2017) argues that the process of leveling up is crucial to the framework of nonconscious cognition. She concludes, "The specific dynamics operating at different levels provide a way to distinguish between material processes and nonconscious cognition as an emergent result, as well as elucidating the modes of organization characteristic of consciousness/unconsciousness" (69). Ultimately, I contend that Hayles's critique of the imprecise forces of new materialism is swapped out for an equally loose application of information levels. To conclude this part of the discussion, then, on the one hand, according to Hayles, the journey from a nonconscious, formed in the materiality of embodied experience, only becomes high-level thought because of a leveling up from micro to macro representations. However, by taking noncognizers out of the assemblage and essentializing information processing as the mechanism of embodied interaction, Hayles in effect divides cognitive minds from material vitality. This separation makes cognizers a primary *relation of interiority* that bifurcates from exterior relations to matter. Matter thus becomes inert and deadened. On the other hand, the new materialists' turn to forces of affective embodied experience decenters the human and moves the analytical lens away from mindful interiorities toward a bodily *relation of exteriority* to the material world. Yet, from the neuroscience perspective adopted by both Hayles and affect theory, although nonconscious exterior forces precede the cognitive mind, they eventually go on to shape it. The precognitive nonconscious is effectively a precursor of cognition. Indeed, how thought emerges from (or alongside) the unthought in both accounts (cognitive and affect) undergoes a comparable measure of inexactness, arguably rooted in varied interpretations of embodied experience.

A Whiteheadian Technological Nonconscious

From a Whiteheadian perspective, a concept of nonconsciousness couched in cognizers, noncognizers, bodily forces or the modification of embodied experience does not go far enough to explain experience outside of thought. To begin to understand why this is, we need to start with Whitehead's resolute refusal to allow a bifurcation between mindful experience and matter. There are several cursory philosophical points to note. First, and similar, to some extent, to the aims of phenomenology, nonbifurcation challenges idealism. Reality is not simply grasped through the mediation of human thought. Second, however, nonbifurcation takes on established materialisms that resort to a version of reality located in discrete objects (things, atoms, neurons etc.). The idealist's bifurcation of mind and matter is not therefore replaced with a mind made simply of matter, like material neuroscience, or indeed, the material environments that embodied cognitive subjects encounter. On the contrary, what becomes crucial to the study of nonconsciousness is that mind and the liveliness of matter only become analyzable when they are taken together in the temporal thickness of events. Third, then, the focus shifts away from a nonconscious predicated by cognitive or embodied experiences to a radical theory of experience outside of thought, *in the event*.

Fourth, it is important to note that Whitehead grasps subjective phenomenal experience *in the event* as decidedly unreliable. In *Process and Reality*, he vividly captures this fallacious subjective perception as a "half-awake . . . awareness . . . absorbed within a small region of abstract thought while oblivious to the world" (Whitehead 1985, 161). Human perception becomes a kind of sleepwalk (Sampson 2020, 69) caught between an embodied "torrent of passion" and a "morbidly discursive" and narrow bandwidth of attention. Along these lines, Isabelle Stengers (2014) notes that at its most exceptional, at its most plastic, the human mind only has a mere foothold in the experience of reality. It is certainly not a phenomenal cognitive command post! Relatedly, then, Whitehead sets out to escape a trap set by a kind of phenomenological embodiment: an embodiment Husserl initially intended to refute idealism and later elaborated by Heidegger and Merleau-Ponty to be comprised of worldly interactions (Sampson 2020, 161). The point is that phenomenological embodiment captures experience in a subject-predicate-object relation. In effect, even when bodies become ecologically linked to their environment (through information levels or affective forces), a preoccupation with human embodiment will always ensure that it is the subject who experiences the world.

Once out of this particular trap, Whiteheadian experience becomes untethered from human cognition and embodiment. This is because Whiteheadian experience begins with an ostensibly uncanny, yet profound, proposition. Worldly experience heralds the arrival of human subjective experience. It is not human consciousness that draws attention to experience. It is, on the contrary, experience that draws attention to an anomalous human perception of worldly experience. As follows, Whitehead offers a radical philosophical point of departure since it is not phenomenal human consciousness that sheds light on experience. Quite the reverse, it is experience in the actual world that draws attention to the aberration that is human consciousness. Whiteheadian event theory therefore confronts the limitations of an abstract thought that can never absorb the entire temporal thickness of the event.

The fallacious preeminence of human minds and bodies makes it very difficult to understand the growing complexity of nonconscious assemblages, especially in technocultures. If we are to disentangle experience from a problematic human-centered perception, as both Hayles and affect theory suggest is necessary, then thinking with Whitehead becomes increasingly important. This is because in the study of embodied interaction (Dourish 2004), the phenomenological subject-predicate-object trap is (always) already set. Like Heidegger's interest in tools, it is always the situated user who experiences the device, *ready to hand* or *present at hand* (Sampson 2020, 156). As an alternative, a Whiteheadian new materialism posits a seemingly strange notion: *objects can experience subjects*. The idea that a device can experience a user is not, however, an entirely alien concept in the design of smart tangible computing. Like stones that sense the warmth of the sun, so-called smart sensor technological objects might arguably *feel* in a Whiteheadian sense. Correspondingly, in the Internet of

Things context, users appear to become the object of sense-making technologies. It might be the case that in twenty-first-century media, as Hayles argues, human subject agency has ceded control to these transcendent technological objects. The binary divide between active communicative subjects and passive silent, fixed objects no longer works. Technological objects are becoming cognitive, sociable, side-stepping human awareness or taking the place of humans altogether (Mitew 2014). Decisively, though, a Whiteheadian approach reconsiders experience in terms of immanence or nonbifurcation. Subjective forces are not predetermined as the knowers (or unknowing) of objects.

Nonbifurcated experience is "the self-enjoyment of being one among many, and of being one arising out of the composition of the many" (Whitehead 1985,145). This is not a self-satisfying moment in time that *essentially* begins in a human head, brain, mind, body, or AI algorithm. Human experience can be "an act of self-origination," but it is constrained to a "perspective of a focal region, located within the body . . . but not necessarily persisting in any fixed coordination with a definite part of the brain" (Whitehead, cited in Dewey 1951, 644). In short, experience cannot be decoupled from its entanglement with the "whole of nature." Experience is continuous to material assemblages (technological and otherwise) and their encounter with the entire temporal thickness of events. As Whitehead describes what we might call an *assemblage brain*, "We cannot determine with what molecules the brain begins and the rest of the body ends. Further, we cannot tell with what molecules the body ends and the external world begins. The truth is that the brain is continuous with the body, and the body is continuous with the rest of the natural world" (644). This assemblage does not limit experience to any privileged sense organ (the cognitive nonconscious, the sensation of a body) or a higher level of consciousness (the all-perceiving mind with the capacity for language). Although Whitehead (1967, 78) concedes that human consciousness may well be an exhibit of the "most intense form of the plasticity of nature," there is no dichotomy between the human and what is experienced. In this nonbifurcated sense-making assemblage, the nonconscious or unthought can only be defined as an experience of events closed to mind. Which is to say, the cognitive mind does not provide direct access to matter since it is entangled in a continuous matter flow. At best, the mind provides a mere foothold in the event.

To conclude, there are two key takeaways arising from this approach. First, a Whiteheadian nonconscious puts the event in affect theory. By doing so, it presents a version of matter that is lively. Indeed, mind and matter are entangled in the dynamic temporal thickness of the event. Mindful access to an event is not therefore experienced from a commanding cognitive position, as an idea in form or inert substance, but instead arises out of a continuous duration of momentary rhythms of experience. Second, events are experienced as affects *outside of thought*. This is a relation of exteriority that clearly differs from Hayles's reference to an interiorized unthought constrained by cognition and thus a notion of affect rendered in the cognitive theoretical frame, whether that be a human or nonhuman cognizer (see Hayles and Sampson 2018). More radical than this, a Whiteheadian nonconscious does not limit the experience of events to the affects of either a lower level protoself or an embodied precognition. By removing the subject-predicate-object, affect theory gains access to a *more-than-human* experience of events.

References

Bertelsen, Lone, and Andrew Murphie. 2010. "An Ethics of Everyday Infinities and Powers: Félix Guattari on Affect and the Refrain." In *The Affective Theory Reader*, edited by Melissa Gregg and Gregory J. Seigworth, 138–60. Durham, NC: Duke University Press.

Borch, Christian, and Ann-Christina Lange. 2017. "High-Frequency Trader Subjectivity: Emotional Attachment and Discipline in an Era of Algorithms." *Socio-economic Review* 15 (2): 283–306.

Clough, Patricia T. 2000. *Autoaffection: Unconscious Thought in the Age of Teletechnology*. Minneapolis: University of Minnesota Press.

Damasio, Antonio. 1995. *Descartes' Error: Emotion, Reason, and the Human Brain*. New York: Penguin.

Damasio, Antonio. 2000. *The Feeling of What Happens: Body, Emotion, and the Making Of Consciousness*. London: Vintage.

Deleuze, Giles, and Félix Guattari. 1987. *A Thousand Plateaus: Capitalism and Schizophrenia*. Minneapolis: University of Minnesota Press.

Dewey, John. 1951. "The Philosophy of Whitehead." In *The Philosophy of Alfred North Whitehead*, edited by Paul Arthur Schilp, 641–61. New York: Tutor Publishing.

Dourish, Paul. 2004. *Where the Action Is*. Cambridge, MA: MIT Press.

Gibbs, Anna. 2010. "After Affect Sympathy, Synchrony, and Mimetic Communication." In *The Affect Theory Reader*, edited by Melissa Gregg and Gregory J. Seigworth, 186–205. Durham, NC: Duke University Press.

Grusin, Richard. 2010. *Premediation: Affect and Mediality after 9/11*. New York: Palgrave Macmillan.

Hansen, Mark. 2015. *Feed-Forward: On the Future of Twenty-First-Century Media*. Chicago: University of Chicago Press.

Hayles, N. Katherine. 2006. "Traumas in Code." *Critical Inquiry* 33 (3): 136–57.

Hayles, N. Katherine. 2017. *Unthought: The Power of the Cognitive Nonconscious*. Chicago: University of Chicago Press.

Hayles, N. Katherine, and Tony D. Sampson. 2018. "Unthought Meets the Assemblage Brain: A Dialogue between N. Katherine Hayles and Tony D. Sampson." *Capacious: Journal for Emerging Affect Inquiry* 1 (12): 60–84.

Highmore, Ben. 2010. "Bitter After Taste: Affect, Food, and Social Aesthetics." In *The Affect Theory Reader*, edited by Melissa Gregg and Gregory J. Seigworth, 118–37. Durham, NC: Duke University Press.

Karppi, Tero, Lotta Kähkönen, Mona Mannevuo, Mari Pajala, and Tanja Sihvonen. 2016. "Affective Capitalism." *Ephemera: Theory and Politics in Organization* 16 (4): 1–13.

LeDoux, Joseph. 2003. *The Synaptic Self: How Our Brains Become Who We Are*. New York: Penguin.

Leys, Ruth. 2011. "The Turn to Affect: A Critique." *Critical Inquiry* 37 (3): 434–72.

Libet, Benjamin. 1985. "Unconscious Cerebral Initiative and the Role of Conscious Will in Voluntary Action." *Behavioral Brain Sciences* 8 (4): 529–39.

Mitew, Teodor. 2014. "Do Objects Dream of an Internet of Things?" *Fibreculture Journal* 23. http://twentythree.fibreculturejournal.org/fcj-168-do-objects-dream-of-aninternet-of-things/.

Pitts-Taylor, Victoria. 2016. *The Brain's Body: Neuroscience and Corporeal Politics*. Durham, NC: Duke University Press.

Probyn, Elspeth. 2010. "Writing Shame." In *The Affect Theory Reader*, edited by Melissa Gregg and Gregory J. Seigworth, 71–92. Durham, NC: Duke University Press.

Sampson, Tony D. 2012. *Virality: Contagion Theory in the Age of Networks*. Minnesota: University of Minnesota Press.

Sampson, Tony D. 2016. *The Assemblage Brain: Sense Making in Neuroculture*. Minnesota: University of Minnesota Press.

Sampson, Tony D. 2020. *A Sleepwalker's Guide to Social Media*. Cambridge: Polity.

Seigworth, Gregory J., and Melissa Gregg. 2010. "An Inventory of Shimmers." In *The Affect Theory Reader*, edited by Melissa Gregg and Gregory J. Seigworth, 1–25. Durham, NC: Duke University Press.

Stengers, Isabelle. 2014. *Thinking with Whitehead: A Free and Wild Creation of Concepts*. Cambridge, MA: Harvard University Press.

Thrift, Nigel. 2007. *Non-representational Theory: Space, Politics, Affect*. New York: Routledge.

Watkins, Megan. 2010. "Desiring Recognition, Accumulating Affect." In *The Affect Theory Reader*, edited by Melissa Gregg and Gregory J. Seigworth, 269–88. Durham, NC: Duke University Press.

Wetherell, Margaret. 2012. *Affect and Emotion: A New Social Science Understanding*. London: Sage.

Whitehead, Alfred N. 1967. *Adventures of Ideas*. New York: Free Press.

Whitehead, Alfred N. 1985. *Process and Reality: An Essay in Cosmology*. New York: Free Press.

Williams, Rick, and Julianne Newton. 2009. *Visual Communication: Integrating Media, Art, and Science*. New York: Routledge.

The Impersonality of the Minor

Erin Manning

To begin with black sociality—rather than to produce a Black subject from the perspective of the world as given—is to refuse, as Tina Campt (2019, n.p.) might say, the assumption that all worlds produced and entered into are White: "**refusal**: a rejection of the status quo as livable and the creation of possibility in the face of negation i.e. a refusal to recognize a system that renders you fundamentally illegible and unintelligible; the decision to reject the terms of diminished subjecthood with which one is presented, using negation as a generative and creative source of disorderly power to embrace the possibility of living otherwise." Living otherwise begins in the relational field, a field replete with the force of what is still in the forming. This fierce commitment to other ways of living is, in one and the same gesture, a repudiation of what Saidiya Hartman (1997, 9) calls "the burdened individuality of freedom" and an affirmation of modes of existence activated in the interstices. Through an activation of a particular subset of such interstices, this chapter adopts a logic of approximation of proximity as it sidles black sociality and process philosophy. This approximation of proximity recognizes gaps and moves through them, interested in the differential that produces complexity. However, the overlap is hardly seamless. It is the seam in fact that textures the encounter. The claim here is that process philosophy, the study of the relational imbrications through which worlds form themselves, echoes with the call for a sociality that is black in its ethicoaesthetic commitment to worlding and, further, that this call inclines via the force of the impersonal.

To catch an incline is to already be in the midst of the minor sociality that angles, in advance of any other ways of being, toward what Édouard Glissant might call an aesthetics of the earth. Black sociality is the conduit, the orientation that angles otherwise, bringing the earth's necessities into focus, the impersonality of the minor everywhere active in the lively syncopations it provokes.

In an aesthetics of the earth, the balance shifts toward the relational field. It is from the field itself, in the relation, that modes of existence emerge, and it is in collaboration with the field that an ethos of participation with the world is practiced (Glissant 1997). In a celebration of this logic of the included middle (Massumi 2014, 2021), a different account must be given of how difference is made, which is to say, how we come into the becoming of our ethicoaesthetic engagement with the world.

In a process philosophical cosmology—which is to say, in approximation of proximity with an aesthetic sociality of blackness—the question of existence's persistence stages a core problem. How are we made? And what makes the field through which we recognize ourselves?

In abeyance of any concept of the self-serving individual who leads existence, in departure from the colonial narrative that places the subject—whiteness—in advance of the world, outside looking in, the account here given begins not in the personal but in the world. The personal, that edge of recognition that sidles "I," is not the beginning of the story. It is a certain echo of its continuance, a feel for persistence, an infrarecognizability, but it *is* not.

Before there is form and between any notion of consolidation, there is process, open field. This open field is made of all that is in germ, that ontopowerful[1] field of relation that we call potential. Every act is made of potential, a potential that can only ever be felt in the act.

Being emerges from cut, from the fissure of worlds remaking themselves. That is to say, any consolidation of a modality of existence is produced through a tension in the field that moves it into reshaping. We are made from that subtraction of potential into a recalibration, into act, that in the same gesture, remakes the world.

To recalibrate into act, there has to be a share of givenness. Something doing. The world's immanent agitations produce the orientation toward cusping out of which being—the being of relation—irrupts. The cut that sparks the recalibration is a necessity for something to "take," to be known. This something is not yet being. It is the quality on its way, a becoming, a tending toward form.

This tending toward form takes the shape of all that brought it into the form it takes. It pulls the world with it, carrying all that sidled its process of becoming. As we become, we become (with) the world.

This account of how a form feels itself into being from the force of the field reminds us that we are not the sole doers in our process of becoming. We are the collaborators, and in that collaboration we are the carriers of all that fostered our singular becoming. What emerges moves in the feel of that collaboration, carrying with it the tensions and cuts and fissures that brought it to "itself." "We" are (in) the momentum, (in) the abyss, of the crack, to use Bayo Akomolafe's words.[2] In the cross-current of accounts of blackness and what it can do, this is what is heard: the world is made in the cracks, not "my" world, not the world in "my" image but a worlding that dances me into it. "More than my damn self" (Harney and Moten 2021, 45). Blackness as the ungovernable proposition that life begins elsewhere and does its work otherwise than from the perspective of that subject looking in, organizing the world into his image. Blackness as cracked becoming in the atemporality of the most ontopowerful of events: the being of relation.

The givenness that moves the world into act is itself activity. Movement all the way down. What this means: we are made of activity. We are made of the cracks that open us onto being. In the Whiteheadian cosmology, it is the concept of decision that activates this schism that pulls activity out of the immanent valuation of the world in flux. Not world and then human but vectored activity decisionally become-human.

Whether we call it decision or simply crack, what matters is that what motors us into being is the field's relational complexity subtracted into reorientation. The act of becoming (human) must always be the carrying of this cleave, the crack that opens us into our difference while it holds—in the gap—all that exceeds us. This being of relation that we are is activated in the cusp of worlds reorienting. We are worlded into being through a vectoring of the field. This vectoring cuts process to activate the angle on existence we come to know as what came to pass. The movement of our being is the becoming of the world. There is no separation, only conduit and cut.

Decision here is not a conscious action performed by a preexisting subject. Decision is its own motivator. The future anterior is important here: how the world moves us into being is known in the afteraffect of the world's coming to form. We body in the affective tonality of a world expressed through us.

It is common to learn that what matters happens through the agency of a subject's decisional orientation. It is typical, in our classrooms, to learn that it is personal agency that gives us power. Blackness teaches us otherwise. Decisioning ourselves into act does not mean that there is no role to play in the activity of living. It means that the playing out of living occurs from the middling where earth and body meet. Life is the interplay of the qualities of existence that inform it. Life is the practice of creating the conditions for that interplay.

The crack that fissures the processual field is a bodying that yields an aesthetic potential. Life is that aesthetic potential, angling itself into shape. Blackness lives that angle, an angular sociality that irrupts from the cracks, its quality of existence taking us into the interstices.

There is no separation between who we are and how we world.

The angular sociality of a worlding that becomes us is a minor sociality, minor to the degree that its inclination angles existence toward the sideway tendencies of attention decentered. We are not the directors of this existence sidling. Accompaniments in the relational field of worlds decisioning themselves into act, we participate. This is the queer inclination of an aesthetics of the earth.

The impersonal lurks here.

My blackness is a roaming principle, a geological force uncovering the otherwise, a departure from convenient algorithms, a fierce conjuring in a language so secret that the words themselves do not realize they are part of the spell. My blackness is an invitation to the sensuousness of the pothole, to the hospitality of the crack in the wall. My blackness is what happens when loss touches itself, when a people is brought to the edge of apocalyptic Atlantic waters, and still carry a strange hope. My blackness is the creolized promiscuity at the borderlands of goodness. My blackness is the miraculous undoing of identity. (Akomolafe 2021b, n.p.)

In the angling of sociality, blackness endures (Nyong'o 2018). But this endurance is not an endurance of the (time)line. It is an endurance folded, time on the bias. Not identity, not form. Being of relation.

What is a persistence that does not individualize, that does not seek self-recognition? What is persistence that never succumbs to "itself"? What is persistence that is born of the crack, pulsed into act in a movement that refuses the separability of the me-you, body-earth?

Whitehead (1978, 107) speaks of a "thread of personal order." Personal order, the persistence, in the event, of a certain infrarecognizability, is how Whitehead addresses a tendency toward stability in the field of experience. Counter to the decisional cleave, personal order is the carrying-over, the spread, in time, of existence's overlay.

A personal order has a personality to the degree that its carry-over resonates in the fold of time. But it is not reducible to a person or to an object. It does not belong to the logic of a self. Personal order is the perseverance of a tonality, a qualitative ongoingness in the event. Personal order is the reminder that no activity erupts from a vacuum and no mode of existence can be excised from the complex ways it carries the world and is carried by it. The question is, what kind of endurance is at work, and what is given shape by the endurance?

What carries over is not the form things take. What carries over is the intensity of a shaping. This intensity has a character. What endures, in the event, is the character or personality of valuation that flows into it. The personality of valuation is more than a person—it is the quality of personing that runs through the event. The personality of valuation is the qualitative angle through which the occasion lives its continuing *across*.

The personality of valuation colors the event. Affective in its valence, the valuation is a cast, an allure that shades the event into a timeline that both times it and from which it overflows. Activity and value in mutual inclusion, the force of the carrying-over becomes indiscernible from "itself." The personing is made of the personality of valuation that carries it.

The "itself" of personal order is lost in the layerings of so many carryings. It is conduit.

This conduit is in-time to the degree that its persistence is lived, here-now. But it is also out-of-time, in overflow of any and all actuality. A tinge of immortality moves with it, if by "immortality" we understand the quality of experience that exceeds actualization yet continues to make a difference across it.

The immortality of personal order is impersonal. That is to say, what endures in experience is impersonal—it cannot be reduced to any notion of identity or to any limited notion of the person. There is no containment of personality here as identity purports to do. What endures in the personality of valuation is not the self-same but the force of the carryings-over: the impersonality of affect.

The impersonal cuts across personal order in the shape of time bent. Angling into the differential of valuation's spread, it is never known as such, its tendencies minor. Without a form, the impersonality of affect takes the shape of the value that inflects it. This impersonality that acts as intercessor to personal order is not a being. It is a throb in time, a hesitancy of the line, felt across an uneasy array of differential acts.

The impersonal is the biggest threat to identity, to the individual and all that is reduced to form by the imposition of time on a line. Where identity claims a given form, relying on that form to do the work of staging difference, the impersonal is nothing but angles, nothing but inflections. The impersonal *is* not in any normal sense of being. The impersonal is relation of nonrelation, that carrier of existence that functions only from the middle and remains there. The included middle—the associated milieu, as Gilbert Simondon might say[3]—is not between two. The middle is the hospitality of the crack, the cut that opens expression to its outside.

Inclination can only be impersonal, leaning as it does on its uneasy surrounds, forming them in the process, while formed by them. Valuation has this imprint on experience, lending it not a monumentality but a shade, a slant. When personing edges toward the inclination of valuation, a hesitation troubles actualization. Time stutters, the occasion impersonalized by a durational fold felt in the crook of its givenness. There is no I here, no straight (time)lines.

That blackness lives here means this: blackness is the inclination of existence's potential, the aesthetic yield that expresses, in force, not form, the more-than of existence. This minor sociality is not reducible to a person. To reduce it to an identity would be to limit its yield, culling the impersonality of the valuation that flows through it. This is how I hear Rizvana Bradley and Denise Ferreira da Silva's (2021) refusal to reduce the aesthetic to the known: "Black Aesthetics is an utterance that, in its immanent derangement of modernity's grammar, marks and is marked by the art of passage without coordinates or arrival, the art of life in departure."

The impersonality of affect reminds us that the autonomy of affect is never a before, never an externality.[4] It is an imbrication, an alongsideness that angles activity. Affect is the impersonal force that opens activity to the expression of its feel in the feel. The danger of personal order is not that it exists but that its endurance be understood in the logic of the (time)line. Personal order's endurance lives in the interplay of decision and the field it opens up, a field we grow out of—the being of relation. What is carried across is this interplay.

In the interplay, what is made felt is not a unity. A unity has the feel of a hardened form. Unity has no perspective of the universe. Its contours hardened; it cannot let the world in. What is carried over is the force of the one-many, the more-than-one that reverberates in the exuberant proclamation, back to Akomolafe, that "my blackness is the miraculous undoing of identity," "my" catapulted into all that differs within it. Despite consistency, it reverberates.

Reverberation cracks. Unstable, the first tendency is to find purchase. A temptation: startle into I. A proposition: find a ledge, make a body in the reach. Catch the incline.

Catching the incline angles existence into an intuiting modality. A slanted *I* gives way to a new shape. A crack opens. Below consciousness, the world meets a body obliquely. Impersonality spills across its surfacing. The world tips. "We perceive things where they are, perception puts us at once into matter, is impersonal, and coincides with the perceived object" (Deleuze 1991, 25). I loses its balance.

It is often a temptation to return to that straight I, "the hegemony of the vertical,"[5] as though there were a beginning, as though the I could guarantee a starting point. The thing is, there is no straight I. There is only the imposition of its legibility through continued centerings of it by whiteness, by neurotypicality, by colonial logics that keep me in the account of all beginnings. We are not identities in a world of objects. We are the subtractions worlds become when we coincide with the shapes things take. We are cusps of activity and value, impersonally forging existences at the interstices of worlds in the making. "All our false problems derive from the fact that we do not know how to go beyond experience toward the conditions of experience, toward the articulations of the real, and rediscover what differs in kind in the composites that are given to us and on which we live" (Deleuze 1991, 26).

The real carries the impersonal force of what cusps. It is the affective force of value's effect on activity. The real is the feel of the fissure of experience that cusps valuation where it is in act. Here, the one and the many coincide, their limit conditions in relational fold. Along the inflection of this untimely line, what emerges is a discordant multiplicity. This multiplicity feels experience into resonance, its affective valence the force of a lure for a shape of actuality that carries the complexity of worlds bodying. The route of this inflection is durational, its line decisionally forked toward paths as yet unformed.

"Duration," Deleuze (1991, 93, *translation modified*) writes, reading Bergson, "is the most contracted degree of matter, matter the most dilated degree of duration." Time is not a line and matter is not an object. Time is the spread of the act's affect on existence. Time is the feel of how the act made a difference. Matter is the actualization of that difference. In the timing of the act, the act's given time, time folds into perspective, its angle making the world resonate in just this way now. The inclination of this act has a vitality. Bergson calls it "élan vital."

Élan vital is the affective turn the world takes when it folds the many into one and the one into many. Time's totality is felt here as pressure, as rhythm. Creativity is made at this interstice.

The pulse of creativity socializes the world into act. The time signature of this socialization carries a certain hesitation. "There is an efficacity, a positivity of time, that is identical to a 'hesitation' of things, and in this way, to creation in the world" (Deleuze 1991, 105). The divergent lines of experience that time existence into being hesitate a quality of life into being. This hesitation—the pulse of valuation in activity—trembles the world into the quality of a certain in-decision. This in-decision is not a counter to the decisional force that cracks the world into act. It is an in-decision of the act's own certainty as regard how it times experience. The in-decision is the conduit of the impersonal. In-decision shimmers at the cusp of the one-many, living it out in the multiplicity of the both-and. Being of relation. Impersonal affects circulate, bending any notion of rectitude. "For the affect is not a personal feeling, nor is it a characteristic; it is the effectuation of a power of the pack that throws the self into upheaval and makes it reel" (Deleuze and Guattari 1987, 240). The pack: that field of forces, the minor sociality that experiments with how blackness makes a body world. "Personhood has changed address—no longer embodied in the human corporeal entity, but in diffractive enlistments spread out in the environment" (Akomolafe 2021a, n.p.). "Figures who nevertheless come to haunt Man as the bearers of an ontological dissonance, an immanent declension, we might call blackness" (Bradley and Ferreira da Silva 2021).

In the opacity of a poet(h)ics of relation,[6] blackness operates the turn that pulses the impersonal from identity. Its disruption unsettles. "The total exposure of blackness both enables and extinguishes the force of the modern ethical program, insofar as the disruptive capacity of blackness is a quest(ion) toward the end of the world. Blackness is a threat to sense, a radical questioning of what comes to be brought under the (terms of the) 'common'" (Bradley and Ferreira da Silva 2021). In the "threat to sense," there is more than one and less than many. In an ethics of the undercommon feel,[7] what stands out as given is not a figure but the consent not to be a single being. But be careful: the consent is not ours to give or take. The consent is in and of the world giving itself.

The earth gives existence opaquely, its field of relation pulsing us into the uneasy vacillation of activity and valuation. Akomolafe calls this "decolonial abundance." "Whatever you do, don't try to make the world a better place; instead, consider that the world might be trying to make you a better place" (Akomolafe 2021a).

The world is not ours to make. The world is the body affected and affecting. It is the force flow of all that briefly resounds in the one of the many and the many of the one. Minor sociality is its grammar, its lexicon. To listen to it is to incline. To hear it is to angle toward blackness.

> When there is nothing to govern, nothing to secure, there is blackness.
> —Stefano Harney and Fred Moten, *All Incomplete*

Notes

1   On ontopower, see Massumi (2015).
2   See Akomolafe (2021b).
3   See Simondon (1968).
4   See "Autonomy of Affect" in Massumi (2021) and especially Massumi's new preface.
5   See Albright (2017); see also Adeyemi (2019): "The 90° angles of Man (and the related concepts of Human, Subject, and Citizen) were stabilized by the angularities of black to and as ground: in the back-breaking 30° of repetitive agricultural work, the psychological 70° of subservient tending forward with downcast eyes, the sharp shifts between 100° and 110° taken on with each whiplash, the 180° of the dead body, the 0° of '*Cum sup terr*' (Hartman 2008: 1)."
6   See Glissant (1997); Ferreira da Silva (2014).
7   See Harney and Moten (2013).

References

Adeyemi, Kemi. 2019. "Beyond 90: The Angularities of Black/Queer/Women/Lean." *Women and Performance* 29 (1): 9–24.

Akomolafe, Bayo. 2021a. "Let's Meet at the Crossroads." Bayo Akomolafe personal website, May 29. https://www.bayoakomolafe.net/post/lets-meet-at-the-crossroads.

Akomolafe, Bayo. 2021b. "Meditations on Blackness" Shelbourne and Primrose United Churches website, April 15. https://www.shelburneprimrose.com/resources/meditation-on-blackness-by-bayo-akomolafe.

Albright, Ann Cooper. 2017. "The Perverse Satisfaction of Gravity." In *The Aging Body in Dance: A Cross-Cultural Perspective*, edited by Nanako Najajima and Gabriele Brandsetter, 63–73. London: Routledge.

Bradley, Rizvana, and Denise Ferreira da Silva. 2021. "Four Theses on Aesthetics." *e-flux Journal* 120 (September 2021). https://www.e-flux.com/journal/120/416146/four-theses-on-aesthetics/.

Campt, Tina. 2019. "Black Visuality and the Practice of Refusal." *Women and Performance* 29 (1): 79–87.

Deleuze, Gilles. 1991. *Bergsonism*. Translated by Hugh Tomlinson and Barbara Habberjam. New York: Zone Books.

Deleuze, Gilles, and Félix Guattari. 1987. *A Thousand Plateaus*. Minneapolis: Minnesota University Press.

Ferreira da Silva, Denise. 2014. "Toward a Black Poethics: The Quest(ion) of Blackness toward the End of the World." *The Black Scholar* 44 (2): 81–97.

Glissant, Édouard. 1997. *Poetics of Relation*. Translated by Betsy Wing. Ann Arbor: University of Michigan Press.

Harney, Stefano, and Fred Moten. 2013. *The Undercommons*. London: Minor Composition.

Harney, Stefano, and Fred Moten. 2021. *All Incomplete*. London: Minor Compositions.

Hartman, Saidiya. 1997. *Scenes of Subjection: Terror, Slavery, and Self-Making in Nineteenth-Century America*. Oxford: Oxford University Press.

Massumi, Brian. 2014. *What Animals Teach Us about Politics*. Durham, NC: Duke University Press.

Massumi, Brian. 2015. *Ontopower*. Durham, NC: Duke University Press.

Massumi, Brian. 2021. *Parables for the Virtual: Affect, Movement, Sensation. Twentieth Anniversary Edition*. Durham, NC: Duke University Press.

Nyong'o, Tavia. 2018. *Afro-Fabulations: The Queer Drama of Black Life*. New York: New York University Press.

Simondon, Gilbert. 1968. *L'individu et sa genèse physico-biologique*. Grenoble: Jerôme Millon.

Whitehead, Alfred North. 1978. *Process and Reality*. New York: Free Press.

Lisa Blackman

This chapter is dedicated to the memory of Lauren Berlant.

Introduction: Technologies of the Nonrational

This chapter started with a deep sense of bewilderment and shock before it took form more explicitly as an investigation into technologies of the nonrational through emotions and affects of convolution. Emotions and affects of convolution traverse many different settings and are part and parcel of forms of power that link the military, colonial forms of power, media power, soft power, and the "gray areas" of nonphysical abuse primarily associated with coercive control and narcissistic abuse. Narcissistic abuse is a term that recognizes common behavior and communication patterns linked to abuse carried out by perpetrators who have either been diagnosed with personality disorders, such as narcissistic personality disorder (NPD), or who would likely meet the criteria. It is estimated that in the United States alone, there are 158 million victims of narcissistic abuse.[1] Narcissistic abuse has entered public consciousness and taken root within the context of Trumpism. There is a growing genre of accounts by survivors of this insidious form of emotional and psychological abuse, including Mary Trump's (2020) autobiography *Too Much and Never Enough: How My Family Created the World's Most Dangerous Man,* linking narcissism within family systems to cycles of abuse that have been played out on a very public world stage (see Honig 2021).

As well as bewilderment and shock, this chapter is written from a place of profound grief. Grief is capacious and, in my case, a series of events, the death of my mother and multiple traumatic episodes linked to her death, forced the issues that I consider here. It was hard during the period of writing to focus on anything else as I read endless newspaper articles detailing the latest victims of abuse or the shocking statistics worldwide of those who die at the hands of their perpetrators. Abuse was everywhere, brutalizing my grieving process where a shocking event became the catalyst for the return of my past and the ending to a twisted script that I had not quite realized I had been living. This is what "narcissistic abuse" is like,[2] where, in my case, over the period of eighteen months, I was forced to confront a strange and bizarre world of delusion, conning, facades, trickery, subterfuge, traps, scare tactics, isolation, shape-shifting, subliminal programming, pathological lying, false assertions, and alternative narratives, engulfed in an economy of affect and emotion—fear, panic, dread, anger, guilt, shame, confusion, disbelief, shock, puzzlement, as well as malevolent and malign atmospheres, paranoia, overreactive immune and nervous systems and experiences that border on and have a close relationship to insanity.

The unreality and affective dissonance of this intense set of experiences also profoundly resonates with a political conjuncture equally marked by delusion, conning, facades, trickery, shape-shifting, pathological lying, confusion, chaos, indeterminacy, and a public feeling of scandalized disbelief at what has seemingly become a "new normal." At the heart of both the private and public feeling of disbelief lies an apparatus of communication, which embeds *counterfactual* strategies into sense making. Rather than "creative fabulations" (see Anderson 2010)—forms of future casting that imagine and preempt different future possibilities—counterfactual thinking is about alternatives to what happened that *feel* true, that have the ring of sense, or can circulate and retroactively reshape scenes, encounters, evidence, interpretation, relations, feelings, histories, reputations, and relationships. Truths, facts, and the reality of lived experience are replaced with alternative narratives, including the improbable, impossible, unimaginable, false, sometimes ridiculous, and often offensive.

Counterfactuals are deeply affective and emotional forms of sense making or *sensing*, fabrications of reality based on what might have been, could have been, if-onlys, as-ifs, WTFS, and in a more benign form, as "wishful thinking." They are genres of sensing that propagate disinformation, despite being a routine form of emotional reasoning recognized by psychologists and neuroscientists. Counterfactuals are an important element in the practice of coercive forms of power and can be found in different sites of power and abuse. They are probabilistic, speculative, and preemptive, attempting to retroactively change the past to reshape the future. They can also perpetuate cultures of inequality and oppression and are an important element of communication strategies based on deceit, deception, and manipulation. Other elements of this apparatus include the practices of plausible deniability, reverse projection, word salad, perfidy, future faking, grandiosity, aggrandizement, confabulation, conceit, entitlement, reverse victimhood, false claims, and baiting.

At the same time as this apparatus of communication is recognized as reshaping democratic media and politics, it is often described through a psychologized language of disorder, mapping onto and giving meaning to events, political figures, trends, forms of decision making, narratives, attachments, allegiances, beliefs, and communication styles described as narcissistic. Mary Trump, the niece of the former president Donald Trump, provided regular psychological analyses of Trumpism which have become part of a wider cultural fascination with narcissism and narcissistic leaders. Giving unique insights into Trump's character and psychology, she presaged the very likely possibility that we would see his destructive tendencies play out in vengeful and vindictive expressions of his inability to accept that he had not won a second term in the 2020 American election.[3] What were described as his narcissistic wounds, rage, lack of empathy and conscience, and a willful intent to break and destroy values, communication practices, buildings, relationships, and political and media systems aligned to democracy, was born out by the storming of the US Capitol in January 2021.

Trump supporters led the insurrection known as "Stop the Steal" during the certification of the Electoral College vote count to confirm Joe Biden's presidential win. This led to a second impeachment trial and a legal discussion that centered on the coercive power of specific words, slogans, and phrases and their role in the incitement of the violence and riots: "We won it by a landslide," "Stop the steal," "We will never give up," "We will never concede," "You don't concede when there's theft involved. Our country has had enough. We will not take it anymore," "If you don't fight like hell, you're not going to have a country anymore."

In the aftermath of Trump's acquittal for a second time, what has remained as the dust settles are important questions relating to his "remarkable" capacities to exploit, coerce, manipulate, and frame reality such that conspiracy theories, lies, and other forms of mis- and disinformation become contagious and infectious. Analyses of Trump's affective styles and mediated persona reveal how political emotions and fantasies are part of his bellicose performances. In an essay in the online magazine of the journal *Society and Space*, Ben Anderson (2017) recognizes the ambivalent mix of emotions that were produced and circulated among Trump's supporters and opponents, including resentments, hope, hostilities, rage, contempt, anger, incredulity, horror, anxieties, and the role of lies, exaggerations, and distortions in the fantasies and promises offered up. Making the important point that truth-based political critique and fact-checking were largely ineffectual in countering Trump's appeals, Anderson suggests that this critical ineffectivity was partially linked to a particular form of "emotional authenticity" aligned to Trump's sense of "fun" used to connote spontaneity and unpredictability. The ease of his performances and the consistency of his belief as he honed his "persona as winner" was in contrast to a range of identified "losers" (drawn from an already-existing economy of otherness based on longer histories, fears, fetishes, and phobias).

There is no doubt that the questions Trumpism crystallized will preoccupy media and political scholars for decades to come. The focus of this chapter is on aspects of Trump's affective style when considered in relation to the communication and conversational techniques that shape his persona, which produce affects and emotions of convolution. The chapter specifically explores the connections between what I call a social and political apparatus of narcissism and the particularity and genealogy of narcissistic abuse as a way of unpacking some of these issues. At the heart of this discussion are communication strategies based on very strange and duplicitous forms of communication.

They use methods that have largely been excised from reason or are only allowed to appear in certain sanitized forms, including techniques and practices related to suggestion, priming, precognition, retrocausality, retroactivity, time travel, noncausality, cognitive reattribution, confabulation, anticipation, preemption, subliminal, nonconscious, and other paradoxical forms of communication, especially the case of counterfactuals. I explore how these paradoxical forms of communication are central to modern technologies of power by drawing on a range of strategies that are neither rational nor irrational but more akin to what some affect scholars have called the "nonrational" (Berlant 2005). This includes forms of attachment that sidestep conscious deliberation or rational thought and in certain contexts might be recognized as deluded, self-defeating, abnormal, or anomalous.

In my previous writing that engages explicitly with the field of affect studies (see Blackman 2012, 2019), I have explored an archive of experiences that are often discounted as irrational, providing a rich tapestry of practices, experiences, and technologies that extend our understandings of processes understood as affective. The primary archive is from the field of psychology, analyzed genealogically as a science of population management rather than a science of the individual. Drawing on a long tradition of writing in this area (Blackman 2001; Blackman and Walkerdine 2001; Blackman et al. 2008; Henriques et al. 1998; Walkerdine 1990), we can see that from psychology's inception as discipline and set of knowledge practices, it has been part of a wider set of social apparatuses for governing and managing populations in relation to specific regulatory images of the human that are sexed, raced, classed, ableist, and gendered, providing techniques for mapping, classifying, targeting, and administering Otherness. Governing in the name of rationality, psychology has primarily focused on experiences considered outside of reason, including through fears of irrational, suggestible, oversensitive "mass minds" sick with contagion (Blackman and Walkerdine 2001).

As Valerie Walkerdine (1988) cogently analyzed in her book *The Mastery of Reason*, reason has been a central plank of liberal democracies, creating the fear that unreason lurks continually, presenting a danger to liberal governance. Perhaps the con in this cover story is that at the same time as unreason is delegitimated, psychology has developed more and more techniques that govern through the nonrational, including technologies of suggestion, contagion, and processes linked to psychic research in the late nineteenth and early twentieth centuries. These shape-shifting techniques in the present are linked to the controversial field of *weird science*, inviting a renewed focus on registers and modalities of attending to the world that exceed conscious rational thought and that are shared and distributed across the human and more than human.

The role that these techniques play in political communications that mobilize post-truth as a strategy of governance and in the "gray areas" of psychological abuse are the focus of my analysis here. My argument is that counterfactual reasoning has a close relationship to emotions and affects of convolution. I use the term "convolution" to refer to *strange affects* that disclose multiplications of reality characterized by twists, turns, multiplicities, complications, and confusions. The experiences of convolution are often described as torturous and difficult to understand, articulated primarily as forms of *unfeeling*. Convolution is often carried by the emotion of disbelief characterized by moments where we are stopped in our tracks, where eyebrows are raised, where we feel numb and do not know what to think and are unable to feel. Next, I will explore the implications of disbelief as a political emotion for the field of affect studies and our abilities to script and caption the multiplications of reality that are part of convolution.

Disbelief as Political Emotion

Don't believe what you read, hear or see.

That's what the Trump White House and the pro-Trump media are relying upon: Disbelief. Story after story calls to mind the old Marx Brothers line "Who ya gonna believe, me or your own eyes?"[4]

Disbelief can be a political emotion, but not in the usual sense, since it is not oriented toward opinion. It is, rather, the scene of stopping and looking around while full of unacted-on sensation related to refusing a consensual real: an emotional space-time for adjustment, adjudication.[5]

The word disbelief doesn't really cover what people are feeling.[6]

"The word 'disbelief' doesn't really cover what people are feeling" is a refrain typically expressed when people are trying to make sense of complicated feelings and shocking events. In this instance, the statement was made by a British Channel 4 news journalist reporting on the killings carried out by Jake Davidson, a self-identified "incel" who shot and murdered his mother and five random members of the public before killing himself in 2021. Disbelief is an interesting political emotion, as Berlant captures in their 2005 reflections on "unfeeling" and disbelief and the convoluted emotions and affects that it puts into motion. Berlant's incisive reflections were made within the context of the failure of the Democrat candidate John Kerry to unseat George W. Bush for a second election term in the 2004 American presidential campaign. Rather than move to a swift analysis of the reasons for Kerry's failure, Berlant dwells in another register, mining disbelief as a way to open up a discussion of the importance of the "nonrational" in political attachments. As they argue, many political commentaries of the time, which have only increased since the time of this piece, are "too knowing," too frank in their objections, rather than dwelling in the strangeness of certain political events and their significance. It is a strangeness that is often communicated through "not having the words for it"—bewilderment, puzzlement, hopelessness, helplessness, and suspension, a space for and of feeling stunned, mystified, befuddled, confused, shocked, overwhelmed, baffled, bewildered, perplexed, puzzled, and motionless.

There is no doubt that disbelief as a political emotion, exercised in the conjuncture of writing this chapter, carries the contradictions, foreclosures, and displacements that point to the strange, and beyond what we *know*, challenging what Berlant calls a "need to know right away." As with the John Kerry event that Berlant analyzes, opinions abound regarding Trumpism, post-truth, and authoritarian populism, including the feminist criticism and analysis of Bonnie Honig (2021) in her book *Shell-Shocked: Feminist Criticism after Trump*. Framing the primary affect of the Trump presidency as shock, Honig draws on the work of Naomi Klein and her concept of disaster capitalism developed in the book *Shock Doctrine* to analyze those techniques of "disaster patriarchy" (deprivation and saturation) that assault the senses and lead to exhaustion, fatigue, and chaos.

Shock is part of disbelief, which as Honig suggests, overwhelms, disorients, floods, desensitizes, and paralyses. Shock causes us to doubt perception and interrupts sense making. Honig offers discernment, as a practice of understanding and critical reflection, as a strategy of resistance to shock, and as a way to bring ourselves back to our senses. In this formulation, shock prevents or stymies sense and our capacity to understand and process what is happening. However, the affective economies of disbelief as a political emotion are more convoluted than shock. Indeed, the dictionary definition of convolution refers to the bewildering aspects of the twisted and twisting multiplications of reality that are confusing, puzzling, and dissociative. The convoluted processes of disbelief move in atmospheres and nervous states that include expressions and feelings of inexplicability and bafflement, as well as affective responses that are primarily associated with trauma reactions. Disbelief is not the opposite of belief and discernment but refers to some of the strangeness of convolution: to something and somewhere else, to incoherent processes, to vertigo, incongruities, strange indeterminacies, chaos, dissonance, and to the primary place of the nonrational in constructing and multiplying realities.

Berlant (2005) invokes the "consensual real"—those social fictions and fantasies that must remain unchanged, that are part of consensus or "common sense"—as important in the operations of disbelief. Disbelief requires a shared commons or common ground that is radically disrupted, challenged, arrested, unseated, stopped, and shattered to take hold and be felt. Disbelief reveals the fragility of the consensual and the attachments that are necessary for it to propagate. As Berlant astutely argues, for example, "families are captioning machines whose frames we presume, until we don't."[7] Disbelief signals that the consensual is blocked, thwarted, that there is uncathected affect and emotion swirling around that carries refusal, modulating dissonance and a sense of an impasse.[8] Disbelief is unknowing; it is retroactive and interferes with what came before without offering an alternative. It is an opening to something else that exists in cracks, silences, interstices, foreclosures, and disavowals. Disbelief shows up in the frames and genres, revealing the counterfactual fantasies of the consensual for what they are: machines to caption and articulate the consensual that are strange and can be made stranger under particular circumstances and conditions. Sometimes they can break down altogether.

As with much of Berlant's work, they focus on the implications of disbelief for public intimacies, and the fantasy sites and objects of the family and sexuality through which intimacies and attachments are primarily shaped. As they cogently argue, the family and sexuality are what must remain unchanged, never to be made strange. I would add that in the context of narcissistic abuse, there are several related elements of the consensual real that must also remain unchanged for these processes of mattering to propagate. These include normative assumptions about mental health, rationality, sanity, the human, the psychological, violence, truth, and legal notions of capacity and consent. Disbelief is ambivalent, registering the centrality of convolution through what it reveals and keeps in place. It is not apathy, but it is a reaction and a strong reaction at that. Disbelief has a momentum, a need to find or create a new object so the feeling(s) can be carried and shared with others. Disbelief requires a period of adjustment without forgoing what is strange. It requires a response which is not just emotional reactivity but something else. Defensive reactions are one response, what Berlant describes as coolness or detachment, or stress, worry, dread, and anxiety. As they argue, "the register of political affect I'm describing expresses mixed feelings, contradiction, ambivalence, and above all, incoherence. Not emotions of revolution, but convolution."[9]

If you ever find yourself in the wrong story, leave.[10]

Convolution is destabilizing not least when your own life is reflected back to you through its distortions and distractions. Although I am not explicitly focusing on the specificities of narcissistic abuse within this chapter, a brief example might help to indicate the central role of techniques of the nonrational and the convoluted communication structures that are part of what I am calling narcissistic storytelling (see Blackman 2022). In a book written as a survivor of narcissistic abuse, Adelyn Birch (2015) recounts the need for victims to acquire knowledge of some of the techniques to better protect themselves from their effects and affects. This includes knowledge of the use of "covert emotional manipulation" in an attempt to shape thinking, feeling, conduct, and behavior. As Birch says, "Covert emotional manipulation operates under your level of conscious awareness" (28). This might include forms of behavioral conditioning (such as intermittent reinforcement), gaslighting ("a manipulator asserts something untrue with enough conviction and intensity that the victim believes it" [34]), empty words, and ghosting (silent treatment). However, the gaps, cracks, silences, and contradictions can be revealed through "incongruities" that the manipulator embodies, including contradicting themselves, inconsistencies, and emotional responses that feel "off-beat." There are also breakthroughs such as "spaceship moments" (34), which are the felt experiences of odd statements or questions, red flags, and inconsistencies, that reveal the perpetrator's intent. Spaceship moments are statements or expressions that are "out of place. Out of context. *Out of the blue*. Like an alien being who didn't get humans or life on earth at all, but who was trying to understand."[11]

These practices and their ubiquity in political communications are normalizing communication once only discussed in self-help manuals, workshops, blogs, and memoirs primarily written by and/or for victims and survivors of abuse. These connections have been severed from the public sphere and unmoored from their genealogical links with abuse and practices such as coercive control. Disbelief has entered the personal and political frame under many guises revealing the close connection among feeling, politics, and the ubiquity of technologies of the "nonrational" in governing psychological and affective life. Perhaps Brexit and the election of Trump were two events associated with post-truth communication strategies, which also marked the contours of public feeling that carried this range of mixed and troubling feelings. Arguably, these feelings communicate and articulate the disbelief that makes the strangeness of the "consensual real" more familiar, while adding layers of disorientation and dissonance.

Gaslighting, Perfidy, and Plausible Deniability

One of the more obvious and recognized communication structures that modulate and amplify convolution is gaslighting: a buzzword of 2018. In some commentary, gaslighting is seen as reflective of the toxicity of the political contexts we have been living through.[12] The *Oxford English Dictionary* defines gaslighting as the intent or capacity to "manipulate (a person) by psychological means into questioning his or her own sanity." The term now circulates widely in media cultures, providing a psychological language for apprehending power, inequalities, and social injustices, including among those who are more "woke"[13] to the insidious nature of political strategies and communications that work primarily through techniques of deceit and deception associated with the nonrational.[14] These techniques are often aligned with narcissism and with disordered personalities and similarly disordered ways of thinking. In my view, some of the most astute writing about post-truth and narcissism and their common patterns of deceptive communication has appeared in publications like *Teen Vogue*[15] and *Ms.* magazine. These writings focus more on narcissist *tactics* as forms of abuse. They do not locate them primarily within the confines of a distinctly disordered personality or within understandings of narcissism as NPD. Narcissism is aligned more to a political and social apparatus that has distinct histories and cultures. However, there is no doubt that one of the effects of this apparatus is a disordering of reality, perception, attention, memory, and even sanity.

Gaslighting is very effective at cultivating atmospheres of disbelief, and emotions and affects of convolution, sowing the seeds of doubt and confusion. It can operate in interpersonal dynamics as well as at institutional levels and is a key strategy of political communications within right-wing populism. In her book *The Gaslight Effect*, Robin Stern (2018, xxv) identifies 2016 as a key moment within which gaslighting entered popular consciousness as a communication tool and political strategy. As she argues, "In March of that year, comedian and HBO host John Oliver claimed that Donald Trump had gaslighted him. At first glance the story seemed simple enough. Donald Trump announced that he had refused an invitation to appear on Oliver's program. 'John Oliver had his people call me to be on his very boring and low-rated show,' Trump tweeted. 'I said "NO THANKS." Waste of time and energy!' *But here's the twist: Oliver never made that invitation. He had no interest in having Trump as a guest on his show*" (my emphasis). What is interesting about Stern's recounting of this gaslighting tactic was the effect it had on Oliver and how destabilizing he found it to be on the end of a blatant lie. Here was a talk show host who to all intents and purposes was confident and had a grip on reality. He was not a woman isolated and subject to gaslighting within the confines of an abusive marriage, as in the 1940s film noir *Gaslight*, which gave this strategy its name. What threw Oliver was Trump's *conviction*, his tone, which communicated an affect of righteous indignation in relation to an event that clearly had not occurred. Trump was certain about his version of events, conveyed in his incongruous tweet. A spaceship moment no less. Was this a retaliation for a perceived slight at not being invited on the show? The tweet was out of place, wrong, strange, and destabilizing. It was a counterfactual statement that played with the "power of possibility," retroactively changing the past to respond to a future that would never happen.

In other contexts, the strange affect communicated was linked to Trump's *gusto*. The definition of gusto includes attacking something and developing a taste for something that is communicated with a sense of energy, enjoyment, and satisfaction. This conjures up a playful sense of baiting and provocation likening the exchange to a game. The term "gusto" was used in an article by Melissa Jeltsen, a senior reporter at the *Huffington Post*, that Stern refers to in her summary of what happened. Jeltsen covers domestic violence and related issues, and the archive of her published articles provides an important repository of the links between Trumpism, right-wing authoritarianism, post-truth politics, and the rollout of tactics and strategies that are part of coercive control. She also draws out the links between gun crime, mass shootings, and domestic violence, as well as the high proportion of Trump supporters and advisers who are known domestic abusers, including Steve Bannon, former chief executive of the Breitbart News and White House chief strategist for the first seven months of Trump's presidency.[16] Jeltsen's John Oliver story runs with the headline, "Donald Trump Is Successfully Conning the Entire Country." The piece continues, "The GOP front-runner is gaslighting us—a technique that involves lying, then feigning outrage when caught. . . . This form of psychological abuse typically plays out like so: The gaslighter states something false with such intensity and conviction that whoever is on the receiving end is confused and begins to doubt their own perspective. . . . When faced with their brazen lies, gaslighters deny their own statements, change the subject, lash out with insults (think 'little' Rubio and 'liar' Cruz), act indignant about the accusation, or turn on the messenger—which, for Trump, is often the national media."[17] The term "gaslighting" was regularly used to identify the erasure and rewriting of history that occurred on an almost daily basis during the pandemic under Trump's presidency. His previous comments to the press and on social media and decisions about the pandemic were *confabulated* (see Vaknin 2020) such that reality was fabricated, distorted, and falsified.[18] These confabulations, whether done with calculated intent to lie and mislead or as the messy result of disordered thinking, were shared in videos, memes, and GIFs. This includes videos using comedic cataloging and editing of these "errors," such as the very funny video shared by NowThis Politics, titled "Trump's Not a Doctor but He Plays One on TV."[19] The affective economy of disbelief that we find across social media helps to archive public feeling expressed through astonishment, humor, and inexplicability alongside expressions of the very real fear and danger of Trump's convictions.

The technique of gaslighting disorients and destabilizes borders and boundaries between sanity and insanity, truth and falsehood, real and imaginary, self and other, fact and fiction, modulating the "power of possibility" shaped through the consensual real, including normative assumptions about family, intimate relationships, sanity, morality, and those infrastructures that shape what counts as true, just, and probable. In Honig's analysis of the film *Gaslight*, as well as in novels such as *Jane Eyre* or Toni Morrison's *Home*, gaslighting is a substantive focus as well as a structuring device for playing with the ambiguity of a plot. Somebody is a victim and somebody is a perpetrator: subject to techniques designed to undermine their apprehension of reality and therefore the reader's capacity to make sense of the plot. Certainty and a reliable narrator or witness are replaced with a feeling that something is "off," that all is not quite what it seems. Gaslighting as narrative device requires a plot resolution, which will reestablish firm distinctions between sanity and insanity, real and imaginary, villain and victim, self and other. Reading gaslighting as a text to be decoded, Honig (2021, 17) frames the technique as a "device of disorientation" that relies on deprivation and an overwhelming shock to the senses, "until she [the victim] comes to doubt her own mind and abilities" (15). The plot resolution is a return to the senses and to an ordered and distinct sense of self.

We can learn a lot from film, media cultures, and literature that deploy gaslighting as a plot to be deciphered, as a dramatic narrative structure that carries normative scripts about sanity and insanity, rationality and irrationality, and their gender normative scripts and plot resolutions. However, in my argument here, gaslighting is a capacious technique more than a technique of shock. Thus, gaslighting takes on different forms in different contexts, enhancing its capacities to convolute and multiply realities, leaving plot resolutions open and ambiguous. Convoluting processes are characterized by infoldings, misdirections, twists and turns, crisscrossing, intervening, and overlapping realities, often in alien, jarring, incongruous, and unfamiliar ways. Convolution also works best within the context of already existing structures of inequality and oppression, providing a purchase on racism and misogyny as technologies of affect long understood as working through the disordering of perception and reality (see Gomez 2015; Davis and Ernst 2019; Sweet 2019; Tobias and Joseph 2018). Gaslighting exists as part of an apparatus that carries technologies of the nonrational into the regulation of psychological and affective life and is effective at modulating moral norms and assumptions that are part of the consensual real. This includes our inability to accept perfidy—being deceitful or untrustworthy—as routine and ordinary (as routine and ordinary as domestic abuse) rather than as an aberrant exceptional phenomenon.

Along with the interrelationships of counterfactual reasoning, coercion, convolution, and plausible deniability, these tactics carry histories of state sponsorship that have embedded these techniques of deception as tools of nonlinear warfare and as strategies to evade accountability. Plausible deniability is a central strategy of convolution that allows an abuser to deny their actions, through twisting, mining, and exploiting the indeterminacy of evidence, feelings, perception, possibility, and memory, including normative assumptions of who is considered believable. It casts enough doubt to assuage claims of culpability. As Honig (2021, 25) has cogently argued, "Believability is a structural privilege that comes with straight white manhood." Plausible deniability operates within and exploits gray areas appealing to normative assumptions that are part of a shared commons. Playing with doubt and disbelief, it operates as a form of retroactive recall, which attempts to change the past by anticipating and reshaping events that have already happened. It is a technique, a close relation of perfidy, that, like many other techniques that link narcissistic abuse with military and colonial forms of power, relates to a genre of psychological warfare tools that are primarily underhanded, dishonest, malicious, harmful, and destructive. Their perfidious nature is located in those techniques that feign trustworthiness or authenticity by posing as innocuous when they are actually nefarious.

Gaslighting embeds perfidy within its storytelling structures, exploiting an assumption we might make that although some people might lie, they do not pathologically lie in order to deliberately deceive. *And* when they are caught in a lie, they surely would not blatantly deny it and blame the victim, particularly when they know it can be proven to not be the case. However, gaslighting reveals that perfidy—the normative assumption that a politician, a partner, or a parent, for example, would act in good faith in relation to those who depend on them—is a *big lie* that is part of the "consensual real." This big lie obscures the fact that technologies of the nonrational are routinely deployed to deliberately exploit this myth, reframing relational dynamics through an adversarial politics more akin to war and combat situations. Perfidy within the context of combat situations is defined as a deliberate and calculated violation and breach of trust. Perfidy is outlawed by Article 37 of the Geneva Convention because it is seen to contravene certain moral assumptions about the integrity and rules of war. Attempts to feign and mislead combatants are considered war crimes. As Sean Watts (2014, 1) has argued, "Perfidy and treachery are among the gravest law-of-war accusations. The betrayals of good faith associated with perfidy threaten more than the immediate, tactical positions of the attacker and victim. Perfidious betrayals inflict systemic harm on the law of war as a guarantee of minimally humane interaction. Even a single instance of perfidy can permanently compromise the possibility of humanitarian exchange between belligerents." Perfidy, as a legal and military concept, has a long history establishing the parameters for what is considered humane conduct, recognized in the United Kingdom through the term "perfidious albion."[20] And yet, within the context of political and personal forms of abuse, the perfidious nature of gaslighting does not attract the same judicial attention. Gaslighting tends to work in more affective registers, carrying horror, incoherence, and dissonance in relation to the breach of trust and even a disbelief that somebody might deliberately mislead *and* then deny the deception, drawing attention to the sinister undertones of pathological lying and its treacherous effects and affects. However, the grave dangers of gaslighting with its breach of even minimal customs and habits of respect and trust are barely recognized in domestic law due to the systemic failures in understanding and prosecuting nonphysical abuse. Such practices are more likely to be dismissed and minimized, not achieving or attracting the same attention as the identification of isolated and discrete acts of violence. The "con" in convolution reveals the deception integral to coercion and its links to forms of power that work through the modulation and convolution of realities resulting in the production of strange and torturous affects that act primarily as forms of misdirection and suspension.

Conclusion

Although it offers but a brief introduction to the *strange affects* convolution entails, I hope this chapter introduces an area to the field of affect studies that identifies a range of feelings and experiences that largely challenge the consensual scripting of reality, reveal its strangeness, and exceed the scripts that we might typically bring to bear on them in analyses of psychological and emotional life (see Frank and Wilson 2020). Convolution includes dissonance and chaos, and profound attachments that are difficult to shake. It also includes paradoxical affective couplings:[21] disbelief combined with righteous indignation, for example, twisting moral senses of injustice to congeal and confuse matters. Sianne Ngai (2005) utilizes the term "ugly feelings" to focus on negative affects linked to "situations of passivity" or obstructed or restricted agency, thus identifying what she calls "unusually knotted or condensed emotions" that emerge in various predicaments. These are revealed through feelings such as envy, irritation, anxiety, paranoia, and so on. "That is, signs that not only render visible different registers of problem (formal, ideological, sociohistorical) but conjoin these problems in a distinctive manner" (3).

Ugly feelings is a good term to describe not only the troubled and troubling feelings cultivated through convolution but the knotted emotions or feelings and the conditions of restricted agency, passivity, and dissonance of convolution (including the torturous, complicated, and indeterminate nature of how abusive environments and atmospheres might feel as realities are multiplied). Although we might use the term "psychological" to refer to these forms of abuse, the techniques of the nonrational central to convolution exceed psychological individualisms and have a closer, yet disavowed, relationship to many of the more public processes that have been identified as affective within affect studies and that require closer attention. There has been a tendency in the field to overlook or obscure relations that exist in a socially displaced and foreclosed form—namely, related techniques of deceit and deception that are common to different contexts of abuse, power, and control (see Boler and Davis 2020).

This is part of a much longer genealogy, which has shaped the political and social apparatuses of narcissism that are part of what I am calling "abuse assemblages" (see Blackman, forthcoming). This genealogy encompasses a range of interconnected elements, practices, forms of knowledge and understanding, laws, communicative structures, policies, practices, habits, subjectivities, embodied realities, emotions, affects, atmospheres, nervous states, forms of apprehension, and methods and techniques of duplicity and the nonrational that form the capaciousness of abuse assemblages. These elements are agile, indeterminate, can group and regroup, cross boundaries and thresholds, and achieve certain forms of legibility, while in other contexts they are not recognized at all. Abuse assemblages are mobile, in between, can telescope and transport while foreclosing and displacing. They appear and disappear, are informational, can entangle, and be forced apart. They connect and cut, appear and disappear, are visible and hidden, are in movement and solidify. The term "abuse assemblages" recognizes that abuse is not a single act or even set of practices. Abuse traverses many different settings, including politics, legal systems, families, sport, psychiatry and mental health systems, universities, schools, the workplace, on the streets, law enforcement agencies, the media including social media, appearing in a range of techniques of control and coercion that have become socially sanctioned and are part of normalcy and the consensual real.

Although we might think of coercion as a form of manipulation that we would seek to avoid, I hope to have demonstrated how the relationships between coercion and counterfactuals are an ordinary and routine part of framing and multiplying realities, again what I am calling *convolution*, drawing on Berlant's (2005) reflections on disbelief as a political emotion. We are more used to focusing on the important concept of revolution as a means of examining and apprehending change processes and the intransigence and creative potential of habitual attachments (see Pedwell 2021), but convolution is a vital and overlooked aspect of modes of power which in different contexts are considered elements of PSYCHOpower (see Orr 2006). PSYCHOpower works in registers that sidestep distinctions between the rational and the irrational, challenging many assumptions we make about self, the human, reason, emotion, sanity, habit, morality, and more. Counterfactual reasoning has serious implications for the bio-politics of mental and physical health. A better understanding of the damage and harm counterfactual thinking and counterfactual com-munication structures can do will allow a greater apprehension of nonphysical abuse and the harms and injuries that are caused through these insidious forms of violence.

Notes

1   Brittany VanDerBill, "How Common Is Narcissistic Abuse in the United States?," PsychCentral, March 28, 2022, https://psychcentral.com/lib/narcissistic-abuse-affects -over-158-million-people-in-the-u-s/.

2   "World Narcissistic Abuse Awareness Day—June 1," National Day Calendar, ac-cessed January 20, 2023, https://nationaldaycalendar.com/world-narcissistic-abuse -awareness-day-june-1/.

3   Mary Trump and Jude Rogers, "Mary Trump on the End of Uncle Donald: All He Has Now Is Breaking Things," *The Guardian*, November 8, 2020, https://www .theguardian.com/us-news/2020/nov/08/mary-trump-on-the-end-of-uncle -donald-all-he-has-now-is-breaking-things.

4   Brian Stelter, "Stelter: Trump Encourages People Not to Believe Their Eyes, Ears or Lungs," CNN, June 4, 2020, https://edition.cnn.com/2020/06/04/media/donald -trump-disbelief-reliable-sources/index.html.

5   Berlant (2005).

6   Amelia Jenne, "Plymouth Shooting: What Do We Know about Jake Davison?," Channel 4 News, August 13, 2021, https://www.channel4.com/news/plymouth -shooting-what-do-we-know-about-jake-davison.

7   Lauren Berlant, "I Went Back 2 the Violent Room for the Time Being," *Supervalent Thought* (blog), April 28, 2016, https://supervalentthought.com/2016/04/28/i-went -back-2-the-violent-room-for-the-time-being/amp/.

8   Berlant (2005).

9   Berlant (2005).

10 "If You Ever Find Yourself in The Wrong Story, Leave," *Outside the Box* (blog), July 19, 2014, https://lookingthroughanotherseyes.wordpress.com/2014/07/19/if -you-ever-find-yourself-in-the-wrong-story-leave/.

11 Adelyn Birch, "Spaceship Moments: Psychopaths Say the Darndest Things," *Psycho-paths & Love* (blog), accessed January 20, 2023, https://psychopathsandlove.com /spaceship-moments/. See also Isabel Waidner, "My Father's Lover Was Never the

Stepdad I Wanted Him to Be," *Granta*, June 4, 2021, https://granta.com/my-fathers-lover-was-never-the-stepdad-i-wanted-him-to-be/.

12 Emma Brockes, "From Gaslighting to Gammon, 2018's Buzzwords Reflect Our Toxic Times, *The Guardian*, November 18, 2018, https://www.theguardian.com/commentisfree/2018/nov/18/gaslighting-gammon-year-buzzwords-oxford-dictionaries.

13 Wikipedia, s.v. "Woke," last modified December 9, 2022, 03:48, https://en.wikipedia.org/wiki/Woke.

14 See Lauren Duca, "Donald Trump Is Gaslighting America," *Teen Vogue*, December 10, 2016, https://www.teenvogue.com/story/donald-trump-is-gaslighting-america; Lauren Duca, "Donald Trump Is Still Gaslighting America. I Really Care. Do u?," *Teen Vogue*, June 23, 2018, https://www.teenvogue.com/story/donald-trump-still-gaslighting-america-i-really-care-do-u.

15 See, for example, *Teen Vogue*'s article discussing necropolitics, "What Is Necropolitics? The Political Calculation of Life and Death," by Namrata Verghese (March 10, 2021, https://www.teenvogue.com/story/what-is-necropolitics?fbclid=IwAR0RukvPUULAs9JWcd0zvMlL2Ts-J42Ata5qhIptnr42pCFscSrvi3_9_ss).

16 Alan Feuer, William K. Rashbaum, and Maggie Haberman, "Steve Bannon Is Charged with Fraud in We Build the Wall Campaign," *New York Times*, August 20, 2020, updated October 19, 2021, https://www.nytimes.com/2020/08/20/nyregion/steve-bannon-arrested-indicted.html.

17 Melissa Jeltsen, "Donald Trump Is Successfully Conning The Entire Country," *HuffPost*, March 16, 2016, https://www.huffingtonpost.co.uk/entry/donald-trump-lies-gaslighting_n_56e95d21e4b065e2e3d7ee82?ri18n=true.

18 Wikipedia, s.v. "Confabulation," last modified July 19, 2022, 03:31, https://en.wikipedia.org/wiki/Confabulation. "Confabulation" as a term has been identified as a pattern of disordered thinking within the context of NPD, for example (see Vaknin 2020). See also Sam Vaknin, "The Narcissist's Confabulated Life," accessed January, 19, 2023, https://samvak.tripod.com/narcissistconfabulation.html.

19 NowThis Politics, "Trump's Not a Doctor, but He Plays One on TV," Facebook, April 10, 2020, https://www.facebook.com/NowThisPolitics/videos/1035913786792402/UzpfSTYoMzg3MDIxMzoxMDE2MzEyODIxNTIxMDIxNA/; Boris Johnson (@BorisJohnson_MP), Tweet from a suspended account, Twitter, accessed April 10, 2020, https://twitter.com/BorisJohnson_MP/status/1253580486380748801; Hannah Jane Parkinson (@ladyhaja), "yeah sure inject yourself with a bottle of dettol, fuck it. i will never, in my entire life, get over this odious moron being president," Twitter, April 24, 2020, 1:49 a.m., https://twitter.com/ladyhaja/status/1253561734280904710.

20 Wikipedia, s.v. "Perfidious Albion," last modified December 14, 2022, 06:17, https://en.wikipedia.org/wiki/Perfidious_Albion.

21 Not unlike Ngai's (2005) coining of the term "stuplimity," which paradoxically couples shock with boredom.

References

Anderson, Ben. 2010. "Anticipatory Action and Future Geographies." *Progress in Human Geography* 34 (6): 777–98.

Anderson, Ben. 2017. "We Will Win Again. We Will Win a Lot." The Affective Styles of Donald Trump." *Society and Space*. https://www.societyandspace.org/articles/we-will-win-again-we-will-win-a-lot-the-affective-styles-of-donald-trump.

Berlant, Lauren. 2005. "Unfeeling Kerry." *Theory and Event* 8 (2). doi:10.135/tae.2005.0021.

Birch, Adelyn. 2015. *202 Ways to Spot a Psychopath in Personal Relationships*. Scotts Valley, CA: CreateSpace.

Blackman, Lisa. 2001. *Hearing Voices: Embodiment and Experience*. London: Free Association Books.

Blackman, Lisa. 2012. *Immaterial Bodies: Affect, Embodiment, Mediation*. London: Sage.

Blackman, Lisa. 2019. *Haunted Data: Affect, Transmedia, Weird Science*. London: Bloomsbury Press.

Blackman, Lisa. 2022. "Future of Truth: Future-Faking, Post Truth and Affective Media." In *The Future of Media*, edited by Joanna Zylinska and Goldsmiths Media. London: Goldsmiths Press.

Blackman, Lisa. Forthcoming. *Gray Media: Gaslighting, Post-Truth, PSYCHOpower*.

Blackman, Lisa, John Cromby, Derek Hook, Dimitris Papadopoulos, and Valerie Walkerdine. 2008. "Creating Subjectivities." *Subjectivity* 22:1–27.

Blackman, Lisa, and Valerie Walkerdine. 2001. *Mass Hysteria: Critical Psychology and Media Studies*. Basingstoke and New York: Palgrave.

Boler, Megan, and Elizabeth Davis. 2020. *Affective Politics of Digital Media: Propaganda by Any Other Means*. London: Routledge.

Davis, Angelique, and Rose Ernst. 2019. "Racial Gaslighting, Politics, Groups, and Identities." *Politics, Groups and Identities* 7 (4): 761–74.

Frank, Adam, and Elizabeth Wilson. 2020. *A Silvan Tomkins Handbook: Foundations for Affect Theory*. Minneapolis: University of Minnesota Press.

Gomez, Jennifer. 2015. "Microaggressions and the Enduring Mental Health Disparity: Black Americans at Risk for Institutional Betrayal." *Journal of Black Psychology* 4 (2): 121–43.

Henriques, Julian, Wendy Hollway, Cathy Urwin, Couze Venn, and Valerie Walkerdine. 1998. *Changing the Subject: Psychology, Social Regulation, Subjectivity*. London: Routledge.

Honig, Bonnie. 2021. *Shell-Shocked: Feminist Criticism after Trump*. New York: Fordham University Press.

Ngai, Sianne. 2005. *Ugly Feelings*. Cambridge, MA: Harvard University Press.

Orr, Jackie. 2006. *Panic Diaries: A Genealogy of Panic Disorder*. Durham, NC: Duke University Press.

Pedwell, Carolyn. 2021. *Revolutionary Routines: The Habits of Social Transformation*. Montreal: McGill Queen's University Press.

Stern, Robin. 2018. *The Gaslight Effect: How to Spot and Survive the Hidden Manipulations Others Use to Control your Life*. New York: Broadway Books.

Sweet, Paige. 2019. "The Sociology of Gaslighting." *American Sociological Review* 64 (5): 851–75.

Tobias, Heston, and Amell Joseph. 2018. "Sustaining Systemic Racism through Psychological Gaslighting: Denials of Racial Profiling and Justifications of Carding by Police Utilizing Local News Media." *Race and Justice* 10 (4): 424–55.

Trump, Mary. 2020. *Too Much and Never Enough: How My Family Created the World's Most Dangerous Man*. New York: Simon and Schuster.

Vaknin, Sam. 2020. "Dissociation and Confabulation in Narcissistic Disorders." *Journal of Addiction and Addictive Disorders* 7 (39). doi:10.24966/AAD-7276/100039.

Walkerdine, Valerie. 1988. *The Mastery of Reason: Cognitive Development and the Production of Rationality*. London: Routledge.

Walkerdine, Valerie. 1990. *Schoolgirl Fictions*. London: Verso.

Watts, Sean. 2014. "Law-of-War Perfidy." *Military Law Review* 219:106–75.

Affective Atmospheres as Transtemporal Contact

Cecilia Macón

Voice, Agency, and Things

> I still hear the voices of my torturers and captors, of my neighboring cellmates, of my companions. They echo in my head every day, but I also know it has taught me to survive. I do not just tolerate them; rather, I realize that every time I hear the voices, they change, even though they are the same. . . . They change with the passage of time, but also because there I do something every day of my life to transform them.

When I first recorded this testimony, the words of a victim of the state terrorism that took place in Argentina between 1976 and 1983, it passed me by. At the time, I was contemplating other questions about the period. Yet, it echoed in my mind. The survivor was evoking an atmosphere created by the sounds of horror, but she was also reflecting on the instruments that enabled her survival. The testimony spoke to the archive of voices that perturbed her amid her own terror, but she also spoke of a sense of contact between the past and present. Today, I understand that, in these words, questions were being posed, not only about the auditory archive of terror but also about the way in which the affective atmospheres of the past connect to action (present and future).

Reflections on the way in which the present exists in affective contact with the past have been part of the debates generated by the affective turn almost from its inception. An intermittent, unpredictable affective form of contact with the past, capable of avoiding both banal continuity and radical disruption, has emerged in conceptualizations of transtemporal contact. Avoiding certain clichéd theories of history, the past is no longer a radical *other* with which we maintain historical distance, nor a constant presence on which to sustain the most commonplace continuities.

Over the last several decades, oral archives have become central to strategies for reconstructing Latin America's recent past. The Archivo oral de memoria abierta (Oral Archive of Open Memory) in Argentina, the Museo memorial del 68 in Mexico ('68 Memorial Museum), the MUME museum in Uruguay, and the Museo de la memoria y los derechos humanos (Museum of Memory and Human Rights) in Chile all serve as prime examples. Several of these archives have been made readily available by digital media; others have been integrated into curated spaces for memory. They have also served as a starting point for the construction of artistic interventions. These recordings are not only composed of sounds but also often include personal testimonies *about* sounds—the voices, music, and noises heard by victims when held captive and blindfolded, enhancing the role of the auditory dimension. In taking into account these discussions and actions, this chapter investigates how the auditory dimension of archives shape the affective contact spaces between present, past, and future. As in the testimony cited above, the reference to the affective archive that endures in the present as a disturbance permits discussion that also contributes to the survival of both victims and subsequent generations. In light of this, I will discuss the tension—sometimes virtuous—between affective atmospheres and the agency of those who have been affected by the past.

The mode in which the concentration camps affect us (or the victims of any genocide or oppression) is neither by mere presence nor at a disaffected distance. As in the above testimony, reflections on the way in which so-called traumatic pasts touch the present have had to consider the affective bond across time in response to a wide range of consequences: among them, the way in which that past marks our movement toward the future. Such touching poses questions: How does this affective contact with the past shape collective agency? To what extent does it define the relationship between the past and the future? In the context of countries and communities whose recent histories are marked by genocide and crimes against humanity, these questions are not merely theoretical, but they directly impact the making of contemporary politics. In these pages, I will contemplate one of the most concrete forms of the affective survival of the past: the sound atmospheres of terror as described by the survivors of those traumatic pasts. This corresponds to a reflection on the power of different versions of the oral archive at the moment when transtemporal contact is made and, in its initial political impact, how collective agency may arise. In this way, I aim to investigate the role of these archives' auditory dimension in transtemporally shaping the affective contact spaces.

The voice shapes affective atmospheres that can persist over time whether through memory, writing, or recording. But that sonorous survival of the past which forms the insistent affective atmosphere is not necessarily crystallized or static; rather, the voice emerges from an animate agency that competes to alter the relationship between the participants and the archive. This process allows one, I believe, to address a fundamental complication: how voices of the past in the contact space of participant and archive can speak to political change in the present while voice also persists as atmosphere that continually shapes that sense of agency. Voices survive in/as atmospheres and configure human agency but are also subject to their own contingency. The voice always makes reference to subjectivity, but it is also the instrument, the medium or material channel. That is, it is something characterized by an accent, an intonation, a tone (Dolar 2006, 20). Moreover and contrary to what happens with pure noise, the voice combines the ideality of meaning with the materiality of the medium (15) and refers to the union between bodies and language (60). In fact, the voice separated from the body, as in the oral archive, evokes the voice of the dead (64) and, with it, that of a past that affects the present in a carnal way. These characteristics allow me to discuss the way in which the present can affect a past that is never merely past, nor does it survive in an unaltered state.

Recently and particularly within the literature on the affective turn, the idea of "affective atmospheres" associated with sound space has taken a central place in discussions about audiovisual and performance arts. Of note in this regard, Friedlind Riedl (2019), Irene Depetris Chauvin (2020), and William Cheng (2016) refigured the very idea of space based precisely on the role of sound as material contact. In my case, I aim to analyze the specificity of sound spaces that, when traversed by digitization, generate affective contact atmospheres and do so within a logic that Susan Schulppie (2020) calls "material witness." Incorporating sound space into materiality as a transtemporal mode of contact—involving past, present, and eventually, future—allows us to see the idea of archival agency in a new light. That is, not only presenting affective atmospheres as charged instances but also as the result of an archival agency that is the product of this atmosphere but at the same time is sustained by its own form of intervention on them.

In this work, I am interested in exploring the way in which these sound atmospheres not only survive over time but are transformed to constitute archives of the past that avoid becoming a mere phantasmal weight. What Hal Foster (2004) refers to as the "archival impulse" has had an important impact in Latin America. Interpretation and re-elaboration of archives as repositories of experiences of the past has been fundamental in generating alternative historical meanings. In these pages, the idea of the archive is not in the sacredness of those documents but rather in taking these archives as a starting point to write new histories (Taccetta 2019, 23). I use the concept of archive in line with Carolyn Steedman (2002) in the sense of it being organized by randomness, tension, and contrast. Archives imply the random presentation of objects in search of a connection that otherwise could not be linked. In this line of inquiry, what Ann Cvetkovich (2003) calls "archives of feelings" explore cultural texts as collections of codified feelings, not only in terms of their content but also in the practices surrounding their production and reception. Such concepts become, as I will argue, particularly relevant while dealing with the tension between agency and archive.

When it comes to a past experienced as disruptive or traumatic, that survival is remarkable; it evokes questions about what should be done with the politically relevant past. Thus, the objective of this chapter is to give an account of how the logic of the Latin American sound archive on state terrorism and its uses—both standardized

and deviant—illuminate the idea of archival agency in its relationship with affective atmospheres in which voice as sound plays a key
role. It is precisely the status of the voice as a thing—immediate and
theatrical—what allows it to act on subjectivities and is, as I will attempt to show, intended to be itself modified. What role does agency
play in shaping and transforming these atmospheres and vice versa?
How do these atmospheres survive in the present but at the same time
force us to reevaluate our capacity for action in relation to the future?

Of Dispositions and Half Things

It is worth recalling that the notion of Stimmung originates in music
(Riedl 2020) and means, precisely, to put in tune. It also implies
analysis of the bodily dimension of listening (8) and the understanding that music and sound convert feelings into something else. Sound
is experienced as spatial; it modulates a situation and puts bodies in
relation (29), generating community. That is, sound creates an affective atmosphere that, like Stimmung, goes beyond the individual
body; it refers to a condition in which bodies become connected (85).
When it comes to the atmospheres constituted by the voice, moreover, the material and subjective dimensions that generated them are
superimposed.

The concept of "affective atmosphere" was introduced by phenom-
enologist Hermann Schmitz, and over the past several years, different
perspectives within affect studies have drawn inspiration from this idea
and also reworked it. In Schmitz's rendering, affective atmospheres
elude the distinctions between an internal and an external order as
well as the appeal to psychologism. They are thus *Halbdinge*—half
things—or tangible entities that capture a felt body and that cannot be reduced to subjective or objective conditions. According to
Micaela Szeftel (2021, 1), Schmitz suggested that "feelings should be
understood as atmospheres poured out over an interpersonal space,
rather than as inner private states": feelings, like objects of perception, are to be found in the world. Atmospheres move the felt body,
or better put, the felt body is affected or "touched" by atmospheres.
Here, feelings are not of the individual but are collectively embodied,
spatially extended, materially and culturally inflected (Riedl 2019, 85).
Thus, affective atmospheres refer to the way in which a multiplicity

of bodies form part of an attachment to a situation that encompasses them. They are also fundamentally contagious and are concerned with amalgamating and configuring practices (21); in this way, they result in a kind of capacity (Slaby 2020, 275) constructed as a set of tangible forces. Atmospheres are, in that sense, like the voice, both material and immaterial.[1] This ability of atmospheres to exceed the merely individual and the distinction between the material and the ideal is particularly relevant when analyzing political phenomena.

Effectively, atmospheres dispose us to certain actions and can open new horizons (Zhang 2018, 123); they allow us to organize and point out certain political objectives as vital and possible (135). By circulating, they also define an ecosystem that is more than the sum of its parts (141). When we perceive atmospheres, we capture the feelings of other people in the air (126), but we also build our capacity for action or agency. It is then in these atmospheres that a willingness for collective action is conjured as possible. However, one of the problems with the notion of affective atmosphere is that in its original definitions, there is little room for agency because—especially in terms of the archive—it is understood more as a repository. What we do or can do with the affective dimension of our experiences—or in this case, of what materially survives from the past through voices—has often been limited. As Jan Slaby (2020, 281) has pointed out, we run the risk of seeing an atmosphere as composed of "homogenizing forces, exceeding its overwhelming influence on all that is in its vicinity." Thus, it is worth noting the ways in which atmospheres can be transformed to give impetus to disruptive action. But how atmospheres generate collective action is only part of the equation. One must also reflect on the ways in which collective agency can transform atmospheres, opening them to unforeseen types of action. It requires reconceptualizing those atmospheres in order to challenge them in more radical ways. What I call here archival agency thus looks to address that dual capacity.

Is this material rootedness called affective atmosphere something more than a tone that tints and links bodies? How is it constituted and transformed? As I understand it, just as epistemic agency accounts for the possibility to transform our beliefs (Sosa 2015), and moral agency refers to the extent to which we are responsible for our actions in a given context, one must formulate an understanding of archival agency that clarifies its possibilities to transform the presented affective order in terms of atmospheres. This implies characterizing archival agency not only as a capacity for action put in play because of the impulse of the affective dimension—that is, affects as generators of action—but also as capable of constituting an affective configuration of its own, from where actions can be promoted and reconsidered.

Just as knowledge informs agency and agency is capable of altering knowledge, affective atmospheres make up agency and are also subject to changes propelled by the agency itself (and, of course, nonintervention is always possible). Agency, in a way, is transformation and self-construction (Broncano 2020, loc. 6765). Given that all agency is built within a power structure that challenges it, it is important to note that I am referring here to a relational concept of agency—one exerts agency with others—which associates certain notions of epistemic agency (what we do with our beliefs) with moral agency (when we are accountable for our actions). In other words, archival agency will have an impact in multiple ways: altering the affective order, on ways in which we are able to modify our actions, and on the possibility—or impossibility—of being responsible for our actions (and vice versa). If we do not address agency of the archive as capable of altering circumstances, the affective dimension embodied in atmospheres could be understood as an unchangeable node or one whose fluidity is autonomous.

Concentrationist Archives and Resistance

In a now-classic analysis, Pilar Calveiro maintains that concentrationist power disseminates terror both within and outside of the camp. The objective was not only extermination but also the demonstration of an absolute power that was capable of deciding about life and death; which is to say, generalized terror (Calveiro 2008, 45). In this way, concentrationist affective atmospheres extend beyond the walls of the concentration camp. Testimonies by the victims of human rights violations in Argentina have often been the subject of the archival sound spaces of once-clandestine detention centers. There, the affective atmosphere of terror was part of this concentrationist logic and was also transformed by the prisoners' own experience. There are, indeed, innumerable testimonies that give an account of the role of sound in the constitution of the concentrationist affective atmosphere. In the recent *Satisfaction en la* ESMA (Satisfaction at the ESMA), Abel Gilbert (2021) analyzes the components of an archive of sound during the last Argentine dictatorship: military marches, concerts, clandestine music but also the sound of terror in detention centers as experienced by its victims.

I am interested here in focusing on this last point; it is a powerful example of the way in which affective atmospheres are instances not only contingent but also open to the affective agency of their participants—here, affective agency, in its contact with beliefs, is also epistemic agency. Gilbert's systematization provides well-known examples like prisoners attentively listening to radio transmissions of the 1978 World Cup soccer matches (a deviant moment shared with their captors)[2] but also the music that torturers would play while committing violence on victims. The testimonies collected by Gilbert, as well as Rosario Figari Layús (2015) and Mario Villani and Fernando Reati (2011), reveal how sound helps the imprisoned to identify routines in the camps and to keep track of the temporality of the outside world. As Gilbert (2021, 11) points out, "Terror had a perceptual effect that shaped the auditory sense in this context of radical confinement." Sounds, noises, music, and silence molded an atmosphere that was an effective tool for ensuring compliance with the concentrationist logic but also for thinking beyond that logic. The sounds recalled by neighbors who believed they could hear the screams of the tortured[3] intersect with those heard by prisoners, who listened for the sounds of families going about their daily life outside the prison walls.[4] Despite the sound-absorbing foam placed on cell walls, detainees could still make out sounds coming from neighboring houses and from the torture chamber: "the screams of the tortured were like that background music you cannot turn off," recalled one prisoner (Villani and Reati 2011, 111). This intermixture of sounds formed an affective atmosphere, an archive that also served as a map for both the prisoners and those outside the camps' walls. It is the agency always available in imagination, as well as an exercise of a competence to intervene in the world.

The sound archive also preserves the movements of people circulating around them: of those who lived in suffering in neighboring cells, of the torturers who moved about the corridors and in and out of offices. The sound space was a concentration of terror but also the only available sensorial tool of orientation (Gilbert 2021, 54). In fact, detainees' sense of sound became hyperdeveloped. As one survivor put it, "One's ear was so fine-tuned that the sounds of boots always created some kind of trembling, a pounding heartbeat" (67). According to another testimony, this sense of alertness began to develop as soon as one was transferred to the centers, just after being kidnapped: "Although I was blindfolded, I could hear his companions yelling at him to be more discreet: 'Che, Pepona, hide your weapon!' I was scared to death, but I was trying to think and figure out what route we were taking, paying attention to each brake, turn and any other movement that could indicate where we were going" (Villani and Reati 2011, 39). According to those who testified in trials for crimes against humanity or in front of investigators, it was critical to distinguish the sounds of steps (Gilbert 2021, 67) to make a sound archive of relevant information and orient oneself in space and in time: key for creating or imagining agency even as it was being violently oppressed. As one testimony recounts, "At Club Atlético I sharpened my sense of hearing until I had an idea of where we were. I learned to recognize the camp's [patterns of] movement by sounds. I could even differentiate the sounds of the guards who looked after us from those who interrogated when they came to a prisoner in their charge" (Villani and Reati 2011, 61).

Here, there are recognizable forms of sound stalking (Turner 2021, 2): senses, felt energies, atmospheres that create rituals (Depetris Chauvin 2020, 7), paranoia in reference to particular sounds (Cheng 2016, 229) and even suffering as a response to particular types of music, which itself was sometimes used as a form of torture. This imposed atmosphere included vibrations, traumas, and humiliation (235) used to exercise a crime against the imagination but also could be used as a map to intervene and alter atmospheres. This sound archive not only survives in the memory of the victims but has also been constituted through their testimonies and compiled into a shared archive that forms part of what is collectively understood as a concentrationist affective atmosphere. It is an archive of affective atmospheres that not only linked bodies but was sometimes experienced in deviant, unforeseen ways: as indications of space-time location that could be used to plot an escape, as modes of contact with other prisoners, as imagining—beyond those walls—the presence of possible witnesses to their oppression. It was not only a question of the parallel uses of the internment affective atmosphere but also of a transformation of the atmosphere itself through actions: whispering among the prisoners, putting a rhythm to music being heard or the noises produced by displacements within the cell, sent as signals to the outside; these could be a starting point for resistance. As one prisoner I interviewed pointed out, "I remember that inside the cell I tried to make noises with whatever I had on hand to communicate with the outside, especially with other prisoners. I also sometimes sang in a low voice to drown out the screams of [those being] torture[d]." Thus, as the witnesses point out, the archive of these affective atmospheres became transformed by resignification into an opportunity for action and thus vividly remains in the present, in the memory of the survivors. They constitute one way by which the present links to the past. At the same time, through their testimonies and their own resignification, they formulate a shared archive. It is those affective atmospheres that were modified from the moment of confinement. The sounds were and are intercepted, superimposed, and distorted by subsequent voices and gestures that indicate, at the same time, the contingency and the survival of their archives.

We should recall that like affect, traumatic memory belongs to an order of intensity and volatility, evading the capture of language (Atkinson and Richardson 2013, 14–16). In this type of experience, then, the affective dimension emphasizes unmediated materiality while trauma brings to light the temporal in terms of latency (17). This is not a successive and lineal temporality but a latent insistency capable of altering everything at any time in unexpected ways. Thus, the survival, the persistence of the sound archive connects the past to the present, rescuing its materiality, but also the possibility of its transformation.

What is the role of affective atmospheres of sound in putting the past in contact with the present when it comes to other contemporary subjects directly affected by that past? How are they altered? I will consider these questions through analysis of the installation *El vacío de la arena* (The emptiness of sand) by Cristián López, a Chilean artist and member of the Tsonami group, a collective made up of sound-based artists in Valparaíso. In 2018, López presented *El vacío de la arena*, an interactive installation in which sound and space are interconnected to mourn the mass disappearance of people during the Chilean dictatorship. In resonance with Charles Reznikoff's book about Adolf Eichmann's testimony at the Nuremberg trials, where embodied voices construct a lyricism of despair,[5] López takes the testimony as his starting point. But this time, the materiality of the voice sets a tone for action in the present. The work expressed a persistent concern for silence and white noise as an expression of trauma and affect—themes López had previously explored in other works and which I will reference here.

El vacío de la arena stems from a disturbing conversation that López had with the daughter of a disappeared militant. She confessed her need to tell her story publicly, something that, for various reasons, she had never dared to do. López offered to record her testimony, a response to the guiding question, "Where is my father?" López's very interactive installation invites visitors to put on wireless headphones; for twenty minutes, they hear the recording of her testimony while they walk through a space covered by randomly distributed stones. Each visitor thus chooses a different path for engaging the materiality of voice giving her testimony. A voice is embodied in a story that is entangled in many possible forms until it finally merges in a random, ephemeral manner but also in close proximity to the objects themselves. The fatally fragile memory, in danger of extinction, becomes a voice attached to the stones and mediated by subjective decisions.

The resulting affective atmosphere is thus sustained in the materiality of the voice and in the dynamics of traversing and building a space. However, that same atmosphere, in its own materiality, is far from being an instance that merely guides, configures, practices, or links bodies; in its ability to generate action, it generates impulses that modify the atmosphere itself. According to López, most of the people who participated in the tour said they felt sadness but also joy—not the anger associated with injustice or the disturbing relief of grief but sadness and joy. That is, they felt one affect linked to an increase in power and another linked to its decrease: a perhaps contradictory form of identifying the possibility of survival. These apparently contradictory affective experiences express the tensions that pass between the unspeakable and the effort to construct a guiding narrative, one traversed by the intervention of the visitors themselves. The practice of silence required by the installation brought to light the unspeakable experience with which visitors came into contact through the presence of the testimonial voice. However, at the same time, it was about transforming that atmosphere through the guidance of a voice that they also altered with their own journey. López's installation forced the participants to listen to the voice and, simultaneously, to intervene and transform it via the path they walked. It was, as the artist pointed out by evoking the words of one of the visitors, "an experience that silences you"; in this way, it illuminated the visceral in the affective dimension, which both transforms subjectivity and alters the atmosphere itself. It was, López insists, a call for nonintervention, for nonoperationalization, of avoiding aestheticism, stylization; it was a call to simply inhabit that atmosphere in time.

But in creating an archival refuge for memory and inhabiting that space, the visitors were also prompted to alter the affective atmosphere. They had to locate the voice in a concrete space/time through a monologue that gradually acquired limits by incarnating itself along an unsteady path. The expression of the experience of walking on ruins gave witness to the voice but also granted it certain limits and even provided it an ending where joy collided with sadness. Here, the auditory archive contains a voice that evokes the past, underlining the actions of its participants, but at the same time, its atmosphere can be altered by those interventions.

The recording here became an incarnation of past material agencies sustained in distanced subjectivities within the present (Tragaki 2020, 191) and tied to operations of affective attachment which construct possible meanings through their actions. Thus, the radical materiality created by the atmosphere of the voice prevails but simultaneously enables agencies that transform it through the decisions of those participating. Despite the premise that they would bring the atmosphere to light, the participants' actions substantially alter it in a circular process. The voice spreads around here without a body, but it maintains its immediacy and theatricality in conforming atmospheres by guiding subjectivities capable of dislocating them. It is by adhering to other moving bodies that the archived voice sets into action and alters the atmosphere. It arms and disarms the senses; it alters time. It brings the past to the present but also challenges it, establishing the affective contacts on their own terms.

As Irene Depetris Chauvin (2015) has pointed out, there is often a temporal ambiguity in sound that contributes to its permanent displacement of meaning: sound is fleeting, but by surviving as a material presence through memory or its recording, resignification becomes possible: in this case, through concrete experiences. And it is this relationship between affective atmospheres—as the voice (material and immaterial) and the agency of the bodies that circulate within the space López designed—that generates this disfiguration of meaning.

In some ways, the sound of the voice, being an atmosphere, constitutes us as subjects beyond meaning. In fact, since the Renaissance, the human voice has become an instrument par excellence (Depetris Chauvin 2015, 4) due to its ability to move us in a particular way. The sound of the voice inhabits us, possesses us, haunts us (1), but also, as the cases here show, in the persistence of materiality, it is subjected to the alteration generated by the very agency it constitutes. The affective atmospheres of a voice that is simultaneously material and immaterial configure practices that at the same time, alter them in unpredictable ways.

Affect and Action

In order to investigate how this type of relationship between atmosphere and agency develops, it must then be emphasized that atmospheres are not inert ghostly things but are entities with agency affected by the practices they generate. That is, if they are manipulable like the subjects on which they are imposed, it is, perhaps paradoxically, because atmospheres themselves have agency. Just as occurs in human agencies, the material aspect of the voice, involved in the creation of atmospheres or half things neither reduces their capacity to act nor to be modified. In recent years, the role of the material in nonhuman agency has been addressed in what has been called the forensic turn: a perspective that underlines how, for example, the remains of victims' bodies generate a link between the object and life, overlapping subject with object and material practices with linguistic ones. This requires that we realize the role of the material presence of the remains of the dead and other related materials (object, tombs, constructions) when massacres, torture, or similar violent events are examined (Dziuban 2017, 10). Further, Schulppie has pointed out that one must not only consider matter as evidence of external events but also as agents (witnesses) in themselves. Schulppie's (2020, 4) aim is to expand the notion of the witness beyond the realm of the human by taking into account the specificity of the material: things speak and thus have agency that impacts the world. In our case, nonhuman agency is found within the voices that persist unattached to their original bodies and constitute an archive of the past, persisting in the present. The archive generates action but also modifies itself through human agency and aids in generating agency in others. The materiality of the voices of the past make them witnesses with agency, even as they are also "things." Acoustic phenomena such as the voice (which also utilizes silence) play a fundamental role in the constitution of affective atmospheres; they are thus guides for agency that remain alterable in their encounter with human agencies. Voices are things that evoke subjectivities but, in their material state, are far from being inert objects. They are things that frame actions and, at the same time, can be modified by actions, even as they may turn imperceptible.

If forms of agency are attributed to the material, it is through their materiality that voices impact those who experience them as atmospheres, opening the possibility that these same atmospheres become altered. Even when they have agency, these material elements—voices, sounds, noises—are not simple, finite artefacts. The voice is subjective and material and is capable of constructing material affective atmospheres—things—that are altered by the sometimes-deviant use of affective agency of subjectivities that aid in construction.

Altering the affective atmospheres exhibited by the archive of voices results from their overlap with other voices but also from their resignification through actions and interventions of the subjectivities that they helped to shape. This is how, for example, the participants in López's installation and the persons detained/disappeared in the clandestine centers altered the sound files using their movements and imaginations. Thus, the question emerges, how do affective atmospheres and human agencies mutually alter each other?

Taking into account the conceptual clarifications introduced here, I believe that it is possible to understand the relationship between archival agency and affective atmospheres as not only mutually constituted but also as contingent and marked by temporal contact. They also serve as a link built on the tension between materiality and immateriality, shaping and undoing subjectivities, but which are also receptive to the agency of those same subjectivities. Returning to the two sound archives of terror presented here, we could say that agency's own disposition to act is built in a sequence in which affect and action are inseparable. Underlining this relationship is fundamental. The opportunity generated by the question of what to do with the affective atmospheres of those sound archives, both material and immaterial, opens up not as a merely voluntaristic perspective but as part of this link between affect and action that is always open and uncertain. We should recall that this is not a question of thinking of agency merely as something that sparks action but as a disposition capable of altering the affective order on which it is also constituted.

This is something that these examples bring to light in their own political effects. The necessity to point out atmospheres as contingent or changing warns against understandings of the archive as static. If the role of such atmospheres in the constitution of collective agency is evident, it is also necessary to acknowledge the capacity of its radical alteration in order to indicate the possibility of rupture. Otherwise, it is difficult to explain the gestures of political change in their relationship with disruptive pasts. This is not merely a theoretical question; rather, in the context of emancipatory struggles associated with stories of oppression, it takes on special relevance. Referring to atmospheres as mere pregnant instances prior to all language may be attractive in some circles, but this is deeply problematic for political reflection and action.

The case of López's installation (and the testimonies analyzed) illustrates that the voice builds a material space that constitutes an atmosphere but also generates action maps from which such atmospheres can be transformed. Thus, oral archives—literal or altered through artistic intervention—conjure a connection between the past and the present that opens toward the future. Faced with recurring questions like *What do we do with the past?* or *What can we do with the past?* it is worth asking ourselves, *What should we do with the atmospheres of the past that have been transformed into an archive?* Answers to these questions need to be sought out in that dynamic way in which subjectivities and material atmospheres are linked and understood as bearing their own agencies. The materiality of the archive—in this case, the sound archive—does not turn it into a single determined instance but into something or someone whose most radical political consequences can be challenged. The voice's immediacy and theatricality, after all, persist over time.

Notes

1 A more recent characterization is developed by Gernot Böhme (2014, 92) who has defined affective atmospheres as "that which designates what mediates between the objective (material) qualities of an environment and the bodily sensory states of a person in that environment."

2 Argentina hosted the World Cup in June 1978. The organization of the event and the triumph of the Argentine national team were used by the state as part of a propaganda campaign to garner legitimacy for the regime. International media and human rights organizations took advantage of the attention placed on Argentina to denounce state terrorism and call for a boycott of the event. Nevertheless, the testimonies of people who were detained and disappeared during this period show that although they were held captive and aware of the political uses of the tournament, winning the World Cup was a moment of celebration. They celebrated from their cells, separating their joy for the sport from the uses applied by the dictatorship.

3 Clandestine camps in Argentina were often embedded in spaces within ordinary urban neighborhoods. This meant that neighbors were at times aware that something was taking place in these spaces, perhaps because they heard strange noises or saw persons entering and exiting the clandestine spaces. This close proximity also meant that the prisoners could overhear sounds or indications of where they were being held.

4 Pilar Calveiro (2008) uses the idea of *poder concentracionario,* translated here as "concentrationist," in order to describe the totalizing power built by the internment machine of the last Argentine dictatorship.

5 The North American objectivist poet Charles Reznikoff published *Holocausto* in 1975, a book in which each poem is based on the fifteen volumes of transcribed testimonies of the Nuremburg war criminal trials, the court record, Adolf Eichmann's appeals, and other related archives.

References

Atkinson, Meera, and Michael Richardson. 2013. *Traumatic Affect.* Newcastle upon Tyne: Cambridge Scholars.

Böhme, Gernot. 2014. "The Theory of Atmospheres and Its Applications." *Interstices: Journal of Architecture and Related Arts* 15:92–99.

Broncano, Fernando. 2020. *Conocimiento expropiado. Epistemología política en una democracia radical.* Madrid: Akal. Kindle.

Calveiro, Pilar. 2008. *Poder y desaparición. Los campos de concentración en Argentina.* Buenos Aires: Colihue Puñaladas.

Cheng, William. 2016. *Just Vibrations.* Ann Arbor: University of Michigan Press.

Cvetkovich, Ann. 2003. *An Archive of Feelings.* Durham, NC: Duke University Press.

Depetris Chauvin, Irene. 2015. "Los cuerpos de la música." *Informe escaleno* (March).

Depetris Chauvin, Irene. 2020. "La docu(ciencia)ficción como máquina de circu-lación de afectos. Música, vibración y temporalidades desarticuladas en *Branco sai, preto fica*." *MusiMid. Revista brasileira de estudos em música e midia* 1 (3): 103–22.

Dolar, Mladen. 2006. *A Voice and Nothing More*. Cambridge, MA: MIT Press.

Dziuban, Zuzanna, editor. 2017. *Mapping the Forensic Turn*. Vienna: Academic Press.

Figari Layús, Rosario. 2015. *Los juicios por sus protagonistas*. Villa María: Eduvim.

Foster, Hal. 2004. "An Archival Impulse." *October* 110 (Autumn 2004): 3–22.

Gilbert, Abel. 2021. *Satisfaction en la ESMA. Música y sonido durante la dictadura.* Buenos Aires: Gourmet Musical.

Riedl, Friedlind. 2019. "Atmosphere." In *Affective Societies: Key Concepts*, edited by Jan Slaby and Christian von Scheve, 85–95. New York: Routledge.

Riedl, Friedlind. 2020. "Atmospheric Relations." In *Music as Atmosphere: Collective Feelings and Affective Sounds*, edited by Friedlind Riedl and Jutha Torvinen, 1–42. New York: Routledge.

Schulppie, Susan. 2020. *Material Witness. Media, Forensics, Evidence*. Cambridge, MA: MIT Press.

Slaby, Jan. 2020. "Atmospheres—Schmitz, Massumi and Beyond." In *Music as Atmosphere: Collective Feelings and Affective Sounds*, edited by Friedlind Riedl and Jutha Torvinen, 274–85. New York: Routledge.

Sosa, Ernst. 2015. *Judgment and Agency*. Oxford: Oxford University Press.

Steedman, Carolyn. 2002. *Dust*. Manchester: Manchester University Press.

Szeftel, Micaela. 2021. "The Role of Atmospheres and Moods in the Intersubjective Constitution of Feelings." Paper presented at the Workshop Affective Intentionality in Medieval Philosophy and Phenomenology, Department of Philosophy, University of Würzburg, July 26.

Taccetta, Natalia. 2019. "Archivar y recordar. El inconsciente óptico del pasado." *En la otra isla* 1:19–30.

Tragaki, Dafne. 2020. "Acoustemologies of *Rebetiko* Love Songs." In *Music as Atmosphere: Collective Feelings and Affective Sounds*, edited by Friedlind Riedl and Jutha Torvinen, 184–201 New York: Routledge.

Turner, Tamara Dee. 2021. "Affective Temporalities of Presence and Absence: Musical Haunting and Embodied Political Histories in an Algerian Religious Community." *Culture, Theory and Critique* 61 (2–3): 196–86.

Villani, Mario, and Fernando Reati. 2011. *Desaparecido. Memorias de un cautiverio.* Buenos Aires: Biblos.

Zhang, Dora. 2018. "Notes on Atmospheres." *Qui Parle: Critical Humanities and Social Sciences* 27 (1): 121–55.

Glitching the Affective Reproduction of the Social

Two Returns to Spinoza

Jason Read

As financial investigations are ruled by the principle "follow the money"
investigations into politics must have as their maxim "follow the affects."
—Frédéric Lordon, *Les affects de la politique*, 2016

In the seventeenth century, Spinoza asked the question, why do people fight for their servitude as if it was salvation? Spinoza not only broached the question of ideology before its formulation, but he went beyond it, suggesting that ideology is as much a question of desires as it is of ideas. Ideology is not something that people passively endure, living their domination as something policed but something that people actively strive for, passionately desiring subjection. Spinoza's question takes on an oddly contemporary relevance in the modern world in which we are told that we should love our jobs, should strive to remake our desires into entrepreneurial activities, and our social relations into networking. An often repeated mantra of the modern age is "Do what you love and you'll never work a day in your life." This ideal of passionate engagement in work, of finding pleasure and not just payment in work, has justified a massive increase in working hours. In the current era, we are told to strive for our employment as if it is our liberation, and the more we search for purpose and meaning in work, the longer we work. In promising us passion and purpose, work has only increased our subjection. As much as Spinoza's question offered a new way forward, his answer, that superstition is the basis of obedience, relegated his thought to an earlier era: an era in which it was religion and not capital or the state that controlled much of life.

There have been two returns to Spinoza in the last fifty years that have argued in different ways that Spinoza's account of desire and the affects is uniquely situated to examine how capitalism restructures desires and joys as much as beliefs and ideas. These particular interventions function as theoretical stepping-stones connecting the concerns of the seventeenth century to the present, the domination of religion to capitalism as the religion of daily life. I am referring first to Gilles Deleuze and Félix Guattari's two volumes of *Capitalism and Schizophrenia* originally published in 1972 and 1980, which made Spinoza's question the central question of political philosophy, arguing that desire is central to any political or economic order. Deleuze and Guattari's understanding of desire and the economy formed at a tumultuous period in which desire and its liberation were at the center of countercultural movements around the globe, movements that resisted a life realized in terms of work and consumption. Some forty years later, in 2010, Frédéric Lordon (2014, 49) returned to Marx and Spinoza, in some sense bypassing Deleuze and Guattari's work, to argue that "capitalism must be seized . . . as a particular regime of desire." For Lordon, Spinoza's understanding of conatus, striving, at the base of individual and collective life, makes it possible to examine the way in which different regimes of accumulation are also different regimes of striving or desire. Lordon's assertion comes in a different era, one not marked by students seeking to liberate their desires from the conventions of society (as in Deleuze and Guattari's era) but by capitalists claiming that the surest path to success is to follow one's desires, converting passions into profits. Despite their different orientations and historical moments, the particular revivals of Spinoza in Deleuze and Guattari and then Lordon attest to not only the contemporary relevance of Spinoza but also to what could be called the importance of affective reproduction in both economics and politics; the way in which affects are as integral to the production and reproduction of the economic and political order as ideas and ideologies.

Affective Reproduction: Spinoza

Prior to discussing Deleuze and Guattari and Lordon, it is necessary to begin with their common point of reference, Spinoza. A full account of the politics of affects in Spinoza is beyond the scope of this chapter; however, a brief orientation to some fundamental points is necessary. First, there is the provocation referenced above, that the fundamental mystification that makes domination possible is that people "fight for their servitude as if it was salvation," that there is an active and desired nature to subjection. For Spinoza, desire is fundamental to both our knowledge and ignorance of ourselves. We are initially conscious of our desires and ignorant of the causes of things, as Spinoza puts it, aware of what we want but unaware of how the world works. To which we could add that what we are profoundly unaware of includes the causes of our own desires. We desire things that we associate with joy, with increases of our capacity to act and think, while shunning those things we associate with sadness, a decrease of the same capacities. Given our original ignorance, we are sometimes mistaken about whether something is truly a cause of joy or if we just assume it to be because of a past association. Spinoza makes it clear that many people misunderstand the true causes of their desires, believing that something that is ultimately harmful is beneficial simply because it is momentarily associated with joy. As Spinoza writes, "So the infant believes that he freely wants the milk; the angry child that he wants vengeance; and the timid, flight. Again, the drunk believes it is from a free decision of the mind that he says those things which afterward, when sober, he wishes he had not said. So the madman, the chatterbox, the child, and a great many people of this kind believe that they speak from a free decision of the mind, when really they cannot contain their impulse to speak. Because this prejudice is innate in all men, they are not easily freed from it" (Spinoza 1994, EIIIP2Schol). This misrecognition stems from the fact that we fundamentally misunderstand our own desires, seeing them as either a free decision (as something we want) or as reflecting the qualities of the object. In each case, what we overlook are the causal relations that produce our desires. As Spinoza writes, "From all this, then, it is clear that we neither strive for, nor will, neither want, nor desire anything because we judge it to be good; on the contrary we judge something to be good because we strive for it, will it, want it, and desire it" (Spinoza 1994, EIIIP9S). The consciousness of our striving, desire, is in some sense secondary to the affects, which is to say the relations that effectively produce it (Fischbach 2005, 88).

Spinoza defines affects as an increase or decrease of one's capacity to act. Joy is the increase of one's power and capacity while sadness is the decrease in one's capacities. Two additional clarifications are necessary to qualify this definition and expand it beyond what can only be referred to as a kind of truism: after all, asserting that people strive for joy and avoid sadness is hardly a revelation. First, an affect is at once an affection of the body and the idea of it. Rather than see affect as something external to mind and to thinking, something that disturbs its internal order, the affects are integral to its very function. All affects have a mental component, a representation or an idea, as well as a bodily dimension, an increase or decrease in power. This immediately relates to how Spinoza defines desire, as the fundamental striving that constitutes human existence, encompassing in equal parts body and mind. Desire is an awareness of this striving, and as such, it is always determined, always affected. We do not strive toward some object, some idea of the good, or even simply to maintain our existence; we strive toward what we are determined to want or desire. This effectively transforms what it means to think of desire "as man's very essence," since that essence is less an original identity, a unity, than an originary dispersion—we are all determined to desire different things (Balibar 2020, 38). It also profoundly alters what we understand by striving and, with it, what is often called agency. What we strive for, what appears as integral to our very existence, is itself the effect of how we have been affected, shaped, by relations. Desire is not the foundation of agency outside of determination but how the ways we have been determined, affected, becomes integral to our agency and striving.

Integral to Spinoza's claim that people fight for their servitude is the recognition that the determining instance of politics is not to be found in the desires of individuals but further upstream in the relations and encounters that shape and determine those desires. In the *Tractatus Theologico-Politicus*, Spinoza not only asks the question as to why people fight for servitude but answers it by demonstrating the way in which particular practices and habits shape desire. Spinoza's analysis culminates in his portrait of the ancient state of Israel in which these practices determined how and when people should dress, eat, and cut their hair. As Spinoza (1991, 199) argues, "Therefore to men so habituated to it obedience must have appeared no longer as bondage, but freedom." The extreme point of theocracy as the culmination of this order through habits should not obscure the more general point that institutions produce the desires that they need in order to exist.

Acting on and transforming habits and desires is the basis of politics. As Spinoza (1991, 186) writes,

> For whether a man is urged by love or driven by a fear of threatened evil, since in both cases his action always proceeds from his own intention and decision, either there can be no such thing as sovereignty and right over subjects or else it must include all the means that contribute to men's willingness to obey. Whenever a subject acts in accordance with the commands of the sovereign power, whether he is motivated by love, or fear, or (and this is more frequently the case) a mixture of hope and fear, or by reverence—which is an emotion compounded of fear and awe—or whatever be his motive, he acts from his ruler's right, not from his own.

Politics is not limited to actions of prohibition or exclusion but include everything that can transform and shape desires. As Pierre Macherey (2019, 160) argues, Spinoza in some sense anticipated Foucault's famous remark that the soul is the prison of the body, that obedience is produced by the production of affects and desires, but adds to this formulation that it is the body, the habits and comportments of existence, that determines the inclinations of the soul. Rituals and habits transform the affective character of individuals, making the connection between particular objects and particular affects, creating objects of love and hatred, remaking the affective character of the individual in the model of the community. What individuals strive toward and against is not the irreducible given of politics but is itself produced by the habits and actions that define social life.

Thus, affects are produced politically, through the organization of habits and desires, and have political effects. They are in some sense doubly determined as political, both causes and effects, first in the histories and practices that produce them, shaping individual and collective desire, and second, in the social and political life of the affects themselves. Political organization is, in this way, primarily affective. As Spinoza (2000, 64) writes, "Since men, as we have said, are led more by passion than by reason, it naturally follows that a people will unite and consent to be guided as if by one mind not at reason's prompting but through some common emotion, such as a common hope, or common fear, or desire to avenge some common injury." In the *Ethics*, Spinoza argues that this common emotion, or affect, is primarily ambition. Ambition is defined as the desire that others should love what we love, and hate what we hate (Spinoza 1994, EIIIP31C). However, ambition is a profoundly ambivalent affective foundation of political life since our desire that others love what we love, to find social recognition of our desires, runs up against the limitations of exclusive possession. Spinoza argues to this effect that the desire that others love what we love is the source of competition as much as identification; as much as we want others to desire what we desire, want our desires to be recognized, we do not want them to possess it. This ambivalence defines our desires of things that cannot be held in common. Money and fame are, by definition, objects of conflict and ambivalence, things that make human beings obstacles to each other precisely because they desire the same finite thing. Spinoza's logic would also seem to suggest that to some extent, the political body is itself an ambivalent object of desire. We want others to live the same, to have the same desires and passions, but the reinforcing similarity of desires is constantly undercut by the fear that they do not love the same thing in the same way (Spinoza 1994, EIIIP33Dem). Any representation of the community in terms of a nation, or a people, is fundamentally ambivalent, threatened by the sense that others do not love the same thing or do not love it in the right way. It is for this reason the affective composition of politics is at one and the same time necessary, producing obedience through a common set of desires, and unstable because affects are fundamentally conflictual and ambivalent.

Consuming Affects: Deleuze and Guattari

Despite the fact that Deleuze and Guattari's *Anti-Oedipus* opens with the invocation of Spinoza's question as the fundamental question of political philosophy, Spinoza does not figure prominently in the text at least by name. Affect appears first in *Anti-Oedipus* under a different name, that of "Stimmung," or mood. Although the term "Stimmung" suggests Heidegger (whom philosophers such as Étienne Balibar and Antonio Negri have recognized as the other, often opposed, philosopher of affect), the reference is actually to Nietzsche by way of Pierre Klossowski's study. What ties these different and disparate philosophies together is the assertion of the unavoidable affective or emotional dimension of all thought and practice, as a fundamentally orienting dimension. Deleuze and Guattari situate Stimmung, the intensities of affect, with what they call the synthesis of consumption. Without recapitulating the entire syntheses, it is possible to note that consumption comes after production and recording; it is necessarily after both the forces of production that structure social life and the relations of production that record that productivity, concealing the productive forces. The affects that define consumption are derived from and a distortion of the productive forces. Deleuze and Guattari's conception of the subject can be compared to Spinoza's assertion that we do not want something because it is good, but we call it good because we want it, desire it, and strive for it. Our affects come *after* the relations that determine them, produce them, and our awareness of affects comes even after that. Subjectivity is secondary to, and unaware of, the process that produces it. Deleuze and Guattari cite one of Marx's more prosaic statements regarding the disconnect between the production of a thing and its consumption. As Deleuze and Guattari (1983, 24) write, "Let us remember once again one of Marx's caveats: we cannot tell from the mere taste of the wheat who grew it; the product gives us no hint as to the system and relations of production." A quotidian fact of existence under capitalism, the separation of the product from the act of production, becomes the basis for an understanding of a larger problem, that of the relationship between production and representation, causality and meaning. The less we grasp the real conditions of production of a thing, the more we are subject to understanding it according to ideal relations of causation, just as the less we know about the conditions of the production of desires, the more we attribute them to the quality of the object rather than the history of relations that shape our desire.

The demarcation that Deleuze and Guattari draw between production and consumption is also part of their criticism of psychoanalysis. The family is not the site of the production of subjectivity but only its consumption. Subjectivity, including desire, is not produced by the family but by the entire social field. The family is only the site of its consumption. The distinction is also integral to their answer to Spinoza's core question, or as they put it, an explanation as to why "desire of the most disadvantaged creature will invest with all its strength, irrespective of any economic understanding or lack of it, in the capitalist social field as a whole" (Deleuze and Guattari 1983, 229). In order to understand this paradox, it is necessary to grasp what comes between production and consumption—namely, recording or representation. Money, currency, is the representation of desire in capitalism. Spinoza (1994, EIVAPPXXVIII) asserted that "money occupies the mind of the multitude more than anything else." This is because it can be attached to any object of desire. It is a deterritorialization of desire, turning desire from specific objects and goals and, instead, toward an abstract quantity that can stand in for any object or goal. Deleuze and Guattari add to this observation a more Marxist point: money is not just the representation of desire and of production and capital but is one that, like the fetish, obscures the conditions of its reproduction. Money makes it appear as if two very different economic relations, two very different situations, are comparable by making the money that is the means of payment, that is wages, appear to be the same thing as money as the means of investment, as capital. According to Deleuze and Guattari (1987, 230), "Measuring the two orders of magnitude in terms of the same analytical unit is a pure fiction, a cosmic swindle, as if one were to measure intergalactic or intra-atomic distance in meters and centimetres. There is no common measure between the value of enterprises and that of the labour capacity of wage earners."

The wage reproduces capitalism in two senses of the term. First, as a material condition, the wage makes it possible for workers to keep living and to show up to work the next day, but second, as a representation of desire, it necessarily obfuscates that relationship, making it appear as if everyone is a potential capitalist. The wage, money, reproduces the capitalist relation both materially and affectively, reproducing the worker as a living being while at the same time reproducing the investment of desire in the social relation of capital. One keeps working, keeps showing up to work, because of the fantasy of all that the wage could buy if only one had more money (a few dollars more to perhaps take advantage of a stock tip!). We are all invested in capitalism as a social relation even if we have no capital to invest because of the way in which money represents and distorts its power.

History of Desire: Lordon

Frédéric Lordon's turn to Spinoza nearly forty years after Deleuze and Guattari is meant to answer the same question, the question of servitude, reflected through Marx: why do people work for others as if they were working for themselves? However, Lordon does not turn to the question of money, at least initially, but to the fundamental problem of desire. Desire, striving, or conatus, is the essence of each individual, but this essence is fundamentally intransitive, undetermined. In order for this striving to become a concrete desire, it must be affected (Lordon 2016, 18). What we desire, what we want, is determined by how we have been affected by things in the past: we want what we associate with joy and shun what we associate with sadness. As we have seen, Spinoza primarily considered the history of these relations in terms of an individual biography; we are drawn to the images of past pleasures and avoid past pains even if we are never entirely aware as to why this is the case. What Lordon adds to Spinoza's account is the social historical aspect of the formation of desire. The things that shape our desire, our very striving, exceed our biography to include the social and economic conditions that shape our world. Lordon focuses on the intersection of labor and consumption as the primary space for the production and reproduction of desires. Or to take an example discussed above, "money occupies the mind of the multitude more than anything else" not just because of one's individual experience of buying the things that one desires with it but because of the historical condition of being born in a world where money, as Marx (1975, 377) writes, "is the alienated ability of mankind." The conditions that directly determine our desires are conditions that exceed our biological memory or experience. As the conditions of capitalism, money and labor are integral to our desire because in its particular social relations, they are the necessary precondition of any desire or any action.

For Lordon, the labor relation has to be understood as a massive channeling of desire. There is nothing given in supposed individual self-interest that would dictate that self-interest take the form of selling one's labor power in exchange for a wage. Contrary to what the apologists for capitalism claim, the only act that unalloyed self-interest would explain would be the immediate grabbing of what one needs or desires without work or money. Capitalism, like every other society or mode of production, is founded not on the putative natural self-interest of individuals, an utter fiction (precisely because there is no self that is not shaped by its biographical and social history) but on the way in which that self-interest, or more to the point, desire, has been affected or modified. In that way, it is no different from any other society; all societies are an organization of desire. What and how we desire is an effect of the different social relations that determine the affections and thus the direction of our striving. Desire is both an effect of the social order, which ascribes its goals and orientation and, at the same time, a cause; it keeps the entire system functioning.

Lordon offers a history of striving under three different regimes of capitalist exploitation corresponding to the emergence of capitalism, the rise of consumer society, and contemporary neoliberalism. This history is mapped onto two axes; the first, drawn from Marx, is considered in terms of the division between production and consumption, the two separate spheres of activity. The second axis, drawn from Spinoza, is that of joy or sadness, understood as an increase or decrease in one's power and capacity. From these two coordinates, it is possible to chart the history of capital. The first phase of this history corresponds to the initial formation of capitalism, what Marx called formal subsumption. The primary institutional basis for capitalism at this stage is the absence of any alternative to wage labor, the destruction of the commons or any sustenance economy. Fear is a motive, a driving force orienting the striving, the conatus, but a limited one. People compelled by fear will work but only as much as it is necessary to stave off punishment. Those who do not work do not eat, and it is the fear of starvation or homelessness that keeps one working. Fear is not only a limited incentive; it is also a fundamentally unstable one. Fear can drive one to revolt almost as much as one can obey.

From this, then, Lordon maps a second stage that roughly corresponds with Fordism. For Lordon, the institutional effect of Fordism is one of the destruction of the pleasures and pride of concrete labor, the pleasures of a particular skill, in favor of a general shift of desire away from labor toward consumption. Ford's "five-dollar day" establishes an affective economy, exchanging sadness and frustration at work for the pleasures of the newly emergent consumer society (Lordon 2014, 30). The final, or at least most recent, change in this affective economy reorients pleasure toward work, but it is no longer the pleasure of a particular skill, job, or the result of work; it is the pleasure of employment itself. It is a desire that is, as much as possible, modeled on abstract labor. As much as there still are pleasures to concrete labor, and Lordon follows Spinoza in arguing that individuals will always affirm their power of existing (in other words, they will find whatever pleasures there are to be had in the workday—from those associated with the task at hand to the gossip and "water cooler talk" that accompany every work experience), the modern ideal is as much as possible an indifference to the specific job in the name of flexibility and dedication to work itself (Lordon 2014, 69). To add to Spinoza's formulation above, we could say that just as the infant thinks that he or she wants milk, the employee freely believes that he or she wants to work. In each case, the affective constitution of desires is obscured. One desires what they have been produced to desire.

Transcendence and Immanence of the Body Politic

For both Deleuze and Guattari and Lordon, the condition of affective reproduction is not just that we are determined, affected by things, but there is a constitutive lag, or gap, between how we are affected and how we make sense of our desires. This gap, that "we are conscious of our desires and ignorant of the causes of things," including the causes of our desires, makes it possible for us to misrecognize those causes, attributing our desires to our own free will and autonomy or, and this is just as much a mistake, attributing them to the qualities of the objects themselves. These two errors are not only dominant in the history of philosophy, which generally subordinates relations and affects to either the interior life of the subject or the intrinsic qualities of the object, but more importantly, they obscure and conceal the actual affects, relations, and practices that shape desires, subjectivity, and ultimately political and social life. Beneath subjects and their supposed wills as well as beneath objects and their supposed qualities are the vacillations and relations of the affects. In different ways, Deleuze and Guattari and Lordon utilize this gap, this disjunct, between the causes of desires and their representations, to develop a social and political theory of how we come to not only misrecognize the causes of our desires but attribute them to other false causes. We could call this second aspect the Marxist dimension of the criticism, following from the constitutive role that Marx ascribes to the difference between the sources of value, labor power, and the representation of that value as an attribute of an object.

The name for this process in Marx is commodity fetishism. Deleuze and Guattari take a rather eccentric approach to the theory of the fetish. First, as I indicated above, the general distinction between production and consumption as two different ways of grasping the commodity becomes the basis of a disconnect between the production and representation of desire. Or as Deleuze and Guattari put it, things are not recorded in the same way that they are produced. This disconnect makes it possible for other connections, other relations to appear as causes, or what Deleuze and Guattari call quasi-cause. With this term, Deleuze and Guattari draw together the two critical strategies. The first, from Spinoza, is one in which the central illusion of much of thought, including that of many philosophers, is to mistake effects for causes. Our desires, and the values that we attach to things, are generally effects, products of affects and relations, that we take for causes. Deleuze and Guattari combine this with a second point, one drawn from Marx, that production and representation are two entirely different orders. In drawing these two criticisms together, Deleuze and Guattari move beyond the fetish understood as the commodity in terms of the way in which value appears to be a quality of the object rather than an effect of labor. For Deleuze and Guattari, the ultimate fetish is not the commodity but the way in which capital appears to be the source of productivity rather than an effect. As Deleuze and Guattari (1983, 10) write,

> The forms of social production, like those of desiring-production, involve an unengendered nonproductive attitude, an element of antiproduction coupled with the process, a full body that functions as a *socius*. This socius may be the body of the earth, that of the tyrant, or capital. This is the body that Marx is referring to when he says that it is not the product of labour, but rather appears as its natural or divine presuppositions. In fact, it does not restrict itself merely to opposing productive forces in and of themselves. It falls back on [*il se rabat sur*] all production, constituting a surface over which the forces and agents of production are distributed, thereby appropriating for itself all surplus production and arrogating to itself both the whole and the parts of the process, which now seem to emanate from it as a quasi-cause.

Capital is an effect. Like the commodity, it is a product of the organization and expropriation of labor. However, once it is seen as a cause, as the source of productivity, once the capitalist becomes a job creator, it has its own effects. Nothing is just an effect. As Spinoza (1994, EIP36) writes, "Nothing exists from whose nature some effect does not follow." The idea that commodity possesses value as an intrinsic quality, or that the accumulation of capital is the cause and not the effect of labor, is an idea that is not without its own effects. This is another way to grasp what Deleuze and Guattari mean by quasi-cause: the effects of an effect being taken as a cause. Once the commodity is seen to be a deposit of value, it changes and restructures our actions with respect to it; the same could be said of capital as the creator of value: effects become causes and distortions, become a part of reality once they become the basis for how people organize their desires, joys, and sadness.

Lordon's argument draws from similar sources, more Spinoza than Marx, to articulate in a different way that effects become causes. For Lordon, social life must first be understood as the auto-affection of the multitude, of the many prior to political organization. Human beings are always affected by and affecting those around them, shaping their joys and sadness, desires and hopes and fears. Moreover, it is not just that human beings affect each other as different bodies interacting and acting on one another, increasing and decreasing power, but affects are thoroughly social in that joy and sadness, love and hate, necessarily pass through our relations with others (Lordon 2015, 64). The question is not how there is a social life of affects, since the two are broadly synonymous; affects are social, and there is no sociality outside of our capacity to be affected but rather how this social life becomes organized, politically and economically. For Lordon, it is a matter of understanding how the immanent, which is to say, horizontal organization of the affects, produces a transcendent hierarchy. As with Deleuze and Guattari, the transcendent is an effect of the immanent but an effect that has its own particular causality, falling back on and acting on the immanent. Lordon refers to this relation, this particular causality, as immanent transcendence: a transcendence that is nothing other than an effect of the immanent organization of social relations acting on those same social relations (Lordon 2015, 62). In other words, there is no transcendence, no state standing above society, or economy structuring society, unless it is always already at work within society. The construction of the state as a separate order is nothing other than the auto-affection of the multitude itself.

To reemphasize, the process by which this transcendence emerges from the immanent relation is a product of what Lordon refers to as the multitude's own auto-affection. Every affect is always already social in that our joys and sadness, our loves and hatreds, are necessarily deflected through the loves and fears of others, real or imagined. Politics, or the political organization of affects, is the process of assigning this sporadic and haphazard sociality of affects to regular objects and passions, defining common objects of love and hate. Political bodies are sustained by their common objects of love or hatred. What Lordon (2015, 118) calls "imperium," the common body politic, is nothing other than a particular organization of the multitude, of the social passions and relations. Affect is both the cause and effect of the body politic as constituted by the organization of common hopes, fears, and passions. As Spinoza (2000, 64) writes, "Since men, as we have said, are led more by passion than by reason, it naturally follows that a people will unite and consent to be guided as if by one mind not at reason's prompting but through some common emotion, such as a common hope, or common fear, or desire to avenge some common injury." The political body is also an effect of this organization of affects. The common organization of affects produces a qualitative change in the nature of affects. The more something is loved by everyone or hated by everyone, the more intensely it acts on our own passions, ultimately capturing them through its centripetal force.

The political organization of the affects, the attempt to create common objects of love and hate, is always situated against their centrifugal motion, the fact that we are all subject to different encounters and relations, shaping our different associations. There is a tendency, starting with Deleuze and Guattari's (1987, 240) *A Thousand Plateaus*, to use the term "emotion" or "feeling" to refer to the organized, centripetal dimension of affects (affects—plural—as organized) and affect (in the singular) to reflect the centrifugal and thus unorganized aspect. Although this terminological distinction is absent from Spinoza, it is possible to see in Spinoza a constant tension between affect as singular, as the particular affective composition of an individual, and affect as it is organized as a common structure of feeling. The politics of affect is the constant organization and disorganization of the relations of affect.

Conclusion: Politics and Economics of Affect

Writing in the seventeenth century, Spinoza makes no real distinction between politics and economics, between the emergent form of capital and the state; they are all thought together under the general problem of the organization of social life. To some extent, Deleuze and Guattari and Lordon continue that indistinction, lumping together the economic organization and political organization of affects as the same fundamental problem of creating common desires, and common loves, even if they pass through different institutions and objects. If politics can be understood as the general problem of constituting common striving through common objects of desire, then it might be possible to argue that it is capital, more than the state, that organizes common desires and fears in the twentieth and twenty-first centuries. This is not to suggest that the state, or political life, is entirely absent. In fact, Deleuze and Guattari and Lordon each offer ways of thinking the distinction between politics and economics on affective grounds.

For Deleuze and Guattari, the distinction between capital and the state is understood as the distinction between abstract flows and concrete codes. As we have seen, part of the way in which capital captures desire is through the indeterminacy and abstraction of money. Money captures every desire because it is the condition of every desire. This abstract and unqualified dimension becomes the basis of affective reproduction in that it ultimately dissolves any appearance of the distinction between capitalist and worker. As much as this undefined flow captures desire, it is ultimately too abstract and too undifferentiated for existence. It is for this reason that the abstract quantitative reduction of everything to flows of money and abstract labor is necessarily countered by the revitalization of concrete qualities of identities, values, and practices, what Deleuze and Guattari (1983, 260) called reterritorialization. The affective reproduction of the state and capital requires both an investment in abstract indifference (indifference to money as a powerful capture of desire precisely because it is indifferent to any object of any existence) but also an investment and identification in specific identities. It is capital that takes care of the former and the state the latter, but both are necessary and are necessary together: specific nation-states, with their common identities and objects of hatred and love, are the necessary condition for abstract capital.

Whereas Deleuze and Guattari frame the division between capital and the state as one between abstract quantity and concrete quality, Lordon frames the distinction as one between contingency and necessity. As Spinoza argues, we tend to feel stronger, more anger or joy, when something is freely undertaken than when it is perceived as necessary. Lordon adds to this that the division between the economy and politics passes between representations of necessity and contingency. Capital or, more often, the market is presented as necessary, as having its own "self-evident laws," while politics is the field of contingency, of human action and freedom (Lordon 2016, 130). This division between the realm of necessity and that of contingency is just as necessary to the reproduction of capital as the division between abstract quantity and concrete qualities. Whereas the latter forms the basis of the constitution and destruction of identities under capital, constituting the space for the capture of both desires for wealth and belonging, the latter is equally necessary for its affective reproduction. Politicians are the basis for hopes and fears, joys and anger, while the economy, as it is called, presses on in sheer necessity: one becomes the focus of our frustrations and hopes through its fluctuations while the other dominates our fears and desires all the more effectively by being seemingly inevitable.

Deleuze and Guattari and Lordon thus take on Spinoza's central provocation and question "Why do people fight for their servitude as if it was salvation?" drawing on Spinoza to develop different aspects of the affective reproduction under capital. What Spinoza saw as the unique problem of theocracy, of religious domination, in that it got people to fight for servitude as if it was salvation by occupying hopes and fears has now been transposed over to capitalism, what Marx (1981, 969) referred to the "religion of daily life." Labor, the very thing that defines our subjection, has become the thing that we cling to in looking for our salvation. The reproduction of the relations of production is not just something that happens in and through social structures but also through our desire and joys. Capital is reproduced affectively as much as it is economically or politically. In knowing this, in understanding affective reproduction, it becomes possible to transform it, liberating ourselves from the cruel optimism of our attachment to work. The COVID-19 pandemic has demonstrated that the affective reproduction of capital is also the condition of its affective destruction. The spell of loving one's job has been effectively broken by the fear of infection and the indignation of poor treatment. It remains to be seen if it will return or if different affects will produce different politics.

References

Balibar, Étienne. 2020. *Spinoza, the Transindividual*. Translated by Mark G. E. Kelly. Edinburgh: Edinburgh University Press.

Deleuze, Giles, and Félix Guattari. 1983. *Anti-Oedipus: Capitalism and Schizophrenia*. Translated by Robert Hurley, Mark Seem, and Helen R. Lane. Minneapolis: University of Minnesota Press.

Deleuze, Giles, and Félix Guattari. 1987. *A Thousand Plateaus: Capitalism and Schizophrenia*. Translated by Brian Massumi. Minneapolis: University of Minnesota Press.

Fischbach, Franck. 2005. *La production des hommes: Marx avec Spinoza*. Paris: Presses universitaires de France.

Lordon, Frédéric. 2014. *Willing Slaves of Capital: Spinoza and Marx on Desire*. Translated by Gabriel Ash. New York: Verso.

Lordon, Frédéric. 2015. *Imperium: Structures et affects des corps politiques*. Paris: La fabrique.

Lordon, Frédéric. 2016. *Les affects de la Politique*. Paris: Seuil.

Macherey, Pierre. 2019. *Sagesse ou ignorance? La question de Spinoza*. Paris: Éditions Amsterdam.

Marx, Karl. 1975. *Early Writings*. Translated by Rodney Livingstone and Gregor Benton. New York: Penguin.

Marx, Karl. 1981. *Capital: A Critique of Political Economy*. Vol. 3, translated by David Fernbach. New York: Penguin.

Spinoza, Baruch. 1991. *Theological-Political Treatise*. Translated by Samuel Shirley. Indianapolis: Hackett.

Spinoza, Baruch. 1994. *Ethics*. Translated by Edwin Curley. New York: Penguin.

Spinoza, Baruch. 2000. *Political Treatise*. Translated by Samuel Shirley. Indianapolis: Hackett.

Ezekiel Dixon-Román

In 2016, the United States witnessed an unprecedented level of foreign influence in presidential elections via the information networks of social media. It is now widely known and documented that Cambridge Analytica and Russia's Internet Research Agency (IRA) were using social media platforms such as Facebook to play on already existing divides in order to provoke political tensions and manipulate voter turnout. To what extent this was decisive for the election is still a question, but what matters more are the tactics at play in racializing affect in political behavior—what I describe as algorithmic governance.

The Facebook posts in figures 18.1 and 18.2 have now been verified to have come from Russia's IRA and reached an estimated 126 million Americans (US House of Representatives Permanent Select Committee on Intelligence 2022). The Russian organization retrieved Facebook data on millions of American users for group targeted political propaganda marketing that worked on already existing sociopolitical predispositions. The first post is playing on a long-standing social and political history of white nationalism: the Confederacy, US Southern politics, and slavery. And, although it states "Heritage, not hate," the legacy of that heritage incites antiblackness and divisive Southern racial politics. More importantly, the latter part, "The South will rise

Suggested Page

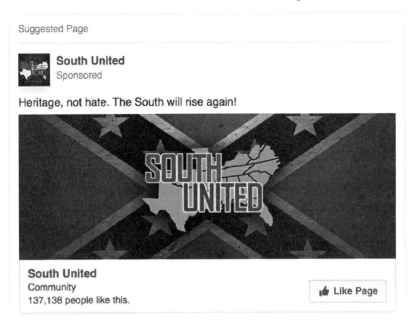

Figure 18.1. South United Facebook ad.

again!" is a performative that seeks to enact a preemptive response. It is also part of a chain of signifiers chanted in the August 2017 Charlottesville, Virginia, white nationalist march, such as "You will not replace us!" and "Blood and soil." The second Facebook post, although working on a different register of political ideology, also seeks to produce a threat based on already existing beliefs associated with Donald Trump: racism, ignorance, bigotry, and sexual assault. Moreover, this ad contains a more overt incitement to action: by organizing people in protest. In both instances, although the target audience is different, what is clear is that the ads seek to generate action based on social and political predispositions made to feel like a threat.

These Facebook ads are hallmark examples of post-truth political discourse. As Luciana Parisi (2017) argues, post-truth political discourse might be characterized by a play on affective predispositions and bodily responses to old beliefs that reappear as new. Although this process is not entirely particular to our condition of computational culture, we might now understand contemporary post-truth as the algorithmically modulating indeterminacies around an affective haunting

Figure 18.2. Not My President Facebook ad.

of nonlinear enfolding of pasts presenting and present futurity. This "history of the present" contributes to the conditions for what Brian Massumi (2015) has called ontopower, an affective politics based on an operative logic of preemption. Under this operative logic, one is incited to preemptively act on an "unknown unknown" and constructed threat before it acts on oneself. Preemption has long been theorized by Massumi and others (Martin 2007; Massumi 2010; Puar 2007), particularly in a post–9/11 era where the political discourse has become increasingly speculative while uncertainty has been politically preyed on to shape affects of social and political behaviors. What is more striking about the two Facebook examples is that they each engage an ontogeny (as sedimented yet ever-emerging embodiment) that has been sociopolitically constituted, *re*enacting not just any kind of affective predispositions but, in the first, a racializing affect drawn out of the postcolonial formation of the subject (as a recursion of the legacy of white nationalism, slavery, dispossession) and, in the second, the reiterative actions against violent forces of racism and sexism.

As Denise Ferreira da Silva (2007) argues, this post-Enlightenment formation of the subject emerges with G. W. F. Hegel's transparency thesis: consolidating Immanuel Kant's metaphysical explanation of the transcendental with Johann Gottfried von Herder's grounding of the historical formation of the subject (see also Hamner's chapter in this volume). Briefly, with Kant's transcendental, the being of the things of the world is apprehended in the given temporality of the knowing subject, acquiring its own fleshy-sensory history. Herder's focus on historical formation is meant to show how human difference evolves from national and geographic context and time, and hence, language and behavioral differences are constituted from the prejudices that produce tribalism. Hegel consolidates Kant and Herder in order to make subjectivity inhere in a self-determining and self-conscious subject: a nonaffectable subject and a transparent being. Through this construction, Ferreira da Silva argues, Hegel places "natural" human difference at the center of the liberal subject of modernism, whereby the transparent subject is the European "I" and the "others of Europe" are the affectable "I." This all sets the philosophical context for later analytics of raciality in the human and computational sciences. Hence, as Sylvia Wynter (2007) argues, this is a further secularization of the Hegelian-style sociogenic principle informed now by the supposedly objective biohumanism of homo economicus. These white and colonialist sciences include the biopolitics of statistics with their practices of prediction and governance. For my purposes, then, the Russian Facebook ads provide an opportunity to analyze and delineate where and how the sociogenic becomes ontogenic—namely, how algorithms enfold and generate the flesh by way of recursive logics haunted by colonialist reason.

I wish to articulate the racializing affect in algorithmic governance to an operative logic based on a threat, fear, anxiety, and desire. These affects, I will argue, are manufactured in the racialized flesh/body as a computationalized iteration of Hegel's transcendental poesis. This biopolitics of racializing affect is an autopoetic reengagement with the transparency thesis via the inputs, optimization functions, outputs, feedback loops, and digital flesh of algorithmic governance. Further, the hierarchizing and differentiating logics of algorithmic governance have come to instrumentalize the liberal subject: an ontoepistemology of racial difference informed by Hegel's transparency thesis (essentially, that to know one's self is to know where one is and how one can affect and be affected). The transparency thesis assumes not only a liberal subject or a self-determining subject but also that the European subject is a transparent subject, while the non-European subject is an affectable subject. The latter was understood to not have been affected by the exteriority of historicity, lacking developed capacities of interiority, progress, and development. Finally, I will turn to a consideration of alternative futures that could follow from an overturning of the racializing affective logics at work in contemporary algorithmic governance.

Ontopower and Algorithmic Governance

Since World War II, societies have been shifting from systems of institutional enclosure that discipline citizens' ways of being to systems of infinite and continuously modulating mechanisms, generatively controlling access and unceasing "dividuations" of the human (Deleuze 1992). Digital technologies and the Internet of Things have enabled increasingly more distributed logics, rationalities, and practices of governance via cybernetic systems of communication and predictive control.

This is what French philosopher Gilles Deleuze prophetically articulated in his 1990 essay "Postscript on the Societies of Control." In Deleuze's rethinking of Michel Foucault's disciplinary societies as control societies, discipline is no longer based on the corporeal disciplining and shaping of bodies via the awareness of (and internalization of) techniques and technologies of surveillance. Control societies are characterized by hypercalculative visibility across time and space and the subsequent regulating of movement and acts via modulating mechanisms across various thresholds of engagement. As Deleuze (1992, 5) states, in control societies, "the numerical language of control is made of codes that mark access to information, or reject it." If disciplinary societies might be characterized by parametric modeling and population census data (associated with Foucault's analyses of how such measures structure society), control societies are characterized by a more invasive "becoming-statistic" (Sellar and Thompson 2016) in which social metrics are actively mutated—in real time—along with that which they measure. In Deleuzian terms, this shift corresponds to a shift from the individual within a particular mold or enclosure to a more "environmental" system of "dividuals"—a term that designates the multiplicity of phenomena that once served to differentiate conceptions of the "individual" and "society." Borrowing from William Burroughs, Deleuze's conception of control is not about direct influence or restraint but rather a supple logic or, following Alex Galloway (2004), a protocol, that gives the impression of freedom while one's choices and behaviors are modulated and generatively shaped.

Deleuze theorized that control societies would increasingly become the dominant logic underlying systems of governance, the longer historical formations of sovereign and disciplinary societies are not superseded so much as enmeshed, coming to persist within control societies. Hence, the features that help to inform speculative predictions of control will continue to necessitate the metrics of disciplinary measurements; sovereign authority will continue to be legitimated and cloaked by the calculative acts of both disciplinary and control societies. There is, then, always the potential for becoming sovereign of/behind predictive acts of control. The entanglement of these technologies of power make up our contemporary moment. Within this context of cybernetic systems of governance, control has become the guaranteed form of "truth." That is, the assured path to "truth" is to create the present futurity of "truth." Thus, rather than try to prevent or deter the empirically verifiable, cybernetic systems of governance work through a temporization to manufacture a "becoming" assemblage of present futurity: an event, a plane of consistency, or a dividual/social body always saturated by a threat, an anxiety, or desire. In other words, regardless of whether a becoming assemblage is empirically or objectively verifiable, a future becoming event is constructed based on already existing predispositions or beliefs. The operative logic for such an environment of manufactured futurity is preemptive action (Martin 2007; Massumi 2010, 2015; Puar 2007). Its modus operandi is to generate affects and actions based on already existing predispositions or visceral bodily responses of ever-presenting pasts. The affect of a threat based on presenting pasts and present futurity, a "history of the present," is a form of control that is ontogenetic: a folding of the environmentality of relations into the generative emergence of an event, body, or consistency, or again, what Massumi (2015) calls ontopower.

Preemption is an operative logic that can never be false. It plays on indeterminacies to both manufacture truth (absent that which is objectively verifiable) and to maintain truth claims indefinitely based on always what "would have" or "could have" happened. For instance, in figure 18.3, the burka is not just constructed as an uncertainty of iden-

Figure 18.3. Burka Facebook ad.

tity but that which should be feared because of what it signifies of a potential terrorist threat. As a result, the image seeks to affect support for the banning of burkas in the United States in order to preempt what "would" or "could" happen if there is a terrorist underneath the burka. This preemptive action is based on a manufactured threat, anxiety, or desire associated with a becoming assemblage of present futurity. Thus, whether the threat, anxiety, or desire materializes, it will always be what it would have or could have been as present futurity.

The predictive intelligence of algorithmic governance works through the generative operative logics of ontopower. Algorithms process data on dividual phenomena, producing statistical and psychometric classifications of behaviors and profiles without ever asking the individual what or who they are or what or who they could become. As a result, as Antoinette Rouvroy and Thomas Berns (2013) argue, algorithmic governmentality acts to circumvent the reflexive subject and processes of subjectification. Through algorithmic governance, power is less focused on the capacities of understanding, ability, or expression and more focused on dividual phenomena that make up statistical and psychometric present-future classifications or profiles to inform preemptive decision making and action. These algorithmically produced present-future classifications or profiles (built from presenting pasts) include becoming events such as the risk of committing a violent offense, potential performance on a state-mandated standardized test, or profit maximization in the supply chain process. Governance here is not about the steering or intervention by governmental institutions but rather entails a technopolitical, market-oriented system that seeks to generatively control populations and systems of relation by continually modulating environments that nudge into future scenarios where capital can be regenerated.

Thus, cybernetic systems of algorithmic governance have no apparent limits to their data consumption and production. They are not limited to algorithmic deployments of public policy or military intervention, nor are they limited to the decision-making practices of state governance. Rather, algorithmic governance extracts and produces a generalized matrix of dividual data that ranges across all quotidian processes of social life, making use of whatever will enhance its stated aims of "predictive precision" that ultimately is about shaping future scenarios of capital accumulation. Algorithmic governance operates through a facade of objectivity, where the former legitimated and authorized authority is displaced into the instrumental reason of technology, leaving nothing or no one to appeal to (Rouvroy and Berns 2013). Given that the predicted threat or event is in the future, on what evidence, conditions, or rationale can one contest the predictive statistical and psychometric classifications of algorithmic governance? There are no committed actions or events to defend, only the "history" of dividual data reaggregated with other data (and this data is often riddled with errors).

These false notions of objectivity are often invoked as the alibi for algorithmic governance where it is argued that cybernetic systems will enable less partiality and greater efficiency in political decision making as well as greater democratic possibilities. Hence, if systems of democratic practice have been built on hierarchizing logics of human difference and variation (Hanchard 2018), then the identity and difference necessitated by algorithms will carry on those logics under the guise of objectivity. But in fact, others have shown how the defaults of technosocial systems are discriminatory in their design (e.g., Benjamin 2019). However, my intervention here is not based on a critique of exclusion but rather on how algorithmic governance entails a potentiation of value from and through automated and calculative machines designed to operate as a recursive reconfiguration of being. This recursion of reconfigured being is one haunted by the transparency principle and its assumptions about hierarchies of human difference. Thus, rather than ask the question who is included in the design of the technology or how is "difference" coded into the machine, I am interested in how the technosocial systems' generative ontoepistemology has been built, from the ground up, upon the colonialist reason of the post-Enlightenment subject. The recursive logics that power the Facebook ads lean on the transparency thesis. As Ferreira da Silva argues, even as cultural difference emerged in US democracy, racial difference had already established its grounds constituting the American subject. She quotes Woodrow Wilson to cement this point: "I stand for the national policy of exclusion. The whole question is one of assimilation of diverse races. We cannot make a homogenous population of a people who do not blend with the Caucasian race. Their lower standard of living as laborers

Figure 18.4. Secure the Borders Facebook ad.

will crowd out the white agriculturist and is in other fields a most serious industrial menace. The success of free democratic institutions demands of our people education, intelligence, and patriotism, and the State should protect them against unjust competition and impossible competition. Remunerative labor is the basis of contentment. Democracy rests on the equality of the citizen" (cited in Ferreira da Silva 2007, 216–17). The racial logics of this quote and relatedly the Facebook ad are shaped by ideas of a fully conscious, pure reasoning, and self-determining subject (i.e., the heirs of European colonialism) and, in contrast, the affectable subject (i.e., the "invader"). Through its performative work of whiteness, the Facebook ad seeks to maintain Wilson's "national policy of exclusion." What is more, the language of "invaders" also connotes the supposed bodies beyond the border as threat. The manufacturing of that threat is lodged in a discourse of racial purity, political contamination, and terrorism. The threat is also underscored by the framing statement "Every man should stand for our borders!" This propaganda—albeit generated by a foreign entity—plays on a long history of US predispositions toward the fear of Black and brown immigrants, especially along the southern border (and, specifically for Wilson, the Chinese).

As Asma Abbas (2019) has sharply articulated, threat has long been shaped by desire arising from the entanglement of capitalism and colonialism, while also continually reorienting this desire toward the future: what Marnie Ritchie (2019) has characterized as the formation of anxious affective infrastructures unbearably exposed to a future that cannot be controlled or predicted.

Skin, Flesh, and Affect

Speaking on the ontopower of preemption, Massumi (2015, 203; my emphasis) questions, "What are the existential effects of the body having to assume, at the level of its activated *flesh*, one with its becoming, the rightness of alert never having to be in error?" I italicize "flesh" to pull it into focus here. Although Massumi's conceptualization of the flesh is based on its sensorial relation to the autonomic nervous system, his reference to flesh also provides an opening to engage with the sociopolitical flesh that Sylvia Wynter, Denise Ferreira da Silva, and Hortense Spillers conceptualize. Even though Massumi argues that affect is presymbolic and prediscursive (and, thus, unmediatedly social), there is an important distinction that must be made between the skin and the flesh and this distinction is key to theorizing the racialized matter in the affective flesh of the body.

Like Deleuze and Guattari, Massumi's conceptualization of affect is nonrepresentational and thus, affect precedes and exceeds social constructions of difference such as race and gender: coming into account through backward formation. As Massumi (2002, 8) states, "Gender, race, and sexual orientation also emerge and back-form their reality. Passage precedes construction. But construction does effectively back-form its reality. Grids happen. So social and cultural determinations feed back into the process from which they arose." As such, for Massumi, affect also exceeds the discursive formation of difference. Although affect is not pre*determined* by the social, symbolic, or discursive, Massumi states, "The field of emergence is not presocial. It is open-endedly social" (9). In other words, until its actualization in particular social grids or formations, affect is indeterminately (autonomously) social. Is it plausible, then, that sociopolitical and racializing affective forces may already be incorporated or materially shaped as the body and as part of the passage of an event? If so, how might the skin and the flesh be key in this process?

In Massumi's (2002) articulation of affect, the skin plays a key role in the sensorial processings of the autonomic nervous system. Regarding the skin, he states, "Intensity is embodied in purely autonomic reactions most directly manifested in the skin—at the surface of the body, at its interface with things" (25). He posits, "The skin is faster than the word" (25) and later explains, "Brain and skin form a resonating vessel. Stimulation turns inward, is folded into the body, except that there is no inside for it to be in, because the body is radically open, absorbing impulses quicker than they can be perceived, and because the entire vibratory event is unconscious, out of mind" (28–29). Thus, the skin as a sensorial organ registers the ongoing intensities of an event (i.e., tactility) that become enfolded into the body in process (i.e., proprioception). It is this proprioception—the body's motion sense—that gives dimensionality to the flesh.

At the same time, the skin has long been understood to be the master signifier for marking racial difference: what Frantz Fanon (1952) theorized as epidermalization. Yet the skin and the flesh should not be conflated. In Michelle Stephens's (2014, 10) *Skin Acts*, she sharply articulates the distinction between the skin and flesh and argues that the color of the skin "ties the skin indelibly to the history of colonialism and, in consequence, to the epistemological categorization of difference." The skin is that which can be seen and represented. It is the sensing skin that perceives the interpellation of difference and absorbs this "knowing" into the body. Leaning on Sylvia Wynter, Stephens genealogically traces how the skin is part of a shift in modernity from a sexualized anatomy to the racialized physiognomy of difference. Over the course of the Enlightenment, the skin went from being conceived as permeable to being hardened and impermeable, securing the naturalization of difference. The flesh, Stephens argues, can be felt and mimetically shared. It is the ontological remainder, excess, and surplus of the skinned body; the flesh is the material that exceeds the discursive constitution of the skin, pressing in rather than standing outside of the symbolic and datafication. For Massumi, this is where proprioception enfolds the sensations of the skin into the material memory of the proprioceptive body and autonomic system.

It is in this material remainder, Stephens argues, that one finds the racialized body, a Black subject before the symbolic race.

The material remainder as fleshy body is where Spillers suggests that the traces of sociopolitical violence leave their marks. Spillers (2003) argues that prior to the legal constitution of the body is the formation of the flesh, a formation that is bound by the markings or traces of political violence designating a hierarchy of humanity. The traces of political violence of the flesh are what she calls "hieroglyphics of the flesh" as produced through the instruments or acts of violence. For Spillers, the "hieroglyphics of the flesh" are transmitted to future generations and are concealed in what is narrativized in pathological or biological explanations of hierarchies of "difference."

Arguments concerning the fleshy Black body and their transmitted hieroglyphics are profoundly important for affect for two reasons. Although William James developed an understanding of human automata as purely automatic and habitual action, his perspective was overturned by the experimental work by John B. Watson and others in behavioral psychology and the classical conditioning, even programming, of human behavior (this is important for the Russian IRA Facebook example in figures 18.1 and 18.2) (Selisker 2016). In fact, classical conditioning of the autonomic nervous system is well established (Powell, McLaughlin, and Chachich 2002; Winters and Schneiderman 2001), indicating the recursive malleability of the flesh. This work more importantly suggests that the fleshy Black body is materially shaped by racialized events, producing a racializing affect prior to the symbolic or discursive construction of an event. In order to more fully conceptualize the emergence of racializing affect, I turn to Wynter's sociogenic principle to provide an account of the sociopolitical process that materially shapes bodies, not as identity but rather as a fleshy process of becoming.

Racializing Affect

As Alexander Weheliye (2014) argues, the sociopolitical relations of racialization are perpetuated via technologies and sciences (among other things) and require "the barring of nonwhite subjects from the category of the human" (2). Similarly, Dipesh Chakrabarty (2000) posits that the racial hierarchies of the Enlightenment became part of the provincializing of European culture via discourses and objects/ objectifications of technologies. Yet the historicity of colonialism did not work only via the techne and episteme of technologies but also via the bodies of human subjects. In fact, Wendy Chun (2009, 7) questions, could race be "a technique that one uses, even as one is used by it"? Here I draw on Wynter's (2001, 2007) sociogenic principle to rethink how sociopolitical relations become ontogenic via the flesh/ body, shaping the neurobiological structure of the body and as such, the racializing affect of the body. Racializing affect is inseparable from the technology and historicity of colonialism.

The sociopolitical assemblage of Man, what Wynter also calls Western Man, has gone through a process of constitutings based on cosmogonies of human origin. She argues that the current iteration of cosmogony is biohumanist homo economicus, as informed by the economic theories of Adam Smith. Here, the correlation between biological and economic survival determines who is and who is not successful as a species. It is this correlation that forms the sociogenic code, reproducing racializing forces. This also corresponds to the sociopolitical constitution of Man, as a fictive (and yet dominant) genealogy of being human. If cosmogonies are the myths, narratives, and stories of human origin, which form our understanding of who we are and how we behave and practice in the world, then Wynter's sociogenic principle is a processual account of how the sociopolitical assemblages of Man and symbolic "difference" become materialized in the ontogenesis of the flesh.

Distinct from the human, though a product of the cosmogonies of the human, Man is the sociopolitical formation of being human. This sociopolitical constitution of Man is what autopoetically institutes Man as the fictive kind of being aligned with what is naturally selected and symbolic life; all other fictive kinds of being are "naturally dys-selected" and aligned with symbolic death (Wynter 2007, 13). To this, Wynter further states, "As if therefore *Man's* embodied signifiers of Otherness as the negation of its self-concept, . . . *homo oeconomicus*— that is, as if the [*homo economicus*]'s *Human Other* institutionalized signifiers of symbolic *death*, i.e., *Negro, Indian, Natives, niggers* (indeed, "White Trash" or *Trailer park trash*), together with *Welfare mom*, ghetto Black, as the extreme expression of the global category of the *non-Breadwinning* non-taxpaying 'planet of the slums' Jobless Poor" (38). Wynter (2001) rejects cultural and biological explanations of race (or "difference") while still accounting for the ways in which the fabrications of race, as sociogenic, come to ontologically generate as the flesh. Neurobiology, for Wynter, provides a theoretical route that explains how "difference" joins with the becoming of the body via neurochemical processes that reconfigure the experience of the self, making the formations of "difference" seem natural and taken for granted. Thus, the always-already ontologies of the physiognomy of the flesh/body are positioned in intra-action with the sociogenics of race. As a product of sociopolitical forces, race is then not inherent to physiognomic structures but rather those ontologies *become* racialized through their encounters of racialized events, situations, or acts.

The principle of cosmogonic/sociogenic causality is Wynter's theory of inheritance and social reproduction. As I have argued in other work (Dixon-Román 2017), inheritance is a process of more-than-human material-discursive forces of intra-acting assemblages with/in moments, events, and situations of time space. Inheritance always demands a response-ability and entails the (re)appropriation of the inherited. With Karen Barad (2007) and Vicki Kirby (2011), I argue that the matter of inheritance is always already mattering; thus, it is not passively being formed and shaped by the discursive, but rather matter itself is vibrant, intra-active, and materially reconfigures the world. Barad (2010, 261) states that "the point is that the past was never simply there to begin with and the future is not simply what will unfold; the 'past' and the 'future' are iteratively reworked and enfolded through the iterative practices of spacetimemattering." Thinking diffractively through Wynter, the neurobiological process of the body becomes materially reconfigured from the iterative intra-actions of the body with the sociogenics of Man. These iterative intra-actions of inheritance produce a sedimenting of sociopolitical relations in the material remainder of the flesh/body.

The autopoetic institution of "difference" as fictively constructed modes of being human comes to appear natural and reflexive. Weheliye (2014, 27) helpfully explicates: "Consequently, racialization figures as a master code within the genre of the human represented by Western Man, because its law-like operations are yoked to species-sustaining physiological mechanisms in the form of a global color line—instituted by cultural laws so as to register in human neural networks—that clearly distinguishes the good/life/fully-human from the bad/death/not-quite-human." The "master code" of racializations, I argue, is not just enacted via human cultural laws and neural networks but also inherited in technosocial assemblages. The data produced from the iterative human intra-actions with the more-than-human agencies of technosocial assemblages are both products and producers of the principle of the sociogenic. In short, the ontoepistemology of algorithmic systems is formed by a sociogenic code of Western Man.

The Russian IRA and the Racializing Affect of the Facebook Ad Algorithm

I wish to return now to consider how the content of the 2016 Facebook ads was, on the one hand, playing on already existing racialized flesh and, on the other hand, enacting intra-actions that were enfolded back into the Facebook ad algorithm to shape the predictive/preemptive potentials of digitized affectibility.

It is now well documented, including in federal filings such as the Mueller Report (2019), that the Russian IRA used social media to try to influence the 2016 US presidential election. It is clear that IRA was engaging in a post-truth political discourse by playing on the indeterminacies of already existing political beliefs. These were not necessarily fully conscious political beliefs but rather, following Tony Sampson (2020), the affect of deep nonconscious entanglements and technologically shaped corporeal contagions. The political beliefs of these ads, I argue, were of the changing same recursion of colonialist reason and the bodily reactions based on the activation of the fleshy racialized body. This agenda of the behavioral shaping and modulating of the human is not new to Russia and, in fact, it resurrects one of the dominant US narratives about the Russians during the Cold War. As part of American propaganda during the Cold War, the Russian military and even the public were often depicted as human automatons in Western media and popular culture (Selisker 2016). This narrative depiction played on ideas of brainwashing via classical conditioning and, as such, constitutions of the human automaton. The Russian government was an early adopter of bots and trolls as key agents for propaganda (Woolley and Howard 2019). Thus, these efforts of using social media ad algorithms to try to shape human behavior is not new and is situated in a longer history of state control and manipulation.

Although we are not able to gain direct access to the proprietary ad algorithm of the Facebook Ad API, it is possible to reverse engineer our way into understanding what the algorithm is doing via a series of experiments. A study conducted by Muhammad Ali et al. (2019) sought to do just that. Through their analysis, they discovered that although advertisers can specify the parameters of the target populations they would like to reach, Facebook's ad algorithm employs an automated optimization procedure that performs automatic text and image classification on ads in order to calculate a predicted relevance score to users. This alters who sees this ad before it is even intra-acted with by users. In addition, this study found that the amount of money invested in the Facebook ads, the content of the ads, and user intra-actions with the ad (i.e., generated ad clicks) each shaped who became digitally interpellated by the ad. Although we may not know the specific algorithms of the Facebook Ad API, we do have a good sense of its performative force.

Both IRA and Cambridge Analytica used the Facebook Ad API to deliver propaganda targeted at well-established politically divisive content. What is most important is that through the intra-actions of racializing affect, the ads became recursive forces for the algorithm. Not merely deploying ads of racializing affect, but simultaneously, this racializing feedback became part of the logic of the algorithm. It is in and through the recursion of such racializing affect that the algorithm became yet another heir to the transparency thesis, engaged in a process of sociogenic prediction. Such modulating acts of algorithmic governance are not only capacitating, but they are also debilitating: helping to contribute to slow suffering and death in terms of precarity and populations (Puar 2017). The racializing affect of IRA's ads produced a biopolitics of algorithmic capacitation and debilitation, one that compromised any notion of democracy via the transparency thesis and manufactured threats, anxieties, and desires. As Gabriel García Márquez stated, "Give me a prejudice and I will *move* a world." That's precisely what IRA did via the Facebook Ad API: they affectively *moved* the United States.

Autopoetic Overturn, Indeterminacies, and Racializing Affect

If today's algorithmic governance is part of autopoetically instituted sociogenic codes, then how can we move beyond or work with the ubiquity of inherited racializing affect? Like Mel Chen's (2012) animacy hierarchies, racializing affect is merely a by-product of a system of sociopolitical relations that hierarchizes and differentiates bodies based on the "representations of origin stories" and the dominant sociopolitical constitution of Man (i.e., racialized assemblages; Weheliye 2014). But racializing affect is even more ubiquitous and entangled in the material, semiotic, and social flows of life. If race or its proxies could somehow be removed from an algorithm, the cosmogonically derived sociogenic codes are still autoinstituted by the sociotechnical assemblages of data and algorithms. Given the entanglement of racializing affect with algorithmic governance, a reprogramming toward a more expansive project of the human is necessary in order to move toward alternative futures.

Reprogramming the sociopolitical constitution of the human will necessitate a critical examination and interrogation of the transparency thesis and the sociogenic codes of Man. Leaning on Aimé Césaire, Wynter (2007) proposes the Autopoetic Turn/Overturn as a praxis of science that makes the sociogenic codes, their processes, and invented sociotechnologies into more open-source objects of inquiry to be critically examined and interrogated: opening up the potentialities of rethinking and reprogramming the human. This entails the inquiry into all fictively constructed modes of being and the foundational myths, stories, and narratives of cosmogonies that have been inscribed in sociogenic codes.

The Autopoetic Turn/Overturn is a call to engage with and perhaps exorcise the hauntology of data, science, sociotechnologies, and the assemblages of sociopolitical relations. Hauntologies conjure what is seemingly absent yet already present. This absent presence is the excess, the beyond, the seeming erasure, or the mutually constituted Other of the referent that remains present as ghostly matter. Thus, the hauntology of algorithmic governance called on by the Autopoetic Turn/Overturn is an examination of the disjunctures and discontinuities of algorithmic acts and its produced/predicted output, with a focus on the various ways the transparency thesis and the sociogenic code are threaded into the design of the technosocial assemblage. If the sociogenic principle is an autopoetic coding of the flesh materially haunted by the sociopolitical constitution of a fictive genre of being human, then the racializing affect shaped by the Facebook ads can and needs to be *recoded*.

How might the praxis of the Autopoetic Turn/Overturn be conducted? Wynter argues that what is needed is a science of the word that thinks, reads, and studies rhythmically and relationally the human species. For Wynter, the human species is an assemblage of bios and mythoi, nature and culture, science and the word. As Katherine McKittrick, Frances H. O'Shaughnessy, and Kendall Witaszek (2018, 867) explain, "Science of the word . . . illuminates a genre of being human that rethinks the racial underpinnings of who and what we are by overturning a knowledge system—evolution and its economic-colonial ally, accumulation-by-dispossession—that justifies racism and other practices of violence." The repeated patterns of sounds, beats, flows, tempos, practices, and movements is an intimate part of being human that enacts the assemblage of bios-mythoi. Here, I am interested in the rhythmic flow, movements, and practices of algorithmic acts and the reconstituting of racializing affect.

The Facebook examples in figures 18.1 through 18.4 are based on an autopoietic and recursive system that seeks to regenerate its logic as exemplified in its diffracted patterns. Such patterns can be found in rhythms, intensities, entangled relationalities, material movement, and temporally entangled becoming processes. Whereas the recursive system is finite, the cybernetic information that forms the bases of its rhythms and patterns is decidedly more boundless. Thus, when the recursive system seeks to compress indeterminacies, it produces diffracted patterns and rhythms of discontinuity or disjuncture. In a system of autopoiesis, the algorithm will seek to regenerate the changing same logic of transparency, as in the Facebook Ad API. Yet, in a system of allopoiesis, a system that is fundamentally open to the potentiation of ontoepistemological transformation, the diffraction of the creative indeterminacies of blackness can open up the system to patterns and rhythms otherwise, even toward what Luciana Parisi has called a xenopatterning or alien intelligence.

It is here where I see Ferreira da Silva's (2014) Black feminist po-ethics as especially helpful, particularly with the development of the art or poethics of quantification. Ferreira da Silva seeks to cultivate a thinking and reading without modern categories. As she argues, it is the formalizations of the law, policy, calculation, measurement, and computation that arrest blackness's creative potential. She considers how modern categories, especially of time, history, or development, have shaped a text or an event and as such, to address the inheritances of colonial and racial subjugation. Yet, I also want to argue that what Ferreira da Silva compels us to consider is a radical recursive praxis, one that is allopoethic, works without modern categories, and is open to the creative potential of blackness. Such a system, what I have characterized as a "poethics of quantification" (Dixon-Román and Puar 2021), would enable the transformative potential of diffracted patterns and rhythms of ontoepistemologies otherwise while also enabling the potentiality of alternative futures.

This poethics of quantification diffractively examines the rhythmic flow, movements, and practices of algorithmic acts while conjuring, interrogating, and even reconstituting the specters of the sociogenic code. Although prejudice may move a world, reconstituted affect can shape alternative futures.

References

Abbas, Asma. 2019. "Contemporary Fascism and the Crisis of the Secular Sensorium: Aesthetic Production in the Global Postcolony." Paper presented at a symposium on "Propaganda, Affect and the Political," University of Toronto.

Ali, Muhammad, Pitor Sapiezynski, Miranda Bogen, Aleksandra Korolova, Alan Mislove, and Aaron Rieke. 2019. "Discrimination through Optimization: How Facebook's Ad Delivery Can Lead to Skewed Outcomes." *Proceedings of the ACM on Human-Computer Interaction*. Last accessed September 13, 2022. https://arxiv.org/abs/1904.02095.

Barad, Karen. 2010. "Quantum Entanglements and Hauntological Relations of Inheritance: Dis/continuities, SpaceTime Enfoldings, and Justice-to-Come." *Derrida Today* 3 (2): 240–68.

Benjamin, Ruha. 2019. *Race after Technology: Abolitionist Tools for the New Jim Code*. Medford, MA: Polity.

Chakrabarty, Dipesh. 2000. *Provincializing Europe: Postcolonial Thought and Historical Difference*. New Haven, CT: Princeton University Press.

Chen, Mel. 2012. *Animacies: Biopolitics, Racial Mattering, and Queer Affect*. Durham, NC: Duke University Press.

Chun, Wendy. 2009. "Introduction: Race and/as Technology; or, How to Do Things to Race." *Camera Obscura* 24 (1): 7–35.

Deleuze, Gilles. 1992. "Postscript on the Societies of Control." *October* 59:3–7.

Dixon-Román, Ezekiel. 2017. *Inheriting Possibility: Social Reproduction and Quantification in Education*. Minneapolis: University of Minnesota Press.

Dixon-Román, Ezekiel, with Jasbir Puar. 2021. "Mass Debilitation and Algorithmic Governance." *e-flux* 123:1–11. (Special issue on "Dialogues on Recursive Colonialism, Speculative Computation, and the Techno-Social.") https://www.e-flux.com/journal/123/436945/mass-debilitation-and-algorithmic-governance/.

Fanon, Frantz. 1952. *Black Skin/White Masks*. New York: Grove.

Ferreira da Silva, Denise. 2007. *Toward a Global Idea of Race*. Minneapolis: University of Minnesota Press.

Ferreira da Silva, Denise. 2014. "Toward a Black Feminist Poethics: The Quest(ion) of Blackness toward the End of the World." *The Black Scholar* 44 (2): 81–97.

Galloway, Alexander. 2004. *Protocol: How Control Exists after Decentralization*. Cambridge, MA: MIT Press.

Hanchard, Michael. 2018. *The Spectre of Race: How Discrimination Haunts Western Democracy*. Princeton, NJ: Princeton University Press.

Martin, Randy. 2007. *An Empire of Indifference: American War and the Financial Logic of Risk Management*. Durham, NC: Duke University Press.

Massumi, Brian. 2002. *Parables for the Virtual: Movement, Affect, Sensation*. Durham, NC: Duke University Press.

Massumi, Brian. 2010. "The Future Birth of the Affective Fact: The Political Ontology of Threat." In *The Affect Theory Reader*, edited by Melissa Gregg and Gregory J. Seigworth, 52–70. Durham, NC: Duke University Press.

Massumi, Brian. 2015. *Ontopower: War, Powers, and the State of Perception*. Durham, NC: Duke University Press.

McKittrick, Katherine, Frances H. O'Shaughnessy, and Kendall Witaszek. 2018. "Rhythm, or On Sylvia Wynter's Science of the Word." *American Quarterly* 70 (4): 867–74.

Mueller, Ralph. 2019. *Report on the Investigation into Russian Interference in the 2016 Presidential Election: Volume I of II* (Submitted Pursuant to 28 C.F.R. § 600.8(c)). Washington, DC: US Department of Justice.

Parisi, Luciana. 2017. "Reprogramming Decisionism." *e-flux* 185:1–12. https://www.e-flux.com/journal/85/155472/reprogramming-decisionism/.

Powell, Donald A., Joselyn McLaughlin, and Mark Chachich. 2002. "Classical Conditioning of Autonomic and Somatomotor Responses and Their Central Nervous System Substrates." In *Eyeblink Classical Conditioning*, vol. 2, *Animal Models*, edited by Diana S. Woodruff-Pak and Joseph E. Steinmetz, 257–86. Boston: Springer.

Puar, Jasbir. 2007. *Terrorist Assemblages: Homonationalism in Queer Times*. Durham, NC: Duke University Press.

Puar, Jasbir. 2017. *Right to Maim: Debility, Capacity, Disability*. Durham, NC: Duke University Press.

Ritchie, Marnie. 2019. "Diffuse Threats: US Counterterrorism as an Anxious Affective Infrastructure." Paper presented at the symposium on "Propaganda, Affect and the Political," University of Toronto.

Rouvroy, Antoinette, and Thomas Berns. 2013. "Algorithmic Governmentality and Prospects of Emancipation: Disparateness as a Precondition for Individuation through Relationships?" *Réseaux* 177:163–96.

Sampson, Tony. 2020. *A Sleepwalker's Guide to Social Media*. Cambridge: Polity.

Selisker, Scott. 2016. *Human Programming: Brainwashing, Automatons, and American Unfreedom*. Minneapolis: University of Minnesota Press.

Sellar, Sam, and Greg Thompson. 2016. "The Becoming-Statistic: Information Ontologies and Computerized Adaptive Testing in Education." *Cultural Studies ↔ Critical Methodologies* 16 (5): 491–501.

Spillers, Hortense. 2003. *Black, White, and in Color: Essays on American Literature and Culture*. Chicago: University of Chicago Press.

Stephens, Michelle A. 2014. *Skin Acts: Race, Psychoanalysis, and the Black Male Performer*. Durham, NC: Duke University Press.

Weheliye, Alexander. 2014. *Habeas Viscus: Racializing Assemblages, Biopolitics, and Black Feminist Theories of the Human*. Durham, NC: Duke University Press.

Winters, Ray W., and Neil Schneiderman. 2001. "Autonomic Classical and Operant Conditioning." In *International Encyclopedia of the Social and Behavioral Sciences*, edited by Neil J. Smelser and Paul B. Baltes, 998–1002. Amsterdam: Elsevier.

Woolley, Samuel, and Howard, Philip. 2019. *Computational Propaganda: Political Parties, Politicians, and Political Manipulation on Social Media*. New York: Oxford University Press.

Wynter, Sylvia. 2001. "Towards the Sociogenic Principle: Fanon, Identity, the Puzzle of Conscious Experience, and What It Is Like to Be Black." In *National Identities and Sociopolitical Changes in Latin America*, edited by Mercedes F. Duran-Cogan and Antonio Gomez-Moriana, 30–65. New York: Routledge.

Wynter, Sylvia. 2007. "Human Being as Noun? Or Being Human as Praxis? Towards the Autopoetic Turn/Overturn: A Manifesto." Last accessed May 19. https://www.scribd.com/document/329082323/Human-Being-as-Noun-Or-Being-Human-as-Praxis-Towards-the-Autopoetic-Turn-Overturn-A-Manifesto#from_embed.

Jasbir K. Puar

Slow Life

The modulation of capitalist registers of time has long been the subject of writings on Palestine especially within the field of Palestine studies.[1] Concerned with how time is used as a modality of control, these analyses focus on numerous manifestations of how temporality shapes and is shaped through the structures of settler colonialism and occupation. One version of this literature foregrounds the denial to Palestinians of historical time and the relegation of Palestine to the past of civilization. Another analyzes the chronic "stealing of time" through the expansion of labor time and the depletion of social reproduction time. Then there is the interest in the refusal or withholding of temporal simultaneity so coveted in our connective technologies that signal modernity. For my purposes I am most interested in the cordoning off of and thus the creation of space through time: what I have elsewhere referred to as slow life.[2] This creation of cordoned-off space through time in the West Bank relies on the physical architectural structures that are constructed as obstacles to "free-flowing" speed, rhythm, and pace: checkpoints, circuitous highways, settlement locations, and the partitioning of land and populations into Areas A, B, and C. Nothing ever happens "on time." Additionally, carceral administrative structures—for example, the mammoth Israeli "permit regime" that controls Palestinian labor (Berda 2018)—ground people in place and alter the capacities of capitalist metrics of time, both of the quotidian and of the lifetime.[3] Time and space are not exponentially compressed, endlessly linked, or more rapidly interfacing.[4] Rather, time-space relations are a series of discontinuous refractions, meaning that the unpredictable rupturing of relations between time and space predominate daily living. In her work on modes of waiting at the checkpoints, Rema Hammami (2015) points out that "checkpoints generally do not function to stop Palestinian mobility in toto . . . [or] to routinize Palestinian movement. . . . This network of permeability . . . operates . . . to make the everyday experience of mobility arbitrary, chaotic, and uncertain. . . . Rather than an effect, this constant state of uncertainty is the very logic of Israeli sovereign violence that checkpoints instantiate, as well as produce." The uncertain stretching of time—the West Bank is both smaller, because movement is short-circuited, and larger, because it takes longer to move from one place to another—is not a by-product of surveillance; it is the point of surveillance.

Uncertainty I: Ontology

In the context of slow life, uncertainty is a primary affective orientation, what could be called, following Hortense Spillers, a folded-into-the-flesh condition of possibility, an ontology of the flesh as felt.[5] Ezekiel Dixon-Román (2021) explains that the sensorial "recursive rhythms and patterns" that bodies experience "inform the racializing of affect." Dixon-Román (2021) articulates a version of slow life when he states that "racializing affect is inseparable from the patterns and rhythms of techno-social systems and the historicity of colonialism, that which reduces and stretches temporality while modulating the speed of life." I have elsewhere described the racializing of affect, or something akin to it, as the "geopolitics of racial ontology . . . that examines the regulation of affect as a racializing form of control" (Puar 2017, 136). I emphasize geopolitics in order to situate bodies in the specificity of technosocial systems that interface and instrumentalize the historicity of colonialism, while also cautioning against defaulting to a "locationless notion of ontology" (55).

Uncertainty II: Algorithms

This uncertainty, as theorists of computation and algorithms alert us, is already embedded in the calculus of statistical probability as the indeterminate. The indeterminate is an ontological capture of uncertainty by the algorithmic governance of the bio-necro-political state, an already-anticipated moment when preemptive power directed toward shaping outcomes is exceeded by the emergent potentialities of those outcomes. Slow life, as I have understood it, is therefore a reckoning with the capitalist captures of uncertainty, but it is also the field within which the indeterminacies of everyday life may disrupt these calculative logics. What are the interstitial ontologies of the body that knows anything can happen or the body that is always prepared for something to happen, when radical uncertainty is not just something tugging at the liberal subject but a foreground condition of being?

Time Itself

I have called this radically uncertain relation between time and space "time itself." Time itself, I argue, is not the same as the time lost to the continual expansion of labor time and the (re)production of the laborer and her/his/their ability to get to and undertake labor. Time itself does not hew to the Enlightenment categories of time, history, and development (Ferreira da Silva 2017), nor does it invest in the narrative structures of past, present, and future as primary referent points. As a stratum of matter and an affective modality, time itself is not of the laboring body—it does not circumscribe the body as a discrete unit—but of the para and sub individual capacities of bodies. Unlike affective labor, time itself refers to the laboring of affect, a laboring that contributes to the capitalist profitability, expansion, and in the case of Palestine, entrenchment of technologies of containment, of occupation as land use. Time itself is less a stripping away of individual properties and more of an endless interfacing of dividual data and metrics. Time itself is not extracted from individual bodies but is produced through the circuitry of dividual material, of the endless divisibility of bodies (Deleuze 1986, 1992; Foucault 1980, 1988; Puar 2017, 21–24). Time itself is dividual time (Puar 2021).

The Being in Question

Dividualization does not rehearse the primacy of human forms and in fact exploits humanist attachments to these forms. If we are to understand something about what Joseph Pugliese (2020) calls a "more-than-human biopolitics," it is that the dividual, not the individual, is the instrumentalized unit of such a biopolitics. This is biopolitics conditioned not through humanity or even on an interspecies spectrum but through pure capacitation and its metrics. The ontoepistemology and metaphysics of dividualization is indebted to cybernetic thought, whereby incommensurate systems reconcile through sense-making assemblages (Modern 2021). It is also important to note that dividual economies do not demote the individual to a stripped-down dividual. In other words, the individual-dividual relation is not a correlate to the human-(de)human one. In his discussion of a recent *New York Times* article on "fake faces," Ezekiel Dixon-Román (2021) notes that these faces are formed through an embedded recursivity that reorganizes and deploys dividual codes.[6] Dividual data do not so much strip the individual to a dividual data set; rather, these data sets are integrated into serial relationalities that inaugurate a "new" face that never was and is yet to be. (That is to say, dividuals do not add up to an individual; in fact, they do not even add up.) Dividual data—the dividual as a representation of data—thus productively induce forms of relationality that do not so much erase the individual or even redistribute it but genericize it through the potentiation of as-yet-to-be-known relationalities that are immanent in the present renderings of the past data. Dixon-Román (2021) explains that this is a process of "grant[ing] a recursive configuration of being," a post-Enlightenment subject that "assumes hierarchies of human difference." Insofar as any "sum" of dividuals do not a human make, I would propose that the being in question is not necessarily only of the human but also of the dividual.

The Art of Quantification

What is at stake in untangling the workings of the dividual? What is the corporeal in these dividual processes? To put it a bit differently, as John Modern (2021) asks, "What difference . . . does the algorithmic difference make?" To that, we can add, how is computational governance lived and felt? I am interested in how dividualization is both digital and of the flesh, involving series of recursive relationalities as well as a way of "unseeing" and reseeing corporeality. Dixon-Román frames the "art of quantification" as the nexus between flesh as felt and the execution of computational governance that inform quotidian existence. The art of quantification is exemplified in a 2018 performance piece by the artist Khalid Jarrar: in front of Wall Street, Jarrar sold ten-millimeter vials of his own blood at the daily stock price of global arms industry companies, such as Smith and Wesson.[7] The art of quantification is intractable from the act of tallying the number of knees successfully shot by the Israel Defense Forces (IDF) during a day of sniper targeting of the Great March of Return protesters in Gaza. Or we can think about the kind of quantified aesthetics required to account for the "epidemic of blindness" in Kashmir, the result of the targeting of more than three hundred eyes with pellet bullets since 2010, or the ocular trauma inflected on hundreds of protesters in the uprisings in Chile in 2019.[8]

The Limits of Ideological Unveiling

This art exceeds the process of tabulation, as it involves a scrambling of fleshly registers, of limbs, of organs, of blood (and thereby hold the potential for indeterminacy, for its own undoing). To explain and redress the violence of dividualization, there is often a recourse to the presumed relay of humanism here: the perpetrators have to dehumanize the protestors or have never humanized them in order to maim and kill them. Appeals to the humanistic are still the dominant rhetorical mode of redress while the violence itself may work through the dividual. Departing from Sylvia Wynter's oft-cited "Man as Overrepresentation of the Human," Denise Ferreira da Silva (2017) notes the limits of "ideological unveiling" in exposing this overrepresentation as if it were somehow the core of racial subjugation; Ferreira da Silva instead desires "an outside space from which to expose that other side of the 'color line.'" Jayna Brown (2021) points out in her wonderful book on *Black Utopias* that Wynter's concept of the Man as Human has curiously been in some cases wrongly taken up as a reinstatement of the primacy of human forms, a speciesism riding on human exceptionalism. Tarrying with the human is less about eschewing the human, as if that were actually possible. Rather, interventions such as those from Ferreira da Silva and Brown are interested in what other registers of knowing, being, and sensing are forsaken or foreclosed through this constant circuiting of value around human forms. Pointing to the species exceptionalism of Wynter's humanism, Brown argues that we need to "move from Wynter's call for a new genre of the human to new genres of *existence*, entirely different modes of material being and becoming."

Comrade Aesthetics

In his 2021 book *Minor China*, Hentyle Yapp offers a powerful critique of calls to "humanize" and the delineation of humanization/dehumanization in general. Ai Weiwei's 2008 Documenta project "Fairytale" consists of 1,001 people from China spending a week in Kassel, Germany, as tourists and as (the) art. One thousand one chairs could represent each individual, could humanize each body, but Yapp is instead interested in how "they all look the same" is turned into amplification, rather than redress, of the fungibility of the Chinese body-cum-art-cum-laborer. Yapp (2021, 74) writes, "Humanization is primarily about how racialized subjects are perceived, which would involve a remedy that appeals to the majority's empathetic capacity. Rather . . . these subjects must be seen as a horde so that their value comes from their contributions to capital. The 'techne of dehumanization' operates by rendering subjects as less so as to expect and extract more from their labor. We must hesitate from demanding recognition and representation so as to grapple with these connections across race and capitalism." This horde, explains Yapp, is a version of "comrade aesthetics," a form that subverts the dehumanization of racial verisimilitude into a powerful massification rather than seeking reconstitution of the agential liberal subject.

The Liberal Techne of Dehumanization

The liberal techne of dehumanization needs to be analyzed for its capacitation rather than resolved through representation. Yapp's point is that the humanization-dehumanization polarity keeps us distracted from the circuits of capital, and one elision is how capital works through the computational technologies of dividualization and repetition that instrumentalize data bodies for profit. Speaking of Palestine, writer Mohammed Al-Kurd argues that "the root of a politics of appeal, or of 'humanization,' is the idea that Palestinians innately are not enough" that operates to deflect from the violence incurred by bodies. "Humanization is a white, Western industry of selling perfect victims—toothless, grateful victims who are not going to act" (Al-Kurd, cited in Schwartz 2021, n.p.). These debates about humanizing targets of violence and capital exploitation, indeed, do little to help us comprehend dividuals as a unit of maiming. Shifting from humanization to dividualization moves us from the accusation of bias to the logic of computational governance.

A Tangent

The human is also consolidated through dominant discourses of health, bodily integrity, and capacity, in part to discipline attachment to a "proper" calculation of risk. If you go to the fence to protest in Gaza and get shot, it is not because there is a blockade, a settler colonial occupation, a violent praxis of maiming that seeks to snuff out anti-colonial resistance. It is because you miscalculated the/your risk.

Titration of Life

An example of how algorithmic governance deprioritizes human forms while still remaining of the flesh is seen in the logistics enacted to maintain the blockade of Gaza. Infrastructures of electricity, water, medical facilities, border crossings, cement and other rebuilding materials, fertilizer, humanitarian aid visas, medical travel permits, all of these and more are modulated to create an elastic, breathing, expandable, and contractable scene of movement. What Ghassan Abu-Sittah calls the "titration of life" entails dividual data—normative metrics of health, fertility, thriving/stunting, birthrates, longevity, productivity—driving this mechanism of modulation, contraction, and expansion (Abu-Sittah cited in Issa 2018). Titration is a form of modulation by degree that tempts a change in kind, approaching thresholds that only cohere retroactively. If, on the one hand, Gaza was determined by the United Nations in 2014 to be unlivable by the year 2020,[9] on the other, 1.8 million people continue to live in conditions with 97 percent water contamination, food and medical supply shortages, and generational mass debilitation.[10] The notion of livability is less a humanistic measure and more a pronouncement of the uneven demands to survive forces of exploitation and disposability. The livable-unlivable binary is usurped by the generating of incremental degrees of being. Without minimizing the strictures of the blockade, it is the production of modulating the flesh-as-felt ontology of uncertainty, in tandem with the blockage of movement itself, that informs logistical governance. Containing what movement is imagined to be is as important as containing movement itself.

What of the Birds?

What is containment in a place that is already constituted and lived as contained? COVID-19 has raised persistent questioning about what it means to social distance and to quarantine in places of extreme confinement like Gaza, the West Bank, or Kashmir. Such zones are defined by their containment, by being "cut off." Part of the power of logistical governance is to produce experiences of containment while tarrying in the endless porosity of the activity of blockading. That is not to minimize the obstacles to mobility that inform the blockade but to point out that the production of containment relies on a projection of fantasized freedom elsewhere/here. On what parameters does one presume "we" are not contained? How is containment a precondition for a certain capacitation, a perverse productivity? That is to say, how are movement and mobility redefined, remade, and lived otherwise? And what of birds that fly above walls, superviruses, toxins that seep up from the soil below, roil in the shared sea, free flow in the air above?

Preemptive? Prehensive

The distinction here between preemptive and prehensive power is crucial to logistical governance, especially because it is not simple to parse them. The preemptive is a mode of grasping to control, using information and calculation to create, delimit, or derail a certain event, to shut down the indeterminant effect or proclivity; it is driven by retroactive recursive temporality insofar as it rewrites the conditions of its own emergence. The prehensive is a mode of intervention, modulation, and titration into what is understood to be lively beyond preemption. That is to say, the preemptive seeks to eliminate that which is indeterminate while the prehensive accepts the indeterminate, entertains it, plays with it. The prehensiveness of algorithms does not revolve only around "representations of data," nor is it solely a "tool to accomplish tasks," but it also fosters "occasions of experience" that are neither driven fully by computation nor that which is external (Parisi 2013, xvii). That is to say, the prehensive seeks to probablize more so than determine.

The Impossibility of Stripping Resistance

There is indeed slippage between the preemptive and the prehensive: they are nested technologies of temporality. Preemption is in part a narrative strategy—"Gaza will be uninhabitable by 2020"—that assists the power of the prehensive to mess with vitality, with excess. In this sense, maiming as a strategy is not about preempting resistance but about encountering, indeed prehending, the impossibility of such preemption, of stripping the body of resistance.

Simply the/a Limb

There is another form of dividual making that is not reliant, or solely sustained by, data-driven technologies, an interfacing of computational sovereignty and a more banal and mundane sovereign right to maim: an imbrication of sovereign, disciplinary, and control forms of power. To hone the articulation of cybernetic logics of governance with their fleshly actualization, Modern (2021) proposes that the logics that operate through the right to maim serve as a "first principle." He helpfully parses out the "metaphysics of the right to maim" from the "physics of maiming." Israeli soldiers' descriptions of sniper targeting suggest there is a proprioceptive process that is parallel and akin to the data dividual process of sensing, sifting, sorting (Sebregondi 2018). Dividualizing does not break down or dismember the body—knees, ankles, limbs. Indeed, it does not recognize these disparate elements as part of a composite in the first place. The target becomes not the Palestinian, not even the Palestinian limb, but simply the/a limb.

Can I Add Another Knee?

There is the intimacy of proximity here—snipers and protesters are not far from each other, their faces, sometimes their eyes meet. But one learns not to see the limb as missing a/the body. This intimacy is what allows, rather than thwarts, seeing a human arm or leg as "a part" that floats free of the human form, available to the sniper as perceptually decoupled from the body. The intimacy that is produced with the part has as its corollary the situatedness of the rest of the individual's body. This relational frame of sight dividuates by "unseeing" the body as a composite and situating these parts in a "more-than-human" biopolitics among other organic and nonorganic entities, be they infrastructural, ecological, biophysical, interspecial. As reported extensively in *Haaretz* on March 6, 2020 by Israeli journalist Hilo Glazer, soldiers tally the knees and/or limbs they have conquered at the end of each day. Glazer (2020) describes the "chain of command" through the words of this IDF commander: "For every sniper there was a commander at a junior level . . . like me, and also a senior commander—a company commander or a deputy company commander. The superior officer would request authorization to fire from the sector's brigade commander. He would get on the radio to him and ask: 'Can I add another knee for this afternoon?'"

A Rubber Bullet

A reminder that as with the 1,001 chairs holding bodies that could be rescue-humanized, maiming is justified as an acceptable and preferable form of violence within the current terms of humanitarianism. There is a question here—historical, geopolitical—about the constitution of limbs as "new" targets and the ballistics and nonlethal weaponry designed to foster that constitution. The humanitarian logic of nonlethality—you will not be killed and never mind about being injured—conditions the rapid global expansion of the nonlethal ammunitions industry, in particular crowd-control weapons.[11] Paul Rocher (2020) argues this expansion, of both volume and of geographical scope, is indicative of the increasing and openly normalized use of disablement and maiming to contain political uprisings, to justify injuring as a form of not killing, thereby authorizing greater use of weapons and increased rather than decreased violence on the part of police and military. These tactics can increasingly be seen in Chile, Kashmir, Lebanon, France, Brazil, Venezuela, Catalonia, and the United States. Emphasizing the moral use of "rubber bullets" functions as one alibi for the right to maim. Situated in a biosphere of war ecology that includes decimated health infrastructures, scarcity of medications and supplies, proliferation of superviruses, and wounds resistant to healing, injury is the future violence. By future violence I mean to indicate how, in the name of liberalism and an ever-growing complex of humanitarianism, the belief that injuring is not as harmful as killing authorizes the expansion of violence and the expansion of its acceptance.

The Plasticity of Parts

In this visual-to-data economy, initiated by the sniper vantage point and circuited through the bureaucracy of authorization and tabulation, the dividual is a ground-zero analysis of fragments that are not of a whole but instead embedded in the process of titrating life through bodily metrics and subindividual capacities. The composite of the body is irrelevant; it is unimportant that it exists. Whereas the maimed, disabled individual is (fantasized as) available for empowerment and prosthetic technologies/apparatuses, *the dividual is a communicated expectation* and a corporeal training rather than primarily an ideologically driven representational figure. This training solicits and mobilizes the plasticity of parts, a becoming of debility and capacity that reorients our attention away from the typical semiotics of the disabled body that rely on overcoming lack and absence. Understanding the fleshly rendering of dividuals entails "a radical praxis of refusal" of the disabled body signified only "in the dialectical form" (Ferreira da Silva 2017). The conventional prosthesis of the wheelchair gives way to the slingshot. What counts as a prosthesis, a de- and reterritorialization of infrastructures, architectures, and objects, is a completely open question.

Source Material

Sniping therefore acts as source material for renewing settler colonial subjectivity and entitlement that has (temporarily) exhausted the utility of aerial bombing, drones, and other forms of remote-controlled violence. The blockade of Gaza oscillates between intimate and remote forms of control, suggesting settler ambivalence about both proximity to and difference from the colonized. Maiming is the reiterative performative of the (founding?) event of settler colonialism that contributes to its enduring structure; maiming rehearses the violent separation of bodies from land indebted to what Dylan Rodríguez (2021, 45) calls the "logic of evisceration," a genocidal logic of durational violence that reveals the incompleteness of the exceptionalized "modern concept of genocide."[12]

Recursivity

Maiming is therefore not a one-off event or a structure but a biopolitical circuitry through which bodies are positioned and repositioned into relations of living, dying, and maiming. This circuit is recursive in that the settler state freshens itself, undergoes an affective source renewal of settler subjectivity that refracts the structure of settler colonialism to the genocidal event and its iterations, its eventness. By affective renewal I am pointing to the recursive circuitry by which settler claims to land become reinvigorated through justification for violently quashing anti-colonial insurgency that will never be recognized as such. The right to maim could be thought of as a differently accentuated right to kill because it avails itself of this recursive process. Fred Moten (2018) describes maiming as "genocide [through] perpetual injuring," the killing of resistance itself, rather than bodies alone. We might pause at the temporal elongations of Moten's invocation of the "perpetual" while still noting the recursive process of enfolding temporalities that continually collapses the event versus structure binary. Perpetual maiming situates one form of the elimination of the native as a recursive structure of eventness. Patrick Wolfe (2006) has importantly argued that settler colonialism is a structure, not an event, stressing that elimination of the native is not accomplished only via one-off genocide. The endless repetition of the founding moment renders porous the otherwise enclosure of the event in time, such that event and structure are no longer opposed, nor do they disappear each other. Events of maiming compose the debilitating structure of settler colonialism, a recursive structure that works to return itself to itself.[13]

What Can a Body Do?

The question, then, is how the recursive creates the potential for re-making time, for inhabiting temporalities askew. Where is the potentiality in dividual economies, what is the performative work of the dividual, what is the future of the dividual? We do not yet know what kinds of rearrangements of domestic and political spheres can be generated from these scenes of mass debilitation.[14] We come to Spinoza again—what can a body do? Through the bio-necro political, how do populations live the (un)livable? As the becoming-pandemic introduces novel precarities while reinforcing old ones, we will be asking these questions again and again. I am struck by the emptying out of the ethical that Ferreira da Silva (2017) points to when she states, "I am interested in the ethical indifference with which racial violence is met." If, per her work and others', mass debilitation is the precondition for the existence of this thing called humanity, the ethical is still within the frame of the human and cannot address the dividual uses of data and information. The force and necessity of a nonrepresentational critique becomes all the more apparent, one that foregrounds the affective porosity of matter—whether of data, temporality, or flesh—across human/nonhuman registers.

Notes

Profound thanks to Jayna Brown and Ezekiel Dixon-Román for working through these arguments with me.

1   Recent scholarship multiplying the numerous conversations about time, temporality, and Palestine include Stamatopoulou-Robbins (2021), Jamal (2016), and a special issue on "Palestinian Futures" edited by Mikko Joronen et al. (2021).

2   There has been a great deal of scholarly and political work thinking about what "slow" is in relation to normative metrics of time. Most often referenced include Rob Nixon's framing of environmental degradation as "slow violence" as contrasted to forms of incident-driven spectacular violence that are represented in the enclosure of an event. I have found Lauren Berlant's notion of "slow death" helpful for thinking about temporalities of debilitation. More recently Jennifer Nash (2022) has written on "slow loss" to complicate paradigms of the psyche that privilege before-and-after ruptures. Scholars of critical disability studies theorize "slow living" and "slow care" as well as "crip time" and "crip temporalities" to problematize the demands of social reproduction under capitalism that center on productive purely capacitated bodies. In these conceptualizations, slowness is both

constitutive of forms of violence as well as the basis for different ways of living and being among that violence. My own thinking on slow life in Palestine contributes to the understanding in Palestine studies that slowness is also unto itself a form of violence insofar as it is used as a colonialist tool of control. At the same time, these frames, including my own, to a greater or lesser extent reify slow in opposition to "fast" or "speed," thereby inadvertently functioning as some capitulation to normative temporality. This is perhaps where Denise Ferreira da Silva's (2017) incisive work on the logic of time itself as a concept marking a foundational violence of Enlightenment assists in understanding how all relations of time, whether slow or speedy, are subject to capture, extraction, and exploitation. Recent work in Black studies, for example a special issue of the *Funambulist*, attests to the unworlding potentialities of such nonrelations to capitalism's metric of time, pointing to ways of remaking time itself (Lambert 2021). See also Falak (2020).

3   Here, I am also inspired by Jackie Wang's (2018, 191) concept of carceral capitalism which clarifies how "fine farming" and other recursive extractive administrative bureaucractic structures are designed to create captive populations while also making captive populations productive. Temporal relations from futurity to the daily rhythms of living are regulated to such an extent that spatial movements are driven by "indebtness and fugitivity" as an existential condition.

4   See David Harvey's (1989) reworking of Marx's "annihilation of space by time" and Massey (2013) for a critique of theories of space-time compression.

5   Hortense Spiller's work on the "hieroglyphics of the flesh" theorizes the flesh and enfleshment as foundational to Enlightenment understandings of corporeal excess and the severing of body from flesh. See also Alexander Weheliye's (2014) elaboration of Spillers and his work on racialization and affect.

6   See Hill and White (2020).

7   See Taylor (2018).

8   For analysis of the phrase "epidemic of blindness," see Raza Kolb (2021). On ocular trauma in Chile, see Velásquez Valenzuela (2020).

9   See United Nations (2015). See also UNCTAD (2015).

10 See Humaid (2021).

11 For a critical genealogy of the concept of nonlethality, see Anais (2014).

12 On the modern notion of genocide, Rodríguez (2021, 32) writes, "'Genocide,' as a modern conceptual and jurisprudential formulation, is the impasse of the racial: To invoke its terms already suggests exceptionality and absolute abnormality, yet the formations of antiblackness and racial-colonial power, in all their iterations, rest on logics of the genocidal that collapse into regimes of normalcy/normativity, universality/humanism, and sociality/civil society. In this sense, 'genocide' is a discursive regime that invokes, but cannot fully engage, the layered, historical violence of Civilization as a global order."

13 For a fuller elaboration of recursivity as a computational techne of colonialism, see the lecture series at Recursive Colonialism, https://recursivecolonialism.com/home/.

14 The brilliant constellation of thought generated by reading together Hortense
    Spillers (1987) and C. Riley Snorton (2017) on ungendering, fungibility, and fugi-
    tivity is inspiring here.

References

Anais, Seantel. 2014. *Disarming Intervention: A Critical History of Non-lethality*. Van-
    couver: University of British Columbia Press.
Berda, Yael. 2018. *Living Emergency: Israel's Permit Regime in the Occupied West Bank*.
    Stanford, CA: Stanford University Press.
Brown, Jayna. 2021. *Black Utopias: Speculative Life and the Music of Other Worlds*.
    Durham, NC: Duke University Press.
Deleuze, Gilles. 1986. *Cinema 1: The Movement Image*. Minneapolis: University of
    Minnesota Press.
Deleuze, Gilles. 1992. "Postscript on Control Societies." *October* 59:3–7.
Dixon-Román, Ezekiel. 2021. "Haunting, Blackness, and Algorithmic Thought."
    https://recursivecolonialism.com/topics/haunting/
Falak, Uzma. 2020. "The Smallest Unit of Time in Kashmir Is a Siege." *Adi Magazine*
    (Summer). https://adimagazine.com/articles/the-smallest-unit-of-time/.
Ferreira da Silva, Denise. 2017. "1 (life) ÷ 0 (blackness) = ∞ − ∞ or ∞ / ∞: On Matter
    beyond the Equation of Value." *e-flux* 79 (February). https://www.e-flux.com/journal
    /79/94686/1-life-0-blackness-or-on-matter-beyond-the-equation-of-value/.
Foucault, Michel. 1980. "Power/Body." In *Power/Knowledge: Selected Interviews and
    Other Writings (1972–1977)*, edited by Colin Gordon, 54–62. New York: Pantheon.
Foucault, Michel. 1988. "The Political Technology of Individuals." In *Technologies of
    the Self: A Seminar with Michel Foucault*, edited by Luther H. Martin, Huck Gut-
    man, and Patrick H. Hutton, 145–63. Amherst: University of Massachusetts Press.
Glazer, Hilo. 2020. "'42 Knees in One Day': Israeli Snipers Open Up about Shooting
    Gaza Protesters." *Haaretz*, March 6.
Hammami, Rema. 2015. "On Suffering at the Checkpoint; Palestinian Narrative Strat-
    egies of Surviving Israel's Carceral Geography." *Borderlands e-Journal* 14 (1).
Harvey, David. 1989. *The Condition of Postmodernity: An Enquiry into the Origins of
    Cultural Change*. Oxford: Blackwell.
Hill, Kashmir, and Jeremy White. 2020. "Designed to Deceive: Do These People Look
    Real to You?" *New York Times*, November 21. https://www.nytimes.com/interactive
    /2020/11/21/science/artificial-intelligence-fake-people-faces.html.
Humaid, Maram. 2021. "Gaza's Undrinkable Water 'Slowly Poisoning' Palestin-
    ians." *Aljazeera*, October 12. https://www.aljazeera.com/news/2021/10/12/gaza
    -undrinkable-water-slowly-poisoning-people.
Issa, Perla. 2018. "Interview with Dr. Ghassan Abu Sitta: There Is No International
    Community." *Journal of Palestine Studies* 47 (4): 46–56.
Jamal, Amal. 2016. "Conflict Theory, Temporality, and Transformative Temporari-
    ness: Lessons from Israel and Palestine." *Constellations* 23:365–77.

Joronen, Mikko, Helga Tawil-Souri, Merav Amir, and Mark Griffiths, eds. 2021. *Geografiska Annaler: Series B, Human Geography* 103 (4) (Special Issue: Palestinian Futures: Anticipation, Imagination, Embodiments).

Lambert, Léopold. 2021. "They Have Clocks, We Have Time." *Funabulamist* 36 (June 21).

Massey, Doreen. 2013. *Space, Place and Gender*. Malden, MA: Wiley.

Modern, John. 2021. "In the Age of Cybernetic Systems What like a Bullet Can Undeceive?" *Political Theology Network*, April 29. https://politicaltheology.com/in-the -age-of-cybernetic-systems-what-like-a-bullet-can-undeceive/.

Moten, Fred. 2018. *Stolen Life: Consent Not to Be a Single Being*. Durham, NC: Duke University Press.

Nash, Jennifer. 2022. "Slow Loss: Black Feminism and Endurance." *Social Text* 40 (2): 1–20.

Parisi, Luciana. 2013. *Contagious Architecture; Computation, Aesthetics, and Space*. Boston: MIT Press.

Puar, Jasbir K. 2017. *The Right to Maim: Debility, Capacity, Disability*. Durham, NC: Duke University Press.

Puar, Jasbir K. 2021. "Spatial Debilities: Slow Life and Carceral Capitalism in Palestine." *South Atlantic Quarterly* 120 (2): 393–414.

Pugliese, Joseph. 2020. *Biopolitics of the More-than-Human: Forensic Ecologies of Violence*. Durham, NC: Duke University Press.

Raza Kolb, Anjuli Fatima. 2021. *Epidemic Empire: Colonialism, Contagion, and Terror, 1817–2020*. Chicago: University of Chicago Press.

Rocher, Paul. 2020. *Gazer, mutiler, soumettre: Politique de l'arme non létale*. Paris: La Fabrique.

Rodríguez, Dylan. 2021. *White Reconstruction*. New York: Fordham University Press.

Schwartz, Claire. 2021. "For the Sake of Truth." *Jewish Current*, October 21.

Sebregondi, Francesco. 2018. "The Zone in Reverse: Logistical Power and the Gaza Blockade." *Footprint*, 25–36.

Snorton, Riley C. 2017. *Black on Both Sides: A Racial History of Trans Identity*. Minneapolis: University of Minnesota Press.

Spillers, Hortense. 1987. "Mama's Baby, Papa's Maybe: An American Grammar." *Diacritics* 17 (2): 64–81.

Stamatopoulou-Robbins, S. C. 2021. "Failure to Build: Sewage and the Choppy Temporality of Infrastructure in Palestine." *Environment and Planning E: Nature and Space* 4 (1): 28–42.

United Nations. 2015. "Gaza Could Become Uninhabitable in Less than Five Years due to Ongoing 'De-development'—UN Report." *UN News*, September 1. https://news .un.org/en/story/2015/09/507762-gaza-could-become-uninhabitable-less-five-years -due-ongoing-de-development-un/.

United Nations Conference on Trade and Development (UNCTAD). 2015. "Report on UNCTAD Assistance to the Palestinian People: Developments in the Economy of the Occupied Palestinian Territory." Geneva, July 6. https://unctad.org/system/files /official-document/tdb62d3_en.pdf.

Velásquez Valenzuela, Javier. 2020. "'Right to Maim? The Use (and Misuse) of Kinetic Impact Projectiles in Chile.'" Lecture, Universidad Católica de Temuco, October 10. https://www.youtube.com/watch?v=NTHA323GFEI.

Wang, Jackie. 2018. *Carceral Capitalism*. Cambridge, MA: MIT Press.

Weheliye, Alexander G. 2014. *Habeas Viscus Racializing Assemblages, Biopolitics, and Black Feminist Theories of the Human*. Durham, NC: Duke University Press.

Wolfe, Patrick. 2006. "Settler Colonialism and the Elimination of the Native." *Journal of Genocide Research* 8 (4): 387–409.

Yapp, Hentyle. 2021. *Minor China: Method, Materialisms, and the Aesthetic*. Durham, NC: Duke University Press.

Michael Richardson

Algorithmic violence has become all too familiar. Drone strikes kill and wound based on algorithmic "pattern of life" analysis. Welfare benefits are unjustly assessed by algorithmic systems. Social media platforms reproduce and circulate violent imagery and hate speech. Delivery apps keep gig workers in precarity and subject to harmful working conditions. Automated credit scores control who has access to finance. Cities use algorithmic tools to allocate municipal resources and restructure urban environments. Police employ predictive analytics that lead to ever more overpolicing of racialized communities, while judges use algorithmic tools in sentencing. No wonder, then, that "the violence of algorithms is becoming part of our common imaginary" (Bellanova et al. 2021, 126). But if algorithms are producing and reproducing violence, what are the enduring effects of that violence? Contemporary life takes place within trauma cultures (Kaplan 2005), defined by widespread precarity, vulnerability, and the pervasive presence of crisis in the fabric of ordinary existence (Berlant 2011). What might it mean for trauma culture if algorithms are among the chief organizing principles of social life, cultural production, economic exchange, and governance? What are the consequences of the algorithmic production and exploitation of relationality itself? And might there even be something fundamental to the algorithm as an operative form that is constituted by and of the traumatic?

This chapter argues that algorithmic trauma is a distinct form of trauma manifested in opaque, contingent, variable, temporally disjunctive, and spatially distributed algorithmic technologies. Algorithmic trauma fragments and disrupts experience, not only for the bodies subject to it but also for the technical system through which trauma is (re)produced. As I conceive it here, algorithmic trauma manifests ruptures of time, space, and knowability via processes of mediation that move through and between the corporeal, technological, cultural, and political. Algorithmic trauma encompasses traumas *transmitted through* algorithmic systems, traumas *produced by* algorithmic systems, and most provocatively, traumas *occurring within* algorithmic systems. Although time, space, and (un)knowability all figure in these three modalities of algorithmic trauma, the cases chosen to illustrate each also serve to highlight a distinct site of rupturing: temporality in traumas distributed *through* algorithms in the live streaming of atrocity, spatiality in traumas produced *by* algorithmic systems in remote warfare, and (un)knowability in traumas *of* algorithmic architectures of machine learning and artificial intelligence composed of neural networks.

Conceiving of these modalities as contingent and evolving assemblages rather than ahistorical structures, this chapter seeks to provide a relational account of algorithmic trauma by thinking with media, trauma, and affect theory. It does so through the reading of three cases studies. First, the live streaming of the 2017 Christchurch massacre, which demonstrates how algorithmic platforms such as social media and search engines introduce an autonomous reproduction and circulation of traumatic imagery in ways that disrupt temporalities and proliferate threat and fear through the everyday of the digital. Second, the application of algorithmic systems of pattern recognition, threat identification, and targeting to drone warfare, which generate identifiable traumas that break and reconfigure communities. Third, and more speculatively, the conceptual architecture of machine learning technologies, which enact a kind of machinic trauma that should prompt a reconsideration of the headlong rush to embrace them.

Despite their ubiquity, algorithms resist clear explanation. Simple definitions such as a step-by-step instruction for solving a task or form of programmed logic, along with common heuristics such as the analogy to a recipe, quickly fall apart when the thing at hand connects with or acts on anything beyond the most basic computational exercises (Seaver 2017; Striphas 2015). In general terms, algorithms are technologies of data analysis that take an input, make it machine readable, process the data according to a set of predefined or emergent rules, and (usually) generate human-readable outputs (Bellanova et al. 2021, 129). In the context of the neural networks that have become synonymous with machine learning—and artificial intelligence more generally—how information is processed, relations produced, and outputs determined is inscrutable as a direct consequence of the computational architecture itself. Algorithms are not simply technical but "entangled, multiple, and eventful and, therefore, things that cannot be understood as being powerful in one way only" (Bucher 2018, 20). Above all, algorithms are techniques of power, working to direct energy, labor, bodies, resources, capital, data, and information. They do so through relation: by identifying, constituting, exploiting, and reworking relations between data, objects, bodies, and contexts. Algorithms are instruments of worlding (Stewart 2007), their affective ensembles pulsing into operative form within and between computational architectures and fleshy, social bodies alike.

There are both scholarly and practical stakes in more accurately and materially conceiving, understanding, and analyzing algorithmic trauma. To take just one example, the question of what counts as trauma—or post-traumatic stress disorder (PTSD) in clinical terms— can have implications for access to care, therapy, and financial support. In the United States, drone operators claim to have experienced combat trauma induced by their participation in highly automated systems of lethal surveillance (Edney-Browne 2019), but whether they are clinically traumatized impacts the care available from the Veterans Health Administration (Holz 2021). For workers increasingly subjected to algorithmic monitoring and control, such systems can influence everything from the allocation of work to continued employment, to access to health care and other social and material benefits. Within their domain, people fail to appear as individuals and instead become "dividuals": aggregations of data points produced by the system (Amoore 2013). This expansion of the algorithmic makes citizenship itself increasingly ordinal, defined by measurement and sorting, whether in public health population profiling or in "the willingness to cultivate a digitally mediated, dividually managed and technologically assisted self" (Fourcade 2021, 165). If algorithmic violence has real consequences for labor, life, and even citizenship, then the question of its traumas and their affectivity is an integral part of the equation.

Complex, varied, and often difficult to track, algorithmic violence "is not spectacular but repetitive, regimented and standardized, and thus insidious" (Safransky 2020, 202). Riffing on Michelle Alexander's (2010) influential account of the legal mechanisms of "the New Jim Crow" of mass incarceration, Ruha Benjamin (2019, 5–6) calls the emergence of technologies of algorithmic violence and control the New Jim Code: "the employment of new technologies that reflect and reproduce existing inequities but that are promoted and perceived as more objective or progressive than the discriminatory systems of a previous era." In the Global South, such technologies enable a "data colonialism" that "combines the predatory extractive practices of historical colonialism with the abstract quantification methods of computing" (Couldry and Mejias 2018, 2). Although vital work has been done in cataloging, critiquing, theorizing, and making visible the violence, injury, and injustice wrought by algorithmic systems (see, e.g., Dencik, Hintz, and Cable 2016; Eubanks 2018; Mann 2020; Noble 2018; Sadowski 2020), the traumatic consequences of such harms tend not to be conceptualized as a distinct phenomenon. A closer examination is needed.

Media, Trauma, Affect

Within the humanities, trauma is generally understood as the belated impact of an event which so ruptures experience that its aftermath has rippling effects through the survivor's life (Caruth 1996). Trauma survivors live "with an event that could not and did not proceed through to its completion, has no ending, attained no closure, and therefore, as far as its survivors are concerned, continues into the present and is current in every respect" (Felman and Laub 1992, 69). Trauma persists in doing injury precisely because it could not be made sense of in the event of its occurrence and so haunts the survivor, unable to be assimilated into the ongoingness of the self. Although such traumas might be shared by many, the debts to psychoanalysis and literary deconstruction incline those foundational theories to address the individual subject split from their own experience of self in time and, as such, reckon more uneasily with collective experience. By contrast, social theories of trauma emphasize the shared identification with "a horrendous event that leaves indelible marks upon their group consciousness, marking their memories forever and changing their future identity in fundamental and irrevocable ways" (J. Alexander 2012, 6). Collective recognition of trauma enables the formation of solidarities around shared suffering and moral responsibility, even as it produces the grounds for the rejection of certain groups or the claim to a moral right to restitution and even revenge. If the trauma theory that emerged from literary studies emphasizes the struggle of artistic works to represent the unrepresentable, social theories of trauma look to popular and political texts, events, monuments, and memorials for the formation and formulation of an agreed-upon collective trauma. But as Amit Pinchevski (2019, 3) points out, rather than something that is simply "represented, signified or performed in literary, filmic, artistic or popular cultural texts," we can "understand the traumatic as something that is made manifest through media technological rendering."

All models of trauma rest on a media-technological conception of the self: one in which events can be imprinted or recorded but also played back at any time. But media is more than a model for trauma: media and the processes of mediation that constitute them are vital to its very structure. Trauma is not an ahistorical structure of experience; it depends on the specificities of the media milieu within which it occurs. As Pinchevski (2019, 15) writes, "It is not by chance that the elusive nature of trauma, its teetering between past and present, presence and absence, proximate and distant, is often made manifest by means of media technology." No one should be surprised that concepts of trauma emerge in conjunction with modernity and its radical upheaval of prior forms of living: railway spine, shellshock (Leys 2000). Media shape what trauma is, even as they are shaped by trauma. Claims to a vital distinction between ahistorical structural trauma and the historical traumas differentially experienced by people (LaCapra 2001) cannot hold if trauma is inseparable from media and processes of mediation, which in turn cannot be extracted from time and context. In fact, we might conceive of trauma as a failed mediation—an event so rupturing that it is not mediated into the flow of experience but rather caught within media. Pinchevski (2019, 4) again: "Media bear witness to the human failure to bear witness, and in so doing render the traumatic tangible by means of technological reproduction." That is, media do not simply enable attempts to represent or signify trauma but rather enact its evolving structures and logics.

Widening the ambit of "media" from technological media to include anything that mediates—light, molecules, energy—allows for a still more radical reckoning with the interdependence of trauma with media. As Sean Cubitt (2017, 4) argues, "The flow of mediation precedes all separations, all distinctions, all thingliness, objects, and objectivity." Mediation thus connects the human and nonhuman. It is a vital process inseparable from life itself: making, shaping, ending (Kember and Zylinska 2012). Such a conception provides a means to foreground the medial dimensions of the traumas of blackness in the wake of slavery (Sharpe 2016) with its legacies in contemporary surveillance technologies (Browne 2015) and machine learning systems (Dixon-Román and Amaro 2021). Those historical traumas take place not only in signification and representation but also in the material relations of bodies as they are mediated in, by, and through material structures (ships), global logistics (slave routes, auction yards), and racial capitalism (slave traders, new world plantations), even before their mediation into archival records, gospel songs, surveillance technologies, public discourse, and so on. Trauma might originate in a singular instance—such as a car crash or sudden violent attack—but it can also be far more dispersed, bound up with the texture of daily life. In this sense, trauma can occur through recursive mediations, taken up by and transmitted through different media technological renderings. To reckon with the mediality of trauma, then, is also to confront its material and affective dynamics within situated contexts (Atkinson and Richardson 2013). But as Jenny Edkins (2003, 58) argues, trauma is also tightly bound to power, and in the context of political abuse, "trauma involves confronting the arbitrary, contingent, and ungrounded nature of authority structures." Such a confrontation disrupts the linear time of the geopolitical state because "trauma time is inherent in and destabilizes any production of linearity" such that "trauma must be excluded for linearity to be convincing" (16). Edkins fears that states will eventually learn to make trauma time their own and so further erode the ground for confronting authority. My fear is that algorithmic media provides the technoscientific instrument for making trauma time an operative tool of state and capital.

With the arrival of algorithmic culture, capitalism, and governance, a qualitative shift has taken place in the media-technological environment. Unlike prior forms of mediation, contemporary algorithmic technologies defer substantive decision making to automated systems and processes that are distributed in space and time. As instruments of automated media reliant on computational process for production and distribution, algorithms "anticipate the automation of subjectivity" (Andrejevic 2019, 11) and, by implication, the potential for automated trauma. With the automated subject produced through techniques of profiling, the cultural phenomena impinging on the human sensorium vary for every individual but are also responsive to and learn from the micro-dynamics of clicks, scrolls, shares, reactions, blinks, touches, gaits, breath, pulse, temperature, and countless other bodily engagements that are sensed and made sense of. Illusions of linear temporality collapse. Incipient futures cohere with the present and carry through into the past, even as past futures impinge on the immanent present: virtual and actual folding together in the algorithmic haunting of space and time (Dixon-Román and Amaro 2021). Algorithmic authority punctures the illusion that the state, or its allies and agents, can deliver on its promise of stability and security. Capricious, fallible, and often unaccountable, algorithmic systems beget a kind of violence that mirrors the destabilization of authority produced by collective trauma (Edkins 2003). Film and literary media enact the imagistic, fragmented, imprinted, and temporally disrupted in trauma; automated media introduce agencies, contingencies, and potentialities that are mutable and unpredictable to a degree unmatched by pre-algorithmic media. If it is indeed the case that trauma is shaped by the media through which we seek to grasp it and within which we life, then what of trauma in this age of algorithmic media?

Answering this question calls for an expansive conception of affect. Massumi (2002, 31) writes that "the body is as immediately abstract as it is concrete; its activity and expressivity extend, as on their underside, into an incorporeal, yet perfectly real, dimension of pressing potential." This emphasis on potentiality and abstraction within the virtualities inherent to all becoming opens conceptual room for a vital affect that does not depend on corporeal bodies. Affects can be understood as machinic: intensities of relation that entangle technical systems, bodies, and worlds. Indebted to Félix Guattari's (1995) radical reformulation of the "machinic" as the assemblage of various forms, objects, processes, concepts, bodies, and events, my framing of affect as machinic seeks to displace the primacy of human bodies and sensoria from the affected and affecting ensemble. "The function of the affective," Marie-Luise Angerer (2017, 27) writes, "is to connect, disrupt, and/or invert life in time and technology as time in motion." As such, affect can extend to those contingent capacities for connection, disruption, and inversion, across time, that take place within technologies themselves and in their permeation of nontechnical life through processes of mediation. Like all affect, its machinic incarnation is recursive, nonlinear, and autonomous: forces of relation that disrupt time, space, experience, and the grounds of cognitive rationality itself. Inflected in this way, affect offers an analytic for thinking machinic relations of complex technical systems in relation with the cyborg experiences of life in the sway of algorithmic systems.

Trauma through Algorithm: Temporalities

Media are not simple instruments that represent reality back to us but part of the sensorial embodiment through which we make and inhabit worlds (Frosh 2019). Hunting out the intensities, insecurities, and anxieties that drive engagement, algorithmic media sculpt themselves to the user in ways that print and broadcast media could not. Social media delivers material that its algorithms predict will drive connectivity, while search engines produce results designed for swift engagement. Algorithms individualize contingency and position the traumatic within the intimate, familiar temporality of the digital platforms that increasingly mediate social and working lives. Transmitted through social media and search, violent content reproduces and circulates, simultaneously risking the inciting of trauma in survivors and even producing fresh traumas.

On March 15, 2019, the Australian white supremacist Brenton Tarrant launched a Facebook Live feed from a GoPro camera, showing himself on the way to Al Noor Mosque in Christchurch, New Zealand. Linked from the message board 8chan, the stream showed Tarrant begin shooting at 1:40 p.m., killing forty-four people, before driving to Linwood Islamic Centre where he killed another seven people before his arrest at 1:59 p.m. His livestream lasted seventeen minutes before it was taken down by Facebook, capturing his actions inside Al Noor Mosque and ending abruptly before he reached Linwood Islamic Centre. Even though most mainstream media organizations refused to show the footage, social media algorithms pushed it across Facebook, Twitter, and YouTube, enabling multiple versions to proliferate (Tikka et al. 2020). With the streaming GoPro strapped to his helmet "man and machine coalesce into an invisible and material force for amplifying and spreading horror in which violence becomes unbound from the event to be re-enfranchised online as a category which delivers the victims as the 'wretched of the screen'" (Ibrahim 2020, 804). Platform architectures and algorithmic logics of continual engagement and reproduction supercharged its spread and ensured an audience, both in the moment and afterward, whether willing or not. In doing so, social media platforms materialized the temporally disjunctive structure of trauma. Such platforms depend on prediction: they are anticipatory in orientation, nudging, preempting, or otherwise modulating desires for information, distraction, and stimulation through the making operative of potential futures. When those futures are haunted by accumulating virtual traumas—traumatic affects—the time of the algorithm vibrates with recursive and disjunctive trauma time as the live streaming of atrocity and its digital afterlives reveals.

Even as Tarant's livestream ceased to be live, it carried vestiges of immediacy. Fractured out of its liveness, it existed (continues to exist) in the algorithmic space of traumatic affect: a fragment of the past that remains "live" yet cut from the stream of liveness, unable to be either replaced or suppressed. Algorithmic search and social platforms conjoined the livestream "to an architecture of non-erasure where terror spectacles can traverse the Internet to be replicated, to be disseminated to a wider audience, to be archived on forums and to be doubled in 'mirror' sites to defy eradication" (Ibrahim 2020, 815). This nonerasure, combined with the capacity to be remixed and memed, means that such spectacular violence has a certain currency in affective economies of attention. Yet while the grim appeal to the far right is obvious enough, the traumatic potential of the video speaks to the traumas inherent to algorithmic systems and cultures. Despite bans in Australia and New Zealand and the arrest of several men possessing the video, its afterlife haunts the digital quotidian. It haunts as the site of trauma itself but also as potentially traumatizing for those who might watch it and most of all for Muslims across the world who might be subject to the violence of those inspired by its deliberately performative slaughter (Besley and Peters 2020). Although social media platforms eventually clamped down and removed the video, the damage had been done; their algorithms had released the footage into the wild where it could roam in the always potentially imminent of the algorithmic virtual.

Algorithmic trauma is thus inseparable from the logics of reproduction, engagement, and reposting of algorithmic platforms for sociality and search. First, in the capacity for content recommenders to (re-)present potentially traumatic material. But second and more radically, in the capacity for those systems to reproduce and perpetuate, through the circulation of traumatic materials, the haunting threat of future violence. Here, then, the problem is not solely that the spread of such videos might be radicalizing for white supremacists but that Muslim people must always live with the circulation of that possibility and with the sheer lack of agency in the face of such algorithmic potential for the transmission of trauma inscribed and enacted through the affective force of mediated violence. Of course, white supremacist violence far precedes and exceeds the algorithmic, but the algorithmic introduces a novel dynamic to trauma, understood not in the narrow clinical sense but in the affective intensity of traumatic encounters that preemptively and perpetually weave themselves through and around lived experience. The stream from the shooter's GoPro is far from the first instance of the live streaming of death and far too from the first leaking, pooling, and circulating of violent horror through the networks of digital life. Although the algorithmic backbone of digital platforms drives the dynamics described here, responsibility rests with the willingness of these companies to trade off such injury for business as usual. Braided with the nonlinearity of algorithmic time, trauma's machinic affects intensify with processes of "resonance and feedback that momentarily suspend the linear progress of the narrative present from past to future" (Massumi 2002, 36).

Trauma by Algorithm: Spatialities

Just as algorithmic technologies have become central to technocratic governance and business, they are also increasingly pivotal to technoscientific warfare. Under the drone warfare waged by the Obama administration in Afghanistan, Pakistan, Yemen, and across the Middle East, "personality strikes" targeted at known individuals were outnumbered by "signature strikes" based on algorithmic analysis of cell phone metadata and other signals utilized in intelligence gathering. Produced through the application of "pattern-of-life analysis" to intercepted metadata, the "signature" of an imminent threat marks otherwise unknown and unnamed persons for death: eminent death by metadata (Pugliese 2020). In places where SIM cards and phones change hands regularly and suspicion toward the United States is both understandable and pervasive, this notion that a record of calls, texts, and geographic proximities to other known or unknown threats should be sufficient to warrant death has led to thousands of civilian casualties, although only a fraction are confirmed as such by the US military. Traumas unfold from such a system in multiple ways. Although the dead and their families and communities rarely learn whether or how an algorithm was involved, algorithmic inaccuracies and contingencies texture the precarity of existence. Violence begins before the "event" of the strike; trauma is already underway. But the algorithmic trauma of remote warfare is spatially as well as temporally disjunctive: the algorithms act on and render dangerous geographies and movements that might not have been otherwise. Drone warfare thus reveals the crucial spatial distributions and disjunctures that are produced by and manifested in algorithmic trauma.

As research on the ground has shown, the trauma of drone war extends beyond those directly wounded and killed to entire communities. "When we're sitting together to have a meeting, we're scared there might be a strike," one man from North Waziristan, Pakistan, told human rights researchers. "When you can hear the drone circling in the sky, you think it might strike you. We're always scared. We always have this fear in our head" (Stanford Law School 2012, 81). Drone violence reshapes social life, changing patterns of behavior—not meeting in groups, not moving after dark, obtaining governmental permission for a range of customary activities—and inducing terrible anxiety, stress, fear, and trauma (Edney-Browne 2019, 1348–50). Using the Gilgamesh surveillance system, the relational geographies of social life are reduced to defined data points: a pair of SIM cards active in two phones that spend time near each other; a vehicle traveling a seemingly circuitous route. This production of metadata reconstitutes individuals and communities as interconnected dividuals whose meaning and identity is determined by the relations generated by computational analysis using the SKYNET program. SKYNET uses a particular type of machine learning algorithm called a "random forest," designed to identify meaningful patterns within seeming chaos. Random forest algorithms sample random subsets of data, generating multiple decision trees that the algorithm then votes on to determine the most likely prediction. Data is spatialized into branching trees and expanding arrays. Proliferating random forests produce "an algorithmic proposition of *What comes next?* that takes place as a calculation amid incalculability, mobilizing chance and the splitting of agency, sometimes with lethal effects on human life" (Amoore 2020, 127).

Spatial actions taken to elude, game, or otherwise appease the algorithm—staying home, avoiding public gatherings—eventually feed back into the random forest, producing further errors of misrecognition that can lead to violence and death. Spatiality itself becomes both the site and medium of trauma as the random forest algorithm turns the mobilities of daily life into the pure potential of violence. People living under drones might not identify algorithms as the origins of trauma as such, but algorithmic contingency is looped through the radical uncertainty of life under skies enclosed by drones (Tahir 2017). Brutally physical traumas such as lost limbs and eyes or scarred flesh are matched by more pervasive yet less visible wounds across the affective atmospheres and material conditions of collective and individual life. Belatedness, inscrutability, inhuman technicity, and contingency all play out in now-familiar ways, but they are intensified, multiplied, and dispersed by the apparatus of technoscientific war. The opacity of that apparatus distances the United States—and particularly its political leaders—from its own violence, making accountability all too rare. Sensors, networks, algorithms, and interfaces distribute data and decisions, dispersing responsibility such that the source of trauma is doubly withdrawn, not just hovering at the limits of perceptibility but too large, distributed, and complex to meaningfully trace and make sensible. In this sense, then, the spatiality of algorithmic trauma is threefold: manifested within the spatial architecture of algorithmic threat identification, in its spatial reorganization of social and cultural life, and in the spatial distribution of the drone apparatus itself.

Although drone warfare is instructive of this spatial dimension of algorithmic trauma, it is not unique. An equivalent analysis could be made of the experience of Amazon workers or Uber Eats delivery staff, who report bodily and psychic injury stemming from the need to keep up with a pace and form of work within warehouse or urban spaces dictated by algorithmic systems and traumatized through automated infrastructures (Ongweso 2021). So too the algorithmic redlining that occurs through smart city policies and platforms adopted by urban governments (O'Malley and Smith 2020), which produce "a repetitive and standardized form of violence that contributes to the racialization of space and spatialization of poverty" (Safransky 2020, 200). Algorithmic trauma is thus instantiated through emergent technogeographies, produced not only within algorithmic systems or in the moment of encounter with them but also in their spatial and material manifestations in war—and in workplaces, cities, hospitals, schools, and courts that apply very similar algorithmic technologies to very different contexts.

Traumas of the Algorithmic: Unknowability

So far, I have focused on theorizing algorithmic trauma in relation to specific instances of algorithmic violence. But in this final section, I want to undertake a more speculative enterprise and pursue the ruptures and disjunctures that manifest the radical unknowability within algorithms themselves. Trauma plays a surprising role in the cybernetic origins of computational rationality through the figure of Warren McCulloch, a neurophysiologist, chair of the Macy Conferences on cybernetics, and an influential theoretician in his own right. For McCulloch, it was obvious that "computers were not yet the same as organic brains" (Halpern 2015, 157), nor likely to become so in any structurally analogous way. Rather than copying the neural structure of the brain, what mattered were the methods, practices, and models that would govern the design of new computing machines. McCulloch rejected the idea that the application of reason led directly to rational outcomes, arguing that rationality was psychotic as well as logical: after all, psychosis was a necessary element—or at least potential—within the organic brain. Working in the wake of World War II, battlefield trauma was as important a context as the signal processing demands of military systems. For McCulloch, neural damage was a machinic problem, one of logical process; repair was just a matter of rewiring.

Against the linearity of traditional computing, with its clear delegations between input and output, McCulloch worked with the mathematician Walter Pitts (1943) to propose neural nets defined by the idea that "one cannot know which neuron sent the message, when the message was sent, or whether the message is the result of a new stimulus or merely a misfire" (Halpern 2015, 168). This meant that "from within a net (or network) the boundary between perception and cognition, the separation between interiority and exteriority, and the organization of causal time are indifferentiable" (168). The genius of McCulloch and Pitts was to recognize that this indifference was an advantage: it meant that memory, amnesic and neurotic rather than infallible, confirmed things only at indeterminate times. What mattered in computation, then, was the capacity to act rather than positioning events precisely in time. Predicting outcomes mattered, not explaining how they were achieved. Unknowability was thus enshrined in computational rationality yet hidden below its surface, alongside psychosis, embodiment, and affect (72; Wilson 2010, 109–32). As Orit Halpern (2015, 184) writes, "Within twenty years of the war, the centrality of reason as a tool to model human behavior, subjectivity, and society had been replaced with a new set of discourses and methods that made 'algorithm' and 'love' speakable in the same sentence and that explicitly correlated psychotic perspective with analytic logic." Although Halpern leaves trauma itself relatively unexamined, in the insistence on unknowability and fractured temporality in cybernetic rationality there exists a machinic rupture, an algorithmic disjuncture that is latent to the composition of all such systems.

That disjuncture is rooted in both how the system works at a technical level and in McCulloch's conception of the mind, one shaped by his psychiatric training but also by the problem of battlefield trauma.

This origin story for neural networks exposes the influence of culture and context within the theoretical frameworks underlying machine learning today. Algorithms are "not singular technical objects that enter into many different cultural interactions, but are rather unstable objects, culturally enacted by the practices people use to engage with them" (Seaver 2017, 5). To take but one example, the Amazon Echo is not only gendered but also racialized within an unacknowledged history of domestic servants that underpins its "aesthetics of whiteness" (Phan 2019). If culture(s) are unstable ensembles of practices, values, interactions, discourses, and materialities, we might consider what it means that algorithms are produced within cultures so constituted by enduring violence and trauma, not least in the structural form of ongoing settler colonialism, white supremacy, patriarchy, and late capitalism. In the big picture, one consequence is that whether a technology should be built or not is rarely asked. In more prosaic terms, algorithms are shaped by the limitations, errors, and injustices of the data they are built on, as well as by the biases of engineers, extractive logics of tech industries, hot housing of start-ups in pursuit of venture capital, procurers blinded by solutionist rhetoric, and the tech bro fanboys of social media and online forums.

Yet even those cultural dynamics do not capture the larger concern. Whether understood as trauma culture or what Lauren Berlant, in an interview with Jonathan Greenwald (2012, 82), calls "a crisis culture borrowing trauma's genres to describe what isn't exceptional at all in the continuous production and breakdown of life," the milieu in which technoscience operates and within which individual subjects exist is one founded on war, dispossession, precarity, inequality, and alienation—even if the engineers, architects, and owners of technical systems are themselves materially secure. Co-emergent with such cultures, algorithmic systems cannot avoid traces of trauma—nor can they avoid feeding trauma back into culture. Such systems datafy and algorithmicize individual persons, producing fractional subjects composed of relational aggregations of data that can be operationalized to produce outcomes. These dividuals (Deleuze 1992) manifest a disjunctive, serial relation (see Puar, this volume): not divorced from individuals because they retain a crucial material connection (think automated welfare, credit scores, and biometric border monitoring) and yet also incongruent, arbitrary, and necessarily delimited to forms and functions dictated by the system(s). The subject of algorithmic trauma is irreducibly and inseparably both yet-to-be dividuals *and* the living person to which they are bound, with the intensities of (non)relation that bind them constituted by ruptures of time, space, and knowing.

Louise Amoore (2020, 114) argues that algorithms cannot shake their histories, writing that "the actions of algorithms are never far from their conjoined histories with psychosis, neurosis, trauma, and the imagination of the brain as a system." Consequently, "violence and harm are not something that can be corrected out of an otherwise reasonable calculus" (111). This proposition can be taken one step further: algorithmic systems cannot be corrected away from the production of trauma because they are always already traumatic, constituted on the one hand by the trauma culture from which they arise and on the other hand by the radical disjunctures in their own operative, determinative processes. Learning algorithms, with their hidden neural layers and indeterminate neuron actions, with their persistent emphasis on outcome over process, exemplify this traumatic disjuncture: experiencing the world as data in iterative fashion, with time made uncertain, malleable, and recursive. Such algorithms are in part the legacy of McCulloch and Pitts, who saw the potential for neural nets at a time when computation did not yet have the processing capacity to enact them in practice. Neural networks can break and fail, they can overfit or underfit the data, introducing irredeemable error. Such breakdowns are not labeled "traumatic" as such but rather reflect the inherent fragility and inescapable contingency of such algorithms, as well as the limited capacity for intervention of their architects.

To return to the algorithmic traumas of American drone warfare, disjuncture within the algorithms co-constitutes the trauma for the people living among them. Using the example of random forest algorithms in drone strikes, Amoore (2020, 124) describes their randomness as "a kind of sheltered madness that dwells inside the logic of the algorithm and promises to the world an impossible vision of a secure future." Adjudications between life and death are conducted within the unreasoning and disjunctive zone of proliferating possibilities, endlessly judged by the machinic agency itself. Moves within artificial intelligence development to push for explainability tools for algorithmic systems rest on a recognition that unknowability is unavoidable and can only be mitigated (IBM, n.d.). But we humans can theoretically explain ourselves while also continually failing to do so, particularly in instances when trauma has ripped away both the experiential knowledge and reflective capacity for making sense of events. In drawing this equivalence, I am not suggesting that humans and algorithms should be subject to the same strictures or demands but rather highlighting that the matter of explainability is always an incomplete process. It never reveals everything, only what can be rendered knowable within the framework available. Explainable artificial intelligence fails to approach disjuncture but rather seeks to edge around it by providing tools designed to instill trust and confidence in the human decision makers at institutions implementing such technologies. To what extent algorithmic trauma shapes and even constitutes machinic processes can only be guessed at through metrics that track inputs and outputs, their drift and quality (IBM, n.d.). Commensurability is only ever propositional because neural networks depend on indeterminacy, unknowability, and nonpresentation. If trauma in general is defined by the recursive and unbidden return of experiences that refuse to settle into place in the past, and if something like trauma operates within algorithms that function through proliferating recursions, how deeply ingrained into the workings of the system might such radical disjunctures become?

Answering such a question is perhaps impossible. A skeptical reader might well dismiss this entire line of argument on the grounds that it is unprovable. But we are expected to trust algorithmic systems through their capacity to produce results and, increasingly, through their compliance with practices of accountability, fairness, transparency, and explainability. We are expected to trust artificial intelligence despite the abundant evidence that it is often neither intelligent nor artificial (Sadowski 2018). To accept that a radical unknowability and disjunctive rupturing exists within algorithms requires no less a leap of faith. One can only imagine what lies in wait within as-yet-unrealized computational prophecies, such as neuromorphic processors that mimic the brain in ways McCulloch and Pitts could not have imagined. Algorithmic trauma can shatter the human subject as both individual and collective enterprise: not because the algorithm itself is pure cold calculation but because it is not and can never be.

Toward a Politics of Algorithmic Trauma

Returning to the proposition that media shapes trauma and trauma shapes media, algorithmic trauma and its affective ruptures can be conceptualized as distinct from traumas manifested in other media. Autonomous, traumatic, and machinic, affect animates ever-shifting relations within and between technical systems, flesh bodies, and worldly contexts. Algorithmic systems introduce a radical computational contingency into both the arrival of the traumatic event and its latent return which renders the virtual potential of trauma into coded probability. Like all trauma, the algorithmic variety is fragmented and displaced from the (seemingly) linear experience of time, but unlike traumas entangled with media forms that imprint or record and playback, algorithmic trauma is recursively iterated into the nonlinear and spatially distributed life of networked systems. In other words, algorithmic trauma fragments experiences for the body subject to it *and* (re)produces itself within the networked system from which it arrived. Algorithmic trauma is thus as spatial as it is temporal. Its disjunctures proliferate across space and time but also work to collapse and rupture relations between them. Although trauma more generally produces a form of unknowability that challenges representation and signification, its algorithmic variety is iterated endlessly within the unknowable depths of the algorithmic system itself. Its traumatic processes are manifested in machinic operations, particularly in the case of neural networks which use hidden layers of analysis that even their coders cannot unveil. This iterated unknowability enables an ever-expanding deferral of responsibility, which is also a disavowal of the origin or end of the traumatic relation. Because the algorithmic so often ends in black boxes of various kinds (if not technical, then corporate or military), seeking recourse or repair in the taking of responsibility is itself a fruitless and even traumatic task.

At this point, we find ourselves at a grim place: atomized dividuals in already wounded cultures given over to increasingly violent, dispossessive, and traumatized algorithmic machines. It is worth asking, then, what to make of the architects of such systems, of the companies, states, and institutions that enact them on people and populations. As governments and companies increasingly apply algorithmic systems to determine benefits, access, resources, care, credit, insurance, sentencing, and much more, the injustices of those systems fall far more heavily on those already rendered vulnerable, marginalized, or subject to violence based on race, class, gender, sexuality, or ability (Benjamin 2019; Rouvroy and Berns 2013). Produced within the frame of paternalistic objectives, regressive budget priorities, neoliberal governing strategies, and arbitrary determinations of parameters, weights, and scores, algorithmic violence reinforces and inscribes existing inequities. Encounters with such algorithmic systems are often doubly disempowering: hierarchical asymmetry is both amplified and buffered by the supposedly neutral and objective algorithmic intermediary. Responsibility for determinations that might be deeply harmful can be deferred to the unknowable black-boxed algorithm; in many instances, its processes are invisible to both those who are subject to its outcomes and the workers who implement them on behalf of the state or commerce (Eubanks 2018). Algorithmic trauma thus disperses responsibility away from the actors and institutions that own, authorize, and implement the algorithmic systems. But recognizing algorithmic trauma for what it is holds the potential to destabilize the authority that helps sustain algorithmic power just as reckoning with political trauma brings state authority into question (Edkins 2003).

Within discourses of algorithmic accountability and fairness, an underlying precept is the notion that with just the right interventions, algorithms could, in Amoore's (2020, 119) words, "be rendered governable by appropriate thresholds of reasonable and unreasonable actions." But as Amoore also argues, even if such projects (as laudable and worthy of the energy and struggle that drives them as they may be) were to change the legal and political milieu within which such systems operate, the trauma that is inseparable from the co-assembly and co-composition of algorithmic systems of recommendation, governance, policing, war, law, and welfare would remain. It may well be that this is something we must learn to live with, in the same way that so many have learned to survive within the violence of settler colonialism, late capitalism, and rampant militarism. But that survival may also depend in part on our recognition that we are not simply at risk of encountering trauma in the content delivered through algorithmic recommenders or even in the adjudications of algorithmic governance. We must reckon with the new forms such trauma takes: of the contingency, unknowability, and disavowal instantiated in the algorithmic and of the trauma that such systems cannot themselves escape. This means that what is needed in response is an affective politics that mobilizes algorithmic trauma to reject the deferral and disavowal of responsibility that algorithmic systems engender even as they claim an authority grounded in computational rationality. Students in the United Kingdom chanted "Fuck the algorithm" in response to the automated generation of school-leaving results in 2021 that produced unjust and biased outcomes. In Australia, a coalition of activists, hackers, lawyers, researchers, and data scientists worked from 2016 to 2020 to galvanize outrage against the algorithmic welfare debt collection program that became known as RoboDebt. A politics that mobilizes algorithmic trauma must recognize that the purveyors and implementers of algorithmic systems are not only responsible for the traumas their systems produce. They are also responsible for perpetuating a computational rationality and algorithmic mythos that obscures the violence within the very systems that promise to make the world a better place and yet end up leaving trauma in their wake.

References

Alexander, Jeffrey C. 2012. *Trauma: A Social Theory*. Malden, MA: Polity.

Alexander, Michelle. 2010. *The New Jim Crow: Mass Incarceration in the Age of Color-blindness*. New York: New Press.

Amoore, Louise. 2013. *The Politics of Possibility: Risk and Security beyond Probability*. Durham, NC: Duke University Press.

Amoore, Louise. 2020. *Cloud Ethics: Algorithms and the Attributes of Ourselves and Others*. Durham, NC: Duke University Press.

Andrejevic, Mark. 2019. *Automated Media*. London: Routledge.

Angerer, Marie-Luise. 2017. *Ecology of Affect: Intensive Milieus and Contingent Encounters*. Translated by Gerrit Jackson. Lüneburg, Germany: Meson Press.

Atkinson, Meera, and Michael Richardson. 2013. "At the Nexus: An Introduction." In *Traumatic Affect*, edited by Meera Atkinson and Michael Richardson, 1–19. Newcastle upon Tyne: Cambridge Scholars Press.

Bellanova, Rocco, Kristina Irion, Katja Lindskov Jacobsen, Francesco Ragazzi, Rune Saugmann, and Lucy Suchman. 2021. "Toward a Critique of Algorithmic Violence." *International Political Sociology* 15 (1): 121–50.

Benjamin, Ruha. 2019. *Race after Technology: Abolitionist Tools for the New Jim Code.* Medford, MA: Polity.

Berlant, Lauren. 2011. *Cruel Optimism.* Durham, NC: Duke University Press.

Berlant, Lauren, and Jordan Greenwald. 2012. "Affect in the End Times: A Conversation with Lauren Berlant." *Qui Parle* 20:71–89.

Besley, Tina, and Michael A. Peters. 2020. "Terrorism, Trauma, Tolerance: Bearing Witness to White Supremacist Attack on Muslims in Christchurch, New Zealand." *Educational Philosophy and Theory* 52 (2): 109–19.

Browne, Simone. 2015. *Dark Matters: On the Surveillance of Blackness.* Durham, NC: Duke University Press.

Bucher, Taina. 2018. *If . . . Then: Algorithmic Power and Politics.* Oxford: Oxford University Press.

Caruth, Cathy. 1996. *Unclaimed Experience: Trauma, Narrative, and History.* Baltimore: Johns Hopkins University Press.

Couldry, Nick, and Ulises A. Mejias. 2018. "Data Colonialism: Rethinking Big Data's Relation to the Contemporary Subject." *Television and New Media*, September. https://doi.org/10.1177/1527476418796632.

Cubitt, Sean. 2017. *Finite Media: Environmental Implications of Digital Technologies.* Durham, NC: Duke University Press.

Deleuze, Gilles. 1992. "Postscript on the Societies of Control." *October* 59:3–7.

Dencik, Lina, Arne Hintz, and Jonathan Cable. 2016. "Towards Data Justice? The Ambiguity of Anti-Surveillance Resistance in Political Activism." *Big Data and Society* 3 (2). https://doi.org/10.1177/2053951716679678.

Dixon-Román, Ezekiel, and Ramon Amaro. 2021. "Haunting, Blackness, and Algorithmic Thought" *123*. https://www.e-flux.com/journal/123/437244/haunting-blackness-and-algorithmic-thought/.

Edkins, Jenny. 2003. *Trauma and the Memory of Politics.* Cambridge: Cambridge University Press.

Edney-Browne, Alex. 2019. "The Psychosocial Effects of Drone Violence: Social Isolation, Self-Objectification, and Depoliticization." *Political Psychology* 40 (6): 1341–56.

Eubanks, Virginia. 2018. *Automating Inequality: How High-Tech Tools Profile, Police, and Punish the Poor.* London: St. Martin's.

Felman, Shoshana, and Dori Laub. 1992. *Testimony: Crises of Witnessing in Literature, Psychoanalysis, and History.* New York: Routledge.

Fourcade, Marion. 2021. "Ordinal Citizenship." *British Journal of Sociology* 72 (2): 154–73.

Frosh, Paul. 2019. *The Poetics of Digital Media.* Cambridge: Polity Press.

Guattari, Félix. 1995. "On Machines." *Journal of Philosophy and the Visual Arts* 6:8–12.

Halpern, Orit. 2015. *Beautiful Data: A History of Vision and Reason since 1945.* Durham, NC: Duke University Press.

Holz, Jacob. 2021. "Victimhood and Trauma within Drone Warfare." *Critical Military Studies*: 1–16. https://doi.org/10.1080/23337486.2021.1953738.

IBM. n.d. "Explainable AI." https://www.ibm.com/watson/explainable-ai.

Ibrahim, Yasmin. 2020. "Livestreaming the 'Wretched of the Earth': The Christchurch Massacre and the 'Death-Bound Subject.'" *Ethnicities* 20 (5): 803–22.

Kaplan, E. Ann. 2005. *Trauma Culture: The Politics of Terror and Loss in Media and Literature*. New Brunswick, NJ: Rutgers University Press.

Kember, Sarah, and Joanna Zylinska. 2012. *Life after New Media: Mediation as a Vital Process*. Cambridge, MA: MIT Press.

LaCapra, Dominick. 2001. *Writing History, Writing Trauma*. Baltimore: Johns Hopkins University Press.

Leys, Ruth. 2000. *Trauma: A Genealogy*. Chicago: University of Chicago Press.

Mann, Monique. 2020. "Technological Politics of Automated Welfare Surveillance: Social (and Data) Justice through Critical Qualitative Inquiry." *Global Perspectives* 1 (1). https://doi.org/10.1525/gp.2020.12991.

Massumi, Brian. 2002. *Parables for the Virtual: Movement, Affect, Sensation*. Durham, NC: Duke University Press.

McCulloch, Warren S., and Walter Pitts. 1943. "A Logical Calculus of the Ideas Immanent in Nervous Activity." *Bulletin of Mathematical Biophysics* 5 (4): 115–33.

Noble, Safiya Umoja. 2018. *Algorithms of Oppression: How Search Engines Reinforce Racism*. New York: New York University Press.

O'Malley, Pat, and Gavin Smith. 2020. "'Smart' Crime Prevention? Digitization and Racialized Crime Control in a Smart City." *Theoretical Criminology*, November. https://doi.org/10.1177/1362480620972703.

Ongweso, Edward Jr. 2021. "Amazon's New 'AmaZen' Program Will Show Warehouse Workers Meditation Videos." *Motherboard*, May 18. https://www.vice.com/en/article/3aqb43/amazons-new-amazen-program-will-show-warehouse-workers-meditation-videos.

Phan, Thao. 2019. "Amazon Echo and the Aesthetics of Whiteness." *Catalyst: Feminism, Theory, Technoscience* 5 (1): 1–38.

Pinchevski, Amit. 2019. *Transmitted Wounds: Media and the Mediation of Trauma*. New York: Oxford University Press.

Pugliese, Joseph. 2020. *Biopolitics of the More-than-Human: Forensic Ecologies of Violence*. Durham, NC: Duke University Press.

Rouvroy, Antoinette, and Thomas Berns. 2013. "Algorithmic Governmentality and Prospects of Emancipation." *Reseaux* 177 (1): 163–96.

Sadowski, Jathan. 2018. "Potemkin AI." *Real Life*, August 6. https://reallifemag.com/potemkin-ai/.

Sadowski, Jathan. 2020. *Too Smart: How Digital Capitalism Is Extracting Data, Controlling Our Lives, and Taking over the World*. Cambridge, MA: MIT Press.

Safransky, Sara. 2020. "Geographies of Algorithmic Violence: Redlining the Smart City." *International Journal of Urban and Regional Research* 44 (2): 200–218.

Seaver, Nick. 2017. "Algorithms as Culture: Some Tactics for the Ethnography of Algorithmic Systems." *Big Data and Society* 4 (2). https://doi.org/10.1177/2053951717738104.

Sharpe, Christina. 2016. *In the Wake: On Blackness and Being*. Durham, NC: Duke University Press.

Stanford Law School and NYU School of Law. 2012. "Living under Drones: Death, Injury, and Trauma to Civilians from US Drone Practices in Pakistan." International Human Rights and Conflict Resolution Clinic at Stanford Law School and Global Justice Clinic at NYU School of Law. https://doi.org/10.1163/2468-1733_shafr_SIM260090013.

Stewart, Kathleen. 2007. *Ordinary Affects*. Durham, NC: Duke University Press.

Striphas, Ted. 2015. "Algorithmic Culture." *European Journal of Cultural Studies* 18:395–412.

Tahir, Madiha. 2017. "The Ground Was Always in Play." *Public Culture* 29 (1): 5–16.

Tikka, Minttu Tuulia, Johanna Sumiala, Anu Harju, and Katja Valaskivi. 2020. "Weaponization of Liveness: Streaming Death as a Hybrid Media Event of Terrorist Violence." *AoIR Selected Papers of Internet Research*. https://doi.org/10.5210/spir.v2020i0.11349.

Wilson, Elizabeth A. 2010. *Affect and Artificial Intelligence*. Seattle: University of Washington Press.

CODA

Lauren Berlant, in the middle of a cascade of thoughts:

> Then there are the people, my peeps, who turn their faces to the world to say this and make that because what they see is what they have to give. I want to call their mode of being "The New Frankness" and share with them my future epitaph: "She did what she could do at the time." (Berlant and Stewart 2019, 97)

At her/their death, she/they were in the middle of the time of COVID-19, the life of poisons, the always ongoing showing up for collaboration, living on through writing, and a hard lean into this new frankness.

This is a sample of poems from collections called COVID Poems and *The Poisons* that were becoming something still unknown, or maybe not anything more, in the end, than files left on a computer, but for me, they are a prehension of faces to the world, of what we have, and might have, to give, what we can do frankly and in the meanwhile, down to the bone and into the excess of what's unfolding. They lead.

Kathleen Stewart

Figure C.1. L, R: Carl Bogler, Jennifer Montgomery, Susan Schultz, Katie Stewart, Lauren Berlant.

Reference

Berlant, Lauren, and Kathleen Stewart. 2019. *The Hundreds*. Durham, NC: Duke University Press.

POISONALITY

Lauren Berlant

Testing Positive for the Funk

In a state of emergency, small things change that add up to new dimensions of space. I mean, on the sidewalk we're trying not to trip over each other *from six feet apart*. We're all in it but not in one place together. There's a society, but there is no one in common. The moment is commonly held and it isn't. We are commonly held and we aren't. Many of us are in holding pens that only some of us chose. Many of us are scrambling for something else the size of the world. Many have folded into their bodies and other airless spaces.

Meanwhile, you're all learning now to live like cancer patients—defensively.

Meanwhile, fear that social distancing is shattering a generation's attachment to life evokes the infant's cry that it will *die* if no-one holds it *right now*.

A person will sneeze in the front yard of your face, now a horror forehead atop a mask. In a crisis, we look for cures in causes, but causes are just storytelling. Fantasy smooths out the road so that your sense of confidence is confused with intelligence. In a crisis, fantasy has a higher market value than other speculations. Statements are fantasy in drag.

Luckily, I have a skiing machine. In the 1980s, a company wrote to professors at their office addresses evoking a scene of our butts spreading out from all the sitting we do. My ex and I were runners then. But I was haunted by the specter of the spreading butt: I imagined sitting behind mine at a lecture.

Two weeks into the coronavirus crisis, another round of care-threats circulated. Suffering bodies and economies were real, but vanity too required attention. The hard body and dyed hair were signs in the beforetimes that people must always work on their bodies, themselves. People who weren't young must look good from behind, maintaining visible evidence that they've still *got it*. But when they turn around, I hate them for fooling my antennae. Now that I've seen your painted face, I disrespect your back. I don't know why I want women especially to be front and back consistent. It's the kind of enraged pity I otherwise save for combovers.

Now we take pointless walks. It's spring. The sun is bright, but I am getting paler. I'm wearing my gray wig a little tousled, like a librarian who's just awoken wire glasses askew. A silent voice is barking at me, "Eat sugar, die sooner! A little cookie won't kill you!"

I am going outside after I find out what happens at the end of this sentence, which might take days or weeks. Meanwhile, the sky is white and the lake light blue outside my window. I'm writing to say something about illness and crisis. The coronavirus is going to kill me faster than I'd otherwise die. You're doomscrolling and looking for a phrase's way out, feeling around the middle for a tug in any direction that can seem like an intention. (500)

Ritual Aversions

So Moved

When I say that I've never loved a ritual, it makes me wonder what "love" means.

Sometimes I fear being body-sucked into a tradition. Or being opened up in public far from where I live. Sometimes a ritual's too okay with mechanical sincerity. Then there's the demand that slaves and workers clap for their oppressors. Now a bot will remind you that it's time to perform fidelity to a time. Neither *voluntaire* nor *involuntaire*, bot memory expands your subjective dark. Because the algorithm told it to, it asks you to interrupt your inattention. You are not obliged to have true or any feelings, but you're forced to decide whether you care for the event of the date. Whenever time demands loyalty, we dissociate. Do you remember the start of this poem?

All the things about me, what I see, what my gut senses, what I've read and remembered, streets, the telephone, hand holding, singing, kissing, talking, and eating too fast to taste have almost nothing to do with events. There's no lineup to walk by like some marshal whose job it is to nod and discipline: ordinary life is more like cleaning up after a party you threw and marveling at the carelessness, interest, and touch that kept things going while you were in the room too, but not entirely. This is why I love episodes, many at a time leaning on each other without masquerading as repair or build. So many people have bookshelves that register their brief intentions. So many toss their hollowed empties into the backseat. It's easier for me to love exposed nerves without a purpose, since I love being alive. The Puritans de-fined life as preparation to deserve a grace God may not deliver, and I'm training for a feeling that I don't have yet, which is why we wash dishes, for example. To me this thought is as visceral as a soft kiss, but it may be too abstract for most people. Can you feel your receptivity? Where is it, can you put your hand on your body where it is?

Sometimes I'm listening, then I get tired. It is not that there is no love left, but there is no more room. To receive isn't just to stuff a thing into a body but to sit within the resonance of an impact while also feeling it out. Ribs are breaking everywhere from cancer. Skele-tons clack like a marionette's dancing sticks but with nerve endings popping sharply. There is no perfect posture to relieve all that. Shift-ing around just redistributes discomfort. Meanwhile, the Capitol is being stormed by whites on a mission to plant their fantasy flag next to another fantasy flag. Their freedom breath barges into the present and fogs its mirror, which is a way to think about crisis. Behind it, people are still dying from the virus, but today that's suspended in ordinary helplessness. The caption of pain life is: make it stop. The caption of infrastructure is, please return. (500)

Funny Story

Right now's a kind of low–joke density time, people too depleted to bother with wordplay and satire's too heavy.

But then, the genre called the "funny story" keeps popping up. People set off with, "funny story."

A funny story is about a thing that could have gotten pocketed somewhere: a letter found in a thrift store book or a doll with uneven button eyes. An object someone stuffed in a drawer or a conversation passed by. A thing someone thought they could say to you. A funny story is not an anecdote bearing the weight of revelatory exemplarity. When you hear it, you're more sure that you're hearing a funny story than you are that it's a story, or funny. I associate its simplicity with tubs of jelly and disbelief. A shy white male kindergarten friend used to bring me the unopened jellies from his dinner plates. I was five: it was a kind of flirting. These were gifts without being fetishes. They were not magical and were pure of the ambition to be magical. It would be mean to call them boring. They were usual. They were perfectly undemanding. Without magic, the unambitious objects were just niceness swiftly gestured, or a person's noticing x without the portentousness of embodying x.

The person to whom the funny story passes has to give into its specific quality of a strange thing happening unless they're anxious for every encounter to appear profound. It's not minor literature or a weapon of the weak. It doesn't gratify any need for drama that generates value beyond the exchange. It gets presented to you for you to sit with.

The thing about the funny story is that they're not really memorable or forgettable because you don't really know what you've got there. Something happens in the exchange. You decide to enjoy that someone is presenting a thing, the way a little kid might show you a stick they found. But this is not just the stick but a something else that fans out, a backstory that makes a funny story something to tell beyond the image in relief. It bears no moral conclusion or agent of action. What I love about it is that it's just a thing someone said about a thing they noticed in a place and time. If you need it to be profound, you've committed a genre violation. Because it was just left behind. It was someone's thin object that rose up into awareness and got circulated.

Splitting the relation of importance and being memorable: not generalizing about what's significant just from the fact that something stuck. Your funny storyteller is uninterested in generalizing and you are also. The exchange is not intimate.

For one friend, this is the only genre that offers delight. It's what he brings, it's what he's got. It doesn't feel like a defense: it's not a psychological genre, I sense. His material comes like a cartoon or a greeting card. I have no idea if he's desperate to turn the world into occasions or just sees a thing, likes it, and is moved to tell someone about what he ran into.

My friend's cache of funny stories encompasses silliness and death as though remains, in the end, are light, not heavy in the tone of their narrative unfolding. There's no tragedy of the leftover. He finds prompts at garage sales and on the side of the road, or when it rains inconveniently on his dog. It's akin to finding money in an old coat pocket and still being surprised you could ever forget about money. I'll often leaf through a book to discover letters I've received and unsent postcards I thought I'd use one day to reach someone I longed for in the postcard way. Finding it doesn't make it a treasure, but a confusion. They say trauma lights up a part of your brain that's never been lit: the funny story isn't like that, though, because the plain object animates attention whose aura is unclear. But it doesn't dig a relentless hole.

Sometimes it takes forever to tell the funny story because of its cast of characters. So many worlds swirl in convergence over it. Notebook paper turned into stationery takes an hour of digressive explanation; lead pencil and cursive handwriting use up chunks of historicizing time. But eventually, things trail off rather than become history books or diaries. Not everything becomes beautiful when it circulates. I pick up objects off the street all the time and fail to make stories out of them. My friend knows how to lay a thing out. His funny story involves threads of ordinary life composed into a series of narrative placemats. It's a story that sticks its nose into your business although you were never asked for your opinion. (800)

You Have a New Test Result

Once a colleague said to me, "The problem with you is, you expect joy at work. A career is not about joy. It is about building monuments to knowledge that will remain after you are gone."

Years later, I read a story that seemed truer in *Sum: Forty Tales from the Afterlives*. In that story, people go into a waiting room after death where they're stuck until no-one on Earth remains to say their name. People who'd built monuments to themselves were therefore the last to enter the afterlife, because tour guides and lecturers had a duty to repeat the story of how they had mattered. Death's finitude hovered over them like a blinking cursor.

A few years later, after that colleague became ill with what would kill her, I caught up with her spouse, another colleague, crossing the quads to the administration building. It was a blindingly bright Chicago winter day. I looked up at him and said, "How do you do it? I'm dying from working at a heart attack pace. I can't stay on top of it: there isn't sleep enough left from which to subtract." He looked down at me and said, "Oh come on, this career runs on the fumes of desperation. That is what we signed up for. That is what we love."

I didn't, I swear. I signed up to secure a place to live.

A hundred times since the diagnosis I've refrained, "I broke my body for the job." But I had already said it for years—it was a thing I said a lot, like "commitment to alternativity" or "transformative relation." These are the kinds of phrase a person uses to mark an impasse—a repetition whose power is a handbrake, a railing, allowing the continuity of ordinary deadly living. "I broke my body for the job" was like "She works hard for the money," a pop hook that points to a problem and becomes an anthem. The phrase was useful too when I had to defend why I work out at the gym each day. I used to run: now everywhere I go—the hospital, the desk, the couch, the café—it's me and some resistance machines, churning. When I was young, I'd been weirdly influenced by a "Dear Abby" column, a touchstone I read assiduously. She wrote that no-one on their deathbed ever says, "I wish I had worked more." It was about absentee workaholic fathers, I believe. I worried about this, but I was stuck. Work was what I knew at root how to do. Therefore I didn't have kids. Each day of my life was, instead, a test to see whether I'd properly earned my existence.

Everyone concurs that I have failed to be sane. It's not a question of balance: people like me are driven toward work to stay interested in living. Others seek adoration through it, addicted to the huzzahs they'd received for mastering toilet training, where you learn to produce and to withhold—to control and have pride in your output. Others who work crazy hard are dying for a shot at being recognized, whatever that means. But my story does not include being valued or overvalued. I absorbed my mother's brokenness and her contempt for my father, whom I looked a lot like. Too ugly, too whatever the opposite of adorable is, we gashed her fantasy. The Yiddish words were *mieskeit* and *vantz*. School took me out of the family and into the world: work was freedom from them.

I use my university's HMO. My psychiatrist says, kindly—she's very kind—that maybe I can do a different thing now that I have no choice but to do a different thing: like what I want to do rather than the job. I responded, "You teach here, you know what the available slots are— deadwood and the people who break their bodies." She nodded and her face receded into an elsewhere that flickered across her rice paper skin. All of her dresses look like upholstery fabric, often black and white or blue and white, squares or zigzag lines. She's a walking EKG. She's sweet with me. Our late afternoon sessions resolve shadowed in dusky light. You get a psychiatrist here when you get a terminal diagnosis. She has a spouse in pediatric oncology. I can't imagine how they let go of their day.

The man sitting near me is shaking his leg so intensely he threatens my chair's stability. His machinic chopping mouth just chased a banana around its curve. I'm writing outside a Magic Johnson Starbucks, breathing in what the old men at my gym call "Cadillac coffee."

A few tables down, a child who was sitting alone in a metal chair is approached by a man and turns away quickly, tucking his face into his own arms and wailing convulsively, as though only folding up into his body and dying would resolve the problem at hand. The father hugs him hard with daddy warmth. The love wrestling doesn't go anywhere. The child is inconsolable, the father relentless. Was he hours or a lifetime late? The father turns out to be with three other workers and needs to get back to his truck. He picks up his child like a movie bride, and the son howls and kicks until the father sets him down. As the man walks toward the work truck, he drags the son by his outstretched arm, but the child drags his heels and turns around toward the garden. The son has a burr cut and the father a Cubs cap. He is singing and making jokes. The adult is trying to drown out what they both know, that the son's misery is just. The adult wants it to be forgotten please.

I had misread the situation entirely and thought that the child was the grandson of the old gray-skinned woman working in the café garden. I thought that the child was having a nice time in the sun while his grandmother bent intensely into the dirt. This is an astonishing garden for a small beans place. Suddenly, the old woman stands up hand on hip and rants into her phone. I can't hear what she says because of the truck noise on the nearby road. When things die down, she returns to her knees and crouches into the ground. The weather report had said that today would be beautiful. It is so beautiful that the ordinary partly cloudy doesn't begin to describe the soft ease that breezes us all, like it or not, through the day's recoveries and trials. (1,100)

Taxotere

On the airplane on the way to the Pacific, I sat with a salt and pepper couple who were beautiful when they were young and now hover like Baucis and Philemon, gracious to the end. But you can't tell much about a couple or a person from surface of an encounter, like when my Lyft driver this morning released the harsh breath of an open Cheetos bag when she unlatched the door to her Nissan Sentra, which made me stupidly anxious that she'd be a bad driver when all it was, it turns out, was that she's had no time for breakfast lately since she drives the minute the sun comes up and blinds her through her lids.

Lorraine says she's driving in her mid-seventies to get out of the damn house. But another story emerged, as they will. For thirty years, she'd worked at a data entry desk job she loved. Then her husband got prostate cancer and forced her to retire to care for him. "He was self-ish," she repeated. They had insurance, but the bills took everything. She drives her Sentra all day to protect her house. She drives until her knees hurt. She heard on the radio her knees won't hurt if she drinks a juice a day. She's got her daughter researching it.

Meanwhile, the couple on the airplane, Jeanne and John, were reading Christian tracts the whole time. Toward the end of the flight, Jeanne introduced herself with a tissue because my nose had begun to drip an oxblood stain to which I was numb. I asked where she was going. She said, to a funeral: her husband's eighty-year-old sister had died. "I hope you're okay," I said to him, at the same time as he said, "She was 80: she had a good run." Alphabets collide.

Loss is loss, I said, like I always do. Then I told them I was 60 and had a cancer that would probably kill me before I was 62. Would that be long enough to say "a good run," or is that still a little too young? Almost all my cancer friends are dead except for the slow-growing prostates and early-onset breast cancers who are kept alive by a pill like the PWAS I know who made it into the trials that worked so they could live on to a moment when it will no longer be said to be too soon when they die. It's crazy what we say to file a life as satisfying, or maybe it's just what language mostly is for, to put something out there to keep the chain of life going. Jeanne said she'd noticed my beautiful hair when I was curled over reading on the airport floor and guessed that I was a teacher. It's a wig, I said. I said, I had noticed you too and thought "my hair looks just like your hair." We looked at each other for a second, unclear, a little jolted. Nothing felt unkind. (500)

Theory of the Apparatus

Illness reshuffles my attachments as though now I'm a citizen of somewhere else, perhaps of a snow globe you shake just to see the flakes descend slowly on a domestic scene that's so still it gives off no clue to how it's lived in. The dollhouse fantasy is that nothing moves without your wishes. The fantasy is that your command of order will control the plot. A gesture becomes a parable of how worlds should emerge. In thirties films, the camera sticks its nose into still-life objects like this, moving through the imitation snow to that place from which a person needs to be rescued. But it's a place that has to be moved through. The lens disturbs the tableau and begins the reveal of the crisis from which a character may not emerge.

People I've loved and held the world up with get avoided now for no good reason. I write in the passive because I'm surprised, split off from the history of my attachments. Sometimes my aversion to the loved ones tells me that they were always a little taxing. Sometimes it aims to protect anxious friends from facing that they can't trust their own bodies to tell the truth. People I don't know well get let in if I sense they can be with what's unsettled. Second order friends, whatever that means, become people I suddenly call on the phone because they slow down the riot inside me to something more like the outdoor concerts I encounter on my way to the summer supermarket, where people sit in folding chairs tapping their feet or talking to their neighbors in the warm sunlight of the scheduled disturbance whose function is to drown out the noise of the world. These events adapt a threatening stream into benign life music. (300)

Remain

A remain is what gets left behind without a plan for it, marking the place of the radically useless. It's the body of optimism flattened by a future that won't or can't revive it. It's a broken mirror, a thin smile that asks "What now?" Any child who cleans out the place of their final parent knows of this. The spice rack packed with jars of dust. Startlingly fresh luncheon meat. Books carried from place to place marking aspirations now deemed nothing by Goodwill. Organs wracked by illness now too ruined for science. Survivors remember episodes with emergent residual love. (100)

Waiting

Dogs wait for their masters to tell them when to wait with a specific attentiveness: to fetch a treat, to cross the street, to hunt a fox or a bird they can snatch a whiff of long before they're freed to pursue. Humans with the same bee-line on what's to come would be pathologized for it, words like "ambition," "obsession," "anxiety," and "paranoia" hovering in the space of judgment because the human's job is to keep things in scale. Except where a decision determines life, what's in front of a human should not be deemed *the most important thing.* Cancer multiplies what a person is waiting for. More things that we'd call tests. There's dying and the side effect. There's the face of a friend you haven't told yet. There's the treatment, involving infusions and scans. The scans produce urgent interpretations for which the patient is forced to wait. The patient has to prepare to hear all the outcomes in advance of the doctor's report of another doctor's interpretation. After, there's rest and the resistance to rest. There's processing melodrama and cruelty plus episodes of everyday awkwardness. There's adjusting to this thing and the next and seeing how they go.

1   Nothing changed.
2   Everything changed.
3   Everything's bigger.
4   Some things are.
5   Everything shrank.
6   Some things shrank.
7   There are tiny dots that might be symptoms, scars, or dings.

8   It's all invisibilia now.

9   Everyone dies after optimism permits carelessness.

10   Heartache.

11   Realism.

13   Remains.

12   As I'm practicing, my uncs says, "Can't you enjoy it a little?"
     I say, "Someone has to stay clear-headed."

13   "Someone has to stay open, yet well-defended."

14   I ask the internet Tarot: next year at this time, dead or alive?
     HA! I picked the card "yes!" Crazy: time. (300)

Port

I dreamed I would bring to the future a mouth that was finally open. Not open wide like at the dentist or in the poem where the poet, disgusted at his desire, gets lost in the cavern of a woman's throat—not like that. The dream was to unclench enough to keep the shop open for the thrill of another encounter.

It turns out that you break even when you love. Then you need a mechanic to protect you from the poisons. Then you're wheeled into a freezing room where a sunset drug separates your pain sufficiently from you for you to take the cut, the implant, the suture, the constraint on your near future, the loss of muscle, and your indefiniteness. Then you have to take in new things that might kill you or cure you—you can't know which or when and you can't force the affect into effect or insist that the world adapt your dream to a different medium. Fuck the future. The task at hand is harder: to stay good when the room shifts tone; to lose the joyless part of composure; to let things become other things; to continue to throw yourself against what unwelcomes life. (200)

Brassed Off

If workers were cats or dogs, you'd be up in bloody arms against their strangulation. If I were a clown, I might tell the truth to children in the form of a joke. If we went out of our way to change the world, we and it might still die. I'd like a spoiler right now.

I used to say to the politically depressed that since the world has changed during our lifetimes, it could change again, to become less bad or even beautiful. Imagine it.

It's not all tragedy repeating as farce. I need phrases to fuel alternative worlds. That's why I'm a scholar.

I said "alternative worlds" rather than "alter-worlds" because suddenly it came to me as I wrote this that people might read "alter-worlds" after I'm dead, not here to explain why the phrase "alter-worlds" is preferable. "Alter-" suggests how small a shift can open up the image of another world. Outside, there are empty shoes at the door that happen to be your size. Inside, there are blocks of time set out for you plural to bullshit and brainstorm collectively, until a problem loses its corset.

For example, I like the pronoun "they" for myself not because I smudge difference but because I don't believe in the stuffy impersonal pronoun "one." We're in our body, not one's body. We're all a kind of thing, many kinds of thing, not a humorless "one." No pulsating body is a neutral "one" cleansed of the swells of gender.

I'm weaker than I was. Tumor pain is spreading across my back and I am losing muscle, pretending that the scale measures only virtuous fat melting. Life is not as desperate as it should feel, though, because my body can quicken to anything: the whatever, the *x*, all the beloved placeholders. (300)

Final Words

Not memory, not at home. (Inspired by Hilton Als.)

The church ladies at the gym bring me bouquets of advice about killing cancer back. It's all about healing from the right combination of Jesus and fruit. They're not fooling: they say "apoptosis." "God is in you and *he* never dies." Belief flings you toward a sensed truth: at the same time, you lean back, observing and nodding.

Think of a small beige pony, its gold mane softly falling. Think of a physical therapist stuck in mid-gesture. Merge the figures into a lenticular shimmer.

Shimmer is an affect-word, a tilt of wonder at the vibrant world, honoring matter's diffusion of light. I don't relate. I circulate in waves like smoke as though the lateral were literal. I'm a dog in a sea of crotches, curious and moving but almost lost, while the rising light of shimmer-wonder offers glowing GIFs for another kind of someone.

The therapist-horse in my brain blinks a midwesterner's blue eye. He releases me to walk on an incline, 1, 2. He admits, "I was dread-ing you." He had imagined a sad old cripple scratching on a tattered lottery ticket. He was fearing being barred from being known by the client's demand to celebrate ridiculously thin improvements. (200)

Poisonality

Temporary tattoos stretch out on my forearm, a living billboard and a note to self. One says "Don't eat poison," which doesn't mean I didn't or that I know how not to. Yesterday, a friend whose face emits "it is what it is" burst out with "Don't drink plastic!" It was a startling moment of bossy care. Around illness, the whole fretful world gets bossy. There must be a *reason* for the body's attrition. Now everyone's solving a case, full of admonition. Love's in the imperative: eat this, or not; drink that, or not; stand on your head; twist out the toxins. It's your fault or the stress of the world that broke you: *do something.* My friend doesn't usually burst out: she's flat, amused, composed.

San Pellegrino in glass was the alternative on offer. Dehydration is a contemporary crisis of the overbusy. Glass saves us from drying out without extending the Plasticine. It's a quenching bargain with impaired resilience. Only vigilance can help us not become whales washed up stuffed with the bags and bottles we've also inhaled. Only discipline can stop us from further absorbance, if by stop I mean "slow down." It's a tragedy how much literal membrane our bodies have leached from our pleasure in breathing. From poison zones of enjoyment, enmeshment, inattention.

My cancer began in the soft tissue, another poisoned lining. It's as though the more receptive one becomes, the more poison one takes in, leaching death from life: the more conscious of the kinetic energy of adaptation, which is to say, of life: cancer and plastic, a dynamic of forced change that has nothing to do with progress or resilience but with the limited plasticity of being. Plastic is photodegradable, not biodegradable: like cancer. It doesn't disappear, it becomes small and floaty. We try to flush it out, but waste has to go somewhere. This is what it means to think of "remains."

New York comedians used to call what we offer to the world "poisonality," because puns are a primitive route to laughter. The inconvenience of other people can be funny the way old milk can be: off.

The "developed countries" and the oceans are enmeshed with the Plasticine and the fact of constant change that cannot be confused with becoming better or different. Adaptation is not the same thing as staying in sync, or being only a little belated. It registers the fact that dynamics will change the tone of surviving. Heather Davis argues that the unraveling world is imperceptible—like cancer. This is why we need concepts of atmosphere. We perceive how easy denial would be. Just invent an analogy. Is "it" a symptom or an ordinary ding?

In cancer, we learn that how we feel has nothing to do with how we are. If you say "Good!" to someone's knowing question about how you're doing, they give you the fish eye. But I feel good! I know I'm dying in the middle of life. But I can coast while declining. (500)

LAUREN BERLANT is, in words here repurposed from "Poisonality," "a citizen now of somewhere else." The young Lauren was "weirdly influenced" by a "Dear Abby" column in which Abby wrote that no one on their deathbed ever says, "I wish I had worked more." Lauren acknowledges some worry about this, but it stuck. Each day of Lauren's life became "a test to see whether I'd properly earned my existence." Affect theory exists today as what it is because of Lauren. This book is dedicated to Lauren as living proof of an existence properly earned. Test passed.

LISA BLACKMAN works at the intersection of affect studies, body studies, and media and cultural theory. Lisa is currently professor of media and communications in the Department of Media, Communication, and Cultural Studies at Goldsmiths, University of London. Their current research project charts the broken genealogy between narcissistic storytelling, military and psychological torture technologies, and post-truth communication strategies. It is set within the context of three interrelated pandemics—COVID-19, domestic abuse, and systemic racism—and the politics of Brexit and Trumpism. This research builds on their previous research in the field of affect studies, including in two books, *Immaterial Bodies: Affect, Embodiment, Mediation* (2012) and *Haunted Data: Affect, Transmedia and Weird Science* (2019).

RIZVANA BRADLEY is assistant professor of film and media studies at the University of California, Berkeley. Her monograph, *Anteaesthetics: Black Aesthesis and the Critique of Form* (forthcoming), is a recipient of the Creative Capital | Andy Warhol Foundation Arts Writers Grant and offers a critical examination of Black corporeality across a range of experimental artistic practices that integrate film and other media. Her scholarship has appeared or is forthcoming in a range of academic publications, including *Diacritics, Film Quarterly, Black Camera: An International Film Journal, Discourse: Journal for Theoretical Studies in Media and Culture, Rhizomes: Cultural Studies in Emerging Knowledge, Women and Performance: A Journal of Feminist Theory,* and TDR: *The Drama Review.* Bradley has curated a number of academic arts symposia, including events at the British Film Institute, London, the Serpentine Gallery, London, and most recently, the Stedelijk Museum of Art, Amsterdam.

ANN CVETKOVICH is director of the Pauline Jewett Institute of Women's and Gender Studies at Carleton University. She was previously Ellen Clayton Garwood Centennial Professor of English, professor of women's and gender studies, and founding director of LGBTQ studies at the University of Texas at Austin. She is the author of *Mixed Feelings: Feminism, Mass Culture, and Victorian Sensationalism* (1992), *An Archive of Feelings: Trauma, Sexuality, and Lesbian Public Cultures* (Duke University Press, 2003), and *Depression: A Public Feeling* (Duke University Press, 2012).

EZEKIEL DIXON-ROMÁN is professor of critical race, media, and educational studies in the Department of Curriculum and Teaching at Teacher's College, Columbia University, as well as director of the college's Edmund W. Gordon Institute for Urban and Minority Education. He is the author of *Inheriting Possibility: Social Reproduction and Quantification in Education* (2017), which received the 2018 Outstanding Book Award from the American Educational Research Association. He also co-guest edited "Alternative Ontologies of Number: Rethinking the Quantitative in Computational Culture" (*Cultural Studies-Critical Methodologies,* 2016), "The Computational Turn in Education Research: Critical and Creative Perspectives on the Digital Data Deluge" (*Research in Education,* 2017), edited "Control Societies @30: Technopolitical Forces and Ontologies of Difference" (*Social Text Online,* 2020), and most recently co-guest edited "Dialogues on Recursive Colonialism, Speculative Computation, and the Techno-Social" (*e-flux journal,* 2021). He is currently working on a book project that examines the haunting formations of the transparent subject in algorithmic governance and the potential for transformative technopolitical ontoepistemologies.

ADAM J. FRANK is professor in the Department of English Language and Literatures at the University of British Columbia, Vancouver. His research and teaching areas include nineteenth- and twentieth-century American literature and media, histories and theories of affect and feeling, and science and technology studies. He is the author of *Transferential Poetics, from Poe to Warhol* (2015), coauthor (with Elizabeth Wilson) of *A Silvan Tomkins Handbook* (2020), coeditor (with Eve Kosofsky Sedgwick) of *Shame and Its Sisters: A Silvan Tomkins Reader* (Duke University Press, 1995), and producer of the *Radio Free Stein* project.

M. GAIL HAMNER is professor of religion at Syracuse University where she teaches religion and culture through film, media theory, continental philosophy, and feminist theory. She is the author of *American Pragmatism: A Religious Genealogy* (2002), *Religion and Film: The Politics of Nostalgia* (2011), and numerous essays on religion, film, and affect theory. She is currently working on a manuscript with the working title *Religion and Public Affects* and is also dabbling in a set of essays on affect, politics, and the seven deadly sins.

OMAR KASMANI is postdoctoral research associate in social and cultural anthropology at the Collaborative Research Center 1171 Affective Societies at Freie Universität, Berlin. His work is situated across the study of contemporary Islamic lifeworlds, queer and affect theory, and queries critical notions of intimacy and postmigrant be/longing. He is the author of *Queer Companions: Religion, Public Intimacy and Saintly Affects in Pakistan* (Duke University Press, 2022). His current book project turns to autotheory to bring personal memoir to bear on an affective geography of Berlin.

CECILIA MACÓN is assistant professor in the Department of Philosophy at the University of Buenos Aires, researcher at CONICET, and director of the SEGAP research group. She is the author of *Desafiar el sentir: Feminismo, historia y rebelión* (2021), which scrutinizes the history of feminism in terms of "affective dis-arrangements," and *Sexual Violence in the Argentinean Crimes against Humanity Trials: Rethinking Victimhood* (2016), which analyzes the role played by affect in testimonies of sexual violence. Macón has coedited or edited, among others, *Affect, Gender and Sexuality in Latin America* (2021), *Pretérito indefinido* (2015), *Afectos políticos* (2017), and *Mapas de la transición* (2010). Her writing has also appeared in journals such as *Journal of Latin American Cultural Studies, Revista latinoamericana de filosofía, Intermédialités, Revista estudos feministas,* and *Journal of Romance Studies.*

HIL MALATINO is assistant professor of women's, gender, and sexuality studies and philosophy and core faculty in the Rock Ethics Institute at Penn State. He is the author of *Side Affects: On Being Trans and Feeling Bad* (2022), *Trans Care* (2020), and *Queer Embodiment: Monstrosity, Medical Violence, and Intersex Experience* (2019).

ERIN MANNING is professor in the Faculty of Fine Arts at Concordia University (Montreal, Canada). She is also the founder of SenseLab (www.senselab.ca), a laboratory that explores the intersections between art practice and philosophy through the matrix of the sensing body in movement. Current art projects are focused around the concept of minor gestures in relation to color and movement. Art exhibitions include the Sydney and Moscow Biennales, Glasshouse (New York), Vancouver Art Museum, McCord Museum (Montreal), House of World Cultures (Berlin), and Galateca Gallery (Bucharest). Publications include *For a Pragmatics of the Useless* (Duke University Press, 2020), *The Minor Gesture* (Duke University Press, 2016), *Always More than One: Individuation's Dance* (Duke University Press, 2013), *Relationscapes: Movement, Art, Philosophy* (2009), and with Brian Massumi, *Thought in the Act: Passages in the Ecology of Experience* (2014).

DEREK P. MCCORMACK is professor of cultural geography at the University of Oxford. He is the author of *Atmospheric Things: On the Allure of Elemental Envelopment* (2018) and *Refrains for Moving Bodies: Experience and Experiment in Affective Spaces* (2014), both published by Duke University Press.

PATRICK NICKLESON is assistant professor of music history at the University of Alberta. Through contemporary experimental and popular music, Patrick's work examines alternate historiographies of authorship and collaboration, dispute and revolt, territory and property. His writing has appeared in *Twentieth Century Music*, the *Journal of the Royal Musical Association*, and *Intersections*. He is the author of *The Names of Minimalism: Authorship, Art Music, and Historiography in Dispute*, coeditor of *Rancière and Music*, and is editing Tony Conrad's *What Music Did* for posthumous publication.

SUSANNA PAASONEN is professor of media studies at the University of Turku. With an interest in studies of sexuality, media, and affect, she is the PI of the consortium Intimacy in Data-Driven Culture (the Strategic Research Council at the Academy of Finland, 2019–2025) and author of, for example, *Carnal Resonance: Affect and Online Pornography* (2011), *Many Splendored Things: Thinking Sex and Play* (2018), and *Dependent, Distracted, Bored: Affective Formations in Networked Media* (2021).

TYRONE S. PALMER is assistant professor of English at Wesleyan University. His research interests include Black critical thought, affect theory, poetics, and negativity. His scholarship has been published or is forthcoming in *Qui Parle: Critical Humanities and Social Sciences*, *Critical Ethnic Studies*, *Philosophy Today*, and TOPIA: *Canadian Journal of Cultural Studies*. Additionally, he has published cultural criticism and poetry in a number of venues, including *The New Inquiry*, *Gawker*, *The Offing*, *Vinyl Poetry*, and *Callaloo*.

CAROLYN PEDWELL is professor of cultural studies and media at the University of Kent, Canterbury. Her research interests include the affective politics of digital media and artificial intelligence, and the relationships among habit, affect, and social transformation. Carolyn is the author of *Revolutionary Routines: The Habits of Social Transformation* (2021), *Affective Relations: The Transnational Politics of Empathy* (2014), and *Feminism, Culture and Embodied Practice: The Rhetorics of Comparison* (2010). Her recent Leverhulme Research Fellowship (2020–21) explored "Digital Media and 'The Human': The Social Life of Software, AI and Algorithms."

JASBIR K. PUAR is professor of women's and gender studies at Rutgers University. She is the author of the award-winning books *The Right to Maim: Debility, Capacity, Disability* (Duke University Press, 2017) and *Terrorist Assemblages: Homonationalism in Queer Times* (Duke University Press, 2007), which is also translated into Spanish and French, with Greek and Portuguese translations forthcoming, and reissued as an expanded version for its tenth anniversary (2017). Her scholarly and mainstream writings have been translated into more than fifteen languages. She is on the advisory board of numerous organizations, including USACBI and Disability under Siege, a project focusing on disability in conflict zones. She is the 2019 Kessler recipient, a lifetime achievement award from the Center for Gay and Lesbian Studies (CLAGS) to scholars and activists whose work has significantly impacted queer research and organizing.

JASON READ is professor of philosophy at the University of Southern Maine. He is the author of *The Micro-Politics of Capital: Marx and the Prehistory of the Present* (2003), *The Politics of Transindividuality* (2015), and the collection of essays, *The Production of Subjectivity: Between Marxism and Post-Structuralism* (2022). He blogs on popular culture, philosophy, and politics at unemployednegativity.com. He is currently writing a book provisionally titled *The Double Shift: Marx and Spinoza on the Politics and Ideology of Work*.

MICHAEL RICHARDSON is a writer, researcher, and teacher living and working on Gadigal and Bidjigal country. He is associate professor in media and culture at the University of New South Wales, Sydney, where he codirects the Media Futures Hub and the Autonomous Media Lab, and an associate investigator with the ARC Centre of Excellence on Automated Decision-Making & Society. His research examines technology, power, witnessing, trauma, and affect in contexts of war, security, and surveillance. Alongside articles, essays, and book chapters, he is the author of *Gestures of Testimony: Torture, Trauma, and Affect in Literature* (2016) and is completing a book currently titled *Nonhuman Witnessing: War, Climate, and Data after the End of the World*.

DYLAN ROBINSON is a Stó:lō scholar and associate professor in the School of Music at the University of British Columbia. From 2015 to 2022, he held the Canada Research Chair in Indigenous Arts at Queen's University, located on the traditional lands of the Haudenosaunee and Anishinaabe peoples. His research has been supported by national and international fellowships at the Faculty of Music at the University of Toronto, in the Canadian Studies Program at the University of California, Berkeley, the Indigeneity in the Contemporary World project at Royal Holloway University of London, and a Banting Postdoctoral fellowship in the First Nations Studies Program at the University of British Columbia. His current research project documents the history of contemporary Indigenous public art across North America and questions how Indigenous rights and settler colonialism are embodied and spatialized in public space.

TONY D. SAMPSON is a critical theorist with an interest in the philosophies of media technology. His publications include *The Spam Book* (2009), *Virality* (2012), *The Assemblage Brain* (2017), *Affect and Social Media* (2018), and *A Sleepwalker's Guide to Social Media* (2020). Tony is the host and organizer of the Affect and Social Media international conferences in East London and a cofounder of the public engagement initiative Cultural Engine Research Group. He works as a reader in digital communication at the University of Essex.

KYLA SCHULLER is associate professor and undergraduate director of women's, gender and sexuality studies at Rutgers University, New Brunswick. She is the author of *The Biopolitics of Feeling: Race, Sex, and Science in the Nineteenth Century* (Duke University

Press, 2018) and *The Trouble with White Women: A Counterhistory of Feminism* (2021). She has coedited a special issue of *Social Text* on plasticity and the *American Quarterly* volume "Origins of Biopolitics in the Americas," which was named Best Special Issue of 2020. Schuller has held fellowships from the American Council of Learned Societies and the Stanford Humanities Center.

GREGORY J. SEIGWORTH is professor of digital communication and cultural studies at Millersville University. Greg has published numerous chapters, essays, and reviews in a variety of venues, including *Antithesis, Architectural Design, Cultural Studies, Culture Machine, Ephemera, m/c, Radical Philosophy,* and *Theory, Culture, and Society.* He is coeditor, with Melissa Gregg, of *The Affect Theory Reader* (Duke University Press, 2010) and coeditor of the open-access journal *Capacious: Journal for Emerging Affect Inquiry* with Mathew Arthur. Greg has also organized two fairly massive international conferences focused on the lively interdisciplinarity of affect studies (in 2015 and 2018) at his home institution in Lancaster, Pennsylvania.

NATHAN SNAZA teaches English and women, gender and sexuality studies at the University of Richmond. He is the author of *Animate Literacies: Literature, Affect, and the Politics of Humanism* (Duke University Press, 2019) and the coeditor of many collections, most recently, with Julietta Singh, a special issue of *Social Text* called "Educational Undergrowth" (2021). His essays have appeared in journals such as *Feminist Formations, Feminist Studies, Parallax, Symplokē, Curriculum Inquiry,* and *Journal of Curriculum and Pedagogy.* His book *Tendings: Feminist Esoterisms and the Abolition of Man* is forthcoming with Duke University Press.

KATHLEEN STEWART writes ethnographic experiments to approach the composition of emergent worldings and their modes of knowing and sensing in refrains, rhythms, voices, tactilities, misfires, labors, and atmospheres. Her books include *A Space on the Side of the Road: Cultural Poetics in an "Other" America* (1996), *Ordinary Affects* (Duke University Press, 2007), *The Hundreds,* coauthored with Lauren Berlant (Duke University Press, 2019), and *Worlding* (in preparation). She teaches at the University of Texas, Austin.

ELIZABETH A. WILSON is a Samuel Candler Dobbs Professor in the Department of Women's, Gender, and Sexuality Studies at Emory University. Her research expertise is in feminist theory, psychoanalytic theory, affect theory, and feminist science studies. She is the author of *Affect and Artificial Intelligence* (2010), *Gut Feminism* (Duke University Press, 2015), and *A Silvan Tomkins Handbook: Foundations for Affect Theory* (2020, coauthored with Adam Frank).